Malta
and Gozo

the Bradt Travel Guide

Juliet Rix

edition
I

www.bradtguides.com

Bradt Travel Guides Ltd, UK
The Globe Pequot Press Inc, USA

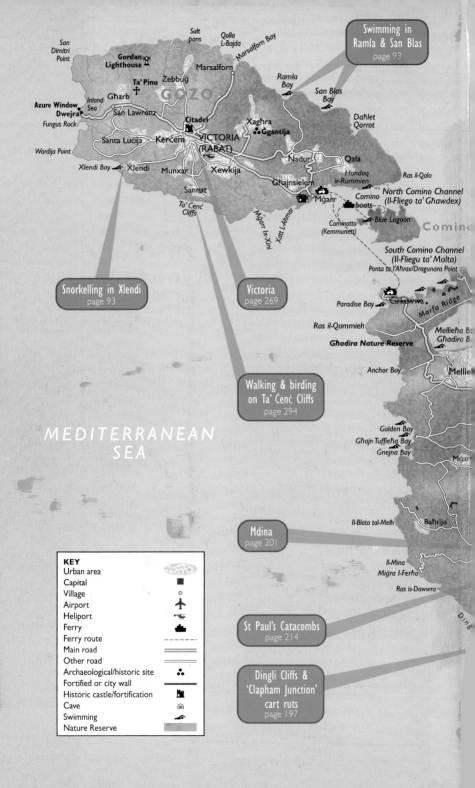

Swimming in
Ramla & San Blas
page 93

Snorkelling in Xlendi
page 93

Victoria
page 269

Walking & birding
on Ta' Ċenċ Cliffs
page 294

Mdina
page 201

St Paul's Catacombs
page 214

Dingli Cliffs &
'Clapham Junction'
cart ruts
page 197

MEDITERRANEAN
SEA

San
Dimitri
Point

Salt
pans

Qolla
L-Bajda

Marsalforn Bay

Gordan
Lighthouse

Żebbuġ

Marsalforn

Ramla
Bay

San Blas
Bay

Ta' Pinu

GOZO

Daħlet
Qorrot

Azure Window
Dwejra

Inland
Sea

Għarb

San Lawrenz

Citadel

Xagħra

Ggantija

Fungus Rock

Santa Luċija

Kerċem

VICTORIA
(RABAT)

Nadur

Qala

Wardija Point

Hondoq
ir-Rummien

Ras il-Qala

Xlendi Bay

Xlendi

Munxar

Xewkija

Għajnsielem

North Comino Channel
(Il-Fliego ta' Għawdex)

Sannat

Ta' Ċenċ
Cliffs

Mġarr Ix-Xini

Xatt L-Aħmar

Mġarr

Comino
boats

Cominotto
(Kemmunett)

Blue Lagoon

Comino

South Comino Channel
(Il-Fliegu ta' Malta)
Ponta ta' l'Aħrax/Dragunara Point

Paradise Bay

Ċirkewwa

Marfa Ridge

Ras il-Qammieħ

Mellieħa Ba
Għadira B

Għadira Nature Reserve

Mellie

Anchor Bay

Golden Bay

Għajn Tuffieħa Bay

Għejna Bay

Mġarr

Il-Blata tal-Melħ

Baħrija

Il-Mina
Miġra l-Ferħa

Ras is-Dawwra

Din g

KEY
Urban area
Capital
Village
Airport
Heliport
Ferry
Ferry route
Main road
Other road
Archaeological/historic site
Fortified or city wall
Historic castle/fortification
Cave
Swimming
Nature Reserve

N

Bradt

0 — 4km
0 — 2·5 miles

MEDITERRANEAN SEA

'um tal-Madonna

St Paul's Island

Qawra Point

St Paul's Bay Qawra
Bugibba
St Paul's Bay

-Simar
ature
eserve

Burmarrad

St George's Bay

bbiegh

Victoria Lines

Gharghur

Paceville

weira
Victoria Lines

Ghargur

St Julian's Bay

St Julian's
(San Giljan)

San
Gwann

Naxxar

Mosta

Sliema

National
Stadium

San Anton
Palace &
garden

Lija

Ta' Xbiex

Ta' Qali

MALTA

Birkirkara

Msida

VALLETTA

Grand
Harbour

Mtarfa

Mdina

Attard

Balzan

Santa
Venera

Pieta

Floriana

L-Isla Birgu

Rabat

St Paul's
Catacombs

Qormi
(San Gorg)

Hamrun

Bormla

Marsa

Zabbar

Dingli

Clapham
Junction
Cart Ruts

Zebbug

Paola

Hypogeum

Tarxien Temples

Marsaskala

Zonqor Point
Marsaskala Bay

Cliffs

Siggiewi

Luqa

Zejtun

St Thomas' Bay

Mqabba

Gudja

Ghaxaq

Kirkop

Marsaxlokk

Il-Hofra z-Zghira

**Mnajdra & Hagar
Qim Temples**

Orendi

Safi

Ghar Dalam

Zurrieq

Birzebbuga

Marsaxlokk
Bay

Delimara Point

**Blue
Grotto**

Wied
Iz-Zurrieq
(boats to Blue Grotto)

Malta
Freeport

Valletta
page 105

The Grand Harbour
page 138

Birgu
page 147

The Hypogeum
page 176

Temples of Mnajdra
& Hagar Qim
page 192

Malta
Don't
miss...

Snorkelling and diving
Malta's clear blue waters are ideal for snorkelling and diving – here at Għar Lapsi on the south coast
(TE) page 96

Neolithic temples and carvings
Aerial view of Mnajdra Temple
(I/FLPA) page 192

Medieval citadels
Gozo's Citadel dominates the surrounding landscape (V/CV) page 271

Gozo
Gozo is quieter and more relaxed than its larger neighbour – pictured here with sweeping views across to Comino (V) page 253

Valletta – Malta's fortified capital city
The bastion walls of Valletta by night with the arches of the Upper Barracca Gardens atop the fortifications (AT) page 105

above **Valletta's bastions/fortifications** (A/D) page 115

left & below left **St John's Co-Cathedral was the main church in Valletta — every inch of the interior is covered in gold, paint or marble** (V & JL) page 123

below right **The hallway in the Grand Master's Palace** (RT) page 127

above left & right A street scene in Valletta with traditional Maltese enclosed balconies (or *gallariji*) — the origins of these balconies remain a mystery (JL & DW) page 130

right The Lower Barracca Gardens offer good views of the Grand Harbour (SL/FLPA) page 138

below The imposing design of the Auberge de Castille testifies to the power of the Spanish and Portuguese Langue (V) page 117

above A traditional game, *boċċi* is a close relation of boules or bowls, but the Maltese version is played a little differently (V) page 292

below Horse racing is a popular spectator sport in Malta with similarities to Roman chariot racing (V/JE) page 33

AUTHOR

Juliet Rix has been a writer and journalist all her working life, in print, radio and television, and on the web. Freelance for most of the time, travel – for pleasure and for work – has played an important part in her life. She spent a couple of years as a BBC correspondent in southeast Asia, and has written on travel – as well as other things – for most of the UK's 'broadsheet' national newspapers. She lives in London with her husband and two sons.

AUTHOR'S STORY

When I mentioned to people that I was writing a book on Malta, most looked a bit blank: they associated Malta with package holidays and not much else. Some would come up with 'The Knights of Malta' or the 'Grand Harbour and World War II'. Only very few knew more. This is not to be critical of my friends and colleagues – a few years ago I was in exactly the same position. It was almost by chance that I discovered just how much this tiny nation really has to offer, and became a bit evangelical about it. So, when I was asked if I would write this book, I had to say yes.

It seems to me that Malta has been hiding its light under the bushel of mass tourism for too long. Malta certainly has sunshine and beautiful clear blue waters in which I love to swim; and Gozo is a great place for a relaxing holiday. But for the main island at least, its USP is surely its history – and prehistory – and the remarkable sites this has left behind.

My first trip to Malta was actually to write about Gozo. My family and I walked the high Ta' Ċenċ cliffs, soaked up the autumn sun and swam at an almost deserted, red sandy Ramla Beach. And we visited Ġgantija Temple – my introduction to one of the least-known and most intriguing aspects of Malta's past: the 'temple culture' that thrived here 5½ millennia ago and left us the earliest sophisticated stone buildings in the world, all now with UNESCO World Heritage status.

I did not get a chance to see any of the other temples on that trip. We had a mere half-day on the main island – a whirlwind press tour that did not include temples. In fact, our first impressions were not great as we drove past serried ranks of modern apartment blocks and hotels. But then we reached Valletta, Malta's tiny, fortified capital city surrounded on three sides by azure sea – a place of real historic charm. Across the Grand Harbour we saw Birgu, the Knights' first capital in Malta, and, in the centre of the island, the walled medieval citadel of Mdina. Historically, I realised, this tiny country punches well above its weight. I knew I would have to return.

And of course I have – criss-crossing the country exploring everything from underground tombs to towering cliffs, welcoming bays to forbidding fortifications, prehistoric temples to high-rise hotels, roadside kiosks to gourmet restaurants. This has only confirmed my view that Malta is seriously undersold by its image as a package-holiday island. I hope readers of this book will enjoy the sun and the sea (as I do) but will also have the pleasure of discovering something of this country's fascinating 7,000-year history.

First published May 2010

Bradt Travel Guides Ltd, 23 High Street, Chalfont St Peter, Bucks SL9 9QE, England
www.bradtguides.com
Published in the USA by The Globe Pequot Press Inc, 246 Goose Lane,
PO Box 480, Guilford, Connecticut 06475-0480

Text copyright © 2010 Juliet Rix
Maps copyright © 2010 Bradt Travel Guides Ltd
Illustrations copyright © 2010 Individual photographers and illustrators (see below)
Project Manager Anna Moores

British Library Cataloguing in Publication Data
A catalogue record for this book is available from the British Library
ISBN-13: 978 1 84162 312 2

Photographs Rupert Blackshaw (RB), Denis Cachia (DC), Chris Cachia Zammit (CCZ), Alex Casha (AC), Daniel Cilia (DC), Craig Durksen (CD), Tamsin Eyles (TE), Ted Geary/World Image (TG), Paul Lewis (PL), Gillian Lloyd (GL), Jorge Lomonaco (JL), Karin Müller (KM), Aron Tanti (AT), Rob Tye (RT), David Winter (DW). From Dreamstime (D): Alexvu (A/D), Leaf (L/D), Marpix26 (M/D), Matokmet (Ma/D), Nemo1024 (N/D), Szirtesi (S/D). From FLPA (FLPA): Robin Chittenden (RC/FLPA), ImageBroker (I/FLPA), ImageBroker/Sabine Lubenow (SL/FLPA), Dietmar Nill/Minden Pictures (DN/FLPA), Paul Sawer (PS/FLPA). From: Visitmalta.com (V): Guido Bissattini (V/GB), Jeremy Enness (V/JE), Gino Galea (V/GG), Peter de Ruiter (V/PR), Alexis Sofianopoulos (V/AS), Clive Vella (V/CV), Bruno Vetters (V/BV)
Front cover Valletta (V)
Back cover San Blas, Gozo (GL), A 5,000-year old porthole doorway in the main temple at Ħaġar Qim Temple (V)
Title page Eye of Osiris on a *luzzu* (V/AS), *Gardjola* on Senglea Point (TG), Maltese bus (PL)
In-text photos Maltese cross (V), *gallarija* (V/Camilla Morandi)

Maps Malcolm Barnes; based on source material under licence from © RMF Publishing and Surveys Ltd (Malta). Temple plans based on site plans from Heritage Malta (all labelling is the author's own).
Illustrations Carole Vincer

Typeset from the author's disc by Wakewing, High Wycombe
Printed and bound in Malta by Gutenberg Press Ltd

Acknowledgements

So many people have helped with this book and I would like to thank them all! Specifically, it could not have happened without the support of the Malta Tourism Authority (MTA). Their London office, particularly Claude Zammit Trevisan, has been extremely helpful, and in Malta Rosanne Sciberras, Maryanne Portanier, Dominic Micallef and Angela Said welcomed me and fielded questions and changes of plan with great equanimity.

Several members of staff at Heritage Malta have given invaluably of their precious time including Suzannah Depasquale and David Cardona of the department of Phoenician, Roman and Medieval Sites, Sharon Sultana, Curator of the Museum of Archaeology and, in Gozo, Nicoline Sagona. Very special thanks go to Dr Reuben Grima, Senior Curator of Prehistoric Sites, who went well beyond the call of duty to ensure that my material on the temples was accurate and up to date (if any inaccuracies remain, they are mine alone!). On this topic I also owe a great debt to Dr David Trump for his excellent book on Malta's temples.

Malta guide, Vince DeBono, introduced me to much of the history of his country, and checked almost all the copy before it went to press. I am very grateful.

Dr Stephen Spiteri, world expert on Malta's fortifications, was kind enough to both brief me at the start and check through the relevant parts of the book when written (again, he bears no responsibility for any errors). Joseph Mizzi of Midsea Books provided me with excellent reading material as well as general advice. Many others took time to answer my questions, including Lorenzo Zahra of the Curia of Malta, Jennifer Wong of the British High Commission, nature guide Annalise Falzon, Petra Bianchi, Catherine Roe, Jay and Alan Jones of Wirt Għawdex, historian Charles Galea Scannura, and Emmanuel Magro Conti, Curator of Malta's Maritime and Military Collections and the staff at Din L'Art Ħelwa.

On the difficult issue of birds and hunting, I am most grateful to both BirdLife Malta, particularly Geoffrey Saliba who was unerring in his careful provision of information (and evidence) and Ray Vella who wrote the text on which birds to see when, and to Francis Albani, secretary to the government's ORNIS advisory committee on the protection of wild birds, hunting and trapping.

Back in the UK, I owe many thanks to Juliet Standing and Wendy Rix for reading the manuscript and, of course, to the Bradt team who have handled everything with perfect good humour and an apparently genuine belief that, even with the very tight turnaround we had to work with, all would come right in the end. Many thanks especially to Hilary Bradt and Adrian Phillips for believing I could write this book in the first place; Daniel Austin for sweet wrapper names that made me laugh (and photo editing) and to Adrian (again) and Anna Moores for actually turning a load of electronic files into a book! And finally, many thanks to my husband Rod and sons Daniel and Luke who put up with my absences (both while I was in Malta and while deep in the computer) and helped with research by contributing their own perspectives on Malta.

Contents

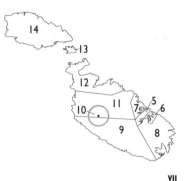

NOTE ABOUT MAPS

Some maps use grid lines to allow easy location of sites. Map grid references are listed in square brackets after listings in the text, with page number followed by grid number, eg: [156 C3].

LIST OF MAPS

Introduction

Malta offers a wonderful combination of sunshine holiday and fascinating sightseeing. Into an area smaller than the Isle of Wight it packs 7,000 years of history – and prehistory. The earliest of its Neolithic temples – little known beyond its shores – are 2,000 years older than Mycenae, 1,000 years older than the Great Pyramids and 500 years older than the famous standing stones at Stonehenge. They all have UNESCO World Heritage status, as does the Ħal Saflieni Hypogeum, an extraordinary underground tomb complex, cut from solid rock, that echoes the architecture of the above-ground temples. And this is just the beginning of the story.

Malta's position in the middle of the Mediterranean and its perfect natural harbours have meant that anyone wishing to control or trade in the Mediterranean has needed access to this country. Almost every major European power in history (and some minor ones) have occupied these islands or tried very hard to do so. Each has left its mark on Malta's landscape and culture. So as well as megalithic temples, carved altars and dramatic underground rooms, Malta has colourful boats adorned with the 'Phoenician' eye of Osiris, Roman mosaics and catacombs, and a still-inhabited medieval walled town of narrow lanes and heavy fortifications.

In the midst of the faded elegance of today's diminutive capital, Valletta, is hidden the opulent St John's Co-Cathedral and many more examples of the Baroque art and architecture of the Knights of St John – the 'Knights of Malta' – who ruled these islands from 1530 to 1798. They were followed (after a brief French occupation) by the British. There are still red letter boxes and phone booths all over Malta, and in Valletta, at noon each day, music of the Band of the Royal Marines is played and a cannon fired beneath a public garden overlooking the vast expanse of the Grand Harbour.

This impressive harbour was the centre of Malta's two famous sieges, both of them critical to the future of Europe: the Great Siege of 1565 when the Ottoman Turks very nearly took the island, and that of 1940–43 when Hitler and Mussolini tried to bomb and starve Malta into submission. The fortitude of the Maltese in holding out against the Axis powers was rewarded by King George VI with Britain's highest award for civilian bravery, the George Cross – the only one ever to be awarded to an entire nation.

This tiny country has absorbed so many influences, and yet Malta is very much Maltese. Ninety-seven per cent of the population was born here and although English is widely spoken, Maltese (or Malti) remains the mother tongue of most of the population. The country has its own cuisine and its own culture. The people of Gozo, Malta's smaller island, pride themselves on being different from the inhabitants of the main island – and Gozo does indeed have its own character.

Taking the 25-minute ferry from Malta to Gozo is like leaving the city for the countryside. Much less built up than its larger neighbour, Gozo has – besides a couple of lovely sandy beaches – rugged coastal landscape described by a visiting

Edward Lear as 'pomskizillious and gromphiberous'. It is thought by some to be the real Calypso's isle, where Homer's Odysseus (Ulysses) remains spellbound by the loving sea nymph for seven years. Gozo is the place to relax.

Malta is welcoming to visitors and some 1.2 million come here each year (over a third of them from the UK). Yet the package-holiday image Malta has lived with – and indeed promoted – for the last three decades undersells this remarkable little country. Malta has great weather (with some 300 days of sunshine a year) and plenty of holiday facilities. There are excellent restaurants, and lots of outdoor activities to enjoy – swimming, snorkelling, diving, boating (of various kinds), walking, sports and spas. But there is also so much that is unique to Malta that has often been overlooked.

This is beginning to change. The government and Malta Tourism Authority seem to have decided to stop hiding their light under a bushel and have begun to promote cultural tourism. UNESCO is helping to preserve the temples and the government is beginning to make them more accessible and to provide (previously sorely lacking) visitor information. A few, mostly British, cognoscenti have long known the hidden gem that is the real Malta, but the time is long overdue for the rest of us to get a look in.

FEEDBACK REQUEST

While the contents of this book are as accurate a reflection as possible of what I found at the time of research, and I have tried to anticipate some developments expected over the next couple of years, other things will certainly change. Hotels and restaurants get better or worse, places open and close, prices go up (and occasionally down), web addresses and phone numbers change. So, if you do find anything that is different from my description (in the text or on the maps), or there is anything you'd like to add, do please let us know. A quick note or email would be great and will ensure that the next edition of the guide includes the necessary updates. Many thanks and enjoy Malta!

Write to: Bradt Travel Guides, 23 High Street, Chalfont St Peter, Bucks SL9 9QE, England; e info@bradtguides.com; ✆ 01753 893444; www.bradtguides.com.

Part One

GENERAL INFORMATION

MALTA AT A GLANCE

Location In the middle of the Mediterranean, 93km south of Sicily, 288km east of Tunisia, 355km north of Libya and 815km west of Crete.

Islands Three inhabited islands: Malta, Gozo and Comino. Three tiny uninhabited islands: Cominotto, Filfla and St Paul's Island, plus the semi-derelict Manoel Island in Marsamxett Harbour due for redevelopment.

Size Total area 316km² with 253km of coastline. Malta 30km (SE–NW) x 11km (SW–NE), area 245.7km²; Gozo 14km x 5km, area 67.1km²; Comino 2.5km x 1.5km, area 2.8km².

Population 410,000 (of which Gozo 31,000, Comino 4).

Status Independent republic. Member of the European Union, the Commonwealth and the United Nations.

Currency Euro

Exchange rate €1 = US$1.4, €1 = £0.90

Climate Mediterranean island – hot dry summers and mild damp winters with chilly winds.

Official languages Maltese and English

Capital Valletta

Religion Roman Catholic (98%)

Time GMT + 2 hours in summer (from the last Sunday in March until the Saturday before the last Sunday in October), otherwise GMT + 1 hour. Always UK + 1 hour.

Economy 35% of GDP from tourism. Manufacturing strong in electronics and pharmaceuticals.

GDP US$23,200 per capita (mid-range for an EU country)

National airline Air Malta

Electricity 230–240V, 50Hz, with British-style 3 square-pin plugs (British visitors don't need adapters).

Telephone codes Into Malta +356, out of Malta 00. Within Malta, no area codes just eight digits.

Weights and measures Mostly metric

Flag Half red (right side), half white, with the George Cross in the top left-hand corner. The cross was added in the 1940s after it was awarded to Malta by George VI for gallantry in World War II (see page 17).

National anthem L'Innu Malti ('The Maltese Hymn') Lil Din L-Art Ħelwa ('To The Sweet Land'), music by Dr Robert Samut, words by Maltese national poet Dun Karm Psaila.

National bird Il-Merrill, the blue rock thrush (Monticola solitariu)

National tree Gharghar/sandarac gum (siġra ta' l-għargħar) (Tetraclinis articulata) – a cypress tree

National sports Football, water polo

Public holidays 1 January (New Year's Day), 10 February (St Paul's Shipwreck), 19 March (St Joseph), 31 March (Freedom Day), Good Friday, 1 May (Workers' Day), 7 June (Sette Giugno), 29 June (St Peter and St Paul), 15 August (the Assumption), 8 September (Victory Day), 21 September (Independence Day), 8 December (the Immaculate Conception), 13 December (Republic Day), 25 December (Christmas Day).

History

OVERVIEW

Malta has had so many masters in its 7,000-year history that it can be useful to have a crib sheet of roughly who was in charge when.

Għar Dalam phase	5000–4500BC
Pre-temple Neolithic	4500–4100BC
Temple culture	4100–2500BC
(Temple building)	3600–2500BC
Bronze Age	2500–8th century BC
Phoenician	8th–6th century BC
Carthaginian/Punic	6th century–218BC
Romans	218BC–AD535
Late Roman/Byzantine	535–870
Arab	870–1090
Norman	1090–1194
Hohenstaufen	1194–1268
Angevin	1268–1284
Aragonese	1284–1412
Castillian	1412–1530
Knights of St John	1530–1798
Napoleonic	1798–1800
British	1800–1964
Independent Malta	1964–present
Republican Malta	1974–present

THE EARLIEST SETTLERS: 5000–4100BC

Divided by pottery types into Għar Dalam (5000–4300BC), Grey Skorba (4500–4400BC) and Red Skorba (4400–4100BC).

The first traces of humanity on Malta have been dated to around 5000BC. We know little about these people except that they were settled farmers who almost certainly came from Sicily, just 93km across the sea. On a clear day, Malta can be seen from the south coast of Sicily, so early sailors knew where they were heading and could get there in a day. They seem to have brought livestock with them and initially set up home in caves including Għar Dalam, meaning 'Cave of Darkness' (page 183), which gives the earliest period of Maltese habitation its name.

Later, villages of oval mud-brick houses were built. A few such huts have been excavated next to the prehistoric temples at Skorba, hence the name of the next prehistoric periods. We know that contact with the outside world was maintained because, as well as tools made from local materials, these farmers had tools of

3

obsidian (a volcanic glass whose exact source can be identified) and flint which were certainly imported, probably via Sicily.

TEMPLE PERIOD: 4100–2500BC

Pottery phases: Żebbuġ (4100–3700BC), Mġarr (3800–3600BC); Temple-building period: Ġgantija phase (3600–3200BC), Saflieni (3300–3000BC), Tarxien phase (3150–2500BC).

In 3600BC the people of Malta seem to have started, quite suddenly, to construct large megalithic stone buildings – known to us as the temples. There is no evidence of earlier simpler stone buildings, although there are rock-cut tombs (including at Xemxija, see page 243) with a lobed pattern some see as a possible forerunner to the design of the temples. The temple builders are not thought to have been new arrivals on the islands. They were probably descended from the same Neolithic people that lived in Għar Dalam. By 4100BC, they had developed several cultural practices – the building of rock-cut tombs and a certain style of pottery – that continued into the temple building phase. Hence the start of the temple culture is dated to 4100BC, even though no temples appear before 3600BC.

The temple-building community lived in mud-brick houses like their predecessors. Only their main community buildings – or temples – were stone. They continued to farm and lived without apparent conflict: their settlements show no concern for defence. Theirs seems to have been a relatively egalitarian society, too, without monarchs and based more on co-operation than coercion. They had no written language and crucially used no metal. Their stone-working and building skills, however, were far beyond anything known at the time anywhere in the world, and the design seems neither to have been learnt from elsewhere nor copied by others.

CONTACT VERSUS ISOLATION Until recently it was thought that the temples were unique because the people that built them had become isolated from the outside world, but archaeological evidence suggests otherwise. The temple people had imported alabaster and red ochre as well as obsidian from Lipari and Pantelleria (volcanic islands near Sicily). And their greenstone axe-shaped pendants came from various locations on the Italian peninsula.

The development of distinct cultures seems to have been a trend across the Mediterranean region at this time, a combination perhaps of the deliberate development of cultural identity and the fact that different peoples had different resources available to them. Malta had vast deposits of limestone – so its people built megalithic limestone buildings.

More than 30 temple sites have been identified, some with more than one temple, as well as the remarkable underground tomb complex, the Ħal Saflieni Hypogeum (page 176) – a kind of temple of the dead. A second hypogeum has recently been uncovered at Xagħra on Gozo (page 278) suggesting there may be others yet to be found.

DATING THE TEMPLES Until the advent of carbon dating it was assumed that these temples were inspired by such famous centres of megalithic architecture as Mycenae and Knossos. It was only with the arrival of the more accurate chemical dating that it was revealed that the Maltese temples were far earlier. The earliest of them (including Ġgantija on Gozo and the oldest temple at Mnajdra) were built some 2,000 years before Mycenae, nearly a millennium before the Egyptian pyramids and 500 years before the famous stone circle at Stonehenge.

This dating made Malta's temples the oldest stone buildings in the world, until the mid-1990s when older stone structures were found in Gobekli Tepe in southeastern Turkey. Malta's temples are vastly more complex and remain far and away the most sophisticated stone buildings of their time. By the time the Great Pyramid at Giza was completed, temple building on Malta, and even the use of the existing temples, had – abruptly and mysteriously – stopped.

BUILDING THE TEMPLES The temples were built of vast lumps of stone, megaliths of up to 50 tons in weight. The largest surviving block is at Ggantija, but there are huge stones of 20 tons or so at several sites. How they were moved has always been open to question. The 17th-century explanation was that the temples were created by a community of giants (obvious really!).

The reality is probably that the stone was found already broken into large chunks, or was cracked along natural fault lines using wedges. Some believe that the blocks were then transported by rolling them along on spherical stones about 30cm in diameter like those found in or just outside several of the temples. Others doubt these stone spheres, made of the same material as the megaliths, could have withstood the weight. We can only presume that some combination of sledges, rollers, ramps and levers was used – and, of course, a great deal of manpower, and perhaps animal power.

SOCIETY The society that built these temples must have been quite sophisticated. Several models and 'sketches' (on stone) have been identified as possible blueprints for the temples – leading to speculation about prehistoric architects. Certainly a degree of planning would have been needed, along with considerable teamwork, to create buildings of this size and complexity. And the craftsmanship of these people is remarkable. They had smart, decorated furniture and produced numerous stone statues and carvings for the temples (best seen in the National Museum of Archaeology in Valletta, page 121). They adorned the temples with spiral patterns as well as images of animals and plants, and the iconic 'Fat Ladies'. These rotund figures (some of which may not in fact be female) range in size from a few centimetres to over 2m tall, their vast hips and behinds often covered in pleated skirts, their short conical legs peeping out below. The most artistically impressive example is the small clay figurine known as the 'Sleeping Lady', found at the Hal Saflieni Hypogeum. She lies on a neat couch and was made at about the time that Stonehenge was begun.

It has been estimated that the prehistoric Maltese islands could have supported a population of up to 10,000, although 6,000–7,000 is considered more likely. Even so, this is a sufficient number of people to provide plenty of contributors to temple building. There is no suggestion of slave labour. More likely is a seasonal local labour force working outside harvest times, perhaps religiously motivated.

HOW WERE THE TEMPLES USED? Nobody really knows. The large forecourts typical of the temples may have acted as a communal gathering place and there is some evidence for ritual activity: equipment for animal sacrifice, holes into which libations (liquid offerings to the underworld) might have been poured, and the constant reappearance of statues of similar figures (the 'Fat Ladies') perhaps representing a deity or at least having some kind of cult status. What appear to be stone phalluses are also common suggesting a possible fertility cult. There is also evidence of secular activity such as grinding corn. We can only make informed guesses. The word 'temple' is applied to the buildings as much because of the way in which monumental buildings were used elsewhere in the world (and at later dates) as because of direct evidence from Malta.

THE END Sometime around 2500BC, all evidence of the temple culture comes to an abrupt end. Not only were no more temples built, but the existing ones fell into disrepair. It seems that the whole temple culture collapsed. Why this happened remains a mystery. Many theories have been advanced from invasion to priestly rivalry (but there is no evidence of conflict), disease (but it is rare for even the most vicious disease to kill off an entire population) to drought or famine, perhaps brought on by over-use of the scarce agricultural land. All that is certain is that this was the end of the society that left us some of the earliest complex stone buildings in the world.

For more on the temples, key sites and a guide to interpreting the sites see *Chapter 4, page 78*. The best book on this period is *Malta: Prehistory and Temples* by Dr David Trump (*Midsea Books; www.midseabooks.com; €25*). There are also a new series of podcasts about the temples available to download free from www.visitmalta.com/podcasts and an excellent website with lots of photos at http://web.infinito.it/utenti/m/malta_mega_temples/indxfram.html.

BRONZE AGE: 2500–circa 8BC

Tarxien Cemetery Phase 2400–1500BC and Borġ In-Nadur 1500–700BC.

The culture that dominated Malta for the next millennium was completely different from that of the Temple people. This has led to the suggestion that the islands may even have been abandoned for a period before the newcomers arrived.

TARXIEN CEMETERY PEOPLE The new people did not bury their dead as the Temple people had but cremated them, storing the ashes in pottery bowls or urns, sometimes with personal items including coloured beads. The urns were kept, perhaps in the islands' various dolmens of this period (structures consisting of a large horizontal stone on a couple of vertical slabs), and certainly at the Tarxien temple complex (built between 3600–2500BC, see page 172) which was reused in the Bronze Age as a crematorium. Most of the archaeological evidence for this time derives from this site so it has given the period its name.

The so-called Tarxien Cemetery People also brought metal to Malta for the first time. They used simple tools and weapons made of copper. They seem to have lived in mud-hut villages though their exact form is unclear. Where they came from remains unknown. Their culture does not accurately match that known anywhere else in the region and cremation has robbed us of much of the physical anthropological evidence.

BORĠ IN-NADUR PHASE By about 1500BC the picture has changed again. The islands are by now more heavily populated, with some well-defended cliff-top settlements of several hundred people. Remnants of one of these has survived at Borġ In-Nadur (page 185), which gives its name to the period. It is not clear who these communities were defending themselves from, but it could have been from each other.

They seem to have produced grain in considerable quantity and fished around Marsaxlokk Bay, still a centre of fishing today. They had looms for weaving and small quantities of imported bronze, possibly traded for textiles or grain. Malta certainly had contact with other nations. Maltese-style pottery has been found in Sicilian tombs of this period and there is one small but crucial piece of evidence for contact with cultures further across the Mediterranean – a single shard of Mycenaean pottery dated to about 1300BC.

The best book on this period is *Malta: Prehistory and Temples* by Dr David Trump; see above for details.

PHOENICIANS AND CARTHAGINIANS: circa 8–218BC

Phoenician 8th–6th century BC, Punic/Carthaginian 6th century–218BC.

The Phoenicians (who came from the land of Canaan in modern-day Lebanon) were the great seafaring traders of the ancient world. Given Malta's position in the middle of the Mediterranean and its sheltered natural harbours it is hardly surprising that Phoenicians settled in Malta sometime around the 8th century BC, and may have visited considerably earlier. These ancient mariners stayed on the islands for over two centuries and the name Malta may come from the Phoenician *malat* meaning 'refuge' (though others source it to the Greek word *melita* meaning 'honey', which the island has long produced). Recent research has shown that some of the Maltese population still have a genetic marker linking them to the Phoenicians, and Malta's colourful fishing boats (which still carry the protective eye of Osiris on their bows) owe much to Phoenician trading vessels (see the boats in Marsaxlokk Harbour, page 180).

The Phoenicians brought the skill of making pottery on a wheel, and reintroduced the practice of burying the dead in rock-cut tombs (a practice that had disappeared through the Bronze Age). They ended Malta's relative isolation — and independence of culture – turning it into an outpost of the wider Mediterranean region, a position confirmed by the rise of the Phoenicians' prosperous colony on the Bay of Tunis, the city-state of Carthage.

The Carthaginians created Malta's first towns, a sophisticated civil administration and the islands' own coinage (some of their coins are in the Mdina Cathedral Museum, see page 207). They planted vineyards and olive groves and stationed a garrison of some 2,000 men on the islands. They constructed temporal and sacred buildings of which, unfortunately, little remains other than a 5m-tall tower in a private garden in the village of Żurrieq (not open to the public). The Carthaginians also seem to have left behind two small carved pillars with dedications to the god Melqart written in both Phoenician and Greek, which in modern times helped in the decoding of the Phoenician alphabet. (one is now in the National Museum of Archaeology, see page 121, the other in the Louvre).

The rise of Rome inevitably brought conflict with the Carthaginians and by 264BC they were at war. There seems little doubt that Malta's harbours would have been used by the Carthaginian quinquiremes (boats with five banks of oars) for rest and repair as the two powers battled it out across the Mediterranean. Malta was raided and pillaged by Rome but by the end of the First Punic War (264–241BC), the islands remained a Carthaginian colony. During the Second Punic War (218–201BC), however, Malta fell to the Romans.

The best book on this period is *Malta: Phoenician, Punic and Roman* by Anthony Bonanno (*Midsea Books; www.midseabooks.com; €25*).

ROMANS AND BYZANTINES: 218BC–AD870

Romans 218BC–AD535, Late Roman/Byzantine AD535–870.

Under the Romans, Malta was once again linked with Sicily as a *municipium* (a municipality with a fair degree of self-government) sharing the Italian island's Roman governor. Roman villas sprang up across Malta and Gozo (the well-preserved mosaic floor of one can still be seen in the Roman Domus in Rabat, page 211). Vineyards and olive groves were tended, high-quality cloth produced and defences built around the main towns, including the largest, Melita. This stood on the hilltop that is now Mdina and spread to perhaps three times the size of the later medieval walled town. With a not unusual combination of Roman and local (Carthaginian) ways of life, the islands seem to have flourished.

In 73BC **Gaius Verres** became governor of Sicily, and therefore Malta, and began a two-year reign of corruption and plunder. Malta and Sicily got together and persuaded **Cicero**, one of Rome's greatest orators, to prosecute Verres. Cicero apparently stayed in Mdina while he wrote his extensive indictment of the corrupt governor. At his trial Verres quickly capitulated, but Cicero went on to publish his Verrines which tell us that Verres – without ever going to Malta – had amassed a considerable collection of Maltese booty including ivory from a temple to the goddess Juno, and large quantities of fine textiles.

Cicero is not the only Classical writer to mention Malta. Homer's Ogygia where **Odysseus** (Ulysses) spends seven years under the spell of the sea nymph Calypso has been identified as Gozo and Ovid writes of Malta ('Melite' to him) as 'the fruitful isle'. The Maltese islanders' favourite story from Roman times, however, is that of the shipwreck of **St Paul** in AD60.

Paul was a prisoner on his way to stand trial before the Emperor Nero in Rome when his ship hit the rocks of Melite (Malta). Whilst warming himself by a bonfire after his ordeal, he was bitten by a viper and miraculously showed no ill effects and it is said that he thus rid the islands of poisonous snakes. Malta certainly has no poisonous snakes, but the less pious amongst the population claim that the venom removed from the reptiles reappeared in the tongues of the nation's women (although Maltese men can be pretty fork-tongued too when they want to be!).

In his three months on the island, St Paul is meant to have converted the then governor Publius (later St Publius) to Christianity. Some say the rest of the population followed and Publius became the first bishop of Malta. This still-devout Roman Catholic country likes the idea that it was one of the first Christian communities, but there is no archaeological or written evidence of Christianity on the islands before the 4th century AD. For the Bible story of St Paul's shipwreck, see page 138.

See *Chapter 4* for more on this period, page 82. The best book is *Malta: Phoenician, Punic and Roman* by Anthony Bonanno (see above for details).

DIVIDED EMPIRE In AD345 the Roman Empire was divided into east and west. Malta seems to have fallen into the eastern half. The period between this division and AD535 when Malta was clearly incorporated into the Byzantine Empire is a dark age in terms of Maltese historical evidence. During the 5th century, Malta may, like Sicily, have been occupied for a while by the Germanic Vandals, who had moved south through France and Spain to North Africa and were active in the Mediterranean (and yes, their behaviour gave us the word 'vandal'), and later by the Ostrogoths, the eastern Goths from the Black Sea area who went on to rule Italy.

There is some evidence that Byzantine Emperor Justinian's top general, Belisarius stopped off in Malta in AD533 on his way to take North Africa back from the Vandals, and again in AD535 *en route* to deal with the Ostrogoths in Sicily. After this both Sicily and Malta were directly incorporated into Justinian's empire.

CATACOMBS There may be little left on paper from the later Roman and Byzantine period but there is a remarkable legacy in stone, almost all of it religious (mainly Christian) underground tomb complexes ranging from large catacombs (St Paul's and St Agatha's, see pages 214–16) to small hypogea of a few individual burial chambers (such as Bingemma, see page 230).

THE ARABS: 870–1090

The rise of Islam through the 8th century saw the Arabs conquer large parts of Africa, Asia and Europe. Malta was quite a late acquisition, taken in AD870. Interestingly, a plaque found in the Aghlabad Arab port of Sousse (in modern-day Tunisia) states that marble columns and dressed stones from Malta were shipped from the islands as booty after the invasion, which may help explain the lack of above-ground material remains from Malta's Roman and Byzantine periods.

Malta was once again ruled from Sicily, by an emir, with a military/naval governor stationed locally on the site of what is now Fort St Angelo (see page 154). The Arabs retained the Roman capital, but instead of Melite, called it Mdina (meaning 'the fortress' in Arabic) and shrank its centre into the smaller, more defensible confines we see today. Rabat (meaning 'suburb') was left outside the walls.

There are few physical remains from this time, apart from some Arab tombstones (see *Roman Domus*, page 211 and *Gozo Archaeological Museum,* page 274). There is an undoubted cultural legacy, however, as most of Malta's place names (other than the names for Malta and Gozo themselves) are Arabic, as are many surnames.

MEDIEVAL MALTA: 1090–1530

In 1091 Count Roger of Normandy invaded Malta and took over the islands. He seems to have had a very light touch, however, and Arab Muslim culture continued to predominate until 1127 when the count's son, Roger II (King of Sicily 1130–54), reconquered Malta and imposed an active European Christian administration. Trade (including burgeoning exports of cotton) began to shift from North Africa to Europe, particularly Genoa, and there is evidence of more Christians on the islands. Yet many Muslims remained and there appears to have been peaceful co-existence until the mid-13th century when the Muslim community seems to disappear.

By this time Malta was part of the Holy Roman Empire under Hohenstaufen Emperor Frederick II (who inherited it along with the throne of Sicily from his mother Constance, daughter of Roger II). For the next 300 years, Malta was a European medieval Christian society (with a small but economically active Jewish population until Ferdinand of Aragon and Isabella of Castile expelled the Jews from all their territories in 1492). Most people worked the land, rearing animals and growing crops – the main cash crop being cotton, mostly exported through Sicily.

Local government was run from Mdina by the Università, a council dominated by a few Maltese noble families, and mostly kept in check by whichever overlord happened to be in charge at the time. As a minor part of the Kingdom of Sicily, the Maltese islands were passed around the royal houses of Europe – Hohenstaufen, Angevin, Aragon and Castile – and, worse, these royal families repeatedly gave or rented Malta to a variety of nobles, despite repeated promises to the Maltese that they would never do so again.

In September 1429, Malta was invaded by a large Muslim force sent by Hafsid, ruler of Tunis. One account describes 70 ships and 18,000 fighting men. Mdina was besieged and may only have been saved by the invaders' fear of seasonal storms. But the Arabs did not leave empty handed. Some 3,000 Maltese were taken into slavery, perhaps 30% of the island's population. This was a taste of things to come.

By the early 16th century, the Spanish had gained control over most of southern Europe and Malta was part of the dominion of the Holy Roman Emperor Charles V. Once again, in 1530, he gave it away – to the Order of St John of Jerusalem (the Hospitallers). This time the deal stuck and opened a new and vital chapter in Malta's history.

The most comprehensive book on this period is *Malta: the Medieval Millennium* by Charles Dalli (*Midsea Books; www.midseabooks.com; €25*).

THE KNIGHTS OF MALTA: 1530-1798

After losing their base in Rhodes in 1522–3 to the Ottoman Turks under Sultan Suleiman the Magnificent, the Hospitaller Knights of St John were homeless. Founded in about 1070, probably by Italian merchants from Amalfi, the Hospitallers were set up, as their name suggests, to care for the sick and give shelter to the poor amongst Christian pilgrims to Jerusalem. At first they did this with permission from the Egyptian caliph and then, after the first crusade had taken Jerusalem (1099), under the Christian patriarch based in the Church of the Holy Sepulchre.

In 1113 Pope Paschal II (1099–1118) issued a papal bull (which is still in the National Library of Malta in Valletta, see page 127) making the Hospitallers an Order of the Church under direct papal protection and control, but with the right to elect their own master. It is shortly after this that the Order begins its military engagement with the Muslims, adding the physical protection of Christian pilgrims to its remit, and soon also the protection of Christian territory.

Those joining the order were obliged to take vows of chastity, obedience and poverty (often giving their property to the Order). As monks and priests they were not allowed to shed blood, but the papacy found a way round this by creating a new class of Knight – or warrior monk – who took the religious vows but was not allowed to take Mass. These knights were remarkably successful in their opposition to the Muslims and whilst the order continued to run hospitals, its primary purpose was soon military. The warrior knights became its undisputed leaders, the grand master always elected from within their ranks.

The renown of the order grew, as did its wealth as donations of money and land came in from across Europe. But when the Muslims retook the Holy Land in 1291, the Hospitallers were obliged to leave. By 1309 they had taken the island of Rhodes (keeping close to the East) and here they remained, built and prospered for 200 years. Surrounded by water, they developed into a formidable naval force and harried the Muslims by sea as well as by land. Needless to say, this did not best please the Ottoman Turks. Twice the Turks besieged Rhodes. The first time the Knights held out, but in 1522 the invaders took the island. After a six-month siege Grand Master Fra Philippe Villiers de L'Isle Adam was forced to seek a truce and Suleiman agreed to allow the Knights to leave. It was eight years before they were once again settled – this time in Malta.

The first contact with Malta came in 1524, when a commission of the Order's *uomi saggi* (wise men) was sent to Malta to report on its suitability as a possible new headquarters. They were not impressed, reporting that the island was barren, with insufficient drinking water for its 12,000 inhabitants, poorly defended and with the one town (Mdina) in a dilapidated condition. It was also, however, an island at the eastern end of Europe and had excellent harbours. More to the point, there was nothing better on offer. So in 1530 – with agreement to pay a symbolic annual tribute of a Maltese falcon – the Knights took control of Malta. Initially, this certainly didn't please all Mdina's noble families, but the Knights brought wealth, organisation and protection from pirates and Turks, and put Malta back on the map of Europe.

The Order's first priority was to strengthen the islands' defences particularly at Birgu (now Vittoriosa) on the south side of the Grand Harbour which they made their first capital. Here they built their *auberges* (usually translated as hostels, but more akin to university colleges) where members of the Order lived and worked in communities of their own language. Each of the eight *langues* (literally, 'tongues') was designated certain jobs and areas to defend. A hospital (Sacra Infermeria) was built, the Knights settled in and the Maltese became used to their presence.

Almost from the start there was a desire on the part of the Knights to strengthen defences by building on Mount Sciberras, the rocky peninsula facing Birgu on the other side of the Grand Harbour (where Valletta now stands), but it seems there wasn't the money. The Order's finances were not helped by Henry VIII appropriating the possessions of the English Langue in 1540 as part of his break with Rome.

The Order of St John and the Turks continued to confront each other. The Knights' galleys harassed Turkish ships across the Mediterranean and the Ottomans made increasingly frequent raids on Malta and Gozo. In 1551 the most successful and feared corsair, Dragut (or Turgut) Reis, attacked Malta. Driven back, he cut his losses and led a devastating raid on Gozo taking most of its able-bodied population into slavery. This made the Knights all too aware that a larger force might follow. A new fort, Fort St Elmo, was rapidly built on Mount Sciberras to provide cross-fire with Birgu's Fort St Angelo but there was neither the time nor the resources to do much more.

THE GREAT SIEGE OF 1565 In May 1565 the Knights' old enemy, Suleiman the Magnificent, now in his seventies, sent a force of some 28,000 men in more than 180 ships to invade Malta. His intention was to oust the Knights from Malta as he

THE GRAND MASTERS OF MALTA (AND THEIR *LANGUES*)

1521–34	Philippe Villiers de L'Isle Adam (France)
1534–35	Pierino del Ponte (Italy)
1535–36	Didier de Saint Jaille (Provence)
1536–53	Juan de Homedes (Aragon)
1553–57	Claude de la Sengle (France)
1557–68	Jean Parisot de Valette (or Jean de Valette de Parisot) (Provence)
1568–72	Pietro del Monte (Italy)
1572–81	Jean L'Evêque de la Cassière (Auvergne)
1581–95	Hugues Loubenx de Verdale (Provence)
1595–1601	Martin Garzes (Aragon)
1601–22	Alof de Wignacourt (France)
1622–23	Luis Mendez de Vasconcellos (Castile)
1623–36	Antoine de Paule (Provence)
1636–57	Jean Paul de Lascaris Castellar (Provence)
1657–60	Martin de Redin (Aragon)
1660	Annet de Clermont de Chattes Gessan (Auvergne)
1660–63	Rafael Cotoner (Aragon)
1663–80	Nicolas Cotoner (Aragon)
1680–90	Gregorio Carafa (Italy)
1690–97	Adrien de Wignacourt (France)
1697–1720	Ramon Perellos y Roccaful (Aragon)
1720–22	Marc Antonio Zondadari (Italy)
1722–36	Antonio Manoel de Vilhena (Castile)
1736–41	Ramon Despuig (Aragon)
1741–73	Manoel Pinto de Fonseca (Castile)
1773–75	Francisco Ximenes de Texada (Aragon)
1775–97	Emmanuel de Rohan Polduc (France)
1797–1805	Ferdinand von Hompesch (German) – in Malta until 1798

had from Rhodes, secure the Mediterranean for Muslim shipping and push back the borders of Christendom.

His soldiers were led by one of his best generals, Mustapha Pasha, the fleet by Admiral Piali, and Dragut Reis – with yet more ships and perhaps another 10,000 to 12,000 men – was to join them as soon as he could get there from Tripoli. The defenders numbered no more than 9,000 spread across Malta and Gozo. In the harbour area Grand Master Jean Parisot de Valette had under his command some 500 knights, 1,100 soldiers (400 of them mercenaries) and about 3,000 Maltese militiamen. He was heavily outnumbered and as soon as the invasion began, he sent word to Sicily requesting help.

The Turks landed first at Marsaxlokk Harbour. The men of St John went to meet them but were overwhelmed by the size of the Turkish force. The invaders' target was Birgu, the Knights' capital, so the colourful armoured column 'like a huge, lovely meadow in bloom' (according, oddly enough, to a Christian chronicler) moved inland and set up camp at the landward end of Mount Sciberras (today's Marsa). The siege began.

The Turks first attacked Fort St Elmo, expecting it to be easily taken. They underestimated the Knights. St Elmo held out for a month and by the time the Turks took possession 1,500 Christians had lost their lives and several thousand Turks – including Dragut Reis. Pasha is reported to have cried, 'What will the parent cost, when the child was won at such expense?' In an attempt to terrify his opponents in Birgu, he mutilated the bodies of some Christians and floated them across the Grand Harbour. The Knights were not to be intimidated. The Grand Master's reply was to cut off the heads of Turkish prisoners and fire them back as cannon balls.

Battle was now joined for Birgu (Vittoriosa), L-Isla (Senglea) and Fort St Angelo. It was a long hard siege through a long hot summer. The Turks had problems supplying troops with sufficient food, and dysentery was rife (possibly caused by the deliberate poisoning of wells by the Order just before the Turks arrived). The Knights held out – just. By early September, both sides seem to have been on their last legs.

Finally, on 7 September, reinforcements arrived for the Knights from Sicily under the command of Don Garcia de Toledo. Believing they had no chance against large numbers of fresh troops, and afraid of losing their ships, the Turks retreated to the sea. When they realised that the new force numbered only a few thousand the fleet returned, anchoring in St Paul's Bay. But the Knights had made good use of the intervening time and it was too late. The invaders finally fled Malta in disarray on 13 September 1565. The end of the siege on 8 September is still celebrated every year.

AFTER THE SIEGE Birgu, and the rest of what we now call the Three Cities, had been badly damaged, Malta's fortifications devastated and both the Order and the Maltese population seriously depleted. Some Knights were in favour of abandoning Malta altogether, but Grand Master de Valette decided to stay and rebuild – in fact to build afresh, creating a new, defendable capital on Mount Sciberras, the city that would bear his name.

The Knights were the heroes of Christian Europe. They had held back 'the Infidel' and Christendom was willing to show its gratitude in financial support. The Pope sent his own military engineer, Francesco Laparelli (a pupil of Michelangelo), to design the city. The peninsula offered high ground with sea on three sides and a narrow entrance overland where Laparelli placed massive defences (mostly still in place).

The first stone of the new capital was laid in 1566. Neither the architect nor the grand master saw the city to completion. Laparelli returned to Italy leaving the project with a Maltese successor, Gerolamo Cassar, and de Valette died in 1568.

Building, however, moved quickly and by 1570 the Knights were able to start the move from Birgu to Valletta.

Valletta flourished and soon took over from Mdina as the Maltese capital as well as that of the Knights. The arts did well, with much embellishing of the new city, both in stone and paint. Another Turkish invasion (albeit much smaller than the Great Siege force) was defeated in 1614 and fortification of the islands continued apace. Coastal watchtowers and defences were built by successive grand masters along with additional fortification of the Three Cities, Floriana (on Valletta's landward side), Mdina and the Gozo Citadel (for more on fortifications see *Chapter 4*, page 84).

The power and determination of the Turks was now on the wane. The last Turkish raid on the Maltese islands took place in the early 18th century, though naval engagements and small-scale attacks on shipping continued. Both the Turks and the Order now turned their minds more to trade than religious zealotry. The Ottomans began to make trade deals with Christian powers. Among the Knights, vows of poverty gave way to comfortable living and much of the fleet was given more to corsairing than crusading.

DECLINE AND FALL On the whole, Malta prospered under the Order of St John and its population rose from 15,000 in 1530 to 48,000 in 1798. By the mid-18th century, however, the Knights, and particularly Grand Master Manoel Pinto de Fonseca, were living a life of luxury and spending as if there were no tomorrow. Francisco Ximenes de Texada became Grand Master in 1773 promising to help the ordinary people, but on taking office he found that there was no money to pay for his plans. The financial situation only worsened with the French Revolution (from 1789) and the sequestration of the possessions of the French *langues* in France (1792). Resentment of the Knights grew both amongst the people and in the Church.

In 1775 a group of disaffected Maltese clergymen took advantage of the absence of the Order's fleet (away raiding Algiers) to mount a surprise attack on the small garrison manning Fort St Elmo. The rebels took the fort and raised the red–and–white flag of the Maltese Università. They presumably hoped to trigger a popular uprising but none was forthcoming and the 'Priests' Revolt' was quickly and brutally put down with the ring-leaders executed.

Tension, however, persisted. The Venetian representative in Malta reported in 1796 that he feared a revolution and in 1797 another plot was thwarted. So by 1798 it is fair to say that much of the population was no longer behind the Knights.

Add to this the fact that world politics was changing: Holy War was now seen as anomalous and small states were losing influence. Much larger powers – including France, Britain, Austria and Russia – were taking an interest in the Mediterranean, with Malta, as ever, at its centre.

On 9 June 1798 General Napoleon Bonaparte, *en route* to Egypt, dropped anchor off Malta and requested entry to the Grand Harbour to fill up with water. Rightly afraid that he was after more than liquid refreshment, the Knights refused, invoking an old rule that only four ships from a belligerent power might enter the harbour at once. Napoleon, with 29,000 men under his command, wasn't taking no for an answer. He met brave resistance in places, but within just a few days, Grand Master Ferdinand von Hompesch capitulated and signed the islands over to Napoleon thus ending the rule of the Knights in Malta.

Why did he give up so easily? Perhaps he could not rely on the loyalty of the Maltese, or indeed of a few of his own in the French *langues*. Others were also ambivalent: they didn't like fighting Christians. Von Hompesch did send word to Lord Nelson requesting help from the British but the message was delayed by bad weather and the grand master seems to have had little confidence that it would bring the necessary relief. Napoleon had control of the sea and far superior

The end of the Knights in Malta was the end of the real power of the Order of St John. Their time had passed. But they do still exist. They have returned to their roots, predominantly doing charity work with the sick. Local branches run or help in hospitals, and take sick and disabled people on pilgrimages (for example to Lourdes). Their name today is the Sovereign Military Hospitaller Order of St John of Jerusalem, of Rhodes and of Malta, often shortened to SMOM (Sovereign Military Order of Malta).

The British Order founded the St John Ambulance Brigade which provides first aid and training. There is a Museum of the Order of St John in Clerkenwell, London (✆ 020 7324 4005) based in the 16th-century gatehouse to the 11th-century priory that was the original home of the English Langue.

Now based in Rome, the Order itself remains a Catholic institution, closer than ever to the Vatican, under no secular government and answerable only to the Pope. Full Knights continue to be drawn from the upper echelons of European society, though there are now few of them. The great majority of the Order's 12,500 members take only a vow of obedience and religious observance. They do not need to be of noble birth and may marry.

The current Grand Master, Fra Matthew Festing, is an Englishman – the second to hold the post after his immediate precessor, Fra Andrew Bertie (1988–2008), a distant cousin of Queen Elizabeth II.

The Order maintains embassies in more than 100 countries. In Malta it is based in St John's Cavalier in Valletta and, coming full circle, has also taken over the upper reaches of Fort St Angelo.

numbers, so von Hompesch may have felt there was little point in sanctioning massive loss of life only to succumb a few weeks later.

Whatever his reasons, the grand master and the administration of the Order of St John left Malta on 17 June 1798, taking with them nothing but three relics: the icon of the Virgin of Philerimos (brought with them from Rhodes), the hand of their patron saint John the Baptist, and the relic of the True Cross. Everything else – archives, treasure, paintings, the lot – they were obliged to leave in Malta.

There are many excellent books on the Knights (see *Appendix 3, Further reading,* page 301).

THE FRENCH: 1798–1800

Napoleon spent just six days in Malta before departing for the Egyptian campaign leaving strict instructions and General Vaubois in charge. It took only three months for the French administration to so alienate the Maltese that they rose against them. The reasons were financial and religious. The French administration had no budget for running Malta, so they raised taxes and refused to honour debts, wages or pensions owed by their predecessors. What really infuriated the Maltese, however, was the looting of churches. This united the most powerful institution left in Malta, the Church, with the populace in open rebellion.

Aware that they could not oust the French alone, the Maltese requested help from the British Royal Navy – by this time in Sicily *en route* to meet Napoleon in Egypt. Admiral Lord Nelson sent ships and men under the command of Sir Alexander Ball, whom the Maltese quickly made President of the National Assembly, de facto leader of the Maltese as well as the campaign against the French.

Soon Vaubois' men were holed up inside Malta's key fortifications and the Maltese (with British help) found themselves besieging and even bombarding their own forts and cities, including Valletta. Crucially, though, the British Royal Navy, with help from the Portuguese, prevented supplies from reaching the islands. This was not much fun for the Maltese, but instrumental in forcing the French into submission. On 5 September 1800 the French capitulation was signed. Napoleon's troops were given safe passage back to France but were obliged to leave their weapons behind.

THE BRITISH: 1800–1964

Who was now to rule Malta? For a while it looked as if – for the sake of good relations in Europe – the British would hand the islands back to the Order of St John. The Maltese were vehemently against this, but realised that they needed the protection of a larger state and so requested that the British remain. At first the British were not especially keen to stay, but Napoleon made it clear to them how much he wanted Malta and they soon discovered what a useful Mediterranean base they had acquired. Also, some of the Knights had gone to Russia when they left Malta and the British were concerned that their return might give the Russians a foothold in the Mediterranean. In 1814 the Treaty of Paris formally handed Malta to Britain and Sir Thomas Maitland became its first civilian and military governor.

Some Maltese felt they had got more than they bargained for with British governors ruling with little local input. In the first few decades of British rule, London was regularly petitioned with requests for greater self-government and in the 1830s a partly elected council was created and freedom of the press granted. The powers of the Catholic Church, including that over education, were left largely undisturbed – the British knew better than to mess with this key institution.

Malta's importance for Britain was always primarily military. The British took over all Malta's defences, maintained them and made additions of their own (see *Fortifications,* page 87). The Grand Harbour rapidly became a key naval base, home to the Royal Navy's Mediterranean fleet, and important for merchant shipping too. Dockyards were built in the Three Cities and this was soon a hub of naval activity, employing large numbers of Maltese. In 1883 a steam railway was built from Valletta to Mdina (closed in 1931) and work on the construction of the breakwaters at the entrance to the Grand Harbour was opened in 1903 by King Edward VII himself.

In 1878 a Royal Commission recommended that English replace Italian as the language of education, culture and the courts, so as to better integrate Malta into the British Empire. The so-called 'language question' became the trigger for the creation of Malta's first political parties: the pro-British Reform Party whose supporters included merchants and dockyard workers, and the Partito Anti-Reformista (Anti-Reform Party) – in whose ranks local clergy and most of the middle class, especially lawyers, showed their support for tradition, Italy and Italian.

WORLD WAR I Politics was put aside as World War I hit Europe, and Malta became 'the Nurse of the Mediterranean'. Before the war, the country had 268 hospital beds. By January 1916 the number had rocketed to 20,000. At the height of the war 2,000 sick servicemen a week were arriving here, including the wounded of Gallipoli. A thousand nurses were required, some brought from Britain, some from the Maltese St John Ambulance, many with little training. Amongst the British contingent was Vera Brittain, who later wrote about her experiences in Malta in *Testament of Youth* (see boxed text, page 16). The French fleet used Malta as its base and so the dockyards too were kept extremely busy, employing at peak, some 10,000 men.

BETWEEN THE WARS The end of the war brought a drop in dockyard jobs and a rise in unemployment. Even those in work felt the pinch. The cost of living rose sharply (due to shortages resulting from the disruption of war) and wages failed to keep pace.

Vera Brittain arrived in Malta in October 1916 sick and miserable. Her fiancé had been killed in France, and her beloved younger brother and two close friends were also in uniform. In 1915 she had abandoned her studies at Oxford to become a Voluntary Aid Detachment nurse, and on the dangerous voyage from Southampton to the Grand Harbour had become seriously ill. She was forced to spend several weeks in Imtarfa (Mtarfa) hospital before taking up her nursing duties at St George's Hospital, two miles west of Valletta, just above St George's Bay. But despite all this, she fell instantly and passionately in love with Malta.

> The place has become for me a shrine, the object of a pilgrimage, a fairy country which I know that I must see again before I die. Looking back through the years to sun-filled memory-pictures of golden stone buildings, of turquoise and sapphire seas, of jade and topaz and amethyst skies, of long stretches of dust-white road winding seaward over jagged black rocks older than history, I am filled with yearning and regret, and I cry in my heart: Come back, magic days!

From Vera Brittain's autobiography Testament of Youth *(Virago; £12.99) included by permission of Mark Bostridge and TJ Brittain-Catlin, literary executors for the Estate of Vera Brittain, 1970.*

Politics raised its head again with nationalists demanding a much greater say in the government of Malta – and showing some impatience about achieving their aims. All this came to a head in the Sette Giugno (7 June) riots in 1919. Thousands of people ransacked government buildings and the homes of those they thought were making money out of the situation. Soldiers were called in to help the police, some were attacked, and when a shot was heard from a building full of rioters, several soldiers opened fire. In total four Maltese were killed and tens of others injured. Since 1989, 7 June has been a public holiday in commemoration of these events.

Political reform, already under consideration before the riots, followed with a new constitution giving the Maltese control over local matters. Elections were held in 1921 and Malta's first Prime Minister, Joseph Howard of the Unione Politica Maltese (later part of the Nationalist Party) took office.

In the early 1930s the 'language question' raised its head again – and again the dispute was about more than language. Italian was still widely spoken amongst Malta's upper and middle classes, English was on the rise and Malti remained the language of the working majority. The British decided to formally drop Italian as the official language of Malta and to replace it with English and Maltese. This alienated a few, who thought Malta should look towards Roman Catholic Italy rather than Protestant Britain, but allied the British with the mass of Maltese.

WORLD WAR II AND THE SECOND GREAT SIEGE Mussolini had made it quite plain long before the war began that he believed Malta should be part of greater Italy. He even claimed that Malti was a dialect of Italian. British–Italian relations had also been soured by the Italian invasion of Abyssinia (Ethiopia) in 1935 which Britain opposed in the United Nations.

As tensions rose, some efforts were made to prepare Malta for war – the governor requested funds to build underground shelters (many of which remain), anti-aircraft guns and some radar were shipped in and details of food and fuel requirements drawn up. But these measures were little and late, partly because the military chiefs in London could not agree on whether Malta was defendable against the Italians, just

90km away in Sicily. The Army and Air Force thought not, while the Navy argued that Malta was essential to the maintenance of a Mediterranean fleet.

Italy remained neutral for the first months of the war, but when Mussolini joined Hitler on 10 June 1940 Malta was ill-prepared. It had only four aircraft, Gloster Gladiator biplanes, which came to be called *Faith*, *Hope* and *Charity* (plus an unnamed reserve) – even these were only in Malta by accident. The biplanes fought alone – and with remarkable effect – for three weeks before reinforcements arrived (what is left of *Faith* can be seen in the National War Museum in Valletta, page 132).

The first bombing raid on Malta came early on the day after Italy entered the war and the first casualties were taken at Fort St Elmo, though most of the damage was to the densely populated residential areas around the docks. The next day a single Italian reconnaissance aircraft flew over to see what the raid had achieved and was shot down. A few Italian sympathisers were interned but the vast majority of the population swung behind Britain and the Allies.

Malta suffered some of the heaviest bombing of the war. Air-raid sirens whined over 3,000 times between 1940 and 1943, tens of thousands of bombs fell and over a million incendiary devices hit the main island. Casualties were remarkably low considering the intensity of the bombardment. People rapidly evacuated the harbour areas or fled underground each time the sirens sounded, scurrying into ancient catacombs, tunnels and purpose-built shelters. The limestone rock of which Malta and most of its buildings are made, was found to be resistant to incendiary bombs and to some extent to explosives as well.

It was no picnic, however. In the first months of 1942 Malta was pounded day after day for months on end – a period of bombing more intense than anything experienced elsewhere during World War II. Electricity failed, disease spread and food began to run short. Malta's importance was now very clear to both sides. Ships were repaired here and submarines made sorties from its harbours. It was from Malta that the Allies disrupted Axis supplies to their armies in North Africa – a crucial prerequisite to the key Allied victory at El Alamein later in the year.

In April 1942 King George VI awarded the George Cross to the nation of Malta. He wrote to the governor that, 'To honour her brave people, I award the George Cross to the Island Fortress of Malta to bear witness to a heroism and devotion that will long be famous in history.' The governor replied, 'By God's help Malta will not weaken but will endure until victory is won.'

Malta, however, was running out of food and fuel. In midsummer it was calculated that the islands could survive only another few weeks. The British sent a large convoy, Operation Pedestal, to relieve the besieged island. Running the gauntlet of minefields, E-boats and bombers, 400 lives were lost and only five of the original 14 merchant ships made it to their destination. But it was enough for Malta to survive. The last of the ships – the oil tanker *Ohio*, full of desperately needed fuel – limped into port on 15 August, the feast of Santa Marija (St Mary) leading the Maltese to call their 'miraculous' relief ships the Konvoj ta' Santa Marija (St Mary's Convoy).

In May 1943 the Axis forces in North Africa surrendered to the Allies and, in July, Malta acted as the base for Operation Husky, the successful invasion of Sicily. On 8 September (the same date that saw the lifting of the Great Siege of 1565) Italy surrendered. The Italian fleet, afraid of being destroyed by the Germans, gave itself up to the Allies in the Grand Harbour. Admiral Cunningham, Commander of the Royal Navy's Mediterranean Fleet, sent a cable to the Admiralty in London: 'Be pleased to inform their Lordships that the Italian Battle Fleet now lies at anchor under the guns of the fortress of Malta.' Malta's War was, to all intents and purposes, over.

There are several excellent books on Malta's World War II; see *Further reading*, page 302.

POST-WAR POLITICS In July 1943 the British governor assured the beleaguered population of Malta that when hostilities ended, home rule would be reinstated. Sure enough, in 1947 a new constitution came into force with provision for universal suffrage over the age of 21, giving women and those without property or education the vote for the first time. The Labour Party won the election, Dr Paul Boffa became prime minister, and income tax and pensions were introduced. A split in the party in 1949 led to its fall from government. The new party leader was Dom Mintoff, Malta's best-known and most controversial politician (see boxed text, below).

Elections in 1950, 1951 and 1953 gave no party an overall majority, but in 1955 Mintoff fought the election on the promise of immediate negotiations with the

DOM MINTOFF

Malta's most famous and controversial politician, Dominic Mintoff, was a maverick socialist firebrand, rarely out of the European newspapers throughout the 1970s. He loved horseriding, reading, *bočči* (see boxed text, page 292) and swimming in the sea near his villa on the Delimara Peninsula. Born in Bormla/Cospicua (next to the docks) in 1916, he was educated at the University of Malta and then as a Rhodes Scholar at Oxford. He was in Britain throughout Malta's war, returning to a devastated urban landscape in 1943.

By 1945 he was deputy leader of the Labour Party, led by Paul Boffa. Mintoff's outspoken character and overt ambition led to a split in the party in 1949. Boffa formed his own Malta Workers Party and Mintoff became leader of the (slightly renamed) Malta Labour Party (MLP). The Labour vote was thus split and it was not until 1955 that they regained power.

Mintoff's policy of full integration into the UK was deeply unpopular with the Catholic Church and created long-term enmity between Malta's most powerful man and its most powerful non-elected institution. The Church even declared at one point that it was a sin to vote for the MLP. Mintoff was equally vitriolic about the Church and, after what he saw as Britain's rejection of his advances, also about the old colonial power he had initially so assiduously courted.

Mintoff's heyday was the 1970s: he was prime minster continuously from 1971 to 1984. A powerful orator with a genuine concern for working people, he made some controversial friends – most notably Colonel Gaddafi of Libya. Nobody in Malta was (or is) neutral on Mintoff – he has always evoked strong feelings.

In 1984 Mintoff chose to resign as prime minster, handing over to his chosen successor, Karmenu Mifsud Bonnici, who led the country until the next election in 1987. The old firebrand still retained his parliamentary seat and was sometimes accused of backseat driving. His outspokenness did not diminish – and was not always in his party's best interests.

The MLP and Mintoff himself were vehemently opposed to the Nationalists' policy of Malta joining the EU. In 1998 Labour was back in power under Dr Alfred Sant, but with a majority of only one. The government wanted to build a yacht marina on the Vittoriosa waterfront to bring in income. Mintoff did not like the limitation this would place on access for local (less wealthy) people. Always one to act on his views – even at the age of 82 – he voted against his own party and brought down the government. In the resulting general election, the Nationalists won and reinstated Malta's application to join the European Union (as well as building the marina).

Mintoff did not return to parliament – though he continued to campaign (unsuccessfully) against EU membership until 2003. At the time of writing, he lives on, truly a legend in his own lifetime.

British government to become part of Britain (in the same way as the Channel Islands), a move expected to significantly improve economic conditions in Malta. Labour won an overwhelming majority in the general election and the referendum on integration that followed. Britain, however, was wary of Mintoff's demand for Maltese MPs at Westminster and when it became clear that the UK (with post-war economic problems of its own) intended to reduce defence spending in Malta (risking the jobs of thousands of Labour voters in the dockyards) Mintoff changed tack. In 1958 he resigned and declared himself and his party for full independence from Britain.

This prompted a political crisis and a brief return to colonial administration, but by the early 1960s (with the Nationalist Party under Prime Minister Ġorġ Borġ Olivier in power) both Labour and the Nationalists were backing independence. It was agreed that some British forces would stay for at least ten years and that London would provide tens of millions of pounds to help Malta rebuild. On 21 September 1964 Malta was declared an independent nation.

INDEPENDENT MALTA: 1964–ONGOING

Queen Elizabeth II remained Malta's head of state until 1974 when Dom Mintoff made Malta a republic, headed by a president appointed by parliament. The last British forces left Malta on 31 March 1979. This was not only the end of a 180-year era it also left a significant hole in Malta's economy. The British forces had been by far the largest employer in the country and Malta now needed to find other sources of income and employment fast.

Tourism was an obvious choice and the rush to attract as many visitors as possible began. Malta also needed manufacturing and trade. It was not self-sufficient in anything much and required the import of oil – most of which came from Libya – and (as ever) food. When the British departed, Mintoff declared Malta neutral and non-aligned (as it remains today) and signed controversial agreements with North Korea, the Soviet Union and Libya.

Mintoff's Labour administration tried to control everything centrally and almost any significant economic activity required a government permit – a state of affairs that encouraged corruption. Tariffs were imposed on all imported goods, leading to the unseemly sight of Maltese families returning from abroad with suitcases containing just a thin layer of clothes covering electronics, foreign toiletries and a year's supply of chocolate – not a policy designed to increase the government's popularity.

In 1987 the Nationalist Party won the election, a feat they repeated in 1992 on a platform that included a commitment to begin negotiations to join the EU. Despite some ups and downs (see box, *Dom Mintoff*, opposite), Malta became a full member of the European Union in May 2004 and joined the Eurozone on 1 January 2008.

2

Background Information

GEOGRAPHY AND GEOLOGY

Malta's geography has been hugely important to its history. Its position in the middle of the Mediterranean and its natural harbours are what has made it desirable and put it on the international map. Malta lies 93km south of Sicily (just visible on a clear day and within a day's sailing) and 355km north of Libya. To the east is Tunisia, 288km away, and to the west is Crete (815km away). The Maltese islands are small (just 316km²), rocky and lack a good source of fresh water, but its harbours are a natural asset that have ensured the strategic importance of the country throughout its history

GEOLOGY Geologically speaking Malta is young. Its oldest rock is less than 30 million years old – so no dinosaurs or dinosaur fossils here. The islands were formed by the buckling up of the seabed as the tectonic plates of Europe and Africa slowly collided – a process also responsible for the formation of the Etna and Vesuvius volcanoes. Malta has no volcanoes and no volcanic rock, although it does suffer occasional earthquakes.

Malta is basically made of limestone (calcium carbonate) and there are five main strata of rock. From the deepest (and oldest) upwards, they are: lower coralline limestone, globigerina limestone, blue clay, greensand and upper coralline limestone.

TEMPERATURE CHART

Month	Average Sunshine (hrs)	Rainfall (mm)	Temp Max°C/F		Temp Min°C/F		Sea	MRH*
January	5.14	89.0	15.2	59	9.5	49	15.2	80
February	6.12	61.3	15.5	60	9.3	49	15.3	79
March	7.21	40.9	16.7	62	10.1	50	15.0	79
April	8.24	22.5	19.1	66	11.9	53	15.9	78
May	9.68	6.6	23.3	74	14.9	59	17.7	74
June	10.93	3.2	27.5	82	18.4	65	21.4	71
July	11.78	0.4	30.7	87	21.0	70	24.5	69
August	10.89	7.0	30.7	87	21.8	71	25.8	73
September	8.68	40.4	28.0	82	20.1	68	24.9	77
October	7.14	89.7	24.2	76	17.1	63	22.6	78
November	6.15	80.0	20.1	68	13.9	57	20.4	78
December	5.03	112.3	16.7	62	11.0	52	17.1	79

* Mean Relative Humidity

Figures from Malta Met office 10 year means.

Coralline limestone is, as its name suggests, formed from dead coral compressed on the seabed. It is hard and durable, relatively little affected by weather. **Globigerina limestone** was formed when the sea was deeper (100–150m). At this depth there is no sunlight or turbulence and fine dust and dead micro-organisms (of which globigerina is one) form the sediment that becomes the limestone. This stone is a wonderful creamy yellow. It is soft and easily weathered, but also easily cut and it is Malta's main building material.

Weather takes its toll even more readily on **blue clay**, but this is another useful layer, giving fertility to the soil. The **greensand** is in a very thin layer on top of the blue clay and is yet more easily weathered. The surface layer of rock is often **upper coralline**, the same type of rock as the bottom layer, resistant to the effects of weather. This can have a dramatic effect on cliffs where the clay and greensand layers weather faster than the rock above them. The upper coralline is left sitting on very little until eventually great boulders fall into the sea.

The southern sea cliffs of Malta and Gozo – such as at Dingli and Ta' Ċenċ – are lower coralline limestone, while those of the west and north of the main island have a strong clay element topped with upper coralline rock. Much of the interior, especially in the centre and east, is globigerina. Comino sits lower in the water than

Wind is a common feature of Malta's weather. Even in summer only about one day a fortnight is windless. The Maltese have names for the winds:

MAJJISTRAL Cool northwesterly, blows nearly one day in five throughout the year.

GRIGAL Dry northeasterly, stirs up the sea so it batters the coast with waves, blows around 10% of days but especially in September and March.

TRAMONTANA Means 'across the mountains' in Italian, this cold north wind from the Alps is the main wind of winter and also blows about one day in ten.

XLOKK The Sirocco. Hot, humid, sometimes dust-laden and unpleasant southeasterly bringing heat from the Sahara and humidity picked up over the sea. May last several days. Strong Xlokks are most likely in March and November.

LBIC Southwesterly similar to the Xlokk.

RIH ISFEL Warm wind from the south that, like the two above, brings sticky oppressive weather.

the other two islands and only the upper coralline is visible.

Gozo is made up of valley areas – mainly globigerina limestone – and flat-topped hills which have the full set of strata, topped with the upper coralline layer. Once you are aware of the five layers (which always come in the same order) you may start to spot them in the landscape.

Limestone Isles in a Crystal Sea by Matyn Pedley, Michael Hughes-Clarke and Pauline Abela (published by Maltese publisher PEG) summarises decades of research on Maltese geology, with colour illustrations and includes a booklet of geological walks.

CLIMATE

Malta, unsurprisingly, has a Mediterranean-island climate, with hot dry summers and mild damp winters with occasional chilly winds. The temperature rarely rises above the mid 30s (°C) or falls below the high single figures. It hasn't snowed here since 1962, and before that 1905. Frost has been recorded only once. Rain is extremely rare in summer, reasonably frequent in winter. Spring is drier than autumn but can be made colder by wind.

NATURAL HISTORY AND CONSERVATION

Nature and wildlife are under tremendous pressure on the main island of Malta, where human habitation has taken over most of the land. Despite this, there are some beautiful areas of countryside here and plenty more on Gozo. There is quite a range of plant life, with wildflowers plentiful in spring. Animals are more limited – not helped by the enthusiasm for hunting amongst some Maltese men.

FLORA Hard though it is to believe, experts say that before people arrived on Malta it had extensive tree cover. This has not been the case now for thousands of years and trees are a rarity, with most species introduced from other countries, including

Aleppo pines, acacia, carob and fig trees, olive trees and a few palms. Tamarisk and oleander bushes add colour. Wild fennel, with its typical aniseed smell and tiny yellow flowers, is all over the place. Caper bushes are common and in spring you may see people harvesting the little green buds used in salads and cooking.

Malta's most typical habitat is the Mediterranean garigue, limestone rock with low shrubby vegetation. The tops of the Dingli and Ta' Ċenċ cliffs and Comino have good examples of coastal garigue with significant endemic flora (unique to the Maltese islands). Wild Mediterranean thyme is often the dominant species, and Malta's national plant, rock centaury, is usually to be seen. Golden samphire is common along with other hardy plants with fleshy fluid-retaining leaves. Others species include Maltese salt tree, sea chamomile and fleabane. More rarely you may find hoary rock-rose, wild artichoke and the scarce endemic Maltese pyramidal orchid.

Among Malta's more unusual plants is the Maltese everlasting, a rare bush up to 1m high flowering yellow in May/June, found only on the western cliffs of Gozo and on Fungus Rock, Dwejra. Also on Fungus Rock (and occasionally on Ta' Ċenċ) is the once much prized plant for which the rock was named (though it is not in fact a fungus) *Cynomorium coccineum* (see page 278).

For more information, www.maltawildplants.com has an index of over a thousand plants found in Malta, many of them pictured.

FAUNA

Land fauna Besides rabbits, butterflies and birds (see below), Malta's main animals are **reptiles**. Lizards are regularly seen: copious **geckos** camouflaged against the limestone or darting across the ground, as well as rounded stumpy **skinks**. There are four kinds of **snake** (two possibly accidentally introduced during World War I and limited to southeast Malta), but no poisonous species. This is credited by some to St Paul who is meant to have miraculously remained unharmed by a viper biting him shortly after his shipwreck on Malta in AD60 (see page 138). The more scientifically minded suggest the snake that bit him was probably Malta's non-poisonous leopard snake.

The snake you are most likely to see is the black whip snake (*Coluber viridiflavus carbonarius*, or in Maltese, serp), found on Malta, Gozo and Comino. The adult has a black back, while the juvenile is dark green with grey and dark brown markings. It grows up to 2m long and lives in rock cracks and under rubble, coming out in the middle of the day to hunt for lizards, rodents and eggs. It hibernates in winter.

Marine fauna There are plenty of fish in the sea around Malta, including some that have died out in more polluted parts of the Mediterranean. Fresh fish are a regular in Malta's restaurants and anyone entering the sea with their eyes down (particularly off rocks and in Gozo) should have no trouble spotting several species in a matter of minutes. Larger fish and a greater variety can, of course, be seen by snorkelling and when diving (see *Snorkelling* page 90, *Diving* page 66 and *Marine wildlife*, page 67).

Birds Malta has very few permanently resident birds, with only 29 species breeding on the islands. This is partly due to destruction of habitat, but also to the continuing popularity of bird hunting (see below). The total species count to date, however, is 384 because Malta is on the central Mediterranean migration, one of the three main routes used by birds to migrate between Africa, where they winter, and Europe where they breed. Multitudes of birds fly over – and may stop for a rest – in spring and autumn. Unfortunately, some of these are also shot, particularly in autumn when certain species can be legally hunted, particularly turtle dove and quail.

You will not see a Maltese falcon in Malta. They were hunted to extinction on the islands in the 1970s and '80s. The Maltese falcon is a sub-species of the peregrine falcon, the fastest bird in the world, more used to hunting than being hunted. From early in the second millennium onwards, the leaders of Europe prized the Maltese falcon above all others for their sport of falconry. When Malta was ceded to the Order of St John by the Holy Roman Emperor Charles V in 1530 the 'rent' was to be paid in falcons. More recently, Malta's *kaccaturi* (hunters) have ensured that birds of prey are now almost completely absent from the islands outside migration times. And some of the migratory ones are – illegally – shot down too.

Spring hunting was stopped in 2008 (under EU legislation) and although a few hunters broke the law, the positive impact of two consecutive closed spring seasons was clearly seen in summer 2009. Nine breeding species extended their distribution, three returned to breed here after long absences – common kestrel, grey wagtail (the first breeding pair in nearly a century) and common cuckoo – and one new species, the pallid swift, colonised the islands.

The most common bird in Malta is the Spanish sparrow which is abundant in towns and villages as well as countryside. The national bird, the attractive blue rock thrush is reasonably easily seen on coastal cliffs. Various warblers live in open country, garigue and valleys, and over the sea Cory's shearwater, and in some places the much rarer and threatened Yelkouan shearwater, can be seen on windy days or at dusk when they gather together like a raft on the water before flying into their cliff nests after dark. Malta has 10% of the world's population of Yelkouan shearwaters and a special conservation project is under way (see page 241).

At migration times, far more birds are visible – songbirds such as finches as well as large birds of prey. Unfortunately any spot that is good for birdwatching is also good for bird hunting (see below).

For more information on birdwatching and related safety issues, see pages 68, 97 and 48 respectively.

HUNTING AND TRAPPING There are around 12,000 licensed bird hunters (*kaccaturi*) in Malta (not all of them active) and 1,266 trapping licences are held. Malta's membership to the EU has changed the situation for hunters, and particularly for trappers, as Malta is now supposed to comply with the EU Birds Directive which rules out trapping and limits hunting to certain species in the autumn season only. There is, however, still enough hunting to have a major impact on Malta's birdlife.

Trapping The Maltese have long kept finches as pets. You can see their little cages hanging outside front doors in more traditional areas, particularly the Three Cities. Trapping of the seven main species of finch (including greenfinch, goldfinch and chaffinch) for this purpose has long been a widespread hobby and until 2009, tens of thousands of finches were caught each year. Presumably as a result, Malta, despite once having had finches breeding here, is the only country in the Mediterranean that does not have a viable breeding population.

When Malta joined the EU it was given special dispensation to phase out rather than just stop the trapping of finches. That grace period ended at the close of 2008 and trapping finches is now illegal. Malta is, at the time of writing, still allowing the trapping of quail and turtle dove during September and the first half of October, and golden plover and song thrush from late October to mid-January. This is strictly speaking against the EU Birds Directive and whether or not it continues to be allowed will depend on how the EU views Malta's excuses for doing it. Trapping of these species was never particularly popular and it seems likely that trapping as a widespread activity is now finished.

Trappers' huts are still very numerous on Malta's coast and in fertile valleys. Built of stone, they have poles or little stands outside to support cages containing captive finches which would sing their wild cousins into the traps. The hides usually have a cleared area outside (sometimes cleared with environmentally unfriendly herbicides) for laying out seeds, and netting the birds. Any trapping sites you see will probably not be in use. If you do see anyone trapping finches, report it immediately to the police on ☎ 112 and BirdLife Malta on ☎ 21347644.

Shooting Hunting has long been popular in Malta and there is a small but significant – and very vocal – minority that regards bird hunting as an inalienable right. They have even claimed that not being allowed to hunt in the spring seasons of 2008 and 2009 has been damaging to their mental health. In order to protect birds on their way to breed, the EU Birds Directive makes spring hunting illegal. Hunters may shoot certain named species during the autumn season only.

After joining the EU in 2004, however, Malta initially chose to exempt itself from this regulation and allowed spring hunting to open. The Maltese government is perfectly entitled to do this under certain conditions and so long as it can justify its actions to the European Commission each year. In 2008 the European Court issued an interim measure ordering Malta not to open spring hunting. For two years this was complied with and, despite some illegal activity, had a very positive impact on Malta's birds (see *Birds*, above). In September 2009 the issue was tested in the European Court of Justice and Malta was found *not* to have been justified in permitting spring hunting.

The hunters have latched onto a small part of the ruling to claim that spring hunting should be reinstated, but at the time of writing, BirdLife and the British RSPB (Royal Society for the Protection of Birds) are confident that Malta would be in clear breach of EU law if it allowed spring hunting to open in 2010 or thereafter. However, do check www.birdlifemalta.org for the latest.

Even assuming that spring hunting stays closed, Malta still has a problem with illegal hunting, both out of season and in terms of which birds are taken in season. In May 2009, a police officer was amongst those apprehended for hunting illegally, and in 2008, 106 protected birds were confirmed shot – and these were only the ones that could be documented. During the autumn 'Raptor Camp' – a two-week gathering of birdwatchers to log migration sightings and discourage illegal hunting – the 59 participants logged 362 illegal incidents including the killing of a lesser spotted eagle. On two days in September 2009 a 'bird cemetery' of over 200 bodies of protected species – including night heron, marsh harriers, falcons, honey-buzzards, a nightingale, hoopoes, nightjar and a golden oriole – was found hidden in one area.

The RSPB points out that Malta's police unit dealing with illegal hunting is under-resourced and therefore not as effective as it could be, and punishment for those caught is often surprisingly light. The hunters are forcefully represented by the FKNK (Federation for Hunting and Conservation; www.huntingmalta.org.mt) whose leader, Lino Farrugia, has a conviction for illegal trapping.

The hunting lobby is strong and anything to do with birds in Malta is a political hot potato. With 12,000 current hunting licences and only 1,580 votes between the parties at the last election, you can see why neither of the main political groups is keen to alienate this block of voters. On the other hand, there are those in Malta who would like year-round access to the country's limited areas of countryside without guns popping around them. A poll in 2007 indicated that some 85% of the population was against the government's decision to defy EU regulations and open spring hunting that year, and when Lino Farrugia stood for the European Parliament in 2004 he gained just 3,308 votes.

There is considerable tension between BirdLife Malta and the hunters. BirdLife's small reserve in Għadira (see page 237) has been attacked several times, trees planted in a reforestation project have been burnt down, and one member of staff has twice been shot. The hunters are particularly incensed by BirdLife's Raptor Camps despite the fact that participants do not interfere with legal hunting and aim only to help enforce the law of the land.

The government position is that the whole thing is just a clash between two hobbies – hunting and birding/rambling – and that the establishment's job is to mediate between them. Both hunters and government officers become quite irritated when foreigners express the opinion that birds should be protected. However, most of the birds the *kaccaturi* shoot are on migration between other places. 'Malta's birds' have in fact been tracked to 47 other countries.

If you see any illegal hunting, you can help by reporting it to the police on ↘ 112 and BirdLife Malta on ↘ 21347644. For additional information, see also *Birds*, above, *Safety*, page 48 and *Birdwatching*, pages 68 and 97.

CONSERVATION Despite rampant development, Malta does have some beautiful countryside – and much of Gozo remains unspoilt. Even in recent years, species of plant and insect new to science have been discovered on the islands and there are several NGOs working hard to try to protect and preserve the habitats and ecosystems of rural Malta. Most prominent amongst these are Nature Trust Malta, BirdLife Malta, Din L-Art Ħelwa (Malta's National Trust) and the GAIA Foundation; see below for details.

FURTHER INFORMATION

BirdLife Malta ↘ 21347646; e info@
birdlifemalta.org; www.birdlifemalta.org. Affiliated to BirdLife International, this is Malta's equivalent of the UK's RSPB. It campaigns for the protection of birds & against poaching & illegal trapping, collect data & have a hugely informative website (inc a section for kids) & multiple publications. It runs 2 small wetland reserves (see *Ghadira* page 237 & *Is-Simar* page 243) as well as a reforestation project in conjunction with Din L-Art Ħelwa. BirdLife also organises data-gathering camps during autumn & spring migration & bird ringing on Comino.

Din L-Art Ħelwa ↘ 21225952; e info@
dinlarthelwa.org; www.dinlarthelwa.org. Malta's National Trust, affiliated to the British National Trust, the primary purpose of Din L'Art Ħelwa is preservation of built heritage – they have renovated numerous sites & opened them to the public. Like their British counterpart they also work to conserve the nation's natural heritage, usually in partnership with the other NGOs named here.

GAIA Foundation ↘ 21584473/4; e director@
projectgaia.org or elysium@projectgaia.org; www.projectgaia.org. Involved in a variety of projects including propagation of native & endemic plants, seabed protection, restoration of sand dunes at Ramla Bay on Gozo & coastal conservation at Għajn Tuffieħa Bay on Malta, as well as organic farming. They have a centre open to the public at Għajn Tuffieħa (near the Radisson Golden Bay Hotel) & a flexible volunteer programme that includes visitors (see page 233).

Malta Nature Tours m 79546987; e info@
maltanaturetours.com; www.maltanaturetours.com. Tailor-made outings for visitors led by people qualified in various areas of Malta's natural environment.

Nature Trust Malta ↘ 21313150; e info@
naturetrustmalta.org; www.naturetrustmalta.org. NGO involved in protection & promotion of Malta's natural heritage. They help manage the Majjistral National Park (*www.majjistral.org*) – an area of mainly rocky garigue in northwestern Malta – as well as 2 forestation projects. They have been involved in protecting the Dwejra region of Gozo & the habitat of the rare freshwater crab. They run occasional nature walks, including at Majjistral.

GOVERNMENT AND POLITICS

Malta is a democratic republic with high popular interest in politics: voter turnout is usually over 90%. The president is the head of state while most executive powers lie with the prime minister who is head of government. The president appoints the cabinet on the advice of the prime minister from the ranks of the 65-seat House of Representatives that sits in the Maltese Parliament in Valletta.

Elections to the House of Representatives take place at least every five years using proportional representation by single transferable vote. Thirteen constituencies each elect five MPs. Occasionally, as at present, 'bonus' MPs are elected in order to ensure that a party gaining a majority of votes nationally has an appropriate majority of seats. Since the election in March 2008 there have in fact been 69 MPs.

Since independence in 1964, Maltese politics has been dominated by two parties: the Nationalist Party (Partit Nazzjonalista) or PN, and the Malta Labour Party (Partit Laburista) or MLP. MLP is an old-fashioned labour movement with strong support in the dock areas of the Three Cities, Marsaskala, Paola and Birżebbuġa. The entrepreneurs, bankers and professionals of areas like Sliema tend to be Nationalist (though there are obviously exceptions). Dom Mintoff, with his pro-Arab policies and deals with the Chinese, did much to alienate the middle classes from the Labour Party. The two parties now have very similar levels of support in the country: the 2008 general election was won by the Nationalist Party with 49.3% of the vote, just ahead of the Labour Party with 48.9%, giving the PN 35 seats, the MLP 34.

The Alternativa Demokratika (AD), Malta's Green Party and Azzjoni Nazzjonaili, National Action (AN), won under 1.5% of the vote each and a handful of other parties received fewer than 200 votes altogether. None of these smaller parties has ever won a seat.

The leader of the majority party in the House of Representatives becomes prime minister. Lawrence Gonzi, a lawyer, took the post in 2009 for the second time, having been prime minister since March 2004. The president is separately chosen by parliament every five years. In April 2009, George Abela (another lawyer, former Chairman of the Malta Football Association and recent contender for the leadership of the opposition Labour Party) took the post. This is the first time a president has been chosen from the opposition party, but Abela is a close friend of the prime minister (going back to university days) and became president with the support of the government.

The Maltese are passionate about politics. Families are often firmly Labour or Nationalist and debate can become quite heated. Part of the reason for this passion is that in a country as small and interconnected as Malta, it can make a real difference who is in power. This is not a corrupt society in the unsubtle sense of brown envelopes full of cash and there is no Mafia here (as in neighbouring Sicily), but nepotism, the favouring of friends and mutual back-scratching, is rife. The saying goes that in Malta it is not what you know that matters, but who you know.

ECONOMY

From the early 16th century until the end of World War II, Malta did not have to stand on its own two feet economically. The Knights and then the British brought foreign money, trade and employment for over four centuries. When Dom Mintoff threw out the last of the British navy in the 1970s, Malta had to fill the resulting economic gap. It has been fairly successful at doing so, though at a price – mass tourism has ruined significant stretches of the coast and countryside. The standard of living in Malta is somewhere in the middle of the EU range and there is universal free education and healthcare, and a life expectancy of 80.

Malta is dependent on imports for key supplies. It produces only 20% of its own food and has no local source of energy, so foreign trade is crucial. Key money-makers are manufacturing for export (especially electronics and pharmaceuticals), financial services and particularly tourism. The tourist industry accounts for some 35% of GDP and is the largest provider of employment.

In January 2008 Malta's currency became the euro and people still complain that this led to a rise in prices. Malta was not as badly hit as some places in the 2008/09 credit crunch but this, combined with the fall of the pound against the euro, has affected tourism with numbers down by about 10% through the peak season of 2009.

PEOPLE AND MIGRATION

With a population of 410,000 in an area of 316km², Malta has the fourth-highest population density in the world. Ninety-four per cent of the people live in urban areas – mainly in the large conglomeration that spreads inland from Valletta, Sliema and St Julian's. There are uncrowded places, however, especially on Gozo and Comino.

Ninety-seven per cent of Malta's permanent population was born in Malta. Emigration and working abroad have long been features of the country's history. Money earned in other countries has sustained many a family in hard economic times (there is a large Maltese population in Australia). Conversely Malta has absorbed Europeans of many nationalities over the centuries.

Yet the Maltese are not used to non-European, non-Christian immigrants from countries poorer than their own, so considerable disruption has been caused by the arrival over the last few years of several thousand destitute North African asylum seekers, some of whom are Muslim. The majority are trying to get to Italy but arrive in Maltese waters. During 2008, 2,775 seaborne migrants arrived in Malta and numbers have kept increasing. Winter 2008/09 was the first in which boats full (often overfull) of Africans kept arriving. This is a genuine problem for a small country, and has also brought to the surface an unattractive streak of racism.

On one level this is an odd place for colour-based racism as the Maltese themselves vary in colour enormously, from northern European white to quite dark. The deep-seated suspicion of anything Arab/Muslim/North African is not just a legacy of the Knights but also of the 1970s and Dom Mintoff's indiscriminate promotion of all things Libyan.

That said, the Maltese are fundamentally a hospitable people. They can be quite unpleasant to each other at times and are not above bearing lengthy grudges, but to visitors they are generally charming, friendly and immensely helpful.

CULTURAL ATTITUDES Malta is conservative, but not formal. Attitudes to women, race, homosexuality and the disabled are all similar to those in Britain a few decades ago. But this is an emotional and religious intolerance rather than stiff Victorian-style disapproval. Family is central to Maltese life. As one gay Maltese man put it: family comes first – if you step out of line with traditional morality you can expect deep disapproval and a constant earful, but you will never be deserted.

Families tend to stay close. A Maltese woman described how, 'I am 40 and my parents still interfere in my life and ask every Sunday if I've been to church and taken my child to church. But if I am sick, or my child needs looking after, they are always there to help.' Women still predominantly stay at home to look after the house, the men and the kids. Working mothers mostly rely on female relatives to look after their children. However, this is changing.

LANGUAGE

Maltese is a Semitic language (in the same family as Arabic and Hebrew), written in the Latin alphabet (the only one that is). However, much of its vocabulary – perhaps up to 50% – is derived from Italian and Sicilian, as well as some from English and a little from French. English words are increasingly incorporated, some of them with Italianised pronunciation; others retain their English pronunciation whilst being spelt the Maltese way, for example: *mowbajl* (as in 'mobile phone').

Maltese derives from Siculo-Arabic, the dialect of Arabic that developed in Sicily, Malta and southern Italy. The first documentary reference to Maltese comes in the mid-14th century followed in 1640 by the first dictionary which was written by one of the Knights of St John, Frenchman François de Vion Thezan Court. The dictionary included phrases necessary for giving orders to soldiers. Most unusually for a European language, written Maltese was not standardised until the 19th century.

During the time of the Knights, Italian and French were the main languages of administration and Italian remained the lingua franca of the upper and middle classes well into the British period. In the 20th century, English took over and in 1934 Maltese (Malti) was formally recognised as an official language of the islands, alongside English. Maltese is also an official language of the European Union (the only Semitic language that is).

Most Maltese people now speak Maltese (Malti) and English. Many also speak Italian. In the 21st century Maltese is increasingly spoken in offices and clubs where English would once have been *de rigueur*, although amongst the highly educated (particularly in Sliema) you will still find some Maltese using English as their primary language. One Maltese told me he speaks Malti with his parents but English with his siblings, friends and colleagues. Another said he generally speaks Malti at home unless he is arguing with his wife. This is done in English 'because it is more nuanced'!

As an English speaker, you are unlikely to find yourself in any great linguistic difficulty. You are not going to need a phrasebook or a dictionary to get around. What is helpful is to know how to pronounce Maltese – particularly place names – so *Appendix 1, Language* on page 297, concentrates on this, as well as giving you a bit of very basic vocabulary as it is always fun to be able to say hello.

In this guide place names are given in a mix of English and Maltese – sometimes one, sometimes the other and sometimes both. This reflects how places are referred to in Malta.

RELIGION

Malta is 98% Catholic and religion remains an important part of both community life and the national sense of identity. Each parish runs a *festa*, the most important celebration of the year (see page 31) and the Maltese are noticeably proud to be a Christian nation. Nearly three centuries of rule by a Christian religious order, whose *raison d'être* was opposing the Muslim 'infidel', has undoubtedly left its mark. A few old Maltese still remember their parents using the Turks like the bogeyman: 'Don't play in the street or the Turks will get you.'

Catholicism is the state religion (though the constitution guarantees freedom of worship) and is taught in all schools. The story goes that from anywhere in Malta you can see a church (not quite) and that you could go to a different church every day of the year (very nearly). There is no doubt that the Church is still a powerful force. It is less so than it used to be – only about half the population now goes to

Mass every Sunday (well down on a decade ago) – but it is still strong. And some members of the clergy are not afraid to comment on political and secular as well as religious matters.

The Church has ensured that abortion and divorce have remained illegal (although foreign divorces are recognised and foreign abortions are obtained in Sicily and Britain). The Church seems to be losing the battle against sex outside marriage, however, as a quarter of babies born in Malta in 2008 were *not* born to a married couple.

There are a handful of Protestant churches in Malta, including the Anglican cathedral in Valletta, and there is one synagogue and one mosque.

EDUCATION

The Church has historically had control over education in Malta and many private schools are still Church run, though there are also some non-religious independent schools. Education is compulsory for children aged five to 16 and state schools are free and open to all. Under the British, most teaching was done in English and in some schools this is still the case, though most now teach in Maltese/Malti with English as the second language.

Secondary education is divided by academic ability into selective junior lyceums (like UK grammar schools) and area secondary schools (for those not passing the 11+ exam). Most schools are single sex and pupils sit O levels at 16 and A levels at 18. There is one university, the University of Malta (*www.um.edu.mt*) in Msida, at the head of Marsamxett Harbour, where women recently reached equal numbers with men.

The literacy rate in Malta has risen dramatically in the last 50 years. Before World War II nearly three-quarters of the population was illiterate. Now 94% can read and write, 99% amongst 15–24 year olds.

ARTS AND CRAFTS

MUSIC Malta has always had a strong musical tradition and a remarkable proportion of the population participates in music making. Each parish has at least one wind **band** (modelled on British brass bands) and some have a small **orchestra** as well. The main musical events of the year are the *festi* (see below), but there are other concerts and events too. Pop music is also plentiful, both live and recorded, and the Eurovision song contest is a national event (*www.eurovisionmalta.com*).

Malta's traditional folk music is *għana*. Sung mostly by men it is peasant music with an Eastern root. There are various forms including one with improvised words in which the song is batted back and forth between two singers, and another in which the song is high-pitched, well above the normal male range. An annual festival of *għana* takes place in July (see *Events* page 35). See also www.allmalta.com – 'The Home of Maltese Għana'.

LITERATURE For many centuries Maltese was the language of the uneducated and so not of literature. The languages of writing were Latin, French, Italian and then English. The earliest known work of literature in Malti is an isolated example: Pietro Caxaro's 15th-century poem, *Cantilena* (also known as *Xidew il-Qada*). The next – a sonnet in praise of Grand Master Nicolas Cotoner by Gian Francesco Bonamico – wasn't written until 1672.

Writing in Maltese only really took hold with the beginnings of nationalist feeling in the 19th century. The first history of Malta in Maltese was not written until 1862 (by Gan Anton Vassallo, who was also a nationalist poet) and the first novel, Anton

Manwel Caruana's *Inez Farrug,* modelled on Italian historical novels, not until 1889. Maltese writers today often write in English or in both Maltese and English.

Dun Karm Psaila (1871–1961) is considered the national poet and he wrote the words to the national anthem as well as poetry documenting the emotional landscape of World War II. Due partly to his influence, poetry was the favourite genre for Maltese writers in the first half of the 20th century. Now there is greater diversity and the most influential contemporary writer, and commentator on matters literary, is Oliver Friggieri, novelist, poet and professor of Maltese at the University of Malta.

VISUAL ARTS The Knights left Malta with a strong artistic heritage and churches full of paintings, some of real quality. There is a lot of work by Malta's top 'Old Master', Mattia Preti (see page 126) and a couple of paintings by Caravaggio in the oratory museum of St John's Co-Cathedral in Valletta (page 124). There is also a thriving contemporary art scene. New private galleries keep popping up in Valletta, and several museums and old buildings (including the Auberge d'Italie in Valletta, the Carmelite Priory Museum in Mdina and the Museum of Fine Arts, Valletta) exhibit changing displays of contemporary art. A useful source of information is the Malta Council for Culture and the Arts (*www.maltaculture.com*).

CRAFTS Lace-making seems to have become established in Malta – and particularly amongst the women of Gozo – in the 16th and 17th centuries. It was given a boost in the 19th century when Genoese lace-makers were brought to Malta to help revive the industry; Maltese lace is therefore a variation on Genoese style. Lace made in Malta, however, often contains the Maltese cross somewhere in the design (see page 32). In Gozo you may still see older women sitting on their doorsteps making lace. (More information at http://lace.lacefairy.com/Lace/ID/MalteseID.html).

The Knights brought the art of **silverwork** to Malta and there are some very fine examples in museums and churches. Many small workshops still produce fine silver filigree and a classic tourist souvenir is a filigree Maltese cross. Other crafts include weaving, knitting and glassblowing. Maltese blown glassware – often in very bright colours – is marketed extensively to tourists, although it is in fact a relatively new addition to Malta's crafts.

FESTA

The *festa* is a hugely important part of Maltese culture – both religious and secular – and the high point of the local community year. Every parish has its *festa* and money is raised and preparations made for it throughout the year. *Festa* is theoretically celebrated on the feast day of the saint to whom the parish church is dedicated, but most are in fact held on summer weekends. From late May to mid-September there is hardly a weekend without at least one *festa* and many weekends with several.

Several days before the big day, the church is decorated with red damask, and the *festa* statue – a more-than-life-size painted figure of the saint – is brought out of its shrine (usually behind glass) to stand in the main body of the church. Other statues are set up on pedestals outside the church and the exterior of the building is decorated with strings of white and coloured lights. Bunting, flags and more lights are hung along nearby streets – you can tell as soon as you enter a town or village if it is *festa* time.

Festa eve – usually a Saturday – is firework time. Most parishes have their own tiny firework factory (with between one and five firework-makers) and there is vehement competition for who can put on the best show. Lija used to have the

THE MALTESE CROSS

The 'Maltese cross' has become a symbol of Malta, though it really belongs to the Order of St John. However, it is correctly 'Maltese' in that, contrary to popular belief, it did not (in its current form) become the universal symbol of the Hospitallers until the mid-16th century, when the Knights were firmly established in Malta.

It has long been believed that the cross was the Order's symbol from the start because it is also a symbol of Amalfi, the city-state thought to be the home of the merchants who started the Hospitallers way back in the 11th century. The 'Maltese' cross still appears on the coat of arms of the city (as well as on the flag of the Italian navy).

A recent survey of the evidence by a British Knight, however, suggests that the current design evolved over the first few hundred years of the Order's existence. Early on, the Hospitallers used a variety of crosses, shared with other crusaders, and particularly a simple Greek cross (with splayed arms but without the V-shaped ends). Only in Rhodes (1309–1522) does the eight-pointed cross emerge as predominant, but still in a less sharp-cornered, thicker-set, design than today's.

It is only in the immediate aftermath of the Great Siege of Malta (1565) that the modern version of the Maltese cross, with its four arrow-head arms coming to a point in the middle, displaces all other designs and starts to appear all over the coinage, art and architecture of the Order (see St John's Co-Cathedral for example). It was even used when depicting scenes from earlier times, helping to plant the idea that it had always been the Knights' emblem.

The symbolism of the cross is certainly Christian. It is a cross as in the crucifixion and the four arms stand for the four cardinal virtues of prudence, temperance, justice and fortitude. The meaning of the eight points is less clear. They were generally understood to stand for the eight beatitudes but may also have come to represent the eight obligations of the Knight: truth, faith, sincerity, humility, justice, mercy, endurance of persecution and repentance of sin.

reputation for the best *festa* fireworks, but Mqabba is challenging for the crown. Fireworks are usually accompanied by music, food stalls and a general festival atmosphere.

On Sunday, the *festa* itself, the day starts with High Mass, usually with an invited preacher and sacred music played by local musicians. Some parishes traditionally play the music of a particular Maltese or Italian composer (or composers). Works may be new or old, on occasion played from handwritten manuscripts dating back as far as the 18th century.

This is followed by the *festa* procession around the local streets. Often accompanied by the setting off of bangers, the procession is led by representatives of local confraternities (like guilds but attached to the Church). Next comes the statue of the saint carried shoulder-high by six or eight men, accompanied by priests bearing church relics, altar boys (still mostly boys in Malta) and members of the public who also line the streets.

As well as, or as part of, the religious processions, there are band marches. Each parish has at least one wind band. These evolved from simple fife and drums in the 18th century under the influence of British military music – and this is the high point of their year. The band marches are usually accompanied by considerable secular celebration and often quite a lot of alcohol; they can occasionally become quite raucous.

The day after the *festa*, usually a Monday, many people take the day off work and go to the beach for a picnic.

ATTENDING A *FESTA* Tourists are always welcome at these feast-day celebrations with their processions, religious services, music, fireworks, food and general jollity. The exact date of each *festa* varies from year to year so check what is happening during your visit by going to www.visitmalta.com/village-festas and clicking through to the *festa* **calendar**, or by contacting the Malta Tourism Authority (↘ *freephone in the UK: 0800 72230;* e *info@visitmalta.com; see page 40 for a list of MTA offices*).

There are a few *festi* in **winter**, but the main *festa* season opens with the feast of St Publius in Floriana in the last week of April. After that (with a brief gap in mid-May) there are *festi* almost every weekend until the end of September. The biggest are public holidays (see page 33). Other particularly popular *festi* include: St Nicholas in Siġġiewi (last Sunday of June), St George in Qormi (same day), St Philip in Żebbuġ (second Sunday of June) and St George in Victoria, Gozo (mid July), which includes *sulky* (horse cart) races up the main street.

SPORT AND ACTIVITIES

FOOTBALL Football is a big thing in Malta. There are over 50 local clubs (*www.maltafootball.com*) and most Maltese males support at least two teams – a Maltese team (run by the Malta Football Association; www.mfa.com.mt) and a British or Italian team. Leagues are followed assiduously and with great passion. The main games in Malta are played at the Ta' Qali National Stadium, while many bars show live international football. The most popular foreign teams – including Manchester United and Liverpool – have their own club houses. Maltese footballer Michael Mifsud plays in the UK and the Malta Tourism Authority sponsors Sheffield United.

WATER POLO Water polo is the next most popular sport, played throughout the summer (in football's closed season). There are lidos in many coastal towns and important matches take place at the Olympic-sized National Swimming Pool (*Maria Teresa Spinelli St, Gzira GZR 06;* ↘ *21322884;* e *asaofmalta@vol.net.mt; www.asaofmalta.org*).

HORSE RACING A popular spectator sport, horse racing here is often more like Roman chariot racing: the driver sits on a *sulky*, a lightweight two-wheeled cart, behind the horse which trots the course. You will occasionally see these vehicles on the street, and in Gozo's capital Victoria, they race along the main road during the July and August *festi*. The national race course is at the Marsa Sports Complex near Valletta (*Marsa Grounds, Aldo Moro St;* ↘ *21233851,* e *info@marsasportsclub.com*).

BOĊĊI Similar to *boules*, this traditional game is played on local pitches, mostly by the older generation (rather like bowls in England); see boxed text, page 292.

NATIONAL/PUBLIC HOLIDAYS AND OTHER EVENTS

NATIONAL HOLIDAYS Malta has more holidays than any other EU country:

New Year's Day 1 January
Feast of St Paul's 10 February. A national winter *festa* commemorating the day
Shipwreck when St Paul, Malta's patron saint, is meant to have been shipwrecked on the rocks of St Paul's Bay in AD60 (see page 138).

The feast day of St Joseph (San Ġużepp)	19 March. Celebrated with Mass in the morning and picnicking in the countryside in the afternoon. Rabat hosts a full *festa* procession in the evening.
Freedom Day	31 March. Remembers the final withdrawal of the British Forces from Malta in 1979. A monument on the Vittoriosa Waterfront commemorates the event.
Good Friday	Churches are decorated and there are processions through the streets.
Workers' Day	1 May. Celebrations mainly by the General Workers Union and Labour Party in Valletta.
Sette Giugno	7 June. In commemoration of serious riots and four deaths that occurred on this day in 1919; see page 16.
Feast of St Peter and St Paul (L-Imnarja)	29 June. Celebrated particularly in Buskett Gardens with music and rabbit stew (see page 196).
Feast of the Assumption of Our Lady (Santa Marija)	15 August. An important *festa* celebrated in many parishes, particularly Victoria and Żebbuġ on Gozo and on Malta in Mqabba, Qrendi, Mosta, Gudja, Attard and Għaxaq. Good view of fireworks from the bastion walls of Mdina.
Victory Day	8 September. Celebrating the victory at the end of the Great Siege of 1565 (see page 11) as well as the Italian surrender in World War II (8 September 1943; see page 17). Also the religious feast of Marija Bambina, the birth of the Holy Virgin, centred on Senglea. Regatta in the Grand Harbour with six harbour towns competing and feasts in Naxxar, Mellieħa and Xagħra (Gozo).
Independence Day	21 September. Celebrating this day in 1964 when Malta became an independent state.
Feast of the Immaculate Conception	8 December. Particularly celebrated in Bormla and well-attended because it is the only *festa* at this time of year.
Republic Day	13 December. Malta became a republic on this day in 1974.
Christmas Day	25 December

OTHER EVENTS Besides the national holidays and numerous *festi*, there are a number of other annual events.

February
Carnival Malta's carnival has existed since at least the 1530s (the time of the Knights) and possibly much earlier. For five days before the start of Lent (usually, but not always, in February), Malta, and particularly Valletta, goes a little crazy. Colourful floats roll through the capital and people in wild costumes populate the streets, cafés and bars. On Gozo, Victoria plays host to the floats while Nadur's carnival, sometimes called the Silent Carnival, is celebrated in stranger fashion. Here there is no organising committee; the whole thing is spontaneous. Costumes are simple (sacks, wigs) and designed for disguise rather than show. Many participants do not speak in order to keep their identities secret (hence the nickname) and some carry placards hand-painted with veiled insults to public (and private) personalities.

Malta Marathon and Half-Marathon Run from Mdina, via Ta' Qali, Attard and Mosta to finish in Sliema. There is also a walkers' half marathon (e *info@maltamarathon.com; www.maltamarathon.com*). Specialist holiday operator,

Sports Tours International, offers trips to this event; see *Chapter 3, Tour operators*, page 43.

March
Opera Festival Held at the historic Manoel Theatre in Valletta, the festival usually consists of two fully staged operas and an opera-related concert. Specialist tour operator, Travel for the Arts, offers packages to this festival; see *Chapter 3, Tour operators*, page 43.

Easter The Maltese take Easter Week very seriously and many processions take place as well as devotional church visits. On Easter Sunday, church is followed by a large family lunch. Children are given Easter eggs and a *figolla*, a pastry filled with almond paste and topped with icing.

Tour Ta' Malta Maltese version of the Tour de France held over four days towards the end of March. Organised by the Malta Cycling Federation (e *info@ maltacyclingfederation.com; www.maltacyclingfederation.com*).

May
Fireworks Festival Annual competition held 1 May with a vast display of foreign and local fireworks over the Grand Harbour.

Mother's Day (Variable date) A great excuse for a large long lunch in a restaurant. If you want to eat out on this day, book well in advance.

P1 Power Boat Race (*www.powerboatp1.com*) A weekend of roaring engines as powerboats race along the Grand Harbour.

July
Ghanafest (*www.maltaculuture.com*) A national folk festival of *ghana* singing (see *Music* page 30) held in the Argotti Gardens, Floriana.

Malta Arts Festival (℡ *21245168;* e *info@maltaartsfestival.com; www.maltaartsfestival.com*) Concerts, opera, theatre, visual arts, food and wine, mainly in Valletta. Also includes the Malta Jazz Festival; see below.

Malta Jazz Festival (*www.maltajazzfestival.org*) Concerts around the Grand Harbour by Maltese and international jazz artists.

September
Notte Bianca (White Night) (℡ *21232515;* e *info@nottebiancamalta.com; www.nottebiancamalta.com*) Date varies, but usually in September or October. Shops and museums stay open all evening and some into the early hours. Historic buildings not normally open to the public welcome visitors and there is a variety of entertainment.

October
Festival Mediterranea (℡ *21550985;* e *info@mediterranea.com.mt; www.mediterranea.com.mt*) Gozo's annual arts festival, based in Victoria. Dominated by concerts and opera but also including talks, walks, art exhibitions, etc.

Malta Military Tattoo (*www.maltaculture.com*) At Ta' Qali Stadium. Precision marching, gymnastics and lots of military music.

Rolex Middle Sea Race Around 70–80 boats take part in this sailing race of 606 nautical miles starting and ending in Valletta's Marsamxett Harbour. Hosted by the Royal Malta Yacht Club (✆ *21333109;* e *info@middlesearace.com; www.rolexmiddlesearace.com*).

November
International Choir Competition and Festival (m *79666149; www.maltaculture.com*) Five days of concerts and choral get-togethers in some of Malta's many churches.

December
Christmas Richly celebrated in this Catholic country, Christmas brings nativity scenes all over the place, decorated churches and lots of carol singing.

For event listings see **www.visitmalta.com** (or contact the MTA – see page 33 for details) and the **Malta Council for Culture and the Arts** (✆ *21245168;* e *info@maltaculture.com; www.maltaculture.com*).

3

Practical Information

WHEN TO VISIT

Malta enjoys some 300 days of sunshine a year and doesn't have a closed season (except in Comino) so you can visit at any time. The weather does, of course, vary through the year and can get wet and windy as well as quite chilly in winter. The best time to visit depends largely on what you want to do.

Summer (which in Malta runs to mid-September) is dry, hot and quite busy. July and August are driest, hottest and busiest. The summer – especially August – is also dramatically more expensive with accommodation prices often double the winter figures. On the other hand there is very rarely any rain from early July to mid-September and the average peak temperature during the day is 30°C. Temperatures can go higher, but on the coast there is usually a breeze to stop it becoming too oppressive.

Watersports – swimming, snorkelling, diving, windsurfing, etc – are most reliable in summer when the water is warm and more likely to be calm. Summer is also *festa* time when each parish has its colourful religious feast day (see page 31). There are feasts almost every weekend in summer and many other events besides (see page 33).

Winter is generally mild and can be warm and sunny. Even in winter there is an average of five hours sunshine a day. There are, however, significant patches of cold wind and rain. When it is very windy and the sea boils up (which can be great to watch) ferries may stop, though rarely for more than a few hours. Even in January (the coldest month) average daylight temperatures are 9–14°C. Winter 2008–09 was unusually cold and wet while winter 2009–10 was particularly mild. The cooler months are generally OK for sightseeing, but not, of course, for swimming. Accommodation is much cheaper than in summer, except over Christmas and New Year, when – although Malta is not busy – prices rise dramatically.

Spring and **autumn** (April–June/late September–November) are ideal if you don't like crowds but would like a bit of sun and are primarily interested in the sights and the countryside. Swimming can be very pleasant from May until the end of October (with the water warmer in the autumn) and on weekdays at least you are quite likely to have the beach to yourself. See also *Climate, Chapter 2*, page 22.

There are some differences between spring and autumn besides water temperature: spring generally has a lower rainfall than autumn and the countryside is greener and full of wild flowers making it the nicest time for walking. Also, in spring, the EU outlaws bird hunting (see page 24), whilst in autumn you are more likely to have to share rural and coastal areas with men taking potshots at migrating birds (see *Safety*, page 48). This is a particular problem for birdwatchers who may find the hunters less than accommodating. Autumn has the greater number of migrants, especially raptors, but spring is definitely the more congenial time to birdwatch (see *Birdwatching*, pages 68 and 97).

HIGHLIGHTS What makes Malta different from other parts of southern Europe is its history – and its prehistory. Malta's **prehistoric temples**, built 3600–2500BC, are unique. There is nothing like them anywhere else in the world and nothing built this early comes close to their sophistication (see pages 4 and 78). If you would visit Stonehenge or Mycenae, then don't miss the temples of Malta.

Malta's other main claim to fame – and far better known – is the art, architecture and fortifications of the **Knights of St John**. A walk around Malta's tiny capital, **Valletta**, is a must, and **St John's Co-Cathedral** (see page 123) is the artistic and decorative highlight. The best way to see fortified Valletta as the Knights and their enemies saw it is from the water (see page 115). This is also the most congenial way to get between Valletta and Sliema, and Valletta and the Three Cities.

In the island's interior is the medieval walled town of **Mdina**. Take a walk around, by day if you plan to go into the museums, otherwise in the evening when the tour groups have gone. **Rabat** (around Mdina) is often ignored, but it is a pleasant place with some amazing late **Roman catacombs**, of which St Paul's is the largest and most accessible (see page 214).

The other period of European history that stands out in Malta is World War II when 'Fortress Malta' played a significant (and locally devastating) role in the Allied victory. There are several underground shelters that can be visited, the **Malta at War Museum** being the most organised (page 147).

Beyond history, many people come to Malta, and especially to Gozo, for the **diving, snorkelling** and **swimming**. Malta could also attract substantial numbers of visitors for **birdwatching** during spring and autumn migration but as mentioned above, the birds are also popular with hunters. **Walking** is great, especially in spring, along the coasts of northeastern Malta and on Gozo. And if you are interested in **churches**, there are hundreds! See page 88 for details on those most worth a visit.

The churches and villages come particularly alive during the *festa* season (mostly May to September but with a few outside these dates, see page 31) when bunting and lights decorate the church and streets, and the whole parish, as well as outside visitors, gather to make music, worship, parade, party, eat, drink and watch fireworks.

Finally, don't miss **Gozo**. It is completely different from the main island, much greener and much more relaxed. The **Citadel** is well worth a visit, there is plenty else to see and the swimming is excellent. A day trip is better than nothing, but really this is a place to spend a few days.

For a list of highlights and suggestions for ways to amuse **children**, see *Malta for families*, page 49. For a list of **public holidays** and **cultural events**, see page 33.

SUGGESTED ITINERARIES

Malta in a day Most one-day visitors are cruise passengers, who arrive at the Grand Harbour's new purpose-built waterfront (*www.vallettawaterfront.com*) in Floriana, just outside the walls of Valletta. If you organise it in advance, you could step straight off your huge modern ship onto a tiny traditional one, a *dgħajsa*, for a 30-minute tour of the Grand Harbour, or board the sea plane for a half-hour airborne tour of the Maltese islands.

If you want to see the historic sights and do not want to do so in a large unwieldy group, then book a guide for the day (see page 41) and ask him/her to arrange a car (or minibus) and driver for the afternoon. Grab a sandwich, so you don't have to stop for lunch, and request something like the following (obviously adapted to your interests and time available):

- Walk around Valletta (1hr)
- Quick look into the National Archaeological Museum (15mins)
- St John's Co-Cathedral (30mins)
- *Dgħajsa* boat tour around the Grand Harbour (30mins)
- If you have time (for instance if you are unable to book a slot at the Hypogeum – below) then take a walk around Birgu (1hr)

Pick up car and driver and head to:

- Mnajdra and Ħaġar Qim temples (1hr 30mins inc travelling time) – if you don't have time for this then replace with the less attractive but still very interesting Tarxien Temples which are close to the Hypogeum.
- Mdina and Rabat – including St Paul's Grotto or Catacombs (1hr 30mins inc driving time)
- The Hypogeum (1hr) – you will not need a guide for this but do need to book well in advance. If few slots are available, you may have to adapt the day's programme to fit in with the slot you are alotted.
- Back to Valletta (20mins' drive)

Malta in five days

Day 1 Wander around Valletta's narrow streets and seafront fortifications, taking in whatever grabs your interest (1–2hrs). Visit the National Archaeological Museum (30mins) and arrive at the Upper Barracca Gardens at 11.45 for the firing of the noonday gun. Bring *pastizzi* (see page 62) with you or some other quick lunch. Visit St John's Co-Cathedral (with the audio guide, 1–1½hrs) then take a (pre-booked, see page 107) traditional *dgħajsa* water taxi around the Grand Harbour (30mins) ending up on Vittoriosa waterfront (Birgu). Visit the Malta at War Museum (page 147) then wander around Birgu and the Knights' area, the Collachio (page 150). Either eat supper early in Birgu or take the water taxi (or bus or car) back to Valletta and its many good restaurants. (This could be done in more depth and in a more relaxed way over two days.)

Day 2 Start at Mnajdra and Ħaġar Qim temples and their surroundings (1½hrs, though it can be done in less), then perhaps a swim and lunch at nearby Għar Lapsi.

Head inland to Rabat to see St Paul's catacombs and grotto and take a stroll around Mdina, perhaps taking in a museum or the cathedral. Hop on bus 81 (if you're not driving) to Dingli Cliffs to explore 'Clapham Junction' with its mysterious ancient cart ruts (page 197) and troglodyte caves. Maybe have a walk and watch the sunset.

If you have a car, you could reverse the order of the last two visits and follow an evening walk at Dingli Cliffs with an atmospheric supper in a historic building along one of Mdina's medieval alleyways (see *Where to eat* in Mdina, page 203).

Day 3 At 09.00 (before the tour groups arrive) head to the Tarxien temples, then walk to the not-to-be-missed underground tomb complex, the Hypogeum (book well ahead; see page 176). In the afternoon take the ferry to Gozo (see page 253) and settle into accommodation before going to Ramla Bay (see page 289) for a swim in good weather, and visiting Calypso's Cave.

Day 4 If you're visiting in summer then make your way to Mġarr ix-Xini on Gozo's south coast (see page 294) to snorkel/swim and visit the tower (check opening times) and for lunch at the diminutive outdoor restaurant. In winter, explore the salt pans and walk along the north coast (see page 284) towards Żebbuġ. Spend the afternoon, exploring the Gozo Citadel and Victoria (see pages 271 and 269).

Day 5 Visit Ġgantija Temple (see page 284) and then relax – sunbathing and swimming or walking (depending on the season).

Needless to say the islands are packed-full with alternatives to the above – see the rest of this book!

CHOOSING A BASE

Malta is not a large place, so if you plan to have your own transport you can visit almost any part of the islands from almost any base. If you want to do a lot of sightseeing and will be using public transport, the ideal place to stay is Valletta/Floriana – although there are fewer good accommodation options here than in the more tourist-oriented areas. The sights of the capital are then within walking distance, with water transport to Sliema and the Three Cities, and easy access to the island's main bus station from which you can get almost anywhere on Malta.

Having said that, the number of direct buses from places other than Valletta – particularly from Sliema and St Julian's – is increasing. Buses may be less frequent and may not run late in the evening, but it is getting steadily easier to stay in these places and sightsee by bus.

Malta often sells itself as 'sun and sea', but the word 'beach' in the tourist brochures can mean anything from a decent stretch of golden sand (not many) to a patch of rock from which to enter the water. Rock swimming can be just as good as (or, for some, better) than sandy beaches but it helps to know what to expect. Ask your operator or hotel and see *Chapter 4, Swimming,* page 90.

Chapter 4 also shows the whereabouts of the main sights for a variety of other special interests, from the historic to the active, which may help you choose where to base yourself. If you are looking for lively restaurants, bars and nightlife then the place to be is St Julian's, or neighbouring Sliema. If you don't like night-time noise and karaoke bars, stay away from Paceville. Valletta is very quiet of an evening, although it has excellent restaurants, and Buġibba and Qawra (which often feature in package deals) are the Blackpool of Malta.

Malta works well as a citybreak, with plenty to see and do and good places to eat, or you can have a more classic holiday with a mix of sunbathing and swimming (pool or sea), outdoor activities and sightseeing. My personal favourite is to spend a few days based in Valletta/Floriana visiting the historic and prehistoric sights of the main island, followed by some laid-back time for relaxed exploring, sun, swimming and snorkelling in Gozo.

i TOURIST INFORMATION

For tourist information on Gozo see *Chapter 14*, page 258.

The **Malta Tourism Authority** (MTA) (*www.visitmalta.com*) has lots of general information as well as a useful list of tour operators that can be searched by requirements, a set of themed interactive maps, weather forecasts, events listings and contacts for guides who speak a variety of languages. Contact MTA direct on **e** info@visitmalta.com or via the offices below.

MTA OFFICES ABROAD

France: Office du Tourisme de Malte, c/o Ambassade de Malte, 50 Av des Champs Elysees, 75008 Paris; ☏ 674670744; **e** info@ visitemalte.com

Germany: Fremdenverkehrsamt Malta, Schillerstrasse 30–40, D-60313 Frankfurt am Main; ☏ 69 284060; **e** info@urlaubmalta.com

Italy: Ente per il Turismo di Malta, c/o Air Malta, Via Gianlorenzo Bernini, 23 Fiumicino, 00054 Rome; ☎ 06 65003335; e info@visitmalta.it

UK: Malta Tourist Office, Unit C, Parkhouse, 14 Northfields, London SW18 1DD; ☎ 020 8877 6990; e office.uk@visitmalta.com

OTHER USEFUL WEBSITES

www.aboutmalta.com All sorts of information aimed as much at locals as foreigners.

www.heritagemalta.org The government's heritage department. Historical & visitor information on many of Malta's historic & prehistoric sites.

www.maltabookers.com Independent commercial website for information & online bookings.

www.malteseislands.com Lots of general information in English, Italian, French & German.

http://maltamedia.com All that's happening in Malta: news, arts, events, etc.

www.maltaweather.com Forecasts & general weather/climate information.

www.starwebmalta.com 'Malta's first on-line concierge' with listings (for locals & foreigners) of restaurants, accommodation, attractions, etc. Tourist locations without their own websites often use Starweb as their presence online.

For websites dealing specifically with Gozo, please see page 259.

TOURIST INFORMATION IN MALTA

Free telephone information line ☎ 80072230; ⊕ 09.00–12.30 & 13.15–17.00 Mon–Fri

Malta International Airport Arrivals lounge, Luga; ☎ 23696073/4; ⊕ 10.00– 21.00 daily★

Valletta 1 City Arcades, Freedom Sq, City Gate, Valletta; ☎ 22915440/41/42; ⊕ 09.00–17.30

Mon–Sat, 09.00–13.00 Sun & public holidays★. Well-informed staff, lots of leaflets & maps. This office may be moving if the planned renovation of this area goes ahead. The phone number will probably stay the same.

★Open most public holidays, closed on Christmas Day, New Year's Day, Good Friday and Easter Sunday.

GUIDES The Malta Tourism Authority keeps a list of **licensed guides** and the languages they speak at www.visitmalta.com/tourist-guides. If you are interested in **history**, then start by contacting Vince DeBono, known locally as 'the Walking Encyclopaedia' (m 79448771; e info@guideinmalta.com; www.guideinmalta.com). For **wildlife and walking** on Malta try Annalise Falzon (m 79472950; e annalise.falzon@gmail.com; natureinmalta.tripod.com).

The MTA has also produced a series of **podcasts** covering the UNESCO World Heritage sites of the prehistoric temples and Valletta. These include content from experts in their field and can be downloaded free (with or without images) at www.visitmalta.com/podcasts.

BOOKS A few key books are recommended within the text of this guide, and a much broader list can be found in *Appendix 3, Further reading* (page 301). Some books on Malta are available from Amazon and from general bookshops in Malta and abroad, but some are harder to find so you may want to try the following websites:

www.maltabook.com
www.maltaonlinebookshop.com
www.midseabooks.com Maltese publisher, covers only their own books, but they publish some of the best.

www.pen-and-sword.co.uk Search 'Malta' for a large selection of this British publisher's books on Maltese military history.
www.wishtoread.com

Once **in Malta**, all bookshops have English-language sections and many of the sights have an interesting selection of relevant books in English. The **Agenda bookshop** in Valletta (*26 Republic St, opposite the National Archaeological Museum;*

✎ *21233621*) has a particularly good range of books as well as well-informed staff to help you choose. Agenda also has a smaller bookshop on the Gozo ferry.

MAPS It is, of course, hoped that the maps in this guidebook will give you most of what you need to get around and sightsee, but if you are planning to drive around the islands or to do extensive walking, you may need more than a guidebook can provide. The best road map I have used is the **Freytag and Berndt Malta and Gozo** (£8.95 from Stanfords online at www.stanfords.co.uk/stock/malta-and-gozo-82032 or from Amazon). **Miller's Gozo & Comino**, and **AA Malta & Gozo** are also quite good. These are available from bookshops in Malta (see above) as well as online.

For the greatest detail of the nation's streets, there is the Malta A–Z, the *mAZe Street Atlas* (€15 from bookshops in Malta or online from www.maltabook.com) which covers Malta, Gozo and Comino, but has street names only in Maltese. If it is detail of topography you are after, the specialist Malta Survey maps produced by MEPA (the Maltese planning authority) are the ones to go for – but they aren't cheap. These can be bought from Stanfords online (*www.stanfords.co.uk/search.html?q=Malta+survey*; Malta £37.95, Gozo and Comino £20.95).

TOUR OPERATORS

Some 200 companies provide travel packages to Malta and most of the large cruise companies stop here. The following is inevitably a small selection of operators. A full list with a useful search facility is available at http://www.visitmalta.com/tour-operator-search.

MALTA SPECIALISTS IN THE UK

Chevron Air Holidays ✎ (UK) 0844 4124343; e malta@chevron.co.uk; www.chevron.co.uk. A real Malta specialist covering only Malta & Gozo, offering 56 different hotels on the islands.
Choice Holidays ✎ (UK) 0800 0918888; e info@choicehols.co.uk; www.choiceholidaysdirect.co.uk. Malta & Italy.

Malta Bargains ✎ (UK) 0800 0912222; e info@maltabargains.com; www.maltabargains.com. Trips from the UK to Malta, mainly to Qawra & Bugibba.
Malta Direct ✎ (UK) 0845 6040035; e maltadirect@holidaymalta.com; www.maltadirect.com. The travel-operator arm of Air Malta.
Mercury Direct ✎ (UK) 0800 0914149; e enquiries@mercury-direct.co.uk; www.mercury-direct.co.uk

OTHER UK OPERATORS OFFERING TRAVEL TO MALTA

Cadogan 0845 6154390; www.cadoganholidays.com
Cox & Kings ✎ 020 7873 5000; www.coxandkings.co.uk
Explore ✎ 0845 0131537; www.explore.co.uk
Kirker Holidays ✎ 020 7593 1899; www.kirkerholidays.com
Martin Randall ✎ 020 8742 3355; www.martinrandall.com
Saga ✎ 0800 0960074; www.saga.co.uk/holidays

The Discovery Collection ✎ 01371 859733; www.discovery-collection.com
Thomas Cook My Travel ✎ 0871 8950055; www.mytravel.thomascook.com
Thomson ✎ 0871 2313235; www.thomson.co.uk
Tui-First Choice ✎ 0871 6649020; www.firstchoice.co.uk
Vintage Travel ✎ 0845 3440460; www.vintagetravel.co.uk/villa_list.cfm?area_id=22. Upmarket Gozo villa holidays only.

ITALIAN TOUR OPERATORS

Holiday Malta ✎ + 39 (0) 95 53 00 00; e info@holidaymalta.it. Italian section of Air Malta's travel operator (see Malta Direct, above).

Il Tuareg ✎ 091 203642; www.iltaureg.com

As well as a few Catholic pilgrimage sites, including St Paul's Grotto in Rabat (see page 211), there are a number of **retreat houses** in Malta. The first dedicated retreat house on the islands, built in 1957 by the Franciscans, was **Poziuncola Retreat House** in Baħar iċ-Ċagħaq (↘ 21374222; e porziun@di-ve.com). With 35 en-suite guest rooms, Poziuncola offers guests the chance to spend time in quiet prayer and contemplation, either alone or in a directed retreat with preaching, counselling and spiritual direction from the friars. The Franciscans also run the **Padova Retreat House** near Mġarr on Gozo (↘ 21563413; e padovarh@di-ve.com). Other retreat houses are listed at www.maltadiocese.org/rh?l=1 and for Gozo at http://gozodiocese.org/institutions/retreat-houses. **Gollcher Travel** offers religious tours such as 'In the Footsteps of St Paul'; see below for full details. Half-day and full-day visits with a religious theme are run by the **Religious Tourism Organisation** (Dar l-Emigrant, Castille Pl, Valletta; ↘ 222644, 240255 or 232545; e mecmalta@dream.vol.net.mt) and **Charisma Travel** organises pilgrimages and other religious cultural tours (see below).

SPORTS AND CULTURAL HOLIDAYS There are some specialist operators that organise trips to specific events in Malta, such as the Malta Marathon and the Opera Festival and a few that specialise in a single sport:

Charisma Travel ↘ 21310517; www.charismatravel.org. A Maltese company which organises pilgrimages & other religious cultural tours.

Gollcher Travel ↘ 21323854/5/6; www.gollchertravel.com. A Maltese tour operator offering religious tours (eg: 'In the Footsteps of St Paul'), many of which take in the main sites from a religious perspective.

Headwater ↘ 01606 720099; e info@headwater.com; www.headwater.com. Offers walking & cycling holidays in Gozo (more details on page 265 for walking & page 226 for cycling).

Ramblers Holidays ↘ 01707 331133; www.ramblersholidays.co.uk. Runs walking holidays to Malta & Gozo.

Sports Tours International ↘ 0161 7038547; e running@sportstoursinternational.co.uk; www.sportstoursinternational.co.uk/running. Offers packages to the Malta Marathon & Half Marathon held each Feb. See Chapter 2, Other events, page 34.

Swim Trek ↘ 01273 739713; e info@swimtrek.com; www.swimtrek.com. British swimming-tours company that runs a 1-week holiday to Gozo (more details on page 267).

Travel for the Arts ↘ 020 8799 8350; e tfa@stlon.com; www.travelforthearts.co.uk. Offers packages to Malta's Opera Festival in March. See Chapter 2, Other events, page 35.

For companies running other activity-based trips, see Sports and activities, page 66.

TOURS WITHIN MALTA There are coach tours available to the main sites of Malta and for day trips to Gozo. These are usually booked through the hotels or your tour-operator rep. Most of the companies providing them do not sell direct to the individual visitor. There is one agent that does: **Maltarama** (↘ 21380200). This company sells excursions both full day (including lunch) and half day. Tours include Valletta (half day €31); Mdina (half day €23, full day €45); the Three Cities (half day €27); Gozo (full day €52 or, in summer only, Gozo by Night €54 inc dinner); 'Ħaġar Qim and Local Lifestyle' – which includes the Blue Grotto and 'an unspoilt Maltese village' (half day €23, full day €48); 'Blue Grotto, Limestone Heritage and Marsaxlokk Market' (extended half day €27); 'The Village Festa' (Jun–Sep, evening, €19.50) and private tailor-made tours (half day for 1–3 people €250, full day €330 – cheaper per head with more people).

3

Other good tour providers are **SMS** (S Mifsud and Sons) and **Robert Arrigo** whose tours are booked through agents and hotels. If you see a tour that is very much cheaper than the above, ask for details. Will you have a separate guide and driver, for instance? You may not want your driver to be holding a microphone with one hand and pointing out sights with the other!

You can, of course, create your own tour by booking a guide (see page 41) and a car (see page 55 or ask the guide to book it), giving you much greater flexibility and avoiding any risk of being herded.

For information on the Malta sightseeing bus, see page 43.

RED TAPE

TRAVEL DOCUMENTS Visitors from the UK and Ireland need a valid passport but do not need a visa. Nationals of EU countries with national identity cards may travel on these instead of a passport. All EU visitors can stay as long as they like in Malta.

Malta is a member of the EU Schengen area giving it the same entry rules as other EU counties (except the UK and Ireland) for visitors from **outside the Union**. No visa is required for a stay of less than three months by those from the USA, Canada, Australia, New Zealand, Japan, or most non-EU European countries (with the exception of Russia).

Other nationalities need to contact a Maltese embassy, consulate or high commission (see below) or where none exists, the embassy or consulate that looks after Malta (often the Italian or Austrian). Further information and downloadable visa application forms can be found on the Maltese Foreign Ministry website at www.mfa.gov.mt/default.aspx?MLEV=53&MDIS=523.

ⓔ MALTESE EMBASSIES, HIGH COMMISSIONS AND CONSULATES ABROAD Please note that not all consulates can issue visas, but the ones listed below should be able to.

Australia & New Zealand 38 Culgoa Circuit, O'Malley ACT 2606; ✆ 0061 (2) 6290 1724 or 6290 1573; e maltahighcommission.canberra@gov.mt; There are also consulates in Melbourne & Sydney.
Austria Opernring 5/1, A-1010 Vienna; ✆ 0043 (1) 586 5010 or 586 5020; e maltaembassy.vienna@gov.mt
Belgium 25 Rue Archimède, 1000 Brussels; ✆ (02) 343 0195 e maltaembassy.brussels@gov.mt
Canada 3300 Bloor West, Toronto ON M8X 2X3; ✆ (416) 207 0922; e maltaconsulate.toronto@gov.mt. Also the embassy of Austria in Ottawa & the Consulate General of Italy, Vancouver.
Denmark, Sweden, Norway, Finland Amaliegade 8B, 2 sal 1256 Copenhagen K; ✆ 3315 3090; e maltaembassy.copenhagen@gov.mt
France 50 Av des Champs Elysées, 75008 Paris; ✆ (1) 5659 7590/99; e maltaembassy.paris@gov.mt
Germany Klingelhöferstrasse 7, 10785 Berlin; ✆ (0)30 263 9110; e maltaembassy.berlin@gov.mt
Ireland 17 Earlsfort Terrace, Dublin 2; ✆ 00353 1 676 2340; e maltaembassy.dublin@gov.mt

Italy 12, Lungotevere Marzio, 00186 Rome; ✆ (06) 687 9990/687 9947; e maltaembassy.rome@gov.mt
Netherlands Carnegielaan 4–14, 2517 KH, The Hague; ✆ (70) 356 1252 or 360 2205; e maltaembassy.thehague@gov.mt
Spain Paseo De La Castellana 45–6 DCHA, 28046 Madrid; ✆ 913 913 061; e maltaembassy.madrid@gov.mt
UK 36–38 Piccadilly, London W1J 0DP; ✆ visa section: 020 7292 4821, switchboard: 020 7292 4800; e maltahighcommission.london@gov.mt (general enquiries), e visa.london@gov.mt (visas); ⊕ 09.30–12.30 Mon–Fri. For visas, you need to make an appointment.
USA 2017 Connecticut Av NW, Washington, DC 20008; ✆ 001 (202) 462 3611/2; e maltaembassy.washington@gov.mt. Also general consulates of Italy in Chicago, Houston & San Francisco.

A full list of Malta's diplomatic missions abroad can be found on the website of Malta's Ministry for Foreign Affairs: http://www.mfa.gov.mt (click the 'missions' tab along the top of the page).

Ⓔ EMBASSIES, HIGH COMMISSIONS AND CONSULATES IN MALTA

Australia Ta' Xbiex Terrace, Ta' Xbiex MSD 11; ✆ 21338201; e aushicom@onvol.net

Austria 143 Palazzo Marina, St Christopher St, Valletta VLT 1465; ✆ 21255379 or 21232241, ext: 541; e austrianconsulate@maltanet.net

Belgium Europa Office Block no 8 & 9, John Lopez St, Floriana FRN 1400; ✆ 21228214; e valletta@diplobel.be; www.diplomatie.be/valletta

Denmark & Sweden 19 Zachary St, Valletta VLT 1133; ✆ 25691790; e consulategeneral@gollcher.com

Finland 63/64 Graham St, Sliema SLM 1711; ✆ 21343790/3; e edgar@oswaldarrigoltd.com or info@oswaldarrigoltd

France 130 Melita St, Valletta, PO Box 408, Valletta VLT 1000; ✆ 22480600; e france@global.net.mt; www.ambafrance.org.mt

Germany 'Il-Piazzetta' Entrance B, 1st Flr, Tower Rd, Sliema SLM 1605; ✆ 21336520 or 21336531; e info@valletta.diplo.de; www.valletta.diplo.de

Ireland Whitehall Mansions, Ta' Xbiex Seafront, Ta' Xbiex XBX 1026; ✆ 21334744, emergencies: ✆ 99911919; e vallettaembassy@dfa.ie

Italy 5 Vilhena St, Floriana FRN 1040; ✆ 21233157/8/9; e ambasciata.lavalletta@esteri.it; www.amblavalletta.esteri.it

Netherlands Whitehall Mansions, 3rd Flr, Ta' Xbiex Seafront, Ta' Xbiex MSD 11; ✆ 21313980 or 21313981; e VAL@minbuza.nl; www.netherlandsembassy.org.mt

New Zealand Malta comes under New Zealand's Italian embassy: Via Clitunno 44, 00198 Rome; ✆ +39 (06) 8537501; e rome@nzembassy.it; www.nzembassy.com/italy

Norway Notabile Rd, Mriehel; ✆ 21448466 or 21448596; e tzcutajar@pcutajar.com.mt

Spain Whitehall Mansions, Ta' Xbiex Seafront, Ta' Xbiex XBX 1026; ✆ 21317365, & for Spanish citizens in Malta also: m 79349191; e emb.valletta@mae.es

UK Whitehall Mansions, Ta' Xbiex Seafront, Ta' Xbiex XBX 1026; ✆ 23230000; e bhcvalletta@fco.gov.uk; www.britishhighcommission.gov.uk/malta

USA Development Hse, 3rd Flr, St Anne St, Floriana FRN 9010; PO Box 535, Valletta; ✆ 25614000, emergencies: m 99203322; e usembmalta@state.gov; www.malta.usembassy.gov

A full list of diplomatic missions and their contacts in Malta can be found on the website of Malta's Ministry for Foreign Affairs: www.mfa.gov.mt.

CUSTOMS AND DUTY-FREE Malta is a member of the European Union so there are no limits on what you may bring in or out for personal use. There are guidelines as to what the receiving country considers reasonable maxima. From **Malta to the UK** these are 3,200 cigarettes, 200 cigars, 3kg tobacco, 110l beer, 90l wine, 20l fortified wine and 10l spirits. Going **into Malta**, the limits are the same except that only 800 cigarettes and 1kg of tobacco are acceptable. Those entering Malta from outside the EU may bring up to 200 cigarettes, 1l of spirits and €430 worth of gifts or goods for personal use.

GETTING THERE AND AWAY

✈ **BY AIR** There is one international airport in Malta, in the southeast of the main island. It is just three hours' flying time from the UK – less from southern Europe. There are numerous direct flights and two low-cost airlines, **easyJet** (*www.easyjet.com*) and **Ryanair** (*www.ryanair.com*) now fly to Malta. easyJet goes from Gatwick, Manchester and Newcastle while Ryanair operates out of Luton, Bristol, Edinburgh, Dublin and Pisa. From summer 2010, **BMI Baby** (*www.bmibaby.com*) will also be flying to Malta on Tuesdays and Saturdays, from the end of May to October, from East Midlands Airport.

The national carrier, **Air Malta** (✆ *0845 6073710; www.airmalta.com*), has services from Heathrow, Gatwick, Birmingham, Manchester and, in summer, once a week from Glasgow, as well as from most European capitals, a few other

European cities particularly in Italy and Germany, and several places in North Africa. **Alitalia** (*www.alitalia.com*) flies to Malta from Italy (Rome) and **Lufthansa** (*www.lufthansa.com*) from Germany.

In addition to the scheduled flights, there are regular **charter flights** out of London and at least seven UK regional airports. The largest charter operators are **Thomas Cook – My Travel** (❧ *0871 8950055; www.mytravel.thomascook.com*) and **Thomson** (❧ *0871 2313235; www.thomson.co.uk*) who also own **First Choice** (❧ *0871 6649020; www.firstchoice.co.uk*).

Getting to and from the airport It doesn't take long to get from the airport to anywhere on Malta (unless it is a rainy rush hour). No part of the main island is more than an hour away by car (longer by bus, of course, because of the stops). It takes 15–20 minutes to get to Valletta, 25 minutes to St Julian's.

Bus no 8 runs between Malta International Airport and Valletta costing just €0.47. The bus stops at the main bus station from where you can walk or take a golf-buggy-style electric citycab to your accommodation in the capital, or a normal taxi if you are staying outside the capital.

Taxis are readily available at the airport and Malta's Public Transport Directorate fixes taxi fares from the airport to each town in Malta (*see www.maltatransport.com/en/new/publictransport/fares.xls*). As a guide, the cost between the airport and Valletta or Marsaxlokk is €13.98, to Sliema or St Julian's €18.63, for Golden Bay or Mġarr €23.29 and to Ċirkewwa (the Gozo ferry terminal) €30.28. It is worth agreeing the fare before you get in.

Malta Transfer (❧ *+356 79646481; www.maltatransfer.com*) is a tailor-made bus service that will take you from/to the airport more cheaply than a taxi and without the hassle of having to drag your luggage to the public bus stop. You need to book at least 24 hours in advance and the trip can be very slow because the bus picks up from multiple places.

Some hotels and self-catering accommodation will arrange airport transfer for you (usually at a price) and hire cars are also available at the airport. It is best to book ahead (see car hire, page 58).

BY SEA Ferries operate to Malta from Sicily and mainland Italy (via Sicily) arriving at the Sea Passenger Terminal on the Valletta Waterfront in Floriana. There are ships most days from Sicily and much less frequently from the mainland. Regularity depends on the season. The shortest journey is from Pozzallo in southern Sicily, to Valletta, taking just 1½ hours. On Saturdays – and other days in high season – you can get a boat direct from Catania (the city next to Mt Etna) to Valletta taking three to four hours. Both are fast catamarans that also carry cars, and are run by **Virtu Ferries** (❧ *(UK) 020 8206 1332, (Malta) 22069022/23491000, (Catania) 095 535711, (Pozzallo) 0932 954062; www.virtuferries.com*). Fares for adults are €80 one-way, €100–125 return (depending on length of stay), and for children €50 single, €68–86 return.

Grimaldi Lines (*c/o Sullivan Maritime, Malta:* ❧ *22995110; www.grimaldi-ferries.com*) also sails from Catania to Malta. They can be cheaper than Virtu but the journey takes longer. With Grimaldi you can also occasionally take a ferry all the way from Genoa to Malta (via Catania, about 36hrs; Malta–Genoa: 27hrs) as well as from Civitavecchia, the port of Rome (also via Catania: 32hrs; Malta–Rome: 27hrs).

✚ HEALTH AND SAFETY

POTENTIAL HEALTH PROBLEMS *with Dr Felicity Nicholson*
Malta is a European Mediterranean country with no special health problems. It is hot in summer, so be sure to drink enough water, have a little extra salt if you are

sweating more than usual and protect yourself from sunburn and the glare of the sun's rays. Sunglasses are essential on water, and also in town where the sun comes off the creamy yellow limestone like a mirror.

Leishmaniasis is a protozoan infection spread by the bite of **sand flies** that have acquired disease most commonly from dogs. Symptoms include a localised swelling or skin ulcer. A serious systemic disease (kala-azar) occurs more rarely. Deet-containing insect repellents will help to prevent sand-fly bites but Deet is a strong chemical that should be used sparingly. It should not be applied to broken skin or used on infants under two months old. If you need to wear it when also requiring sunscreen then apply the sunscreen first and the Deet second.

DRINKING WATER The tap water is theoretically drinkable, but it is very heavily chlorinated and you are likely to be advised – by middle-class locals as well as hotels – to drink bottled water. This is sensible advice. The tap water is not dangerous, however, so you do not need to worry about salad washed in it, ice, ice cream or cleaning your teeth.

SWIMMING There are only two things likely to keep you out of the water in Malta: **bad weather** and jellyfish. It is highly inadvisable to swim off rocks when there are waves or even a significant swell – you might find yourself bashed against sharp edges or unable to get out of the water. Some beaches also have occasional rip **currents**. These usually occur during or after windy weather and can be difficult to detect. Most Maltese beaches do not have flags or lifeguards, so take local advice. In summer the Maltese will swim almost anywhere where they can get safely into and out of the water (as well as off boats), so if there is nobody swimming, you might want to find out why before doing so yourself.

There is little marine wildlife in Malta likely to do a swimmer any harm. A huge shark was caught off Filfla by a fisherman in 1987, but the last shark attack on a person was over half a century ago and this was some way out from the shore. The main problem is **jellyfish,** purple stingers with see-through bodies patterned with purple and tentacles perhaps 10–15cm long. A bay may be clear one day and the next these irritating creatures will be floating around. They are quite pretty to look at but do not make good swimming companions. Being stung by one jellyfish hurts but will do you no lasting damage (though it may take kids a while to go back in the water); jump into a mass of them and you could end up in hospital. So when you arrive at a beach, take a look around. If there is a gaggle of people on the shore and few in the water, it may signal jellies. Ask.

If there are only one or two jellyfish you may want to remove them from the water (with a net or bucket) and leave them in a marked spot on the sand to dry out. Do not damage them in the water, or you may leave stinging tentacles behind. If one beach is plagued with jellyfish, try another, preferably one facing in a different direction. There is almost always somewhere that is not infested.

Jumping into the water off rocks is a favourite summer pastime of the local youth and can be great fun. Just make sure you know what is beneath you – even in deep water there may be rocks sticking up.

The greatest danger to swimmers and snorkellers, however, is **boats**. Almost every year someone is hit and seriously injured or killed. Just remember: boats can't see snorkellers and swimmers. Stay inside the buoys that mark the swimming areas where boats are not allowed, or take an **inflatable buoy** to mark your presence, as divers should also do. These can be bought from dive shops. If swimming from a boat, stay close, swim in a group or be aware of what is around you (which is hard as a snorkeller, head down in the underwater world!).

On a more trivial note (but one that may make a significant difference to enjoyment) Maltese **rocks** can be very sharp and many beaches are stony – it is worth having something to cover your feet when you swim if you don't want to discover of an evening that you have a host of random cuts. Shoes will protect you from sea urchins as well.

For diver safety, see page 67.

ROAD SAFETY When it comes to Malta's roads the key is to expect the unexpected. Like the UK, Malta drives on the left and most of its road rules are the same as in the UK – officially. What drivers actually do varies widely. The local joke is that the Maltese drive in the shade. The reality is even less predictable – they drive to avoid the many pot-holes. The bottom line is that as a pedestrian or a driver, you need to look in all directions. See also *Driving*, page 58.

FIREWORK FACTORIES Most parishes in Malta have a firework factory making *festa* fireworks (see page 31). These are usually small buildings standing alone on the outskirts of villages. If a red flag is flying it means keep away; they are working with explosive material. Accidents do happen – an average of one person a year over the last century has been killed making fireworks. These are, of course, manufacturing accidents not accidents at displays!

BIRD HUNTING If you are out in the Maltese countryside in the autumn – particularly early in the morning or from mid-afternoon, you are likely to come across men popping guns at passing bird life. This is very much less likely at other times of the year. Malta has 12,000 licensed hunters and a proportion of them are deeply wedded to their sport. Accidents involving people other than the hunters themselves are rare, but it is obviously worth being aware of what is going on around you.

If you are a birdwatcher with binoculars or a camera with a long lens around your neck, be conscious too that some hardcore hunters have a deep antipathy to your hobby. They see it as a threat to their own pastime, and a few are willing to go to some lengths to defend their patch. You may see signs, often hand painted, saying 'RTO', meaning 'reserved to owner'. The land may or may not be genuinely private, but it is best to treat it as such. You are unlikely to be the subject of anything worse than shouting, but confrontation is best avoided. If you see anything illegal or threatening, don't try to deal with it yourself; call the police on ↘ 112 and BirdLife Malta on ↘ 21347644.

CRIME AND TERRORISM Crimewise, Malta is an ordinary European destination. Crime against tourists is rare. Simply take the same common-sense precautions you would at home or in any western European country: don't leave valuables visible in parked cars; keep an eye on your belongings; and if you plan to wander the streets in the early hours, take advice from locals or hotel reception as to where is safe and where is not (most places are safe).

If walking alone (especially as a woman) late at night, the lower end of Valletta (towards St Elmo) is considered less safe than the upper end (though neither is exactly 1960s Harlem). Gzira has a red-light district making it a less salubrious place for women alone at night, and the strip of parkland outside the Phoenicia Hotel has a reputation as a gay cruising area (though, if so, it is very discreet). St Julian's seafront in summer has so many late-night establishments that it is generally considered safe at most times of day and night.

The British Foreign Office classes the threat of terrorism in Malta as low (at the time of writing) – better than most of Europe – and there are no particular conflicts or unrest. There is a degree of racism, but it is extremely unlikely to affect a tourist, least of all in any dangerous way. For up-to-date travel advice, see www.fco.gov.uk/en/travelling-and-living-overseas/travel-advice-by-country/europe/malta.

In the unlikely event that you have problems, call the police on the international emergency number: ✆ 112.

THE HEALTH SERVICE The public healthcare system in Malta is described as 'acceptable' by the British Foreign Office and it is free to EU citizens carrying an **EHIC** (European Health Insurance Card, www.ehic.org.uk) and an EU ID document. The UK has long had a reciprocal arrangement with Malta that means that British citizens do not officially even need an EHIC (although a passport to prove you are British is necessary). There is some confusion about this arrangement, however, so it is advisable to carry your EHIC.

Emergency hospital treatment and consultations at health centres are covered by EHIC. Medicines (other than in-patient medication and that prescribed for the first three days after discharge from hospital) and non-urgent treatment and repatriation are not. If in doubt about what is covered, contact the Entitlement Unit of the Maltese Ministry of Health (*24 St John's St, Valletta;* ✆ *22992515;* e *entitlement.mhec@gov.mt;* ◷ *09.00–12.30 Mon, Wed, Fri*).

There are eight primary care **health centres** on Malta and one on Gozo. Many Maltese, however, use the inexpensive **private GPs** who are often attached to local pharmacies. These are not covered by EHIC, but cost only a few euros for an appointment.

The **main hospital** in Malta is the brand-new 825-bed Mater Dei Hospital in Msida (✆ *25450000;* e *mdh@gov.mt; www.materdeihospital.org.mt*). Gozo has its own general hospital in Victoria (✆ *21561600/21562700*). There are also numerous **private medical facilities** which are not covered by the EHIC and may or may not be covered by your travel insurance (which is always worth having). There are no private beds in public hospitals.

MALTA FOR FAMILIES

Malta is a great place for a family holiday, especially with older children. Flying time is short (3hrs from London), there are no long transfers, it is a safe and easy place to be with no particular health or hygiene problems, English is very widely spoken and there is plenty to see and do.

This is not an ideal country for toddlers. There are too many cobbles, steps and rough ground to want to be pushing a buggy, and too many sheer drops (off fortifications as well as cliffs) around the tourist sites for toddlers to be safe without constant supervision. And only a few beaches are suitable for the very young. Ideally, wait for a trip to Malta until children are old enough to walk, talk and understand what they are seeing.

If travelling with kids in summer, try to have access to a swimming pool. Sightseeing can be hot and bothersome for children and a nice cool pool to plunge into when you get back makes all the difference. Check with the hotel that youngsters are welcome and their activities not too restricted – you don't want to be hushing your children all the time. Gozo is a particularly good place for a relaxed family break, being more laid-back than Malta and with plenty of places to swim and lots of good-quality self-catering accommodation. Restaurants tend to be relaxed and family-friendly too.

A children's activity book, *Exploring Malta* (*Miller;* €*4.50*), suitable for kids aged about four to ten, is available in bookshops, usually including the one on the Gozo ferry.

WHERE TO GO AND WHAT TO DO WITH KIDS IN MALTA

Valletta A child-sized capital, Valletta is a great to wander around and explore with narrow alleys and few cars. Stop for an ice cream at Caffe Cordina in the middle of town (page 111); admire the fortifications (Valletta is one big castle!); and hear the cannons fired at the Upper Barracca Gardens (page 118). Take a horse-and-carriage ride and maybe go to the Malta Experience for an accessible 45-minute filmic introduction to the country and its history (page 137).

Boat trips Most kids like boat trips and Malta has plenty to offer: try a crossing of the Grand Harbour in a traditional *dgħajsa* (page 115), the Two Harbours Tour to admire the fortifications (page 115), or a boat round Gozo and Comino with swimming stops (page 265).

Sea plane If budget will allow this could be a really memorable experience. Taking off from the waters of the Grand Harbour, enjoy a 10-minute flight to Gozo or a longer round-trip sightseeing flight (page 106).

Malta at War Museum, Birgu Descend into the subterranean world of this large World War II shelter. Excellent guides bring it all to life for children (it's even relevant to the British National Curriculum!). Take a look at the fortifications of Birgu on the way out (more castles). See page 147 for full details.

Il-Barri and the Mġarr Shelter Take the kids for a good, inexpensive Maltese lunch in this family-friendly restaurant then take them downstairs (maybe without telling them why) and they will find themselves in the long underground corridors of a World War II shelter; see page 228.

Fort Rinella You may not want to do the full tour (it is long and detailed), but some youngsters would love the chance to light the fuse to fire a cannon. See page 158.

Mnajdra and Ħaġar Qim The most child-friendly of the temple sites with lots of space, three temples, a watchtower and a visitor centre with infomation and toilets. See page 192.

The Hypogeum Extraordinary underground tomb complex which should interest older kids. No children under six. See page 176.

Clapham Junction and the troglodyte caves Cliff-top area with loads of space. Seek out and follow the mysterious cart ruts then take a look at caves with rock-cut shelving. People lived here until a couple of centuries ago; see page 197 for further details.

Mdina The ancient capital of the Romans, Arabs and medieval Maltese, smaller than Valletta. A maze of narrow alleys to get lost in. No cars during the day. Another castle city. See page 201.

St Paul's Catacombs An underground maze of late Roman tombs. Great for those with an interest in history or who just like exploring! See page 214.

Fort St Elmo If your child plays 'Age of Empires', he may have defended this fort against the Turks. See page 131.

Birding Kids are welcome at BirdLife Malta's reserves (pages 237 and 243) and staff will make an effort to interest them. Those accustomed to bird reserves may, however, find them unimpressive. BirdLife Malta's website has a kids' area with information and games: www.birdlifemalta.org/kids/did_you_know.

On Gozo Ramla Bay is the best beach for younger kids, and **Calypso's Cave** is fun to climb into (keep hold of young children – it is on the edge of a cliff); see page 289. In the middle of Gozo's capital, the **Citadel** (page 271) is another massive fort (or very small city) with high fortified walls and narrow car-free streets. Pop into the **cathedral** for a surprise (page 273).

Get **snorkels** for older children, or just **paddle** and look with the very young. There are lots of fish within a few feet of the shore, especially at Xlendi Bay (page 295) and Mġarr ix-Xini (page 294). Xlendi is easier with the youngest kids.

DISABLED TRAVELLERS with Mark Davidson

Malta has made great strides in recent years to improve conditions for those with disabilities and many hotels and restaurants are now wheelchair accessible. The nature of the country's towns, villages and countryside, however, does not make it an easy place for those with limited mobility or a wheelchair to get around and historic sightseeing can be a problem.

PLANNING AND BOOKING There are specialist travel agencies running trips to Malta. Companies such as **Disabled Access Holidays** (✆ 0845 257 0113; www.disabledaccessholidays.com) have a number of locations on Malta available for those wishing to travel there.

GETTING THERE AND AROUND Assistance is on offer with facilities for getting on/off the **aircraft** and there are disabled toilets. These services do have to be booked in advance. Contact the airline you are travelling with directly for any service needed on the aircraft. For further information contact Malta International Airport (✆ +356 21249600; e mia@maltairport.com; www.maltairport.com). When travelling to the island of Gozo, the **ferry** is fully accessible with lifts from the car to passenger decks. (✆ +356 21556114; e admin@gozochannel.com). If driving (or being driven) you can use your blue badge to park in designated disabled bays. These are listed in the sixth edition of the mA–Ze map book (Uptrend Publishing, 2007). Wheelchairs can be rented from www.maltabookers.com.

ACCOMMODATION There are quite a few **hotels** which are accessible to people with a disability. The main hotels in resort areas have ramps and wide doorways – for example the **Hilton International** (see page 167) – and there are less expensive options too, including bungalows at the **Mellieħa Holiday Centre** (see page 236). However, in more historic buildings and the more remote parts of the country, there is limited scope for wheelchair access.

EATING OUT There are many restaurants which are easily accessible although it is worth checking beforehand. The following website gives a comprehensive guide to restaurants and offers a section on accessibility: www.restaurantsmalta.com.

SIGHTSEEING Modern buses have access for people with a disability but the older buses, of which there are still many, do not. The waterfront at Valletta is accessible for those in wheelchairs, but many of the historic sites and buildings may cause problems for wheelchair users. Valletta, for instance, is a city of cobbles, hills and steps. Likewise the Three Cities are full of stone staircases. The streets of Mdina and the Gozo Citadel are also uneven, narrow and sometimes steep.

TRAVEL INSURANCE AND HOSPITALS There are a few specialist companies that deal with travel to Malta. A number of operators deal with pre-existing medical conditions, for example **Travelbility** (✆ *0845 338 1638; www.travelbility.co.uk*) and **Medic Travel** (✆ *0845 8800168; www.medicitravel.com*).

If you need **hospital treatment**, the new hospital on the main island, the Mater Dei Hospital in Msida (✆ *25450000;* e *mdh@gov.mt; www.materdeihospital.org.mt*) is fully accessible to wheelchairs with ramps and lifts.

FOR THE ADVENTUROUS Several **dive centres** in Malta offer scuba diving for the disabled; contact the **International Association for Handicapped Divers** for information (*Malta co-ordinator: Shaun Connell:* e *uk@iahd.org; www.iahd.org*).

FURTHER INFORMATION You can contact the **Malta Tourism Authority** (MTA) in London (✆ *0208 8776990;* e *info@visitmalta.com*) and the **National Commission for People with Disabilities** (e *helpdesk@knpd.org; www.knpd.org*). Bradt Travel Guides' *Access Africa: Safaris for People with Limited Mobility* is aimed at safari-goers, but is packed with advice and resources that will be useful to all disabled adventure travellers.

GAY MALTA

By Gattaldo, owner of Valletta G-House (www.vallettahouse.com) and Indulgence Divine (www.indulgencedivine.com)
The gay scene in Malta is not conspicuous, but it has blossomed considerably since the 1980s. Young gay men and women now rub shoulders confidently with their heterosexual peers in public, though it is best to keep overt shows of affection to a minimum. Any recognition of gay partnerships by the state is still off the map due to the strong hold of a conservative Catholic Church.

ENTERTAINMENT AND NIGHTLIFE

Klozet Club/Klozet Lounge Ball St, Paceville; m 79842184; e info@klozetclub.com; www.klozetclub.com; ◷ Wed–Sun from 22.00. Gay bar/club in Malta's nightlife capital. DJ nights & drag shows on Fri & Sat.
My Bar Racecourse St, Marsa; m 7946165; e bonellofoca@hotmail.com; www.wix.com/mybarr/mybarr; ◷ after 21.00 Fri & Sat. A bar & club frequented by transvestites & transsexuals, a mixed rowdy crowd. A place to walk on the wild side & meet some of the more colourful characters. Regular cabaret nights.

Station2Station Events m 7927260; e info@station2stationevents.com; www.station2stationevents.com. Events organised in various venues around the island by the S2S duo Frankie & James. Dancers, fire eaters, drag artists – the lot. These people know how to party.
Tom Bar 1 Crucifix Hill, Floriana; ✆ 21250780; e tombarmalta@yahoo.com; www.tombarmalta.webs.com; ◷ from 20.30 daily. Gay bar founded in 1995, now under new management. Close to Valletta Waterfront. Friendly staff & warm ambience. Outside patio popular in summer.

BEACH Ġnejna Bay (Bus 652 for Għajn Tuffieħa, then face the sea, turn left and walk for about 15 minutes) is a stunning rocky bay with rugged natural beauty, just secluded enough for private encounters, though be aware that even nude bathing is illegal in Malta. Take refreshments with you as the walk itself makes for thirsty work.

FURTHER INFORMATION

Malta Gay Rights Movement & Helpline 32 Parish St, Mosta; ☏ 99255559; e mgrm@maltagayrights.net; www.maltagayrights.net. Young NGO started in 2001 which has gained prominence & clout quickly.

Organises the (still small) annual Gay Pride march every July & runs the **National Gay Helpline** (☏ 21430006).

Maltese Australian Joseph Carmel Chetcuti recently wrote a history of gay Malta entitled *Queer Mediterranean Memories* (*Lygon St Legal Services, A$65 (approx £33) from www.queermalta.com*).

WHAT TO TAKE

British travellers will not need electric plug adapters as Malta uses plugs with three square pins as in the UK and a similar voltage. Those from continental Europe will need adapters, and American devices require adapters and transformers.

Walking in Malta is best done in sturdy shoes. Trainers will do for short walks, but if you plan to spend hours stomping over rough rock (and the most beautiful walking spots in Malta and Gozo have rough rock underfoot) you will need something with a tougher sole and some ankle support, preferably walking boots.

Sunglasses, sunhat and sunscreen are a must (except in winter, though you may need sunglasses even then), and a small pack each of tissues and wipes can be handy as public loos are sometimes not fully equipped. A torch is an important item if you intend to explore caves, tombs or catacombs. Swimming (often off rocks or with stones in the sand) can be more comfortable if you have something to wear on your feet in the water. Don't panic if you forget something – you can buy almost all standard items in Malta.

$ MONEY AND BUDGETING

Malta joined the euro on 1 January 2008. Although all prices are in euros they are sometimes quoted in Maltese pounds or lira (Lm) as well, so if a price looks too good to be true, then check the currency. There are 0.43 Lm to the euro. Many locals still translate into Lm, and euro prices are sometimes still not round numbers and have clearly been directly translated from Lm (eg: €4.66 appears quite often, presumably replacing Lm2).

There are no limits on the money that can be brought in or out of countries within the EU. If crossing the EU border, however, then anyone lucky enough to be in the possession of more than €10,000 (in any form – including cheques, money orders, etc) must declare it.

BANKS, ATMS AND CHANGING MONEY Banks in Malta usually open Monday to Friday 08.30–13.30 (later on Fridays) and Saturday mornings. A few larger branches have recently started to open again from 16.30 to about 19.00. There is an HSBC or Bank of Valletta (often both), usually with an ATM, in every town and many villages. On Gozo, banks and ATMs are less widespread but are available in Victoria and in tourist centres like Xlendi and Marsalforn, as well as a few of the villages. For BOV branches, see www.bov.com/page.asp?p=10842&l=1 and for HSBC www.hsbc.com.mt/1/2/find-a-branch. There are bureaux de change in the most touristy areas, and these open later than the banks, particularly in summer. At the airport, you will find 24-hour banking.

Credit cards Most places take credit cards, but some restaurants, smaller guesthouses and village shops do not.

BUDGETING The cost of living as a visitor in Malta depends heavily on when you go because accommodation costs vary so much between high and low season. Even within a season it is well worth shopping around as most hotel prices rise and fall by the day according to occupancy. The cost of eating in Malta is less variable – but the quality varies a great deal. Other than at the two extremes of price, you can eat very well indeed or not very well at all for the same money – so do take a look at the restaurant sections of this guide.

The following costs are based on per-day rates for two people and are broken down so that you can take out or add parts (for instance swapping buses for car hire in the middle-of-the-road budget, or hiring a car for a day in the shoestring option) and adjust for the prices you actually find. These are, of course, only examples.

Top whack

Good double room & breakfast in a top 5-star hotel	€350
Large car with driver	€120
Lunch in a good restaurant (2-courses & coffee)	€60
3-course supper in top restaurant with bottle of good wine	€125
Sundries (museum entry, water, tips, snacks, etc)	€25
Total	**€700**

Comfortable middle-of-the-road

Accommodation (5-star low season/special offer, or 3–4-star summer/full price)	€150
Small car, self-drive	€25
Petrol	€15
Light lunch out	€20
Restaurant supper with glass of wine	€55
Sundries (museum entry, postcards, snack, water, etc)	€15
Total	**€275**

Shoe-string

Accommodation	€30
Public transport	€5
Bread & cheese lunch	€6
Supper out (pizza/pastas/single dish)	€20
Sundries (as above)	€15
Total	**€73**

Costs of some common items Note: some prices will vary from shop to shop, town to village.

Loaf of Maltese bread	Around 60c
6-pack of large bottles of water	€2.60–3.60
33cl can of Cisk lager (in a supermarket)	85c
1l of milk	72c
Postcard	Around 30c
Marguerita pizza (take-away)	€3.50–5.50

TIPPING Tipping is usual practice in Malta and a tip of 5–10% is appreciated when reasonable service has been received, for instance in a restaurant or taxi. Service will sometimes be added to bills, in which case nothing additional is required. Hotel porters in four- and five-star hotels expect a few euros (depending on the number of bags) and most people will tip parking attendants at makeshift car parks €0.70–1.50.

GETTING AROUND

BY PUBLIC TRANSPORT Public transport on Malta is very good. There are no trains but you can get buses to almost everywhere on the main island, and there are plenty of taxis. The ferry between Malta and Gozo is frequent and takes under half an hour. It goes from the very north of Malta about 40–45 minutes by car from Valletta, a little less from St Julian's (unless it is raining or rush hour).

Fares are mostly set by the Public Transport Directorate and can be found at: www.maltatransport.com/en/new/publictransport/fares.xls (click on the tabs at the bottom for different kinds of fares). Some guide fares are given below.

Buses Buses are inexpensive, and on the main island they are frequent and go almost everywhere, including the airport and the ferry terminal. Many of Malta's buses are 1950s British Leyland vehicles repainted in yellow and orange. 'Boneshakers' they may be, but they are also a lot more fun than their modern replacements increasingly being insisted upon by EU legislation. Bus buffs should see *The Malta Buses* by Joseph Bonnici and Michael Cassar (*BDL;* €17.50).

Disconcertingly, a few older Maltese people still cross themselves when they get onto a bus, although the bus is almost certainly safer than a car (see page 58). Unless you are in a huge hurry or going somewhere off the beaten track, buses are a great way to travel. The **standard fare** is €0.47, €0.23 for children aged between three and ten. Very short trips within the same town or village cost just €0.16 and journeys before 08.00 (except on Sundays and public holidays) are €0.30. If you travel across two zones (see map on page 56) the fare goes up to €0.54 and across three zones, to €0.58. 'Direct' buses (those not originating in Valletta) cost about twice as much. It is worth keeping some coins handy for fares.

The **main bus station** is just outside Valletta's City Gate and the vast majority of buses start from here. The bus station can get busy and quite confusing. A map showing which bus goes from which stop can be obtained, along with other information, from a little kiosk staffed by the Department of Transport. If no-one is there (which does happen) then ask bus drivers or members of the public, most of whom will go out of their way to be helpful.

All stops other than bus stations are request stops so you need to stick your arm out to board the bus and pull the old-fashioned wire above the seats to get off. No buses run inside the capital as most of it is pedestrianised, but the bus station is only a few minutes' walk from the centre of town and bus 198 runs all the way around the city, just outside the walls, every hour.

Gozo also has a reasonable network of bus routes but the buses are much less frequent, especially outside the summer months. Unlike on Malta, you cannot rely on buses on Gozo. Don't assume that a bus will arrive within a reasonable waiting time – you really do need to check. The main bus station is in the centre of Victoria, a very few minutes walk from the main square It-Tokk. Bus fares are mostly the same as on Malta, but in summer it costs €0.82 to travel to Gozo's coastal tourist centres of Dwejra and Ramla Bay (Ramla I-Hamra). See page 256 for a route map of Gozo's bus system.

Bus timetables for Malta and Gozo as well as other details are available from ATP, the Public Transport Association (21250007/8/9; e atp@atp.com.mt; www.atp.com.mt/atp/html/index.html). At the time of going to print, Transport Malta are in the process of introducing radical reforms to the bus network. See http://updates.bradtguides.com for the latest information.

Taxis Despite some fares being set by the Transport Department (see web address, above), it is advisable to agree fares before using a taxi, water taxi or

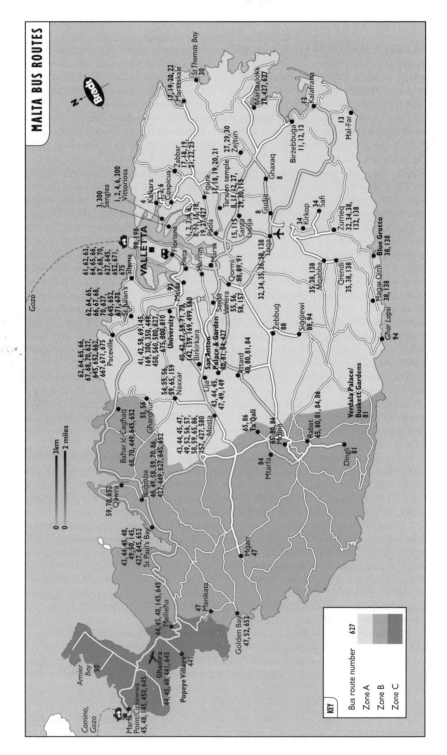

MALTA BUS ROUTES

This hop-on-hop-off open-topped bus service covers much of the island on its two tours – North and South (see below) – taking in most of the main sights and some minor ones too (including the Binġemma Gap, page 230, where public buses do not go). The tour lasts three hours if you stay on the bus. Get off, and the next bus will be along an hour later. Tours cost €15 for adults, €9 for children aged 5–15 and under-fives are free. Book both tours and the price falls to €13 each, and there is usually a special offer giving you a free Two Harbours Cruise (usually €15, children €10) with the bus tours. A night tour is also available (Mar–Nov) as is a Gozo tour (not hop-on-hop-off, €20, children €10, lunch €8, ferry and museum entry excluded) and on Saturdays throughout the summer the company will take you on a Festa Firework trip to whichever parish has the best display that weekend (adults €7, children €5, trips start at 20.00 or 21.00 and finish roughly at 00.30). Commentary is available in a choice of eight languages (English, Maltese, Italian, French, Spanish, German, Danish, Japanese). All tours leave from Sliema Ferries on the hour from 09.00 to 15.00 Monday–Saturday and at 10.00 to 13.00 Sundays and public holidays.

Malta sightseeing bus: ☏ *21694967;* e *info@maltasighseeing.com; www.maltasightseeing.com.*

horse-drawn cab. Apart from journeys to and from the airport, which are fixed separately (see page 46), the main island's official white taxis (*www.maltataxi.net*), sometimes known as 'the white sharks', are supposed to charge €1.40/km for the first 8km, and €1.16/km thereafter. Once 20km has been travelled the cost should fall to €0.47/km. Waiting time should be charged at €4.66 per hour or part of an hour.

Taxis gather at strategic points, often by tourist sites and bus stations, and ply the streets. They can also be ordered by phoning ☏ 21823017 or 23696071. If booking a cab in advance most Maltese seem to prefer to use one of the **private taxi firms**, that will do short journeys as well as offering hourly/day rates. These companies set their own fares.

Marshall Group ☏ 21691007; m 99497228; www.marshallgroup.com.mt. Cars to coaches, chauffeur driven & self-drive.
Wembley Cars ☏ 21374141/27374141; e wembleys@maltanet.net; www.wembleys.net. 24hr taxi service based in Paceville close to St Julian's.

Zarb Coaches ☏ 21489991/2/3; e info@ zarbcoaches.com; www.zarbcoaches.com. 40 vehicles from cars to coaches (& a minibus catering for special needs) with good drivers.

For taxis on Gozo see *Chapter 14*, page 258, and for water taxis, Valletta city cabs and horse-drawn carriages see *Chapter 5, Valletta* page 107.

Ferries Travelling between Malta and Gozo is easy with regular ferries taking less than half an hour. Between mid-March and mid-November, boats also operate to the tiny island of Comino from both Malta and Gozo – see *Chapter 13 Comino*, page 57. The only other regular ferry service is between Valletta and Sliema (see *Chapter 5*, page 106).

Sea plane and helicopter You can hop between Malta and Gozo by tiny sea plane (see page 106) – a ten-minute flight with wonderful views and not as expensive as you might think. The sea plane also does **tourist flights** over the islands for half the price of the helicopter tours.

At the time of writing, helicopter transfers from Malta airport to Gozo are expected to be on offer shortly. The helicopter – which can only take three passengers at a time – can already be chartered for tailor-made trips and the **Platinum Tour of Malta** runs from the airport giving you a 20-minute scenic flight over the sights of the main island for €125pp (✆ 2369442; e helitours@heli-link-malta.com; www.heli -link-malta.com).

🚗 **DRIVING** The Maltese love their cars. They will always drive rather than walk – even if it's just a few hundred metres – and there is lots of interest in the best new model. There are therefore lots of cars on the roads with some of them going rather faster than you might wish. Malta drives on the left (like the UK) – at least in theory. As one local put it: 'We drive on the left ... or on the right, or in the middle of the road.' The standard of driving in Malta is described by the British Foreign Office as 'poor' and it can be very erratic. The per capita death toll is actually lower than the UK's, but the accident rate – and certainly the scrape rate – is higher. If you hire a car, make sure you will not be stung for some massive excess if someone 'eases' past you. Should you have an accident, call the police on the international emergency number: ✆ 112.

Anyone driving in Malta needs to be aware that the Maltese do not like to give way – even at roundabouts. They are not generally inattentive drivers, but they don't like slowing down, let alone stopping. Overtaking happens on all sides and in almost any place so it may be worth beeping on blind bends. The speed limits are 80km/h on highways and 50km/h in urban areas – and they are enforced. Perhaps unfortunately, the locals mostly know where the cameras are and only slow down accordingly. Seatbelts are mandatory except where there are none available in the back seat, and so are crash helmets on mopeds and motorbikes.

Malta's main roads are in reasonable condition, but side roads are often pot-holed. When it rains, some roads flood and main routes are often jammed. Getting into Valletta in the morning rush hour when it is raining can be very slow indeed.

If you are planning to tour by car, you are likely to need a road map; please see *Maps* (page 42). Driving on **Gozo** is much easier and much less hair-raising (see page 258).

Car hire Many car-hire companies in Malta require you to be aged 25 or over, although a few will hire to over-21s. If you are 70+, you may be asked for a medical certificate to prove fitness to drive. Prices can vary considerably from company to company, as can the insurance excess (and the cost of removing it), so do shop around. Some companies also charge extra for a second driver.

Avis rent-a-car ✆ (airport office) 25677550; www.avis.co.uk/CarHire/Europe/Malta-Gozo. 24hr office at Malta International Airport, plus several other offices in Malta.

Europcar ✆ 25761000; www.europcar.com/ car-MALTA.html. Several offices including an airport branch.
Supercar hire ✆ 21446004, m 79446004; e duncan@supercarhire.com. Local company with 200 vehicles.

Parking Parking can be a nuisance on Malta but tends not to be a problem in Gozo except in Victoria. The usual yellow lines and driveway restrictions apply and some towns have restricted parking areas where you can only stay for a certain length of time. These are signed with a blue clock and require you to place a cardboard clock on the dashboard showing the time of arrival. Make sure you are given one when hiring a car. There is no charge but fines apply if you overstay or fail to display your arrival time. If you have to park and don't have the necessary clock, you could try writing a note to the parking attendant with the time of arrival on it – this is sometimes accepted (but no guarantees).

Sliema and Floriana (just outside Valletta) each have a large multi-storey car park, and there is a big open car park at the airport. Otherwise it is a matter of using car parks attached to tourist sites (where they exist) and the small, less formal, open car-parking spaces (where attendants expect a fee of between €0.70 and €1.50) or finding unrestricted areas.

CYCLING I would not recommend cycling as a way of getting around the main island of Malta (Gozo is different; please see page 266). Not only are some roads very pot-holed, but the traffic can also be fast and unpredictable (see *Driving*, opposite). There are a few cycle lanes, but don't expect them to contain only bikes or to extend the whole length of the road. In Malta's main towns there are charming metal stands shaped like small bicycles especially for locking up your two-wheeler; I have never seen a single bike attached to one. In fact, it is very rare to see a bike on the roads at all – let alone with a local riding it. A few tourists do come to Malta to cycle as recreation and there are some areas in the north that are quite rural and a bit more like Gozo. If you want to cycle in Malta, there is an excellent little book *Cycle Malta & Gozo* by Joseph Montebello (*RMF Publishing; €6; www.cyclemaltaandgozo.com*) and www.maltabookers.com also runs guided cycling tours and rents out bikes. The sports cycling body in Malta is the **Malta Cycling Federation** (e *info@maltacyclingfederation.com; www.maltacyclingfederation.com*) which organises the annual four-day Tour Ta' Malta (as in Tour de France), usually in March.

ACCOMMODATION

Malta has nearly 200 hotels and other forms of accommodation and over 38,000 guest beds. More than half of these beds are in hotels rated four- and five-star. Several of the five-star hotels would match provision anywhere in the world; the four stars are more variable and some would be classed as three-star in the UK.

Many of the 'top' accommodation options are modern chain hotels. If you are looking for this level of comfort, but would like something with a bit more character, look at the **Xara Palace** (page 203), a historic boutique hotel and the only hotel inside the walls of the ancient capital Mdina. For something a bit less expensive and with gardens and swimming pool, try the **Corinthia Palace** (page 221) which is tucked right away from the tourist crowds in a traditional residential area near the home of Malta's president in San Anton Gardens.

Less expensive still are some good self-catering options – particularly useful in Valletta where there is little choice of hotel accommodation, and in Birgu where there is none. For the lowest budgets, there are a few pleasant value-for-money guesthouses – particularly in Gozo – and a couple of hostels. The NSTS (National Student Travel Service, page 163) hostel in Sliema is a particularly good low-budget option in a very convenient location. There is little provision for camping: just one campsite in the far north of Malta (see page 241), and a small patch of land for pitching tents on Comino (see page 252).

For information on **religious retreat houses**, see page 43 and for details on **spa hotels** see page 100.

PRICES AND DISCOUNTS Many of the hotels' published room rates are way above what you should expect to pay and, on the whole, the more expensive the hotel, the more dramatic the reductions can be. Some establishments are more straightforward about this than others, admitting that rates rise and fall daily according to occupancy. This is particularly true in the main tourist centres like St

Julian's and Paceville where five-star hotels sometimes offer discounts that put them mid-range on price. It is always worth checking the website and/or emailing or phoning for the best available rate.

Booking in advance can also gain you substantial discounts, and low season prices may be less than half the August highs. Hotels vary as to when they consider high season to begin, so some offer winter rates into June, while others are already charging as if it were August. Given all this, the prices listed in this book are inevitably only examples and it is crucial to check exactly what is available.

SEA VIEWS Many hotels in Malta charge extra for a sea view. It is often worth paying if you can. When considering a non-sea-view room ask in detail about how much window you will have, what it will look over and how noisy it is likely to be. If you say you are trying to choose between sea view and non-sea view (rather than between hotels) they may give you the truth about the non-sea views!

SMOKING Smoking is not allowed in public buildings including restaurants and the communal areas of hotels (as in the UK) and this is surprisingly well adhered to. Of course, many people do smoke and some hotels (especially the larger ones) designate certain bedrooms or whole floors to smokers. These rooms may stink of tobacco, so it is worth making clear when booking whether you want a smoking or a non-smoking room.

AIR CONDITIONING AND CENTRAL HEATING Summers in Malta are hot. Most hotels have air conditioning, but budget accommodation and self-catering properties (especially in old buildings) may not. If you want air conditioning, it is worth checking availability and price. Winters are generally mild so central heating is rare. There are, however, times when it is wet and cold and being in an unheated room, especially one designed to stay cool in summer (as most Maltese buildings are), can be miserable. It is worth asking what heating and bedding will be provided.

SWIMMING POOLS If travelling in winter, especially with children, it is worth checking the size and warmth of indoor pools, and whether children are allowed. Indoor pools are sometimes part of the spa and under-16s may be barred from entry. If you want your children to be able to relax and play in the pool, it is also worth checking whether balls and inflatables are allowed and how many families use the hotel.

✖ EATING AND DRINKING

FOOD The Maltese love to eat – almost as much as they hate to exercise. This unfortunate combination makes Malta a European record-breaker for both obesity and diabetes. Yet their love of food has a positive effect – Malta has a substantial number of very good restaurants, almost all serving locals and visitors alike.

Maltese food is heavily influenced by Italy. Pasta – usually fresh – is omnipresent, usually as a starter or 'light' lunch. Mains are mostly meat or fish. Few people in Malta understand vegetarianism – and that goes for most of the chefs as well. Malta's cuisine is Mediterranean so it is no good being shy of olive oil or garlic, unless you are eating the excellent and copious fresh fish, in which case you can ask for it simply grilled or steamed. Meat is mostly pork, beef and rabbit (the national favourite). After World War II Malta was advised to reduce the number of sheep and goats on the islands. The result has been less lamb on the table, but more vegetation in the countryside.

Many restaurants in Malta offer local specialities. Here are a few to look out for.

SOUPS Traditional soups include:

Aljotta Fish soup with a thin base rather like a fish minestrone with lots of bits of fish.
Minestra Vegetable soup much thicker than Italian minestrone and often including one or more pulses.
Soppa ta l-armla ('widow's soup') Meant to be cheap to make: a mix of potatoes, cauliflower and onion with a fresh *gbejna* (or a lump of ricotta) and sometimes an egg dropped in at the end.

MAIN COURSES

Fenek Rabbit in almost any form (fried, stewed, in wine, with tomato, as pasta sauce).
Braġioli Slices of beef wrapped around a mix of minced beef and herbs. Sometimes called 'beef olives' because of the shape (there are no olives in it).
Laham taⵊ-ⵊiemel Horse meat, usually steamed or fried.
Zalzett tal-Malti Maltese sausage. Short, fat, rough-cut pork sausage.
Lampuka The national favourite among the many fresh fish served in Malta (see box, page 182). *Lampuki* pie is particularly popular when *lampuki* are most plentiful. Chopped *lampuki* fillet is mixed with tomato, onion, spinach and olives.
Sawrell Mimli il-forn Baked stuffed mackerel. Mackerel, breadcrumbs, anchovies, olives and parsley between layers of potato and onion.
Laham il-forn Baked meat. Slices of pork or beef between layers of onion and potato, often with fennel seeds.

PASTA AND OTHER BAKES Pasta, in all the usual forms, comes with sauces ranging from octopus and sea urchin to rabbit.

Ravjul Ravioli. Fresh homemade ravioli are widely available with fillings from rabbit to ricotta, spinach to minced meat and, in Gozo, local cheese. Usually large and priced by the dozen.
Ghaġin il-forn Baked pasta, usually macaroni, with cheese, tomato sauce and minced meat.
Ross il-forn Similar to the above, but made with rice.
Ghaġin bl-inċova Crispy spaghetti with anchovy sauce.

VEGETABLES The Maltese for vegetables is *haxix* (pronounced *hashish* – not to be confused!)

Patata l-Forn Literally baked potáto, but actually layers of potato and onion with fennel or caraway seeds baked in the oven. Meat is often cooked underneath this.
Haxix Mimli Stuffed vegetables. Courgette, aubergine, peppers, tomatoes, cabbage leaves, etc filled with ricotta, local cheese, minced meat and herbs, or fish of various kinds.

Homemade cakes and puddings are very popular, often delicious and rarely sickly sweet. There is excellent local ice cream (try fig or passion fruit) which is widely available. Meals are generally accompanied by fresh Maltese bread (*ħobż Malti*, see boxed text, page 291), a crusty loaf rather like a French *pain de campagne*.

Ftira is a low-rise ring-shaped loaf usually eaten with fillings (a Maltese sandwich). Gozitan *ftira* is more like pizza and comes open (like normal pizza) or folded over (like calzone but the folding is from all edges so it stays round). Unlike pizza, Gozitan *ftira* has thin slices of potato directly on top of the crust. One traditional version is topped with sardine (or tuna if you don't like sardine), potato, fresh tomato, onion, capers and olives. The most traditional (and delicious) closed Gozitan *ftira* is filled with Gozitan cheese which puffs up so it is almost like a crusty savoury cheesecake.

All the usual pizzas are also readily available.

Many Maltese cannot get through the morning without a snack – almost always *pastizzi* (confusingly translated as 'cheesecakes'). These savoury mini-pasties filled with ricotta cheese or mushy peas are sold in almost all cafés, as well as tiny shopfronts known as *pastizzeria*.

Snacks and fast food The most Maltese snack you can get is *pastizzi* (see above), but there is also the delicious traditional sweet snack *imqaret* (pronounced Im-*aart*), which is a pastry filled with date paste and fennel seeds and deep fried. There are good date stalls at Valletta's City Gate (page 115) and in Marsaxlokk market (page 180). For fast food, **pizza** is readily available, and even the street-side slice is usually a cut above their northern European counterpart. Malta does not escape Mcdonalds and Burger King either.

Vegetarian food The Maltese are not much into vegetarian food as main courses and even in top restaurants the vegetarian option may be rather dull. There are, however, some excellent vegetarian appetisers and antipasti and you can of course ask for vegetarian pasta sauces and pizza. Common local appetisers include *bigilla* – a tasty rough paste made from crushed broad beans and garlic, usually served with *galletti* (thin crackers sometimes with herbs); and *ħobż-Malti* which literally means 'Maltese bread' but in this case comes with fresh tomato, local olive oil, salt and pepper.

Local **cheese** – often called Gozitan cheese although it is also made on Malta – is usually made from sheep and goat's milk, and comes in three main forms: fresh (soft, like an extra-smooth ricotta, with which it is sometimes mixed or replaced in recipes); peppered (dried hard with pepper on the outside) and semi-dried (in between, without pepper). The dried sometimes comes 'pickled' in vinegar. The cheese is usually produced in small roundels an inch or two across known as *ġbejna* (usually translated as 'cheeselets').

Books For more on Maltese cuisine, try *A Guide to Maltese Cooking* by Darmanin Francis (*Jumbo Publications, Malta*) or *The Food and Cookery of Malta* by Anne & Helen Caruana Galizia (*Pax Books*).

DRINK The drinking age in Malta has recently been raised from 16 to 17, but nobody takes much notice of it, particularly in Paceville. Malta produces its own wine (see below) and beer – most popularly **Cisk lager** (pronounced *chisk*). There is also a national soft drink, **Kinnie** (pronounced *Keeny*) which is a little like Coke but less sickly sweet (more like the traditional English dandelion and burdock). A new 'Zest' version has an edge of orange. Kinnie is drunk by kids and adults alike and is sometimes used as a mixer with spirits. Malta's favourite local **liqueurs** are limoncello – lemon zest, alcohol, water and sugar – and Bajtra, a very sweet liqueur made from prickly pears.

Wine There are a number of wineries in Malta. Many make wine both from their own grapes and from grapes imported, usually from Italy. Until recently it was difficult to know which was which but wine made from foreign grapes bottled after 2007 has to be clearly labelled as such. A form of quality control, similar to that in Italy, has also been introduced. DOK is the equivalent of the French Appellation Controllée, while IGT is like a Vin de Pays. Both must be made from grapes grown in Malta.

Five wineries produce wine with DOK and IGT certification: **Delicata** (*www.delicata.com*) – the largest and oldest, drawing grapes from 650 small independent vineyards; **Marsovin** (*www.marsovin.com.mt*), the largest until a few years ago, has some vineyards of its own, produces a broad range of wines and seems to have the widest distribution; **Camilleri** (*www.camilleriwines.com*); **Montekristo** *(www.montekristo.com)*; and **Meridiana** (*www.meridiana.com.mt*), the smallest winery next to its single vineyard near Mdina, making some excellent wines, including some particularly good reds.

A Comprehensive Guide to the Quality Wines of Malta by Bill Hermitage (a Brit with many years wine trade experience in the UK and Malta) is published each winter (*€14.95 from Agenda bookshops*). It does not review wines (he can't – he works for one of the wineries), but lists all the DOK and IGT wines, recommends ageing potential and makes food pairing suggestions. It also has a list of wine bars as does his website (*www.maltawinebars.com*).

In August each year, the **Delicata Classic Wine Festival** (✆ *21825199;* e *info@delicata.com; www.delicata.com*) is held first in Valletta and later in the month on Gozo. Buy a wine glass for €10, then taste (and drink) as many wines as you like.

RESTAURANTS Malta has some excellent restaurants and you can eat extremely well here. Many restaurants are closed on Mondays or Sundays and some do only lunch or only dinner. Outside the main tourist areas, restaurants often do not stay open late, so if you need to eat after 22.00 check ahead. The Maltese like their food, so portions tend to be generous. Even top-end restaurants with nouvelle-cuisine-style presentation tend not to have nouvelle-cuisine-sized portions ('our local clients would not stand for it'). Be warned though, restaurateurs have got wise to people ordering starters as main courses and will often slap an extra couple of euros on the bill.

The restaurants recommended in this guide are mostly establishments that offer at least some Maltese or Mediterranean food on the grounds that most people do not come to Malta to eat Asian or Chinese (although Chinese food is popular with the Maltese). If you are desperate for a taste of the East, you can find good places to go on Malta's restaurant website (see below). The listings in this guide also concentrate on independent restaurants; hotel restaurants are included only if there is a particular reason to do so. Those Maltese that can afford it love to eat at the restaurants of the five-star hotels, but for visitors the independent restaurants tend to be more interesting and better value for money.

The Definitive(ly) Good Guide to Restaurants in Malta and Gozo is published annually (*www.restaurantsmalta.com; €9.20 in shops*). Based on votes from Maltese restaurant goers, it rates food, ambience and service and has useful indexes/searches by location, opening times, type of food and even wheelchair access. Five-star hotel restaurants feature disproportionately so a few of the featured restaurants may be overpriced, but they will not be bad.

🛍 SHOPPING

Most shops are open from 09.00 (often earlier) until 19.00, with a three- or four-hour break in the middle of the day. In tourist areas shops will often stay open later than 19.00 in summer and close considerably earlier in winter and may not close at lunchtime. Most shops are shut on Sundays though some in tourist resorts are open, particularly in peak season.

With the pound sterling to euro exchange rate as it stands at the time of writing, Brits are unlikely to go to Malta for shopping. Most things you can get in Malta, you can get at home for a similar price or less. **Souvenirs**, however, are a different matter.

CRAFTS Local crafts include gold and particularly silver filigree, lace, glass, pottery and woollens. See page 31 for additional information.

Artisan Centre 9–10 Freedom Sq, Valletta; ✆ 21246216/5236; e artisans@keyworld.net; ⏰ 09.00–19.00

Ta' Qali Craft Village On the old airfield at Ta' Qali (page 226); ⏰ 09.00–16.00 Mon–Fri, ⏰ until 13.00 Sat

SOUVENIR FOOD Some of Malta's specialist foods – including mini-cheeses, local honey and antipasti – can be bought packed for long-distance travel.

Caffe Cordina Republic Sq, 244/5 Republic St, Valletta; ✆ 21234385; e info@caffecordina.com; www.caffecordina.com

Casa Rocca Piccola 74 Republic St (between St Christopher St & St Dominic St), Valletta; ✆ 21221499; www.casaroccapiccola.com

SOMETHING DIFFERENT OR FOR CHILDREN Small 'pocket money' items – including miniature versions of the colourful painted wooden **Eye of Osiris** seen on the traditional boats – can be found on Marsaxlokk Market (especially on Sundays, page 180) and other markets and small shops. For something completely different, the Early Learning Centre on Merchants Street in Valletta sells **Malta Monopoly**, as does the Agenda bookshop on the Gozo Ferry (but it is very expensive at up to €60).

For shopping on Gozo, see *Chapter 14*, page 264 and for books see above, page 41.

🎭 ARTS AND ENTERTAINMENT

The Maltese love **music** and there are concerts and festivals of all kinds of music in churches, historic buildings, and outdoors in summer (see *Events*, page 34) as well as at the **Manoel Theatre** (page 134) and **St James Cavalier Centre for Creativity** (page 118) in Valletta. There are two **opera festivals** each year (one in March at the Manoel Theatre, and one in Gozo, usually in October) as well as a summer **jazz festival** and a **festival of traditional music** (see *Events*, page 34). Music – classical and popular – also plays a major part in the Maltese *festa* (see page 31), a mix of religious and secular celebration held at least once a year by each parish in the islands.

The **Manoel Theatre** is one of the oldest theatres still in use in Europe having been founded by the Knights of St John. It has performances most days except in summer when it is too hot and the theatre is closed for maintenance work. The **Malta Amateur Dramatic Club** (*MADC, www.madc.biz*) is very active. Begun by the British Forces in 1910 it stages several productions a year including a panto at Christmas and a Shakespeare play outdoors in the summer. There are occasional theatrical performances too at **St James Cavalier** – a modern arts centre in a historic building – which also houses an arts cinema and large, interesting gallery spaces with changing exhibitions.

Contemporary art is displayed and sold in some public buildings including the Auberge d'Italie (page 121) and the Valletta Museum of Fine Arts (whose collection is otherwise less modern and definitely not for sale), as well as in the Carmelite Priory Museum in Mdina (page 208).

There are three commercial **cinemas** showing the usual Hollywood fare: the Embassy Complex in Valletta (*St Lucy St/Triq Santa Luċija;* ↘ *21227436 or 27227436;* e *info@embassy.com.mt; www.embassycomplex.com.mt*); the Empire in Buġibba (*Pioneer Rd;* ↘ *21581787 or 21581909;* e *info@empirecinema.com.mt; www.empirecinema.com.mt*) and The Eden in Paceville (↘ *23710400; www.edencinemas.com.mt*) which is next to the Intercontinental near the Bay Street shopping centre and opposite the Eden Superbowl. The **Eden Superbowl** is Malta's only bowling venue (↘ *23710777; www.edemsuperbowl.com;* ⊕ *10.00–23.00 daily; standard rate €6pp for first game but prices vary*) and also has free Wi-Fi and an internet café on site (*expect to pay €2 for 1hr & €5 for 3hrs*).

THE CLUBS No, not nightclubs, **band clubs**. Every parish in Malta has at least one band (of the musical wind instrument variety) and usually an associated band club. These are often in the main church square, and may have an interesting façade. They frequently include an inexpensive bar, café or restaurant – of very variable quality – as well as a snooker table and a television, which seems to perpetually show live English and Italian premier league football. In Valletta, two central band clubs have large restaurants that do a roaring trade (see page 111).

Many towns also have **political clubs** – Nationalist and Labour, the latter often being the more prominent. Here again there are usually cheap bars and restaurants, often occupied by semi-resident groups of older men smoking, chatting and drinking (and watching football). The Labour Club on Republic Street in Valletta (see page 111) has a sign saying tourists are welcome. At other clubs, check that they are open to non-members before settling in. **Football clubs** offer a similar atmosphere and facilities but are dedicated to sport – some even have a sign prohibiting discussion of politics!

The clubs vary hugely in their congeniality, and – outside the capital at least – they are a side of Malta most tourists never see.

NIGHTLIFE Most of Malta goes pretty quiet after about 21.00. There are lots of excellent restaurants (see page 63), but don't expect to be served at midnight. Even in Valletta most restaurants close by 23.00 and in the villages it may be even earlier. There is, however, plenty of nightlife for those who want it in St Julian's and particularly in neighbouring Paceville. Here there are streets full of fast-food joints, pubs, bars and clubs where the booming bass thuds until four in the morning (it used to be six or seven but the government has recently clamped down).

Paceville tends to attract a very young teenage crowd (many under the official drinking age of 17) that can, particularly on summer weekends, become rowdy and fractious. Around midnight the age may rise into the 20s (even early 30s) at some of the clubs and there is one live music venue, the long-established **BJ's jazz and blues club** (see page 168 for venue details) that is frequented by the over-35s.

There is some nightlife elsewhere. In summer, bars stay open late in Buġibba and Qawra but Brits run an even greater risk here than in Paceville of being embarrassed by alcohol-fuelled compatriots. The large hotels also have their own bars and restaurants some of which stay open well into the night.

Far more fun – and more interesting – though, is to get involved in a *festa* (see page 31): eat Maltese snacks, watch fireworks and enjoy congenial local nightlife under the stars.

MUSEUMS AND HISTORIC SITES

Malta has a remarkable range of museums and historic sites ranging across its 7,000-year history. The temple sites and many of the key museums are run by the government body **Heritage Malta** (⟍ *22954000;* e *info@heritagemalta.org; www.heritagemalta.org*). Most of their sites are open from 09.00 to 17.00 with last entry at 16.30; there is plenty of information on their website. The **Hypogeum** – the extraordinary 5,500-year-old underground temple of the dead – must be booked through Heritage Malta preferably well in advance (see page 176) – but at all other sites you can pay for entry on arrival. Independent museums each have their own ways of doing things and these are covered in the guide chapters of this book.

SPORTS AND ACTIVITIES

⚓ SWIMMING Malta has no shortage of places to swim in beautiful clear blue waters. In summer, the Maltese will swim anywhere they can safely get in and out of the water. Beware of finding your own spots – there are hidden currents in some areas and getting out of the water onto rocks is not nearly as easy as getting in. Be guided by what the locals do.

'Beach' in Malta merely means a place to swim. It may be sandy, rocky or even concrete. The most common is rocky and, as long as you are all competent swimmers, these can be the pleasantest places, and good for snorkelling too. With young children you may want sand, a gentle slope into the water and shallows to paddle in (see *Chapter 4* page 90 for swimming locations).

Topless and nude sunbathing and swimming are illegal and if someone complains you could find yourself in trouble. Any swimwear is acceptable by the water, but it is appreciated if you put something on before wandering around town, the inside of hotels or restaurants.

Please see also *Health and safety,* page 47.

⚓ DIVING Some 50,000 people a year visit the Maltese islands for diving. The water is warm in summer and autumn and diveable even in spring and winter; it is known for its clarity, with visibility of up to 30m in undisturbed sea. The water is also cleaner than in some other parts of the Mediterranean. There are nearly 100 dive sites around the Maltese coast, about half of them accessible from the shore. There are sites suitable for beginners as well as deep-water challenges for the very experienced. Seasoned divers tend to come here for the underwater landscape of dramatic rock formations and caves, as well as for the wrecks (including nine deliberately scuttled), rather than for the fish, but there is plenty of marine wildlife too. For details of wrecks around the Maltese coast (as well as other Malta diving information) see www.marinefoundation.org. Night dives are also popular and many local divers are involved in underwater photography. Advice on this is available through dive centres and also in Peter Lemon's excellent dive guide (see below).

Malta's islands are small and offer a wide variety of dives quite close together. If one site is too windy, there is almost always an alternative not far away. Established dive companies offer instruction ranging from children's taster sessions (age eight plus) through beginners' Open Water Diving courses right up to specialist and instructor qualifications. If you have PADI Advanced, BSAC Sports Diver or equivalent qualification – and can show your certificate – you can also hire

Tens of thousands of foreign students a year study English in Malta. In 2007, 7% of all tourists arriving in Malta, 11% of summer arrivals, were language students, mostly Europeans aged 16 and 17. English courses range from a week or two to a few months, though most are short, and some combine lessons with outdoor activities such as diving and sailing (all taught in English). Students stay in hostels, hotels or homestays. A list of government-recognised language schools can be found at www.visitmalta.com/language-schools, or if you want to be on Gozo, there is a choice of four schools: www.visitmalta.com/lang_schools_gozo. Further information is available from the Federation of English Language Teaching Organisations in Malta (FELTOM, ☏ 27445422; e executive@feltom.com; www.feltom.com).

equipment to dive independently, though if it is your first time in Malta it may be wise to take a guide at least at first. When diving, please always leave wildlife and underwater heritage as you find them.

Choosing a dive centre There are nearly 50 dive centres in Malta, 12 of them on Gozo, licensed by the Malta Tourism Authority (MTA; www.visitmalta.com/diving-malta). It is important to dive with one of these; any other company is acting illegally. Malta's Professional Diving Schools Association (www.pdsa.org.mt) only admits licensed operators and many of the top Maltese dive centres are also registered with PADI International (www.padi.com) and/or with the British Sub-Aqua Club (BSAC, www.bsac.com). If a company does not appear on at least one of these four websites, don't use it.

Exactly which dive centre you choose will depend on where you want to stay, your level of experience and what kind of diving you wish to do. Gozo is a particularly good place for diving and there are several well-established dive centres there (see *Chapter 14, Gozo diving*, page 266). There is also a PADI-registered dive centre on Comino (see *Chapter 13*, page 252).

Diver safety During the summer the number of motorboats around the coast of Malta can be considerable and they are a real danger to divers (and snorkellers) so do make your presence obvious with a surface marker buoy, or an 'A' flag if diving from a boat.

The Mediterranean is almost tideless but there can be currents around the coast of Malta particularly during or after windy weather (though note that the currents may go in the opposite direction to the wind). Seek local advice.

Finally, if despite your best efforts the worst should happen, there is a decompression chamber at Malta's main hospital. There is also a decompression chamber on Gozo, but at the time of writing it is not fully staffed and therefore is not always available in an emergency. Helicopter airlift the few kilometres to Malta is more likely.

There is little in the water to present a serious danger to divers, but there are a few species that should not be touched including scorpion fish, bristle worm (fireworm), jellyfish, snakelock anemone, weaver fish and stingray.

Marine wildlife Malta does not offer the rainbow kaleidoscope of the tropics, but there is plenty to see at all levels of diving – and indeed snorkelling. Species divers are likely to see include barracuda, wrasse and bream (of various kinds), damsel fish, parrot fish, cardinal fish, painted combers, groupers, bogue, amberjack, octopus (especially on night dives), red mullet, meagre, stingrays, flying gurnard

Practical Information **SPORTS AND ACTIVITIES**

3

and squid. Conger eel and moray eel are often found around wrecks and John Dory is sometimes spotted, usually in winter.

You are very unlikely to see 'big game'. Dolphin, tuna and turtles are rare and dangerous sharks almost unheard of. Sea horses can occasionally be seen, usually in July, but they are shy and well camouflaged and once a location is known may be taken by locals to sell. Malta has a small minority of people who enjoy hunting marine wildlife, so if you find anything rare, be careful who you tell.

Dive guide *Scuba Diving Malta, Gozo, Comino* by Peter G Lemon (2nd edition) is an excellent guide to diving in Malta with details and maps of over 90 dive sites as well as photographs and general information (£18.99 + £2 p&p from *www.scubadivingmaltagozocomino.com or from Waterstones bookshops in the UK and dive centres and the airport in Malta*).

For more on diving see *Chapter 4*, page 93 and for diving on Gozo, page 266.

BIRDWATCHING Malta should be an excellent place for birdwatching in spring and autumn. With few resident birds there is little to see in summer, but Malta sits on one of the main migration routes between Africa and Europe and whilst the birds are not quite as abundant as in Israel or Sicily, some 170 species are reliably seen during migration. There is one major drawback to birding here, however, especially in autumn – bird hunters. See also *Birds* (page 23), *Hunting* (page 24) and *Safety* (page 48).

In autumn it is legal for hunters to shoot certain species (most notably quail and turtle dove). Spring hunting is outlawed by the EU Birds Directive although it is worth double checking before heading out. If you see hunters shooting birds of prey or other protected species at any time of year, report them to the police on ❧ 112 and BirdLife Malta on ❧ 21347644.

There are two tiny bird reserves on Malta, Għadira (page 237) and Is-Simar (page 243), both run by BirdLife Malta, and the whole of Comino is also classed as a bird reserve with no hunting allowed and a BirdLife ringing station set up there during migration. The other best places to bird are mainly on the top of cliffs on Malta and Gozo where tired birds make landfall, and high points in fertile valleys. For more on exactly what to see when and a **map** of some of the best birding spots see *Chapter 4*, page 97.

Further information

Birding in Malta e birdinginmalta@gmail.com; www.birdinginmalta.com. Excellent new website run by 2 birdwatching Maltese students.

BirdLife Malta ❧ 21347646; e info@ birdlifemalta.org; www.birdlifemalta.org. Malta's equivalent of the RSPB. Hugely informative website, includes a section for kids.

Both organisations are happy to help visiting birders and would be interested to know about your sightings. BirdLife Malta produces a *Checklist of the Birds of Malta* (€1) which lists all 381 species seen in Malta with their English, Maltese and scientific names, their local status and a tick-box for twitchers. Also, http://schoolnet.gov.mt/tanti/birds.html displays clear colour photos of many of Malta's birds with the English, Maltese and scientific names. For other birding publications, see *Further reading*, page 304 and the BirdLife Malta website, above.

⚠ SAILING

Yachting with your own boat Malta has been a stopping place for people sailing around the Mediterranean for many hundreds of years – the only difference now being that most are leisure sailors. The country's natural harbours are as good today as they were for the Phoenicians and the Knights of St John, and facilities for yachts are improving all the time. **Grand Harbour Marina** on Vittoriosa Waterfront (⟍ *21800700;* e *info@ghm.com.mt; www.ghm.com.mt*) is the Mediterranean's newest super-yacht marina, but there are four other yacht centres.

The largest, **Msida** (*Ta' Xbiex Waterfront on Marsamxett Harbour, the other side of Valletta;* ⟍ *21332800*) and **Mġarr** on Gozo (⟍ *21558856/7*) are both run by the Malta Maritime Authority (e *info@mma.gov.mt; www.mma.gov.mt*); **Manoel Island Marina** (⟍ *21338589;* e *info@manoelislandmarina.com; www.manoelislandmarina.com*) and **Portomaso Marina** (*St Julian's;* ⟍ *21387803;* e *info@portomasomarina.com; www.portomasomarina.com*) are privately owned.

Online Maritime Directory (*www.maritimedirectory.com.mt*) covers everything from navigational rules to a list of chandlers. *Yachting in Malta* is a printed directory of yachting services and facilities (m *99071949;* e *yim@ anatlus.com*) and there is always the **Royal Malta Yacht Club** in Marsamxett Harbour (*Ta' Xbiex Seafront, Ta' Xbiex;* ⟍ *21333109;* e *info@rymc.org; www.rymc.org*) which has reciprocal arrangements with many other yacht clubs around the world and also organises the annual Rolex Middle Sea Race in October (see *Events*, page 36).

Sailing courses, boat hire and charter You can of course sail without having your own boat. Dinghies can be hired and yachts chartered for day trips or longer – including sailing to Sicily. Tuition is also available. Charters, particularly in peak season, should be booked well in advance.

BoatLink Msida Marina; m 99882615; e jonathan@boatlinkmalta.com; www.boatlinkmalta.com. Courses in sailing dinghies & yachts (from €200 for a beginner's course), small boat hire & yacht charters with skipper (from €210/day for a 29ft yacht – €500 for 50ft).
Fairwind Sailing Portomaso Marina & St George's Bay (near St Julian's); ⟍ 21459398; m 79552222; e pauldebono@onvol.net; www.fairwindsailing.com.mt. A sailing school offering adults & children instruction in dinghy sailing, windsurfing & yachting as well as boat hire to the experienced. Dinghy hire starts from €20/hr, €40/day.
Malta Sailing Academy & **Malta Yacht Charters** 10 St Lawrence St, Sliema (but boats based at Msida); ⟍ 21339655; m 79432526; skype: Michael.gauci1; e info@maltasailingacademy.com or info@maltayachtcharters.com; www.maltasailingacademy.com or www.maltayachtcharters.com. RYA yachting courses,

from Start Yachting to Yachtmaster, & tailor-made yachting trips/charters. All tuition in English. Price for example: 2-day Start Yachting Course €233.
S&D Yachts Sea Breeze, Triq Giuseppe Cali, Ta' Xbiex; ⟍ 21320577 or 21331515; e info@sdyachts.com; www.sdyachts.com. Acts as a broker for chartering yachts – access to a great many.
Windy Shack Marfa Rd, Mellieha; m 99515360; e info@windy-shack.com; www.windy-shack.com; ⊕ 1 Apr–1 Nov. Rents out dinghies, catamarans & windsurfers & offers group & individual lessons for adults & children. Dinghy hire costs from €15/hr (€20 for 2 people), catamaran €20/hr (+ €5 for each additional person). Private lessons: dinghy €25/hr, catamaran €35.
Yachting Malta m 99821460 or UK 7958391198; e info@yachtingmalta.com; www.yachtingmalta.com. A small British-Maltese Yacht charter company. Prices from €450/day with skipper for up to 6 people.

🖍 **WALKING** Many people – even in Malta – think there is so little countryside left that walking is not a realistic pastime. This is not true. There are some lovely walks, especially in the north/northwestern part of the main island, and Gozo has excellent walking (for which see page 265). Most of the best walks are coastal, although there are inland walks as well – including along the Victoria Lines on Malta (see page 231) and up some of Gozo's flat-topped hills (see page 281).

The MTA produces eight *Countryside Walks* booklets each detailing a long walk (*download free from www.visitmalta.com/e-brochures, or expect to pay about €2 from tourist information offices*). They are well mapped out with lots of information and all start and end at public transport. With your own car, you can cherry pick the best bits (although you will either need a driver or have to backtrack to fetch the car).

The **Ramblers Association of Malta** (e *ram205@gmail.com; www.ramblersmalta.jointcomms.com*) runs a regular programme of walks and is happy to help visiting walkers. It can also organise a whole programme for rambling groups visiting Malta.

The **Majjistral Nature and History Park** (e *info@majjistral.org; www.majjistral.org*) covers the coast from Golden Bay (ir-Ramla tal-Mixquqa) to Anchor Bay (Il-Prajjet) along the west coast towards the north of the island – an area of rocky garigue, cliffs and clay with some rare plants. Organised walks, about 6km long, with an informed guide run most Sundays. They are free but must be pre-booked (e *walks@majjistral.org*). Walks are also occasionally organised by **Nature Trust Malta** (✆ *21313150*; e *info@naturetrustmalta.org; www.naturetrustmalta.org*).

British companies **Ramblers Holidays** (✆ *01707 331133; www.ramblersholidays.co.uk*) and **Headwater** (✆ *01606 720099*; e *info@ headwater.com; www.headwater.com*) run walking holidays to Malta and Gozo.

FISHING Malta is naturally an ideal place for coastal and deepwater fishing from boats. Tuna, swordfish, barracuda, dorado, bream, wrasse, grouper and snapper can be caught, amongst others – depending, of course, on how far from the shore you go and on the season. Many of the boating companies will hire out a boat and boatman for fishing trips. Those listed here provide a specialist service including all the fishing gear you will need and an experienced skipper. It is advisable to book well in advance.

Aquatica Sport Fishing Charters ✆ 21579753, m 79063462; e daryl@fishingmalta.com; www.fishingmalta.com. Tailor-made fishing trips for up to 4 people in 1 boat, offshore (from €128pp for 6hrs or €400 for the whole boat) & coastal (4hrs, €85pp, €300 boat).
Fishing Mania ✆ 21632595; m 99822012; e fishingmania@keyworld.net;

www.mol.net.mt/fishingmania. Sports fishing charters, day or night for up to 6 anglers (though 4 is more comfortable) from €400 for 8hrs.
Luzzu Cruises m 79064489 or 99474310; e luzzucruises@onvol.net; www.officialluzzucruises.com. Year-round fishing trips, max 10 people; 3hr trip, adults cost €60, children €35.

For up-to-date information from other fishermen in Malta go to the online **Malta Fishing Forum** at www.maltafishingforum.com.

ROCK CLIMBING Rock climbing is increasingly popular and Malta certainly has plenty of rock to climb! There are some 1,300 routes on the islands in about 30 locations ranging from fairly straightforward to very challenging. For the adventurous, there is plenty of scope for bouldering, deep-water soloing and sea-level traversing. Not all equipment is easily found in Malta, so do bring your own.

The Malta rock-climbers bible is *Malta Rock Climbing: The Comprehensive Guide* by John Codling, Andrew Warrington and Richard Abela (*Moonstone Communications*; €28.50 + p&p) with details of 1,200 routes. The book is available from www.climbmalta.com, which is also the home of Malta's **Climbing Club**.

Further information can be found at www.malta-rockclimbing.com and in *The Adventure Guidebook to the Maltese Islands* by Xavier Hancock (*www.gozoadventures.com; €16.95*). Xavier is an experienced climber who runs an adventure holiday company in Gozo (☎ *21564592;* m *99241171;* e *info@gozoadventures.com*).

OTHER SPORTS AND OUTDOOR ACTIVITIES MTA lists companies and clubs offering sporting and outdoor activities of all kinds at www.visitmalta.com/sports-contacts and much can also be found in *The Adventure Guidebook to the Maltese Islands* by Xavier Hancock (see *Rock climbing,* above) which covers watersports, mountain biking, diving and walking. For **cycling**, see also *Getting around,* page 59 and for cycling in Gozo page 266.

Besides sporting facilities in hotels, there are various local sports and leisure centres around the country. By far the largest centre for land-based sporting activity, however, is the **Marsa Sports Club** (*about 4km from Valletta;* ☎ *21233851 or 21232842;* e *marsport@maltanet.net; www.marsasportsclub.com; visitor membership is €5/day, €25/week*), which began life as the British colonial club. Here you will find 18 tennis courts, five squash courts, a gym and sauna, polo and cricket pitches, several football pitches, a racetrack and a swimming pool. It is also home to the **Royal Malta Golf Club** (*Aldo Moro Rd, Marsa;* ☎ *21223704, 21227019 or 21239302;* e *sales@royalmaltagolfclub.com; www.royalmaltagolfclub.com*) with its 18-hole course (no beginners) and mini-golf. One 18-hole round costs €60–65, although there are sometimes special offers on the website.

Watersports – including windsurfing, waterskiing and canoeing – are catered for on many of Malta's beaches, particularly the main sandy ones like Golden Bay and Mellieħa Beach, as well as by most large and five-star hotels. **Windsurfers** favour Mellieħa Bay and St Thomas's Bay. There is information for experienced windsurfers on www.holidays-malta.com/windsurf and a new site, www.windsurfmalta.com, was under construction at the time of writing and looked promising. **Fairwind Sailing** (see *Sailing,* above) also offers windsurfing courses.

Rugged Coast Adventures (☎ *2129251;* m *79926734;* e *ruggedcoastadventures@ yahoo.com; www.seakayakmalta.com*), based in Mellieħa and run by an enthusiastic American, offers **sea kayaking** around the coast of Malta. Courses can be taken (from €70) or accompanied trips of anything from two hours (€30) to a few days arranged. Sit-on-top kayaks can be hired from €10/hour or €40/day for independent canoeing.

Horseriding is available from riding schools at Golden Bay (☎ *21573360;* m *99856862; www.goldenbayhorseriding.com).* and Bidnija Riding School (☎ *21414010;* m *79992326;* e *info@bidnijahorseriding.com; www.bidnijahorseriding.com; note: no public transport*). Rides are usually one or two hours accompanied by instructors. All equipment is provided and no prior experience is required. Prices from about €20.

PHOTOGRAPHY

Most of the time Malta has marvellous light for photographs. The only problem can be that the sun is very bright and therefore contrast is generally high. Most sights and museums allow photography so long as the flash is switched off (the bright light can damage some exhibits). Tempting though it is, please don't climb over ropes at prehistoric and ancient sites to get a better picture: the ropes are there to protect the fabric of the site and the archaeological evidence it holds.

If you need to empty your memory stick or want a back-up, Primatel on Triq Wilga in Paceville will download your pictures onto a CD (€3.50 for 700MB).

TELEPHONE To **phone Malta from abroad** you need the exit code for your country ('00' from the UK) plus '356' for Malta, followed by the number. Within Malta, there are no area codes, just the phone number which usually has eight digits. The first two numbers are geographically indicative but are always used. To **dial out of Malta**, the code is '00'.

Malta still has some functioning phone boxes – often British red ones. Although a few take coins, most now only take cards which can be bought at the airport (€2, €5, €10). As most Maltese own a mobile phone the cards tend not to be readily available from newsagents.

Primatel in Paceville (Triq Wilga) offers internet phone calls at fantastically cheap rates: UK and Italy €0.07/min; Australia, France and Germany €0.08.

The Malta **phone book** is online at www.go.com.mt or **directory enquiries** can be called on ❱ 1182 or 1187. The **talking clock** is on ❱ 195 and **weather forecasts** on ❱ 50043848. The **emergency number** is ❱ 112.

MOBILE PHONES There are three main mobile-phone networks in Malta: **Go** (*www.go.com.mt/gomobile*), **Melita** (*www.melita.com/landing.aspx?id=4851*) and **Vodafone Malta** (*www.vodafone.com.mt*). UK and other European mobiles work in Malta. If you want to make calls at local rates, you can buy a Maltese pay-as-you-go SIM card to insert into your phone (available from the airport, mobile-phone outlets and some newsagents). Most Maltese have mobile phones and mobile numbers start with a 7 or a 9.

PHOTOGRAPHIC TIPS   *Ariadne Van Zandbergen*

EQUIPMENT An SLR camera with one or more lenses is recommended for serious photography. The most important component in a digital SLR is the sensor; either DX or FX. The FX is a full-size sensor identical to the old film size (36mm). The DX sensor is half size and produces less quality. The type of sensor will determine your choice of lenses as the DX sensor introduces a 0.5x multiplication to the focal length. FX ('full frame') sensors are the future, so I will further refer to focal lengths appropriate to the FX sensor.

Always buy the best lens you can afford. Fixed fast lenses are ideal, but very costly. Zoom lenses offer good flexibility with composition. If you carry only one lens a 24–70mm or similar zoom should be ideal. For a second lens, a lightweight 80–200mm or 70–300mm or similar will be excellent for candid shots and varying your composition. Wildlife photography requires at least a 300mm lens. For a small loss of quality, teleconverters are a cheap and compact way to increase magnification: a 300 lens with a 1.4x converter becomes 420mm, and with a 2x it becomes 600mm. NB 1.4x and 2x teleconverters reduce the speed of your lens by 1.4 and 2 stops respectively.

For ordinary prints a 6-megapixel camera is fine. For better results, the possibility to enlarge images and for professional reproduction, higher resolution is available up to 21 megapixels.

It is important to have enough memory space. You should calculate how many pictures you can fit on a card and either take enough cards or take a storage drive onto which you can download the cards' content.

Remember that digital camera batteries, computers and other storage devices need charging. Make sure you have all the chargers, cables and converters with you.

DUST AND HEAT Keep your equipment in a sealed bag, and avoid exposing equipment to the sun when possible. Digital cameras are prone to collecting dust particles on the

ⓔ INTERNET ACCESS There are internet cafés in most major population centres – and particularly in tourist areas. Internet access usually costs about €2 per hour (less if you buy several hours). There are also a growing number of Wi-Fi hotspots where you can connect through your own equipment for free.

Some **hotels** offer free internet access in the lobby or bar, either via Wi-Fi or through a couple of broadband computers, but most charge for using the web. The cost is roughly in proportion to the published cost of rooms so five-star hotels may charge up to €19/day, while hostel and guesthouse fees tend to be more in line with internet cafés.

Internet cafés Internet cafés, like bars, have a tendency to come and go, but a few are quite well established (see below). There always seem to be several internet cafés along **Tower Road** in Sliema and around **Sliema Ferries** so you should never have trouble getting connected in this area.

Ghall-Kafe/Primatel Triq Wilga, Paceville; ➦ 21380901, 21359684 or 21319686; e info@melita.net.mt; ⏲ 24hrs. Lots of computers, Wi-Fi, phones (see above) & download (eg: of photos) to CD/DVD (€3.50 for 700MB). **Superbowl** St George's Bay, Paceville. See *Arts and entertainment* above.

Ziffa Business Centre 194 Strait St, Valletta (cnr of South St, opposite Trabuxu wine bar); ➦ 21224307; www.ziffa.net/ziffa-business-centre; ⏲ 09.00–23.00 (22.30 on Sun) daily. 28 PCs, Wi-Fi, scanning, colour photocopying, download to CD/DVD & internet phones.

For internet cafés in **Gozo**, see page 264.

sensor which results in spots on the image. The dirt mostly enters the camera when changing lenses, so be careful when doing this. You can have your camera sensor professionally cleaned, or you can do this yourself with special brushes and swabs, but note that touching the sensor might cause damage and should only be done with the greatest care.

LIGHT The most striking outdoor photographs are often taken during the hour or two of 'golden light' after dawn and before sunset. Shooting in low light may enforce the use of very low shutter speeds, in which case a tripod/beanbag will be required to avoid camera shake. The most advanced digital SLRs have very little loss of quality on higher ISO settings, which allows you to shoot at lower light conditions. It is still recommended not to increase the ISO unless necessary.

Generally, it is best to shoot with the sun behind you. When photographing animals or people in the harsh midday sun, images taken in light but even shade are likely to look nicer than those taken in direct sunlight or patchy shade.

PROTOCOL In some countries, it is unacceptable to photograph local people without permission, and many will refuse to pose or will ask for a donation. Don't try to sneak photographs. Even the most willing subject will often pose stiffly when a camera is pointed at them; relax them by making a joke, and take a few shots in quick succession to improve the odds of capturing a natural pose.

Ariadne Van Zandbergen is a professional travel and wildlife photographer specialised in Africa. She runs 'The Africa Image Library'. For photo requests, visit the website at www.africaimagelibrary.co.za or contact her direct: ⓔ ariadne@hixnet.co.za.

Practical Information **MEDIA AND COMMUNICATIONS**

3

Wi-Fi In Valletta the **Marks and Spencer** café just off Palace Square (St George's Sq) offers free Wi-Fi or, if you prefer surfing in the sun, the whole square has recently been made into a Wi-Fi hotspot. The café in the **Manoel Theatre** (page 134) offers free Wi-Fi as does **Café Jubilee** (*www.cafejubilee.com*; see also *Where to eat* page 111 and page 263) – with branches in Valletta, on the Gzira waterfront and in the main square of Victoria in Gozo. If you can cope with the strong whiff of burgers while you browse, all Malta's branches of **McDonalds** (*www.mcdonalds.com.mt*) offer Wi-Fi too. Locations include Republic Street, Valletta; Sliema Ferries, Islet Street, Buġibba; Bay Street shopping centre, Paceville; Valley Road, Birkirkara; and the Arkadia shopping centre, Victoria, Gozo (all branches are listed on the website).

In Paceville both **Primatel** (see above) and the **Superbowl** offer free Wi-Fi in their internet cafés. For somewhere quieter and more comfortable there's **Café Juliani** (in the Juliani Hotel, see page 167) on St Julian's Waterfront. In Sliema the bar of **Pebbles** apartments (page 163) has Wi-Fi; get a free password from the barman with your drink. Mdina has one of the most charming and historic Wi-Fi hotspots in the **Caremelite Priory Café** (see page 204).

✉ **POST** Post is reasonably reliable in Malta and there are small post offices dotted across the country. All are open in the morning, usually Monday to Saturday, and some also open in the afternoon on weekdays. Full details can be found at www.maltapost.com/page.asp?p=7176&l=1.

NEWS Malta has several English-language newspapers which also have a strong presence online:

The Times of Malta & The Malta Sunday Times www.timesofmalta.com. By far the most comprehensive daily coverage. The useful website features its own articles with blog comments on them (which can be quite revealing about the mood in the country). The paper does voice criticism of government, although in the run up to elections it tends to support the Nationalist Party.

The Independent & Independent on Sunday (no connection to the UK paper) www.independent.com.mt. Much smaller daily paper with fewer resources. Much weaker link to the establishment.
Malta Today www.maltatoday.com.mt A midweek & a Sun edition. Fiercely independent & critical.
Business Weekly www.maltabusinessweekly.com.mt. From the same stable as *The Independent*.
Sunday Circle www.sundaycircle.com. Women's magazine with current affairs content.

There are also several news websites:

di-ve www.di-ve.com. Sport, business & entertainment.
MaltaMedia http://maltamedia.com. Independent online news service.

MaltaSport www.maltasport.com
Malta Star www.maltastar.com. Online Labour newspaper.

TELEVISION Maltese television has a mix of programmes in both Maltese and English. **TVM** is the national station which is mostly in Maltese but also airs British programmes from the BBC and ITV as well as American shows and news in English. **One TV** (*www.one.com.mt*) is affiliated to the Labour Party and **Net TV** (*www.nettv.com.mt*) to the Nationalists. Cable is also widely available and includes two independent Maltese channels, **Smash** (*www.smashmalta.com*) and **Favourite** (*www.favouritechannel.tv*) as well as a range of international, American, British and Italian channels including BBC World, CNN, Al Jazeera, Discovery, UK and a range of sports channels. The cable programme schedule can be found at www.melita.com/content.aspx?id=541.

RADIO There are numerous radio stations in Malta, some in English and most based around popular music, much of it fairly easy listening. Some have names you might recognise such as **Malta's Magic** (91.7MHz, 'more music, less talk') and **Kiss FM** (91.3MHz). **Bay** (89.7, *www.bay.com.mt*) is a popular music and entertainment station and **Vibe FM** (88.7, *www.vibefm.com.mt*) specialises in dance and R&B. The national public service channel, **Radio Malta** (93.7), is mainly in Maltese but takes news in English from the BBC three or four times a day (usually 06.00, 09.00, 11.00 and 15.00), and **Campus Radio** (103.7) is a 24-hour station run by Malta University which includes substantial content from the BBC World Service and the UK's Classic FM.

BUSINESS

Nearly 5% of foreign visitors to Malta (in 2007) were conference delegates. Some 24 of Malta's four- and five-star hotels (including those that are part of international chains like Intercontinental, Corinthia Hotels, Radisson and Kempinski) have meeting and conference facilities, some extensive. The **Hilton Malta Conference Centre** in St Julian's (❧ *21383383; www.hilton.co.uk/malta*) is particularly large with a capacity of 1,400.

There are also 22 non-hotel conference centres including the grand historic Mediterranean Conference Centre in Valletta which was once the hospital of the Knights of St John (❧ *21243840/3; www.mcc.com.mt*).

Destination management companies (DMCs) can organise team-building and incentive activities from film-making to historic treasure hunts, beach Olympics to walking, as well as the more common sports.

As the UK is the main source of conference bookings in Malta, the **Malta Tourism Authority** has a dedicated unit in London (❧ *020 8877 6993*).

The world of business in Malta is male-dominated. Although there are increasing numbers of working women, the glass ceiling is still generally in place and some Maltese career women complain of feeling invisible in meetings. Although Malta is not corrupt in a 'brown-envelope' way and there is no mafia of any kind here, doing business in Malta does tend to rely on who you know.

Most offices full of educated people used to function in English, but government offices in particular are run more and more in Maltese. Everyone you are likely to deal with will, however, speak English, so there is no actual language barrier. Office hours are generally from 08.00 (sometimes 09.00) until about 17.00. Most people do not work late into the evening and in summer the civil service and some other firms may only work until 13.00.

BUYING PROPERTY

Malta is increasingly seen, mostly by Brits, as a potential place for a holiday or retirement home, as well as being something of a tax haven. Gary Neville has a house here and Billy Connolly spends much of his time on Gozo. But it is not just the mega-rich and famous who are getting into Maltese property, although the collapse of the pound against the euro post-credit crunch has not helped those whose money is in sterling.

Foreigners from EU countries may freely buy property in Malta if they are planning to make it their primary residence. If the property is to be a second or holiday home then the price paid for it must be above a set minimum (at the time of writing €104,510 for apartments/maisonettes and €174,138 for houses) and a permit is required which usually takes about six weeks to get. The property must be for personal/family use. Renting it out requires an additional permit.

Further information can be found on the websites of two of the more established estate agents in Malta: Frank Salt (✆ *23794554; www.franksalt.com.mt*) and Perry's (✆ *21310800; www.perry.com.mt*).

CULTURAL ETIQUETTE

Malta is conservative, but not formal. The Maltese don't much like to see people in **swimwear** on the streets of Valletta or Mdina (let alone in restaurants) but bikinis on the beach are fine. **Topless bathing** is (despite what you might occasionally see) illegal (see also *Swimming*, page 66). Smart casual, including jeans, is perfectly acceptable in almost all **restaurants**, even the top ones, and shorts are fine by day. In **churches**, however, you need to cover knees and shoulders. A few churches provide wraps for the purpose, but most do not. Suitably dressed, you are always welcome to attend services, but this is obviously not the time to wander around the interior of the church sightseeing.

Greeting is usually by handshake – or perhaps a kiss on each cheek if you know someone better. **Public displays of affection** are frowned upon, though walking arm in arm or holding hands is common. **Gay couples** need to be a little more discreet than heterosexuals (see page 52). The age of consent for both groups is 18.

See *Cultural attitudes* for further information, page 28 and *Money and budgeting*, page 54, for information on **tipping etiquette**.

TRAVELLING POSITIVELY

Malta is a moderately well-off European country, so not a place where you can help by stuffing your rucksack with pencils or hard-to-get foods. What you can do is support its efforts to care for its remarkable historic heritage and its environment.

HERITAGE Join, or donate to, one of the NGOs active in the renovation and care of historic properties, and in opening them to the public. These organisations also act as lobby groups with government for the protection of places of historic importance. If you are going to be in Malta for a long time, offer to help at one of their sites. There are many foreigners, mainly Brits, already volunteering with these organisations.

Din L-Art Helwa ✆ 21215222 or 21225952; e info@dinlarthelwa.org; www.dinlarthelwa.org. Malta's National Trust with annual membership €20, youth €5 & life €200. Responsible for quite a few small properties including Knights'-period towers on Malta, Gozo & Comino.
Fondazzjoni Wirt Artna ✆ 21800992 or 21809713; e info@wirtartna.org; www.wirtartna.org. The Malta Heritage Trust offers foreign membership for €35 or

£25. Several military properties plus a large World War II shelter & the Neolithic Kordin III temple.
Wirt Ghawdex e info@wirtghawdex.org; www.wirtghawdex.org; you can chat to Jay Jones (a British volunteer) on ✆ 21563839. Gozo Heritage with annual membership fees of adult €11.50, senior €7, student/child €4.50, family €23 & life €115. Projects from Knights' fortifications to an old Gozo ferry.

ENVIRONMENT
BirdLife Malta ✆ 21347646; e info@ birdlifemalta.org; www.birdlifemalta.org. Malta's equivalent of the British RSPB & runs two small nature reserves & a reforestation project as well as working to protect birds. Overseas membership is €23.29 for up to two adults at the same address. If you go birdwatching in Malta, BirdLife would be

pleased to have a copy of your sightings. You can also volunteer for the **Raptor Camp** (e raptorcamp@birdlifemalta.org) which runs for a couple of weeks each spring & autumn. Birders from across Europe gather to observe & note sightings of migratory birds & to help keep illegal hunting in check.

GAIA Foundation ☎ 21584473/4; e director@ projectgaia.org or elysium@projectgaia.org; www.projectgaia.org. Add a tree to the Maltese landscape for €14. The GAIA foundation will plant it, water it & maintain it; if anything happens to it, they will replace it. The Foundation also runs a volunteering programme for locals & visitors. Placements can be short or long & may be on any of the NGO's projects. You could help with tree-planting, organic farming, designing visitor information, seed-gathering or helping wardens on beach watch in summer.

For more on natural history and conservation issues, see *Chapter* 2, page 22.

4

Planning for Your Interests

This chapter aims to help you organise your trip to suit your particular interests. The idea is to provide a bit of extra information, highlight top locations (each section is accompanied by a map with relevant sites plotted) and make it easier to find relevant material elsewhere in the book. It is, of course, worth reading any general material in *Chapters 2* and *3* first.

PREHISTORIC MALTA AND THE TEMPLES

Malta's temples are unique. They are some of the oldest stone buildings in the world and by far the most sophisticated for their time (the fourth and third millennium BC). Despite having UNESCO World Heritage status, the sites haven't, until recently, been especially well looked after, and have had no visitor information worth mentioning. This is now changing and at Mnajdra and Ħaġar Qim (page 192) a EU-funded project has allowed the building of a new visitors' centre, as well as the construction of two vast canopies over the temples to protect them from sun and, crucially, rain. Projects of this sort will follow at other temples in due course, but it takes time and money. For now, information is still a little short, so, as well as a map of the temple locations, there follows a brief general guide to interpreting Malta's prehistoric temples.

INTERPRETING THE TEMPLES

Location and orientation The temples are generally located on south-facing slopes in areas favourable to agriculture and with access to the sea. You don't find them on the top of Malta's many high rocky cliffs, but in the rare places where the coastline dips down closer to sea level and boats might feasibly land nearby. They may face south in order to bring in light and to keep out the prevalent northerly winds.

Often two or more temples are found together. The reason for building additional temples on the same site remains a mystery but we do know that they were usually built at different times and the new ones were additional rather than replacements for the older ones. Older temples continued to be used alongside new ones.

Construction, exteriors and doorways Temple construction is sophisticated and follows a roughly similar pattern – though with many variations. Typically the temple has an **oval forecourt**, big enough perhaps to gather the whole community. The substantial **concave façades** usually face south or southwest.

The **doorways** are interesting. Some are made of a single stone with its centre cut out to allow passage through. Such **'porthole' doorways** are found at main entrances (as at Mnajdra; see page 194) and internal doorways as well as connecting apses to side chambers. Smaller portholes (more like windows) are also found in many temples and are often known as 'oracle holes'. Portholes are not easy to make so it seems likely that the space behind them was important in some way.

Many of the temple doorways are not portholes but constructed of **slabs of stone**. Most appear to be simple trilithons, two uprights with a lintel or capstone. They are, however, often more sophisticated than this. Most have a 'box within a box' construction with the lintel also touching (and occasionally even rebated into) two further, taller, uprights. This ingenious system helps to support the megalithic walls that are pushing in on the doorway space and makes the whole construction much stronger and able to support the immense weight of the roofed apses either side.

In temple doorways you will also often see large **'hinge holes'** indicating that there would have been a closing door of some kind, as well as occasional larger holes that look as though they were meant to house the end of some kind of bar that would have blocked the doorway or carried a drape or curtain.

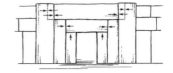

Holes may also be found in the threshold stones at your feet and just inside or outside entranceways. These have become known as **libation holes** (where liquid offerings are poured into the underworld) because they have been identified as such in ancient architecture elsewhere in the world (though in all cases less ancient than this). There is, however, no direct evidence as to what they were for.

At each corner of the façade (where the corners survive) you will usually find a particularly **tall upright stone**. The outer walls of the temples are built of large close-fitting stone slabs known as **orthostats**, topped with smaller blocks. Often there is a bench-like structure along the base of the façade. Where you see part of a wall built from a mass of small stones or capped with concrete this is usually reconstruction (mostly from the 1950s).

Building materials The temples are all built of local limestone. Malta has little wood, but plenty of stone. There are two main types of limestone used in temple building: **globigerina** which is soft, workable and smooth – the best for creating decoration but easily weathered; and **coralline** which is harder and weathers better, but is rougher looking and harder to carve.

Most temples are built of the stone most locally available – although some built on coralline deposits still have a few internal features of the more attractive globigerina limestone. It was clearly thought worth the effort to transport relatively small quantities of the smoother stone for decorative purposes.

Ta' Ħaġrat is constructed from coralline, likewise Skorba and Ġgantija are mainly so. Mnajdra South has the perfect combination – its outside is coralline, the inside globigerina. Meanwhile, Ħaġar Qim, which is a mere 500m from Mnajdra, is constructed entirely from globigerina, the rock on which it sits. It seems even 500m was considered a long way to drag 20 tons of stone!

(For the formation of these limestones see *Geology, Chapter 2,* page 20.)

Temple roofs There are no surviving temple roofs, but archaeologists believe they must have existed because the plaster (sometimes painted with ochre) known to have covered many internal walls, and indeed internal globigerina stone carvings, would not have survived being open to the weather. Carved decorations at both Ġgantija and Mnajdra were seen to weather badly, even in a few decades, when they were left open to the skies following excavation in the early 19th century (most carvings have since been moved to the National Museum of Archaeology in Valletta or the Gozo Archaeological Museum; see pages 121 and 274 respectively).

Nobody is quite sure how the roofs would have been **constructed**; the likelihood is that there were several techniques. It seems probable that some temples were roofed with flat slabs of stone or possibly wood. Another technique was more sophisticated: a corbelled stone roof with concentric circles of stone blocks getting smaller and higher towards the centre. The ceiling of the 'Holy of Holies' – an inner room of the Ħal Saflieni Hypogeum – is carved to look like a corbelled roof. Since there are many other architectural echoes of the above-ground temples in this underground tomb complex, it seems logical to conclude that the roof is another. It is also possible to see the beginnings of corbelling (stones starting to lean in) at the top at some temple walls, particularly at Mnajdra. Roofs could of course have been a mix of corbelling and slabs, with a few layers of corbelled stones topped by slabs closing the remaining, smaller, hole.

Inside the temples Inside the temple entrance there is usually a **corridor or central space** off which are internal chambers, D-shaped or oval rooms known as **apses**. Often (but not always) these are laid out in a trefoil pattern, sometimes with a second corridor leading to further apses. The apse floors were usually made of **torba** – crushed and pounded limestone that could be smoothed and, confusingly for archaeologists, sometimes looks like bedrock.

The temples are constructed with an outer and inner wall. The gap between the two is usually filled with earth and rubble, although in a few places there are small subsidiary 'rooms' between the walls.

Altars, reliefs and statuary Inside, most of the temples have what are known as **altars**. Some are solid blocks of stone, others constructed of trilithons (three megaliths, two upright supporting one horizontally across the top creating a door or table-like construction) or groups of trilithons. Still others consist of a single slab on a pedestal or are smaller and mushroom-shaped. Some of the larger slab altars are so tall that a person can hardly reach the top, which makes it seem more likely that the inside was used rather than the top surface. One at Tarxien (see page 172) is a likely candidate for animal sacrifice as it has a cubby hole with a carved door that was found to contain animal bones and a flint knife.

Some experts have identified stone 'rings' (holes going right through the corner piece of stone often seen at entrances) as tethering points for animals. Others think the holes may have been used to attach ropes when hauling the stones to the temple site. They could of course have been used for both.

Some altars are **decorated** with pitting (creating a dotted pattern) and/or with carvings of spirals and occasionally animals and plants. The remarkable **temple statuary** is usually found close by. Most of these statues are of some version of the 'Fat Lady', with huge hips and rear ends, conical legs, and variable upper bodies (some of which may even be male). There are also many phallic symbols in stone and clay. These two together suggest a possible fertility cult, perhaps with the fat figures as a deity or deities.

Most of the carvings and statues seen at the temple sites are copies, the originals having been removed to the safety of the National Museum of Archaeology in Valletta (see page 121) which is a real must-see for anyone interested in the temples.

WHERE TO VISIT The key temple-period sites are as follows; locations are plotted on the map opposite.

① **Mnajdra and Ħaġar Qim** (on one site) The most scenic on Malta, two of the best preserved and with interesting contrasts in design. The only ones with full visitor services. See page 192.

② **The National Archaeological Museum in Valletta prehistory galleries** (see page 121) – home to most of the best statuary and carvings and contains some useful information.

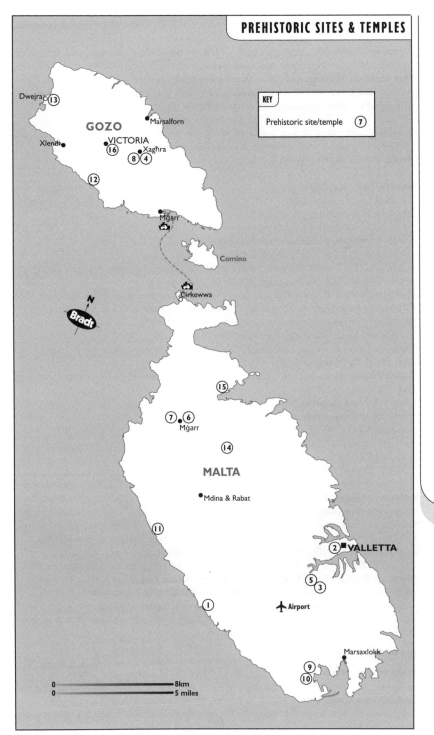

PREHISTORIC SITES & TEMPLES

KEY

Prehistoric site/temple ⑦

Dwejra ⑬

GOZO

●Marsalforn

Xlendi●

VICTORIA
⑯
⑧ ⑭Xaghra

⑫

Mgarr

Comino

Cirkewwa

N
Bradt

⑮

⑦●⑥
Mgarr

⑭

MALTA

●Mdina & Rabat

⑪

②■VALLETTA

⑤
③

⑤
③

①

✈ Airport

●Marsaxlokk

⑨
⑩

0 _____ 8km
0 _____ 5 miles

③ **The Tarxien Temples** The latest, most complex site with the greatest decoration. Not the loveliest location. See page 172.
④ **Ġgantija Temples** Xagħra, Gozo. This is the oldest of the well-preserved temples, and has the largest megalith. Set in a pleasant location. See page 284.
⑤ **Ħal Saflieni Hypogeum** An extraordinary underground tomb complex in Paola whose design echoes the above-ground temples. Book well in advance to be sure of getting in, although some tickets are sold the day before. See page 176.

If you see the sites above, you have seen the best and most interesting of the prehistoric temples and anything else is a plus. Three other, smaller, temple-period sites are open to the public:

⑥ **Skorba** See page 229.
⑦ **Ta' Ħaġrat** See page 228.
⑧ **Xagħra Hypogeum** See page 287.

Other important prehistoric sites include:

⑨ **Għar Dalam** This is the cave where some of the first people in Malta settled in about 5000BC. See *History*, page 183.
⑩ **Borġ In-Nadur** Bronze Age site (and cart ruts – see box page 197). See page 185.
⑪ **Clapham Junction** At Dingli Cliffs you will find the greatest concentration of Malta's mysterious cart ruts, see page 197 and the box text on page 198.
⑫ **Ta' Ċenċ** Gozo. Cart ruts; see page 294.
⑬ **Dwejra** Gozo. Cart ruts; see page 277.
⑭ **San Pawl Tat-Tarġa** Naxxar. Cart ruts; see page 224.
⑮ **Xemxija graves** Early rock tombs that may have been models for the temples. See page 243.
⑯ **Gozo Archaeological Museum** Within Victoria's Citadel, displaying prehistoric (and other) finds made on Gozo including some remarkable small-scale figures. See page 274.

ROMAN/BYZANTINE MALTA

The most interesting sites of this period are underground – the late Roman/Byzantine catacombs that undermine several areas of Malta – although there are also a few places to see above ground. All the tomb complexes are referred to as 'catacombs' even though strictly speaking the smaller ones are 'hypogea' (a collection of individual tombs, or those of a single family or guild, rather than of a whole community).

Some sites – including the largest and most impressive – are regularly open to the public; others are opened only on request and with an extra payment to Heritage Malta (↘ 22954000; e *info@heritagemalta.org*; *€50/hr to open the sites plus normal entry fees of €5 adult, €3.50 student/senior/child 12–17 & €2.50 child 6–12*).

See also the boxed text on page 214 for an introduction to Roman burial practices in Malta. For more information on open sites see the page numbers below. Request sites are described here.

WHERE TO VISIT
Open to the public
① **St Paul's Catacombs** The largest and most accessible; a must-see. See page 214.
② **St Agatha's Catacombs** Large, with frescoes. See page 216.
③ **Wignacourt Museum Catacombs** Originally part of the same catacombs as St Paul's, but accessed from the museum. See page 213.

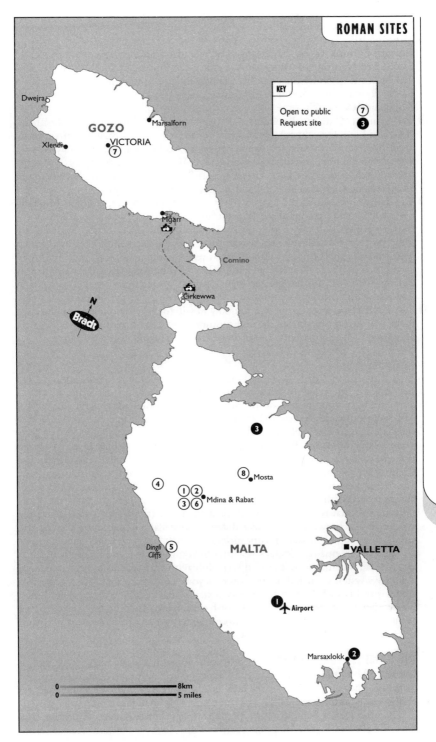

KEY

Open to public ⑦
Request site ❸

Dwejra

GOZO

Marsalforn

Xlendi

VICTORIA
⑦

Mgarr

Comino

Cirkewwa

N

Bradt

❸

⑧ Mosta

④

① ②
③ ⑥ Mdina & Rabat

Dingli
Cliffs ⑤

MALTA

■ VALLETTA

❶ ✈ Airport

Marsaxlokk ❷

0 ————— 8km
0 ————— 5 miles

④ **Binġemma** Always open, hillside tombs. See page 230.
⑤ **Dingli Cliffs** Three punic graves. Always open. See page 198.
⑥ **Roman Domus** Mosaics and statuary on site of 1st century house. See page 211.
⑦ **Gozo Archaeological Museum** A few unusual Roman artefacts. See page 274.
⑧ **Ta' Bistra Catacombs** Expected to open to the public in 2011/12. See page 226.

Request sites

❶ **Tal-Mintna Catacombs** Located beneath Pjazza Tal-Gublew Tad-Djamanti (Diamond Jubilee Square) in Mqabba (near the airport). Under an ordinary, modern street lie these three Roman hypogea (early for Malta, possibly AD4-6). They are small but particularly well preserved. With excellent examples of window tombs, scalloped decoration, an exceptionally well-preserved triclinium (*agape* table), triangular lamp holes and arched and pointed doorways.

❷ **Tas-Silġ** Just northeast of Marsaxlokk is a multi-period site, running from the prehistoric to the medieval via Phoenician, Roman and Byzantine. Tas-Silġ is a modern name taken from the nearby church of Our Lady of the Snows. Very important site for archaeology (excavation is ongoing every summer), but laymen will need an expert to point things out so when booking ask for a well-informed member of Heritage Malta to open it up for you. The most striking feature here is obvious – the red Roman flooring – *opus signinam* – made from crushed pottery and lime and white marble mini-tiles.

❸ **San Pawl Milqi** Just west of Burmarrad you will find the sparse remains of a large Roman 'villa' occupied from the 2nd century BC to the 4th century AD, now partly beneath a 17th-century church. Evidence of olive pressing was found here.

FORTIFICATIONS

For anyone interested in fortifications, Malta is a dream destination, with a tremendous concentration of remarkable fortifications in a very small area. Although the name 'Fortress Malta' came to prominence only during World War II, it applies equally well from the late 16th century onwards. Malta has four dramatically **defended historic capitals**: **Valletta**, a small fully fortified coastal city; the hill-top citadels of **Mdina** (the old capital of Malta) and **Gozo**; and **Birgu**, first capital of the 'Knights of Malta', divided (along with its neighbours Senglea and Bormla) from the surrounding countryside by a monumental set of defensive walls (the Santa Margarita and Cottonera lines). Add to this the 19th-century wall that runs the full width of the country (the Victoria Lines) and the system of watchtowers and smaller defensive installations that dot the coast and you have a veritable feast of fortifications.

There are fragments of defensive structures dating back to as early as the Roman and Arab administration of the islands (mainly remnants of Mdina walls), medieval defensive systems (including the street layout of Mdina and parts of Fort St Angelo) and British-built 19th-century installations, including the Victoria Lines, which divide the main island into north and south. But the great majority of fortifications – and by far the most interesting to look at – date from the period of the Knights of St John (1530–1798).

THE KNIGHTS' FORTIFICATIONS The Knights were in a semi-permanent state of war with the Ottoman Turks and so in almost constant fear of being attacked and besieged. They very nearly lost the islands in the Great Siege of 1565 (see page 11) and were determined thereafter never to come close to defeat again.

The Order of St John drew its members from the aristocracy of Europe and, after the Great Siege, Malta was seen as Christianity's bulwark against Islam.

So when fortifications were built here, they were the best and most up to date. Malta's defences were designed by the top military architects in Europe. The Italians dominated the field through the 16th and 17th centuries (Francesco Laparelli da Cortona, for instance, produced the blueprints for Valletta); by the 18th century the top men were from France – like François de Mondion who, in the early part of the century, reshaped (and redecorated) many of Malta's defences, as well as renovating Mdina.

Many of Malta's fortifications make use of its natural landscape, digging down into the bedrock to create defensive ditches, and using the stone quarried there to build upwards. In some places, including the landward fortifications of Valletta and Fort Manoel, a large percentage of the very walls themselves are carved out of bedrock making them far stronger than anything that could be built. It is worth remembering in this context that the Knights' workmen used no machinery: pick-axe marks can still be seen on the surface of the stone.

The defences were designed not only to be strong but to *look* strong. Today's leading expert on Malta's fortifications, Stephen Spiteri, describes Fort St Elmo – at the entrance to the Grand Harbour – as 'propaganda as well as physical defence'. Fortifications that deterred the enemy and never had to be used, were the most successful fortifications of all. Walk, drive or take a boat around Valletta and the deterrent effect is obvious.

The coastal towers Fortifying the Grand Harbour and the main cities was all very well, but the rest of the coast needed protection too. From the start of the 17th century, a series of coastal towers were constructed. Thanks to four grand masters – Alof de Wignacourt (1601–22), Jean Paul de Lascaris (1636–57), Martin de Redin (1657–1660) and Nicolas Cotoner (1663–80) after whom the towers are often known – Malta had, by the end of the century, an interlinked system of towers right around the coast of the archipelago. These provided both an effective early warning system as well as small-scale physical defence to ward off enemy landings. They communicated by means of flags and fire and if you travel the North Coast Road it is easy to see how it was possible to pass messages from one tower to the next.

These towers remain a feature of the Maltese coast and some have been renovated and opened to the public. The most rewarding to visit are the **Wignacourt Tower** (page 224), the **Red Tower** (page 239), **Comino Tower** (page 251) and, on Gozo, the **Dwejra Tower** (page 278) and **Mġarr ix-Xini Towers** (page 294).

During the 18th century the Order continued to strengthen its shoreline, building batteries, redoubts and entrenchments in an attempt to secure every bay around the islands. Resources were running short, however, and the project was not completed by the time Napoleon arrived in 1798 and ended the rule of the Knights in Malta.

Spiteri points out that, ironically, all the Order's amazing fortifications could not in the end protect it. Napoleon was the catalyst, but the Order had lost the confidence of the Maltese population and had run out of money as well as morals. High walls could not defend them from themselves (see page 13).

The best book on the Knights' fortifications is *The Art of Fortress Buiding in Hospitaller Malta* by Stephen C Spiteri (*published by BDL, Malta*).

Where to visit (map overleaf)
① *Valletta key sites*
- The walls from outside: City Gate and Great Siege Road (see page 115) and Hastings Gardens (see page 135).
- The walls from above: Upper Barracca Gardens (see page 118).

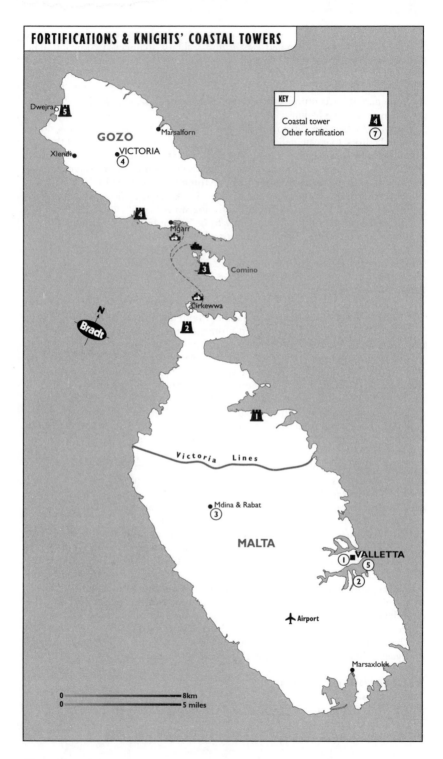

FORTIFICATIONS & KNIGHTS' COASTAL TOWERS

Dwejra 5

GOZO

Marsalforn

Xlendi

VICTORIA 4

4

Mgarr

3

Comino

Cirkewwa

2

N

Bradt

1

Victoria Lines

Mdina & Rabat 3

MALTA

1 VALLETTA 5

2

Airport

Marsaxlokk

KEY

Coastal tower 4
Other fortification 7

0 _____ 8km
0 _____ 5 miles

- Walk the walls: walk right round the edge of Valletta (see pages 135–9).
- The walls from the water (as the enemy saw them): the Two Harbours Tour (see page 115) and Fort St Elmo (see page 131).

② **Three Cities key sites**
- Walk the fortifications of Birgu and Senglea (see pages 147, 154 and 155).
- Take a look at the Margarita Lines (page 156) and the Cottonera Lines (see page 158).

③ **Mdina key sites**
- See it from a distance, straight-sided above the surrounding countryside.
- The gates and the walls to either side of the gates (see page 204).
- Bastion square (see page 210).

④ **Gozo Citadel key sites**
- See it from a distance dominating the land around it.
- Walk the walls (see page 271).
- The Knights' gunpowder store (see page 275).

Coastal towers key sites The following are all open to the public, but do check opening times to avoid disappointment. Travel the North Coast Road to see how the towers could communicate along the coast.

1 Wignacourt Tower (page 224)
2 The Red Tower (page 239)
3 Comino Tower (page 251)
4 Mġarr ix-Xini Tower, Gozo (page 294)
5 Dwejra Tower, Gozo (page 278)

A **Fortifications Information Centre** is scheduled to open in Valletta in 2010 or 2011. See page 136.

BRITISH FORTIFICATIONS In the 19th century new technology completely changed what was required of fortifications. Monumental walls were little use against 100-ton guns and defensive installations became all about weaponry rather than strongholds. It was the guns that now defended the island rather than the walls.

The **Victoria Lines** (see page 231) – the 12km barrier built along a natural ridge across the entire width of the main island in 1870–97 – were the last gasp of the old defensive style, and within a few years they fell into disuse. They remain interesting to look at, and the infantry walkway along the top of the walls makes a scenic footpath.

The British took over many of the Knights' fortifications, maintaining them to a varying degree, and using them, though not always for the original purpose. The colonial administration also built a few new forts and batteries, mostly for coastal artillery. The best surviving example is **Fort Rinella** (⑤) with its 100-ton gun (see page 158).

The glossary on page 299 explains key terms you may come across in relation to fortifications.

WORLD WAR II

Malta's greatest moment on the modern world stage was its part in World War II for which the whole country was awarded the George Cross. 'Fortress Malta' hung on through some of the heaviest bombing of the war (by some reckonings, *the* heaviest) and through siege conditions leading to shortages of food and fuel, to make a genuine difference to the Allied campaign. The **Grand Harbour** was of course the star location. Here, mostly in the Three Cities, British naval vessels were hidden, re-supplied and repaired, the wounded were brought ashore and healthy servicemen given a break. And here too 'Operation Pedestal' broke the siege of Malta in August 1942.

Besides the harbour itself, which is best seen from the Upper Barracca Gardens in Valletta (see page 118) and from the water (see *Harbour Cruises*, page 115), the most interesting World War II sights are listed below:

WHERE TO VISIT
Underground shelters (see also boxed text, page 149)
① **Malta at War Museum** In Birgu, this is the most organised and informative visit to a World War II shelter. See page 147.
② **Mġarr Shelter** Based in Mġarr, this one is the most personalised – you may be shown round by a man born in the shelter. See page 228.
③ **Wignacourt Museum** Situated in Rabat, there is a shelter under the museum (as well as a Roman catacomb). See page 213.
④ **Casa Rocca Piccola** Regular tours of the house also take you underground to see the first World War II shelter built in Valletta, by the far-sighted grandfather of the present owner. The only World War II shelter in the capital. See page 131.

Other World War II sites
❶ **Lascaris War Rooms** From where the Allies controlled the Mediterranean fleet. See page 119.
❷ **National War Museum** In Valletta, see page 132.
❸ **Malta Aviation Museum** In Ta' Qali, see page 226.

CHURCHES

Anyone interested in churches is spoilt for choice in Malta. There are over 350 of them ranging in age from the little medieval chapel of Ħal Millieri (see page 191) built in the mid-15th century, to cavernous 20th-century constructions. Yet the majority of Malta's churches, tiny wayside chapels to lavish cathedrals, were built during the reign of the Catholic Order of St John, the Knights Hospitaller, who ruled here from 1530–1798. A few were built by the Order itself, most notably St John's Co-Cathedral in Valletta (see page 123), but most were the work of the local diocese and often paid for by public subscription.

The Knights' earliest churches and the first chapels of their *langues* (language groups; see page 117) were plain, almost brutal in style, often designed, along with the rest of their buildings, by military architects. The advent of the Italian Renaissance left some imprint on church architecture in Malta, but it was the Baroque that became the dominant style resulting in the many opulent churches still seen today.

The 19th and 20th centuries saw a few churches built in neo-Gothic style, including the **Church of Our Lady of Lourdes** in Mġarr on Gozo (page 268), and the construction of several Neoclassical buildings, most famously the **Mosta Dome** on Malta (page 225) and **The Rotunda** in Xewkija on Gozo (page 293) and **Anglican cathedral** in Valletta (page 134). The only conspicuous attempt at a truly modern style – **St Theresa's in Birkirkara** – is sadly hideous (see page 219).

Some of the most important churches are geared up for tourists, opening throughout the day. Others open only for worship, usually first thing in the

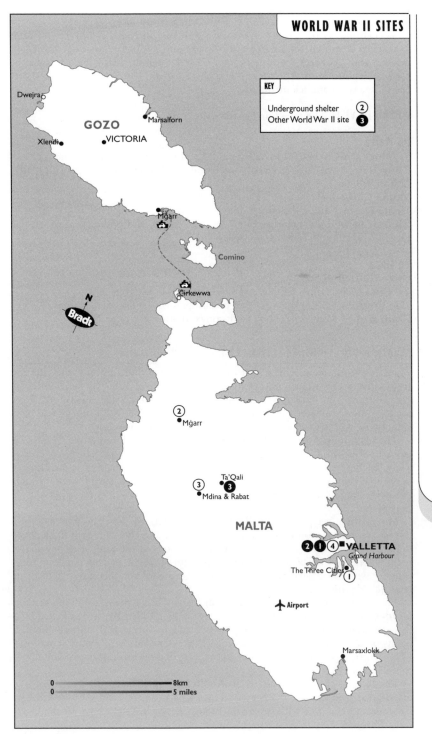

KEY

Underground shelter ②
Other World War II site ❸

GOZO

Dwejra

Marsalforn

Xlendi

VICTORIA

Mġarr

Comino

Ċirkewwa

N

Bradt

② Mġarr

Ta'Qali
③ ❸
Mdina & Rabat

MALTA

❷❶④ ■ VALLETTA
Grand Harbour
The Three Cities ●
①

✈ Airport

Marsaxlokk

0 ——————— 8km
0 ——————— 5 miles

morning and in the early evening. Rural chapels are often kept closed except on special occasions. Visitors are always welcome in Malta's churches so long as respect is shown for services, and knees and shoulders are covered. Mass times and contact numbers for each parish can be found at www.maltadiocese.org/parishes?l=1. For more on the Anglican Church in Malta, see www.anglicanmalta.org.

WHERE TO VISIT The top churches for visitors are as follows:

On Malta
① **St John's Co-Cathedral** In Valletta, the Knights' main church. See page 123.
② **Church of St Paul's Shipwreck** Celebrating St Paul's miraculous stay on Malta. Also in Valletta. See page 139.
③ **Mdina Cathedral** See page 207.
④ **Mosta Dome** One of the largest domes in Europe. See page 225.
⑤ **Church of St Lawrence** In Birgu, on the site of, and with remnants of, the Knights' first church in Malta. See page 152.

On Gozo
⑥ **Gozo Cathedral** See page 273.
⑦ **Ta' Pinu** Malta's most famous and favourite shrine. See page 280.
⑧ **The Rotunda** In Xewkija – another of Europe's largest domes. See page 293.
⑨ **Church of St Mary** In Żebbuġ for its onyx interior. See page 282.

SWIMMING, SNORKELLING AND DIVING

There are some wonderful places to swim in Malta, but the brochures do not always give a very honest impression of what to expect. You may be promised a 'private beach' and find a rocky foreshore. Nothing wrong with swimming from rocks – unless you were expecting to build sandcastles. The following should help you choose where to go and key sites are plotted on the map, page 92.

The main tourist centres of **St Julian's**, **Paceville** and **Sliema** (see *Chapter 7*), as well as **Buġibba** and **Qawra** (see pages 159 and 244) are basically rocky coasts. Many Maltese prefer swimming off rocks because the water is usually clearest here, much clearer than around sandy shores. This makes it ideal for snorkelling, but swimming from rocks may not so good for young children or those nervous of deep water.

Marsalforn (see page 282) and **Xlendi** (page 295), the two bays where Gozo's tourist accommodation is concentrated, are also rocky, although each has a small sandy beach along the head of the bay to complement the long stretches of flat rocks where most people base themselves. Xlendi's beach is tiny but the swimming is lovely with lots of shallow water as well as deep areas and plentiful fish that can be watched with ease.

There are several good sandy beaches in Malta. On the main island, the best are **Golden Bay** and **Għajn Tuffieħa** (see page 232). Golden Bay is dominated by a five-star hotel, but is nonetheless pleasant, and in spring and autumn there is plenty of sand to play on. In summer it gets very crowded. Neighbouring red-sand Għajn Tuffieħa, is much quieter due to the long flight of stone steps leading down to the beach.

The longest beach on Malta is on **Mellieħa Bay** (Għadira Bay, page 235). It offers great sand and sea, but is marred by a long main road and summer crowds. There are several bays with some sand along the northwestern coast by the Gozo ferry. **Paradise Bay** (page 239) is by far the best of them.

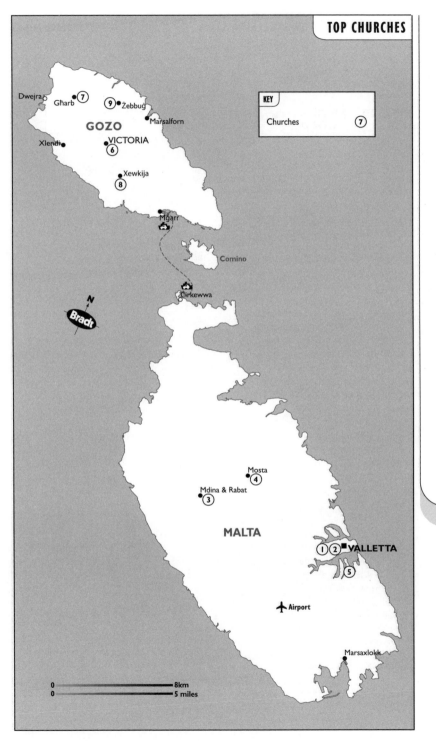

KEY

Churches ⑦

Dwejra
Gharb ⑦
⑨ Żebbug
Marsalforn
GOZO
Xlendi
VICTORIA
⑥
Xewkija
⑧
Mġarr
Comino
Ċirkewwa

N
Bradt

Mosta
④
Mdina & Rabat
③
MALTA
① ② ■**VALLETTA**
⑤
✈ Airport
Marsaxlokk

0 ——————— 8km
0 ——————— 5 miles

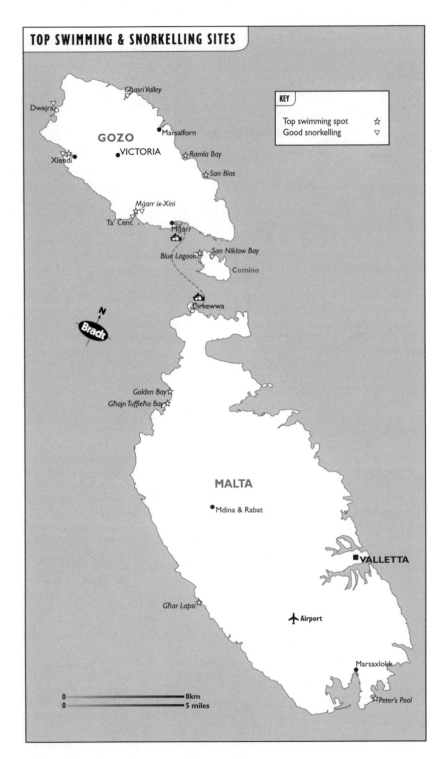

TOP SWIMMING & SNORKELLING SITES

KEY

Top swimming spot ☆
Good snorkelling ▽

Ghasri Valley
Dwejra
GOZO
Marsalforn
VICTORIA
Ramla Bay
Xlendi
San Blas
Mġarr ix-Xini
Ta' Ċenċ
Mġarr
Blue Lagoon
San Niklaw Bay
Comino
Ċirkewwa
N
Bradt
Golden Bay
Għajn Tuffieħa Bay
MALTA
Mdina & Rabat
VALLETTA
Għar Lapsi
Airport
Marsaxlokk
0   8km
0   5 miles
Peter's Pool

92

On Gozo, **Ramla Bay** (page 289) is the largest and most popular sandy beach. Easily reached by car or bus, it has two large cafés well tucked away and rocks to explore at either end. It is a great place for families and so gets crowded in summer. Nearby is the much less accessible **San Blas Bay** (page 290) – a beautiful red-sandy cove surrounded by cliffs and greenery. It never gets too crowded because of the precipitous track leading down to it – and, of course, up again, which is heavy going in the heat of summer.

If you are looking for **swimming** and snorkelling rather than sand and sunbathing, **Mġarr ix-Xini** (page 294) – a long, secluded inlet on the south coast of Gozo – is the perfect spot. Almost never crowded, it is a beautiful, protected stretch of clear blue water with a little coarse sandy shore where you can get into the water gently, as well as rocks to jump off and a set of 'swimming pool' steps. The snorkelling is excellent.

Peter's Pool (page 182) on the Delimara Peninsula (near Marsaxlokk on Malta) has insalubrious wider surroundings, but is itself a delightful rocky cove, rarely crowded because it is not on a bus route and is a few minutes' walk from the nearest available parking. If you prefer somewhere less remote, with parking space, people and somewhere to eat, **Għar Lapsi** (page 190) is a popular place to swim on the south coast, close to the temple sites of Mnajdra and Ħaġar Qim.

Malta's most sought-after swimming spot – the target of flocks of tourists each day in summer – is the **Blue Lagoon** (page 249) on the coast of Comino. This is a glorious area of clear blue sea over white sand surrounded by picturesque caves. Note that it has little shore and gets horrendously crowded in summer.

There are quite a number of bays around the islands' with rock and concrete shorelines and sometimes a little sand where the Maltese congregate to swim on summer weekends. These places are not always beautiful to look at, but the water is generally clear and inviting. Not necessarily places to seek out, they may be useful swim-stops between sights (sightseeing in summer can get very hot and sweaty!) so they are mentioned in the relevant chapters of the text.

For additional information on swimming and swimming safely, see pages 60, 66 and 47.

SNORKELLING The best places to snorkel naturally overlap with recommended swimming spots, but are not always the same. Snorkelling is generally best near rocks, and you will see something through your mask if you swim close to almost any rocks around Malta's coast. At **Xlendi** on Gozo (see page 295), where the sand is close to the rocky shore, quite a few fish can be seen in the sandy shallows. At **Mġarr ix-Xini** (see page 294) there are fish to be seen in water barely up to an adult's knees (though this is over stones rather than sand).

DIVING This is clearly not an activity you can do entirely on your own. Even if you are very experienced, you will need to find a good dive centre, hire equipment and take much more advice than can be provided here. So this is just to give you an idea of some of the more interesting dive sites available, and where they are on the islands.

You will notice that there is a concentration of good shore dive sites around Gozo. This is a very congenial place to be based while diving, with short travelling times between dive centres and dive sites. Many divers choose to base themselves here (more on Gozo diving on page 266). See also *Diving* page 66 and *Diver safety*, page 67. The dives listed below can be accessed from the shore unless otherwise stated.

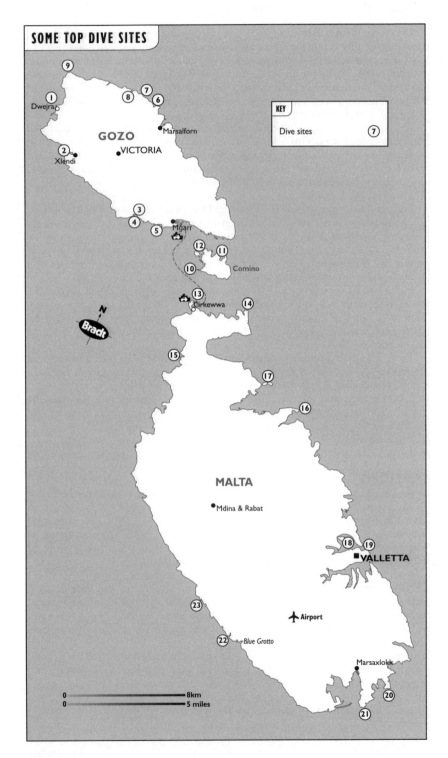

SOME TOP DIVE SITES

KEY

Dive sites (7)

Dwejra (1) (9)

GOZO (8) (7) (6)

VICTORIA Marsalforn

(2) Xlendi

(3)
(4) (5) Mgarr

(12) (11)

(10) Comino

(13) Cirkewwa (14)

N

Bradt

(15)

(17)

(16)

MALTA

Mdina & Rabat

(18) (19) VALLETTA

(23)

Airport

(22) Blue Grotto

Marsaxlokk

(20)

(21)

0 —————— 8km
0 —————— 5 miles

Recommended dive sites

① **Dwejra** (see page 277) Several key dives attracting more divers than anywhere else on Gozo. Spectacular underwater landscape, plus fish (including grouper and perhaps barracuda), corals and marine flora. The famous **Blue Hole** drops 16m to the seabed where there is a cave and a 'window' letting you look out into the open water of **Dwejra Point** and towards the great rock column of the **Azure Window** (see page 278). From the **Inland Sea** you can dive through the 80m tunnel that connects it to the open sea (beware of the shoals of motorboats carrying tourists) emerging through a cliff face falling 40m to the seabed. Other rocks, including **Crocodile Rock** (best accessed by boat) also offer a focus. **Fungus Rock** (always a boat dive) falls 45m to the seabed and is surrounded by boulders where groupers may hide. The rock itself is covered with coloured corals and other marine life. The dives here are mainly deep dives for experienced divers.

② **Xlendi Bay** (see page 295) An easily accessed reef, 50m-long underwater tunnel, barracuda, octopi and moray eels and abundant other fish. The bay is also used for training beginners.

③ **Mġarr ix-Xini** (see page 294) Two caves at 10m and 16m and a chance in summer of spotting sea horses.

④ **Fessej Rock** A boat dive: about 400m from the entrance to Mġarr ix-Xini a column rises 15m out of the water and drops some 50m below. The column is full of holes inhabited by corals, tube worms and octopi and there are plenty of fish passing by.

⑤ **Xatt l-Aħmar** A protected bay with a shallow reef, a drop-off and a couple of caves as well as three deliberately scuttled wrecks at about 45m – **MV Xlendi**, an old Gozo ferry (do not enter); and **MV Karwela** and **MV Cominoland**, 1940s and 1950s passenger ferries once owned by Captain Morgan Cruises. NB: there has been some dispute over use of the road down to this bay so you will need to take advice about the best way to get there. Access by boat is unaffected.

⑥ **Xwejni Bay near Marsalforn** (see page 283) There are several dives here: **Double Arch**, a very unusual double stone arch some 200m offshore (NB: local divers call the entry point for this dive 'the washing machine' – for the very experienced only); **Anchor Reef**, a reef, but no anchor – deep, with possible groupers; **Reqqa Point** with a spectacular drop-off, reef, boulders and lots of fish at depths up to 50m; and in the shallows by the **salt pans** the less experienced can have fun following a maze of channels in 5–7m of water. Beginners can also dive directly into the bay.

⑦ **Billinghurst Cave** A boat dive: 120–130m tunnel with two caverns (maximum depth 27m). Plentiful coloured corals, anemones and sponges but no light after 30m. Torch and experience required.

⑧ **Cathedral Cave, Ghasri Valley** (Wied il-Ghasri) (see page 282) Nearly 100 stone steps must be descended to get to the starting point for this dive in a deep ravine. In calm weather only, the Cathedral Cave or Blue Dome dive takes you into a vast cave with a dome (in which it is possible to surface) as big as that of St Paul's Cathedral with iridescent blue from sunlight entering via a crack in the rock.

⑨ **San Dimitri Point (Barracuda Point)** A boat dive: at Gozo's westernmost point with vast boulders creating a remarkable underwater landscape with plenty of wildlife possibly including grouper, barracuda and passing tuna. Can be adapted to varying levels of experience and even snorkellers.

⑩ **Lantern Point** Comino Boat dive: a dramatic and popular dive down a steep drop-off with a reef, chimney (4m–18m) and massive boulders (at 30–50m) with plenty of wildlife, which can include groupers, bream, barracuda, moray eels, cuttlefish and octopus.

⑪ **Santa Marija Caves (Comino Caves)** A Comino boat dive: a dive much enjoyed for its interconnecting caves and large numbers of bream that divers feed creating a writhing mass of fish (10–16m).

4

⑫ **Cominotto Reef (Anchor Reef)** A Comino boat dive: a drop-off and long wall with plenty of marine life in its nooks and crannies. This Anchor Reef actually has an anchor (at 38m), a World War II relic now taken over by sponges and corals.

⑬ **Ċirkewwa (Marfa Point)** Malta's most-dived location, has five different dives, but beware of boat traffic including dive boats anchoring. **Ċirkewwa Arch** is at about 12m (seabed 20m), some distance – via a cave – from the shore. Amberjack are sometimes seen here as well as groupers and moray eel. There are two wrecks in the area: at 30m there's *Tugboat Rozi* (at a maximum depth of 34m) which was scuttled in 1992 as an artificial reef and is much dived; likewise *Patrol Boat P29* (38m down). The **Madonna Statue** (at 18m) often surrounded by cardinal fish, and the **Sugar Loaf**, an 8m rock on the seabed, are often dived together. There is also plenty of underwater scenery to explore: reef, boulders, drop-offs, caves, etc, including around **Paradise Bay**.

⑭ **L'Aħrax Point** (see page 240) Malta's most northerly point and much less crowded than Ċirkewwa. Can be dived from shore, but often a boat dive. The reef is at 10–12m, there is a curving tunnel at 8m, and over the edge depths reach 23–30m. Best dived in the morning when sunlight colours the reef.

⑮ **Anchor Bay** (by Popeye Village; see page 238) Depths of 2–12m within the bay make this a training site. Further out, depths fall to 20m. Named for the anchor to which barges moored during the building of Popeye Village, the heavy anchor chain now attracts marine wildlife. There's a cavern at 10m inside which you can surface to admire its domed shape; there's a sunken barge at 20m.

⑯ *Imperial Eagle* Another boat dive: about 38m down lies this 45m 1930s British boat that served as a Gozo ferry from the 1950s to the 1970s. Deliberately scuttled in 1999.

⑰ **St Paul's Island** This is where St Paul is meant to have been shipwrecked in AD60. There is nothing of this period, but there is a valley to explore between the two above-sea parts of the island, a reef, and the scuttled wreck of a small ferry.

⑱ *X127 Water Lighter*/**Carolita Barge** Built for the Gallipoli campaign in World War I and sunk during World War II, the wreck lies with its bows in 5m and its stern in 22m of water. Interesting to explore but do not enter.

⑲ *HMS Maori* Half a British navy destroyer which was involved in Malta convoys in 1941 and 1942. Sunk in 1942 in the Grand Harbour, it was cut in half and moved to deeper water in 1945.

⑳ **Blenheim Bomber** This is the wreck of a British World War II bomber that ditched in the sea after attack by an Italian plane in 1941 (the crew were rescued); it now lies, with wings intact, in 42m of water. An interesting dive beloved of underwater photographers. Experienced divers only.

㉑ **Delimara Point** Two main reefs and plenty of underwater landscape, flora and fauna down to 30m and deeper. Currents can be a problem here.

㉒ **Wied iż-Żurrieq** The tanker *Um el Faroud*, scuttled here in 1998 to a depth of 38m, is regarded by some as the best wreck dive in Malta. An explosion on board the 110m tanker in the Grand Harbour killed nine dockyard workers to whom there is a brass plaque in the centre of the bridge. There is also a reef near the ship. Experienced divers only. There are two other **reefs** at Wied iż-Żurrieq with drop-offs, ledges, boulders, and, of course, fish. These are considered good night- as well as daytime dive sites. Beware of boats taking tourists to the Blue Grotto (see page 191), fishermen's lines and currents.

㉓ **Ghar Lapsi** (see page 190) There are several dives around this popular summer swimming spot including **Finger Reef**, shaped as you would expect, and **Crib Reef**, home to an almost life-size metal nativity scene (at 22m), both of which lead to a narrow entrance to a substantial cave system.

BIRDWATCHING

As noted in *Chapters 2* and *3* (page 23 and page 68) Malta has great potential for birdwatching. This section will give you a more detailed guide to what to look out for and when – as well as highlighting the best spots from which to do it. Please be sure, though, to also read the information on hunting and trapping (page 24, and *Health and safety* page 48 respectively) as anyone birding in Malta, certainly in the autumn, is likely to come across hunters.

MIGRATION BIRDWATCHING IN MALTA *by Ray Vella (BirdLife Malta)*
Situated between Europe and North Africa, Malta is on the migratory route for many species and, being quite small, it acts as a magnet for birds crossing the Mediterranean in both spring and autumn seasons. Over 350 bird species have been recorded, including vagrants from as far away as North America, Africa and Asia.

Spring The first spring migrants sometimes appear as early as **late January**. These are usually house martins and barn swallows already heading north. In February the first marsh harriers can be encountered usually quartering the wheat fields and the airport vicinity (to its south side or even opposite the terminal building), while hoopoes are also quite frequent.

It is in **March**, however, that the migration starts in earnest. Hirundines are passing in good numbers while herons and waders can be spotted feeding and resting at the small wetland areas of Għadira, Salina and Is-Simar, all located in the north of the island. Keep an eye out for falcons as lesser kestrels are frequent in spring.

Usually around the **full moon phase of March** very good numbers of pintail and garganey, together with ferruginous ducks and northern shovelers, can be seen resting in the Gozo Channel just off the Ċirkewwa ferry terminals. These usually congregate all day in the sea during the day, waiting for the evening when they then fly off through the channel in flocks, comprising sometimes hundreds of birds. Since hunting in spring has been banned, the flocks tend to remain unmolested and can now be seen quite easily from the ferry landing. In some years, upwards of 15,000 birds may pass through the channel.

Around this time, expect to see small numbers of waders, common cranes, slender billed gulls and glossy ibises which are found migrating in the same area. Strong northwesterlies also bring large numbers of Cory's and Yelkouan shearwaters close to land, the latter already feeding their chicks while the former are just arriving to nest on the western cliffs of the islands.

April is the month that brings the largest number of passerines to the islands, especially with southeasterlies and rainy weather. Turtle doves – although far fewer in number than 30 years ago – are still seen regularly, while golden orioles are encountered frequently feeding in valleys, together with common whitethroats, subalpine, wood and willow warblers. Barn swallows, house martins, red-rumped swallows, as well as common, alpine and pallid swifts can be seen hawking insects in the calm skies during April. In the open areas whinchat and northern wheatears are common. Woodchat shrikes are seen regularly in shrubs and low trees as well as all flycatcher species – including collared, pied, semi-collared and spotted.

A trip to the island of Comino is well worth the effort at this time of the year as it sometimes acts as a bottleneck for many of the passerines, which seem to take cover in every tree and shrub on the island.

In **May** there are still many passerines migrating while small numbers of red-footed falcons and honey-buzzards soar over the hillsides. Waders, especially curlew sandpipers, are frequently seen feeding at Għadira and Salina, together with

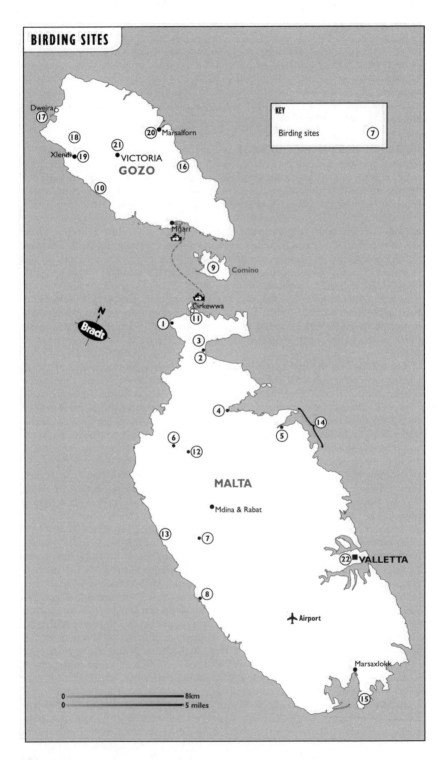

BIRDING SITES

KEY

Birding sites   ⑦

Dwejra ⑰
⑱
Xlendi ⑲   ㉑   VICTORIA
GOZO   ⑯
⑳ Marsalforn
⑩

Mġarr

⑨   Comino

Cirkewwa
①   ⑪
③
②

④
⑤   ⑭

⑥
⑫

MALTA

Mdina & Rabat

⑬   ⑦

㉒ VALLETTA

⑧

✈ Airport

Marsaxlokk

⑮

N
Bradt

0 _____ 8km
0 _____ 5 miles

little and Temminck's stints, and the calls of European bee-eaters overhead herald approaching hotter weather.

Autumn Autumn migration in Malta starts early, with **late June** bringing the first common redshanks already migrating south. While the beaches are packed solid with locals and tourists soaking up the hot rays, waders are already winging their way towards Africa. **July and August** bring wood, common and green sandpipers, while little ringed plovers, ringed plovers, curlew sandpipers and black-winged stilts are all common migrants at the Salina salt pans and Għadira.

Subalpine warblers are already heading south in early August, while hoopoe and common kingfisher arrive throughout the month. By the **end of August** the first marsh, Montagu's and pallid harriers are soaring over Buskett in the afternoons, while large flocks of little egrets and grey, purple and night herons are seen migrating high up in formation.

September at Buskett Gardens (where shooting is not allowed) is highly rewarding for honey-buzzards, ospreys and Eleonora's falcons. The birds can be seen quite close and a recent ban on shooting throughout the islands after 15.00 from 15–30 September gives the birds a chance to get to Buskett to roost and rest. Bans on hunting are obeyed by most hunters, but occasional poaching unfortunately continues, especially of the larger and rarer birds prized by the poachers for their taxidermy collections. Up to 3,000 birds are usually seen around this time at Buskett. These include almost all species of medium-sized birds of prey. In recent years, lesser spotted eagles have been sighted more regularly, along with black storks.

At least two **Raptor Camps** run during the month of September; one organised by BirdLife Malta (see page 76) and another, parallel camp is run by Animal Rescue and a German organisation named CABS (Committee Against Bird Slaughter, *www.komitee.de/en*). These camps keep an eye on the migrating raptors and make sure that any infringements of the law are dealt with by ALE (Administrative Law Enforcement), a specialist unit of the Maltese police.

In **October** the first of the seven finch species migrating south pass through in flocks. These were trapped in huge numbers until the end of 2008; since then a complete ban on finch trapping has come into force due to pressure from the European Union. It is hoped that this will bring more birds to winter on the islands and lead to an increase in breeding birds, although the first years may be difficult as some people might not wish to change their habits overnight.

It is in October, too, that vagrants are normally seen. Yellow-browed warblers are spotted annually while red-breasted flycatchers are also regulars. In this period, sea watching can bring some surprises as many species may be encountered, especially on the east coast of the islands. Great crested grebes are sometimes seen in the bays with black-necked grebes. Some numbers of the latter species winter at BirdLife Malta's nature reserves at Għadira and Is-Simar. A few duck species also winter regularly in the reserves, including common shelduck, common pochard, mallard, Eurasian wigeon and pintail.

The wintering species, such as black redstart, meadow pipit, grey and white wagtails, common stonechats and very large numbers of robins, arrive at this time. Song thrush, skylark and golden plover are common at this time of the year, together with woodcock – these are the main target species for the hunters and are very much persecuted.

There's an interesting roost of white wagtails in Valletta, in front of the Law Courts, which attracts up to 5,000 birds from 17.00 onwards. These may be seen approaching the city from a westerly direction, heading into town to roost in the ficus trees, to shelter from the cold and windy nights which can be typical of Maltese winters.

TOP BIRDWATCHING SITES

1. **Qammieh** (by the Red Tower, see also page 239) Coastal garigue, cliffs and clay slopes. Qammieh Point offers views of the channel between Malta and Comino.
2. **Għadira Nature Reserve** See also page 237.
3. **Ta' Biskra and Cumnija** Typical garigue with cliffs at the coast, next to Għadira Nature Reserve (the part directly around the reserve is a buffer zone where hunting is not allowed).
4. **Is-Simar Nature Reserve** See also page 243.
5. **Salina** Salt pans with degraded marshland (hunting prohibited). See page 244.
6. **Dwejra** (Malta) **and Binġemma** (see also page 230) Natural ridge surrounded by fields, garigue and some planted trees. Particularly good for migrating birds of prey September to mid-October.
7. **Buskett** Mature, semi-natural woodland park (hunting prohibited). See also page 196.
8. **Għar Lapsi** Coastal cliffs with low vegetation and caves. See page 190.
9. **Comino** The whole island is a bird sanctuary (hunting prohibited). See *Chapter 13*, page 249.
10. **Ta' Ċenċ** Sheer cliffs topped by typical garigue – privately owned but open to the public. The owners do not allow hunting. See page 294.
11. **Ċirkewwa** Near the Gozo ferry.
12. **Nadur** (Malta) High point offering good views of migrating birds of prey in autumn. See page 231.
13. **Dingli Cliffs** Cliff-top coastal garigue. Popular with hunters. See page 197.
14. **The Qawra–Għallis–Baħar iċ-Ċagħaq coast** Good place for watching seabirds flying along the coast. A telescope is helpful. See *North Coast Road*, page 247.
15. **Delimara Peninsula** See also page 182.
16. **Ramla Valley** Winding valley of terraced fields leading down to Ramla Bay in Gozo. Migrants funnel through the valley. See page 289.
17. **Dwejra** (Gozo) Coastal garigue, cliffs and inland sea. Breeding blue rock thrush and warblers plus migrants including seabirds. See page 277.
18. **Lunzjata Valley** Running south from Fontana (page 276), here is a reedbed, fields and year-round stream (unusual in Malta). Rarities have been seen here. The land is private, however, and birdwatching has to be done from the road.
19. **Xlendi Valley** Inland from Xlendi Bay, this is a deep valley with rocky heights and fertile base. See page 295.
20. **Marsalforn Valley** One of Gozo's largest valleys running from the heart of the island down to Marsalforn (see page 282). Good for migrants during southeasterly, southerly and northeasterly winds.
21. **The Gozo Citadel** High point from which to watch for migratory birds, especially birds of prey. Also good for blue rock thrush. See page 271.
22. **Valletta** A roost of white wagtails gathers in front of the Law Courts. See page 123.

SPAS

Among Malta's many modern four- and five-star hotels are a number with spas attached. In fact, Malta claims the largest hotel spa in Europe: the five-star **Fortina Spa** (see below) which offers over 250 different treatments and boasts Europe's first 'Spa Bedrooms'. The hotels listed below are all five-star unless otherwise stated and all are also included in the hotel listings where you will find more general information about them.

Be aware that most spas do not admit children under 16. Note also that many hotels claim to have a spa, but it's worth asking what facilities are actually included; they vary from a couple of treatment rooms to full expert-run spa facilities.

🏠 **Athenaeum Spa, Corinthia Palace Hotel,** De Paul Av, Attard BZN 9023; ☎ 21440301; ✉ sananton@palace.corinthia.com; www.corinthiahotels.com. See also page 221. In a building of its own in the hotel garden, the Athenaeum Spa offers thalassic therapies along with OKKAIDO (herbal steam bath), as well as a solarium, sauna garden & fitness room. A wide range of massages & classical beauty therapies is available & there's even music & art therapy, physio, osteopathy, chiropractic & more.

🏠 **Fortina Spa** Tigné Seafront, Sliema SLM15; ☎ (UK) 0800 917 300 & ☎ (Malta) 23462346/0000; ✉ info@fortinasparesort.com; www.fortinasparesort.com. See also page 161. Full spa facilities including swimming pools & wet & dry therapy rooms. 250 different treatments from around the world: Balinese body scrub to thalasso, Le Stone therapy to Thai massage – or try 'Cleopatra's bath' (yes, in asses' milk – well, horses'). The large, designer, 'Spa Bedrooms' (35 in all) have their own mini-spa with jacuzzi, spa bath, 2-person walk-in shower/steam room & Dermalife 'pod' meant to detox the body using infra-red rays, steam & vibration. Also smaller 'wellness rejuvenation rooms' (of which there are 11) with magnetic therapy beds, water & air purification systems plus a Vibrogen which claims to give your body a full gym workout in 15mins with no effort from you! No children are allowed in the spa or spa bedrooms.

🏠 **Grand Excelsior Hotel** (269 rooms, 167 suites) Great Siege Rd, Floriana FRN 1810; ☎ 21250520; ✉ info@excelsior.com.mt; www.excelsior.com.mt. Le Grand spa direct: ☎ 2319 2115; ✉ spa@excelsior.com.mt. See also page 108. Le Grand Spa next to the terrace overlooking Marsamxett Harbour has a large indoor swimming pool, sauna & steam room, as well as offering a variety of beauty & massage therapies.

🏠 **Kempinski San Lawrenz Spa** Kempinski Hotel, Triq ir-Rokon, San Lawrenz SLZ 1040, Gozo; ☎ 22110000; ✉ info@sanlawrenz@kempinski.com; www.kempinski-gozo.com. See also page 259. An extremely pleasant & professionally run spa with a very warm indoor swimming pool & many & varied treatments from algae wraps to the aphrodisiac! Partially refurbished at the start of 2010, the spa also boasts of being the only Ayurveda & Marine Cure Centre in the Mediterranean. Ayurvedic treatments are overseen by the resident Indian Ayurvedic doctor & include everything from one-offs to a full 3-week detox programme of treatments &

an Ayurvedic diet prescribed by the 'doctor' & cooked up by the hotel kitchens.

🏠 **Lotus Spa, Le Meridian Hotel** 39 Main St, St Julian's STJ 1017; ☎ 23110000/2810/0001; ✉ intolmsj@lemeridien.com; www.lemeridienmalta.com. See also page 166. The hotel's Lotus Spa (a Myoka spa: www.myoka.com) styles itself 'one of the best hotel spas in Malta' & it is. A large warm, well-landscaped, indoor swimming pool takes centre stage. There are a couple of jacuzzis & a steam room. The changing rooms are a bit basic & a little chilly in winter, but the upstairs treatment rooms are staffed by well-trained therapists who know how to massage.

🏠 **Myoka Five Senses Spa at the Hilton** Portomaso, St Julian's PTM01; ☎ 21383383 or 21386386; ✉ sales.malta@hilton.com; www.hilton.co.uk/malta, www.myoka.com. See also page 167. The multi-national team of therapists in this smart spa treat rather than merely relax you (or if necessary instead of relaxing you). A wide range of treatments is offered in the 9 spacious treatment rooms, from an Ashiatsu (backwalking) massage to facials (inc one specially for men), wraps, water treatments & a couple's duet massage in the same room with its own jacuzzi bath. Downstairs is a steam room & sauna along with a large indoor swimming pool, naturally lit through huge windows.

🏠 **Radisson SAS Golden Sands Spa** Golden Bay MLH 5510; ☎ 23561000; ✉ goldensands@radisson.com.mt; www.radissonblu.com/goldensandsresort-malta. See also page 232. 1,000m² spa & leisure centre. Several swimming pools & plentiful sports facilities accompany the Myoka spa (www.myoka.com) which has glass walls overlooking the bay, wet & dry therapy rooms & a range of massage & beauty treatments.

🏠 **Riviera Resort & Spa** (230 rooms, 2 suites) Marfa MJH 9069; ☎ 21525900; ✉ info@riviera.com.mt; www.riviera.com.mt. See also page 241. The Elysium Spa specialises in thalasso therapies & also has a wide range of massages (from Swedish to Chinese, aromatherapy to reiki) & beauty treatments.

🏠 **Ta' Ċenċ Hotel Wellness Spa** (83 rooms, 13 suites) Sannat SNT 9049, Gozo; ☎ 21556819/6830/8199 or 2156152522/3; ✉ tacenc@vborg.com; www.vjborg.com/tacenc. See also page 259. Swimming pool (part inside, part out), jacuzzi, steam room, sauna, solarium, & a small selection of massages, facials, pedicures & manicures..

Part Two

THE GUIDE

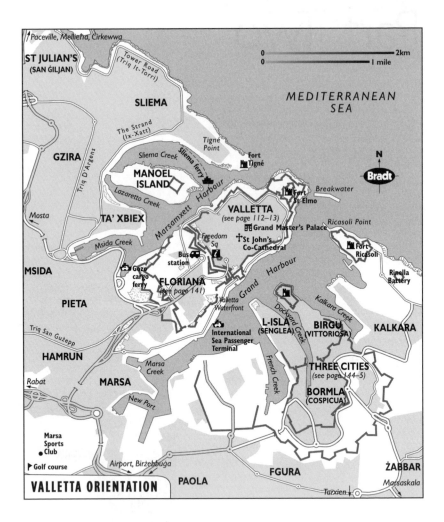

VALLETTA ORIENTATION

5

Valletta

Valletta must be the easiest capital city in the world to explore and is probably the most charming. A UNESCO World Heritage Site and due to be European Capital of Culture in 2018, it is just 1,000m by 600m and sits on a peninsula surrounded on three sides by the sea and on the fourth by the suburb of Floriana. On all sides it is enclosed by massive 16th- and 17th-century bastion walls. Initiated by, and named after, Grand Master of the Order of St John, Jean Parisot de Valette, who led the Knights to a victory in the Great Siege of 1565 (see page 11), the city was begun in 1566 with the clear intent that it should withstand any future attack by the Ottoman Turks. It was designed by military engineers, the first city since Roman times to be built from scratch on a grid system. Valletta remains fundamentally the Knights' city. The layout is little changed and many of their buildings – the *auberges* where the Knights lived and worked in their eight *langues* (language-based groups; see page 117), the churches and fortifications, and the Grand Master's Palace – are still standing.

The grid layout makes the city easy to navigate and offers glimpses of bright blue water at many crossroads. The warm limestone of the old buildings is set off by painted wooden *gallariji* (closed balconies) that hang out over the narrow streets. Much of Valletta is pedestrianised and even some of the shabbier streets towards the edge of town have charm.

Republic Street (Triq Ir-Repubblika) runs right down the middle from City Gate (and the island's main bus station) to Fort St Elmo on the seaward tip, passing along the brow of the hill (Mount Sceberras). This makes it the easiest route to walk, free from the dipping and rising of the streets on the hill's slopes. Republic Street is also the busiest and when a large cruise ship pours out 1,000 people or more (often on Wednesday or Friday) you may want to escape to a parallel street (a mere 10m or so either side). The hordes rarely venture beyond the main drag.

At one time or another, it is worth taking all the main routes through Valletta (there aren't very many!) as well as the diminutive side streets, some of which are little more than a stone staircase. Valletta is not a great city for wheelchairs or buggies, but for anyone able and willing to walk (even a few hundred metres) it is a hugely rewarding place packed with things to see and do.

There is a **combined ticket** to four Heritage Malta museums in Valletta: the National Archaeology Museum, the Museum of Fine Arts, the Palace Armoury and the Palace State Rooms (*tickets available from the sites: €20 adults or €30 with audio guides, €15/24 students & children aged 12–17, €10/19 children 6–11, children under 6 go free; more details at www.heritagemalta.org*). It saves you a bit of money but you have to visit them all to make it worthwhile and the ticket is only valid for one day. Another combined ticket includes a tour of the Saluting Battery, Lascaris War Rooms, Malta War At Museum and Fort Rinella.

HISTORY

After the 1565 siege, the Knights and the Maltese were seen as heroes across Christian Europe for holding back the Turks. The Order had long wanted to build a fortified city on the Mount Sceberras peninsula (where Valletta now stands) but had not had the money. Now funds flowed in from many Christian quarters and Pope Pius IV sent not only cash but his favourite military engineer and architect Francesco Laparelli da Cortona. It was he who conceived the design for Valletta and its defences before departing Malta in 1569 leaving the project in the hands of Maltese architect Gerolamo Cassar.

The first stone was laid – at the Church of Our Lady of Victory – by Grand Master de Valette on 28 March 1566. He did not live to see his city completed (dying, aged 74, in 1568) but he made sure his connection with the city lived on by officially naming it Humilissima Civitas Valletta – 'The Most Humble City of Valletta'. Needless to say the 'humble' bit was never used!

Much of the work was done by labourers brought over from Sicily (including many Maltese) with promises of good pay, as well as by the Order's slaves who served on the galleys in summer and worked on the construction sites in winter. The Knights built fast; they never wanted to leave a fortress unfinished through the summer fighting season in case it was taken, completed and used against them. Initially the architecture was plain, even severe; elegant, but military rather than decorative. The almost omnipresent Baroque embellishments were added later, as were the *gallariji* (painted wooden balconies).

Despite heavy bombing in World War II, a remarkable amount of the original city remains. Valletta was famously described in the 18th or 19th century (though by whom is contested) as 'a city built by gentlemen for gentlemen' and it still has a refined and elegant, albeit somewhat faded, air.

The resident population of the capital is small. During World War II, when the Grand Harbour was being heavily bombed, most residents moved out (the wealthy to summer houses in Sliema, the rest to the villages) and many never returned. Valletta has a thriving working population by day but by night the numbers fall to about 6,900. This is beginning to change as young Maltese (as well as a few foreigners) realise the delights of Malta's tiny capital.

GETTING THERE AND AWAY

BY AIR

Sea plane If you feel like splashing out (hopefully not literally!) then **Harbourair** (*Sea Passenger Terminal, Valletta Waterfront, Floriana;* ✆ *21228302 or 21228309;* e *info@ harbourairmalta.com; www.harbourairmalta.com*) operates a little 14-seater De Havilland Canada Turbine Single between Valletta and Gozo. It takes off from the Grand Harbour and lands just outside Mġarr Port, Gozo – it is a ten-minute flight with fabulous views. Expect to pay €44/38 adult/child, or €65 to sit next to the pilot! Harbourair also offers 30-minute **scenic flights** (€90/66 adult/child) up the northwest coast, right round Gozo and back along the southwest coast, crossing back to the Grand Harbour over Mdina and Mosta.

BY WATER The **Sliema ferry** [112 C2] links Valletta with Sliema on the other side of Marsamxett Harbour (*Marsamxetto Steamferry Services,* ✆ *23463862;* e *info@ captainmorgan.com.mt; www.captainmorgan.com.mt/ferry_service.htm*) about every half an hour until mid-afternoon in winter and late afternoon in summer. The ferry takes five minutes as opposed to the half-hour bus ride, and in good weather it is a pleasure in itself.

On the other side of Valletta, **water taxis** using the traditional *dgħajsa* (open, painted harbour boats) link Valletta with the Three Cities on the far side of the Grand Harbour (usually landing at Vittoriosa Waterfront or Senglea and at Valletta Waterfront or Customs House). In the mid-19th century well over 1,000 of these boats plied the harbour. Now there are only a handful, mostly dedicated to the tourist trade. The ten-minute crossing of Malta's most famous stretch of water is much more fun than the bus – and quicker – if a little more expensive. Water taxis also offer tours of the Grand Harbour.

A&S Water Taxis ❯ 21806921; e info@
maltesewatertaxis.com; www.maltesewatertaxis.com.
Working from a kiosk on the Vittoriosa Waterfront,
A&S can also be booked by phone to meet you at
the Customs House or Valletta Waterfront. €4pp. Min
2 people, max 6.

Waltar Ahar & the Dgħajsa Cooperative
m 79620034 or ask for Walter in Il Barklor
pizzeria or Manchester Bar at 36 Triq Ix-Xatt Juan
B Azopardo, Senglea. Walter will take you from any
landing stage to any other in the Grand Harbour.
Usually €4pp but check before booking/boarding.

Ferries from Sicily also arrive just outside the walls of Valletta, at the Sea Passenger Terminal in Floriana (see page 46 for details).

BY BUS Valletta is the easiest place to get to and from on Malta. Just outside its main gate (City Gate) is the island's public transport hub – the central bus station [112 A4] with regular buses to and from almost everywhere on the island including the airport and the Gozo ferry terminal.

BY CAR Coming towards Valletta in the morning rush hour (approximately 07.00 to 09.00) can be slow – if it rains it is very slow indeed. You cannot drive far into Valletta as much of it is pedestrianised. You can, however, get quite close to most places by driving along the main road just outside the walls. You will almost certainly need to park outside the city, too. One option is the CT car park opposite the Phoenicia Hotel; another is to leave the car at the free Park and Ride car park (Horn Works Ditch/Crown Works Ditch, National Road, Blata l-Bajda) and take the free minibus to Freedom Square. This car park is open 24 hours a day and the bus runs 06.00–01.00.

For a list of car-hire firms operating on the island, see page 58.

BY TAXI The island's official white taxis gather at most of Valletta's entrance/exit points including the bus station, or you can book a car from one of the private firms that most Maltese use (see *Chapter 3, Getting around*) to meet you outside the pedestrian zone.

GETTING AROUND

The best way to get around Valletta is **on foot**. Should you need wheels, there are **City Cabs** (❯ 21333321), little electric taxis like golf buggies carrying up to three passengers, that run anywhere within the city walls for a fixed fee of €2 per person.

Horse-drawn cabs or *karrozzin* also offer tourist transport around the streets. They gather in St George's Square (by the Grand Master's Palace) and sometimes at City Gate and near Fort St Elmo. Expect to pay from €6.99 and always agree a fare before boarding.

For information on **harbour cruises** which are a great way view Valletta's fortifications, see page 115.

TOURIST INFORMATION

Valletta's tourist information office is on Freedom Square [112 B4] (*1 City Arcades;* ✆ *22915440/41/42;* ⏰ *09.00–17.30 Mon–Sat, 09.00–13.00 Sun & public holidays*), but may be moving shortly if the planned renovation of this area goes ahead. The phone number will probably stay the same. The staff are well informed and there is a good range of maps and leaflets available.

VALLETTA AUDIO GUIDE AND PODCASTS You can pick up an informative 55-minute audio guide from the National Archaeological Museum (see page 121) or the Palace Armoury (see page 128) from 09.00 each day for €8. It comes with an excellent map that guides you around the main buildings of Valletta. The tour is available in English, Maltese, French, Italian, Spanish, German and Dutch and includes occasional brief interventions from the ghost of Jean Parisot de Valette. Handsets must be returned by 16.30.

Alternatively, the MTA has recently produced a series of short podcasts covering various aspects of Valletta's history and culture. These can be downloaded free from www.visitmalta.com/podcasts.

WHERE TO STAY

There is not a great deal of accommodation available in Valletta. There are two five-star hotels just outside the walls – both very conveniently located. Within the fortifications the very few hotels – all mid-range in terms of price – are of mixed quality, as are the guesthouses. An increasing number of self-catering properties are offering a very useful alternative.

TOP END

⌂ **Grand Hotel Excelsior******* [112 A2] (436 rooms) Great Siege Rd, Floriana; ✆ 21250520 or 21250522; e info@excelsior.com.mt; www.excelsior.com.mt. Large new business-style hotel right up against the bastion walls of Valletta looking over Marsamxett Harbour. Convenient location, very spacious, great views, psychedelic carpets in public areas, free Wi-Fi, good-sized indoor & outdoor swimming pools, private yacht marina & excellent food. See page 101 for details of spa facilities. *Dbls from €121 (winter), €175 summer with sea-view balcony €160–231.*

⌂ **Phoenicia Hotel******* [112 A3] (136 rooms) The Mall, Floriana; ✆ 21225241 or 22911024, freephone from UK ✆ 0808 2381 710, skype: Phoenicia.hotel; e info@phoeniciamalta.com or res@phoeniciamalta.com; www.phoeniciamalta.com. An ideal location just outside the city walls of Valletta, next to the bus station (which causes no problems with noise). Comfortable 1930s-style hotel, newly renovated (apart from the bedroom windows). Long, narrow garden leading to sunny swimming pool (heated when necessary) beneath Valletta bastion. *Dbls officially from €300 (room only), but prices on request/website can be less than half that B&B, even in summer.*

MID RANGE

⌂ **Castille Hotel***** [112 B5] (38 rooms) Castille Sq; ✆ 21243677/8 or 21220173; e info@hotelcastillemalta.com; www.hotelcastillemalta.com. Perfect location between Castille Square & the Upper Barracca Gardens, the Castille has bright rooms with views, friendly helpful staff & an excellent rooftop restaurant. By far the best mid-range hotel in Valletta. *€40–50pppn B&B (in sgl or dbl).*

⌂ **The Osborne Hotel***** [112 B2] (60 rooms) 50 South St (at Vassilli St); ✆ 21243656/7; e osbornehotel@onvol.net; www.osbornehotel.com. Welcoming public areas, simple en-suite rooms mid-refurb at the time of writing, but many have no window or only a tiny floor-level window. 6 rooms on 4th & 5th floors have views. Dinner can be unreliable. *Standard dbl €68.40 (room only), €73 (B&B).*

⌂ **The British Hotel**** [112 B5] (40 rooms) 40 Battery St; ☎ 21224730 or 21239022/3; e info@britishhotel.com; www.britishhotel.com. 1970s-style furniture dominates (probably original) – the hotel is in need of renovation, but it is a friendly option. Excellent location, free Wi-Fi & fantastic views of the Grand Harbour from the bar, restaurant, terraces & sea-view rooms. Some AC (for €7). *Inland twin €45–50, sea view €65 (child under 12 sharing €14).*

⌂ **The Grand Harbour Hotel**** [112 C5] (30 rooms) 47 Battery St; ☎ 21246003, 21237197 or 21242219; e info@grandharbourhotel.com; www.grandharbourhotel.com. Just round the corner from The British. Similar décor problems & without the light or views from public rooms. Some AC (for €10). *Dbls B&B €49, €56 with view (min 3 nights' stay).*

BUDGET

⌂ **Asti Guesthouse** [112 C5] (8 rooms) 18 Ursula St, close to the Upper Barracca Gdns; ☎ 21239506 or 21227483; Run by the elderly, but house-proud Mrs Galea, Asti may be basic but it is a very well-kept guesthouse in an ideal location. Some rooms have balcony, all have basin. Showers & WC shared. Book well ahead; this place is popular. *B&B from €18pppn (winter), €20 (summer).*

⌂ **Coronation Guesthouse** [112 C2] (9 rooms) 10E Mikiel Vassalli St (between South St & Melita St); ☎ 2124294; m 99406080. On a street of stone steps near Hastings Gardens, even more basic than the Asti but clean & cheap. Rooms have tiled floors, basin & strip lighting. 4 rooms have own shower. Helpful Charlie, the owner, is here during the day (sometimes with his French wife) to let you in & out, but you are given a key for the evenings. *€15 pppn (winter), €17 (summer) B&B (b/fast very basic).*

SELF-CATERING ACCOMMODATION Self catering can be a great option in Valletta, particularly if you really want to feel part of the place. These apartments are all in old buildings and/or great locations with real character and offer much more style and space than similarly priced hotels.

⌂ **Felix Street Apartment** ☎ +20 104088752; www.holidaylettings.co.uk/rentals/valletta/51444. Situated in the centre of Valletta, just off Merchants Street by the market, this 1-bedroom apt in a house built in the 1730s has its own *gallarija* & a trendy, modern interior, sunken bath at the foot of the main dbl bed & a Moroccan-style bathroom. There's a dbl sofa-bed in open-plan living room so there's space for an extra 2 people. No smoking, no pets, not suitable for children or the less mobile. *£80–5/night, £375–95/week (Christmas/New Year £495).*

⌂ **Maison la Vallette** 2 St Patrick's St (just off St Mark's St); m 79488047; e stay@maisonlavallette.com; www.maisonlavallette.com. In an unassuming street in the Mandragg, a red door leads into a stylish 1-bedroom apt that cleverly mixes Maltese tradition & contemporary design. Small modern kitchen, entrance hall/living room with CD, DVD, TV, Ipod-dock & books. *€81–3/night, min 3 nights' stay.* Free airport transport if booking for a week or more.

⌂ **Palazzo San Pawl Apartments** St Paul St; m 99423110; e nshaw@onvol.net; www.livinginvalletta.com. 4 1-bedroom apts in newly restored Palazzo San Pawl. Old building, modern facilities. Central heating, fans, open walkways.

€65–75pn plus €30/stay. Sofabed can take up to 2 extra people (+€20pppn). Min 3-night stay.

⌂ **Valletta G House** North St & Republic St; m (call Aldo) 79815145; www.vallettahouse.com. Part of a 16th-century house at the rougher, but more residential end of town (plenty of local food shops) & set over 2 levels with stone walls & floors. The apt is airy & cool (if a little dark) with its own *gallarija*, interesting wooden furniture, modern kitchen, low ceilings, helpful owner. Guests must be 20 or over. *£490–524/week or €535–72.*

⌂ **Valletta Nobile** m 79488047; e info@vallettanobile.com; www.vallettanobile.com. Owned by the same people as Maison la Vallette, above, Valletta Nobile is a 2nd-floor, 1 dbl-bedroom apt with a *gallarija* overlooking Merchants Street (at the Fort St Elmo end). Even more contemporary than its sister apt. *€85/night.*

⌂ **Valletta Studios** ☎ 27021656; m 99895827; e mimer24@hotmail.com; www.vallettastudios.com. 2 studios (1 dbl bed in each) on Battery Street, just below the Upper Barracca Gardens. Wonderful views over Grand Harbour. Modern interiors – 1 has its own wooden *gallarija*, the other an open balcony. Great value. *Sgl €45–50; couple €55–65pn.*

5

Valletta has some excellent restaurants. Most are in the middle to upper expense bracket, though they compare well with other places in Europe in terms of the quality for the price. There are also places – like Trabuxu wine bar and the Band Club restaurants (see below) – where you can eat home-cooked food at very reasonable prices. Booking is advisable in the more upmarket restaurants to be sure of a table, although it is often not necessary.

RESTAURANTS

✕ **Ambrosia** [112 D4] 137 Archbishop St; ☎ 21225923; ⏱ 12.30–14.30 & 19.30–22.00 Mon–Sat, closed Sun. Friendly place on a narrow Valletta side street. Busy at lunchtimes, quieter in the evenings. Imaginative, changing, blackboard menu of Mediterranean & Maltese dishes. The patron's English wife runs front-of-house. *Starters €5.50–9, mains €14–22.*

✕ **D'Agostino** [112 D4] 63 Republic St (St Elmo side of St George's Sq); ☎ 21225197; ⏱ 12.00–15.00 Mon–Sat & 19.30–23.30 Wed–Sat (closed 15–22 Aug), closed Sun. Very good Mediterranean food in a lovely old building with modern art on the walls. Can be very busy at lunchtimes. *Starters €6.80–9.20, mains €13–20.*

✕ **Fumia** [112 D3] Old Bakery St; ☎ 21317053; e fumia@maltanet.net; ⏱ 12.30–14.30 & 19.30–22.30 Tue–Sun. Next to the Manoel Theatre, very expensive, very good Italian restaurant specialising in seafood. If you don't like fish, don't waste your money as a meal will set you back €50+/head. No children under 5.

✕ **Fusion 4** [112 B3] St John Cavalier St; ☎ 21225255; e fusion4@malta.net; ⏱ 12.00–14.00, 19.30–23.30 Tue–Sun, closed Mon. Built into a sloping tunnel inside 400-year-old fortifications. Trendy, but relaxed with excellent fusion food. Outside terrace tucked in between the bastion walls, sunlit by day, floodlit by night. Byzantine hemispheric catapult boulders (found inside the cavalier) decorate the terrace & inside is the 'Traditions and Crafts of Malta' exhibition – a Maltese street scene complete with waxworks, mechanical motion & sound effects, showing life a century ago. Short regular menu plus daily specials, all from fresh ingredients. *Starters €7.50–8.95, mains around €15.*

✕ **Giannini** [112 B2] 23 Windmill St, St Michael's Bastion; ☎ 21237121; ⏱ 12.00–14.30 & 19.00–22.30 Mon–Fri, 19.00-22.30 Sat, closed Sun. 3rd floor of a townhouse on the edge of Valletta with great views across to Manoel Island from inside & from the terrace. Pricey but good Italian & Mediterranean food. Highchairs available. *Starters €4.75–8.25, mains €14.50–25.*

✕ **La Cave Pizzeria** [112 B5] Castille Sq; ☎ 21220161; e reservations@hotelcastillemalta.com; ⏱ 12.00–15.00 & 18.00–23.00 daily (24.00 Sat), closed Sun & 11–31 Aug. In a 400-year-old cellar underneath the Castille Hotel, friendly atmosphere, bright tablecloths, highchairs available, pasta, salads, wide range of pizzas plus 100 local & foreign wines. *Pizza €5–8.90, pasta/salads €6.50–8.50.*

✕ **Malata** [112 D4] St George's Sq/Palace Sq (opposite the Grand Master's Palace); ☎ 21233967; ⏱ 12.00–14.30, 19.00–23.00 daily. Outdoor tables in the square & inside cellar full of caricatures of Maltese politicians – many of whom eat here. Excellent unfussy Mediterranean & French food, great fish. Live jazz Tue & Fri evenings. *Starters €5.90–10.50, mains €9.50–19.80.*

✕ **Rubino** [112 D3] 53 Old Bakery St/Triq Il-Fran; ☎ 21224656; e mjdiacino@onvol.net; ⏱ 12.30–14.30 Mon–Fri & evenings on Tue, Thu, Fri & Sat 19.30–22.45, closed Sun. A tiny old-fashioned black-&-gold shopfront leads into this charming Valletta favourite. Excellent Maltese & Mediterranean food, white tablecloths & walls decorated with wine bottles & jars of pickle. Intimate, friendly atmosphere. No printed menu – the options are listed on a small blackboard & via the waiter. Tue night is rabbit night, & their Cassata Siciliana (a traditional desert made of moistened sponge cake, ricotta cheese & candied fruit) is rightly famous. *Prices vary from day to day (& are not listed on the board), but a starter & main usually totals €25–30. Book in advance.*

✕ **Spezzo** [112 D4] St George's Sq/Palace Sq (on the St Elmo side); ☎ 21228500; ⏱ 12.00–14.30 Tue–Sun & 19.00–23.00 Tue–Sat, closed Mon. Orange interior with interesting fabrics on the chairs (zebra stripes, batik) & modern art on the walls. Mediterranean/Italian food. *Starters/salads/pasta €8.50–11.50, mains €18–21.*

✕ **The Carriage Restaurant** [112 B3] Valletta Bldgs, South St; ☎ 21247828; e thecarriage@gmail.com;

⏱ 12.00–15.00 Mon–Sat & 19.30–23.00 Fri & Sat, closed Sun. Highest-rated Valletta eatery in Malta's 2009 *Good Restaurant Guide*. The entrance looks like an office block but the restaurant is at roof level with a large terrace & views over the rooftops. Seasonal French Mediterranean food. Young kids not encouraged. *Starters average €8, mains €16.*

✗ **Trabuxu** [112 B3] 1 Strait St (at the end of South St); 🕿 21223036; e info@trabuxu.com; www.trabuxu.com; ⏱ 12.00–14.30 Tue–Fri & 19.00–24.00 Tue–Sun. Friendly little winebar in a traditional stone barrel-vaulted cellar decorated with brass musical instruments & contemporary paintings which change monthly. Small, blackboard menu of excellent, inexpensive & beautifully presented home cooking. *Mains €6.95–9.50, extensive local & international wine list from €2.50/glass.*

✗ **Trattoria da Pippo** [112 C4] 136 Melita St; 🕿 21248029; ⏱ 12.00–15.00 Mon–Sat, closed Sun. Cosy, busy, popular lunch-only eaterie hidden away off Republic Street (look for the Xerox sign on the shop next door). Large portions, fresh fish, traditional pasta & other Italian/Sicilian dishes that change daily according to what is fresh on the market. Booking essential. *Starters & pastas €6, mains €10–19.*

✗ **Two Twenty Two** [112 C2] 222 Great Siege Rd; 🕿 27333222; e info@two-twentytwo.com; www.two-twentytwo.com; ⏱ 18.30–24.00 daily, sometimes as late as 02.00 on Fri & Sat. Built into the bastion walls of Valletta. Ultra-modern, black-&-white minimalist design, this is an example of 'reversible architecture' – it could be removed leaving no ill effect on the historic site. Open-plan upstairs bar/lounge with projected archive images of Malta (particularly Valletta). Small menu of nouvelle-cuisine-style meat & fish – but portions are not nouvelle cuisine-sized (the Maltese don't do small meals). Food a bit overpriced. *Starters average €10, mains €18.50–20.*

VALLETTA'S CLUBS There are two band clubs (see page 65) in Valletta that serve decent inexpensive food as well as a couple of other clubs.

✗ **King's Own Band Club** [112 C4] 247 Republic St. Strong on traditional Maltese food & at the time of writing it has a particularly good chef. *Starters €3.80–5.90, mains €7.90–16, 3-course set menu with wine & coffee €14.90.*

✗ **Labour Party Bar** [112 C4] Republic St. Very male 'Old Labour'. Full-English b/fast €3.50, omelette & chips €5.90, mains €7.95–13.95 including glass of wine. English Premier League & Italian Serie A football on TV.

✗ **Restaurant La Vallette** [112 C4] Occupies the traditional building of the San Pawl band club towards the City Gate end of Republic Street. It has snooker tables & a large canteen-style dining room open all day (09.00–22.00) serving sandwiches on Maltese bread from €1.30, ravioli €4/dozen & a set menu from €9.

✗ **The Anglo-Maltese League** [112 C4] 221 Merchants St. Founded 1935, this club serves a 2-course daily set menu for €8.50.

CAFÉS

✗ **Café Jubilee** [112 D3] 125 St Lucy St/Triq Santa Luċija; 🕿 21252232; e jubilee@maltanet.net; www.cafejubilee.com; ⏱ 08.00–23.00 daily. Café/bar, decorated with old newspapers, adverts & wonky posters, & an upside-down table & chairs on the ceiling. Fun place for an inexpensive drink or light meal. Cosy in winter. Free Wi-Fi. There is also a Café Jubilee on Gozo; see page 263.

✗ **Café Teatro** [112 D3] 115 Old Theatre St; 🕿 21222618 or 21246389; e info@teatrumanoel.com.mt; ⏱ 08.30–20.00 Tue–Sun. Charming café in the 18th-century courtyard of the Manoel Theatre. Covered with a retracting roof in winter. A little oasis that also serves as the theatre bar. Free Wi-Fi.

✗ **Caffe Cordina** [112 D4] 244–5 Republic St (Republic Sq/Queen's Sq); 🕿 234385 or 241359; e info@caffecordina.com; www.caffecordina.com; ⏱ 08.00–19.00 daily, closes at 15.00 on Sun. A Valletta institution, perfectly located in the heart of the city, selling pastries, light meals & snacks (inc *pastizzi*; see page 62) & very good ice cream. Sit outside by the statue of Queen Victoria

✗ **Inspirations** [112 B4] St James Cavalier; 🕿 21241224; e inspirations@maltanet.net; ⏱ from 09.30 daily. Closes at 20.00 Mon–Wed & at 23.00 Thu–Sun. Snacks, light meals, wine & smoothies.

✗ **282 Coffee Garden** [112 C4] 282 Republic St; 🕿 21222111; ⏱ all day (approx 08.30–19.30). Not special but pleasant & conveniently located right in the middle of Republic Street just where you might run out of steam. Decent snacks, coffee & light meals.

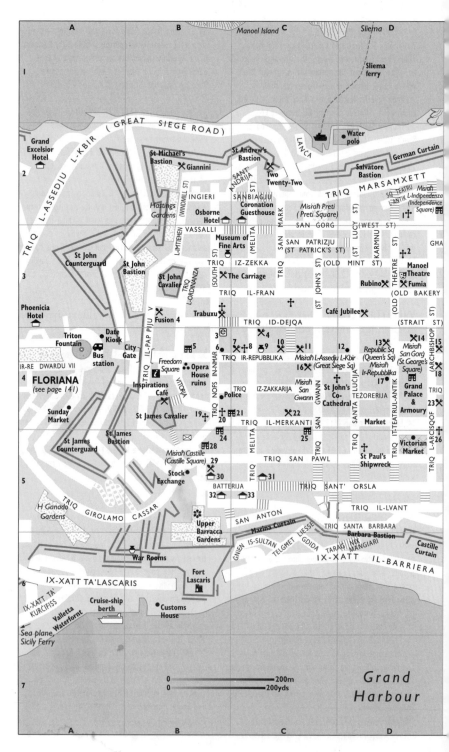

Manoel Island **C**   *Sliema* **D**

Sliema ferry

Water polo

GREAT SIEGE ROAD

L-KBIR

TRIQ L-ASSEDJU

Grand Excelsior Hotel

St Michael's Bastion ✕ Giannini

St Andrew's Bastion

Two Twenty-Two

SANT' ANDRIJA

LANCA

German Curtain

Salvatore Bastion

TRIQ MARSAMXETT

SQ TEATRU ANTIK

Misrah L-Indipendenza (Independence Square)

INGIERI

Hastings Gardens

WINDMILL ST

Osborne Hotel

SANBIAGJU

Coronation Guesthouse

Misrah Preti (Preti Square)

SAN GORG

SAN MARK

SAN LUCIJA (WEST ST)

KARMNU

GHA

L-IMTIEHEN

VASSALLI

Museum of Fine Arts

(MELITA)

SAN PATRIZJU (ST PATRICK'S ST)

St John Counterguard

St John Bastion

St John Cavalier

TRIQ L-ORDINANZA

TRIQ IZ-ZEKKA

(SOUTH ST)

SAN JOHN'S

(OLD MINT ST)

(ST JOHN'S)

THEATRE

Manoel Theatre ✕ Fumia

Rubino ✕

Phoenicia Hotel

IR-RE DWARDU VII

Triton Fountain

Date Kiosk

Bus station

City Gate

TRIQ IL-PAP PIJU V

✕ Fusion 4

Trabuxu ✝

TRIQ IL-FRAN

Café Jubilee ✕

TRIQ ID-DEJQA

(STRAIT ST)

(OLD BAKERY ST)

FLORIANA
(see page 141)

Freedom Square

Inspirations Café

TRIQ VITORIA

Opera House ruins

TRIQ NOFS IN-NHAR

Police

3 📧

7 ✕4

6 ✕8 ✕9 10

✕11

12

TRIQ IR-REPUBBLIKA

Misrah L-Assedju L-Kbir (Great Siege Sq)

16 ✕

13 ✕

Republic Sq (Queen's Sq)

Misrah Ir-Repubblika

14 ✕

Misrah San Gorġ (St George's Square)

15

18

ARCHBISHOP

IZ-ZAKKARIJA

Misrah San Gwann

SAN GWANN

St John's Co-Cathedral

TEŻORERIJA

17 ✝

Grand Palace & Armoury

TRIQ

23 ✕

Sunday Market

St James Counterguard

St James Bastion

St James Cavalier

19 ✝

20

✝ 21

22 ✕

Market

TRIQ IT-TEATRU-ANTIK

SANTA LUCIJA

24

28

Misrah Castille (Castille Square)

29

Stock Exchange

30

TRIQ IL-MERKANTI

MELITA

25

TRIQ SAN PAWL

St Paul's Shipwreck ✝

Victorian Market

26 ✕

TRIQ IT-TEATRUL-ANTIK

TRIQ IL-ARCISQOF

TRIQ GIROLAMO CASSAR

H Ganado Gardens

31

BATTERIJA

32 33

TRIQ SANT' ORSLA

TRIQ IL-LVANT

Upper Barracca Gardens

SAN ANTON

Marina Curtain

GNIEN IS-SULTAN

TELGHET LIESSE

GDIDA

TARAH

TRIQ SANTA BARBARA

Barbara Bastion

NA MANGIARI

IX-XATT IL-BARRIERA

Castille Curtain

War Rooms

Fort Lascaris

IX-XATT TA'LASCARIS

IX-XATT TA KURCIFISS

Valletta Waterfront

Cruise-ship berth

Customs House

Sea plane, Sicily Ferry

0   200m
0   200yds

Grand Harbour

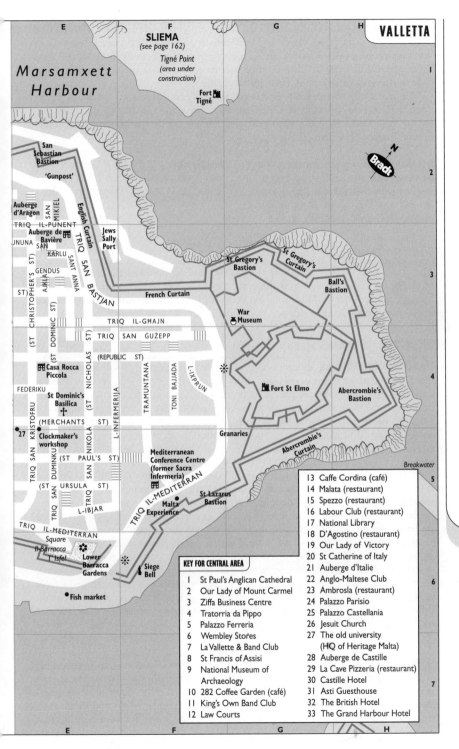

SNACKS AND SELF-CATERING SUPPLIES There are plenty of places for a *pastizzi*, or if you fancy something sweet and different try *imqaret* (see page 62 for more information on both). Apart from Wembley Stores (see below), most of the food shops are towards the St Elmo end of Valletta where more people live. Vans also park in this area selling fresh fruit and vegetables.

The main Valletta market is open each morning on Merchants Street, or in the ditch just outside the walls at City Gate on Sundays. If you like to cook fish and are an early riser, there is a wholesale fish market on the harbourside below the Lower Barracca Gardens (⊕ *approx 04.30–06.30*).

Date Kiosk [112 A4] City Gate bus station. Sells the tastiest cheap sweet snack around, *imqaret*, deep-fried pastry filled with date paste & fennel seed. Best when freshly cooked (& not too often if you are worried about cholesterol!); 20c each.

Wembley Stores [112 B4] Cnr of Republic St & South St, just off Freedom Sq; ☎ 21225147; ⊕ Mon–Sat 08.00–19.00. All-round grocery shop.

OTHER PRACTICALITIES

The main **post office** [112 B5] is situated on Castille Square (⊕ *08.15–15.15 Mon–Fri, 08.15–12.30 Sat*) and there are banks – with ATMs – along Republic Street. Internet cafés and locations with free (or free-with-a-drink) Wi-Fi are listed in *Chapter 3*, page 73. For *Arts and entertainment*, please see *Chapter 3*, page 64.

WHAT TO SEE AND DO

WANDER AND WONDER Valletta is a lovely place to wander. You will happen upon many of the main sights – *auberges*, churches and museums – as well as historic buildings marked with plaques which, happily for tourists, the Maltese love. Nothing is far away so you can always double back to take in anything you miss. If you are following the text below, be sure not to have your nose too firmly in the book or map. It is worth looking up and around, both at the architecture and to allow for chance encounters: a woman lowering a basket from her *gallarija* for a pint of milk, perhaps, or a silversmith at work by an open door.

If you have time, walk the streets at different hours of the day and you will see at least three different Vallettas. First thing in the morning (around 06.30–08.00) all the church doors are open as people drop in for early Mass (often audible from the street). You can drop in too as long as you are quiet. Small workshops and bakeries are just opening up (and you will notice them, which you may not in the midday bustle) and the market will be setting up in Merchants Street near St John's Square/Misraħ San Gwann.

In the middle of the day, everyone is out and about, and, of course, the museums, cafés, sights and shops are all open. Then it suddenly goes quiet, sometimes as early as 16.00 or 17.00 (when the large tour groups disappear) and certainly by nightfall. Valletta has no bright lights at night, other than floodlighting of ancient fortifications and historic buildings. Nightlife here consists of a peaceful walk, the occasional concert or other performance and some very good restaurants (see *Where to eat*, above).

SEEING THE SIGHTS If you follow the text below it will take you – albeit with a bit of inevitable zig-zagging and doubling back – to all the main sites of Valletta, as well as many more minor ones. This is just one way of seeing the sights, however, and there are many other ways of walking around Valletta. Particularly as Valletta is so small and since opening times vary, you may well find yourself viewing things in a different order.

To see Valletta's fortifications in their full glory – as they would have been seen by a potential invader – you need to be outside the city. Walk from the City Gate bus station down **Great Siege Road** and turn right into the ditch in front of St Michael Bastion. You'll be left in no doubt about the difficulty of scaling these walls.

To see the whole of the city walls, follow the road all the way round Valletta. This can be walked (though it is quite a main road) or driven, or you can take bus 198 which does the full circuit.

HARBOUR CRUISES The other great way to see Valletta and its harbours is from the water. Tours of the Grand Harbour and the creeks of the Three Cities in traditional harbour boats can be arranged with the water taxi companies listed under *Getting there and away*, page 107. **A&S Taxis** are well organised and their boats are canopied in summer against the sun. The old-fashioned pair of Venetian-style oars is still used to manoeuvre into and away from land, while an engine speeds things up around the harbour. Half-hour tours take you out to the harbour wall and into each of the creeks (€8pp, min 2 people). **Walter's Co-Op** does similar tours.

These boats are, however, too small to take outside the harbour so if you want to cruise both the Grand Harbour and Marsamxett Harbour – or would like a full English commentary – you need a larger boat. These cruises start from Sliema (see page 164) which is just a five-minute, less than €1, ferry from Valletta (or ten minutes in a water taxi). Alternatively, **Luzzu Cruises** will pick you up from the Valletta side of the Sliema ferry (m 79064489 or 99474210; e luzzucruises@onvol.net; ⊕ year round, weather permitting; €15.75/12.25 adult/child).

City Gate, Freedom Square and the Opera House Most people arriving in Valletta come through **City Gate** [112 B4] (though if you arrive by boat or car there are other ways through the fortifications). The original Porta San Giorgio was locked each night and the drawbridge raised. There are plans for this area to be completely revamped (see below) but at the time of writing the gate is an ugly 1960s construction, Freedom Square just inside is a car park (not public) with souvenir shops and the tourist information office (see above) and it is all a bit of a mess. The fortifications, however, are extremely impressive with a deep ditch and huge walls leading to vast bastions and two massive Knights-period gun platforms, **St James Bastion and Cavalier** [112 B4] to the right (see below) and **St John Bastion and Cavalier** [112 B3] to the left.

Inside the gate, in Freedom Square, the ruin ahead of you was Valletta's **Opera House** [112 B4], designed by Edward Middleton Barry (architect of the Royal Opera House, Covent Garden). Built in 1866, it was razed to the ground by German bombing in 1942 and has lain largely untouched ever since, becoming something of a national icon.

The redevelopment plan includes a new gate, Malta's first purpose-built parliament and redevelopment of the opera house. At the time of writing, it is hoped that Italian architect Renzo Piano (co-designer of the Pompidou Centre in Paris) will lead the project with his design for an outdoor theatre in the opera house ruin (retaining the existing structure), an open-topped gate that returns to the proportions of 1633, and an unashamedly modern (but mainly stone) ultra-'green' parliament building replacing the car park.

Castille Square/Misraħ Kastilja/Pjazza Kastilja [112 B5] If you turn right out of Freedom Square and walk up South Street/Triq Nofs In-Nhar you will reach the

CHURCHES AND CATHEDRALS
Church of Our Lady of Victory [112 B4] Pages 116–17.
Church of St Catherine of Italy [112 B4] Page 117.
Church of St Francis of Assisi [112 C4] Page 121.
Church of St Paul's Shipwreck [112 D5] Pages 139–40.
Old Jesuit church [112 D5] Page 140.
Sanctuary Basilica of Our Lady of Mount Carmel [112 D2] Page 134.
St Dominic's Basilica [113 E4] Page 121.
St John's Co-Cathedral [112 D4] Pages 123–6.
St Paul's Anglican Cathedral [112 D2] Page 134.

MUSEUMS AND GALLERIES
National Museum of Archaeology and the Auberge de Provence [112 C4] Pages 121–3.
National Museum of Fine Arts [112 B3] Page 135.
National War Museum [113 G3] Pages 132–3.
St John's Co-Cathedral Museum [112 D4] Pages 125–6.

PARKS AND GARDENS
Hastings Gardens [112 B2] Page 135.
Lower Barracca Gardens [113 E6] Page 138.
Upper Barracca Gardens [112 B5] Page 118.

OTHER PLACES OF INTEREST
Casa Rocca Piccola [113 E4] Page 129.
Fort St Elmo [113 G4] Page 131.
Grand Master's Palace [112 D4] Page 127.
Knights' auberges See box, opposite.
Lascaris War Rooms [112 B6] Page 119.
Manoel Theatre [112 D3] Page 134.
National Library/Biblioteca [112 D4] Page 127.
Sacra Infermeria – the Knights' Hospital [113 F5] See page 137.
St James Cavalier [112 B4] Page 118.
The Malta Experience [113 F5] Page 137.
Unfinished Tunnels [112 B6] Page 120.

attractive **Castille Square** with a central roundabout lush with large palm trees and flowers. Just before you enter the square you will have the small, but historically important **Church of Our Lady of Victory** on your right, and on your left is the main church of the Italian Knights of St John, the **Church of St Catherine of Italy.**

Along the city side of the square (on your left as you enter from City Gate and South Street) is the **Auberge de Castille**, while along the side closest to City Gate are the main **post office** (see page 74) and the entrance to **St James Cavalier**.

On the other side is the former British garrison church, now the Malta Stock Exchange, and to its left just beyond the square is the entrance to the **Upper Barracca/Upper Barrakka Gardens**.

Church of Our Lady of Victory [112 B4] (⊕ *for Mass in the morning at around 08.00 & early evening*) This delightful, peaceful little chapel was the very first public building in Valletta – dedicated in thanks for the newly won victory in the Great

Siege. Built in 1566 to the design of Gerolamo Cassar it served as the Knights' church until the completion of St John's in 1577. This chapel was also the first burial place of Grand Master de Valette, until he was moved to the crypt of St John's (now the Co-Cathedral). The interior paintings by Alessio Erardi and the Baroque façade, including the bust of Pope Innocent XI (1676–1689) above the door, are 18th-century additions.

Church of St Catherine of Italy [112 B4] (*The church is rarely open, except for lunchtime concerts on Thu at 12.30; entrance by donation of €5*) Also a 16th-century work of Girolamo Cassar, with a Baroque façade added in the early 18th century, the octagonal interior has a fine dome and an altarpiece by Mattia Preti (1613–99), the distinguished Italian artist who spent four decades in Malta and is represented in many of its main churches (see boxed text, page 126). This was the church of the Italian *langue* of the Knights and was originally attached to the Auberge d'Italie behind it on Merchants Street (see below page 121).

Auberge de Castille [112 B5] (*Castille Sq/Pjazza Kastilja; only visible from the outside except on Notte Bianca – for details see page 35;* e *info@nottebiancamalta.com; www.nottebiancamalta.com;* ✆ *21232515*) Now the office of the prime minister, the

THE KNIGHTS, *LANGUES* AND THEIR *AUBERGES*

The Order was divided into eight *langues* (literally 'tongues') within which the knights lived and worked with others who spoke the same language. Each *langue* took responsibility for certain areas of administration and defence. The Italian-, German- and English-speaking knights had one *langue* each. There were two from what is now Spain: Aragon, which included Catalonia and Navarre; and Castile, which shared its *langue* with Portugal. What is now France was divided into three: Provence, France and Auvergne (central-eastern modern France). Traditionally named in French, each *langue* had its own *auberge* (usually translated as 'hostel', but perhaps more like a university college) and many of these buildings remain. The earliest are in Birgu (see page 150) where they are mostly concentrated into a small defensible area of town known as the Collachio. The later (post 1570) *auberges* in Valletta – where the defensive walls go all around the city – are much more spread out.

THE VALLETTA AUBERGES

Auberge d'Aragon [112 D2] On Independence Square, this is now the Ministry of Justice (page 133).

Auberge d'Auvergne [112 C4] Destroyed in World War II, this *auberge* stood where you now see the law courts in Great Siege Square.

Auberge de Castille [112 B5] Located in Castille Square, now the prime minister's office; see above and overleaf.

Auberge d'Italie [112 B4] On Merchants Street, now the HQ of the Malta Tourism Authority (page 121).

Auberge de Provence [112 C4] Situated on Republic Street, now the National Archaeological Museum (page 121).

English None after Birgu until 1783 when the English joined with Bavaria in a shared *auberge* (the Auberge de Bavière), now government offices (page 136) [113 E3].

French [112 B3] Destroyed by World War II bombing. Stood on the corner of South Street and Bakery Street where the General Workers Union now stands.

German [112 D2] Demolished to make way for the Anglican cathedral.

Auberge de Castille with its cannons, broad steps and imposing Baroque stone façade testifies to the power of this *langue* of the Spanish and Portuguese. The main doorway is topped with a bust of Portuguese Grand Master Manoel Pinto de Fonseca (grand master from 1741 to 1773) – who was responsible for the Baroque embellishment of the building – and surrounded by symbolic stonework and coats of arms. This site (at the high point of Valletta) was originally intended for the palace of the grand master, but Grand Master Pietro de Ponte (who succeeded de Valette) became impatient to move to Valletta and so took over a house in the centre of the city, later extended into the Grand Master's Palace we see today (see page 127).

St James Cavalier [112 B4] (*Castille Sq;* ☎ *21223200;* e *info@sjcav.org; www.sjcav.org*) This most solid of buildings formed a major part of Valletta's original landward defences. Along with its twin, St John Cavalier the other side of City Gate, it was designed by Francesco Laparelli da Cortona. The cavaliers were raised gun emplacements that guarded the city's main entrance and, should the enemy somehow get in, also had guns that could shoot down into the town. Walk around the outside to get a feel for the strength of the building. This was built just after the Great Siege and the Knights were not taking any chances.

When the British arrived, the building became first an officers' mess, then a water tower fed from Wignacourt's Aqueduct (see page 220) and finally the forces' food shop, the NAAFI. The building has now been imaginatively converted into a **Centre for Creativity**, focusing on contemporary arts. You enter up a long stone stairway in an original limestone tunnel (well floodlit) to find an arthouse cinema, a theatre and plenty of exhibition space – including stone-vaulted galleries and a central cylinder (once a water cistern) with a cylindrical lift to match. It is a great space with regularly changing art to view.

The **Inspirations Café**, with a stone-vaulted ceiling inside and a stone terrace outside overlooking the bombed-out opera house, is very pleasant and reasonably priced (see *Where to eat*, page 111).

Upper Barracca Gardens/Upper Barrakka Gardens, the Grand Harbour and the Saluting Battery [112 B5] Just off Castille Square on the opposite side from City Gate is the Upper Barracca Gardens [112 B5]. This arcaded public garden stands at Valletta's highest point offering stunning panoramic views of the Grand Harbour and the Three Cities. It is also the setting for the daily firing of the noonday gun – accompanied by rousing British military music.

Look down from the Floriana end of the gardens (the furthest corner from where you enter) to get a vertiginous sense of the strength of Valletta's defences. From here you can also see the Valletta Waterfront, newly developed from the Knights' old warehouses into the landing stage for cruise ships, bars, restaurants and souvenir shops.

Looking straight out from the main wall of the gardens you can take in the full sweep of the Grand Harbour. It is primarily this harbour and its natural hidden creeks that has made Malta so attractive to any power that wished to control the Mediterranean, and so has dictated Malta's history.

From the breakwater (built in 1903) at the harbour mouth and Fort Ricasoli guarding the entrance (opposite Fort St Elmo) moving right you see several peninsulas: Kalkara (not part of the Three Cities but part of the same district) dominated from here by Bighi Hospital, a grand old British-era building, now offices; Vittoriosa/Birgu with Fort St Angelo on its tip; then Senglea/Isla, with Cospicua/Bormla at the head of the creek.

High up here on the bastion walls, there is usually a breeze freshening the gardens' walkways, flower beds and fountain. Built in 1661 (to the design of Italian Knight Flaminio Balbiani) the arcades were once roofed. The story goes that Spanish Grand Master Ximenes de Texada (1773–75) suspected shady goings on and ordered the roofs be removed.

There is a little snack bar with tables within the gardens and a full-scale café just below it on the Valletta side.

The monuments The gardens are dotted with monuments, mostly to Maltese and British military men – including Churchill and Battle of Trafalgar hero Sir Thomas Fremantle – along with others, bizarrely including Albert Einstein who has no link with Malta other than the admiration of a Maltese influential wealthy enough to commission the memorial!

Taking centre stage is **Lord Strickland** (1861–1940), an Anglo-Maltese politician, UK peer and Malta's fourth prime minister. At the landward side stands the Malta Stock Exchange and in front of it a statue of painter **Giuseppe Cali** (1846–1930) whose work features in many of Malta's churches. Finally, the sculpture, *Les Gavroches* ('The Urchins'), is by Antonio Sciortino (1879–1947), Malta's most famous modern sculptor. This is in fact a copy; the original is in the Museum of Fine Arts (see page 135).

The Saluting Battery Directly beneath the public gardens and visible from them, is the Saluting Battery, reached by steps down in front of the fountain. The battery, its guns overlooking the Grand Harbour, was part of Valletta's original defences and the terrace would at first have held bronze cannon firing stone cannonballs. The battery was in continuous use (with 21 different kinds of cannon over the years) until 1960, although in its last 100 years its use was primarily ceremonial.

The battery also acted as the city clock. It fired at sunrise, noon and sunset, signalling the opening and closing of the gates of this fortified city as well as the start and end of the military day (reveille and retreat). From the second half of the 18th century, the noon gun provided the all-important marker by which ships set their chronometers (crucial for navigation).

The battery now consists of eight renovated two-ton 1807 British cannons looked after by an NGO. **Guided tours** in English – with great detail about the weaponry – are available at 11.00 and 12.15 (❧ *21225277, 21800992 or 21809713;* e *info@wirtartna.org; www.wirtartna.org; €5 adults, €4 students/seniors, €3 children under 16, €13 family of 2 adults & 3 children*). The 11.00 tour participants can stay on the battery for the noonday firing, but you can see (and hear!) it just as well from the gardens above and a short introduction (sufficient for most people) is given through the loudspeakers before the firing.

A **combined ticket** is available for this tour, Lascaris War Rooms (see below), the Malta at War Museum (see page 147) and Fort Rinella (page 158), including transport between them (*€22/19/48 adult/child/family*).

Lascaris War Rooms [112 B6] (*Lascaris Bastion, almost beneath the Upper Barracca Gardens – from the Upper Barracca Gdns, turn right into Battery St then right down steps signed to the war rooms; run by Fondazzjoni Wirt Artna:* ❧ *21234717, 21800992 or 21809713;* e *info@wirtartna.org; www.wirtartna.org;* ☉ *daily 10.00–17.00, guided tours & film shows on the hour. Closed to the public for renovation at time of writing but will be open by the time you read this. Price is likely to be around €7 for adults with cheaper concessions. Combined ticket as for Saluting Battery, above.*) Dug deep into the rock under the Upper Barracca Gardens and the Saluting Battery, is the World War II control centre of the British and Allied Mediterranean forces, officially called the

Lascaris War Rooms but commonly known to troops as 'The Hole'. Named after French Grand Master Jean Paul de Lascaris Castellar (1636–57), the tunnels were originally built by the Knights as living quarters for their galley slaves. These dank corridors became the nerve centre of successful campaigns to disrupt the Axis powers in North Africa and to invade Sicily, achieving the surrender of Italy. They were also an important listening post for Military Intelligence.

The services had begun the war in a range of locations from Fort St Angelo to the Auberge de Castille (see page 117), but these all became too dangerous once serious bombing got under way and they withdrew to the depths of the Lascaris Bastion. Numerous operations rooms for all three forces – with vast maps and plotting tables as well as dummies in uniform – give a sense of the work that went on here. Overlooking a huge map is a little room from which General Dwight Eisenhower (Supreme Commander of the Allied forces in the Mediterranean) directed the invasion of Sicily.

The Unfinished Tunnels [112 B6] (*Next to Lascaris War Rooms; viewed by appointment with Fondazzjoni Wirt Artna:* \ *21800992 or 21809713;* e *info@wirtartna.org; www.wirtartna.org*) Beneath Valletta lies an underground city of caves, military tunnels, reservoirs, cisterns, sewers (some 16th century) and World War II shelters (often adapted from one or more of the former). Next to the Lascaris War Rooms is a labyrinth of broad tunnels and cavernous subterranean rooms apparently dug by NATO at the end of World War II. The complex, at least 50ft underground, was never finished and rails and trucks used in its construction lie abandoned. Exactly what this secret underground space was to be used for is unclear, but they are now due to be cleaned up and opened to the public. If visiting before this, be sure to take a torch and wear old clothes (it's very dusty) and trainers or walking shoes. Not recommended if you have asthma.

Merchants Street/Triq Il-Merkanti [112 C4] (*Back on the City Gate side of Castille Sq, Merchants St leads off into the city*) After Republic Street (see below) Merchants Street is Valletta's main street, running almost the entire length of town from the Church of St Catherine of Italy (see above) and the **Auberge d'Italie** (see below) to the edge of Fort St Elmo.

Merchants Street is one of the few roads in Valletta to retain the name given to it by Napoleon in 1798 (though he said it in French, of course) in his mass renaming of Valletta's streets. For most of his few days in Malta he stayed here, opposite the Auberge d'Italie at **Palazzo Parisio** [112 B5], now the foreign ministry (not to be confused with Palazzo Parisio in Naxxar, which belonged to the

MALTA'S WORLD WAR II IN NUMBERS

- 16,000 tons of bombs were dropped on Malta – four times as many as on Dresden.
- 26,000 aerial sorties were flown over Malta.
- There were nearly 3,000 bombing raids.
- Between January and June 1942 there was only one 24-hour stretch without an air-raid alert.
- In April 1942 alone there were 282 air raids.
- 1,468 Maltese people were killed (surprisingly few considering the level of bombing).
- 3,720 Maltese people were injured.
- 50,000 were made homeless.

above	Lija has traditionally held the reputation for the best *festa* fireworks although competition is fierce (V/GG) page 220
right	Good Friday is a national holiday in Malta — churches are decorated (a few in the traditional black damask of mourning) and there are processions along the streets (AT) page 35
below left	Village *festa*: the statue of the patron saint of the parish is carried through the streets at shoulder height followed by priests, musicians, parishioners, and visitors (V) page 31
below right	Victory Day in Xagħra celebrates the end of the Great Siege of 1565 and the Italian surrender in World War II (GL) page 34

above left & right　Strawberry farming in the Majjistral National Park, north Malta (both AT)

below left & right　Lace-making became established in Malta in the 16th and 17th centuries with designs often including the Maltese cross (both V) page 31

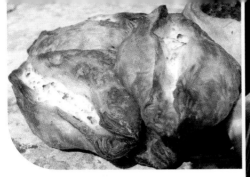

above   *Pastizzi* — a traditional Maltese snack (V) page 62

right   A master carpenter at work on a model of a traditional Maltese boat — such skills are becoming increasingly scarce in Malta (AT)

below left   Many Maltese run workshops from their garages; this man carves stone for fireplaces (GL)

below right   A fisherman prepares his nets, Marsaxlokk (AT) page 180

above left The Mosta Dome is arguably the third-largest unsupported church dome in Europe (V/AS) page 225

above right Verdala Palace is perched above Buskett Gardens which were once the Knights' private hunting ground (N/D) page 196

below Marsaxlokk, on the southeast coast, is the hub of traditional fishing (AT) page 180

top left   Malta's bus system allows you to explore almost anywhere on the island (PL) page 55

top right   The Church of St Lawrence in Birgu is the site of the Knights' first church in Malta (V) page 152

above   St Paul's Catacombs in Rabat are the most impressive of all Malta's catacombs — and the most accessible (KM) page 214

right   The winding streets of Mdina are a pleasure to explore (CD) page 201

top   Carvings at Tarxien Temples: the remains of the largest 'fat lady'; a procession of animals (foreground); a spiral-decorated 'altar' in which instruments of sacrifice were found; and a stone sphere, perhaps used in the transportation of megaliths (DC) page 172

above   The Sleeping Lady, perhaps a ritual image of death, was found in the Ħal Saflieni Hypogeum (page 177) and can now be seen in the National Museum of Archaeology (DC) page 121

right   The temples have semi-circular rooms known as apses; here at Ħaġar Qim (DC) page 192

same family). When offices are open you can see into the central courtyard; the interior is only open to the public during Notte Bianca each October (see page 35).

A little further down Merchants Street is **Palazzo Castellania** [112 C5] (1760) once the Law Courts of the Order of St John – hence the allegorical figures of Justice, Truth and Fame on its façade. It is now the Ministry of Health.

Where Old Theatre Street crosses Merchants Street, is Valletta's **market,** which each morning (except Sunday) fills the street here outside the Victorian covered-market building. It sells everything from food to clothes. The larger Sunday market is held in the ditch just outside the city walls at City Gate.

On the corner of St Dominic Street is **St Dominic's Basilica** [113 E4] originally built in 1571 and dedicated to the Madonna of Porto Salvo ('safe haven') by whose name it is often still known. The church was made the mother church of Valletta by Pope Pius V (1566–72), infuriating the other monastic orders. It is still Valletta's largest parish. The present richly decorated building dates from 1815 and contains a 17th-century wooden polychrome statue of St Dominic that is a particularly fine example of the genre. In Holy Week, the church's oratory is turned into a tableau of the Last Supper.

Auberge d'Italie [112 C4] (*Merchants St;* ☎ 22915000) The Auberge d'Italie on Merchants Street, with a British red letter box just outside, was built in 1574, and enlarged in 1683. The bust above the door is Italian Grand Master Gregorio Carafa (1680–90). The *auberge* is now the head office of the Malta Tourism Authority (MTA) and is not officially open to the public, but you can go in and have a look around the ground floor. The central courtyard is home to a small Italian triumphal arch and the walkway around it often houses exhibitions of contemporary Maltese art, which can usually be bought.

Italy was responsible for the Knights' ships and their leader was always the Admiral of the Fleet. The room straight ahead of you through the reception area (to the right of the main door) was once the meeting room of the Order's Congregation of the Galleys, the fleet's ruling body. On the wall is a 1655 inscription (with an English translation) lauding Carafa for leading seven Maltese galleys that helped Venice to victory in the battle of the Dardanelles. It states proudly that he took 360 Turks as slaves and rescued 2,600 Christians.

Republic Street – Upper (City Gate) end [112 B4] Republic Street is Valletta's main street – and its backbone: it runs straight down the middle of the city from Freedom Square (City Gate) to Fort St Elmo; see page 131 for the lower end.

Coming from the City Gate end you will first pass **Palazzo Ferreria** [112 B4] on the corner of Ordnance Street/Triq L-Ordinanza, with shops on the ground floor and the Ministry for Social Policy above. This fine 19th-century Valletta building was the largest to be built as a private palace other than the Grand Master's, and the first to fully integrate *gallariji* into the design of its stone façade. A few metres further on is the **Church of St Francis of Assisi** [112 C4]. Built in 1598–1607 but altered in 1681 with the dome added in the 1920s, it has one of the earliest Baroque interiors.

About 200m down the road from City Gate is one of Malta's most important – and under-visited – sights, the the **National Museum of Archaeology**, housed in the **Auberge de Provence**, home of de Vallette's *langue* (see below). The road opens out into Valletta's three central squares, the narrow Great Siege Square, the slightly larger Republic Square and the true centre of Valletta, St George's or Palace Square (see below).

The National Museum of Archaeology and the Auberge de Provence [112 C4]
(*Republic St, between Melita St & St John's St/Triq San Gwann;* ☎ 21221623;

www.heritagemalta.org/museums/museums.html; ⊕ *09.00–19.00 daily;* €*5 adult,* €*3.50 over-60s/children aged 12–17/students,* €*2.50 child (6–11), children under 6 go free; combined ticket available inc entry to other Heritage Malta museums, see page 105)* The Archaeological Museum is a must for anyone remotely interested in Malta's prehistoric temples as this is where all the most important finds from the temples reside – including the iconic 'Sleeping Lady'. Even before you pay to go in, there are two monumental upright panels with polished surfaces decorated with pitting and spirals, and two vast pots, one a full metre in diameter (all from the Tarxien temple complex, see page 172). The museum will soon also include galleries on the islands' Phoenician, Punic and Roman periods.

Auberge de Provence The museum building was the Auberge of the Knights of Provence – de Valette's *langue* – built in 1571 and probably designed by Gerolamo Cassar. The original *auberge* took up the whole block and included stables and a bakery making it almost self-sufficient in the event of a siege. Upstairs is the **Grand Salon** – the Knights' banqueting hall – with an unusual wooden ceiling and richly painted walls. The room was painted in the Knights' time and it is unclear how close the present Victorian paintings are to the originals. The **minstrels' gallery** is a British addition. The room is open to the public when temporary exhibitions are held here and occasionally in between.

Neolithic Galleries The ground floor of the museum is given over to the period from **first settlement** of the Maltese islands by around 5000BC to the end of the temple period in 2500BC. The exhibition begins with the time when people lived in caves including that at Għar Dalam (see page 183). It shows the changes in style of pottery over the first $1\frac{1}{2}$ millennia of settlement and includes shell pendants, biconical limestone 'sling stones', and a few very early animal and human figures including one with a triangular head, like those in Cycladic art but around a millennium older.

The real highlights though are architectural and artistic artefacts from the **temples** (3600–2500BC) – which are likely to be more evocative to those who also visit the temple sites. **Don't miss**: the highly decorated little altar from Ħaġar Qim; the stone slab carved with low-relief fish from Buġibba; friezes of animals from Tarxien; animal design pottery and pendants; clay fish from the Hypogeum; and several monumental stone blocks decorated with a variety of spirals and geometric patterns. There is also a little model of a temple found at Ta' Ħaġrat (ie: made at the time the temples were built) and an interesting display on the debate about how the temples were roofed.

Here too is the place to see Malta's **'Fat Ladies'** (some of which may not in fact be female). The largest – now reduced to the lower body and pleated skirt – would once have stood 2m or more in height. It was found at Tarxien, as was the smallest 'fat lady'. The 'ladies' come in a variety of styles (some very obviously female) including eight seated figures from Ħaġar Qim, one with traces of paint, another with exceptionally delicate hands, all with vast bums and thighs. (A well-rounded local woman once pointed out to me that it is only in the last 20 years that the Maltese have begun to move away from seeing the 'very well fed' female as the most attractive.)

In a smaller side room is the lovely **Sleeping Lady**, a delicate naturalistic little clay model of a fat lady asleep on a couch (even the base of which is rendered in detail). She was found in the Ħal Saflieni Hypogeum and is thought to be a personification of death (if so, a very peaceful death) or a deity, but nobody actually knows.

A variety of **phallic symbols** has also been found in the temples (and several are displayed here) adding support to the theory that the fat ladies may have been the central figures or deities of a fertility cult. Other female figures (not always obese) are shown with one hand on their (sometimes rounded) bellies. The so-called **Venus of Malta**, a 15cm headless clay figure is the most famous of these.

Further information There is a very good **guidebook** to the Neolithic Galleries by the curator. Sharon Sultana: *The National Museum of Archaeology: The Neolithic Period (Insight Heritage Guides; €6.99)*. A **podcast** on the museum's highlights by Senior Curator of Prehistoric Sites, Reuben Grima, can be downloaded free from www.visitmalta.com/podcasts.

Bronze Age to Roman At the time of writing work is under way to convert the first floor of the museum into a new permanent exhibition dedicated to this period. As well as artefacts not seen by the public for 60 years or more, displays will include an exploration of Malta's mysterious cart ruts (see boxed text, page 198), a reconstructed Phoenician tomb, and a gallery dealing with the multi-period site of Tas Silġ (see page 84). There will be modern interactive and audiovisual interpretation and a children's room with quizzes and workshops. These galleries are likely to open in 2011.

At the time of writing, the only object on display from this era (on the upstairs landing, so may only be accessible when the Grand Salon is open) is the important 'Rosetta stone of Malta', a *cippus,* or marble **candelabrum.** On its base is an inscription in Phoenician with a shorter Greek version. The inscription is a votive text from two brothers to Melqart (Herakles), protector of the Phoenician city of Tyre. Comparison of the two was crucial to the 18th-century deciphering of the Phoenician language just as the famous Rosetta stone had been instrumental in the translation of Egyptian hieroglyphic script. The candelabrum originally formed one of a pair, but Grand Master de Rohan (1775–97) gave the other to King Louis XVI of France in 1780 and it is now in the Louvre in Paris.

Great Siege Square/Misraħ L-Assedju I-Kbir A short way down Republic Street from the Museum of Archaeology, the road opens out into **Great Siege Square** – which looks more like a widening of the road than a real square. Along one side is the columned façade of the **law courts**, built on the site of the Auberge d'Auvergne which was destroyed during World War II. Opposite is the **Great Siege Monument** (1927) designed by Malta's most respected 20th-century sculptor, Antonio Sciortino, and behind that is the side wall of **St John's Co-Cathedral** where you will find the tourist entrance (see below). The façade and main doors of the church (used to enter for Mass) are in St John's Square/Misraħ San Gwann round the corner along St John's Street/Triq San Gwann.

St John's Co-Cathedral [112 D4] *(St John's Sq/Misraħ San Gwann; ☎ 21220536; stjohnscocathedral.com [no www]; ⊕ 09.30–16.30 Mon–Fri (last admission 16.00), 09.30–12.30 Sat; no narrow-heeled shoes (they damage the floor); €5.80 adults, €4.65 over-60s, children under 12 (accompanied by an adult) go free. Admission inc an audio guide – in English, French, Italian, Spanish, German & Maltese – which is well worth having.)* This was the Order's church in Valletta, with a chapel for each *langue.* Begun in 1572 by Girolamo Cassar (a military architect by training), it started life as a large, plain limestone building completed in 1577 and consecrated in 1578. The oratory and sacristy were added in 1604 under Grand Master de Wignacourt, who was also responsible for handing the chapels over to the individual *langues* to decorate. As Baroque fashion took hold in the second half of the 17th century the serious aggrandising of the interior began with Italian artist Mattia Preti's redesigns and his painting of the six-section barrel-vaulted ceiling (1661–66). The Knights continued to lavish artistic attention (and money) on their church and the *langues* competed for superiority until St John's became what it is today – the most opulent church you could imagine, every inch covered in gold, paint or marble. In 1816 (after the Knights had left Malta) Pope Pius VII gave the church cathedral status so that the single diocese of Malta had two cathedrals (the other being St Paul's in Mdina) – hence the term 'co-cathedral'.

The church The **façade**, flanked by two bell towers, has a balcony, used by the grand master to address the people, and a copy of a bronze Christ by Alessandro Algardi (1598–1654), the remarkable original of which can be seen close up in the cathedral museum (see opposite). The sculpture was brought here from a church in the Grand Harbour in 1853.

Inside, the **cathedral floor** consists entirely of colourful inlaid marble tombs (though many are covered for protection). They date from the early 17th century to the end of the Knights' time in Malta in 1798. Symbolic images recur, particularly a sickle-wielding skeleton (Death) and the angel of fame blowing a trumpet. The Knights blew their own trumpet right enough and this image appears on the memorial monuments of a number of grand masters – most of whom are buried here.

Preti's ceiling paintings, done with great skill, start from the lunette over the main door and represent (unsurprisingly) scenes from the life of St John the Baptist, patron saint of the Order. They are not frescoes but painted with oils direct onto the stone. Notice the *trompe l'oeil* of the figures at the base of the ceiling vaults. They are so three-dimensional that they look like sculptures and with some figures, like the one opposite the main tourist entrance to the church, Preti has actually painted their shadows onto the gold stone carvings next to them. The ceiling decoration was paid for by Raphael and Nicolas Cotoner – brothers who were both grand masters and who can be seen by the lunette above the main door.

The **chapels of the *langues*** are all richly decorated – with altarpiece paintings (several by Mattia Preti), carvings and monuments, some of real artistic merit. The Italian chapel has recently been fully restored with money from the Italian government and all are worth a visit.

The **Chapel of Our Lady of Philermos** used to house the Knights' most precious icon, carried with them since their time in Jerusalem. In preparation for battle they would pray before this painting and, if victorious, bring the keys of the captured fortress to the chapel. A few keys still hang here (though they are not easy to see). The icon left Malta with the Knights, and was taken to St Petersburg. After the Russian Revolution, it disappeared for some years. It now hangs in the Museum of Fine Arts in Montenegro and St John's has a copy.

The Oratory The highlight of a visit to the oratory is **Caravaggio**'s vast *Beheading of St John* (1608) – his largest painting and his only signed work ('Fra Michaelangelo' scrawled in the Baptist's blood). It is worth noting that when Caravaggio was here the church was still in its original austere unembellished state (Mattia Preti and the Baroque came later) and the oratory was newly built. The painting was commissioned by Grand Master de Wignacourt who wanted a devotional picture for the Order's novices who used the oratory.

Although already in his mid-thirties, Caravaggio was one of these novices, training to become a knight, hoping to escape his violent past in Italy (see boxed text, opposite). The painting is a powerfully realistic portrayal of the story with a total absence of religious iconography (no angels, God, etc). The spare composition is painted in a limited palette lending extra power to the splash of red that is St John's mantel.

Also in the oratory is Caravaggio's **St Jerome**, another very human image, this one of an old man writing (St Jerome translated the Bible from Greek into Latin). The painting was a private possession of the knight-patron (you can see his coat of arms on the work). After his death, his property passed to the Order (as was usual) and the painting was placed in the Italian chapel. When the painting was moved to the oratory, a copy was put in its place and still hangs in the chapel.

The Cathedral Museum The museum's most treasured possession is a set of 29 **Flemish tapestries** (1697–1700), the largest such complete set in the world. Made

---

CARAVAGGIO AND MALTA

Born Michelangelo Merisi in 1571, a middle-class boy in the town of Caravaggio, the artist-to-be lost his father to the plague at the age of five and his mother in his teens. He took his inheritance and departed for Rome, never to return. This brilliant but hot-headed young man was soon making waves with his painting and with his violence. In 1606 things came to head when he killed a well-connected Roman in a duel. He fled south, a wanted man, and a year later boarded a galley belonging to the Order of St John heading for Malta. *En route*, word came of Turkish ships lying in wait off Gozo and all men were armed and made ready, but it was a false alarm and Caravaggio arrived safely in the Grand Harbour in July 1607.

On the same voyage to Malta was Knight Ippolito Malaspina (a personal friend of the grand master). He soon became the owner of Caravaggio's *St Jerome* which now hangs in St John's Oratory. Grand Master de Wignacourt too recognised Caravaggio's talent and commissioned him to paint his portrait (now in the Louvre). He also accepted him as an unlikely novice of the Order of St John. Caravaggio was neither noble-born, nor of good character, but Wignacourt petitioned the pope for special dispensation and received it. While a novice, Caravaggio painted the powerful *Beheading of St John*, now the highlight of the co-cathedral's art collection (see opposite).

Caravaggio was formally admitted to the Order as a knight on 14 July 1608. His studies over, he left the confines of the church and within weeks was involved in a brawl with six other Italian knights in the house of the church organist. A high-ranking knight was shot and seriously wounded and Caravaggio was imprisoned in Fort St Angelo. A risky escape (perhaps aided by powerful friends) using ropes to scale the fort's massive walls, saw the artist on a boat to Sicily. This was a bridge too far for the Order and on 1 December 1608, in the Oratory of St John's with the artist's painting hanging on the wall, Caravaggio was, 'like a rotten and fetid limb', cut off from the Hospitallers.

From Sicily he returned to Naples, and by early 1610, after more than a year on the run, he was in a bad way. He painted *Salome with the Head of John the Baptist* showing his own head on the platter and sent it to Wignacourt. With hopes that powerful friends in Rome might succeed in extracting a pardon from the pope, Caravaggio took a boat north but died mysteriously, probably from a fever, a few days before the pardon was forthcoming.

His effect on European painting is hard to underestimate and, despite the fact that he spent little over a year in Malta, his effect on painting here is clear to see in the friezes in the State Rooms of the Palace of the Grand Master (completed shortly after his departure; see page 128) and in the work of many of his admirers, including Mattia Preti.

A podcast on Caravaggio in Malta by a local art historian can be downloaded free at www.visitmalta.com/podcasts.

by Jodicus de Vos from cartoons, many of which were by Peter Paul Rubens, the tapestries were Spanish Grand Master Ramon Perellos y Roccaful's contribution to St John's and they used to be hung in the church on feast days.

The museum also has some huge **illuminated choral books** (16th- and 17th-century) and a silver-and-gilt monstrance (sacred receptacle, 1686–89) which once held a relic believed to be part of St John's forearm – the arm that baptised Christ. Napoleon pinched the gold from it and the Knights took the relic with them when they left Malta.

Richly embroidered vestments that once belonged to several grand masters are followed by a picture gallery which includes the original altarpiece of the church by Matteo Perez d'Aleccio, pupil of Michelangelo, paintings by Mattia Preti and an interesting portrait by Antoine de Favray of Grand Master Manoel Pinto de Fonseca (1747) in an ermine cape which is meant to be reserved for royalty.

Also most enjoyable is the walk through the long *gallarija* overlooking Merchants Street and the raised walkway between Merchants Street and an internal courtyard on the way to the vestments hall.

Mass Mass is said at 07.30 and 08.30 each weekday. On Sundays at 09.15 there is High Mass in Latin with organ and full choir – quite an experience. There is no charge for entering the church for Mass, but you cannot wander around and sightsee while the service is on.

Further information There's an informative official guidebook to St John's by the curator Cynthia de Giorgio (*Insight Heritage Guides;* €6.99) available at the cathedral.

Republic Square/Misraħ Ir-Republikka [112 D4] A few metres from Great Siege Square is Republic Square, also known as 'Queen's Square' because of the statue of Queen Victoria that stands at its centre looking down on the denizens of Valletta sipping coffee (or licking ice cream) at the capital's most famous café. **Caffe Cordina** (see *Where to eat*, page 111) has attracted locals and visitors alike since the

---

MATTIA PRETI

Although Italian, Mattia Preti is arguably Malta's most important painter. He spent 40 years here and is represented in numerous churches – particularly St John's Co-Cathedral where he painted the vast vaulted ceiling (see page 123). Born in Calabria in 1613 and later known as Il Cavalier Calabrese, he trained in Naples and Rome (where he was influenced by the work of Caravaggio) before travelling to Venice and all over Italy absorbing the work of many of Europe's greatest painters. He developed an eclectic style, carried out numerous commissions and made influential friends before being admitted as a Knight of the Order of St John in 1642.

A few years later he received a commission from Grand Master de Redin for a painting depicting St Francis Xavier. The following year, 1659, he travelled to Malta where he spent most of the rest of his life. Art historian Nicholas Pevsner credits Preti with the creation of High Baroque art, identifying as seminal works his altarpiece in the Church of St Catherine of Italy (see page 117) and his decoration of St John's (see page 14). Preti went on to paint numerous other altarpieces and private commissions, mostly of a religious nature.

He died in Malta in 1699 and is buried in St John's. His memorial plaque of coloured marble can be seen in the side chapel that leads to the sacristy (just to the right of the main door looking from the inside).

19th century. Locals will often suggest meeting here as a central Valletta landmark – as well as for a coffee. In the arcade behind the café tables is the **National Library**.

The National Library/Biblioteca [112 D4] (↘ *21243297/5303/3297 or 21236585/ 2961/6585; www.customercare.nlm.gov.mt or www.libraries-archives.gov.mt; ⊕ to the public on production of ID 1 Oct–15 Jun 08.15–17.45 Mon–Fri, 08.15–13.15 Sat; 16 Jun–30 Sep 08.15–13.15 Mon–Sat. Accessing books & documents requires a research ticket – contact the library in advance.*) This was the last important building to be constructed by the Order in 1796, two years before Napoleon arrived. They needed a new home for the massive collection of papers and books accumulated through the Order's statute that forbade the sale of any of a deceased knights' books. Napoleon ordered the contents of the library destroyed. Fortunately, he was not obeyed and today the library houses over 300,000 books and 10,000 manuscripts, some dating back to the 12th century. These include the written records of the Order from 1107 to 1798 as well as a letter from Henry VIII proclaiming himself head of the Church of England, the Act of Donation in which Charles V gave Malta to the Knights and the papal bull of 1113 that first recognised the Order of St John. Convincing copies of these last three can sometimes be seen in a polished wooden showcase in the atmospheric old library, but maybe they're put away to make way for temporary exhibitions of varying interest to the visitor.

St George's Square/Misraħ San Ġorġ/Palace Square [112 D4] Right next to Republic Square is St George's Square, more commonly known as Palace Square because one side of it is taken up with the **Grand Master's Palace** (see below). The palace houses Malta's parliament and for a long time the square has been used as the MPs' car park. It has, however, just been refurbished with new paving, no cars, free Wi-Fi and a decorative fountain – low to the ground to allow it to be marched over during the national ceremonies that take place in this square.

St George's is the heart of the city. It was here, for instance, that the ceremony for the awarding of the George Cross to the nation of Malta was held in September 1942 and here that visiting dignitaries are officially received.

The Grand Master's Palace [112 D4] (*St George's Sq; ↘ 21249349; www.heritagemalta.org; ⊕ see below for details; joint admission to the State Rooms & Armoury: €10 adults, €7 over-60s/children aged 12–17/students, €5 child aged 6–11. If the State Rooms are closed, entry to the armoury alone costs €6/4.50/3; combined ticket available inc entry to other Heritage Malta museums, see page 105*) The first building on this site was built under Grand Master Jean de la Cassière (1572–81) and designed by Gerolamo Cassar along with much of the rest of Valletta at the time. It had a simple, almost severe exterior, now a little softened by some ornamentation and the long corner *gallarija* (a real gallery this one), which may have been responsible for starting the craze for these closed balconies across the city and the country (see boxed text, page 130). With numerous grand masterly extensions and additions, the palace reached its present shape in the mid-18th century.

Grand masters were based here until Napoleon took over in 1798. The palace subsequently became the headquarters of the British Governors of Malta and is now the office of the president, home to Malta's parliament (based in the Knights' original armoury) and to the Armoury (now in the old stable block).

When, or if, the planned renovation of the City Gate area is complete and the new parliament building opens, the MPs will move out of the Grand Master's Palace. The Armoury will then be able to move back to its original location (currently the parliament chamber) and more of the palace will be opened to the public.

The State Rooms (☉ *10.00–16.00 (last admission 15.30) daily, except Thu & when the president is using them*) There is (at the time of writing) no information for visitors at the State Rooms, so you may want to take this brief guide with you.

Up a winding, wooden staircase you enter a **painted gallery**, with a 19th-century coloured-marble floor, which runs round three sides of **Neptune's Courtyard**. The courtyard is named for the statue at its centre, moved here during British rule from its original position below the Upper Barracca Gardens (now a road) where it was part of a fountain installed in 1615 by Grand Master de Wignacourt to celebrate the completion of his aqueduct (see page 220). Beneath the statue, known locally as *Il-Ggant* ('The Giant') and said to resemble Wignacourt, was a waterspout from which the Knights' ships could fill up with water (see *Maritime Museum*, page 153).

The gallery is flanked by suits of armour and adorned with portraits of grand masters – quite telling as to what they thought of themselves. Nicolas Cotoner, for instance, sits severely in tall black hat and robes of the Order pointing at a map of the Mediterranean with fortifications all along its European coast. Doors off the galleries are the MPs' entrances to the Chamber of Parliament (not open to the public) and the five State Rooms.

Room I: Tapestry Room Named after the set of French Gobelins tapestries that hangs here. Known as the *Teintures des Indes,* they were made for the room in 1708–10 to exotic designs originating in a gift from a Dutch prince to Louis XIV of France. This is the only surviving full set of its kind.

The room itself – with its original coffered ceiling and paintings of naval battles against the Ottoman Turks – was the centre of the government of Malta for some four centuries. It was the meeting place first of the Council of the Order of St John, then of the Legislative Council under British rule and finally of Malta's Parliamentary Assembly (which began under British rule in 1921). The parliament continued to meet here after independence until it outgrew the room and moved in 1976 to the Knights' Armoury (the arms being removed to their present location; see page 128).

Room 2: Dining Room Rebuilt after a bomb hit it during World War II, this room now houses portraits of Malta's heads of state since Independence in 1964 – including Queen Elizabeth II who was Queen of Malta until it became a republic in 1974.

Room 3: Throne Room The grand master's ceremonial chamber was built in the reign of French Grand Master de la Cassière (1572–81). The coffered ceiling is original and the wall paintings showing scenes from the Great Siege of 1565 are by Italian artist Matteo Perez d'Aleccio (1547–1616), a pupil of Michelangelo who worked with him on the Sistine Chapel.

Under the British the room became known as the 'Hall of St Michael and St George' after the chivalric order created for the Maltese and Ionian islands. The minstrels' gallery is not original to the room and was probably moved here from the palace chapel. Like the Tapestry Room, the Throne Room has long retained its original function and is today still used by the President of Malta on state occasions.

Room 4: Pages Room (also known as the 'Yellow Room') This room originally linked the grand master's private quarters with the Throne Room and here the grand master's many young pages would await their orders. These boys of noble birth worked from age 12 on the promise that at 18 they could apply to be Knights.

Around the top of the walls are scenes from the history of the Order prior to its arrival in Malta. These pictures were painted in 1609 and the solidity of the figures along with the general style shows the influence of Caravaggio who was in Malta 1607–08. The narrative of the frieze can be followed through the Ambassadors' Room to link with the images of the Great Siege in the Throne Room.

Room 5: The Ambassadors' Room (also known as the 'Red Room') This was the grand master's audience room, used for meeting and greeting visting ambassadors and other dignitaries. It serves a similar purpose today for the President of Malta. The portraits (which are sometimes hard to see) are of 17th- and 18th-century monarchs and dignitaries.

The Armoury (⊕ *09.00–17.00 daily; audio guide inc in the entry fee, available in English, Maltese, French, German, Spanish or Italian*) Arms galore! If you are interested in period weaponry this place ranks high. It was a working armoury, intended to keep the Knights and their militias kitted out with the best European equipment, until Napoleon arrived in 1798. In fact, the Knights had just bought a whole batch of state-of-the-art weaponry for their militias in the 1780s which Napoleon no doubt found very useful. Certainly he depleted the collection, as did his British successors, and there is now a preponderance of hunting equipment over weapons of war.

One of the two rooms is dominated by armour, mainly European but with a little Ottoman as well. There is a fabulous black suit embossed with gold made for Grand Master de Wignacourt (1601–22) as well as a very fancy 16th-century cuirass engraved to look like a buttoned waistcoat. Other curiosities include helmets with eye shades to keep off the sun (looking rather like Darth Vader, but in fact dated 1600–30) and breastplates with a little lever that can be pulled out to act as an arm rest when metal-covered limbs get tired.

The Order's militiamen were issued with a helmet, a back plate and a breast plate (all on view here). A leather or quilted jacket was worn underneath for comfort, though with most campaigns fought in summer they must have been horrendously hot. If you were fat, your sides were left exposed – unless you were wealthy enough to order a made-to-measure suit of armour like the one at the end of the gallery on the left.

In the Ottoman showcase are some vast cannonballs (perhaps 45cm across). These were fired from a Turkish Great Siege battery in the area that is now Castille Square. At the end of the siege the Turks tipped their bronze cannons into the sea. The Knights recovered them and melted them down to cast the bells of St John's Co-Cathedral.

The other room is mostly weapons – from huge cannon to spears, swords, muskets and crossbows, thin guns that could be poked through defensive walls, and a flintlock rocket launcher (that looks like a mere rifle). There is a matchlock gun that could have been used in the Great Siege and a vast weighing machine for cannons, as well as some beautifully engraved horn powder flasks.

Republic Street – Lower (Fort St Elmo) end [113 F4] Below St George's Square and the Grand Master's Palace, Republic Street continues down towards the tip of the peninsula. Here you will find the unobtrusive entrance to Casa Rocca Piccola, the remaining section of a traditional 16th-century Maltese aristocratic townhouse open to the public, before reaching Fort St Elmo.

Casa Rocca Piccola [113 E4] (*74 Republic St between St Christopher St & St Dominic St;* ☏ *21221499; www.casaroccapiccola.com;* ⊕ *Mon–Sat for guided tours in English on the hour between 10.00 & 16.00 – written translations of the main points available in Italian, French, German, Spanish, & Hungarian;* €*7 adults,* €*3.50 students, children (under 12) free. There's* *a pleasant café/Italian restaurant, Bocconci, located in the old kitchens:* ☉ *11.00–16.00 & 19.00–22.00.*) The house is part of an original Valletta *palazzo* built around 1580 for Don Pietro La Rocca, Italian Admiral of the Order. He left it to the Langue of Italy, from where it passed into private hands when the Knights left Malta. In 1918 it was bought by the grandfather of the present owner and became the home of a distinguished Maltese noble family. If you are lucky you will be shown round this treasure trove of Maltese history by the 9th Marquis Nicholas de Piro (9th Baron Budach and a Knight of St John) – who describes the house as representing Maltese aristocratic 'aspiration, ambition and pretension' – or by his English Marchioness, Frances. Both are wonderfully well informed and full of good stories.

The house Highlights include a set of silver surgical instruments from the Knights' **Sacra Infermeria** (see below), dated to around 1780, and possibly the only remaining set; a Maltese **Knights-period chess set** with a grand master as king and a crownless queen to mark the Order's celibacy; and an almost new-looking golden **sedan chair** belonging to a French knight and former Captain of the Galleys, Fra Nicholas de Vachon Belmont. The knight was old and unwilling to leave Malta in 1798; the British found him penniless having sold his belongings (probably including this chair) to continue his charity work. He was given a small pension and eventually buried in the French chapel of St John's.

Amongst the **furniture** are a beautifully inlaid bureau constructed in 1640 and marked with the double-headed eagle of Grand Master Lascaris; a painted portable

THE MALTESE *GALLARIJA*

The Maltese *gallarija* is the enclosed painted wooden balcony with glass windows that is such a prominent feature of Malta's towns and villages. Yet, despite now being so closely associated with traditional Maltese architecture, when Valletta was first built in the 16th century, there were almost certainly no *gallariji* at all, only open stone balconies.

The origins of the *gallarija* are obscure. People used to think they were an Arab phenomenon pre-dating the Knights, but Maltese historian Judge Giovanni Bonnello points out that not only are all the names for the various parts of the balcony derived from Italian rather than any Semitic language, but the first evidence of a *gallarija* in Valletta is not until 1675, the date of the earliest known painting of the long *gallarija* of the Grand Master's Palace.

It seems quite likely that this was the first *gallarija* in Malta, which would explain the name; *gallarija* means 'gallery' not 'balcony' (Italian for 'balcony' is *balcone*) and the *gallarija* of the Grand Master's Palace is indeed a gallery – a long wooden walkway linking several of the palace rooms (see above). The grand master apparently strolled up and down here keeping an eye on the goings on in the streets and squares below.

This might also explain the sudden popularity of the enclosed wooden structures. If the palace has one, naturally everyone else wants one too! They might not be able to manage a whole gallery – but a shorter version, perhaps superimposed on an old stone balcony, is better than nothing. The craze lasted. While there are enclosed wooden balconies elsewhere in the world, the Maltese have made the *gallarija* their own.

chapel; and a wooden chest decorated with the cross of St John (the 'Maltese cross'; see page 32) which is reputed to be the oldest piece of Maltese domestic furniture in existence. Amongst the smallest items on display, don't miss the earrings given to the family by the Bishop of Gozo after they donated land for the building of the pilgrimage church at Ta' Pinu (see page 280).

There are some important **paintings** including interesting portraits and works by Mattia Preti (see page 126) and Antoine de Favray, and an exhibition of **Maltese costumes**. The *gallarija* is worth a visit too. It is one of the very few that still has the covered hole in the floor through which to check on who is arriving at the front door (do you wish to be in or are you diplomatically 'out'?) as well as a little shuttered window at child's eye level.

'Quarry', 'wells' and World War II shelters When Valletta was built, the stone for its buildings was mostly quarried on the spot – creating foundations as the stone for the house was removed. At Casa Rocca Piccola, beneath the house you can see part of the area from which stones were cut.

Valletta was always short of water, so every house had to have a 'well' – actually a cistern or stone tank where rain water collected from the roof was stored underground. Visitors can now walk down into Casa Rocca Piccola's largest cistern – a vast conical stone room – which was later used as part of a World War II shelter.

Nicholas de Piro's grandfather was convinced as early as 1935 that war was inevitable and built for his family the first shelter in Malta, a zigzag corridor (to protect from bomb blasts), and a tiny room with steps up into the house's little garden. Later, two much larger shelters were added offering protection to some 150 people.

Further information and souvenirs Nicholas de Piro has written an excellent short **guidebook** to the house and his family: *Casa Rocca Piccola (Insight Heritage Guides; €6.99)*. He is also the author/editor of several books on Maltese art and history (see *Further reading*, page 301). These, along with souvenirs, can be bought in the house shop.

Fort St Elmo [113 G4] (*Not generally open to the public but can be viewed from the outside. Occasional re-enactments take place inside the fort allowing access to it – see below*) At the bottom of Republic Street on the tip of the Sciberras Peninsula is Fort St Elmo. A watchtower and a chapel (dedicated to St Elmo) stood on this point from 1488 (before the Knights arrived) and in 1552 this solid star-shaped fort was built in anticipation of attack by the Turks. The fort was indeed the first target of Ottoman attack in the Great Siege of 1565 and despite heavy bombardment from three sides it held out for a month. Fort St Elmo fell on 23 June with the loss of 1,500 men including all the defending Knights. Nine Maltese swam across the Grand Harbour to safety. The Turks suffered far heavier losses including their greatest corsair and strategist Dragut Reis who may have been killed by what we would now call 'friendly fire'. After the siege, Fort St Elmo was rebuilt and incorporated into the fortifications of the new capital, Valletta.

In the Priest's Uprising of 1775 the fort was seized by the rebels. The Maltese flag flew briefly over Fort St Elmo and St James Cavalier, but the Knights' reaction was swift and the flags were soon replaced with the heads of three of the conspirators. Napoleon turned the place into a French prison but the British returned it to its defensive purpose. Malta's first victims of World War II fell here, casualties of the first Italian bombing raid. The fort was instrumental in repelling an attack by E-boats (small enemy gunboats that were then the fastest on the water) on the Grand Harbour in 1941.

Fort St Elmo is now the Maltese police academy and can only be viewed from the outside, except when there is a re-enactment (see below). The National War Museum (also below) is in part of the lower fort but it does not really show you anything of the building. Just outside the fortress gates is a large flat forecourt. The substantial round slabs of stones raised from the ground here are openings to the Knights' granaries or fosse – stores for the crucial grain that Malta has, since at least Roman times, had to import for its staple diet of bread.

For the media-minded, the lower bastion (now closed to the public even during re-enactments) was used as the Turkish prison in the 1970s film *Midnight Express*, and in the strategic computer game *Age of Empires III* you can defend Fort St Elmo against the Ottoman Turks.

Knights-period re-enactments in Fort St Elmo (*Performances are trilingual – in English, French & German; dates from the Malta Tourism Authority* ⤴ *21237747; e info@ visitmalta.com; www.visitmalta.com; €5 adults, €3 children & students*) Re-enactments take place occasionally at 11.00 on the central parade ground, flanked by 18th-century barracks whose balconies make a shady place from which to watch the performance. The gates are opened about 45 minutes early for ticket-holders to explore the fort. There is a little barrel-vaulted chapel on the site of St Elmo's Chapel. It is now dedicated to St Anne and is a mix of late Renaissance and Baroque. The fortified structures are mostly in quite poor repair, but you certainly get the defensive idea!

There are two different re-enactments:

In Guardia A 40-minute performance of an inspection by the Grand Bailiff of the Order to ensure the fort was battle ready. It is all in Knights-period costumes with pikemen, swordsmen, musketeers, ensigns of the various *langues* and demonstrations of weapons. It starts off a bit slowly (particularly due to the repetition of commentary in three languages) but the cannon-fire towards the end is impressive.

Alarme Held less frequently, this is a 55-minute re-enactment of a military encounter between Maltese militias and French forces (1798–1800).

National War Museum [113 G3] (*Lower Fort St Elmo;* ⤴ *21222430; e info@ heritagemalta.org; www.visitmalta.com/national-war-museum-map, www.heritagemalta.org;* ⊕ *09.00–17.00 daily; €6 adults, €4.50 over-60s/children 12–17/students, €3 children, children under 6 go free; combined ticket inc entry to other Heritage Malta museums, see page 105*) Newly refurbished, the War Museum covers the two world wars from both a general and Maltese perspective with lots of information and a number of interesting exhibits.

The small World War I section looks at Malta's role as the 'Nurse of the Mediterranean' (*see Chapter 1, History*, page 15), the tension between the British and the French (the latter had been given the job of controlling the Mediterranean), and German prisoners of war in Malta who included Rudolf Hess and Admiral Karl Doenitz (who at the end of World War II briefly succeeded Hitler as the Führer).

The World War II displays are more extensive and include the Gloster Sea Gladiator plane *Faith* (minus wings) which was one of only four planes in Malta when Italy declared war in June 1940. They were nicknamed *Faith*, *Hope* and *Charity* (plus an unnamed reserve) and by February 1941 only *Faith* survived. She lost her wings in the bombing of a nearby hangar. There is a copy of the George Cross and the letter from George VI that came with it, as well as *Husky* – the jeep used by General Eisenhower when he was based in Malta.

At this point you can of course choose to explore the sites next to Fort St Elmo on the Grand Harbour side (The Malta Experience, Knights' Hospital, etc – see page 137) and indeed walk along the fortifications beyond them (page 138) back towards City Gate. You could, of course, also turn the other way and follow the fortifications overlooking Marsamxett Harbour (page 135 – although they are listed from the other end coming towards Fort St Elmo). If you take the Grand Harbour side first, you could do a full circuit of the fortifications following the text down the Marsamxett side, returning to this point to pick up the next part of the route into the middle of town.

Interesting archive footage plays on television screens giving a sense of the damage the island suffered. Gozo was hardly bombed, but there is a small display explaining its role in (somewhat reluctantly) providing grain to sustain the country in its second Great Siege, relieved only with the arrival of the Pedestal convoy in August 1942.

A milestone with its information scraped out is a reminder of the British policy of removing all geographic information to confuse any enemy who might land on the island. You may see such milestones around the country.

Strait Street/Triq Id-Dejqa [112 D3] Running on the other side from Merchants Street, parallel with Republic Street, is Strait Street, known in the days of the British Navy in Malta as 'The Gut'. The street had a dubious reputation even in the days of the Knights when it was the favourite place for a duel, but it really came into its insalubrious own as the place where British sailors came to relax. At the lower end (nearest Fort St Elmo), it was Valletta's red light district full of bars, dance halls and establishments of ill repute. The life of The Gut came to an abrupt halt when the last of the Royal Navy departed in 1979. Some of the prostitutes moved to Gzira (next to Sliema) and Strait Street is now an ordinary – if rather grubby – street.

Turning off Strait Street into **Archbishop Street** (towards Marsamxett Harbour) you pass the **Archbishop's Palace** (the building with two large columns taking up the pavement), designed by Tommaso Dingli in 1622 (with the second storey added in the 1950s), before you reach **Independence Square**.

Independence Square/Misraħ Independenza [112 D2] This square is dominated by St Paul's Anglican Cathedral, built on the site of the Auberge d'Allemagne (home of the German Knights), which was pulled down to make way for it in 1839. Directly opposite stands the Auberge d'Aragon which, of all the surviving *auberges*, has remained closest to its original state.

The Auberge d'Aragon [112 D2] The Auberge of Aragon, Catalonia and Navarre to give it its full name, is the only surviving *auberge* not to have received the Baroque treatment. It is largely untouched and its plain façade and simple courtyard give you an idea of what all the *auberges* would originally have looked like. The building is now the Ministry of Justice and during office hours you can go into the front hall and look into the central courtyard. This used to be the office of the prime minister (1921–72) before he moved to the Auberge de Castille (see page 117) and there is a plaque listing all of Malta's prime ministers up to that point, as well as one naming the Knights' 'venerable drapers' (1539–1796) – always members of the Langue D'Aragon.

Valletta **WHAT TO SEE AND DO**

5

St Paul's Anglican Cathedral [112 D2] (*St Paul's Pro-Cathedral, Independence Sq;* *21225714;* **e** *anglican@onvol.net; www.anglicanmalta.org;* ⊕ *08.30–17.00 approx*) This Neoclassical cathedral was built in 1839–44 after the Dowager Queen Adelaide, widow of William IV (and Queen Victoria's aunt), visited Malta and was horrified to find no proper Anglican church. The Anglican congregation (or those who could fit in) met in a room in the Grand Master's Palace. Queen Adelaide put up £20,000 and work began immediately – the old Auberge of the German Langue being knocked down to make way for the new church. Its 200ft spire can now be seen from all over Valletta.

In the very plain interior are memorial plaques naming all the units of British and Commonwealth forces that took part in World War II in Malta. Army, navy and air force are listed on oak panels around the sanctuary, Merchant Navy on the north wall and submariners on a plaque outside facing northwest towards Manoel Island, where the submarines were based.

There is **sung Eucharist** in English every Sunday at 11.00 as well as other services (details at http://www.anglicanmalta.org/b.services.html).

Old Theatre Street/Triq Il-Teatru L-Antik [112 D3] If you walk one block up West Street/Triq Il-Punent (towards City Gate) from Independence Square and turn left into Old Theatre Street you will come to the Santuary Basilica of Our Lady of Mount Carmel, an odd combination of old and new, and then to the Manoel Theatre, one of Europe's oldest functioning theatres (see below).

The Sanctuary Basilica of Our Lady of Mount Carmel [112 D3] (*Old Theatre St,* *between Old Mint St & West St;* ⊕ *06.00–12.00 & 16.00–19.30; entry fee (not for Mass)* €*1*) This is Valletta's newest church built between 1958 and 1981, but its history goes back 400 years. The first church on this site dated from 1570, but it was so badly damaged in World War II that total reconstruction was needed. The new church, with its 42m-high elliptical dome, was designed to ensure that the spire of a Protestant church (the Anglican cathedral) did not alone dominate the skyline of Valletta. The façade is very unassuming and the interior cavernous and quite plain. The church contains several paintings by Mattia Preti (see page 126) and the 17th-century picture of Our Lady of Mount Carmel above the high altar (curtained off except when the church is open to visitors and on special occasions) is considered to have miraculous powers.

Manoel Theatre [112 D3] (*115 Old Theatre St, between Old Mint St & Old Bakery St;* ↘ *21246389;* **e** *bookings@teatrumanoel.com.mt; www.teatrumanoel.com.mt. Free podcast* *about the theatre at: www.visitmalta.com/podcasts. Tours of the theatre run every 45mins from* *10.15 to 17.30 Mon–Fri, 10.15–12.30 Sat;* €*4pp. Performances throughout the year except* *in summer, when the theatre gets too hot.*) One of the oldest theatres still in use in Europe, the Manoel was commissioned by Grand Master Antonio Manoel de Vilhena in 1731 and run by the Knights for their own and the population's 'honest entertainment'. The interior, with tiers of gilded boxes, has legendarily accurate acoustics and is best enjoyed at a performance. A tour, however, is the only way to see the **museum** which displays among other things costumes, old sound-effects machines and early programmes (some painted on silk). There is a delightful little **café** in the courtyard which has a retracting roof making it suitable for all weathers (see *Where to eat*).

Old Mint St/Triq Iz-Zekka [112 D3] Walk 200–300m up Old Mint Street to the junction with South Street/Triq Nofs-in-Nhar and you will come to the **National Museum of Fine Arts** (see below). At the end of Old Mint Street is **St John**

Cavalier, twin to St James Cavalier (on the other side of City Gate; see page 118). St John Cavalier is smaller and now houses the Embassy of the Knights of St John in Malta (not open to the public). Beyond the cavalier, and a little to the right between St John's and St Michael's bastions, you will find **Hastings Gardens**.

The National Museum of Fine Arts [112 B3] (*South St, cnr with Old Mint St;* \ *22954341 or 21225769;* e *info@heritagemalta.org; www.heritagemalta.org;* ⊕ *09.00–17.00 daily; €5 adults, €3.50 over-60s/children aged 12–17/students, €2.50 children aged 6–11, children under 6 go free; combined ticket available inc entry to other Heritage Malta museums, see page 105*) Originally built in 1571 for a prominent knight, and remodelled in 1761 for another, this *palazzo* was later home to the British naval commander and so from 1821 to 1961 was known as Admiralty House. It became a museum in the 1970s and now houses an extensive collection of paintings, sculptures, objets d'art and furniture, particularly Maltese and Italian.

On the ground floor is a room of **British artists'** impressions of Malta. Amongst these are a handful of evocative little watercolour sketches by **Edward Lear** (1812–88) who spent time on both Malta and Gozo in the 1860s, as well as a single watercolour by **J M W Turner**. This is Turner's only painting of Malta, a country he never visited. It is done from a view by another artist, probably George Philip Reinagle (1802–35). The scene looks at Valletta from Ricasoli Point on the far side of the Grand Harbour and was done for a series of engravings of places visited by Lord Byron (who was in Malta in 1809 and 1811). Perhaps for this reason, the picture is precise and lacks any sign of Turner's more impressionistic work.

Upstairs is an excellent and substantial collection of the work of **Mattia Preti** (see boxed text, page 126 and www.maltaart.com/pretismall) including his large *Martyrdom of St Catherine of Alexandria* and a *St Sebastian* that clearly shows the influence of Caravaggio. Also a wonderful *St Francis of Paola* by Jusepe de Ribera (1591–1652).

In a side room on the ground floor and all around the courtyard at lower-ground level are exhibitions of work by **contemporary Maltese artists** (some of high quality) which change monthly. Also on the lower ground is *Les Gavroches*, a sculpture of street urchins by Malta's most famous modern sculptor **Antonio Sciortino** (1879–1947) which used to stand in the Upper Barracca Gardens (see page 118) and has been moved here for conservation reasons. A copy stands in its original place.

Hastings Gardens [112 B2] (*Entrance on Ordnance St/Triq L-Ordinanza*) A pleasant public garden and a great place to get a sense of Valletta's defences: look back towards Valletta at the twin cavaliers (St James and St John) guarding its landward side, then stand looking away from the city for the view of the defender. Note how thick the walls are and the several large cannons that still point out through their own firing channels (embrasures) towards Floriana. Further along (away from City Gate) are views of Marsamxett Harbour (see below).

At the centre of the garden is a colonnaded **monument** with a reclining figure of the first Marquis of Hastings, a distinguished British soldier, Governor General of India and Governor of Malta 1824–26 who died at sea in the Mediterranean and is buried here.

Fortifications on the Marsamxett Harbour side From Hastings Gardens you can follow the fortifications round past **St Michael's Bastion** [112 B2] (in the equivalent position to the Upper Barracca Gardens on the other side of town) to **St Andrew's Bastion** [112 C2]. Just inland from here, in the 1580s Biagio Steps

Building, on St Mark Street and Melita Street, a **Fortifications Information Centre** is expected to open late 2010 or 2011. It will contain models, interactive exhibits and a user-friendly database covering all of Malta's defences. In the meantime, an **MTA podcast** on Valletta's fortifications, with Stephen Spiteri, the top expert on the subject, can be downloaded free at www.visitmalta.com/podcasts.

The main road that starts as **Great Siege Road** running round the outside of the city walls from Floriana, enters Valletta here through the fortifications (which house the **Two Twenty Two Restaurant**; see *Where to eat*, page 111) becoming **Marsamxett Street/Triq Marsamxett**. A steep slope leads down from here to the **Sliema ferry** (see page 106) and a **water polo lido**.

This area, around today's **Mattia Preti Square** [112 C2], used to be known as **The Mandragg** and sometimes still is. The Knights planned to dig a vast hole here to create a sheltered harbour (a *manderaggio*) to serve the same function for Valletta as the natural creeks of the Three Cities had served in Birgu (Vittoriosa). The project was soon abandoned and the semi-sunken area became a slum. At the start of the 20th century some 2,500 people were living here in a space the size of 2.5 football pitches. It was cleared and redeveloped into social housing in the 1950s.

Continuing, you pass along the **German Curtain Wall** [112 D2] (the part of the fortifications that were the responsibility of the German Langue whose *auberge* was nearby in Independence Square; see page 133) to **St Sebastian Bastion** and the **Gunpost**, a World War II gun tower that now contains a small bar.

There are clear views of **Marsamxett Harbour**, **Manoel Island** and the ugly modern developments on the Sliema Waterfront, including the massive building site that (at the time of writing) surrounds **Fort Tigné**, a late Knights' fort built in 1792. The fort sits on the tip of Sliema known as **Dragut Point** after its use by Turkish leader Dragut Reis to position cannons to attack Fort St Elmo during the Great Siege.

The walls now become the **English Curtain** [113 E2] breached by the **Jews Sally Port**, an unobtrusive way through the fortifications for Knights' sorties. It is unclear why the Jewish connection – the gateway has had this name since at least the 1580s and although some people say it was so called because it was the only entrance through which Jews visiting Valletta were allowed to pass, there is no actual documentary evidence to say this.

Opposite the English Curtain is the **Auberge de Bavière** (see below) – a late addition to the Knights' *auberges*. Past the English Curtain the French took over responsibility for defence and the **French Curtain** leads to **Fort St Elmo** (see above page 131).

Auberge de Bavière [113 E3] (*31 Marsamxetto Rd, cnr of West St opposite the English Curtain, can only be viewed from outside*) The Bavarians had long wanted their own *langue* (separate from the rest of the Germans) when in 1782 the grand master finally gave his permission. However, the Knights did not want to raise the number of *langues* above the existing eight. Since there were hardly any English knights, the Bavarian king persuaded the Hanoverian George III to combine forces and, in 1783, Palazzo Carnerio, built as a private house in 1696, became the *auberge* of the Anglo-Bavarian Langue. The English continued to defend the English Curtain (see above) and the Bavarians were put in charge of the St Lazarus Bastion just the other side of Fort St Elmo. The *palazzo* is now government offices.

Mediterranean Street/Triq Il-Mediterran [113 F5] If you walk away from Fort St Elmo towards the **Grand Harbour** you pass the **St Lazarus Bastion** [113 F5] (on your left overlooking the harbour) before reaching a small clutch of other sights right next to each other.

The Malta Experience [113 F5] (*St Elmo Bastions, Mediterranean St/Triq Il-Mediterran;* ℡ *21243776 or 21251284; www.themaltaexperience.com; shows on the hour: 11.00–16.00 Mon–Fri, 11.00–13.00 w/ends (14.00 Oct–Jun); €9.50 adults, €6.50 students, €4.50 children under 14. Commentary available in 15 languages.*) The Malta Experience is the best of the various audiovisual shows around the country. Though a bit expensive, it offers a very good 45-minute introduction to the country, a romp through Malta's 7,000-year history and some great photography. The cinema is actually part of the Knights' Hospital, the Sacra Infermeria (see below), though the way in to this is now across the road. There is a **café** at the entrance and if you go through to the terrace on its far side you can avoid the crowds and enjoy marvellous views over the Grand Harbour.

Sacra Infermeria – the Knights' Hospital [113 F5] (*Mediterranean St/Triq Il-Mediterran, at the end of Merchants St, opposite the Malta Experience. To look around (subject to use by conference delegates), ask the doorman nicely or pay for the Knights Hospitallers heritage attraction, open ⊕ 09.30–16.30 Mon–Fri, 09.30–16.00 Sat, Sun & public hols;* ℡ *21417334;* m *99494590;* e *r.cassar@global.net.mt; www.knightshospitallers.com.mt; €4.30 adults, €2.90 students/seniors, €2 children, children under 7 go free*) Now the Mediterranean Conference Centre (℡ *25595215;* e *sales@mcc.com.mt; www.mcc.com.mt)*, the Sacra Infermeria was built in 1574. This was the Knights' hospital, central to the Order and known throughout Europe for its quality of care. In the early days, all knights – even the grand master – took their turn caring for the sick. All medical instruments and dishes were silver because the Knights knew it had anti-infection properties, patients had a bed each (unusual at the time) and there was a lavatory by each bed (unusual even today!).

The 155m **Long Ward** is one of the longest halls in Europe, its unsupported roof recognised at the time of its construction in the 16th century as a serious architectural feat. It is on the ground floor next to the main entrance so you may be allowed a peep in here even when other parts of the building are shut.

In winter the ward used to be hung with 131 (insulating) tapestries, in summer with paintings by Mattia Preti. All classes and nationalities were treated – though in different wards – but no women. Non-Catholics wishing to stay on the Long Ward (the best ward) for more than three days had to accept religious instruction, though there is no record of any conversions.

Off the Long Ward is a small **chapel** (1712) next to the **Sallette** – the ward for the dying. The **central courtyard** of the Infermeria has been roofed over and is now the 1,400-seat **Republic Hall** – the main venue of the conference centre – but you can still see some of the original arches. The vaulted **Magazine Ward** in the basement is used for dinners as well as housing **Knights Hospitallers**, a 'heritage attraction' consisting of recreated scenes from the time of the Knights.

When the Knights were thrown out by Napoleon in 1798, the hospital was declared to be for French troops only and when the British took over it became the British Military Hospital. So it remained until after World War I, in which it played a significant role. It was badly bombed in World War II and remained largely unusable until its award-winning renovation and conversion in the 1970s.

The Siege Bell Memorial [113 F6] At the far end of the Sacra Infermeria, overlooking the Grand Harbour is the Siege Bell memorial that honours the 7,000 service personnel and civilians who died during the 'Siege of Malta' that took place from 1940 to 1943. A Neoclassical cupola containing a 12-ton bell that tolls daily at noon (mind your ears), the memorial was unveiled by Queen Elizabeth II in 1992 – the 50th anniversary of the award of the George Cross by her father to the people of Malta. Between the bell and the water is a **monument to World War II**

5

sailors lost at sea – a bronze statue of a sailor being prepared for water burial. On the other side is a *boċċi* **club**. *Boċċi* is a traditional Maltese game a little like boules (see boxed text, page 292).

Lower Barracca Gardens/Lower Barrakka Gardens [113 E6] Just beyond the

Siege Bell monument is the Lower Barracca Gardens, a colonnaded public garden smaller than the Upper Barracca Garden (see page 118) and – funnily enough – a little lower, but still affording good views of the Grand Harbour, as does much of this side of the bastion walls of Valletta (see below). The central **monument** is to Sir Alexander Ball, the British captain, later admiral, who was instrumental in taking Malta from the French. He went on to become Malta's hugely popular first governor.

Below the Lower Barracca Gardens (outside the city walls on the harbour side) is Valletta's wholesale **fish market** (⊕ *approx 04.30–06.30*).

The Grand Harbour fortifications: Lower Barracca to Upper Barracca

Continuing up **Mediterranean Street/Triq il-Mediterran** [113 E6], you follow the **Castille Curtain** [112 D6] (the part of the bastions defended by the Langue of Castille). Stay next to the Grand Harbour and you will find yourself on **St Barbara Street/Triq Santa Barbara** [112 D6] and **St Barbara Bastion** [112 D6], a lovely row of 19th-century houses looking straight out over the Grand Harbour – one of the most sought-after addresses in Valletta. The fortifications

THE BIBLE STORY OF ST PAUL'S SHIPWRECK ON MALTA

Paul is a prisoner on a ship *en route* to Rome where he is to be judged by Caesar and this account is said to be by his travelling companion St Luke:

ACTS 27: 20–24, 36–39, 41–44

And when neither sun nor stars in many days appeared, and no small tempest lay on us, all hope that we should be saved was then taken away.

But after long abstinence Paul stood forth in the midst of them, and said, 'Sirs, ye should have hearkened unto me, and not have loosed from Crete, and to have gained this harm and loss.

And now I exhort you to be of good cheer: for there shall be no loss of any man's life among you, but of the ship.

For there stood by me this night the angel of God, whose I am, and whom I serve.

Saying "Fear not, Paul; thou must be brought before Caesar: and, lo, God hath given thee all them that sail with thee."'

[...]

Then they were all of good cheer, and they also took some meat.

And we were in all in the ship two hundred threescore and sixteen souls.

And when they had eaten enough, they lightened the ship, and cast out the wheat into the sea.

And when it was day, they knew not the land: but they discovered a certain creek with a shore, into the which they were minded if it were possible, to thrust the ship.

[...]

And falling into a place where two seas met, they ran the ship aground; and the forepart stuck fast, and remained unmoveable, but the hinder part was broken with the violence of the waves.

And the soldiers counsel was to kill the prisoners, lest any of them should swim out, and escape.

But the centurion, willing to save Paul, kept them from their purpose; and commanded that they which could swim should cast themselves first into the sea, and get to land:

continue from here up to meet the high walls supporting the Saluting Battery and the Upper Barracca Gardens (see above, page 118). If you have already been here, however, turn inland up St Lucy Street/Triq Santa Luċija to find one of Malta's most important churches.

Church of St Paul's Shipwreck [112 D5] (*St Paul St, tourist entrance from St Lucy St/Triq Santa Luċija;* ⊕ *09.00–19.00*) The Church of St Paul's Shipwreck celebrates the stormy arrival of St Paul on Malta in AD60 – an event many Maltese see as the foundation of the nation's Christianity (see *History*, page 8). First built in the 1570s, the present church dates to later in the 16th century. It is large and richly painted with coloured marble tombstones along the nave, marble columns and multiple domes.

The polychrome wood and gilt **statue of St Paul** (in the niche to your left as you enter the church from the sacristy) was carved in about 1657 by Maltese sculptor Melchiorre Gafa (brother of Lorenzo Gafá who redesigned the church in 1680, as well as designing Mdina Cathedral). It is the one carried in procession for the important feast of St Paul's Shipwreck on 10 February – when tradition has it that it always rains!

In the **Chapel of St Joseph** to the right of the high altar is an important relic: 'the right wrist-bone of St Paul' contained in a golden forearm. Here too is a piece of marble column topped with the severed head of St Paul in silver. The stone is said to be part of the 'pillar of St Paul' on which the saint was executed. It was given

And the rest, some on boards and some on broken piece of the ship. And so it came to pass, that they escaped all safe to land.

ACTS 28: 1–11

And when they were escaped, then they knew that the island was called Melita.

And the barbarous people showed us no little kindness: for they kindled a fire, and received us every one, because of the present rain, and because of the cold.

And when Paul had gathered a bundle of sticks, and laid them on the fire, there came a viper out of the heat, and fastened on his hand.

And when the barbarians saw the venomous beast hang on his hand, they said among themselves, 'No doubt this man is a murderer, whom, though he hath escaped the sea, yet vengeance suffereth not to live.'

And he shook off the beast into the fire, and felt no harm.

Howbeit they looked when he should have swollen, or fallen down dead suddenly: but after they had looked a great while, and saw no harm come to him, they changed their minds, and said that he was a god.

In the same quarters were possessions of the chief man of the island, whose name was Publius; who received us, and lodged us three days courteously.

And it came to pass, that the father of Publius lay sick of a fever and a bloody flux: to whom Paul entered in, and prayed, and laid his hands on him, and healed him.

So when this was done, others also, which had diseases in the island, came, and were healed:

Who also honoured us with many honours; and when we departed, they laded us with such things as were necessary.

And after three months we departed in a ship of Alexandria which had wintered in the isle...

From the Authorised King James *version of* The Bible.

to the church by Pope Pius VII in 1817 in recognition of its work during the plague of 1813.

There are various **paintings** of the life of St Paul. The most important, the altarpiece from the original church by Matteo Perez D'Allecio (1580), is unfortunately ill lit and quite hard to see. The **side chapels** are interesting: each belongs to a particular confraternity (guild) and there are signs explaining their roles and their contributions to the church. The cobblers for instance made an annual donation of one pair of shoes to the rector.

St Paul Street/Triq San Pawl and back to City Gate Running most of the length of the city just to the Grand Harbour side of Merchants Street (see page 120), St Paul Street is the only street in Valletta to have retained its original 16th-century name.

At number 22 [112 C5], on the corner with St Christopher Street, is the workshop of one of the few remaining **Maltese clockmakers**. Maltese clocks are sizeable wall clocks with brightly painted faces and much gold leaf. They traditionally have only one hand ('The Maltese aren't that bothered about time' a local jokingly explains). Here you can watch Pierre Darmanin at work (m *99822281;* e *dittadarmanin_gilders@yahoo.com*). He is the fifth generation of his family to make clocks and his daughter is now joining the business.

Also on St Paul Street, though with the public entrance round the corner in Merchants Street, is the **Old University** [112 C5], now the offices of Heritage Malta and others. Built as a Jesuit college (Collegium Melitense) in 1595–1602, it offered the first higher education in Malta (albeit, of course, primarily religious). During Carnival of 1639 some over-excited knights attacked the building which led to Grand Master Lascaris making himself and the Jesuits very unpopular by severely limiting future carnival celebrations.

In 1676 Grand Master Cotoner founded Malta's first medical school here and in 1769, after the Jesuits had been expelled from the country for political interference, it became Malta's first university.

Next door is the old **Jesuit church** [112 D5] (⊕ *09.00–12.00 & sometimes early evening*). Originally 16th century, the church was rebuilt in the 1630s and '40s after an explosion at a nearby powder store damaged both it and the college. It was designed by Italian military engineer Francesco Buonamici to echo the plan of the Jesuit church in Rome. In the fourth side chapel on the left are an altarpiece and lunettes by Mattia Preti.

From here, to get back to the City Gate area, you can either walk towards the Grand Harbour and up the steps past some lovely (if faded) old buildings on **Ursula Street/Triq Sant'Orsla**, or simply follow St Paul Street or Merchants Street back to Castille Square (page 115 above), South Street and Freedom Square.

FLORIANA

Floriana is Valletta's suburb sitting just outside City Gate filling the gap between the defensive walls of Valletta and the later fortifications, the **Floriana Lines**. It is not a must for visitors but there are a few places of interest. Places to stay in Floriana are detailed along with Valletta accommodation (page 108). Strictly speaking, both of 'Valletta's' five-star hotels are in Floriana, along with the Valletta Waterfront where the sea plane and the Sicily ferry dock.

WHAT TO SEE AND DO

The Floriana Lines In 1634 Grand Master Antoine de Paule became convinced that the Turks were planning another attack on Malta and appealed to the Pope for

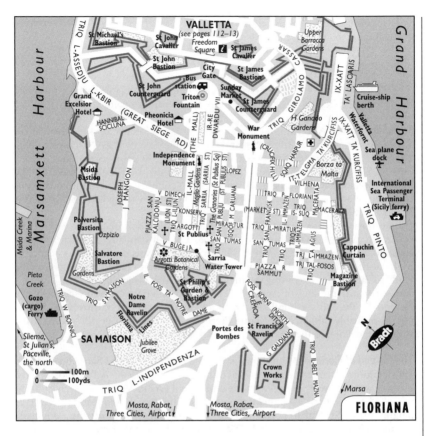

help to strengthen Malta's defences. Pope Urban VIII sent Italian military engineer, Pietro Paolo Floriani, to help. Floriani designed a hugely ambitious plan for a defensive system spanning the Sciberras Peninsula on Valletta's landward flank – and set to cost more than all of Valletta's existing fortifications put together. Work began in 1636, but by 1638 Floriani was fed up with constant criticism of his expensive plans and returned to Italy where he promptly died.

His successor, Vincenzo da Firenzuola, was more concerned with the defence of the south side of the harbour and work shifted to the **Margarita Lines** enclosing the Three Cities. Progress on the Floriana Lines resumed in 1640 after a visit from Giovanni de' Medici; the defences were eventually completed with the help of French military engineer De Tigné. There is a good view of the Floriana Lines from **St Philip's Garden** (see below).

The town The town was planned in 1724 under the rule of Grand Master de Vilhena. Although it suffered enormous damage during World War II, the layout remains largely original. Floriana centres on two parallel streets, **The Mall** and **Sarria Street**, which run straight from the Triton Fountain by City Gate bus station to the defensive walls at the other end of town, a few hundred metres away.

The narrow strip of garden between them is **Maglio Gardens**, originally created by Grand Master de Lascaris (1636–57) as a place for young knights to exercise. He had this inscribed in Latin on the wall:

Here perish sloth, here perish cupid's darts
Knights, on you this place I now bestow
Here play your games and harden your warrior hearts
Let not wine, women or dice bring you low.

The closest thing to his games ground remaining is the neighbouring (and much used) football pitch on what was once the British parade ground.

St Publius Square Also running almost the length of Floriana, on the other side of Sarria Street, is St Publius Square, commonly known as 'Il-Fosos' ('The Granaries'). It is dotted with raised circular stones (the same as the ones outside Fort St Elmo above) which cover the openings into the Knights' stores for the island's precious grain. Some 5,000 tons of grain could be stored in the conical pits beneath this square – crucial at times of siege. They were reused during World War II and are still in good repair.

The huge Floriana parish **Church of St Publius** dominates one end of the square. It was originally built in 1733–68, but substantially restructured after sustaining bomb damage in World War II. St Publius was the Roman governor of Malta at the time of St Paul's shipwreck and was said to have been converted by Paul to Christianity, becoming the first Bishop of Malta (see page 8). This church's *festa* – towards the end of April – opens the summer *festa* season (see page 31). Behind St Publius's Church is the much smaller circular **Church of Sarria** (1676) probably designed by Mattia Preti (see boxed text, page 126) who, at the very least, decorated the interior.

The far end of Floriana Beyond this, at the end of The Mall and Sarria Street is the 19th-century botanical **Argotti Gardens** (⊕ *09.00–19.00 daily*) and a 17th-century **water tower**, carved with the emblem of Grand Master de Wignacourt to whose Mdina–Valletta aqueduct it was once attached (see boxed text, page 220). In neighbouring **St Philip's Gardens** is the **Wignacourt Fountain**, originally created in St George's Square in 1615 to celebrate the arrival of the first water along the aqueduct. The gardens sit atop **St Philip Bastion** with a great view of the Floriana Lines and the **Portes des Bombes,** through (and now around) which all road traffic must pass to get into Floriana and thence Valletta. The gate was built in 1697–1720 as a single arch with a drawbridge, but was extended in the 19th century when the defensive walls around it were dismantled to improve traffic flow.

6

The Three Cities

Across the Grand Harbour from Valletta are the Three Cities. They lie around Dockyard Creek (called Galley Creek by the Knights), one of the natural hideaways that have made Malta so attractive to maritime powers through the ages. Behind Fort St Angelo lies **Birgu** (pronounced *Beergoo*), the Knights' first capital in Malta which still oozes history from its narrow streets. It was renamed Vittoriosa after the Great Siege victory of 1565, but locals have never really taken to the 'new' name. On the other side of the creek is **Senglea** (pronounced *Sengleea*), originally called L-Isla (pronounced *Leezla*). Between Senglea and Birgu at the head of the creek is the relative newcomer, and these days the poor relation, **Cospicua** or Bormla.

Each of these 'cities' is actually a small town only a few hundred metres across with little other than a length of military ditch to divide them. The three really became one when they were enclosed together within the Knights' improved 17th-century defences, the Margarita Lines and the massive Cottonera Lines, which still run 5km around the landward side of the cities. This enclosure led to the area being known as the Cottonera District. The name the 'Three Cities' was coined much later by Napoleon's General Vaubois in 1798.

The Three Cities were at the centre of both Malta's historic sieges. In 1565 it was from Birgu and L-Isla that the Knights resupplied Fort St Elmo and held out against the Turks. In World War II, the cities' proximity to the Grand Harbour meant that they bore the brunt of the bombing (it has been estimated that in one month – April 1942 – over 3,156 tons of bombs fell on the Three Cities). It is amazing how much of Birgu has survived, whilst, in each of the sieges, Bormla/Cospicua was more or less destroyed.

For the rest of the 20th century, the Three Cities deteriorated, not helped by the departure of the Royal Navy in the late 1970s and the closure of the dockyards. By the 1990s the area was in a sad state. A revitalisation project for Birgu has made a significant difference with the renovation of some of the Knights-period buildings, a new yacht marina and the Vittoriosa Waterfront now full of cafés and restaurants. Senglea has received less attention and Cospicua almost none.

GETTING THERE AND AWAY

GETTING THERE

By bus Buses 1, 2, 4 and 6 go from Valletta bus station to Birgu stopping at the bus station just outside the defensive walls, next to the main fortified entrance (the Three Gates). The 1, 2 and 6 go on to Cospicua, the 4 to Kalkara. Bus 3 goes from Valletta to Senglea and the 300 links Birgu and Senglea directly with Żabbar and Paola.

By car Cars can be parked outside the Three Gates or driven into town via the Gate of Provence, a modern breach in the defences further along the walls (there is parking on the streets).

6

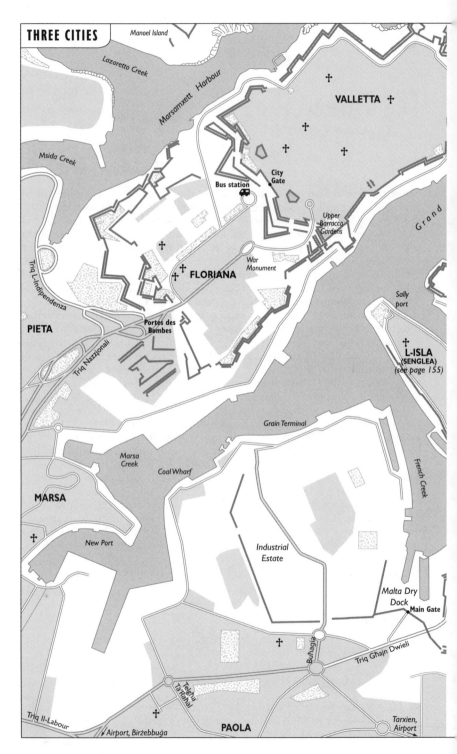

THREE CITIES

Manoel Island

Lazaretto Creek

Marsamxett Harbour

Msida Creek

VALLETTA ✝

Bus station

City Gate

Upper Barracca Gardens

FLORIANA

War Monument

Triq L-Indipendenza

Grand

Sally port

PIETA

Portes des Bombes

L-ISLA (SENGLEA) (see page 155)

Triq Nazzjonali

Grain Terminal

French Creek

Marsa Creek

Coal Wharf

MARSA

✝

New Port

Industrial Estate

Malta Dry Dock
Main Gate

Buhagia

Triq Ghajn Dwieli

✝

Tarxien, Airport

Triq Il-Labour

✝

Telgha Ta' Rahal

PAOLA

Airport, Birżebbuġa

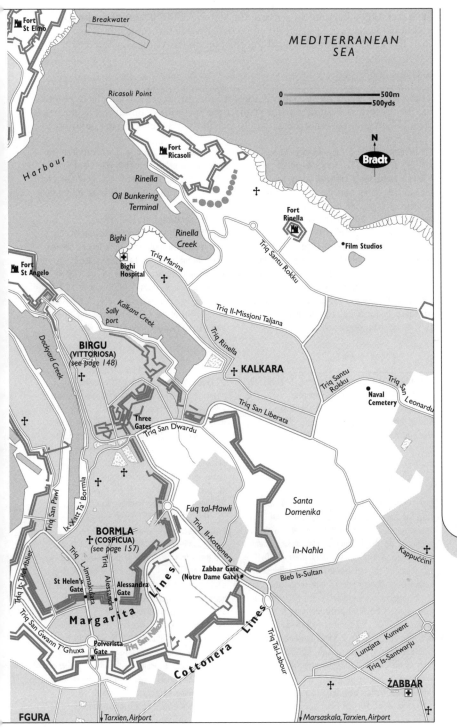

MEDITERRANEAN
SEA

Fort
St Elmo

Breakwater

Ricasoli Point

Harbour

Fort
Ricasoli

Rinella

Oil Bunkering
Terminal

Bighi

Rinella
Creek

Fort
Rinella

•Film Studios

Triq Santu Rokku

Bighi
Hospital

Triq Marina

Fort
St Angelo

Kalkara Creek

Sally
port

Triq Il-Missjoni Taljana

BIRGU
(VITTORIOSA)
(see page 148)

Triq Rinella

KALKARA

Triq Santu
Rokku

Triq San Leonardu

Naval
Cemetery

Dockyard Creek

Three
Gates

Triq San Dwardu

Triq San Liberata

Triq San Pawl

Ix-Xatt Ta' Bormla

Fuq tal-Ħawli

Santa
Domenika

Triq Il-Kottonera

In-Naħla

Kappuċċini

BORMLA
(COSPICUA)
(see page 157)

Triq L-Immakulata

Triq L-Alessandra

Zabbar Gate
(Notre Dame Gate)•

Bieb Is-Sultan

Triq Ir-Tmien Ibliev

St Helen's
Gate

Alessandra
Gate

Lines

Lunzjata Kunvent

Margarita

Triq Is-Santwarju

Triq San Gwann T'Ghuxa

Polverista
Gate

Triq San Nikola

Cottonera Lines

Triq Tal-Labour

ŻABBAR

FGURA

↓Tarxien, Airport

↓Marsaskala, Tarxien, Airport

N

Bradt

0 ────── 500m
0 ────── 500yds

145

By water taxi Alternatively, arrive at the Vittoriosa/Birgu Waterfront by *dgħajsa*, a traditional water taxi. See page 107 for a list of water-taxi companies; A & S Water Taxis has a little kiosk with tourist information on the Vittoriosa Waterfront.

🏠 WHERE TO STAY

There are no hotels in the Three Cities. A boutique hotel has long been planned for the Vittoriosa Waterfront but at the time of writing, building has not even begun. This is, however, a great place to stay in the few self-catering options:

🏠 **Indulgence Divine** 6 Pope Alexander VII St, Birgu; m (UK) 0781 398 8827; www.indulgencedivine.com. A historic house, newly converted into a holiday let, just round the corner from the Inquisitor's Palace in the heart of Birgu. Same owner as Valletta G-House (see page 109). 1 dbl bedroom that used to be a chapel & has votive graffiti of ships on the wall, roof terrace, kitchen, bathroom & sitting room. Modern decoration themed on the religious & the secret (inc a bit of historic erotica). Not suitable for children. *£500–600/week; shorter stays negotiable.*

🏠 **Marina Apartment** St Angelo Mansions, Vittoriosa Waterfront (British owned); m (UK) 0779 516 4379; e topeurolet@yahoo.co.uk;

www.holidaylettings.co.uk. In a new waterfront apt building just behind Fort St Angelo. 3 bedrooms (sleeps up to 6), long balcony with great views, own underground parking. *£550–750/week; shorter stays negotiable.*

🏠 **Templar House** Nelson St, Cospicua; m 99892041; e info@templarhousemalta.com; www.templarhousemalta.com. On a historic alleyway where Nelson is said to have been billeted, technically in Cospicua but close to the edge of Vittoriosa, & a few mins from the waterfront. English-owned, 3 bedrooms (sleeps up to 6), 3 bath/shower rooms, views of the marina from the roof terrace. No under-5s. *£595/week Apr–Oct, £475 Oct–Mar.*

✖ WHERE TO EAT

✖ **Del Borgo** St Dominic St, Vittoriosa; ☎ 21803710; m 99280000; e delborgo@onvol.net; ⏲ 18.00–01.00 Mon–Sat, 12.00–24.00 Sun. Popular wine bar in the 18th-century cellar of the Prince of Wales Band Club. Over 300 wines, Maltese food with a modern touch & traditional Maltese puddings. *Starters generallly €8–10, mains €11–13.*

✖ **Don Berto** The Treasury, Vittoriosa Waterfront; ☎ 21808008; m 79808008; e info@donberto.com; www.donberto.com; ⏲ 12.00–23.00 daily, Sat stays open until midnight. For a different perspective on the waterfront sit up here on the balcony of the Old Treasury building looking down at the water & along to the clock tower (1810) that separates the Old Treasury from the British Naval Bakery. Modern interior with comfortable sofas. Lift for buggies & wheelchairs. Varied Mediterranean menu. *Starters €6–8.50, pizza (evenings & Sun lunch only) €7.50–9.25, mains €15.95–21.95.*

✖ **Il-forn** 26–27 North St/Triq il-Tramuntana, Birgu; ☎ 21820379; ⏲ 19.30 onwards, Tue–Sun. In the heart of the Collachio, this cosy wine bar, which doubles as a small contemporary art gallery, is popular with locals. *Good ftira (€6.50–9.90) & platters for 2 (€8.50–16). Glass of house wine €2.30.*

✖ **Lupanara Wine Bistro** Sea Gate Vaults, Fort St Angelo; m 99526500; e info@lupanarabistro.com; www.lupanarabistro.com/lupanara; ⏲ 20.00–23.30 daily & Sun lunch. This World War II shelter under Fort St Angelo has been tastefully converted. Also tables outside on the water's edge. Delicious food, beautifully presented. Each standard menu choice comes with a wine recommendation & there are lots of specials. *Starters average €9, mains €20.*

✖ **Riviera Della Marina** Vittoriosa Waterfront; ☎ 21807230; m 99997973; e riviera@tritonmalta.com; ⏲ summer 11.00–14.30, 19.30–23.00 daily (variable in winter; call to check). The menu tells the history of the building which was the Knights' Treasury. Small attractive interior, large outdoor terrace on the waterfront. At the back is a quiet open courtyard. Best known for fish dishes. *Starters €6–10, mains €11–18.50.*

✖ **Sottovento** Vault 2, Old Treasury Bldg, Vittoriosa Waterfront; ☎ 21808990; ⏲ 10.00–23.30 daily. Particularly good for sitting outside on the edge of Dockyard Creek & popular with families. Highchairs are available. Broad menu of Mediterranean & Italian food, including tasty pizza. *Starters & pasta around €7.25, pizza €6.25–10.25, mains €11.50–18.75, kids' menu around €6.*

The oldest of the Three Cities, Birgu or Vittoriosa is a wonderful place to wander and has a few significant sights around which to plan a visit. When the Knights arrived in Malta in 1530, Birgu (or Il Borgo, meaning 'the town') was a fishing settlement and mercantile port with a fortress, Fort St Angelo, which the Knights regarded as thoroughly inadequate. It was, however, the main centre of population outside Mdina and its position next to the Grand Harbour made it the natural place for the maritime Knights to settle, particularly as the Sciberras Peninsula on the other side of the harbour (where Valletta now stands) was at the time a barren hillside.

The Hospitallers enlarged, embellished and fortified Birgu into their capital. Its layout remains largely unchanged with narrow streets radiating out from the central Victory Square and there are many old buildings dating from the period between the arrival of the Order (1530) and their post-Siege move to Valletta (1570s).

WHAT TO SEE AND DO

The Three Gates This is the original fortified entrance to Birgu/Vittoriosa, and until the building of the modern road, it was the only way into the city. The **Advanced Gate** with its carved crossed cannons was rebuilt in 1722 and leads into a courtyard with entrances to British barracks which later became the local police station and now house the Malta at War Museum (see page 147).

On the far side of the courtyard is a defensive ditch, now a little public garden, which was used as a location for the film *The Gladiator* with Russell Crowe. Crossing the bridge over the ditch (which would originally have been a drawbridge) you pass through the second gate, the **Couvre Porte**. Steps lead up onto the ramparts from where there are great views of the fortifications and the final **Main Gate** into Birgu. Alternatively, turn right after the second gate and join the road that enters the town through the Gate of Provence.

Malta at War Museum (*Couvre Porte;* ℡ *21225277 or 21896617;* e *info@wirtartna.org;* www.maltaatwarmuseum.com; ⊕ *10.00–17.00 daily, tours on the hour;* €8 adults, €7 students/seniors, €6 children under 16, €22 family (2 adults, 3 children). A combined ticket with Fort Rinella (page 158), Saluting Battery (page 119) & Lascaris War Rooms (page 158) costs €22/19/48 adult/child/family inc transport between them.) This is not really a museum at all, but an excellent guided tour in English (with written handouts in other languages) through one of Malta's largest World War II underground shelters (see boxed text, page 149), plus a remarkable historic film.

Led by a guide in British military uniform, you enter through a (replica) gas curtain down into the hand-dug shelter deep in the rock. Being right next to the Grand Harbour, the Three Cities were heavily bombed and this shelter regularly held 500 people overnight. There was theoretically electricity down here but by the time the *Luftwaffe* had bombed the power system a few times, only one bulb was kept functioning – the one in the tiled birth room. As you walk the hundreds of metres of corridors, the enthusiastic guide, full of facts and anecdotes, brings Malta's extraordinary wartime experience to life.

The audiovisual presentation is not to be missed. It includes an original 20-minute film, *Malta G.C.*, made in 1942 on the orders of King George VI who had just awarded Malta the George Cross (see *Chapter 1, History*, page 17). Voiced by Laurence Olivier, it is rousing stuff: a marvellous example of wartime propaganda and, through the archive footage, a real insight into the destruction that Malta suffered between June 1940 and September 1943.

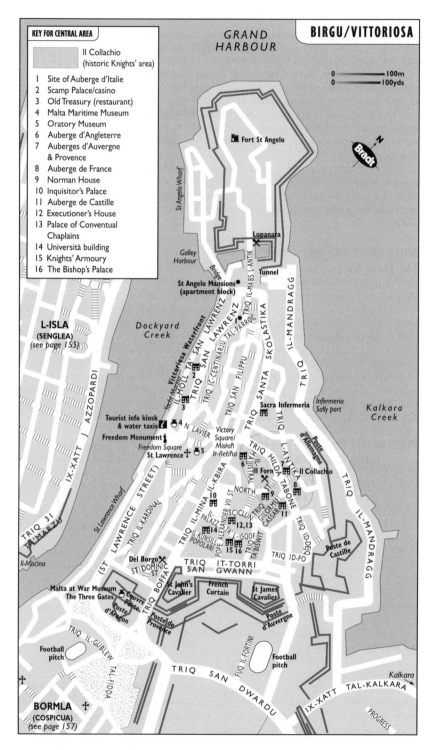

GRAND HARBOUR

KEY FOR CENTRAL AREA

Il Collachio
(historic Knights' area)

1   Site of Auberge d'Italie
2   Scamp Palace/casino
3   Old Treasury (restaurant)
4   Malta Maritime Museum
5   Oratory Museum
6   Auberge d'Angleterre
7   Auberges d'Auvergne
    & Provence
8   Auberge de France
9   Norman House
10 Inquisitor's Palace
11 Auberge de Castille
12 Executioner's House
13 Palace of Conventual
    Chaplains
14 Università building
15 Knights' Armoury
16 The Bishop's Palace

0 ———— 100m
0 ———— 100yds

Bradt N

Fort St Angelo

St Angelo Wharf

Lupanara

Galley Harbour

Bridge

Tunnel

St Angelo Mansions
(apartment block)

L-ISLA
(SENGLEA)
(see page 155)

Dockyard Creek

Vittoriosa Waterfront

IX-XATT I AZZOPARDI

TRIQ 31 TA' MARZU

Il-Macina

St Lawrence Wharf

(ST LAWRENCE STREET)

TRIQ IL-KARDINAL

TRIQ SAN LAWRENZ

IL-MOLL TAL-MINA

Torri Mandra

TRIQ ICCENTINARJU TAL-PARROC

TRIQ IL-HABS L-ANTIK

TRIQ SAN FILIPPU

TRIQ SANTA SKOLASTIKA

TRIQ IL-MANDRAGG

Sacra Infermeria

Infermeria Sally port

Kalkara Creek

Tourist info kiosk
& water taxis

Freedom Monument

Freedom Square

St Lawrence

Victory Square/ Misrah Ir-Rebha

N LAVIER

TRIQ IL-MINA L-KBIRA

TRIQ SAN LAWRENZ

Il Forn

TRIQ L-ANTIKA

Poste d'Allemagne

Il Collachio

TRIQ HILDA TABONE

NORTH

TRIQ GILORMU CASSAR

TRIQ IL-PALAZZ

IL-PALAZZ

SCICLUN

POPE ALEXANDER VII ST

TRIQ IL-KUNSILL POPOLARI

IL-ISQOF

TRIQ IT-TORRI GWANN

TRIQ SAN BOFFA

ST DOMINIC ST

Del Borgo

TRIQ TA BISWIT

TRIQ ID-DEJ

TRIQ ID-FO

Poste de Castille

TRIQ IL-MANDRAGG

Malta at War Museum
The Three Gates

St John's Cavalier

Œuvre
Poste
d'Aragon

Poste de Provence

French Curtain

St James Cavalier

Poste d'Auvergne

Football pitch

TRIQ IL-GUBLEW

TAL-FIDDA

TRIQ SAN DWARDU

FUQ IL-FORTINI

Football pitch

Kalkara

IX-XATT TAL-KALKARA

PROGRESS

BORMLA
(COSPICUA)
(see page 157)

The Inquisitor's Palace (*Main Gate St;* ✆ *21663731 or 21827006;* e *info@ heritagemalta.org; www.heritagemalta.org;* ⊕ *09.00–17.00 daily, last admission 16.30; €6 adults, €4.50 over-60s/children aged 12–17/students, €3 children 6–11, children under 6 go free*) One of few inquisitor's palaces to survive anywhere, this was originally the law courts of the Order of St John from the 1530s until the courts moved to Valletta in 1571. Today only the left-hand ground-floor rooms and the vaulted courtyard remain from this period. It became the Inquisitor's Palace with the arrival of the first inquisitor on the island in the mid-1570s and remained so for over 220 years, through 61 inquisitors, until Napoleon kicked out both the Knights and the Inquisition in 1798.

In the basement are the **cells**, rebuilt for greater security in 1698 after a prisoner had managed to dig his way out eight times in one year. On the walls, prisoners have carved graffiti including names, a boat and a beautiful rose. The occupants were a very mixed bunch, among them a newly Christian slave who told his wine merchant owner he would have been better off staying Muslim, a Sicilian priest (and convicted murderer) who was tortured and found guilty of 'satanic magic', a couple of female British Quakers (in the 1650s) and various prostitutes and bigamists.

The civilian warden, sworn to secrecy about the workings of the Inquisition, was responsible for the prisoners' routine. His room can be visited and just outside it on the exterior wall of the building is a little **sundial**, carved in 1730 by a warden who needed a clock.

MALTA'S WORLD WAR II UNDERGROUND SHELTERS

Until 1944, Malta was the most bombed place in Europe, hit by some 16,000 tons of bombs (see boxed text, *Chapter 5*, page 120). Underground shelters were obviously essential. At the start of the war there were only five (including part of the Malta at War Museum shelter) but by the time it was over the entire population could be housed underground – albeit in far from ideal conditions.

Some people sheltered in old wells (cisterns), catacombs or tunnels but many of these needed to be extended and plenty of shelters were dug fresh from the rock. All the work was done by hand and the walls are lined with chisel marks. Fortunately Malta was a nation of quarrymen and stonemasons skilled in techniques that had been in use here for centuries if not millennia. Two parallel channels were cut, then the stone between broken up with sledgehammers. During the war everyone, from the Royal Engineers to local children, was involved.

The standard pattern for a shelter is long corridors with rooms off to the sides. The corridors were the public shelter, where most people waited out the air-raid alert and, when necessary, slept. The rooms were 'private'. Better-off families paid for a stretch of wall 6ft long into which to build a family shelter. These rooms offered some privacy and elbow room but little protection from the diseases that spread in the crowded corridors (tuberculosis, scabies and dysentery) and they were as rough, damp and dark as the rest of the shelter. If conditions became too overcrowded, even the private rooms had to be shared.

When it rained, water seeped quickly through the porous limestone, and in the deeper corridors people were sometimes knee-deep in water. Some shelters had electricity but enemy bombing often interfered with supply. Candles were used briefly, but Malta imported its candles from Italy, so the Maltese were soon reduced to burning olive oil in hollowed out bowls in niches in the shelter walls (much as the Romans did in the catacombs 1,000 years earlier). The oil was smoky but effective: 500ml of olive oil would burn for two days. This, like much else about the shelters, was not ideal – but it worked.

The accused who did not immediately admit his or her 'crime' risked torture in the chamber on the back stairs (between the prison and the Tribunal Room). **Torture** was usually by stretching and here you can see the hooks, ropes and pulleys designed for the purpose. Records show that those tortured included a Flemish member of the Order accused of keeping prohibited books (1573), a Maltese person 'with a love of magic', a Sicilian 'blasphemer' and a French sailor who had converted to Islam (1641).

On the first floor a low door connects the stairs to the **Tribunal Room**. This ensured that prisoners always arrived in front of the inquisitor looking suitably supplicant. The flimsy little stool for the accused contrasts sharply with the heavy, carved dark-wood bank of thrones on which the inquisitor and his officials sat.

The rest of the first floor is now the **Museum of Ethnography** (focusing particularly on objects of domestic religious devotion), but the rooms remain little changed. In the Chancery there is a frieze around the top of the walls with the coats of arms of Malta's inquisitors – two of whom became pope: Fabio Chigi (Pope Alexander VII 1655–67) and Antonio Pignatelli (Pope Innocent XII 1691–1700). The neighbouring **audience hall** has pink walls and *trompe l'oeil* windows.

The museum shop sells three short but detailed **guidebooks** by Kenneth Gambin: *The Inquisitor's Palace, Torture and the Roman Inquisition* and *The Prison Experience at the Inquisitor's Palace (Insight Heritage Guides; €6.99 each)*.

Victory Square/Misraħ ir-Rebħa

This was originally two squares with lower buildings than today's and a watchtower from which Grand Master Jean Parisot de Valette directed some of the battles of the Great Siege. The square was the rallying point for the Knights' troops and de Valette is said to have moved out of his palace into a tavern on the square to be closer to the centre of operations. Bomb damage in World War II meant that the tower had to be knocked down and the two squares were merged into one.

At the centre of today's square are two monuments: a white statue of Birgu's patron saint **St Lawrence** (1880) and the **Victory Monument**, erected in 1705 to commemorate the defeat of the Turks in the Great Siege 150 years earlier. The railings make the Order's position very clear with a repeated pattern of the cross of St John atop a sword that points down on the crescent of the Ottoman Empire. At the corner with La Vallette Street is a wall-mounted lamp and small **shrine** by which is a plaque marking the spot where **public executions** took place in the 16th century.

The wonderfully ornate building with a splendid *gallarija* and intricate white wrought-iron balconies is the **San Lawrenz Band Club** (in British times, the Duke of Edinburgh Band Club). Almost next door is the site of the **German Auberge** (7 Victory Square, marked with a plaque) which was (ironically) destroyed by Axis bombing in World War II and is now a modern building. This was on the edge of the Collachio (see below) and the granite bollard marks the start of the Knights' private area of the capital.

The Collachio and the Knights' *auberges*

Just off the square are the narrow stone-paved streets which were Il Collachio, the area reserved for the Knights. Here their *auberges* were concentrated, the idea being that keeping them close together made them easier to defend in times of trouble. A surprising number have survived. The interiors are not open to the public but the buildings are marked with marble plaques.

Triq Hilda Tabone (which the Knights called Strada della Castiglia) was the main street of the Collachio. Here you will find four of the Knights' first *auberges*:

- 17–23: shared **Auberge d'Auvergne et Provence** – structurally changed by subdivision of the middle of the façade into smaller houses.

- 24–7: **Auberge de France** – larger and a little grander than the others because at this time the French were the largest and most influential group. Grand Master de L'Isle Adam (grand master at the time the Knights arrived in Malta) was a Frenchman and the French *langue* ran the Sacra Infermeria. The Knights continued to use this *auberge* up until 1586 in addition to their new *auberge* in Valletta which was destroyed in World War II.
- 28–30: **Auberge d'Aragon** – almost unrecognisable due to modern alterations
- 57–9: (on the corner of Triq Gilormu Cassar) **Auberge de Castille et Portugal** – a large portion of the building was destroyed in World War II but the corner is original.

The **Auberge d'Angleterre** is round the corner in Mistral Street/Triq Il-Majjistral (numbers 39–40). Recently restored, this is the only true English *auberge* in Malta. Henry VIII broke with Rome shortly after the Knights' arrival here and seized their property in England in 1540. This left the English Knights in an awkward, and financially compromised, position. Mary Tudor reinstated the Order in 1557 but the *langue* never really recovered and when the Order moved to Valletta no English *auberge* was built. The few English Knights that remained (and at times there were none) had to find other accommodation until the late 18th century and the creation of the shared Auberge of Bavaria and England (Auberge de Bavière, page 136). Even in Birgu the relationship between the German and English *langue* was close, with their *auberges* connected at the back.

The site of the **Auberge d'Italie** is a couple of hundred metres away towards Fort St Angelo at 1–6 St Lawrence Street/Triq San Lawrenz. The head of the Italian *langue* was also the Admiral of the Fleet so the *auberge* was built closer to the ships and the naval headquarters at Fort St Angelo.

Other historic buildings you might pass Like the *auberges*, the following buildings are of historical interest, but can only be viewed from the outside.

Sacra Infermeria (*Santa Scholastica St/Triq Santa Skolastica overlooking Kalkara (Calcaara) Creek*) This large early Renaissance building was the Knights' first hospital in Malta, built in 1532, and as Hospitallers it was central to their mission. Part of the building (on Saint Scholastica Street) was pulled down to make way for modern housing. When the Order moved into its new hospital in Valletta in 1604 this building became a Benedictine convent and so it remains today. Next door is the small **Benedictine Church of St Anne** (1679) designed by Lorenzo Gafá with an altarpiece by Mattia Preti. Close by at 19 Observer Street is an old house that was the residence of the Chief Medical Superintendent of the hospital.

The Norman House (*10–11 North St*) Almost all that is left to be seen of pre-1530 Birgu, this house was reputedly built in the 13th century. The first-floor window and façade frieze are 15th century.

The Executioner's House (*6 Pope Alexander VII St, cnr with 17 Pacifico Scicluna St*) This was the grace and favour home of the Knights' official executioner.

Palace of the Conventual Chaplains (*7–9 Pope Alexander VII St*) Home of the Order's chaplains of St Lawrence Church until the move to Valletta.

The Università building (*36–7 Popular Council St*) Built in 1538 this was home to the Birgu Università – local council – until the British took over.

The Bishop's Palace (*26–9 Bishop's Palace St*) Built in 1542 and enlarged in 1620 by the last bishop to be based in Vittoriosa. When the Order moved to Valletta they did not want the bishop to move with them, so this palace and St Lawrence Church remained his second base after Mdina.

St Lawrence Church (San Lawrenz) (⏰ *mornings early for prayer & 09.30–12.00 for visitors. Reopens around 16.30/17.00 for prayer prior to 18.00 Mass (you can pop in if you are quiet), 09.15–11.00 Sun. Festa in Aug.*) Immediately to the left inside the visitors' door to the church is a red-and-grey **monument** with the cross of the Order of St John and a Maltese flag. It commemorates the 900th anniversary of the parish (1090–1990) for which John Paul II made a visit. The first church here is believed to have been built in the time of Roger the Norman, and whilst the Knights were based in Birgu (1530–71), the church on this site was the main religious centre of the Order. It was here that Grand Master de Valette gathered his Knights and the people of Birgu on the eve of the Great Siege in May 1565, and here that those that survived met again in September when victory was finally theirs.

The present building, built in 1681–97, was designed by Baroque architect Lorenzo Gafá (also responsible for the cathedrals of Mdina and Gozo). The left tower was added in the 18th century, the right only in 1930. The church – including Gafa's dome – was badly damaged in World War II, but has been faithfully restored. The huge altarpiece of *The Martyrdom of St Lawrence* is thought to be Mattia Preti's largest painting. The detail is, as so often in churches, frustratingly hard to see. If the painting is unlit, ask the warden if he could switch on the lights for a short while.

In front of the church on the waterfront is the **Freedom Monument** which was unveiled on the eve of 31 March 1979 when the British Armed Forces departed from Malta. The **precincts** to the side of the church were once a burial ground for people killed during the Turkish insurgency of 1551, as well as a few of the dead from the Great Siege. Here too is the entrance to the oratory dedicated to St Joseph which houses a small but interesting **museum** (see below for details) including items rescued from the church and other parts of Birgu after they suffered serious bomb damage in 1942.

St Lawrence Oratory Museum (⏰ *approx 09.30–12.00 daily; free entry*) Most Mondays the museum is manned by Lorenzo Zahra, the archivist of the curia of Malta, who knows the collection backwards and is full of fascinating information. He's sometimes here on other days too and is the perfect guide to this Aladdin's cave of historic documents and objects.

Most famous amongst them are the hat and sword of Grand Master de Valette – which hang in the chapel, originally a small Greek parish church. The hat is black and wide-brimmed and the functional sword is said to be the one de Valette wore during the victory ceremonies after the Great Siege. He apparently left them in the church in pious thanks for victory and was given a richly decorated replacement sword by Catholic King Philip II of Spain in gratitude for the body blow his Order had dealt the Turks. Only a picture of this ornate sword hangs on the wall here; the original was taken by Napoleon and is now in the Louvre in Paris.

Amongst other items in the museum are a 15th-century Gutenberg incunabulum (a book printed before 1501 in Europe), a 1777 bill of lading for a Knights' galley (in Italian), the Grand Inquisitor's Pectoral Cross, a copy of the first newspaper ever published in Malta (1804, after the British took over, although the paper is in Italian and French), a cap from an SS uniform (hidden amongst other World War II memorabilia 'so as not to offend German visitors'), and a rare early atlas published in Venice in 1598 using the maps of ancient Greek geographer

Ptolemy (AD90–168) a copy of which Christopher Columbus is assumed to have used on his famous voyage.

Malta Maritime Museum *(Ex-Naval Bakery;* ✆ *21805287;* e *info@heritagemalta.org; www.heritagemalta.org;* ⊕ *09.00–17.00 daily; €5 adults, €3.50 over-60s/children aged 12–17/students, €2.50 children aged 6–11, children under 7 go free)* This building, next to the Freedom Monument on the Vittoriosa Waterfront, is the old **British Naval Bakery** in which steam-driven machinery produced 30,000lbs of bread and biscuits a day for the Mediterranean Fleet. The building was designed by William Scamp and built in 1842–45 in place of the Order's Galley Arsenal. Its façade was apparently inspired by Windsor Castle.

The highlight of the museum for most people will be a large (about 3.5m long) mid-18th-century model of a ship of the line of the Order of St John. The model was probably used by the Order's nautical school and gives a good idea of the sort of vessels that once dominated the creeks and harbour outside the museum. There is also a variety of smaller contemporary models of the Knights' ships, as well as of a couple of opulent grand masters' barges.

All sorts of objects take you through Malta's maritime history: cannons, anchors, hand-held weapons, manuals, documents, paintings and uniforms including the Order's extremely smart 18th-century naval garb of knickerbockers and long red jackets. The old dark wood Customs cupboard is here too, full of weights and measures, some still marked with the coats of arms of grand masters. A marble waterspout in the shape of a cannon barrel used to be part of a harbourside fountain fed by the Wignacourt Aqueduct (see page 220) from which the Knights' galleys filled up with water. Its Latin inscription reads: 'Why are you afraid little boat? There is no fire here, but water instead of shot.'

An extensive gallery is devoted to 200 years of the British Royal Navy in Malta: from a portrait of Sir Alexander Ball (one of Nelson's admirals who helped the Maltese see off the French in 1798–1800 and became first British governor of Malta) to a uniform, documents and photographs of Admiral Sir Nigel Cecil, last Commander of the British Forces in Malta (1975–79).

There is a brightly painted figurehead from HMS *Hibernia* (1805) and for ship buffs a case of over 250 tiny models showing the evolution of Royal Navy warships from HMS *Victory* through to today. There are also four barmaids' (for which read prostitutes') licences – like large coins – probably used in the notorious Valletta street nicknamed 'The Gut' (see page 133). Back by the entrance is the final gallery which covers the arrival of steam and modern ship propulsion, displaying a variety of machinery including a working triple expansion steam engine.

Vittoriosa Waterfront The wharf which faces Dockyard Creek (Galley Creek) has always been at the centre of Birgu's activities. It was the first place to be inhabited on the Grand Harbour (as far back as Phoenician times) before becoming the Grand Marina of the Order and then the Royal Navy's base in Malta. It is now a modern yacht marina and its old buildings have been renovated and turned into cafés, restaurants and a (well-disguised) casino.

Vittoriosa Waterfront offers the best views of **Senglea** – from its tip in the Grand Harbour, along its fortifications and Number 1 Dock to the start of Cospicua. This is also the best place to look at Il-Maċina, a large crane once used to turn ships over for cleaning and repair. During the Great Siege a pontoon bridge was laid across the water to speed up resupply of Fort St Michael (which then stood on the Senglea side towards the head of the creek), and a great chain linked Fort St Angelo to Senglea Point to prevent enemy ships from entering the creek.

6

The wharf (with very limited access for motor vehicles) starts at the Malta Maritime Museum (see page 153) which abuts the **Order's Old Treasury**. After the move to Valletta, this became a centre for the manufacture of galley rigging and sails. Its arched arcade has now been sympathetically converted into restaurants with waterfront terraces (see *Where to eat*, page 146).

The casino is in **Scamp Palace**, once the residence of the Order's Captain General of the Galleys and later the office of the British Admiralty. It was named after the architect of the British Naval Bakery who was based here during its construction. Next along is a patch of wasteland. Here stood the palace of the head of the Order's arsenal until it was bombed in World War II. The site is earmarked for the Three Cities first hotel, but work has yet to begin. By St Angelo Bridge (leading to the Fort) is a new apartment block, St Angelo Mansions, built on the site of the Order's slave cells.

Fort St Angelo Cut off from the rest of Birgu by a moat, Fort St Angelo is a dominating presence at the tip of the Vittoriosa Peninsula. It was documented as the Castrum Maris ('Castle by the Sea') as early as 1274 and was probably fortified long before. The medieval Castellan (governor of the fort) lived here, administering the area for his overlord in Sicily, and his 15th-century house still stands at the high point of the castle. The first Grand Master of the Order of St John in Malta, Phillippe Villiers de L'Isle Adam, converted the house into a palace for himself.

Expanded and strengthened by the Knights to withstand cannon fire, the fort played a crucial role in the Great Siege of 1565, and, nearly 400 years later, withstood over 60 direct hits in World War II. Under the British, the fort became the Malta HQ of the Royal Navy and was listed in 1933 as HMS *St Angelo*.

In 1998 the Maltese government signed a 99-year lease handing over the top half of the fortress to the modern Sovereign Military Hospitaller Order of St John of Jerusalem, of Rhodes and of Malta (to give it its full name). Two hundred years after its expulsion, the Order has returned.

The fortifications From Fort St Angelo the fortifications of Birgu/Vittoriosa run all along the water's edge on the Kalkara Creek side and then along the landward flank of the town back to the Three Gates. It is an interesting route to walk.

Each *langue* took responsibility for a stretch of Birgu's defences (a *poste* or post) as they did later in Valletta. The first length of fortifications along Triq Il-Mandragg is the **Poste d'Angleterre**, which runs as far as the **Bighi Sally Port**, also called the **Infermeria Sally Port**. Originally the bastion walls on this side of Birgu rose straight from the water. The only way to land or leave was through small sally ports (hidden entrances/exits from which the Order's troops could 'sally forth').

From here there are good views across the creek to Kalkara and the **Bighi Royal Naval Hospital** with its tall tower containing a lift that carried the sick directly to the hospital from the ship below. The building now houses a government Restoration Centre and Edward de Bono's World Thinking Centre.

The next stretch of wall is the **German Post** (Poste d'Allemagne) which seems to be a favourite dog-walking spot so watch where you tread. Where the fortifications turn the corner is the **Poste de Castille**. During the Great Siege, the Turks stormed the ramparts here (spawning its nickname, *Il-breccja* – 'the breach'). It looked as though the day was lost for the Knights until Grand Master Jean Parisot de Valette arrived personally leading reinforcements. A plaque marks the spot where he was wounded in the leg in the subsequent fighting. The need to reinforce the defences at this corner was clear and the outer fortifications you now see are mainly 18th century.

The landward fortifications centre on **two cavaliers** (massive raised gun platforms) – called, as in Valletta, St James and St John. Both were the responsibility of the French Langue and are joined by the French curtain wall. The present structures are post-siege. **St James Cavalier** was planned in 1588 but only built in 1723–30. It is uncared for but always open. The (closed) tunnel underneath was a World War II shelter. **St John's** (also 1723–30) is closed to the public. It is hoped that both cavaliers will be restored in the near future.

Next to St James Cavalier is the Knights' **Old Armoury** (on Triq L'Arċisqof Mikiel Gonzi (Archbishop Michael Gonzi Street) at the top of Triq Il-Palazz tal-Isqof (Bishop's Palace Street). Probably originally mid-16th century, this was the Knights' main weapons store in Birgu and served as a makeshift hospital during the Great Siege. The first floor was added in 1636 and under the British it was a military hospital and residential quarters (gaining it the name Il-Kwartier). It is now government offices.

L-ISLA/SENGLEA

The hunting grounds of L-Isla became the village of Senglea in the 1550s when Grand Master Claude de la Sengle offered a plot of land to anyone willing to build a house. He also strengthened its fortifications, which proved to have been a prudent move when the Turks attacked a decade later. Senglea's main fort, Fort St Michael, was demolished in 1922 so the British could expand the docks, but the fortifications at Senglea Point and along the side of French Creek remain. Whilst it has fewer specific sights than Vittoriosa, Senglea is well worth wandering around. You can circle the peninsula along the water's edge, with views across the creeks and the Grand Harbour, and perhaps duck inland briefly to see the parish church and a few of the more attractive older streets.

WHAT TO SEE AND DO
Safe Haven Garden (*Senglea Point, end of Victory St*) Right at the tip of the

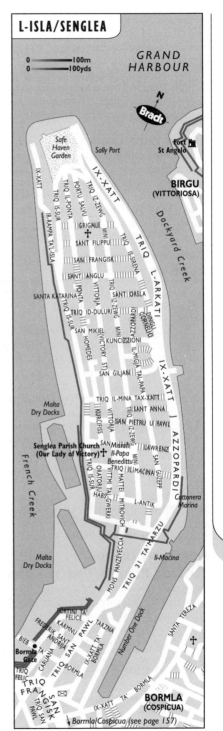

L-ISLA/SENGLEA

peninsula is Senglea Point and a small public garden with spectacular views over the Grand Harbour and across to Valletta. The Upper Barracca Gardens are clearly visible atop the bastion walls of the capital. There are great views too of Fort St Angelo and Vittoriosa.

On the wall of the gardens overlooking the Grand Harbour is a stone *gardjola,* a rebuilt Knights-period sentry box, carved with an eye and an ear to remind the guards to be vigilant. It was from just below here that the Great Chain (see *Vittoriosa Waterfront,* above) ran across the mouth of the creek to Fort St Angelo.

Senglea Parish Church (⊕ *early until 12.00 & then 16.00–19.00*) The substantial **Church of Our Lady of Victory** was built in 1743 but had to be reconstructed in the 1950s after it was severely damaged in 1941 by bombs meant for the British aircraft carrier HMS *Illustrious* anchored in Dockyard Creek. The church is chiefly known for its statue of **Christ the Redeemer** (*Gesù Redentur*) – in the chapel to the right of the altar. This unusually emotional polychrome statue of Christ on his hands and knees under the weight of the cross is believed to have miraculous powers. The parish has two feast days – in March and June.

BORMLA/COSPICUA

Bormla was given the title Citta Cospicua (Italian for the 'conspicuous' or 'distinguished one') in the early 18th century on account of its recently completed massive, eye-catching fortifications (see below).

Bormla suffered terribly in both Malta's sieges. Just before the start of the Great Siege, Grand Master de Valette ordered that the few homes in the area (then outside any fortifications) be razed to the ground so that they could not be used by the invading Turks. Bormla was largely destroyed again in World War II, this time by enemy bombing. One of the few buildings to survive was the vast, ornate **Church of the Immaculate Conception** (built in 1584, enlarged 1637) which sits at the top of a long flight of steps staring down at the dock. It is at the centre of a large *festa* in December. The **monument** at the bottom of the steps is to the fallen of World War II and there are a few old streets around the church that are worth exploring. Narrow **Nelson Street** is possibly the oldest of many streets around the world named after the British admiral – in this case in thanks for his efforts to free Bormla and Malta from Napoleon's troops.

To add to Bormla's woes, it suffered disproportionately from loss of employment in the second half of the 20th century as the British Navy departed and ship repair yards closed. Today Bormla's narrow, stepped streets are among the poorest urban areas in Malta.

WHAT TO SEE AND DO

The Santa Margarita/Firenzuola Lines Bormla/Cospicua is surrounded on the landward side by the Margarita Lines – four bastions joined by curtain walls breached by two gates. Begun in 1638 to designs by military engineer, Vincenzo Maculano da Firenzuola, these were intended to protect the rear of the Three Cities. Even after the move to Valletta, the creeks here remained home to the Knights' ships as the new capital had no such harbours. Protecting the landward side of the Three Cities was therefore very important at a time when fear of Turkish invasion remained high. The Order's concern was not without reason: Turkish raids took place in 1641 and 1645, though never with the force of 1565.

Work on the Margarita Lines stopped before the project was finished and although additions continued to be made into the 18th century, they were never fully completed. The attention of the Knights' defence teams had moved to the

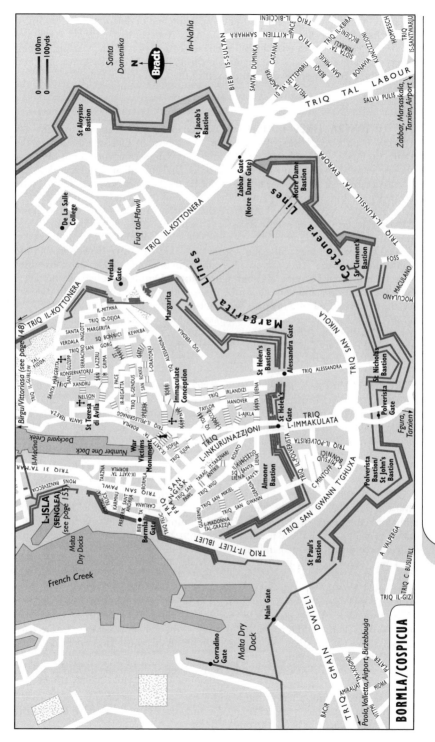

BORMLA/COSPICUA

St Aloysius Bastion

St Jacob's Bastion

Santa Domenika

In-Nahla

Zabbar Gate (Notre Dame Gate)

Notre Dame Bastion

BIEB IS-SULTAN

SANTA DUMINKA

TRIQ IL-BICCIENI

TRIQ IL-KITTIEN SAHHARA

PACE

BRBAL TAL SETTEMBRU 8 OTT

HELITA TAL SETTEMBRU 8 OTT

SAN MIKIEL

BONAVIA

TRIQ IL-KBIRA

HIRAKLI

SIDTA TA' SAHHTAR

CATANIA

BICCIENI

TRIQ KUNCIZZJONI

HOMRESCH

TRIQ IS-SANTWARJU

TRIQ TAL LABOUR

SALVU PULIS

Żabbar, Marsaskala, Tarxien, Airport

De La Salle College

Fuq tal-Hawli

TRIQ IL-KOTTONERA

Verdala Gate

Cottonera Lines

St Clement Bastion

FOSS

TRIQ IL-KUNSILL TA' L-EWROPA

MACULANO

MOCULANO

Margarita Lines

Margarita

IL-MITHNA

TRIQ ID-DEJQA

SANTA VERDALA

SQ BONNICI

KEWKBA

Birgu/Vittoriosa (see page 48)

TRIQ IL-KOTTONERA

TAL FIDDA

SANTA MARGERITA

TRIQ IL-GUBLEW

SAN GUŻEPP

SERRACINO INGLOTT

SQ GORG

L-LAZZU

IM-GRIMA

GAFFI

L-ORATORJU

FUQ VERDALA

TRIQ ALESSANDRA

St Helen's Bastion

Alessandra Gate

TRIQ ALESSANDRA

TRIQ SAN NIKOLA

St Nicholas Bastion

Polverista Gate

KONSERVATORJU

SAN XANDRU

NELSON

St Teresa di Avila

SANTA TBEŻA

L-REGATTA

IR-REGATTA

TRIQ IL-GENDUS

SAN RONKU

PACE

Immaculate Conception

TAIFI

TRIQ ALESSANDRA

IRLANDIZI

TAYLOR

HANOVER

SANTA HENA

SANTA LENA

L-AJKLA

St Helen's Gate

TRIQ L-IMMAKULATA

Polverista Gate

Fgura, Tarxien

Dockyard Creek

TRIQ IL-PELLEGRINAGG

BORMLA

TRIQ IL-PELLEGRINAGG

MIN'U

TOL'S-SITT

L'LUN

SOFIJA

MIN'U

L-INKURUNAZZJONI

ROSATO

IL-MINCHI

DIZELMINTI

TRAG IT-TAŻNARI

ANTNU

SQ LIENA

SANTA LENA

C MINTOFF BONNICI

TRIQ IL-POLVERISTA

Polverista Bastion/ St John's Bastion

War Victims Monument

Number One Dock

TRIQ 31 TA' MAR

IL-H'Macina

MONS PANZAVECCHIA

TARŻNA

TRIQ SAN FRANGISK

IX-XATT TA' BORMLA

TRIQ WIGI

TABAG

TRIQ SAN PAWL

SQ LIEN

SANTA LENA

GUILERMU

TRIQ SAN MIKIEL

TRIQ SAN GWANN

A VALPERGA

TRIQ SAN GWANN T'GHUXA

SAN PAWL

KARMNU

FREBRIK SANT ANDRIJA

L-MADONNA TAL-GRAZZJA

St Paul's Bastion

L-ISLA (SENGLEA) (see page 153)

Malta Dry Docks

French Creek

PRINCIPESSA FELICE

SANT'ANDRIJA

VINCENZ

CARAANA

OBORMA

TRIQ FELIC

Bormla Gate

BIEB TA' BORMLA

TRIQ IT-TLIET IBLIET

Corradino Gate

Malta Dry Dock

Main Gate

GHAJN DWIELI

TRIQ IL-GIZI

TRIQ C BUSUTILL

BACIR

TRIQ AMIRALJAT

VITTMI

MIDMA

PLATER

C BUSUTILL

Paola, Valletta, Airport, Birzebbuga

0 —— 100m
0 —— 100yds

Brackt

N

157

creation of an even larger, more all-encompassing line of defence, the **Cottonera Lines** (see below). **St Helen's Gate**, with its stone mortars, carved scroll and decorative columns, is a good place to start to see a stretch of the Margarita Lines. Note that although this is the main gate through the Margarita Lines, its Latin inscription commemorates the completion of the Cottonera defences.

AROUND THE THREE CITIES

THE COTTONERA LINES In 1669 the Venetian city of Candia (modern-day Heraklion on Crete), then the easternmost outpost of Christianity, fell to the Ottoman Turks, leaving Malta next in line. The Knights put the nation on a war footing expecting a repeat of the Great Siege. Italian military engineer Antonio Maurizio Valperga was loaned to the Order by the Duke of Savoy and in 1670 he created an ambitious master plan for the defence of the Grand Harbour area. The only parts that were actually built were the Cottonera Lines (named after Grand Master Nicolas Cotoner), Fort Ricasoli (which languishes, battered by the sea at the entrance to the Grand Harbour) and some additions to the Floriana Lines.

The Cottonera Lines still stand – a massive 5km defensive barrier around the landward side of the Three Cities. There are eight bastions and two demi-bastions. The monumental Baroque **Żabbar Gate/Notre Dame Gate** is still the tallest building in Bormla and still one of the main routes into town. It now houses the headquarters of the **Fondazzjoni Wirt Artna** (*Malta Heritage Trust;* ℡ *21800992 or 21803091;* e *info@wirtartna.org; www.wirtartna.org*) and tours of the building can be arranged with them (€5pp). If driving (or walking, though be aware this is not the most salubrious spot in Malta) turn left inside the gate and follow the walls along for a good sense of the Cottonera Lines.

FORT RINELLA (*St Rocco Rd, Kalkara;* ℡ *21809713, 21800992 or 21809713;* e *info@ wirtartna.org; www.wirtartna.org or www.maltaheritagesites.com;* ⊕ *10.00–17.00 Tue–Sun; tours in English on the hour;* €10 *adults,* €8 *students/seniors,* €5 *children under 16,* €25 family (2 adults, 3 children); additional tour with weapons demonstrations daily at 14.30 (for an extra €5pp). To get there take bus 4 from Valletta (25mins; 09.30–16.55 only) or transport booked with Fondazzjoni Wirt Artna by calling:* m *99495734. A combined ticket with Saluting Battery & Lascaris War Rooms (Valletta, page 119) & Malta at War Museum (above, page 147) inc transport between them costs* €22/19/48 adult/child/family.) Fort Rinella, the world's first fully mechanised fort, was built by the British in 1878 to house the new 100-ton gun, then the largest cannon available. This monster gun with its bizarre (but authentic) pink camouflage, still stands pointing menacingly out to sea. With a range of eight miles, it could penetrate 65cm into steel armour and was so heavy that it had to be turned, cleaned and loaded by steam-powered hydraulic machinery.

There were originally two such guns in Malta, the other at Fort Cambridge (see *Sliema,* page 165) now largely demolished. The guns were intended to fire alternately, keeping up a devastating bombardment of the sea at the entrances to Valletta's harbours. They were never used in anger.

An interesting film explains why this gun was needed. The short version is that its British inventor sold it to the Italian navy so the British Navy then had to have it too! Some 135 men were stationed here: 100 to guard the landward side of the fort, 35 to operate the gun.

The 14.30 **extended tour** includes demonstrations of musketry and pre-radio naval communications (morse code, semaphore, etc) as well as a firing of the only 6-ton howitzer cannon left in the world. This was the sort of gun that defended the Victoria Lines (see page 231) and for an extra €15 you can have the slightly unnerving privilege of being the one to fire it!

7

Sliema, St Julian's and Paceville

Most of Malta's top hotels, and many others, are in this built-up area along the northern coast across Marsamxett Harbour from Valletta. The rocky shoreline is backed with apartment blocks and hotels and, particularly in summer, life goes on into the early hours.

Sliema is the area closest to Valletta (with the Sliema ferry linking the two). At Balluta Bay, Sliema seamlessly blends into St Julian's, which itself morphs unnoticeably into Paceville on the other side of Spinola Bay. Despite this lack of clear borders between the three areas, they each have their distinct characters. Sliema is upmarket with Malta's most prestigious shopping area and expensive residential areas as well as the popular seafront promenades. St Julian's is the main centre of upmarket mass tourism on the island with lots of seafront restaurants, and Paceville is its brasher, noisier and younger neighbour.

PRACTICALITIES

There are plenty of **shops** (standard European fare), **banks** and ATMs in this built-up part of Malta, as well as several **internet cafés** along Tower Road. These tend to come and go so are not listed individually, but there are several along the waterfront including at Sliema Ferries. There is a **post office** in St Julian's (*Lombard Bank bldg, Triq, Paceville;* ⊕ *w/day mornings*) and a sub-post office in Sliema (*7 Triq Ċensu Xerri, Tigné;* ⊕ *08.00–13.00 Mon–Sat with additional opening w/ends 16.00–18.00*).

SLIEMA

Sliema isn't just a place, it's a type (like 'Sloane' in London). If you are 'Slimiz' you are likely to be a well-educated, English-speaking member of the professional classes with a cosmopolitan outlook and, although not necessarily rich, certainly not poor. Sliema is the place where Maltese families can still be heard speaking English in preference to Maltese, or unselfconsciously mixing the two into 'Manglish'.

Sliema began as a fishing village and by the 19th century was the place for well-off Vallettans to have a summer house (there is good swimming off the rocks). During World War II, many of these people left Valletta to escape the bombing and based themselves full-time in Sliema. With the capital a mere five-minute ferry ride away, most didn't bother to return to Valletta when the war ended. The population duly shrank and that of Sliema swelled towards its present 14,000.

The once-elegant 3km seafront promenades along The Strand and Tower Road are now lined with unattractive modern apartment blocks and hotels. Tower Road is still *the* place in Malta to stroll of a summer evening and you will find the Maltese of all ages promenading here as the heat of the day diminishes.

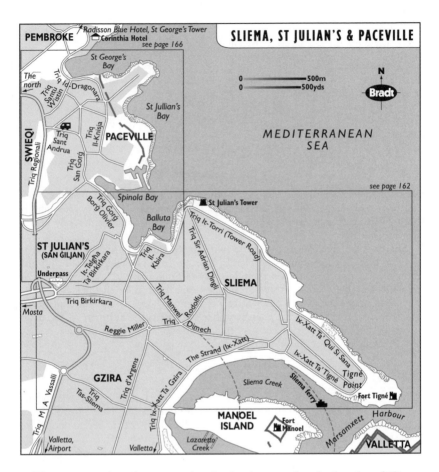

Radisson Blue Hotel, St George's Tower
Corinthia Hotel
see page 166

St George's Bay

The north

Triq Santi Wistin

Triq Id-Dragonara

St Jullian's Bay

SWIEQI

Triq Sant Andrua

Triq Il-Knisja

PACEVILLE

Triq San Gorg

Triq Regjonali

MEDITERRANEAN SEA

N

Bradt

0 — 500m
0 — 500yds

see page 162

Spinola Bay

Triq Gorg Borg Olivier

St Julian's Tower

ST JULIAN'S
(SAN ĠILJAN)

Balluta Bay

Triq It-Torri (Tower Road)

Triq Sir Adrian Dingli

Underpass

Ix-Telgha Ta' Birkirkara

Triq Il-Kbira

SLIEMA

Triq Birkirkara

Triq Manwel Dimech

Rodolfu

Mosta

Reggie Miller

Triq Dimech

Ix-Xatt Ta' Qui Si Sana

The Strand (Ix-Xatt)

Ix-Xatt Ta' Tigné

GZIRA

Triq d'Argens

Triq Tas-Sliema

Triq Ix-Xatt Ta' Gzira

Sliema Creek

Sliema ferry

Tigné Point

Fort Tigné

Triq M A Vassalli

Valletta, Airport

Valletta

Lazaretto Creek

MANOEL ISLAND

Fort Manoel

Marsamxett Harbour

VALLETTA

The coast may have been overtaken by development but the interior of Sliema is largely untouched – a quietly elegant residential area with some lovely old buildings, colourful *gallariji*, churches and pretty squares.

Sliema is also Malta's premier shopping area. It has most of the European high street chains plus a few independent shops of its own, occasionally elegant, rarely cheap.

GETTING THERE AND AWAY Lots of buses connect Valletta and Sliema. Numbers 61, 63, 627 and 652 stop at Sliema Ferries, as do bus 70 (which goes to Baħar iċ-Ċagħaq, Buġibba and Qawra), number 645 (which goes to Ċirkewwa) and the 65 (which stops at Naxxar, Mosta, Ta' Qali and Mdina). Buses 62, 63, 64, 66, 67, 68, 70, 652 and 671 stop along the Sliema Waterfront. Many of these buses also stop at St Julian's and Paceville and the 675 only goes as far as Paceville.

The best option for getting to and from Valletta though (as long as the weather is reasonable) is to take the Sliema ferry – a pleasant five- to ten-minute crossing (see page 58 for details).

Parking on the streets in Sliema requires a parking clock (see page 106) and can be very difficult, but there is a multi-storey car park just inland from the Sliema ferry (*113 High St, SLM 16;* ✆ *21335800 or 21339541;* e *cccp@onvol.net; www.cccp.com.mt*) where you can park for €1/30 minutes (€0.60 *after 20.00 & most of Sun*).

GETTING AROUND The key thing to remember with Sliema is that if you want to cross town quickly, cut through the middle rather than taking the coast road. This is obvious on the map but not so obvious on the ground. Sliema ferry to St Julian's is perhaps a 15-minute walk through the centre but can take 45 minutes along the seafront. There are, however, plenty of buses running the length of Tower Road if you want to ride along the coast to St Julian's.

BOAT TRIPS Sliema is the starting point for numerous boat trips, including the excellent 1½-hour to 1 hour 50 minute **Two Harbours Cruise** which offers full English commentary on a circuit of the Grand Harbour and Marsamxett Harbour with great views of Valletta and the Three Cities (€16 adult, €13 children under 12). There is also a range of coastal cruises. Boats may leave from slightly different points along the Sliema Waterfront.

Captain Morgan Cruises ☎ 23463333; e info@captainmorgan.com.mt; www.captainmorgan.com.mt

Luzzu Cruises m 79064489 or 99474210; e luzzucruises@onvol.net

⌂ WHERE TO STAY
Top end
⌂ **Fortina Spa******* (140 rooms) (not to be confused with the older Fortina 4-star next door) Tigné Seafront; ☎ 23462346 or 23462162; e info@fortinasparesort.com; www.fortinasparesort.com. 17-storey skyscraper & (at time of writing) next to the Tigné Point building site. Rooms, however, are very well designed. Gorgeous views of Valletta from upper-floor seaview rooms. The 1st hotel in Europe to have spa rooms with their own spa bath & treatment machines. 6 restaurants, largest spa in the Med (see Spas page 101), indoor & outdoor pools. Standard dbls B&B pppn based on 2 sharing €40 (winter)–€80 (summer), spa rooms €148–188, wellness rooms €58.75–98.75 (sgl supplements €23.30 on standard & wellness rooms, €46.60 on spa rooms).

⌂ **The Palace******* (153 rooms) High St; ☎ 21333444 or 22621000; e business@thepalacemalta.com; www.thepalacemalta.com. Tucked into the quiet residential heart of Sliema, this new urban hotel has a designer lobby & modern rooms, well-heated indoor pool & unheated rooftop infinity pool, gym & small spa. Easy walk to both seafronts & Sliema Ferries. Helpful staff. Temperamental & expensive Wi-Fi but 2 free broadband computers in the lobby. Avoid rooms beneath the 9th-floor restaurant. Standard dbls officially €330 (room only) but website prices can be less than a third of this.

Mid range
⌂ **Cambridge Place Hostel** (58 rooms of 2–6 beds) Tigné St; ☎ 21332044; m 99332044; e info@cambridgeplace.com; www.cambridgeplace.com.mt. Not in fact a hostel, but the remains of the 5-star Crown Plaza Hotel in a building that was the British barracks for Fort Cambridge (see page 165). Now it's more like a 3-star hotel. Spacious rooms, bright b/fast room, fresh clean public rooms. May be full of students in summer. Currently next to the Tigné Point building site so ask for a room on the opposite side. Dbls B&B €39.60pppn (Jul/Aug), €29.70pppn (May/Jun).

⌂ **The Imperial***** (95 rooms) 1 Rudolph St; ☎ 21344093 or 21336471; e info@imperialhotelmalta.com; www.imperialhotelmalta.com. Deep in residential Sliema, the grand 19th-century staircase & armour in the lobby set the old-fashioned tone. Clinical corridors. Rooms variable. Clean, tiled floors, some rather 1970s, lit with fluorescent strips. Garden-view rooms the best. Pleasant gardens, smallish outdoor pool & paddling pool. Cheerful restaurant. Standard twin B&B €90 (summer), €40 (winter), child discounts.

⌂ **The Victoria****** (120 rooms) Gorġ Borġ Olivier St; ☎ 21334711 or 22623205; e victoria@victoriahotel.com; www.victoriahotel.com. The Palace's older & more traditional sister hotel shares its spa, gym & pool facilities. A little faded in places, but most rooms are fine & the staff are excellent. Standard dbls officially €147 but website offers can be half that.

Seafront hotels There are numerous modern three- and four-star (mainly Malta four-star) hotels along and near the seafront. They have little character and are

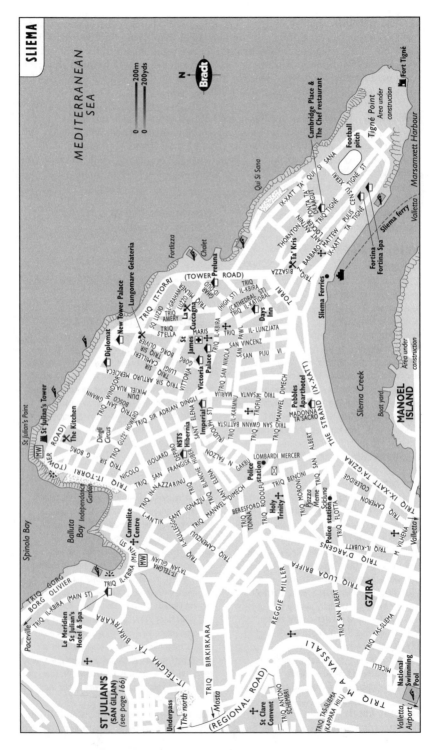

MEDITERRANEAN SEA

0 200m
0 200yds

N

Bract

St Julian's Point

Spinola Bay

Balluta Bay Independance Garden

Paceville

TRIQ BORG OLIVIER

TRIQ IL-KBIRA (MAIN ST)

Le Meridien St Julian's Hotel & Spa

ST JULIAN'S (SAN ĠILJAN) (see page 166)

Underpass
The north

TRIQ IT-TELGĦA TA' BIRKIRKARA

Mosta

TRIQ BIRKIRKARA

St Clare Convent

TRIQ ANTONO SCHEMBRI

(REGIONAL ROAD)

REGGIE MILLER

Valletta, Airport

TRIQ M A VASSALI

TRIQ TA'SLIEMA (KAPPARA HILL)

National Swimming Pool

MICELLI

GZIRA

TRIQ TA'SLIEMA

TRIQ SAN ALBERT

TRIQ IL-KUBATT

M VILLHENA

Valletta

TRIQ D'ARGENS

TRIQ LUQA BRIFFA

TRIQ FLOTTA

TRIQ CAMERON

TRIQ COLERIDGE

TRIQ IX-XATT TA'GŻIRA

THE STRAND

MANOEL ISLAND

Boat yard

Sliema Creek

Area under construction

Marsamxett Harbour

Sliema ferry

Valletta

Fortina Fortina Spa

Sliema Ferries

Days Inn

TORRI

IX-XATT TA' TIGNE

TRIQ TIGNE

LOCANTA PONTA
TIGNE ST

PULIS CENSU

BARBARO MATTEW

THORNTON

IX-XATT TA' QUI SI SANA

Qui Si Sana

Football pitch

Tigné Point Area under construction

Fort Tigné

Cambridge Place & The Chef restaurant

Ta' Kris

BISAZZA

Pretuna

(TOWER ROAD)

TRIQ IT-TORRI

Fortizza

Chalet

Lungomare Gelateria

New Tower Palace

Diplomat

TRIQ SQ LUŻJU

TRIQ GRAHAM

TRIQ MILNER

GĦAR ID-DUD

TRIQ STELLA

La Cuccagna

St James

Victoria Palace

TRIQ IL-KBIRA

(HIGH ST)

(CATHEDRAL ST)

TRIQ IL-KATIDRAL

TRIQ IL-KBIRA

SAN PAWL

SAN VINCENZ

TRIQ IL- LUNZJATA

SAN PUU VI

TRIQ SANTA MARIJA

TRIQ MANWEL DIMECH

Pebbles Aparthotel (IX-XATT)

MADONNA TA'SACRO

TROFIM

TRIQ SAN ĠWANN BATTISTA

TRIQ KARMNU

TRIQ MANWEL DIMECH

TRIQ SAN ALBERT

LOMBARDI MERCER

TRIQ BENCINI

Piazza Sciuma

Meme Scicluna

TRIQ MORONI

Holy Trinity

Police station

TRIQ RODOLFU

BERESFORD

TRIQ TONNARA

TRIQ CAMENZULI

TRIQ MANWEL DIMECH

TRIQ MANWEL ELENA

Police station

LOMBARDI

TRIQ N TALŻON

St Maris

TRIQ VITTORJA

TRIQ ĠORĠ BORĠ OLIVIER

TRIQ SIR ARTURO MERCIECA

TRIQ CAMILLERI

LUIGI

TRIQ WINDSOR

DUN MIKIEL XERRI

BOSCO

TRIQ GUŻE HOWARD

Dingli Circus

Imperial

Hibernia

NSTS

SANT ELENA

TRIQ SIR ADRIAN DINGLI

RUDOLPH

TRIQ SIR ADRIAN DINGLI

NICOLO

ISOUARD

TRIQ SAN FRANĠISK

HUBER

N. NAZZARINU

L'ANTIK

SANT IGNAZJU

BLANCHE

TRIQ IN-NAZZARINU

TRIQ SAN ĠILJAN

Carmelite Centre

St Julian's Tower

The Kitchen

(TOWER ROAD)

TRIQ IT-TORRI

TRIQ SIR G BORĠ

The Kitchen

mostly used by package-holiday operators; however, with the rise of the internet, individuals are also booking direct.

🏠 **Preluna****** (280 rooms) 124 Tower Rd; ☎ 21334001, 21339366 or 21342292; e info@ preluna.com; www.preluna.com. Large high-rise hotel spread over 3 buildings. Rooms mostly bright & clean with good-sized windows even on the town side. Indoor spa & pool. Outdoor pool by the sea across the road. *Standard twin inland room B&B €105 (summer), €63 (winter). Special offers can give up to 30% off.*

🏠 **The Diplomat****** (108 rooms, 21 sea view) 173 Tower Rd; ☎ 23497000 or 23491782; e sales@diplomat.com.mt; www.diplomat.com.mt. Convenient (if built-up) location in the middle of

Tower Road. Pleasant & clean. Even non-sea-view rooms are OK. Swimming pool on 8th-floor roof. *Twin room, side-sea view around €99 (room-only, summer) €46 (winter), less if you book well in advance. Web booking may be cheaper.*

🏠 **The New Tower Palace***** (62 rooms) Tower Rd; ☎ 21337271 or 21311235; e info@ newtowerpalacehotel.com; www.newtowerpalacehotel.com. All rooms have a little balcony. The hotel is on a junction so some rooms may be a bit noisy. Helpful staff. 8th-floor roof terrace with small pool. *Town-view dbls €80 B&B (summer), seaview €90, €50/70 (winter).*

Budget

🏠 **Days Inn***** (100 rooms) 76 Cathedral St; ☎ 21339118 or 21331162; e info@ daysinnmalta.com; www.daysinnmalta.com. Inland on a quiet street near Sliema's shopping area. Basic, but clean & friendly. Small pool on the roof. 2 family rooms. *Dbls B&B from €20pppn (winter), €27pppn (summer). Balcony/front room an additional €1 pppn, sgl supplement €10. 50% off for children 2–12.*

🏠 **New Strand Pebbles Aparthotel**** (27 apts) 89 The Strand; ☎ 21311889 or 21316907; e pebbles@ keyworld.net; www.maltaselfcatering.com. On the Sliema promenade. Wi-Fi in the bar. *Studio apt for 2 with sea view €50, on the back €40. Jan–Mar €40/€30.*

🏠 **NSTS Hibernia Hostel** (40 rooms) De Piro St ☎ 25588340 (mornings), NSTS HQ 25588233 or 21333859; e nsts@nsts.org; www.nsts.org. Great budget option. Excellent location just off the seafront near Balluta Bay. Good-sized bright, clean rooms (though older showers & toilets) with 2–8 beds & kitchenette. Communal lounge, TV, computers (small charge) & canteen serving a good cold b/fast buffet. NSTS also has a branch with 121 rooms in Msida. *Published prices winter/summer: dbl €22/€29, trpl €17/22, sgl 24/49, dorm (6 or 8 beds, genders divided) €11/15. Discounts up to 35% available for walk-in/direct contact (except on dorms).*

✖ WHERE TO EAT

✖ **Ta' Kris** 80 Fawwara La; 21337367; m 99847713; www.PlanetSoftPages.com/takris; ⏱ 12.30–15.00 & 19.00–22.00/23.00 daily. On a tiny alley off Bisazza Street (one of Sliema's main shopping streets). Converted from a traditional Maltese bakery, the oven is still here & the warm orange walls are decorated with baking implements. Service can be a touch slow, but chef Kris produces excellent Maltese/Mediterranean food artistically presented & keeps the prices sensible. Families welcome. Highchairs available. Book in advance, it gets busy. *Starters €5–6.85, mains €7.80–11.55. 'Dad's famous braġioli' (see Food, page 61) €10.15.*

✖ **La Cuccagna** 47 Amery St/Triq Amery (just off the seafront); ☎ 21346703; m 99490550; www.starwebmalta.com/cuccagna.htm; ⏱ 19.00–24.00 Tue–Sat & 12.00–14.30 Sun. Welcoming, popular, inexpensive (for Sliema) pizza & pasta place. Recently doubled in size. Colourful hand-painted tile tables. Gluten-free pizza & pasta available with 24hrs notice.

Good for families. Highchairs available. *Maltese pizza & green salad for under €10, pasta €5.90–8.50.*

✖ **The Chef Wine Terrace & Bistro** Dragut Point St (Cambridge Pl); ☎ 21332044; m 79060808; e camilleri.mart@gmail.com; ⏱ in winter from 19.00 Wed–Sat & Sun lunch, in summer Tue–Sat evenings. Newly opened bistro in an attractive ex-pizzeria with stained glass & brightly coloured plates. The patron was chef of the 5-star hotel that occupied the building before the start of the Tigné Point development. He has also been the Captain of Malta's National Chef's team. There are rumours that it might move to Kalkara so check the website. *Soup €3, pastas €6.45–8.50, national platters €8.50–12.90 & always a slow-cooked roast.*

✖ **The Kitchen** 210 Tower Rd, Sliema; ☎ 21311112; e thekitchen@onvol.net; ⏱ 19.00–23.30 daily & lunch Thu–Mon, closed Jan & Aug. This small restaurant with an unprepossessing exterior & no outside seating won top award in Malta's Good

Restaurant guide for providing healthy options as well as being generally highly rated. Unusually, the menu includes interesting vegetarian dishes. *Starters €7.50–10.50, mains €17–22.75.*

✕ **Lungomare Gelateria** Cnr of Windsor & Stella Maris sts, by the waterfront. For a good ice cream on the go. Loads of flavours (& even a sugar-free one & a soya option).

WHAT TO SEE AND DO

Tigné Point Sliema has two waterfronts: The Strand (facing Valletta) and Tower Road which leads up to St Julian's. Between them is Tigné Point, which at the time of writing is a vast and hideous building site. It is supposed to be turning into a luxury development with a renovated Fort Tigné at its tip on Dragut Point. There is for now (and will be for some time to come) no access to **Dragut Point**, named for the fearsome Turkish corsair who harried Malta through the middle of the 16th century. Some accounts say that this is where he was mortally wounded during the Great Siege of 1565. Until the building work is completed, the best views of Tigné Fort are from Valletta.

Tigné Fort, constructed in 1792–5, was the last of the Knights' defences and one of the first truly polygonal forts in the world. It was intended (rather belatedly) to partner Fort St Elmo in the defence of Marsamxett Harbour. Just six years after it was built, Napoleon arrived, expelled the Knights and took Valletta. The Maltese rebelled and (with British help) found themselves firing the cannons of Fort Tigné at Fort St Elmo and their own capital.

The Strand The main attraction of The Strand is the great views of Valletta, especially impressive at night when the bastion walls of the capital are floodlit. The Strand also leads to the **Sliema Ferries**, not only the landing stage for the ferry and for many tourist boat trips, but also an area of shops, banks and other facilities. If you keep going along The Strand you come into Gzira, a less salubrious version of Sliema (home to the local red light district, though not on the waterfront) and the bridge to Manoel Island.

Manoel Island This island in Marsamxett Harbour was home to the **quarantine hospital** set up by the Knights in 1643 after bubonic plague had hit Malta twice, in 1592 and 1623. By the middle of the 18th century 1,000 people could be processed here at one time and ships could be quarantined for several weeks. The maximum penalty for breaking quarantine was death. This strictness seems to have paid off: Malta didn't suffer another serious outbreak of plague until 1813 and that was its last.

Fort Manoel was built on the orders of Grand Master Antonio Manoel de Vilhena (1722–36) to protect Marsamxett Harbour (this was before Fort Tigné was built). Some French troops were held here after their defeat in 1800 before signing away any rights to Malta and being sent back to France aboard ships of the British Royal Navy.

You can cross the bridge from Gzira to visit the island, but there is little to see besides decaying shipyards. The Tigné Point developer (see above) has Manoel Island next on his list, but given the time Tigné Point is taking it could be years before anything happens. Restoration work on the fort, however, is under way.

Tower Road Tower Road runs right along the northwest coast of Sliema to St Julian's, with a promenade along the seafront next to the rocks and the sea. There are few specific sights. This is a place for **strolling**, **swimming** and watching or joining the Maltese at play. There are cafés and bars varying from the brash and noisy to the calm and peaceful, as well as several ageing lidos (with changing rooms and showers) and a vast swathe of flattish rocks on which to picnic, sunbathe (if you can find a comfortable patch) and swim. The swimming is directly into deep clear water so best for competent swimmers and ideal for **snorkellers**. Be guided on exactly where to swim by where the locals choose.

There are two small historic forts, one at each end of the main stretch of promenade, Il-Fortizza at the Tigné Point end, and St Julian's Tower on the border with St Julian's. **Il-Fortizza**, also known as Sliema Point Battery or Għar Id-Dud, and now Fortizza Pizzeria, was built by the British in 1872–76 though in a Gothic style that makes it look much older. The observation tower was added in 1905. Originally equipped with artillery guns, these were replaced with searchlights after the 100-ton guns came into service at Fort Rinella (see page 158) and at Fort Cambridge. Fort Cambridge faced out to sea from the Sliema end of Tigné Point, but the gun was scrapped in the 1950s and the fort largely demolished so the site could be used for a five-star hotel. Most of this has also now been torn down to make way for the Tigné Point development, leaving only a listed British barrack block which was a military hospital in World War I. This has now become the Cambridge Place Hostel (see *Where to stay*, page 161).

St Julian's Tower is one of a system of coastal watchtowers built by Grand Master Martin de Redin in 1658–9 (see *Fortifications*, page 85) – later turned into a coastal battery in 1715. Its seafront terrace is now a snack and pizza bar with fresh fish and chips for a (rather steep) €14.95. Next to the tower is a colourful little **children's playground** and below, the Paradise Exiles terrace bar and café with a concrete lido and steps down from the rocks for **swimming** in deep water at the mouth of Balluta Bay.

ST JULIAN'S (SAN ĠILJAN) AND PACEVILLE

St Julian's covers the area from Balluta Bay to Spinola Bay, including both bays. Walk 100m up St George's Street (Triq San Ġorġ) from Spinola Bay to Spinola Gardens and you are in Paceville. On your right here is the shiny new and expensive Portomaso/Hilton complex. Keep going along St George's Street and you come to the heart of Paceville – full of bars, pubs, clubs, fast food and pounding bass: brasher, louder and cheaper.

GETTING THERE AND AROUND Buses 62, 64, 65, 66, 67, 68, 627 and 675 all go to St Julian's and Paceville (many of them also to Sliema; see page 160). Bus 65 joins both St Julian's and Paceville with Naxxar, Mosta, Ta' Qali and Mdina, and bus 70 runs along the north coast to Baħar iċ-Ċagħaq, Buġibba and Qawra. Bus 671 and 652 both also go to St Julian's and the 662 and 667 to Paceville. The 645 goes to Ċirkewwa.

Parking in St Julian's and Paceville can be difficult, particularly at weekends, but there is a large underground car park in the Portomaso complex (in front of the Hilton Hotel) and another by the Westin Dragonara Hotel where you can park for a few euros. Some, but by no means all, hotels have parking for their guests (and it may be charged as an extra) so if you are planning to stay here and hire a car it is worth checking.

Taxis are readily available in St Julian's and in Paceville; they gather both at Spinola Gardens next to the Portomaso complex and in St George's Bay by the shopping centre. Wembley Cars (*24hr taxi service;* ✆ *21374141 or 27374141;* e *wembleys@maltanet.net; www.wembleys.net*) is also based on St George's Street opposite the bus stop by Spinola Gardens.

WHERE TO STAY
Top end
Corinthia, St George's Bay ***** (250 rooms) St George's Bay; ✆ 21374114 or 21374039;

e stgeorges@cbr.corinthia.com; www.corinthia.com. Not to be confused with the Corinthia Marina, also

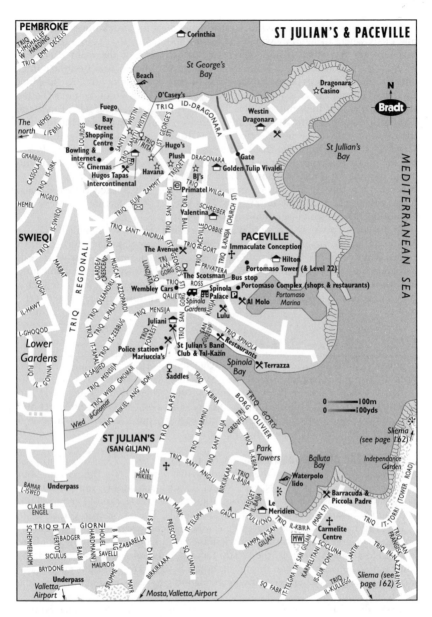

ST JULIAN'S & PACEVILLE

PEMBROKE

TRIQ L-IMGHALLEM
W HARDING
TRIQ EMM DECELIS

Corinthia

St George's Bay

Beach

O'Casey's

N

Bradt

Dragonara Casino

Westin Dragonara

St Jullian's Bay

MEDITERRANEAN SEA

The north

NEMES
LIEBRU

GHARBIEL

CASSOLA
TRIQ IS-SIRK
MIGBED

HEMEL

Fuego

Bay Street Shopping Centre

Bowling & internet

Cinemas
Hugos Tapas
Intercontinental

SANTU SANTI WISTIN
TRIQ SANTI WISTIN
TRIQ IS-RITA

Hugo's

Plush

Havana

BJ's

TRIQ GEORGE'S STR

TRESOTA

TRIQ ID-DRAGONARA

DRAGONARA

Gate

Golden Tulip Vivaldi

TRIQ WILGA

SWIEQI

SQ LOURDES

TRIQ ELIJA ZAMMIT

Primatel

TRIQ SAN GORG

TRIQ BALL

SCHREIBER

Valentina

DOBBIE

PACEVILLE

Immaculate Conception

IS-SWIEQI

TRIQ SANT' ANDRUA

TRIQ PACEGORT

TRIQ KNISJA (CHURCH ST)

Hilton

MARBAT

TRIQ REGIONALI

GARDEN CRESCENT

TRIQ MUSCAT AZZOPARDI

TRIQ IL-PALM

The Avenue

TRIQ SAN GORG'S

LUNZJATA

TRIQ PRIVATERA

ROSS

Portomaso Tower (& Level 22)

Bus stop

Portomaso Complex (shops & restaurants)

ILOUGH

IL-HAWT

L-GHOQOD

Lower Gardens

FUQ IL-GONNA

TRIQ OLEANDRU

TRIQ IL-PALM

QALIETA

The Scotsman

Wembley Cars

Spinola Palace

MENSIJA

Spinola Gardens

TRIQ SAN KNISJA

Al Molo

Lulu

Portomaso Marina

IT-TAMAR

TRIQ IZ-ZEBBUG

Juliani

TRIQ FOREST

Police station
Mariuccia's

St Julian's Band
Club & Tal-Kazin

TRIQ SPINOLA

Restaurants

Spinola Bay

Terrazza

IS-SAJJIED

Saddles

TRIQ WIED GHOMAR

TRIQ MIKIEL ANG BORG

Wied il-Gnomar

TRIQ LAPSI

TRIQ IL-KARRNU

BORG OLIVIER

TRIQ GORG

0 ————— 100m
0 ————— 100yds

Sliema
(see page 162)

ST JULIAN'S
(SAN GILJAN)

TRIQ SANT ANGLU

TRIQ IL-KBIRA

BIRKIRKARA

Park Towers

Balluta Bay

Independance Garden

SAN MIKIEL

Waterpolo lido

Barracuda &
Piccola Padre

BAHAR
L-ISWED

Underpass

TRIQ SAN MARK

IT-TELGHA TA GAUCI

TREQET IL-BAJJA

PULLICNO

Le Meridien

Carmelite Centre

TRIQ IT-TORRI (TOWER ROAD)

CLAIRE E
ENGEL

TRIQ TA' GIORNI

SCHEMBERHOM

BADGER

HOUEL HARDMANN

ZABARELLA

PRESCOTT

SQ CIANTAR

MAIN ST

RAMPA TA SAN GILJAN

KARMELITANI

SCICLUNA

IS-SUR FONS

LANTIK

TRIQ IN-NAZZARINU

TRIQ SAN FRANGISK

SICULUS

BALBI

SAVELLI

BIRKIRKARA

Sliema (see page 162)

BRYDONE

MAUROIS

Underpass

Valletta,
Airport

MUMME

Mosta, Valletta, Airport

IT-TELGHA TA SAN GILJAN

SQ FABR

TRIQ IL-KULLEGG

on St George's Bay, this is a typical modern, large resort hotel on the edge of St George's Bay. 3 swimming pools (1 indoor), gym & games room, 3 restaurants. *Dbls from approx €130 (winter), €220 (summer) room only (full buffet b/fast €16pppn), but see website or contact hotel.*

⌂ **Intercontinental** ***** (451 rooms) St George's Bay; ☎ 21377600 or 21372222; e malta@ intercontinental.com.mt; www.intercontinental.com.

Good hotel in a neon location — opposite the neon-lit Bay Street shopping centre, Paceville. Extensive paved 'garden', large indoor & outdoor pools. Private area of St George's Bay beach. *Dbls in Aug officially €199 (€238 B&B), but regular offers can cut this dramatically.*

⌂ **Le Meridien** ***** (276 rooms) 39 Main St, St Julian's; ☎ 23110000/0001/2810; e infolmsj@ lemeridien.com; www.lemeridienmalta.com.

International-standard, modern 5-star hotel right on Balluta Bay. Great place to be inside looking out: lovely views of St Julian's & the sea. Comfortable terraces, good-sized indoor & outdoor pool, spa (see page 101), fresh & spacious rooms. Rooms on the higher floors are better. Daytime kids' club. *Room rates vary daily & can fall as low as €82 for a dbl, room-only basis (min 5 nights) even in summer.*

🏠 **Radisson Spa Bay Point** ***** (124 rooms, 28 suites, 9 apts) St George's Bay; ✆ 21374894 or 21374895; e info@radisson.com.mt; www.islandhotels.com. Large resort hotel just beyond St George's Bay to the north. 3 outdoor pools, 1 indoor pool (heated in winter) & a children's pool, sauna, tennis, courtesy mini-bus. 3 restaurants (4 in summer), families welcome. *Standard dbls from €110 (winter), €160 summer (higher if high occupancy). Check website or call for best rates.*

🏠 **The Hilton** ***** (373 rooms, 31 suites) Portomaso; ✆ 21383383 or 21386386; e sales.malta@hilton.com; www.malta.hilton.com. Probably the top modern 5-star hotel in Malta. The Hilton is on the edge of Paceville in the shiny, expensive, Portomaso complex: 98m tower, private yacht marina, cafés & restaurants. The hotel has 4 outdoor & 1 indoor swimming pools, 2 children's paddling pools, a small rocky 'beach' (not open in

winter), jacuzzi, fitness centre, spa (see page 101), tennis & squash. Choice of classic or contemporary décor in rooms (the contemporary are newer), all with balconies overlooking the sea, swimming pools or yacht marina. Also 6 new studio apts/family suites (sleeping up to 4) that are quite a good deal if you need extended high-end hotel accommodation *(1–6 months €2,500/m, 6 months–1 year €1,950/m with use of hotel facilities but no meals).* The hotel has its own desalination plant so the tap water is drinkable & 99% of water is recycled. *Dbls officially from €385 (room only), but offers & advance booking can cut this by about 40% in summer, over 50% in winter.*

🏠 **Westin Dragonara Resort** ***** (340 rooms) Dragonara Rd, St Julian's; ✆ 21381000 or 21381347; e westin.dragonara@westin.com; www.westinmalta.com. Pompous exterior, but spacious recently renovated rooms with attractive bathrooms, good-sized balconies & sea views. Although on the edge of Paceville, rooms are quiet as they all face away from the town. Family rooms, kids' club & small outdoor children's play area. Private rocky 'beach'. Large sea-view terrace. Indoor, outdoor & children's pools. *Dbls from around €100 (winter), €230 (summer), but check the website or contact the hotel.*

Mid range

🏠 **Golden Tulip Vivaldi** **** (205 rooms) Dragonara Rd, St Julian's; ✆ 21378100 or 21378101; e sales@goldentulipvivaldi.com; www.goldentulipvivaldi.com. On the edge of Paceville opposite the Westin Dragonara. Typical modern high-ceilinged marble, wannabe 5-star-hotel lobby. No character but pleasant rooms (no views) & good service. Sauna, gym, cards to operate lift to keep out intruders. A few non-smoking rooms. *Dbls B&B €151.20 (summer), €102.90 (winter).*

🏠 **Hotel Valentina** *** (40 rooms, due to expand to 100) Schreiber St, Paceville; ✆ 21382232 or 21382406; e info@hotelvalentina.com; www.hotelvalentina.com. In one of the quieter parts of Paceville, this lovely hotel has more real style than many of the 5 stars. Fun, colourful, welcoming designer lobby, bar & restaurant with comfortable cream sofas

& bright cushions. Discounts at the Avenue (see *Where to eat*, below) which has the same owner. *Dbls B&B €54–114 (depending on season).*

🏠 **Juliani** **** (44 rooms) 12 St George's Rd, St Julian's; ✆ 21388000 or 21387800; e info@hoteljuliani.com; www.hoteljuliani.com. Overlooking Spinola Bay in the centre of St Julian's. City boutique hotel with smart but relaxed public areas full of comfortable seating, modern art & a cave enlarged into a World War II shelter that is now part of the bar. Cafe Juliani does particularly good salads & a children's menu (€4.50). The hotel's Asian restaurant, Zest, is very highly regarded (⏱ 19.00–23.00 Mon–Thu, 23.30 Fri–Sat). Rooftop terrace with small, tiled swimming pool. *Dbls €80–150 (room only) but prices vary with occupancy.*

✕ WHERE TO EAT

✕ **Al Molo** Portomaso Marina; ✆ 21384300 or 21372918; e info@marinarestaurants.com.mt; ⏱ 19.00–23.00 daily (closed Sun, Oct–Mar). Elegant modern fine dining Italian restaurant beside the Marina. Attentive, helpful service, excellent food immaculately presented. *Starters €9–15, pasta/risotto*

€10.50–15, mains €21–30, puds not always as described but delicious €6–7.50, cover charge €1.60.

✕ **The Avenue** Gort St, Paceville; ✆ 21351753 or 21378731; e info@hotelvalentina.com; www.theavenuemalta.com; ⏱ 18.00–23.30 daily &

7

12.00–14.30 Mon–Sat. Always buzzing, this popular family restaurant is 'cheap & cheerful' with plenty of choice. Highchairs available. *Kids' menu €3.80, pizza & pasta average at €7, mains €12.*

✗ **Barracuda** 194–5 Main St, St Julian's; ☎ 21331817; e barracuda@wgc-group.com; ⊕ from 18.30 daily. Elegant restaurant in an early 18th-century seaside villa with wonderful views of Balluta Bay. The restaurant is in what was once the drawing room & the conversion won an award from Din L-Art Ħelwa (Malta's National Trust). Excellent Mediterranean cuisine specialising in carpaccio & fresh fish. *Starters €9–11, mains 17–19.50, veg & salads €3.90–4.40, cover charge €2 (well, the amuse bouche was very tasty), min charge €14.*

✗ **Hugo's Tapas** St George's Bay, Paceville; ☎ 21383634; e info@hugostapas.com; www.hugostapas.com; ⊕ 12.00–23.45, 00.45 at w/ends. With the same owner as Hugo's (see *Bars and clubs*, below), this is a Paceville café-bar where you can actually hold a conversation. A chill-out modern interior with large chandeliers, but low light. *Tapas dishes €5.25–12.75.*

✗ **Lulu** 31 Church St/Triq Il-Knisja, Paceville/St Julian's border; m 79495007; e info@lulurestaurant.com; ⊕ 12.30–14.30 daily (closed Sat in winter) & 19.00–23.00 Mon–Sat. Smart, but relaxed modern restaurant with comfortable chairs & sofa-style benches. Large front window looks onto lit walls of Spinola Palace. The starters are a meal in themselves. Small menu. Good fresh fish. *Starters around €10, mains about €19, good puds €5, cover charge €1.25.*

✗ **Mariuccia's** 1 St George's Rd, Spinola Bay, St Julian's; ☎ 21384066, m 79497973; e marriuccia@tritonmalta.com; wwww.tritonmalta.com; ⊕ 19.00 onwards daily & Sun lunch. Newly opened restaurant under the same ownership as the Riviera della Marina in Vittoriosa (see page 146). In a traditional Maltese townhouse (of which there are few left in this area) with marble stairs & painted tiles, this restaurant serves only traditional Maltese food (inc rabbit, swordfish, octopus, pork & fresh fish) as well as offering a kids' menu of homemade fish fingers & chicken nuggets. Dine inside or out. *Starters around €5–6.50, mains €11–20, kids' menu €4.50.*

✗ **Piccolo Padre** 195 Main St (just into St Julian's from Sliema); ☎ 21344875; e piccolo@wgc-group.com; ⊕ 18.30–22.45 daily (23.30 in summer), 12.00–15.30 Sun winter only. Descend as if to go underground, but emerge into an attractive relaxed family-run pizzeria with uninterrupted views of the bay. For seats on the edge of the terrace or by the large windows, book or arrive early. Same ownership as elegant Barracuda upstairs (see above). Tasty thin-crust pizzas, pasta & seafood. Great for families. Highchairs available. *Pizzas €6.20–8.30.*

✗ **Tal-Każin** St Julian's Band Club (Banda San Ġiljan), St George's St, Spinola Bay; ☎ 21354361, m 99251459; ⊕ 18.00–22.30 Tue–Sat & for Sun lunch: 12.00–15.30/16.00. Cosy, traditional, inexpensive restaurant with football on TV. Local specialities, fresh fish & daily specials. *Soups €3, starters €3–6.25, mains €6–9.80.*

✗ **Terrazza** Spinola Bay, St Julian's; ☎ 21384939; e info@terrazzamalta.com; ⊕ 12.00–15.00 & 18.00–23.00 daily. Pass by the line of glitzy eateries along the side of Spinola Bay, leaving the hubbub behind, & instead sit high on the peaceful terrace of Terrazza (my favourite St Julian's restaurant). Lovely views, informal atmosphere, friendly knowledgeable staff & great food. Service is not fast but who cares: relax. *Starters/salads/pastas €5.25–9.50, mains €13.75–18.95. (steaks more), 'mini-man' kids' dishes €3.25–5.65. 4-course set menu €19.95.*

ENTERTAINMENT AND NIGHTLIFE

Bars and clubs A lot of the venues in Paceville change hands and names so regularly that there is little point in listing them. That said, there are some which have survived long enough to suggest they may still be there when you get there! The clubs of Paceville tend to have no entry fee and drinks mostly cost €2–2.50 (unless otherwise stated).

☆ **BJ's** Ball St/Triq Ball, Paceville; ☎ 21337642; m 99493534; ⊕ 22.00 daily until the early hours. Quite unlike anywhere else in the area, this congenial club is dedicated to live music, particularly jazz & blues, & it's the only place in Paceville where the average age is likely to be over 30. Younger people call this club 'retro' but it is actually original. Owner-manager Philip Fenech has run BJ's for 30 years & is still here almost every night. If things are quiet, sit at the bar & have a chat about jazz, business or current affairs. Unless there is a special guest, Mon–Wed is usually piano/acoustic, Thu jazz, Fri salsa, Sat classic rock & Sun young & up-&-coming or veterans. Past performers include John McCloughlan,

Aldi Maoila & Dee Dee Bridgewater, & (at his own request while filming in Malta) Bon Jovi. Starting on Easter Mon each year, the club runs BJ's Live Music Marathon (*www.bjslivemusicmarathon.com*) when a relay of musicians plays continuously for a week raising substantial sums for charity.

☆ **Fuego** St George's Bay (in the middle of the road between Bay St shopping centre & the Intercontinental Hotel); www.fuego.com.mt; ⊕ 22.30–04.00. Lively bar & disco with rainforest theme & windows with water bubbling through them. Free salsa classes Mon to Wed 20.30–22.00. Bouncers on the door & a multi-cultural clientele depending on which tourists are in that night. More Maltese people at w/ends. No entry fee. *Cocktails* €5–6.

☆ **Havana** St George's St, Paceville; ✆ 21374500; e carlo@havanamalta.com; www.havanamalta.com; ⊕ 20.00–04.00 daily. Large soul & R&B club with 6 bars on 2 floors & loads of room to dance. Also here is Flashback, playing music from the '60s to the '90s.

☆ **Hugo's** Santa Rita St/Triq Santa Rita, Paceville; ✆ 21382264. In the heart of Paceville, Hugo's has 3 floors. The ground floor is Hugo's Lounge (*www.hugosloungemalta.com*;

⊕ 11.00–02.00/03.00), a trendy sushi restaurant (*6-piece dishes from about* €7). The middle floor is a club with loud music, DJ & dancing from about midnight as well as a small outside terrace where you can just about hear yourself shout. The top-floor club is for over-21s & is open only at w/ends. The clubs open 20.00–04.00.

☆ **Level 22** Top floor of the Portomaso Tower; ⊕ 21.30–04.00 Wed–Sun (may close early on quiet nights), lounge bar Wed, Thu & Sun; club with DJ Fri & Sat. Upmarket venue on the 22nd floor of the tower next to the Hilton Hotel with fantastic views & a large screen showing music videos (rather than the usual football). On lounge bar nights it is candlelit, comfortable & the music is quiet enough to allow conversation. On DJ nights the dance floor is used. *Cocktails* €7–13.

☆ **Plush** St George's St, Paceville; ⊕ 20.00–04.00. Very dark, long bar-lounge in shiny black with red lights & disco. Pounding bass (even on the street outside). No chance of communications beyond the purely physical. Feels rather '80s though the teens of Paceville think it's very now. 1st-floor windowed gallery like a modern *gallerija* from which to observe the goings on in the street below.

Pubs There are quite a few 'pubs' – styled as English, Irish and Scottish. **The Scotsman** (*St George's St, Paceville;* ⊕ *11.00–late daily*) is a long survivor and **O'Casey's** (*Santa Rita St; Paceville;* ⊕ *09.00–04.00*) includes the Red Aroma restaurant that serves reasonably priced food, starting with breakfast (until 13.00; €7.50 for the works). **Saddles** (*see the neon sign; Spinola Bay, St Julian's;* ⊕ *09.00 until after midnight*) has a cosy pub atmosphere with table football as well as football on television. Popular first port of call for those starting the evening in St Julian's before heading up into Paceville.

Other entertainment There is a cinema and a bowling alley in St George's Bay, Paceville (see *Arts and entertainment*, page 65).

ST JULIAN'S Not so long ago St Julian's was a delightful little seaside fishing town. Unsympathetic development has changed all that, although if you look carefully at the two bays (Balluta Bay and Spinola Bay) – especially on a quiet night and with your back to the vast Meridien Hotel – you can still see what they once were. The 19th-century Carmelite church and priory (with 'gothic' windows added in the 20th century) look particularly impressive lit up after dark. During the **Festa of Our Lady of Mount Carmel** in late July you can get a great view of the fireworks from the Level 22 bar in Portomaso Tower (see above).

So long as you are expecting a modern resort town, St Julian's is quite pleasant and, along with neighbouring Paceville, it has some of the island's top modern five-star hotels and some excellent restaurants. You can swim in Balluta Bay and Spinola Bay, but there is no beach. A water polo lido sits to one side of Balluta Bay and many of the hotels have swimming pools as well as 'private' rocky 'beaches' from which to get into the sea. The nearest sand is at St George's Bay the other side of Paceville (see below).

Historically, the coast around St Julian's was largely uninhabited because of the fear of Turkish invasion. It was here that Dragut Reis anchored 15 ships when he arrived to join the Great Siege of 1565 and indeed here that Napoleon's General Vaubois disembarked in 1798. When the Royal Navy came to help remove the French, St Julian's became a British ship-repair yard and supply base. Development began later under the British, with the construction of a few seaside residences, but it went mad only in the 1970s with Malta's headlong plunge into mass tourism.

PACEVILLE Beyond Spinola Gardens, you enter the heart of Paceville (pronounced *Pachéville*), one of Malta's least peaceful areas with all the downsides of St Julian's and none of the residual charm. This is an area of bars, pubs, discos, clubs, hotels, fast-food outlets and restaurants all crammed together with the noise and the clientele spilling out onto the narrow (and fortunately part-pedestrianised) streets.

Paceville is most popular with teenagers (some certainly below Malta's official drinking age of 17), though the age rises into the 20s after about midnight. There is little to recommend this area to anyone older (or younger, or calmer) other than the live jazz and blues club BJs (see above, page 168) and a couple of restaurants. It might also attract a football addict in need of a fix as many of the bars show live television coverage of the English and Italian premier leagues – although these can also be found elsewhere.

On summer weekends Paceville can get not only busy, but rowdy and occasionally violent. The government has recently made it illegal to carry open glass bottles here or to drink alcohol on the streets and has started to enforce a 04.00 closing time.

On the St Julian's side of town, there are a few older buildings worth noting. **Palazzo Spinola** was built by an Italian Knight, Paola Raffaele Spinola, in 1688 when it was the first significant building in the area. It was enlarged by his great-nephew, another high-ranking Knight, Giovanni Battista Spinola, in 1733. It is now the Malta home of the Parliamentary Assembly of the Mediterranean and is not open to the public. The former stables of the palace house a Pizza Hut and the loggia that was originally boat houses built by Spinola for local fishermen, is home to a number of restaurants. Spinola Sr also built the nearby **Church of the Immaculate Conception** (1688).

The **Dragonara Palace** – now a casino – holds a commanding position on Dragonara Point. The point is named for the legend that the roars emanating from its rocks were those of a dragon. They were of course the roar of the sea. A colonnaded folly with Egyptian-style statues at its entrance, the palace was built in 1870 by a wealthy banker Emanuele Scicluna who, five years later, was made a marquis for lending money to the pope. His nephew inherited the palace and also created Palazzo Parisio in Naxxar (see page 222). During World War I the Dragonara Palace was an officers' hospital taking in the wounded of Gallipoli, and in World War II it housed people made homeless in the bombing. The casino opened in 1964 and the Westin Dragonara Hotel now stands in what was the palace gardens.

At the far side of Paceville is **St George's Bay** where you will find the Superbowl, cinema, shopping centre, and the only sandy beach in the area, a smallish stretch next to the road that is regularly topped up with imported coarse-grained sand.

The Intercontinental Hotel (see *Where to stay*, page 166) keeps it clean in return for having its private beach at one end. This is (at the time of writing) Malta's only Blue Flag beach (*www.blueflag.org*) and gets heavy use in summer.

The bay has the Westin Dragonara resort on the St Julian's side and the Corinthia hotels on the other (see *Where to stay*, page 165). The promenade is being extended to join the Corinthias to the existing prom (due for completion in 2011).

8

Southeast Malta

Outside the Cottonera Lines that enclose the Three Cities (see *Chapter 6*, page 143), urbanisation has now claimed an area far larger than that within the fortifications and consumed a number of historic villages along the way. In most of these suburban areas there is little to draw the visitor, but hidden amongst the houses are two of the most important sites in Malta – the **Tarxien temple** complex and the **Ħal Saflieni Hypogeum**. Further southeast is a site that takes you back even further – **Għar Dalam**, the cave occupied by Malta's first-known settlers. On the other half of the same large bay is **Marsaxlokk**, long the centre of fishing in Malta and now also of fish restaurants. Less on the tourist map, but with their own interest and historical importance, are Żejtun and Żabbar.

ŻABBAR

Żabbar lies just outside the Three Cities, the other side of the Żabbar Gate (see page 158). During the Great Siege, rural Żabbar had little protection and it was in the fields around here that the Turks established themselves to besiege Birgu. Only after the building of the huge Cottonera fortifications and the lessening of the threat from the Turks in the late 17th century did the population of Żabbar begin to grow. Today it is the fourth-largest population centre in Malta with over 14,500 people.

In the middle of a roundabout along the road from the Żabbar Gate stands the rather forgotten-looking **Hompesch Arch**, once the main entrance to Żabbar. It was built to celebrate the elevation of the village into a town by Grand Master Hompesch (1797–8), the Order's last Grand Master in Malta. Żabbar is still officially known as 'Citta Hompesch'.

In the centre of town is the heavily decorated parish church, the **Sanctuary of Our Lady of Divine Grace** (tal-Grazzja, *festa* in September). Originally built between 1641 and 1696, it has been subjected to copious later adjustments and additions. The altarpiece of Our Lady is Crowned (making it particularly sacred in Catholic eyes) and has long been the object of pilgrimage and requests for intercession. There is a significant collection of ex-voto paintings (see boxed text, page 280) in the small purpose-built **Sanctuary Museum** (⊕ *9.00–12.00 daily*). Most are connected with seafaring at the time of the Knights. Also in the museum are sedan chairs, an 18th-century model of a ship of the line, a plague hearse (1813), silverware, coins and religious paintings by Mattia Preti and Giuseppe Calí amongst others. A small exhibition recalls the explosion of an RAF Vulcan bomber over Żabbar in 1975. Some locals regard the fact that only one resident died, despite the debris landing around a packed school, as a veritable miracle.

GETTING THERE AND AWAY Buses 17, 18, 19 and 21 link Żabbar and Valletta, and bus 22 goes to Marsaskala. Parking is possible on the streets but be aware of the usual restrictions.

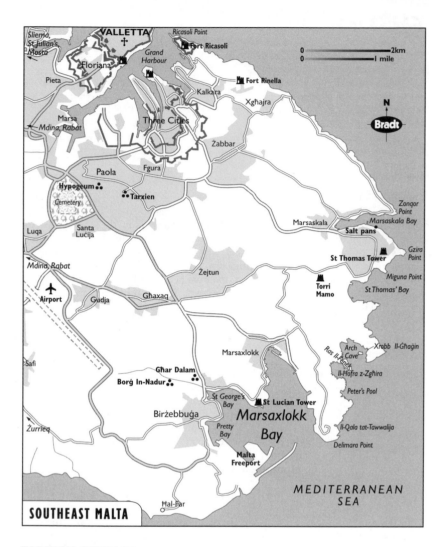

SOUTHEAST MALTA

TARXIEN TEMPLES

(Neolithic Temples St, Tarxien PLA11; ✆ *21695578;* e *info@heritagemalta.org;* *www.heritagemalta.org;* ⊕ *09.00–15.00 daily (last entry 16.30);* €6 *adults,* €4.50 *over-60s/children aged 12–17/students,* €3 *children aged 6–12, children under 6 go free)* This is the most complex of the temple sites, and was the most decorated. Tarxien is the source of many of the outstanding carved reliefs and statues now in the National Museum of Archaeology in Valletta (see page 121), represented on site by copies. The Tarxien site is not picturesque, walled around as it is with an unattractive modern suburb, but it is of huge archaeological importance and there is plenty to see.

Rediscovered by local farmers in 1913–14 when their ploughs kept hitting large lumps of stone, the site was excavated by 'the father of Maltese archaeology' Temi Zammit (see boxed text, page 176) in 1915–19. The remains of four temples were revealed, the earliest (Tarxien Far East) dating from the first phase of temple building (from 3600BC) with the South and East temples added in the period named after them, Tarxien phase (3000–2500BC) and the Central one slotted in between them. Changes and embellishments seem to have continued until the temple culture disappeared in 2500BC.

The South Temple (the first temple you reach) was reused as a crematorium/cemetery in the early Bronze Age (2500–1500BC) – leaving evidence of a very different culture from that of the temple people. The Tarxien Cemetery People burnt their dead, storing the ashes in urns, and made use of copper weapons. The Romans also reused the site, and a medieval oven was constructed in front of the East Temple before soil covered the area until the 20th century.

GETTING THERE AND AWAY Buses 8, 11, 12, 13 and 27 come to the temples from Valletta, and number 427 from Buġibba or Marsaxlokk. The 1, 2, 3, 4 and 6 (from Valletta) stop in Paola's main square, a short walk to the temples – take Church Avenue before turning right into Neolithic Temples Street. The temples are a few minutes' walk from the hypogeum (where bus 15 stops) and the ticket offices at both the Tarxien Temples and the hypogeum should be able to give you a little map showing how to get between the two. There is free parking on the street outside though it is not always easy to find a space.

PRACTICALITIES The ticket office sells a few books about the temple culture including a **guidebook**, *The Tarxien Temples* by Anthony Pace (*Insight Heritage Guides;* €6.99) which contains quite detailed information and an excellent aerial photo. There are toilets here too, but no other facilities. There are shops close by if you are in need of snacks or water.

EXPLORING THE TEMPLES

Tarxien South Built between 3000BC and 2500BC, Tarxien South was probably the most richly decorated temple on the islands. It was first built as a four-apse temple but had various structural changes made during prehistory as well as after. Entering the Tarxien site, the path runs along beside the reconstructed west end of the façade of the South Temple to the **monumental entrance** rebuilt in 1960 (thank goodness they don't do that anymore!). In front of the temple are some **stone spheres** (about the size of cannonballs) and a picture of how the temple builders might have used them as rollers to transport building blocks. Given that we know that the temple people had animals, some experts believe animals, rather than people, would have pulled the stones. Others doubt that these stone spheres were used as rollers at all, believing they could have had ritual significance, perhaps as votive offerings.

To the right of the doorway, a bit of the **original façade bench** survives, and at the far end of the façade is a massive stone with its centre carved out to create a kind of three-sided box. Its floor is punctured by five holes. This may have been a **shrine** and the holes could have been libation holes through which to pour offerings to the underworld.

Going through the reconstructed doorway, you enter what was probably once the most elaborate area of any temple on the islands. In the right apse stood a '**fat lady' statue** more than 2m high, the largest known from Maltese prehistory. Only the lower half of the body – its conical thighs and pleated skirt – survives. A copy stands here now; the original is in the National Archaeological Museum in Valletta (see page 121). On the left in this same apse is a very interesting '**altar**' (also a copy, the original is in the museum). It consists of a large block decorated with spirals with a flat table-like top on which stands a small shrine (or niche) made of cleanly cut rectangular stones. Look carefully at the front of the base block and you will see that there is a semicircular stone that is removable. The inside is in fact hollow. When first discovered by Temi Zammit the plug stone was held in place with two

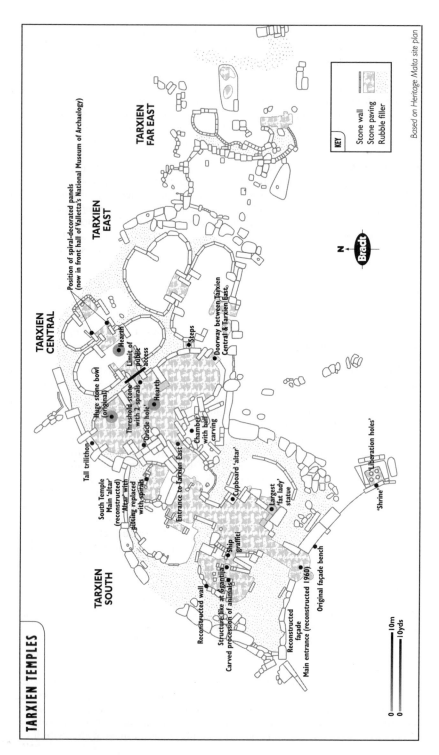

TARXIEN TEMPLES

TARXIEN CENTRAL

Position of spiral-decorated panels
(now in front hall of Valletta's National Museum of Archaelogy)

TARXIEN EAST

TARXIEN FAR EAST

Hearth

Limit of public access

Huge stone bowl (original)

Threshold stone with 2 spirals

Oracle hole

Hearth

Steps

Doorway between Tarxien Central & Tarxien East

Chamber with bull carving

Tall trilithon

South Temple Main 'altar' (reconstructed)

'Altar' with spirals replaced with spirals

Entrance to Tarxien East

Cupboard 'altar'

Largest 'fat lady' statue

Liberation holes

'Shrine'

TARXIEN SOUTH

Reconstructed wall

Structure like at Ggantija

Carved procession of animals

Ship graffiti

Reconstructed façade

Main entrance (reconstructed 1960)

Original façade bench

KEY

Stone wall

Stone paving

Rubble filler

N

Bradt

Based on Heritage Malta site plan

0   10m
0   10yds

174

small wedges and within the **'cupboard'** were found a 4½-inch flint knife, oxen and sheep bones, marine shells, a bone spatula and fragments of pottery. The knife and bones are the best evidence so far of animal sacrifice in the temples.

Other spiral stones decorate this apse and the one opposite it, where, on the floor, can be seen an oblong stone carved with a procession of domestic animals. The semicircular threshold stone flanked by two spiral-decorated screens that fronts this apse is almost identical to a structure in the first right apse of the South Temple at Ggantija (on Gozo, see page 284), attesting to close links between Malta and Gozo during the time of the temple culture. The back wall of this apse is partly reconstructed; the small stones are modern. Some believe this western wall may not in fact have collapsed but removed deliberately during prehistory. The first section of this temple is also where Bronze Age **cremation urns** were found.

In the doorway to the next apses are large hinge holes suggesting this was once a closable entrance. Similar arrangements can be seen on other doorways. The **inner apses** are less adorned than the first two, but the **central altar** is decorated with pitting which has been partially replaced with spirals. This is more easily seen on the original preserved in the museum in Valletta. The right-hand apse was restructured in prehistory to give access to the next temple, Tarxien Central.

Tarxien Central The only surviving six-apse temple, the layout of Tarxien Central is quite hard to fathom on the ground so do take a look at the plan opposite. Immediately visible is a **low bowl**, partly reddened by fire, probably a hearth. In the left apse is a **much larger and more impressive bowl** – an original – carved of globigerina limestone. This would not have withstood fire (and is not reddened) and its use is unknown. Also in this apse are a **porthole doorway** and a very **tall trilithon** (uprights with a top stone across them) that could possibly be a blocked doorway.

The walls of large close-fitting stones (orthostats) in this apse are reddened by fire which may date from the Bronze Age when the temple was a crematorium, or from an earlier destructive fire. Some say this apse is structurally unsuited to a corbelled stone roof and may have been roofed with wood or not at all. The discolouring due to fire and the fact that the floor is paved with stone slabs, may be evidence that this part of the temple was open to the sky.

The first apse on the right has a chamber off it containing original **carvings** of two bulls and a sow with piglets (more evidence of the importance of domesticated animals). They are badly weathered and hard to make out but the images are known from a plaster cast (now in the Museum of Archaeology, Valletta) taken in the 1950s before the carving became so faint. Their poor state makes clear the necessity for the plastic roofing that now covers them.

The **innermost part of the temple** is (at the time of writing) closed to the public. It is separated from the first two apses by a vertical threshold stone, carved with two spirals. It has been suggested that this partial barrier marked the start of a more sacred area of the temple or a part with a different function. The second two apses beyond this point were once screened by the large spiral-decorated slabs now in the front hall of the museum in Valletta. Should this section of the temple reopen to the public, look in the inner-left apse for a little set of shelves that could almost have been built yesterday.

Back in the first right apse is the way out of Tarxien Central and into Tarxien East. Just to the left of this doorway (before going through) is a hole in the paving through which a stone sphere (like those at the front of the temple) can be seen. One school of thought sees its presence here – tucked under one of the massive paving slabs – as evidence that it was used to roll the stone above it into place.

Tarxien East To the left just inside this temple is an unusual **flight of steps** which must have led to a second floor or perhaps to the roof. The flooring at ground level is of torba (ground limestone) rather than stone slabs so this temple would almost certainly have been roofed. At the time of writing you cannot enter this temple but you can admire the way the huge vertical building blocks (orthostats) fit so closely together.

Tarxien Far East Beyond and separate from the three linked temples is the earliest building on the site, a much less well-preserved five-apse temple. It was built of smaller, rougher blocks; less stable than the huge orthostats of the later temples and more easily carted off for other uses. You may be able to make out the raised threshold which was once the main entrance at the centre of a concave façade.

HAL SAFLIENI HYPOGEUM

(*Burial St, Paola PLA 1116;* ✆ *21805018/9;* e *info@heritagemalta.org; www.heritagemalta.org; pre-booked tours only, on the hour 09.00–16.00; €20 adults, €15 over-60s/children aged 12–17/students, €12 children aged 6–11. Children under 6 not admitted. Numbers are limited to 10/tour to protect this UNESCO World Heritage site, so book well in advance (weeks ahead in peak season). Tickets available online. Any problems, contact* e *hypogeum@gov.mt; tickets for the 12.00 & 16.00 tours are not sold online, but on a first-come-first-served basis at 09.00 the day before the tour at the Museum of Fine Arts in Valletta for €25pp (see page 135). Essential audio guide available in English, French, German, Italian, Japanese, Maltese & Spanish, & soon as text for the hard-of-hearing.*) An unobtrusive doorway in a suburban street is the unlikely entrance to this extraordinary prehistoric site – a complex underground burial chamber, a temple of the dead that echoes the architecture of the above-ground temples. Built on three levels (Upper 3600–3300BC, Middle 3300–3000BC, Lower 3150–2500BC), the Hypogeum probably served the same community as the Tarxien Temples – and perhaps also the nearby Kordin Temples (see page 177). Protected from weather and human interference, the hypogeum offers a unique insight into the art and culture of the temple people.

Discovered in 1899, the find was not reported until four years later when a workman digging a cistern broke through into the hypogeum again. The site was first examined by a Jesuit priest and historian of Maltese antiquity, Father Manwel Magri. Unfortunately, in 1907 he was called away to do missionary work in Tunisia where he died and the records of his excavation have never been found. Temi Zammit (see boxed text, page 176) took over in 1910 and his report on the site is still a key document. It was he who estimated that the hypogeum once held some 7,000 bodies. This might seem a lot on an island whose entire prehistoric population was probably around that figure, but it is not excessive bearing in mind that the hypogeum was in use for nearly 1,000 years.

GETTING THERE See *Tarxien Temples*, page 173.

EXPLORING THE SITE The hypogeum tour starts in a small **museum** displaying a few items found amongst the burials. The most important finds, however, including the iconic Sleeping Lady, are in the National Museum of Archaeology in Valletta (see page 121). A highly informative film tells the history of the site, before you descend into the maze of underground passages, halls and interconnecting chambers – particularly atmospheric because, for preservation reasons, lights only come on for a limited time at each stop.

The tour starts on the **upper (oldest) level**, which would once have had a monumental entrance and possibly been marked with a stone circle. As it sits at the edge of the Tarxien plateau, this would have made it visible from the Grand Harbour. The people who dug this complex – particularly the later parts – were sophisticated geo-engineers, using natural fault lines to achieve the strongest and smoothest walls. And they carved and smoothed them further, creating illusions of architecture: pitted columns, windows and doors, benches and even – in the so-called Holy of Holies – a corbelled roof (excellent evidence that this system of roofing was used above ground). The corners and lines of these architectural features are as clean and sharp as if they had been made machine-made yesterday, yet they were made entirely by hand some 5,000 years ago.

In a few places, painted decoration can be seen – red ochre spirals, a plant-like structure (a tree of life?) and something not seen above ground: a chequered pattern of black-and-white squares. In the **'oracle chamber'** a concave stone has a bizarre effect on the male voice. Low-pitched sounds are amplified, reverberating around the subterranean complex. Whether this is deliberate and perhaps used in ritual, or a chance effect, we can only guess.

There are also a few stone spheres of the type some experts believe were used to roll stones into place. The sceptical cite their presence underground – where the architecture is cut from the rock not built of blocks – as evidence that the balls were not rollers but had some other significance.

One other underground tomb complex has been found, the much smaller and rougher Xagħra Hypogeum on Gozo (see page 287) and research is beginning to try to locate further hypogea that may have been linked to other known temple sites.

KORDIN III TEMPLES

(*Next to the Capuchin church in Paola which has a huge purple cross outside, & opposite the country's only mosque; ⊕ by appointment with Fondazzjoni Wirt Artna;* ✎ *21800992 or 21809713;* e *info@wirtartna.org; www.wirtartna.org;* €*6pp; there are no facilities at the site at all*) There were originally three temple complexes in this area (hence the name), but only this one survives. At the time of writing the site is badly overgrown so it is difficult to make out the features of the temples and is only for the very interested. There are, however, plans to clear it up and open it more regularly to the public. For now, it will help a lot to have the **guidebook** (*The Prehistoric Temples at Kordin III* by Nicholas Vella, Insight Heritage Guides; €6.99) with its aerial photo and explanations. Better still, the company of a knowledgeable person who can point things out (ask when booking entry as the FWA has well-informed staff but may just send someone with a set of keys).

GETTING THERE AND AWAY Buses 1, 2, 4 and 6 from Valletta will get you here or you can park in the large church car park for free. The site is about 1km from the hypogeum. If asking for directions, or for the right bus stop, ask for the mosque. It is the only one on the islands so everyone knows it.

EXPLORING THE TEMPLES There are **two temples** on this site. The one to the **left** is the better preserved and here it should be possible to make out the line of the concave façade and the entrance with a sill, a raised threshold over which you must step to enter. It is a three-apse globigerina limestone temple built in about 3600–3200BC (Ggantija phase; see page 4). The apses have been walled off, probably during the Tarxien phase about 3000BC – something that is also seen at the Skorba Temple site (see page 229). Unusually, both the courtyard outside the temple and the inner court are paved (though you won't see this until it has been weeded!).

The most interesting (indeed unique) feature of this temple is a large **trough** made from a single piece of coralline limestone (probably hauled from an outcrop about a kilometre away near Żabbar) with seven compartments carved out of it, separated by narrow walls of stone. The trough lies across the threshold of part of the left apse and is thought to be a quern for grinding grain – evidence of at least some secular activity in the 'temple'.

The **right-hand temple** (closer to the entrance) is of a similar age but has just two apses. Behind it, almost impossible to make out at present, are traces of elliptical torba-floored huts (perhaps 3800BC) suggesting the presence here (again, as at Skorba) of a village before the temples were built.

ŻEJTUN

Originally the main village in the area, Żejtun has (by virtue of being further from the urban centres of Valletta, Sliema and the Three Cities) retained some integrity. Named for its production of olive oil (*żejt* means 'oil') Żejtun was right in the path of the invaders in 1565 at the start of the Great Siege. Fortunately Grand Master Jean Parisot de Valette had the foresight to evacuate the population and their livestock to within the fortifications of Birgu. The cavalry left to patrol the area were the first to engage the Turks. Two young knights were captured and the lies they told under torture led the Turks to the wrong strategic conclusions and helped the Order towards its eventual narrow victory. The two knights paid with their lives.

At the centre of the town today is the fine Baroque **Parish Church of St Catherine** with Classical pilasters and an octagonal dome. It was designed by Lorenzo Gafá (architect of the cathedrals of Mdina and Gozo) and built between 1692 and 1728. The *festa* here in held in June.

The parish of Żejtun goes back long before this church was built and was one of the original ten Maltese parishes listed in 1436. At that time the parish church was the much smaller Old Church of St Catherine of Alexandria, usually known as the **Church of St Gregory** (*San Girgor; St Gregory St;* ✆ *21677187*) which had just been built. Its low dome, now thought to be the oldest in Malta, was added in 1495. The Knights made their own alterations and additions but apart from the 16th-century Renaissance portal, the façade is 15th century. The interior frescoes, however, were lost when the Royal Engineers (who really ought to have known better!) whitewashed the church for use as a storeroom after World War II.

If you look at the main door you will see that it is off-centre. This was intended to prevent the devil – who apparently only walks in straight lines – from disrupting services! There is also a more macabre oddity: up a narrow stone spiral staircase are two secret passageways hidden between the inner and outer walls of the church. These passageways were discovered in 1969 and found to contain the bones of a few tens of people. Nobody knows who they were or how they got there. Some suggest they were locals who hid here during the Turkish raid of 1547 and were overpowered by smoke when the Turks set light to the inside of the church. Others, noting that the bones were neatly stacked when found, say they may have come from elsewhere. The passageways can be visited by arrangement with Connie Apap at the church.

GETTING THERE AND AWAY Buses 29 and 30 come here from Valletta via the Tarxien Temples and the Hypogeum. Number 27 comes from Valletta and goes on to Marsaxlokk, and bus 110 goes to Birżebbuġa and Marsaxlokk. **Parking** is possible on the streets, but beware of the usual range of restrictions.

MARSASKALA/MARSASCALA

This small harbour town (whose name is sometimes shortened to M'Skala) with a mix of traditional and modern small boats in the water has a pleasant-enough seafront promenade. There the rest of the town feels a bit run-down and the bars at the bus-station end of the seafront can be noisy. There are no sights within the town – though a few nearby (see below) – but there are several good restaurants.

GETTING THERE Buses 17, 19 and 20 will bring you here from Valletta, while number 22 links Marsaskala with Cospicua in the Three Cities. The main bus station is in the middle of town on the seafront by Grabiel's restaurant (see *Where to eat,* below). Parking is free.

✘ WHERE TO EAT

✘ **Grabiel** Mifsud Bonnici Sq; ☎ 21634194 or 21636368; ⊕ 12.00–14.00 & 17.00–22.00 Mon–Sat. Traditional trattoria-style restaurant that you know is good the minute you enter just from the smells. A painting of the harbour on glass separates the entrance from the restaurant. Mainly Italian cuisine, specialising in fish. The kitchen separates Grabiel from Terrazza (see below) – the café with the same owners. *Starters €8.50, mains €13.85–19.00.*

✘ **La Favorita** Triq il-Gardiel; ☎ 21634113; ⊕ 12.00–14.30 daily & Mon–Sat 19.00–23.00. Almost next door to Tal-Familja (see below), this restaurant is also family run & although it looks less prepossessing, the food is at least as good &

prices lower. Emphasis on fresh fish & seafood. Families welcome. *Starters €3.50–8.50, pasta €5.75–7.75 (+€2.50 for main), mains €12.50–19.50, many puddings €2.75.*

✘ **Tal-Familja** Triq il-Gardiel; ☎ 21632161; ⌂ 99473081; www.talfamiljarestaurant.com; ⊕ 12.00–15.00 & 18.00–23.30 daily. Up a seedy road alongside a stagnant canal beyond the seafront. Popular family-run & family-friendly restaurant. Traditional décor, unpretentiously stylish, specialising in fish & Maltese food. Highchairs available. Singer/guitarist Sat evening & Sun lunchtime. *Starters €6–10.50, pasta €6–8.50 (+€3.50 for main), mains €10–23, kids' menu €5–9, 4-course Maltese set menu €17.50.*

X **Terrazza** Mifsud Bonnici Sq (see Grabiel for contact details, above); ⊕ all day. Same owner as Grabiel next door, this Formica-table-style café offers live football on TV without the rowdiness of the bars over the road. *Pizzas, wraps & salads €5.75–9.50, kids' menu €3.50–3.90 & ice cream €1.75.*

WHAT TO SEE AND DO AROUND MARSASKALA

St Thomas's Tower On the Il-Gzira headland between Marsaskala Bay and St Thomas's Bay this substantial tower was built after the last full-scale Turkish invasion of Malta which landed at Marsaskala in 1614. The 5,000-strong force was beaten back, but only when it reached Żejtun. St Thomas's Tower was part of Grand Master de Wignacourt's scheme to strengthen coastal defences that included the building of six new watchtowers. The exterior of this tower has been recently renovated and now looks very fine. At the time of writing the derelict hotel opposite mars the scene, but it is apparently to be pulled down and rebuilt. You can go inside by appointment with Fondazzjoni Wirt Artna (❧ *21800992 or 21809713;* e *info@wirtartna.org; www.wirtartna.org*), but there isn't much to see – better to visit one of the towers that are regularly open to the public (see *Chapter 4,* page 85).

St Thomas's Bay Not picturesque, but if you are hot and need a cooling dip in the sea, this bay might fit the bill. Locals crowd in on summer weekends and there is a café pizzeria next to the rocks. From here, it is possible to walk to the next bay (see *Xrobb Il-Għagin,* below) in about half an hour.

Torri Mamo (*Triq id-Damla Ta' San Tumas, about 10mins' walk from the Marsaskala bus station. Restored & run by Din L-Art Ħelwa (Malta's National Trust):* ❧ *21225952;* e *info@dinlarthelwa.org; www.dinlarthelwa.org;* ⊕ *09.30–12.00 Thu–Sun; free entry*) A very unusual fortified home built by the Mamo family in 1657. The house is shaped like the cross of St Andrew giving it 16 sides. Inside is a domed central room with four rooms off it (the arms of the cross). A staircase leads to the roof which has views as far as St Thomas's Bay – the most likely source of the pirates against whom the house was fortified. It originally had a drawbridge across the 2m ditch that runs right round the building and in the ditch is a 4th-century Roman tomb, possibly first used in Phoenician times.

MARSAXLOKK

A few of Malta's traditional brightly painted boats can be seen in many of the country's harbours, but the place to see them *en masse* is Marsaxlokk, a pleasant fishing village with a long harbourfront full of cafés and restaurants, mostly specialising in fish fresh off the boats.

At one end of the harbour is the village square with its parish church (*festa* at the beginning of August) and on the harbourside itself is a daily market – relatively small Monday to Saturday but quite substantial on Sundays – selling everything from pungent fresh fish to local honey, clothes and souvenirs. There is also a stall making *imqaret* (pronounced *im-aart*), a delicious deep-fried sweet snack of pastry, date paste and fennel seed.

HISTORY Marsaxlokk has always had a good harbour. Prehistoric Maltese people almost certainly fished from here, and at the start of the Great Siege, 181 Turkish galleys sailed in with 35,000 of Mustapha Pasha's men on board (see *History,* page 11). Over two centuries later, in 1798, this was one of five places where the French landed by night for their successful invasion (but short-lived occupation) of Malta. The British duly followed, using the bay to resupply their forces and repair their ships. In December 1989, in the midst of a wild winter storm, US President George

In Malta, it being an archipelago in the middle of the Mediterranean, boats have necessarily played a crucial role in both culture and survival. Even today, traditional boats find their place alongside modern yachts and motorboats. The old boats are easy to spot as they are made of wood and painted in bright colours, particularly blue, red, yellow and green and most have a black 'moustache' across the bow.

Luzzu An open, traditional fishing boat with a high pointy prow and stern. Sea-going, but for day trips rather than lengthy voyages. Traditionally used to catch *lampuki*, the national fish, and sometimes sporting the 'eye of Osiris' on the prow to ward off evil and bring good luck. Traditional *luzzus* are no longer built but many survive.

Kajjik (*caiques*) A smaller fishing boat with a high pointy prow, but a flat stern. Traditionally only about 4m long and intended for coastal fishing; later versions were bigger and often went well out to sea. A popular fishing craft. In 1920, more than half of Malta's 760 registered fishing boats were *kajjiks*.

Dgħajsa A traditional harbour boat for transport rather than fishing. Originally rowed – from a standing position Venetian-style. Now most also have motors. A host of these boats used to ply the waters of the Grand Harbour. Most disappeared when the Royal Navy left and there were no longer sailors needing transport to and from their ships. A few survive as water taxis, mainly for tourists.

Dgħajsa tal-Latini or the 'Gozo Boat' The first Gozo sailing ferry, an oversized, strongly built, version of the *dgħajsa* with two masts. With the later addition of a motor, it ran between Malta and Gozo until the 1960s. One of the last Gozo boats, *Sacra Famiglia*, is being renovated and will eventually be on display in Mġarr, Gozo.

Bush Sr and Soviet President Mikhail Gorbachev held their ground-breaking end-of-the-Cold War Malta Summit here on board Soviet cruise ship SS *Maxim Gorky*.

GETTING THERE AND AWAY Bus 27 comes to Marsaxlokk from Valletta, while buses 427 and 627 come from Buġibba. The 427 also stops at Mosta and St Anton Gardens, and the 627 comes via St Julian's and Sliema. There is **parking** on the streets.

WHERE TO STAY

Duncan Guesthouse (8 studios) Rooms above Duncan restaurant; 21657212; e info@ duncanmalta.com; www.duncanmalta.com. The only tourist accommodation in Marsaxlokk. 8 very good-value, spacious studio rooms, 7 with balcony, all with modern shower rooms, TV, fridge & microwave. Guests have use of a washing machine & the flat roof. Some rooms can sleep 4, even 5. From €32 for 2 (no balcony, low season) to €45 (with balcony, summer). Children 3–12 €12, small charge for cots (free if staying a week). B/fast available in café (see below) from 08.00.

WHERE TO EAT Marsaxlokk is where the Maltese come to eat fresh fish (although restaurants elsewhere also do excellent fish). The restaurants along the harbour here (most of them indoor) display whole fresh fish on trays or trolleys so you can select your own. They are usually simply grilled or steamed. You have to take the whole fish so you will need two (or more) people (or a large appetite and a deep pocket) if you choose a big beast. What is on offer varies by season, with Malta's national favourite – *lampuki* (dolphin fish) – usually available mid-August until December. The price of a fish dish depends on the species and the weight. Most main courses come in at about €12–16 but do ask (the main course prices quoted below are necessarily for other main courses). All the eateries recommended here are on the road along the harbourfront, Xatt is-Sajjieda, so only building numbers are given in the individual entries.

✗ **Acqua Pazza** No 43; ☏ 21651190; ⏰ 19.00 onwards Tue–Sat & for lunch on Sun (from 12.00). A small smart but relaxed restaurant at the far end of the harbour from the square. Excellent service, pressed white tablecloths & white walls with splashes of bright modern art. Excellent fresh fish, pastas (inc with lobster or sea urchin sauces) & particularly tasty vegetables. *Starters around €8, mains average €16.*

✗ **Duncan bar & restaurant** No 32; ☏ 21657212; ⏰ 10.00–16.00 daily & 19.00–22.00/23.00 Wed–Sun in summer, Fri–Sun (winter). Fresh fish isn't cheap so if you are on a tight budget, Duncan's, on the corner of Church Square, is the place to get a filling pasta dish. Tables inside & out. *From €3 (starter size), €4.50 (main).*

✗ **La Capanna** No 60; ☏ 21657755; ⏰ 12.00–15.00 & 19.00–22.30 daily. Pine & beamed interior & a few outside tables, highly rated by the Maltese in Malta's *Good Restaurant Guide*. Prefers children to be over 5. *Starters average €7, mains €9–19.*

✗ **Ix-Xlukkajr** no 47; ☏ 21652109; m 99247365; e vivian.deb@hotmail.com; ⏰ 10.00–11.30 daily, 12.00–16.00 & 19.00–22.30 Tue–Sun. Considerably more expensive than some of the others but with more space outside as it is on the corner of the church square. Highchairs available. *Starters €6.40–9.90, mains €8.95–20.90.*

✗ **Ir-Rizzu** No 52; ☏ 21651569/0492; www.ir-rizzu.com; ⏰ 12.00–15.00 daily, 18.00–22.30 Mon–Sat. Large, busy, family-run & noisy when full. Service is efficient rather than attentive. Chips & salad rather than fancy veg. Prominent Maltese eat alongside foreigners & locals of all ages (highchairs to wheelchairs). *Pasta starters €6–7, mains €10–20, kids' menu (nugget-style) €5.*

✗ **Ron's** No 54; ☏ 21659382; ⏰ 11.30–16.00 daily, 19.00–22.00 Fri & Sat. A small upstairs restaurant with a couple of tables outside. Gregarious owner with some keen regulars. *Starters €4.50–8, mains around €12.*

DELIMARA PENINSULA AND SWIMMING

The Delimara Peninsula is a few kilometres outside Marsaxlokk. It is walking distance (30–40 minutes) to the swimming places below, but in summer it is a hot and not especially nice walk. Otherwise you need a car or taxi to get here.

On the Marsaxlokk side of the peninsula is Malta's largest power station. On the other side are some of the best swimming spots in the area. A single road runs the length of the peninsula. You can park almost anywhere along it.

PETER'S POOL A delightful spot to sit and to swim, Peter's Pool is signposted from the road but you cannot drive all the way to it – one reason it remains so nice! Walk five minutes through small agricultural fields and caper bushes then down some rough stone steps to reach this rocky cove. High sides block out views of the power station and the water is clear and inviting. Deserted on spring and autumn weekdays. Even in summer, Peter's Pool is rarely overcrowded. Be warned, it is not safe to swim here if there is any swell or choppiness. Blissfully free of any commercialisation so you will need to bring your own water and refreshments.

DELIMARA BAY/IL-QALA T-TAWWALIJA Further along the peninsula towards the point is another set of stone steps down to a quiet rocky bay. A derelict restaurant mars the view but there are rocks to swim off and deep clear water. The huge chunks of rock in the water fell during winter storms, so beware overhangs.

DELIMARA POINT At the point is **Delimara Lighthouse** and a very unlovely view of the massive **Freeport** across the bay with all its cranes, metal and concrete. Right at the tip of the peninsula (beyond the lighthouse) is a good place for **birdwatching** especially during spring and autumn migration. This of course also makes it a great place for bird hunters and trappers and the point is littered with their debris. See *Chapter 2, Hunting*, page 24 and *Chapter 3, Safety*, page 48 for further details and advice.

On the Marsaxlokk side of the point is **Delimara Fort** built low into the rock by the British in 1881. It was used as a cowshed until about ten years ago and is now deserted and in a very poor state.

RAS IL-FENEK AND XROBB L-GĦAĠIN At the base of the Delimara Peninsula on the opposite side from Marsaxlokk are two bays divided by Ras il-Fenek (Rabbit's Headland). The rock of this peninsula has a picturesque hole in its tip that gained it its name, and in summer boats make the trip to the bays for **swimming** (it can get quite crowded). It is apparently also possible to walk through the hole in the rock (at your own risk!).

If you don't have access to a boat, you can drive round to Xrobb l-Għaġin. Here there is a small bay, a few salt pans, deep clear water and rocks to swim off (in dead calm only). You can also walk down from here into the closest of the Rabbit's Head bays.

BIRŻEBBUĠA

This unattractive town is itself of little interest to the visitor and lies in the shadow of the vast industrialised area of the Freeport to its south. On the north side is the headland that separates Birżebbuġa from Marsaxlokk and here stands **St Lucian Tower**, originally built in 1610–11 as one of Grand Master de Wignacourt's six coastal defence towers (see *Fortifications*, page 85). The British expanded it into a small Victorian fortress with a defensive ditch and a curved entranceway (allowing a clear line of fire on enemies attempting to enter). It is now houses Malta's Centre for Fisheries Sciences.

The town has two bays, **St George's Bay** (not to be confused with the one near St Julian's) and **Pretty Bay**, which is moderately pretty, with its white sandy beach (topped up with imported sand), so long as you keep your eyes firmly turned away from the cranes and concrete of the Freeport. Birżebbuġa is, however, worth a visit for the two prehistoric/ancient sites on the edge of town.

GĦAR DALAM (*Birżebbuġa Rd, BBG9014;* ✆ *21657419;* e *info@heritagemalta.org; www.heritagemalta.org;* ⊕ *09.00–17.00 daily (last entry 16.30);* €*5 adult,* €*3.50 over-60s/children aged 12–17/students,* €*2.50, children aged 6–11, children under 6 go free*) This natural cave (pronounced *Ar Dalam* and meaning the 'Cave of Darkness') was one of the first places in Malta to be inhabited by man. There were people here by

5200BC and the cave gives its name to the islands' earliest archaeological phase (Għar Dalam phase 5200–4500BC; see page 3). The presence of these early people is known from human remains, animal bones in rubbish pits and pottery. The pots have simple geometric decoration made by etching into the wet clay and are of the same style seen in Sicily during this era, suggesting that the first Maltese came from the neighbouring island 93km away.

The cave has also revealed animal remains dating from 180,000–130,000 years ago – including bones of hippo, elephant, brown bear, fox and wolf as well as a giant dormouse. A **guidebook** by Nadia Fabri (*Insight Heritage Guides; €6.99*) is available from the ticket desk.

Getting there and away Buses 11, 12 and 13 from Valletta take about 45 minutes (though travel times vary greatly) and drop you right outside. If travelling by **car**, the site is on the main road into Birżebbuġa and is signposted. There is parking less than 100m from the main entrance.

The museum The 'Old Museum' to the right of the entrance is lined with traditional tall glass-fronted dark-wood 1930s-style cabinets packed full of Pleistocene hippo bones and prehistoric elephant molars. There are also slightly younger deer bones and antlers.

On the other side of the entrance is a modern museum explaining the significance of the cave and its contents. Most intriguing is the development of dwarfed and gigantic prehistoric animals. During the Pleistocene era (1.8 million years to 10,000 years ago), the last part of which is commonly known as the Ice Age, animals travelled south from continental Europe to Sicily and Malta (then linked, at least intermittently, by a land bridge) in search of warmer climes. At this latitude the 'Ice Age' was merely a rain age and some animals settled and thrived.

When sea levels rose again, the islands were cut off and these creatures evolved separately from their relatives in the rest of Europe, with some species changing quite dramatically in size. While the continental elephant stood 4m to the shoulder, the Maltese equivalent was a mere 1m tall. Hippo, deer, brown bear, fox and wolf all shrank. But some smaller animals grew, so Malta had tortoises nearly as big as today's Galapagos giants and dormice the size of modern guinea pigs.

The garden As you leave the museum building, on the ground to your left is a pair of Malta's ancient or pre-historic cart ruts (see boxed text, page 198). Ahead, the long flight of shallow steps leading from the museum to the cave has been landscaped with native Maltese plants. Amongst them (on your left) is the national plant of Malta, the rare little bush, rock centaury (*widnet il-baħar, Cheirolophus crassifolius*), and to the right is the national tree, the sandarac gum tree (*siġra ta'l-għ argħar, Tetraclinis articulata*) a member of the cypress family. Amongst many others are a carob tree (brought here in ancient times when the Phoenicians and Romans used the seed as a unit of weight), oleander and a caper bush.

From the steps you can see across the valley to a microcosm of Malta's historical landscape: almost straight ahead is a Knights' watchtower and, just above it, a World War II pillbox. Above and to the right of the towers, next to a gate and an orangey limestone wall stands Tal-Kaċċatur, the site of a Roman villa with the largest Roman cistern found on the island (not open to the public).To the left, a cross on the top of a hill marks the Bronze Age settlement of Borġ In-Nadur (see below). There are plans to build a walkway across the valley and link all of these sites into a heritage trail.

The cave The triangular rock with a hole in it that stands at the entrance to the cave is a tethering stone from the days when the cave was used as a cattle pen, as it was

above left and right   Maltese rock centaury is Malta's national plant and the sandarac gum tree is the national tree (both AT) pages 23 and 184

right   The buds from the caper bush are harvested for use in cooking and salads (AC) page 23

below left   Maltese everlasting is a rare bush that grows up to 1m high and flowers yellow (AC) page 23

below right   Prickly pear is found all over Malta and its fruit is used to make a local liqueur (AT) page 63

Malta sits on one of the main migration routes between Africa and Europe and as such is an excellent place for birdwatching, especially in spring and autumn page 97

top left The European bee-eater is one of the brightest-coloured European birds (AT) page 99

top right Blue rock thrush – Malta's national bird, readily seen on clifftop garrigue (DC) page 24

above left The first marsh harriers of the season can be seen as early as February (PS/FLPA) page 97

above Cory's shearwaters gather on the surface of the sea at dusk before flying in to their cliff-face nests (RC/FLPA) page 24

below left Honey buzzards soar over the hillsides in May and September (AT) page 99

below Little bittern have been known to nest at Is-Simar Nature Reserve (AT) page 243

above   **A flock of Squacco herons settling in Marsa** (AT) page 97

right   **Hoopoes pass through early in spring and autumn** (CCZ) pages 97 & 99

below left   **A colourful spring migrant, the golden oriole** (DN/FLPA) page 97

below right   **A male Sardinian warbler, a common species in Malta all year round** (AT) page 240

above & left **St Paul's Island — named for the saint who was shipwrecked on Malta in AD60** (both AT) page 242

below **Off the coast from Għadira Bay** (AT) page 235

above & right While Malta is very built up in places (such as around Valletta and Sliema, above), there are also some beautiful wilds, especially along the west coast (both AT)

below Situated on the Delimara Peninsula, Peter's Pool is a lovely rocky cove from which to take a swim (IB/FLPA)
page 93

left   **Xlendi is a peaceful village with wonderful swimming and snorkelling** (AT) page 295

below   **Almost everyone coming to Gozo arrives at Mġarr** (V/GB) page 268

bottom   **Salt has been produced in Gozo's salt pans since Roman times** (Ma/D) page 283

above left The Azure Window — a popular spot with tourists, snorkellers and divers (M/D) page 278

above right Ta' Pinu Sanctuary is Malta's most important pilgrimage site (V) page 280

right Because of its secluded location, San Blas is much quieter than Ramla Bay (GL) page 290

below The Ta' Ċenċ plateau is a fantastic spot for walking and birdwatching as well as tracking cart ruts (AC) page 294

above   Comino Tower was built by Grand Master Wignacourt in 1618 and was part of the Knights' earliest attempt at a national defence system (S/D) page 251

left   Comino ferries regularly bring day trippers and hotel guests across to the island from both Gozo and Malta (AT) page 250

below   The Blue Lagoon is Malta's most popular swimming spot, Comino (L/D) page 251

right up until the start of excavations in the 19th century. The cave also served as a World War II shelter in 1940 and then as a military fuel store. Fast minelayers would come into the nearby harbour under cover of night, off-load fuel and other supplies and disappear again the following night.

The cave itself is a broad tunnel 145m long (though the far end is closed for safety reasons). It was formed by water percolating through the rocks. The river that flowed above it eventually deepened and broke through its roof (at the point at which we now enter) probably bringing with it the earliest animal bones found here. The walkway leads past still-forming stalactites, nests of Spanish sparrows in the cave walls, and the excavation pits. A mound and pillar have been left to show the various excavated layers and what was found in them.

BORĠ IN-NADUR (*Birżebbuġa–Għar Dalam Rd. Most of the Bronze Age & modern parts of the site are always open, but the temple ruins (which are not extensive) are only open by private (& expensive) arrangement with Heritage Malta;* ↘ *22954000;* e *info@ heritagemalta.org; see page 82 for how such requested openings work*) On a natural plateau above the surrounding countryside, Borġ In-Nadur is an interesting multi-period site, though not the easiest to interpret. It has sparse ruins of a Tarxien-phase prehistoric temple and the remains of a Bronze Age settlement, as well as being the centre of a small modern-day Christian cult.

Borġ In-Nadur gives its name to the Bronze Age phase of Maltese archaeology (1500–700BC) and is also the site of some important cart ruts (see boxed text, page 198). These ran right up to the village and led one of the experts in the field, Dr David Trump, to believe that the cart ruts originated in this period. Unfortunately these ruts are very difficult to find without help.

Getting there Borġ In-Nadur is on the main Birżebbuġa–Għar Dalam road on the edge of the town, about 1km south of Għar Dalam and it is not difficult to **park**. By public transport, take **bus 11** towards Birżebbuġa and ask the driver or another passenger to tell you which stop to get off at.

The Bronze Age and modern parts of the site can be reached freely by following a **path** from the main road signed 'Il-Madonna ta' Lourdes'.

The temple The temple site is approached via a duck farm and a weird modern stone carving of a face – do not be put off. Large megaliths mark the unusual fact that this temple's forecourt was surrounded by a high wall. The rest is quite hard to make out but does in fact form the ground plan of a typical four-apse temple. There must have been a temple-period village in the area, from which people presumably fished in Marsaxlokk Bay, and there are known to have been other temples nearby at Tas Silġ (see page 84) and at Xrobb il-Għaġin. The Borġ In-Nadur temple was probably long abandoned by the time the Bronze Age settlers built their village here.

Bronze Age settlement At least 1,000 years after the temple people deserted this site, Bronze Age settlers developed a thriving community covering the whole of this rocky spur. A great deal of pottery has been found along with oval huts (now covered over again). Many more Bronze Age huts are assumed to lie below the modern fields.

The most notable feature today is the 4.5m Bronze Age stone wall. The plateau is naturally defended on three sides. This wall defended the fourth. The big stones are original while the smaller rubble is reconstruction.

The large mound outside the wall is spoil from the 1880s archaeological dig. On top of it stands a modern cross. Since 2006 a local man has claimed to see visions of the Madonna on this spot, starting a minor cult with worshippers regularly gathering here to pray.

Outside the site On the path down from the Bronze Age settlement to St George's Bay is a gate in the stone wall that takes you into a pretty little 'Garden of Peace' (which pre-dates the hilltop cult) with flowers, benches, shade and a little shrine.

St George's Bay At the bottom of the path is the head of St George's Bay with its own evidence of prehistoric activity. On the triangular terrace below the promenade you can see two covered raised stone circles, and on the rocky foreshore are several fair-sized holes, some plugged, some open and some flooded with seawater. All of these are probably **Bronze Age grain silos** linked to the Borġ In-Nadur community which may have used this bay as a harbour for overseas trade.

There is also a pair of **cart ruts** that runs into the water. This is most unlikely to be because the carts ran into the sea; more likely it is due to rising water levels. It is thought that these ruts are Bronze Age and may have been made by vehicles carrying grain to and from the silos.

For a bit of more recent history, turn your back to the water to see a **Knights-period redoubt** (mini-fort) that defended the bay. It now has a chapel built onto it. These redoubts usually come in threes and you can see another (now a private home) on the other side of the bay. The third has been destroyed.

9

South Malta

This southern region is the heartland of traditional Malta. Villages like Żebbuġ and Siġġiewi are snapshots of what Malta used to be, with their church squares, band clubs, old limestone houses and little gaggles of elderly (and sometimes not-so-elderly) men sitting outside on benches or in the local café chatting the day away.

You won't find many tourists here; these villages are not on the main visitors' maps. Except Żurrieq, that is. Even here, though, most tourists simply pass through on their way to the Blue Grotto caves boat ride (see below page 191).

Beyond the villages, along the south coast, are two major sights – the prehistoric temples of Mnajdra and Ħaġar Qim (see page 192) and the Dingli Cliffs (with a variety of things to see, page 197) – as well as a popular rocky swimming spot.

GETTING THERE AND AWAY

There are buses to each of the villages (noted below the place name) but it is certainly easier to explore the villages by car since you won't necessarily want to spend hours in each one. You shouldn't have any trouble parking.

ŻEBBUĠ

(*Bus 88 from Valletta*) This attractive peaceful village naturally centres around the church square, Misraħ San Filep (St Philip's Square), with its Baroque parish church. The **Church of St Philip** (1599–1659 with finishing touches added by Maltese architect Tommaso Dingli) has a double bell tower and ornate interior with a mass of golden arches above the altar. In the square, the church is complemented by the colourful *gallariji* and traditional decorative wrought iron of the village's two band clubs. *Festa* is held quite early here – usually towards the end of April.

Żebbuġ was one of Malta's first ten parishes listed in 1436 and its name – which means 'olives' – goes back at least to the 14th century, although there have been olive groves here since Roman times. The British tried to replace this industry with cotton. They had limited success but Żebbuġ did become a centre for the making of sailcloth and in the 19th century supplied the Royal Navy and other ships over in the Grand Harbour.

Żebbuġ is a traditional residential area, popular with wealthy Maltese. It was the birthplace of Dun Karm, Malta's national poet who wrote the words of the national anthem, and of Anthony Sciortino, Malta's most famous modern sculptor. Nowadays, it seems to be lawyers, doctors and the like who have the money to buy the beautiful centuries-old traditional stone houses. And the French government; its ambassador's residence sits on a quiet street just behind the church.

At the roundabout between Żebbuġ and Siġġiewi is the **de Rohan Arch** (1777), once the monumental entrance to Żebbuġ. Grand Master de Rohan visited the *festa*

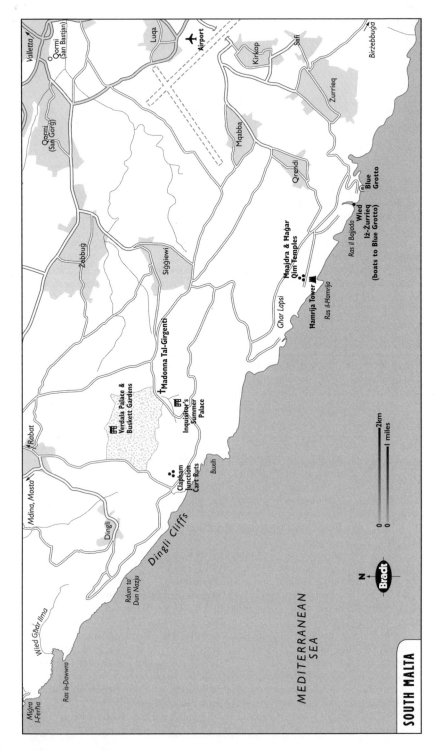

SOUTH MALTA

MEDITERRANEAN SEA

Valletta

Qormi (San Bastjan)

Qormi (San Gorg)

Luqa

Airport

Kirkop

Safi

Birzebbuga

Zurrieq

Mqabba

Qrendi

Blue Grotto

Wied iż-Żurrieq (boats to Blue Grotto)

Ras il-Bajjada

Żebbuġ

Siġġiewi

Madonna Tal-Girgenti

Għar Lapsi

Mnajdra & Ħaġar Qim Temples

Ħamrija Tower

Ras il-Ħamrija

Verdala Palace & Buskett Gardens

Inquisitor's Summer Palace

Rabat

Mdina, Mosta

Clapham Junction Cart Ruts

Buxiħ

Dingli

Dingli Cliffs

Rdum ta' Dun Nazju

Ras is-Dawwra

Wied Għar Ilma

Migra l-Ferħa

N

Bradt

2km

1 miles

0

0

of St Philip in Żebbuġ in 1776 as part of his policy of re-engaging with the Maltese population (see boxed text, below). The villagers asked to be given the status of a town and the grand master agreed. Żebbuġ gained the honorific Citta Rohan and built an arch to commemorate the event.

SIĠĠIEWI

(*Buses 89 from Valletta & 94 to Għar Lapsi in summer*) A classic southern Maltese village, Siġġiewi was one of the first ten Maltese parishes listed in 1436 and is now a mix of long-time residents, mostly involved in local agriculture, and well-off families moving out of the urban sprawl. Tourists often make it to the edge of the village – to the Limestone Heritage Centre (see below) – but rarely bother with the place itself.

Siġġiewi has a large double church square – an L-shape sloping down from the large highly decorated parish **Church of St Nicholas** (1675–93) whose *festa* is held towards the end of June. The tall thin mid-19th-century dome of this church can be seen from miles around. The church's Baroque triple-arched façade (with angels keeping a watchful eye over the main entrance) is part of the original church designed by Lorenzo Gafá (architect of the Mdina and Gozo cathedrals). Inside, the altarpiece of St Nicholas is thought to be Mattia Preti's last, and unfinished, work.

GRAND MASTER EMANUEL DE ROHAN POLDUC (1775–97)

The penultimate grand master of the Order of St John in Malta was, like nearly half his predecessors, a French aristocrat. Unlike many of the Order in his time, however, he was both clever and conscientious. By the second half of the 18th century, the Order as a whole had slipped into self-satisfaction and self-gratification. Their monastic vows of poverty (not to mention chastity) had long been ignored and the Order's relationship with the Maltese was at an all-time low. The Ottoman Empire was in decline so the Order was no longer a crucial bulwark on the borders of Christendom. The Knights had run out of money and de Rohan was reduced to selling ships to the kings of Naples and Spain to raise cash.

The new grand master tried to reintroduce a moral and administrative structure. He took the fleet off a war footing and formalised its role in commerce. He reformed taxation and modernised the legal system, abolishing the worst forms of torture. The Code de Rohan, his two-volume constitutional law book, is still a part of Maltese law.

De Rohan was responsible for the building of the National Library in Valletta to house the Knights' archives, records and book collection. He also ordered the construction of Fort Tigné to pair with Fort St Elmo in defending Marsamxett Harbour.

In his efforts to improve relations with the local population he created ten new Maltese noble titles and visited villages around the country. The Maltese recognised his efforts and developed a great respect for him. For the Order, though, it was too late and de Rohan didn't help matters with his politically ill-considered, though loyal and generous, support for his beleaguered monarch.

In 1791 de Rohan sold most of the Order's silver to help fund Louis XVI's ill-fated flight from revolutionary Paris. When Napoleon arrived in Malta seven years later (a year after de Rohan's death) the Order tried to claim it was a neutral religious community that should be left in peace. The French general reminded them of their grand master's actions, helped himself to what was left of their silver and kicked the Knights out of Malta.

Below in the square, a tall statue of St Nicholas stands as if addressing a crowd, and at the head of the lower arm of the square (where the buses stop) is the much smaller **Church of St John the Baptist** (1730), also known as the Church of the Beheading of St John because of a gory painting of this event inside.

LIMESTONE HERITAGE *(Mgr M Azzopardi St;* ╲ *21464931;* e *info@ limestoneheritage.com; www.limestoneheritage.org;* ⊕ *09.00–15.00 Mon–Fri, 09.00–12.00 Sat, 09.00–11.30 Sun; €6/€2.50/€5 adults/children under 12/students. The centre is a few mins' walk from the centre of Siġġiewi. Bus 89 (from Valletta) stops here & there is plenty of free parking on site.)* Limestone really is a major part of Malta's heritage. The buildings – from the prehistoric temples, through the Knights' forts and churches to today's houses – are mostly built of limestone because, quite simply, it is what Malta is made of. This well-designed centre, created and run by a family of quarrymen and stonemasons in a disused quarry, sets out to show how limestone has been sourced and used over the years.

An eight-minute **film** introduces a short audio guide (both multi-lingual) which takes you round a series of **tableaux** of stone-working, tools and vehicles. The story starts 100 years ago (when techniques had in fact changed little for 1,000 years) and leads up to mechanisation, which only happened fully during the 1950s dash to rebuild after World War II. More stone was quarried in the 40 years after the war than in the previous 700.

The **original quarry** wall can still be seen, and there are examples of different kinds of stone building from a *girna,* the ancient circular rubble-built farmer's hut (some of which are still in use today), to a traditional Maltese home. Inside are a geological map and some original Victorian tools.

You can also watch **stonemasons** at work or even have a go yourself. Carve out a line picture of a flower (€3, about ½hr) or make your own seated fat person (€8, 1hr+). In the garden are peacocks, chickens and a donkey as well as a **Punic tomb** that has been reused as a cistern.

As well as limestone carvings, the **souvenir shop** has a small, but well-chosen selection of **books** including *Limestone Heritage* by Vincent Zammit *(Insight Heritage Guides;* €6.99) with lots more detail about stone working in Malta.

GĦAR LAPSI

(Bus 94 from Siġġiewi (summer only); there's free parking although it gets busy on summer w/ends) On the coast south of Siġġiewi is this popular place for **swimming** on windless summer days (it isn't safe when there are waves). The rocks here form protected little lidos and, despite the length of concrete shore (part of which has collapsed), it is an inviting place to enter the clear blue water. It can get very crowded with locals (and a few tourists) on summer weekends.

Għar Lapsi is also a very popular place for **rock climbing**. Some 400m above the village is a great arc of cliffs where the intrepid (and properly equipped!) can be seen like little insects working their way up the rock face. (For more on rock climbing see page 70.)

✘ **WHERE TO EAT** There are two sizeable restaurants in Għar Lapsi, one of which is particularly nice and is listed below (though also more expensive than the other).

✘ **Blue Creek Bar & Restaurant** ╲ 21462800/2786; e info@bluecreekmalta.com; ⊕ 12.00–15.00 & 19.00–23.00 Wed–Mon. The fresh, stylish interior in marine blue, green & white, links nicely to the sunny terrace overlooking the sea. Families welcome. Highchairs available. Summer Sundays get very busy – be sure to book. Starters & pastas €6.40–9.30, mains €15.15–24.45. Starter-only +€2.

ŻURRIEQ AND THE BLUE GROTTO

(*Buses 32, 34 & 'express' 132 from Valletta. Numbers 38 & 138 head to the Blue Grotto itself. There is parking at the top of the little hill that leads down to the boats.*) Żurrieq is the largest village in the south of Malta and, whilst vast numbers of tourists go through it *en route* to the Blue Grotto at Wied iż-Żurrieq, few stop. There is not a vast amount to make them do so, except perhaps the **Church of St Catherine of Alexandria** (1634–59) containing six paintings by Mattia Preti, who lived here for a while, and the late-17th-century **Knights' Armoury** in Mattia Preti Square, although this is quite ordinary looking. Żurrieq's *festa* is held in late July.

AROUND ŻURRIEQ

Ħal Millieri Chapel (✆ *1st Sun of each month 09.30–12.00 or by appointment with Din L-Art Ħelwa (Malta's National Trust):* ✆ *21225952/0358/52222;* e *info@ dinlarthelwa.org; www.dinlarthelwa.org*) Just north of Żurrieq is this wayside Chapel of the Annunciation. Ħal Millieri was a medieval settlement and this little church dates from about 1450. Inside is Malta's only surviving medieval church art – 14 frescoes (some damaged) of Byzantine saints. The paintings are somewhat old-fashioned even for their time and it has been suggested they may be copies of earlier local frescoes, created to provide continuity of devotional activity when, for whatever reason, the earlier frescoes disappeared.

Wied iż-Żurrieq On the road from Żurrieq to Wied iż-Żurrieq there is a viewpoint at the side of the road from where you can look down on the **Blue Grotto**, and, in the right light, see the luminous blue that gives the place its name. In decent weather, though, it is still worth taking the Blue Grotto boat trip (see below) to see it, and other caves, close up.

Wied iż-Żurrieq lies 3km from Żurrieq and is a little fishing village-turned-tourist-site. It has survived the transformation quite well with just a small street of souvenir shops and cafés leading down to the boats. On the other side of the road is an open 'garden' area with views out to sea towards the uninhabited island of **Filfla** (see boxed text, page 191) and a **Knights' watchtower** built under Grand Master Lascaris (1636–57).

Blue Grotto boat ride (✆ *09.00–17.00 daily (approx – weather permitting);* €*7/3.50 adult/children 3–10. Price inc any commentary; boatmen should not ask for extra.*) Follow the road downhill to the ticket office and the landing stage in a protected inlet. From here an endless stream of colourful little boats (seating up to nine passengers) putters out around the coast to explore the caves and rock formations. The Blue Grotto is the largest and most impressive of these: a high double-arched

---

FILFLA

An uninhabited island some 5km offshore, Filfla seems to have been named from *felfel*, the Arabic for 'pepper', though the reason isn't clear. The island is a mere 350m across, standing 60m out of the water at its highest point. A chapel was built here after a major storm in 1343 but was destroyed around 1575. The British and NATO used the island for bombing target practice. It is now much more peacefully used by a breeding colony of storm petrels and, between February and October, a couple of hundred breeding pairs of Cory's shearwaters. There are also quite a lot of yellow-legged gulls (which unfortunately feed on petrels). The island is a nature reserve with no access for people.

cave with a pedestal/column between the arches. When the light is right – on sunny mornings – the sun bouncing off the white sandy seabed turns the water a bright luminous blue. Glimpses of this can also be seen in some of the other caves and even when the light is not right the trip is still enjoyable. At peak times of year, it can get horribly busy so try to arrive first thing.

MNAJDRA AND HAĠAR QIM

(Triq Ħaġar Qim, Qrendi QRD 2502; ℡ *21424231;* e *info@heritagemalta.org; www.heritagemalta.org;* ⏰ *09.00–17.00 daily (last admission 16.30); €9 adults, €6.50 over-60s/children 12–17/students, €4 children aged 5–11, under 5s go free. Buses 38 & 138 from Valletta come to the main entrance & there is plenty of free parking.)* Mnajdra and Ħaġar Qim are the most atmospheric temples to visit. They sit in an idyllic location well away from Malta's urban sprawl, surrounded by blue sea, grey rock and, in spring, greenery and flowers. The view from a distance is now disturbed by two vast cream-coloured canopies that have been built to protect the temples from sun and rain, but there can be no doubt that this was necessary (see boxed text, opposite).

These are the first temples to be the subject of a concerted effort to both conserve the buildings and make the temples more accessible to visitors. The European Regional Development Fund has ploughed €4.7 million into the project, funding the creation of a new visitors' centre (well tucked into the landscape so that it does not intrude too much) – with an exhibition, toilets and refreshments – as well as the two protective canopies.

Mnajdra and Ħaġar Qim are separate but neighbouring temple complexes, now with one visitor entrance. It is not clear in what way they were originally connected but we do know that they were used simultaneously and right up until the end of the temple period (2500BC). They are, however, quite different from each other: the Mnajdra temples show well-preserved examples of many of the common characteristics of Malta's temples (see page 78), while Ħaġar Qim has some very unusual features. A pleasant 500m stroll separates the two; Mnajdra is usually less busy because coach parties often don't make it that far. Also see *Temples history* page 4 and *Chapter 4*, page 78.

MNAJDRA **Three temples** stand along one curved side of an oval forecourt or plaza 30m across. All three have outer walls of coralline limestone with inner parts in the smoother, more decorative (but more easily weathered) globigerina limestone.

The first temple The first temple you come to, up a few steps, is the smallest and oldest (started c3600BC). It has an unusual **triple entrance** and a typical trefoil (three-lobed) design, although the central lobe is very shallow so it looks almost like a mere niche. The walls include a lot of 20th-century reconstruction (in limestone rubble).

The central **'altar'** has pitted decoration and on the inner face of the uprights (particularly on the right) are a few lines of dots. It has been speculated that these are tally holes relating to the appearance of certain constellations, perhaps making a crude calendar (though many, including one of the leading experts, are sceptical).

The South Temple The furthest temple (closest to the sea), known as the South Temple, was built around 3000BC. It is much larger and more complex than the first temple, with a well-preserved **concave façade** that extends some way beyond the temple walls around the edge of the forecourt. The **'bench'** along the façade is clearly visible and wide enough here that it could have been a walkway. In front and

After 5,000 years, why should these temples suddenly require canopies to protect them? The answer is that for the first 1,000 years or so the temples had roofs and for most of the rest they were buried under soil. Ħaġar Qim was uncovered in 1839, Mnajdra in 1840. Since then significant damage has been done by weathering (quite obvious when photos from the 1890s are compared with what is seen today). Action was necessary and urgent. A covering that protects the stones without affecting the integrity of the buildings seems an appropriate response. The canopies do not touch the temples and are completely removable.

These two temples have received primary attention because here there was the most to lose. They are well preserved so far and were deteriorating fast. Ħaġar Qim is built entirely of soft, easily weathered, globigerina limestone, while Mnajdra is mainly globigerina with harder coralline limestone on the outside. Ġgantija (on Gozo), for instance, is of less concern as it is mostly made of the tougher coralline stone. The Tarxien Temples are also built of globigerina and are next in line for a canopy (hopefully by 2012).

Despite somewhat damaging the view from outside, the canopies have a positive effect once you are inside the temples, making them feel more like the roofed buildings they once were (though without losing air or light as the canopy is high above you and open sided). It is easier here than at sites open to the skies to appreciate the internal structure of the temple, to walk its 'corridors' and be in its 'rooms'. The canopies also protect visitors from rain and remove the glare of the sun making it easier to see details on the stones and to take photographs.

The canopies' supporting structures are carefully positioned to ensure that the view from the front of the temples is not obscured and the line of the sun's rays at solstice and equinox still falls where they were (probably) intended to fall.

to the left of the main doorway is a so-called **'tethering point'** (where animals may or may not have been tied up) and the threshold has a dark band across it – a natural feature of the stone, but clearly chosen as decoration for an important entrance.

Inside, look back at the **main entrance** – it has an architecturally sophisticated double trilithon construction (two uprights with a topstone repeated one inside the other; see page 78) giving it extra strength. It is also a good place to compare the two limestones from which the temple is constructed. The inner trilithon of the doorway is of globigerina while the outer is coralline.

The **left apse** is a good place to see how cleanly and tightly the stones of the walls are fitted together. There is also a framed **'porthole' stone** (with pitted decoration) through which you can see a large **pedestal altar** in a further 'room'.

The temple has an interesting alignment to the sun at sunrise. On the equinoxes (the first day of spring and autumn), sunlight beams straight through the front door of the temple and down its central axis. On the winter solstice (between 20 and 23 December) the light hits the outer edge of the pitted upright to the right of the inner doorway. On the summer solstice (Midsummer Day) the beam seems to strike a similar distance to the other side of the doorway just missing the now damaged upright. Perhaps it once just hit the stone, or maybe it was always intended to carry on through the small doorway to land on the pedestal altars.

The **right apse** has the best surviving example of corbelling with the stones leaning progressively inwards towards the top of the walls. There are a few 'oracle holes', like windows through the walls, and a porthole doorway up a small flight of steps leading to a chamber between the apse wall and the outer perimeter wall.

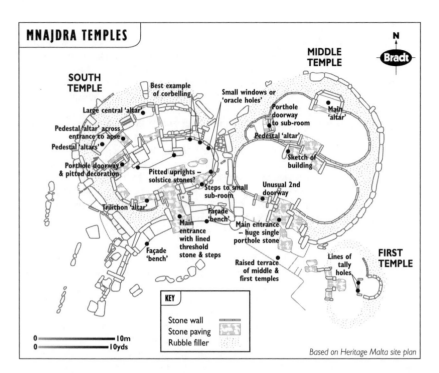

MNAJDRA TEMPLES

SOUTH TEMPLE

MIDDLE TEMPLE

FIRST TEMPLE

N

Bradt

Best example of corbelling

Small windows or 'oracle holes'

Large central 'altar'

Porthole doorway to sub-room

Main 'altar'

Pedestal 'altar' across entrance to apse

Pedestal 'altars'

Pedestal 'altar'

Porthole doorway & pitted decoration

Sketch of building

Pitted uprights – solstice stones?

Steps to small sub-room

Unusual 2nd doorway

Trilithon 'altar'

Façade 'bench'

Main entrance with lined threshold stone & steps

Main entrance – huge single porthole stone

Façade 'bench'

Raised terrace of middle & first temples

Lines of tally holes

0 ▬▬▬▬▬ 10m
0 ▬▬▬▬▬ 10yds

KEY

Stone wall
Stone paving
Rubble filler

Based on Heritage Malta site plan

At the far end of the temple is a **central altar** with huge verticals. The **last pair of apses** is sometimes roped off, but if they are open, the right apse is quite plain while the left is filled with pedestal altars, which are also part of the structure of the temple. The large two-level ones look like vast shelves.

The middle temple The middle temple, tucked in between the other two, is the latest (3000–2500BC). It has a similar internal structure to the South Temple with two pairs of apses, but its shape is simpler and its interior plainer. Entrance is from a raised terrace through a **large porthole doorway** (made of one massive stone, now broken) with an unusual extra door next to it.

Inside, to the left of the doorway leading to the second pair of apses, is a little engraved drawing of a temple with a triple entrance. As you pass through this central doorway, look back at its strong double-trilithon or 'box-within-a-box' construction (see page 78). You can see where the lintel was rebated into the outer uprights for extra strength. The temple people were really quite sophisticated builders!

BETWEEN MNAJDRA AND HAĠAR QIM The 500m path between the two temple sites is lined with wild fennel, looking like yellow cow parsley in summer and smelling of aniseed. On the surrounding garigue are several stone huts. These are **trappers' hides** where Maltese men traditionally hid to net finches during autumn and spring migration (see *Trapping*, page 24).

Towards the sea is a small **cenotaph to Walter Norris Congreve** – a British World War I general and governor of Malta in the 1920s who died in office and is buried at sea halfway between here and the uninhabited island of Filfla (see above). The channel between the two islands is named the Congreve Channel after him.

Just beyond the cenotaph on the cliff edge is **Ħamrija Tower** built in 1659 as part of the chain of coastal defence and communications towers commissioned by

Grand Master de Redin. It is not open to the public, but makes a good starting point for a wander along the coast. If you are nimble and have a head for heights, you can get down nearly to sea level here, and there is an attractive rock arch just offshore.

You may also notice small quarries dotted across the landscape. These are not prehistoric, but if you walk up the rocky terrain above Mnajdra Temple you will find the **misqa tanks**, which almost certainly are. To get there, go 250m north of the temple and follow a path between a low wall and the higher boundary wall of the site. When you come to a flat barren area of rock, watch where you are treading and keep hold of children because there are circular holes cut into it – the openings to large tanks dug into the rock beneath. They were probably built as water tanks – and still collect rainwater – but their exact use is unknown.

HAĠAR QIM Ħaġar Qim is unusual. It sits on a kind of acropolis and seems to have no specific front. You approach a clear concave façade (like that at other temples), but if you walk around the building there is another on the other side along with a second monumental entrance, complete with 'libation holes'.

The exterior It is as if it looks out in all directions. The **'bench'** goes almost all the way round and there are doorways at both ends. There is also an external **'shrine'** – a semicircular recess in the outside wall that may have had a ritual use. To the left of the 'shrine' is one of the largest stones in the temple – a 20-ton megalith. Also visible from the outside, on the other side of the building, are the legs of two **'fat lady'** statues (signposted). Returning to the main entrance, you can see a large **'tethering point'** (which may alternatively have been where ropes were attached when transporting the stone) before entering through the tunnel-like entrance.

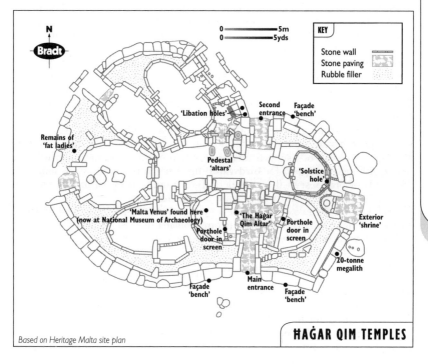

HAĠAR QIM TEMPLES

Based on Heritage Malta site plan

The interior The **main building** at Ħaġar Qim has a confusing arrangement of rooms. It is as if a much smaller four-apse temple has had large rooms added onto one side (see the site plan, page 195). The **first apses** are screened from the main passageway and each has a porthole doorway. The two doors are positioned such that from just inside each one you cannot see through the other.

Copies of **decorated stones** can be seen (the originals are in the National Archaeological Museum in Valletta; see page 121) including 'the Ħaġar Qim Altar' which looks like an ornate stone stool with leaf-like patterning up the pedestal. The second right apse shows evidence of corbelling and has a hole through which the sun beams on the summer solstice.

The apse on the left here contains a complex assortment of **'altars'**. Some seem ill suited to being altars (due to their shape and height). Two, however, are strong candidates for being sacrificial altars. They are mushroom-shaped and the round-top stones once had rims around the edge (now badly weathered) which would have controlled the flow of any blood or other liquid on its surface. Four **'fat ladies'** (or possibly gents, now in the Valletta museum) were found here. Where you would normally expect the 'main altar', Ħaġar Qim has its second entrance/exit and views to the world outside.

BUSKETT GARDENS (IL-BUSKETT) AND VERDALA PALACE

(*Bus 81 from Valletta, also connecting to Ta' Qali, Rabat & Dingli. If you are in a car you can drive into & through the gardens & park inside*) Malta's only substantial patch of woodland was deliberately planted by the Knights in the 17th century and stocked as a private hunting forest. The deer are long gone, but this is a popular place for the Maltese to meet and picnic or eat in one of the two café-pizzerias.

By the main gate is a **milestone**, with its place name and distance scraped out – a wartime measure intended to hinder spies or invaders trying to find their way around the island. As you enter the gardens along a long driveway, you can see the castle-like **Verdala Palace**, perched above the gardens (there are even better views from the approach to Clapham Junction – see below). Built in 1586 as a summer retreat and hunting lodge for French Grand Master Hugues Loubenx de Verdalle, it was designed by Girolamo Cassar, the military engineer who designed much of early Valletta. Despite its four turrets and dry moat, it was a place primarily for leisure rather than defence, although it was intended to be able to withstand 24 hours of siege in case senior Knights were caught out here during a corsair attack. Today it is the summer residence of Malta's president and is not open to the public.

The **gardens** are now a public park of trees and paths with a stream flowing through in winter. For visitors from northern Europe this is nothing to write home about, although it is good for **birdwatching** at migration times when songbirds and birds of prey rest in the trees here. Bird hunting is illegal in Buskett even during the open autumn season when it is legal elsewhere.

Each year on the eve of 29 June, the popular **Feast of St Peter and St Paul**, better known as Mnarja or Imnarja (from *luminarja* meaning 'light') is celebrated in Buskett with an agricultural show followed by traditional music and rabbit stew late into the night.

GIRGENTI

(*No public transport*) On the edge of this pretty valley about 4km from Siġġiewi sits the **Inquisitor's Summer Palace (the Girgenti Palace)** built by Inquisitor Horatus Visconti in 1625 (the chapel added in 1760). The palace is just one room deep, its seven rooms sitting in a line along a narrow ridge overlooking the countryside below. Abandoned for many years, it has now been restored and is the summer residence of the prime minister. It is not open to the public.

Further down the valley is a peaceful **outdoor chapel** with stone bench pews, a large wooden cross and a statue of the Madonna in white robes and a blue mantle. This is the **Madonna Tal-Girgenti** (*www.ourladyofconsecration.org*) and the shrine is dedicated to Our Lady of Consecration – a title not known before it was used here. This Marian shrine was built in 1986 as a result of two visions claimed by a local woman, Guza Mifsud. She said she had been told by the Madonna to spread devotion to the new title, and also claimed that during a break from farming her family's land in the Girgenti Valley, the Madonna had appeared to her dressed in white with a blue mantle. The shrine is visited by pilgrims and is always open.

Another modern Christian landmark is the **Laferla Cross**, up on the Hill of the Cross (Tas Salib), 218m above sea level. The cross, visible for miles around, was erected in 1903 to celebrate the start of the 20th Christian century. It was destroyed in a storm, but replaced in 1963. Whilst the cross itself is of no more interest close up than from a distance, the hill affords panoramic views of the surrounding area. On Maundy Thursday the cross is floodlit and crowds of people make their way up the rough track.

THE DINGLI CLIFFS AND CLAPHAM JUNCTION

(*Bus 81 from Valletta. Free parking on the roads.*) The highest place in Malta, the Dingli Cliffs fall a sheer and impressive 250m into the sea. Their flat rocky top is a great place for **walking** (except in the midday heat) and there is usually a breeze up here. It is also possible to drive along the edge of the cliff for some distance. The views of the Mediterranean are spectacular and this is a popular spot from which to watch the sunset. In spring the area is covered in wild flowers. Even in summer wild fennel and caper bushes flourish, and the smell of thyme wafts up as you brush the greenery underfoot.

Less romantically, you may find yourself treading on the cartridge cases littering the rocks. These are left by Malta's bird hunters whose stone hides dot the area along with the paraphernalia of bird trapping. During migration these cliffs are the first land many migrating birds have seen for hundreds of miles so they are an ideal place for **birdwatching** (and therefore bird shooting). Under EU law trapping is now very restricted and hunting is only allowed in the autumn. In season, hunters frequent the cliffs in the early morning and late afternoon (see *Safety*, page 48 and *Hunting*, page 24).

Alone on the edge of the cliff stands the little **Chapel of St Mary Magdalene** (1646), occasionally the target of vandals, but otherwise a peaceful spot from which to survey the sea and look out towards the uninhabited island of Filfa (see boxed text, page 191). The chapel can be reached by car along a roughish track. It is closed except on 22 July when evening Mass is said here on St Mary's feast day.

CLAPHAM JUNCTION (*Bus 81 from Valletta, Rabat or Ta' Qali to Buskett & walk 500m following signs to cart ruts. Free parking on the road.*) On the rocky plateau on top of the Dingli Cliffs is this bizarre sight: over 40 pairs of **cart ruts** (see boxed text, overleaf) running along the rough rock, dividing and combining, parallel and criss-crossing, disappearing (where the surface of the rock has been eroded) and reappearing. Some can be followed for many metres. You can see how the place got its name.

Most of the ruts have a gauge of about 1.4m, although one pair is much wider. The most recent research suggests that these (though not all Malta's cart ruts) were probably made for, and further eroded by, vehicles carrying stone from the ancient

Punic/Roman quarries (now masked by modern fields). The vehicles would have followed the ruts across the rocky plateau to a surfaced road. The depth of the channels varies enormously and debate still rages about what kind of vehicle ran in them.

PUNIC TOMBS There are three shaft-and-chamber tombs close to the cart ruts (one in fact is cut across by a pair of ruts, which has played a part in dating the ruts). The tombs are surrounded by little modern dry-stone walls and are found by walking from the (signed) cart ruts across the rock, up an incline going away from the sea, towards the (signed) troglodyte caves (see below). The tombs are open squarish holes in the ground a couple of metres across and of a similar depth. They are obviously manmade and at the base of the main hole is the entrance to a chamber cut into the rock which would have held the body (or bodies). Take a torch if you want to look in.

GHAR IL-KBIR TROGLODYTE SETTLEMENT A little further up the slope (going away from the sea) is a complex of natural caves extended by people, now partially collapsed. This was a troglodyte settlement from perhaps as early as the Bronze Age until possibly as late as the 19th century.

There is documentary evidence of an established community in the caves in 1536, and in 1647 27 families (117 people) are listed as living here. A description from 1637 tells how the caves were lit through shafts in the roof and how dry-stone walls were used to create façades across the cave entrances and to divide the caves internally between different families. There is still evidence of this and, particularly in a cave through a narrow passageway to the right, you can see how the inhabitants improved their subterranean homes with cupboards, alcoves and seats carved out of the rock walls.

In 1678 a Dutch visitor noted that the people living here were tall and healthy and the women remarkably good looking. Keith Buhagiar (in his thesis on the settlement) describes how the people were vegetarian, raising animals only for dairy produce and for sale and how the community spoke a dialect closer to Arabic than is Maltese.

There is some dispute over how the community disappeared. It is usually said that the British found the place unhygienic and in 1835 moved the reluctant population to Siġġiewi. Some even say that the troglodytes were so keen on their caves that they kept returning until the authorities deliberately collapsed the roof. Buhagiar, however, believes that the roof collapsed naturally after the people had drifted away.

THE COAST NORTHWEST OF DINGLI CLIFFS Dingli is not the only place for walking. There are lovely **walks** along the coast to its northwest where the landscape is quite different from Dingli and where few people go. You will need your own transport. Try parking at **Migra Feħra** and walking south along the coast. There is a narrow path on the edge of the cliff (take care and don't bring young kids). Much

WHAT MADE THEM? In the past the suggestion has been made that these are not cart ruts at all but were created to collect rainwater. In some cases (including the ruts at San Pawl Ta' Targa outside Naxxar, page 224) the channels have been used for this purpose but this is almost certainly a secondary use. It seems fairly clear that the cart ruts are just that – made by, or for, some sort of vehicle. One suggestion is that many of the ruts were first cut by hand, ie: that they were deliberately created to help a vehicle pass more easily over the rough rocky terrain. The ruts would then have been further carved out by use, and suffered additional natural erosion after they had been abandoned. Others, however, believe that wear and weathering are wholly responsible for the ruts.

So what sort of vehicle ran along these tracks? Sledges, wheeled carts and slide cars have all been proposed. Sledges seem least likely because straight runners would not have been able to take the sharp corners seen in several sets of ruts. A simple cart with wooden wheels is more likely. It would have had to have a loose axle in order to run in ruts whose distance apart varies significantly, and the wheels would have needed to be large to cope with the depth of some of the ruts. Slide cars fit the profile too. They are made of two long thin pieces of wood set diagonally along each side of a load-bearing platform. One end of the wooden poles would have been pulled by man or beast while the other – perhaps tipped with hard stone or metal – slid along the ground, a movement likely to create a clear line of wear in the rock. How and when the cart ruts were made remains the subject of research and heated debate.

THE BEST PLACES TO SEE THE CART RUTS See map of prehistoric sites in *Chapter 4* (page 81).

FURTHER INFORMATION A recent compendium of research is to be found in *The Significance of Cart Ruts in Ancient Landscapes*, edited by Joseph Magro Conti and Paul C Saliba, published by Midsea Books and Heritage Malta. This is, however, by no means the last word on the subject.

of the rock here is weathered smooth, shining bright creamy-white in the sunshine. In spring it is set off magnificently with greenery and wild flowers. The area teems with butterflies and the national bird, the blue rock thrush is a not uncommon sight.

This place is good for **birdwatching** – and therefore also for bird hunting and trapping (see page 24). There are lots of stone hides and cleared trapping areas. Trapping is now heavily restricted so most sites are likely to be abandoned, but you may still meet hunters, particularly early on autumn mornings.

If you keep walking along here you will come to a bay, **Ras id-Dawwara**, at the head of which is a **small waterfall** – a real rarity in Malta – at Wied Għar Ilma. From about November to April (depending on rainfall) water flows over the edge of the cliff plunging into the sea above a large sea cave.

✘ WHERE TO EAT

✘ **Bobbyland Restaurant** Panoramic Rd, Dingli Cliffs (just along the cliffs from the chapel. Bus 81 passes directly outside); ☎ 21452895; m 79206065; e aynor@hotmail.com; www.bobbyland.eu. As a small boy, owner Reno used to bring sheep & goats to graze here. He got to know some of the men working at the Royal Air Force signal station (which stood where the restaurant kitchen now stands), one of whom was called Bobby. So when the cast of the film

Eyewitness which was shot here in the '70s encouraged Reno to open a bar & coffee shop in an old air force Nissen hut, it became Bobbyland. Now much extended & run by Reno's daughter, Aynor, it serves generous helpings of Maltese food (chef's speciality: rabbit in garlic sauce), pasta & kids' meals. Dine on a bamboo-fringed beachside-bar style terrace or inside. *Starters €4.15–8.75, pasta €5.50–9.50, mains €14.75–19.50.*

10

Mdina and Rabat

In the centre of the island a natural ridge rises from the countryside and on top of it sits Mdina, the old capital of Malta. It is easy to see why this was the capital in the days when all danger of invasion came from the sea and natural defences were the starting point for manmade defences. Around Mdina lies the town of Rabat (meaning 'suburb'), missed by many tourists, but with some very interesting historical sites of its own both from the late Roman and Knights' periods.

A **multi-site ticket** can be bought for all Heritage Malta's properties in the area: the Roman Domus, St Paul's Catacombs and the National Museum of Natural History (*www.heritagemalta.org; €12 adults, €9 children aged 12–17 & students, €6 children 6–11, children under 6 go free*). This only saves you money if you visit all three sites and the ticket is only valid for one day. Tickets can be bought from any of the three sites.

MDINA

Mdina is a medieval walled town, but its history goes back far earlier. This was Malta's first capital, its main town from at least Roman times, when it was called Melite, until the arrival of the Order of St John in 1530. The Knights needed to be closer to their ships and so based themselves in Birgu (Vittoriosa) on the Grand Harbour. The Maltese aristocracy, however, remained in Mdina and it continued to be an important centre.

This is an extraordinary place. Strategically perched on the edge of a plateau 150m above the surrounding countryside, it is a striking sight as you approach by road: sitting on top of its rock, impenetrable, lording it over all it surveys. Within its fortified walls, there are very few shops and offices; it is mainly *palazzi* (grand old houses) and religious buildings set in a labyrinth of narrow streets, many of them (wonderfully) too small to take a car. There are almost no vehicles by day and just a few in the early evening as some of Mdina's 400 residents (the only people allowed to drive here) come home from work. Mdina's nickname, the Silent City, remains well earned.

It is not so silent when the tourist groups are out in force, however, but you can always duck down a smaller alley to get away from the crowds. Alternatively, come back in the evening: take a stroll along the cobbles in the twilight, have a meal in one of several good restaurants, watch *festa* fireworks from the top of the bastion walls (on summer weekends), and return through peaceful darkness, back to the 21st century.

HISTORY With its obvious natural advantages, this site has been inhabited since at least the Bronze Age, becoming the main town and administrative centre of the island under Punic or Roman domination. The sizeable fortified Roman town of Melite spread into today's Rabat almost as far as St Paul's Church. Under Arab rule, in the late 9th or 10th century, the town was reduced to its present and more

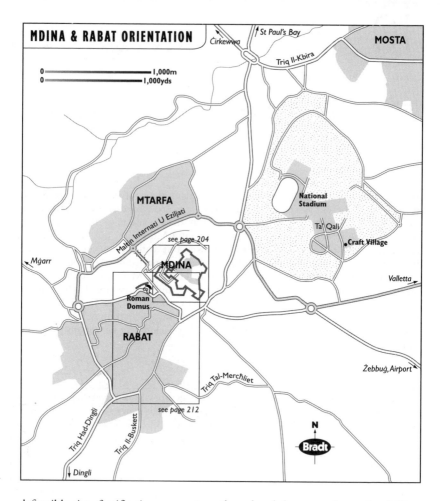

defensible size, fortifications were strengthened and the name changed to Mdina (Arabic, *Medina*).

As the Arabs gave way to the Normans and subsequent medieval rulers, Mdina was repeatedly remodelled and refortified, and became the place where noble families built their *palazzi*. The streets were deliberately kept narrow and angled to protect against invasion. When in 1429 the Saracens attacked and laid siege, the population of Mdina held out apparently inspired by a vision of St Paul riding a white stallion and waving a flaming sword. They earned the town the soubriquet Citta Notabile from its overlord of the time, Aragonese King Alfonso V.

When the Order of St John arrived in Malta in 1530, Mdina's role as the capital ended, although it initially remained important both in terms of defence and as the seat of the Maltese nobility. Whilst the Knights' first priority was to strengthen the fortifications of their harbour-side capital Birgu (Vittoriosa), they also improved Mdina's defences. During the Great Siege of 1565, troops of the Order made sorties from the safety of Mdina, helping to weaken the Turkish invaders.

After the building of Valletta, Mdina became known as Citta Vecchia ('The Old Town') and its influence waned. Its buildings fell into disrepair and in 1693, when a strong earthquake hit the central Mediterranean, Mdina was particularly badly damaged. Many houses and the cathedral had to be rebuilt and in the early 18th century Grand Master de Vilhena commissioned a major refurbishment led by French military engineer Charles François de Mondion.

When the French arrived in 1798, Napoleon's troops looted Mdina's churches. Having already taken much of the treasure from the Carmelite priory church, the soldiers unwisely returned for more. This was the last straw and the local people ran riot. They threw the French commander out of a first-floor window and began the rebellion that eventually brought France's brief rule in Malta to an end and ushered in the British. The British naturally centred their administration in Valletta and Mdina retired gracefully to become the wonderful living museum that it is today.

GETTING THERE AND AWAY Buses 80 from Valletta, 86 from Buġibba and 65 from Sliema drop you close to the Main Gate through the walls of Mdina. The journey may take longer than you expect because of all the stops (eg: Sliema to Mdina can take an hour). There is plenty of **parking** by Mdina's Main Gate.

AUDIO GUIDE A very informative **audio tour** is available (*Discover Mdina Audiotour:* ☏ *21455951; www.discovermdina.com;* ⊕ *09.00–16.00;* €*8pp,* €*6 over-60s from the Vilhena Palace ticket office; see page 205*) lasting 1½ hours. The tour is annoyingly presented as an argumentative conversation between a young female guide and a pompous elderly 'baron'.

⌂ WHERE TO STAY

⌂ **The Xara Palace Relais et Chateaux*******
(17 rooms, mostly suites) Misraħ Il-Kunsill; ☏ 21450560 or 21452612; e info@ xarapalace.com; www.xarapalace.com.mt. The only hotel within the walls of Mdina, this is a place of real character: a converted 17th-century palazzo with an air of calm, furnished with antiques,

original Maltese paintings & historic objects. A book on its history is due out in 2010. Some suites have terrace & outdoor jacuzzi. Past guests include Bruce Willis & family, senators McCain & Lieberman, Sharon Stone & Brad Pitt. *Dbls from €200 Mar–Nov, €125 Nov–Mar (except Christmas) room only.*

There are also places to stay in Rabat (see below) that are only a few minutes' walk from Mdina.

✗ WHERE TO EAT

✗ **Bacchus** Inguanez St; ☏ 21454981; e reservations@bacchus.com.mt; ⊕ 09.00–23.30 daily. 2 vaulted chambers built as gunpowder magazines in 1657–60 now make up this large restaurant that also has open-air tables on the Mdina bastions with panoramic views. Long menu of main meals & snacks. Highchairs available. *Starters €7–8, mains around €15.*

✗ **Ciappetti** 5 St Agatha's Esplanade; ☏ 21459987; e ciappetti@kemmunet.net.mt; ⊕ 12.00–15.00 & 19.00–22.00 Tue–Sat, also Sun lunch, closed 10 Jan–10 Feb. Tucked away in a quiet corner of Mdina, Maltese/Mediterranean restaurant with a peaceful internal courtyard where it grows its own herbs, a bastion terrace with wide-ranging views & 2 art-filled interior rooms. Kids are 'welcome', but parents beware – sign outside reads: 'unattended children will be sold as slaves'! *Starters*

€4.65–7.40, mains €13.60–19.50 (starter only, add €2.20).
✗ **De Mondion Restaurant** Xara Palace Hotel (see above for contact details). This elegant establishment, the top-floor restaurant of the Xara Hotel, won the top award from the Maltese *Definitive(ly) Good Guide to Restaurants* (2009). It is very expensive, but genuine fine dining. The excellent French/Mediterranean/Maltese food is beautifully presented & service is attentive without being intrusive. Summer terrace with panoramic views, indoors with open fire in winter. Small menu. *Starters €17–30, mains €30–38.45.*
✗ **Fontanella** 1 Bastion St (just off Bastion Sq); ☏ 21454264; ⊕ winter 10.00–18.00 Mon–Fri, 10.00–22.00 w/ends; summer 10.00–23.00 daily. Famous for cakes & views. The terrace is on top of Mdina's bastions with a 180° panorama, & the

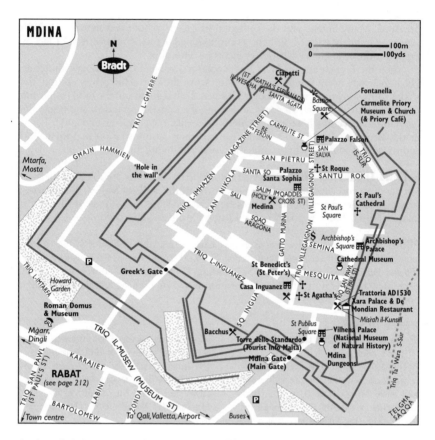

MDINA

The map shows labels including: N, Bradt, 100m, 100yds, TRIQ L-GHARREB, GHAJN HAMMIEN, Mtarfa, Mosta, 'Hole in the wall', TRIQ L-IMHAZEN, SAN NIKOLA, SALI, (MAGAZINE STREET), (ST AGATHA'S ESPLANADA) IL-WESGHA TA' SANTA AGATA, SANTA AGATA, Ciapetti, Bastion Square, Fontanella, Carmelite Priory Museum & Church (& Priory Café), CARMELITE ST, RE FERDIN, SAN PIETRU, SAN SALVA, Palazzo Falson, TRIQ IS-SUR, St Roque, SANTU ROK, (VILLEGAIGNON STREET), SANTA SO, Palazzo Santa Sophia, SALIM IMQADDES (HOLY CROSS ST), Medina, SOAQ ARAGONA, GATTO MURINA, St Paul's Square, St Paul's Cathedral, Archbishop's Square, Archbishop's Palace, SEMINA, Cathedral Museum, TRIQ VILLEGAIGNON, St Benedict's (St Peter's), TRIQ L-INGUANEZ, TRIQ MESQUITA, TRIQ SAN PAWL (ST PAUL ST), Casa Inguanez, St Agatha's, SQ INGUA, Trattoria AD1530, Xara Palace & De Mondian Restaurant, Misrah il-Kunsill, Greek's Gate, P, TRIQ L-IMTARFA, Howard Garden, Roman Domus & Museum, Mgarr, Dingli, TRIQ IL-MUSEW (MUSEUM ST), KARRAJIET, Bacchus, St Publius Square, Torre dello Standardo (Tourist Info Malta), Mdina Gate (Main Gate), Vilhena Palace (National Museum of Natural History), Mdina Dungeons, TRIQ TA' WARA S-SUR, RABAT (see page 212), TRIQ SAN PAWL (ST PAUL'S ST), LABINI, BARTOLOMEW, RONDA, Town centre, Ta' Qali, Valletta, Airport, Buses, P, TELGHA SAQQA

chocolate cake is known countrywide. Some of the other cakes are just as good & there is a long list to choose from (*€2.50 for a large slice*). Also serves sandwiches & light meals. Can get very busy (with long queues for the toilet!).

✕ **Medina** 7 Holy Cross St; ☎ 21454004; e info@medinarestaurant.com; www.mol.net.mt/medina; ⏲ 19.00–22.30 Mon–Sat. Atmospheric, historic setting in a lovely stone-vaulted medieval building in a quiet Mdina side alley just off St Paul's Square. Sink into sofas in the bar for a Maltese *aperitiv*. In winter eat in the cosy candlelit interior with open fire & in summer, in the traditional stone courtyard hung with oleander & vines, kept cool by fans. Classic & imaginative Mediterranean food presented with true artistry. Highchairs available. Smart casual. Families welcome. *Starters €7.25–9.85, mains mostly €15–25.*

✕ **Old Priory Café** Carmelite Priory, Villegaignon St; ⏲ 10.00–17.00 daily, lunch served 12.00–15.00. Bright, white, fresh modern café with original 17th-century ceiling (surprisingly not in the least incongruous) serving snacks including Maltese bread pudding, soup & filled *ftira* (traditional Maltese bread rolls). *From €2.85, main lunches €6.50–16.*

✕ **Trattoria AD1530** Misraħ Il-Kunsill; ☎ 21450560; e info@xarapalace.com.mt; ⏲ 10.30–22.30 for drinks & snacks, meals served 12.00–22.00. Owned by the same people as the Xara Palace & De Mondion, this is the casual everyday version. A welcoming vaulted interior & tables outside in the quiet little square. A mix of light meals, pizza, pasta as well as more imaginative dishes, including vegetarian options. Highchairs available. *Starters €5–6, salads/pizza/pasta around €9, mains €15–25, sandwiches & pastries from €2.25, kids menu €5.80.*

WHAT TO SEE AND DO

The gates There are three ways of passing through Mdina's walls and into the town:

The **Greek's Gate** (Porta Graecorum) is the oldest – the only complete medieval gateway left in Malta. It was always a secondary entrance, opening as it does into the front ditch, but it would once have had a wooden drawbridge. From the outside what you see is early 18th-century de Mondion, but from the inside you can see the typically medieval pointed horseshoe shape. The arch has now been partly filled with a scene of the baptism of St Publius and the wooden doors are Knights period, but the walls to either side are medieval ramparts some 3m thick and 10m high. It is possible to distinguish between the different aged walls: the purely vertical are usually medieval, while the slanted ones, which are reinforced at the base against cannon fire, were built by the Knights.

The **'Hole in the Wall'** (Magazine Street) was created in the late 19th-century so that residents of Mdina could get quickly to the station of the Mdina–Valletta railway. The railway closed in 1931 but the gate remained open.

The **Main Gate** is where most people first enter Mdina as it is closest to the bus stop and the car park. In the Knights' time, this was where a newly appointed grand master would formally meet the Università (the Maltese governing council) to guarantee their freedoms – at least in theory – and receive the key to the city. The present gate was built a few metres along the walls from its predecessor (whose outline is just visible to the right) in de Mondion's 1724 refurbishment. It is decorated with the coat of arms of the grand master of the day, Manoel de Vilhena, who also ordered the restructuring of the Grand Master's Palace, just inside the gate, that bears his name (see below).

St Publius Square Looking back at the gate from inside the walls, you see (left to right) St Publius, St Paul and St Agatha, Mdina's three patron saints. The little square you are in is named after Publius, the Roman governor of Malta at the time of St Paul's shipwreck here (later St Publius, see page 8). The governor's residence was in Melite (Mdina).

On the left as you come through the gate is the **Torre dello Standardo** (Tower of the Standard), used by the Knights to flag up danger of corsairs or Turkish invasion to people living in the surrounding countryside and to communicate with other towers. The tower now contains a **tourist information** office. On the right are the Mdina Dungeons (see below) and the Vilhena Palace.

Vilhena Palace and the National Museum of Natural History (St Publius Sq;
↘ 21455951; info@heritagemalta.org; www.heritagemalta.org; ⊕ 09.00–17.00 daily (last entry 16.30); €5 adults, €3.50 over-60s/children 12–17/students, €2.50 children 6–11, children under 6 go free) Just inside the main gate of Mdina to your right is this lovely Baroque building with its peaceful courtyard. It was commissioned by Grand Master de Vilhena and was the last of the island's grand masters' palaces to be built. Designed by de Mondion, it replaced the original building of the Maltese Università (governing council). Vilhena was not a modest man and his coat of arms tops the gate and his bust the door. He would come here particularly in summer when Mdina's altitude and narrow streets shadowed by buildings made it cooler than Valletta's. During British times the palace became a military hospital, before being taken over by the Maltese government and turned into the National Museum of Natural History.

The museum The collections include 15,000 rocks and minerals, 4,000 birds and birds' eggs, a couple of hundred each of mammals and fish, thousands of insects and a few fossils. Some of the stuffed birds are a bit scruffy, but they do offer a close-up look at some of the birds that might be seen on Malta if habitats were protected and there were no hunting. The museum takes a very clear line against the killing of birds and other wildlife and is a useful educational resource in this respect. There are informative displays on Malta's geology, its minor islands and the Wignacourt Aqueduct (see page 200), as well as some attractive shells and polished stones.

Mdina Dungeons (*St Publius Sq;* \ *21450267;* e *thekeeper@dungeonsmalta.com; www.dungeonsmalta.com;* ⊕ *09.30–16.00 daily;* €*4 adults, students &* €*2 children*) The underground prison cells of Vilhena Palace – some of which date back to the days of the Università when the palace was also the law courts – have been turned into the Mdina Dungeons 'attraction'. This revolting exhibition is a series of tableaux of waxworks being subjected to some of the hideous tortures that have been used here through the ages.

Villegaignon Street This is Mdina's main street, running the length of the town from just off St Publius Square to Bastion Square. Most of the key sights are on or very close to this street – but do stray off it at some stage in your wanderings (especially if there are crowds around) to get a real feel for Mdina. If you start up Villegaignon Street, you will come across the following sites before you reach Bastion Square.

St Agatha's Chapel (*1st cnr of Villegaignon St, coming from Publius Sq*) This tiny, recently renovated, little chapel was first built in 1417 and reconstructed after the 1693 earthquake to a design by Lorenzo Gafá (who also rebuilt the cathedral). St Agatha is a patron saint of Mdina and regarded as protector of the city after the part she is meant to have played in repulsing a Turkish invasion force in 1551 (see boxed text, below).

Close to St Agatha's Chapel is the **Church of St Benedict** (also called St Peter's), first built in 1418 and reconstructed in 1625. It has an altarpiece by Mattia Preti (see page 126). Opposite is **Casa Inguanez**, the palace and private home of the oldest titled Mdina family. Created barons in 1350 for putting down a Gozitan rebellion against the Aragonese king, the family led the Università until the arrival

THE LEGEND OF SAINT AGATHA

St Agatha was brought up in a wealthy family in Sicily under Roman rule. As a young woman she was asked to marry the Roman Governor Quintianus. She refused, raising the wrath of both the governor and the Emperor Decius. She fled to Malta, arriving in AD249 and is said to have lived in Mdina and prayed at the site that is now St Agatha's catacombs in Rabat (see page 216). Her insistence that she would remain a virgin married to God and her attacks on Roman polytheism did little to improve her reputation back home. In AD251 she returned to Sicily where she was imprisoned and had her left breast (or some say both breasts) cut off, before being stripped naked and burnt to death.

Medieval Malta took this story to its heart. St Agatha became a patron saint of Mdina and is frequently depicted, usually either covering her left breast or holding a pair of shears. She became even more beloved of the people of Mdina after apparently seeing off a Turkish attack on the city – led by fearsome corsair Dragut Reis – in 1551. A nun had a vision telling her that the statue of St Agatha (which today still stands in the saint's church in Rabat; see page 216) should be paraded by the population around the walls of the city. Whether due to St Agatha's intervention or because of the sight of so many people on the ramparts, the Turks turned tail and Mdina was saved. Unfortunately for Gozo, the Turkish force headed there instead and enslaved most of the smaller island's population!

of the Knights. The *casa* was originally built in 1370 but most of what you see now is much later.

St Paul's Square/Misrah San Pawl This is Mdina's central square. The cathedral fills the far end of the square, while to the right is **Banca Giuratale**, the public records office where the Università met after Grand Master de Vilhena took over its previous base for his palace. In 1798, Banca Giuratale became the first headquarters of the rebellion against the French, and it was from here that the Maltese sent to the British requesting help.

Mdina Cathedral *(St Paul's Sq;* ↘ *21456620 or 21454136;* ⊕ *09.30–16.30 Mon–Fri, 09.30–15.30 Sat; tickets are bought from the museum (on the left side of the square as you look at the cathedral) & cover entry to the cathedral & the museum: €2.50 adults, €1.75 students, under-12s go free.* **Festa** *at the end of Jun/early Jul)*

The exterior Designed by Lorenzo Gafá, Mdina's St Paul's Cathedral was completed in 1702 just before its architect died. The simple façade is set off by two bell towers and two clock faces – one telling the time, the other the date. The dome, visible across much of Malta, cannot be seen from directly in front of the church. The cathedral is dedicated to St Paul, and legend has it that it is built on the site of Roman governor Publius' house, where St Paul is said to have healed the governor's father and converted Publius to Christianity in AD60 (see page 8). St Publius, the story goes, is buried beneath the high altar.

The visitors' entrance to the cathedral is in the side wall to the right of the main door, in Archbishop's Square.

The interior The interior is the most impressive in Malta after St John's Co-Cathedral in Valletta. Here too the floor is a rich symphony of coloured marble tombs and memorials – and you can actually see more of them than at St John's because fewer are covered. One marble tomb on the floor just to the right of the main door is to Alyosius Deguara, a priest at the cathedral and author of its **guidebook**, *The Metropolitan Cathedral Mdina (Insight Heritage Guides;* €6.99). His birth date is there (1928) but his death date is absent. The reason is that (at time of writing) he is still alive!

In the **Chapel of the Blessed Sacrament** to the left of the high altar is an **icon** of the Madonna and Child. This was long believed by locals to have been painted by St Luke when he was on Malta after being shipwrecked with St Paul; it is actually 13th century. To the right of the altar, between the organ loft and the painting, is a small **oval window** that allows the bishop, without leaving his palace, to keep an unseen eye on proceedings in the cathedral.

Looking at the **main altar**, the two oval pictures of St Peter (left) and St Paul may look like paintings; they are actually mosaics (1873). The main altarpiece, the *Conversion of St Paul*, is by Mattia Preti (see page 126) as is the mural above it of St Paul's shipwreck. The other paintings in the choir are all by Preti and his studio.

A few items remain from the earlier (pre-earthquake) church. The heavy early **16th-century carved timber door** to the sacristy was the main door of the old cathedral, and the **marble font**, supported by caryatids and topped with a highly decorated octagonal carved wooden lid with St Paul at its peak, is 15th century.

The museum This building was originally a Baroque seminary (1733–40) and was built on the site of the house where Cicero is believed to have stayed while writing his indictment of Gaius Verres, corrupt Roman governor of Sicily and Malta (see page 8).

Mdina and Rabat MDINA

10

There is a real mix of exhibits here, some more remarkable than others. The excellent numismatic collection starts with some extraordinarily well-preserved 4th-century BC Carthaginian **coins** and has examples of currency from every subsequent administration on the islands right up to the 20th century.

Other displays include a room dedicated to Malta's **national poet**, Dun Karm Psaila (1871–1961), who wrote the words to the national anthem, and an impressive collection of **Maltese silverware**, vestments, **illuminated religious tracts** and grand masters' **swords**. The many pictures are of variable quality but include some by **Mattia Preti** and a collection of over 50 woodcuts and copperplates by **Albrecht Dürer** (1471–1528). In the chapel is a medieval 'picture book' of saints with a case full of little relics that belonged to Grand Master de Villeneuve (1270–1346).

Downstairs is a handful of interesting historic documents including a 1507 declaration from King Ferdinand II of Spain that Malta would remain 'attached to his crown' in perpetuity. This followed the leasing of Malta to a Spanish nobleman, Consalvo de Monroy, for 30,000 florins. De Monroy's imposition of excessive taxes on the Maltese led to an uprising. The population raised almost the full 30,000 florins and begged the king to let them buy Malta back. He eventually agreed and assured them in this document that 'any future deed of alienation or cession will be null and void'. This did not, of course, stop Charles V from handing Malta over to the Knights a mere 23 years later.

Palazzo Santa Sofia Back on Villegaignon Street, almost immediately on your left is Palazzo Santa Sofia, the ground floor of which is thought to be the oldest building in Mdina and carries a date of 1233. The first floor, however, was built no earlier than 1938. You can only see it from the outside; it is not open to the public.

Carmelite Priory Museum and Church (*Villegaignon St;* ✆ *27020404;* e *carmelitepriorymuseum@gmail.com;* ◔ *10.00–17.00 daily; €4 adults, €3 over-60s/children aged 12–17/students, children under 12 go free; tours 11.00 & 15.00. An audio guide is in production at the time of writing. Concerts are often held Sat 12.00 (free with entrance, but donations for the restoration fund appreciated). Also, Old Priory Café (see* Where to eat, *page 204) & gift shop.*)

The Priory Museum Recently opened, this museum is a gem of a place and the curator, Michelle Galea, is an inspirational guide. Set around a peaceful garden courtyard (*carmel* is Hebrew for 'garden') the museum takes up the ground floor of the restored 1670s Carmelite Priory. The few friars who live here today occupy the second floor.

The **refectory**, where the friars ate in silence, is largely original. Note the pulpit high on the wall from which the Bible was read during meals, and the stone *lavabo* (basin). The ceiling was painted by a Carmelite friar around 1750 and is (at the time of writing) awaiting restoration. Friars were not allowed to enter the neighbouring 17th-century **kitchen** where lay staff cooked for them on the limestone stove. Everything here, including all the copper pots and pans, is from this priory kitchen. In the **pantry** you can see traditional clay pots (*il-baqra*) for cooking rabbit and little baskets for making *gbejna* (small round cheeses).

The **oratory** houses the first altar from the church (1670) and the *Virgin of Mount Carmel with St Simon Stock* by Mattia Preti. The priory was surprisingly democratic. On the table in the **chapter hall** is a ballot box. Each friar had two marbles – one black and one white – which he dropped invisibly into different compartments of the box in order to vote for or against the motion in question.

A surprisingly large **friar's cell** is set up as it would have been in the 1940s and there is a painted bier used to carry dead friars who were traditionally shrouded rather than put in a coffin. The intricately embroidered vestments on display were made by cloistered nuns – though not here. This institution was (and is) all male. The priory has an artist-in-residence programme so there is often also some **contemporary art** to be seen here as well as, perhaps, the artist working.

The fine 1780 **silver altar front** – made by hammering the metal over a wooden 'mould' – is used during the **Feast of Our Lady of Mount Carmel** on the first Sunday after 16 July. It is one of the very few items of value from the church to have survived the French army's ransacking in 1798 (the altar front was away for renovation). The **French** paid dearly for their thefts from the Carmelites, however. Having already stolen the silver, the troops returned for the rich red damask that covers the church during *festa*. The locals locked the church. Some boys ran up the belfry and rang the bells rallying the population who chased the French troops through Mdina killing their commander and beginning the rebellion that eventually led to the defeat of the French in Malta (see *History*, above).

The church (☉ *via the museum & for Mass at 07.00 daily & 17.30 Wed*) Built between 1660 and 1675, this was the first elliptical church and dome in Malta. The altarpiece is the original 1677 *Annunciation* by Stefano Erardi and there are several paintings – including the four Carmelite saints above the small chapels – by Giuseppe Cali (1910). The painted wooden processional statue of Our Lady of Mount Carmel dates from 1765. At *festa* time (in July) it is apparently very amusing to watch the difficulty her bearers have manoeuvring her through Mdina's narrow streets! The original damask, although rescued from the French, has sadly disappeared.

Palazzo Falson (*Formerly known as the Norman House; Villegaignon St;* ✆ *21454512;* e *info@palazzofalson.com; www.palazzofalson.com;* ☉ *10.00–17.00 Tue–Sun, extended to 20.00 summer w/ends. Last entry an hour before closing.* €*10 adults,*€*5 over-60s/children aged 12–17/students, children aged 6–12 go for free, no children under 6. Entrance fee inc informative 45min audio guide (in English, Italian, Spanish, French, German), necessary as there are few labels. Free children's activity book. Touch tours available for the blind. Great café on site.*) The second-oldest building in Mdina, dating in parts from the mid-13th century, Palazzo Falson is named for its early 16th-century owner, Vice Admiral Michele Falsone, but its eclectic contents come from the 45 collections of its last private owner, soldier, shipping magnate and philanthropist Captain Olof Gollcher (1889–1962).

The main door is closed with a 700-year-old medieval lock and in the basement is a **slave cell** surrounded by Gollcher's formidable collection of **weapons**. Here too is a **chastity belt** – either a medieval original or perhaps a Victorian model of what they thought a medieval chastity belt should look like!

There is an important 80-piece **oriental rug collection** and an extensive display of **silver**, including a couple of wonderful 19th-century wheeled galleons that carried cutlery and condiments along the dinner tables of the wealthy. The shipping theme continues upstairs with a collection of harbour- and sea-battle pictures and shipping ornaments. There is lots of **antique furniture** (some beautifully inlaid), **paintings** by significant artists including Mattia Preti, **jewellery** and **coins** (starting from the 3rd century BC). Amongst these smaller objects, the highlight is a 1791 **French ten-hour pocket watch**. French Revolutionary time divided the day into ten hours, each of 100 minutes, but this didn't catch on and there are only three watches of this kind in the world.

10

On the roof of the building is the **museum café**, probably the highest coffee shop in Malta, with views over Mdina's roofs to the cathedral dome and across the countryside to the Mosta Dome and the sea. It serves snacks, 'hot drink and a cake' (€3.35) and local beer (€1.50/half pint).

Bastion Square At the top of Villegaignon Street is Bastion Square from where you can survey the surrounding countryside. On the plain below Mdina is the **Ta' Qali National Football Stadium** and Meridiana winery's main **vineyard**. Straight ahead is **Mosta** with its prominent dome. **Valletta** can just about be picked out to the right by finding the distant (and hence tiny) tall dome of the Basilica of Our Lady of Mount Carmel, beyond the vast urban sprawl.

On a close hilltop (slightly left) is **Mtarfa** (or Imtarfa in British spelling), the former military town that housed troops patrolling the stretch of the Victoria Lines from here to Binġemma (see page 230) and the military hospital where British writer Vera Brittain spent several weeks recovering from a mystery illness before she could take up her World War I nursing duties (see page 15). The bastion walls here are so thick you can sit, walk or even lie on them. Beware, though: they can be slippery when damp and they slope towards a long sheer drop!

RABAT

Rabat is Arabic for 'suburb' and this is indeed Mdina's suburb, the undefended area outside the walls that could evacuate to Mdina in times of trouble. It is often overlooked in favour of its fortified neighbour but it is actually a very attractive place to wander and has some significant sights of its own. The town centres on Parish Square/Misraħ Il-Paroċċa where St Paul's Church stands; everything is within walking distance from here.

Several of Rabat's sights are underground. The town sits on a honeycomb of tunnels and caverns. Most are catacombs – Romano-Christian tomb complexes dating from the late Roman or Byzantine period (4th–8th century AD). A few are natural caves, earlier burials (Phoenician/Punic) and tombs of other faiths, and there are also World War II shelters.

GETTING THERE AND AWAY Buses 80, 81 and 84 from Valletta come to Rabat and any Mdina bus will drop you just a few minutes' walk from the centre of Rabat. There is plenty of **parking** next to the main gate of Mdina and some on the streets.

WHERE TO STAY

Point de Vue Guesthouse (12 rooms) 2/7 Saqqajja Sq; \ 21454117; e reservations@ pointdevuemalta.com or pointdevue@nextgen.net.mt; www.pointdevuemalta.com. Just across the car park from the main gate of Mdina, well-kept guesthouse with plain clean rooms, all but one en suite (shower), 2 with balconies. €35pppn B&B Apr–Sep, €25 Oct–Mar, children 0–5 go free, 6–12 €10 discount.

WHERE TO EAT

Cosmana Navarra 28 St Paul's St/Triq San Pawl; \ 21450638; e cosmananavarra@onvol.net; www.cosmana.com; ⏰ 12.00–16.00 daily, 18.30–22.30 Thu–Sun. This 16th-century building was once owned by the woman who paid for the construction of St Paul's Church, opposite. Her pious-looking 17th-century portrait hangs on the stone staircase, & the place has been sensitively converted retaining its historic (though not pious!) atmosphere.

Stylish, but relaxed with some enjoyable nooks & corners. Antipasti from €3.50, mains from €11 & €5 kids' menu.

Crystal Palace St Paul's St (at the Mdina end). A tiny little workmen's café famous for its puffy pastizzi (28c) straight from the oven. Also milky tea & coffee Maltese-style out of a glass.

The Grotto Tavern 9–12 Parish Sq; \ 21955138; e grotto@onvol.net; ⏰ 12.00–14.30 & 19.00–22.30

Tue–Sun. Run by a French–Maltese couple, popular centrally located subterranean restaurant, offering Maltese & fusion main dishes. Highchairs available. Small pizzas €5, pastas from €5.95, mains €12.

WHAT TO SEE AND DO

The Roman Domus (*Il-Wesgha Tal-Muzew (just outside Mdina's Greek's Gate)*; ✆ *21454125* or *22954000*; e *info@heritagemalta.org; www.heritagemalta.org*; ⊕ *09.00–17.00 daily (last entry 16.30); €6 adults, €4.50 over-60s/children aged 12–17/students, €3 children aged 6–11, children under 6 go free*) This is the best-preserved and most excavated of Malta's Roman villas and houses – and the only one regularly open to the public. Standing just outside the walls of Mdina, it would have been well within the fortifications of the Roman town of Melite. We know where the Roman town ended because part of the surrounding ditch survives behind St Paul's Church (see below) and because we know where the catacombs are (Roman burials were always just outside the city walls).

There is not much left of the structure of this Roman townhouse (*domus*), but the foundations and some well-preserved mosaics remain, along with a variety of Roman artefacts: coins, bone hairpins, vessels, architectural fragments, and some remarkable examples of Roman glass including beautiful little coloured perfume bottles and (amazingly) an intact glass amphora some 50cm tall.

A few **Islamic gravestones**, with Kufic inscriptions, are also on display. They come from a few of the 245 Muslim graves found in the archaeological layer just above the Roman floors. Like the Romans, the Muslims bury their dead outside the city, but Mdina was smaller in the time of Arab rule. The Muslim graves yielded few objects but there is displayed an 11th-century silver signet ring found on the finger of one of the skeletons.

The highlight of the Domus is the Roman **floor mosaics**, dated to between 125 and 75BC. They include complex geometric patterns, some using optical illusion, and at the centre of the courtyard mosaic are two delightful 'drinking doves' – a popular Roman motif.

Interesting too are a finely **carved head of Emperor Claudius** and a toga-clad boy thought to be his adopted son (later the Emperor Nero). These, along with other high-quality 1st-century AD marble statuary suggest that by AD50 the house may have had some official function. Certainly, the Domus did not stand alone. Remains have been found of numerous Roman buildings behind this house.

St Paul's Church and Grotto (*Parish Sq/Misraħ Il-Parocca;* ⊕ *09.00–17.00; no entry fee.* **Festa** *in early Jul*) Known as St Paul's Outside the Walls, this church sits in the defensive ditch that surrounded the Roman walls of Melite, now in the central square of modern Rabat. The marvellously named Bishop Hilarius mentions the church as early as 1336, but the present building was constructed in the 16th century with funds from a local noblewoman Cosmana Navarra who lived on the corner opposite the church (see *Where to eat,* opposite). It was completed with the addition of the dome by Lorenzo Gafá in 1683. This dome collapsed (fortunately during the night) in the early 20th century and was rebuilt in 1926.

The vast altarpiece is a highly regarded *Shipwreck of St Paul* by Stefano Erardi (1683) depicting dramatic seas and the newly shipwrecked St Paul miraculously unharmed by the viper that has just bitten him (see page 138).

Next to the church is the **Sanctuary of St Publius** built in 1617 through the efforts of a pious Spanish hermit of noble birth who also looked after the grotto beneath it. This is meant to be where St Paul spent most of his three months in Malta. He is variously described as imprisoned here (and it was used as a prison at sometime during the Roman period), choosing to live in simplicity or just coming here to preach. He may of course not have been here at all.

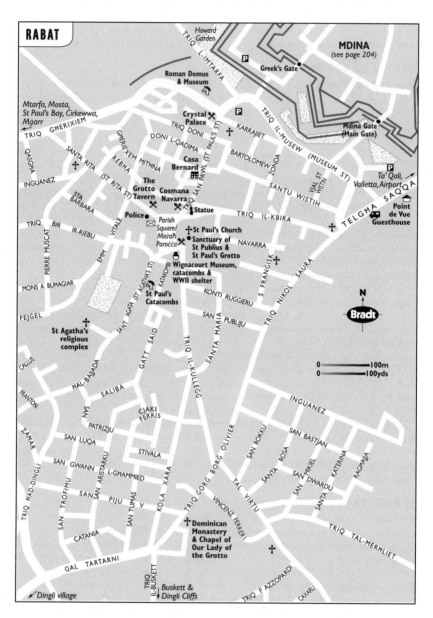

MDINA
(see page 204)

Howard Garden

TRIQ L-IMTARFA

Greek's Gate

Roman Domus & Museum

Mtarfa, Mosta, St Paul's Bay, Cirkewwa, Mgarr

TRIQ GHERIXIEM

GHERIXEM MITHNA

REBHA

SANTA RITA (ST RITA ST)

QASGHA

INGUANEZ

Crystal Palace

TRIQ DONI

DONI L-QADIMA

KARRAJIET

TRIQ IL-MUSEW (MUSEUM ST)

Mdina Gate (Main Gate)

Ta' Qali, Valletta, Airport

TELGHA SAQQA

Point de Vue Guesthouse

Casa Bernard

BARTOLOMEW

ZONDA

SANTU WISTIN

VIAL ST WISTIN

The Grotto Tavern

Cosmana Navarra

Statue

SAN PAWL (ST PAUL'S ST)

STA BARBARA

VITALE

EMM

TRIQ BIR

IR-RIEBU

PIERRE MUSCAT

MONS A BUHAGIAR

FEJGEL

CALLUS

FRANTON

ZAHAR

Police

Parish Square/ Misraħ Paroċċa

St Paul's Church

Sanctuary of St Publius & St Paul's Grotto

TRIQ IL-KBIRA

NAVARRA

S FRANGISK

TRIQ NIKOL SAURA

Wignacourt Museum, catacombs & WWII shelter

KATAKOMBI

St Paul's Catacombs

SANT AGATA (ST AGATHA'S ST)

GATT SAID

KONTI RUGGIERU

SAN MARIA PUBLJU

SANTA MARIA PUBLJU

N

Bradt

St Agatha's religious complex

TRIQ IL-KULLEGG

HAL-BAJJADA

SALIBA

CJAKI FERRIS

0 ———— 100m
0 ———— 100yds

INGUANEZ

SAN PATRIZJU

SAN LUQA

STIVALA

KOLA XARA

TRIQ GORG BORG OLIVIER

SAN ROKKU

SANTA ROSA

SAN BASTJAN

SAN MIKIEL

SAN DWARDU

SANTA KATERINA

RAGHAJJA

SAN GWANN

SAN ARISTARKU

L-GHAMMIED

SANJA PIJU

SAN TUMAS

V

TAL VIRTU

VINCENZ FERRERI

SAN TROFIMU

CATANIA

QAL TARTARNI

Dominican Monastery & Chapel of Our Lady of the Grotto

TRIQ IL-BUSKETT

Buskett & Dingli Cliffs

TRIQ TAL-MERHLIET

TRIQ F AZZOPARDI

CAXARU

Dingli village

What is for sure is that the people of Malta had created a Pauline cult around this place even before the arrival of the Knights in Malta, and that Grand Master Wignacourt (1601–22) decided to tap into this belief and turn the place into a destination for international pilgrims. He succeeded, and even today the sanctuary and grotto are visited by both secular tourists and Catholic pilgrims.

The **grotto** is cut into the bedrock and because of the biblical story of St Paul's miraculous immunity to snake venom, the rock became regarded as an antidote to poison. Perhaps to assuage the guilt of those who chipped away at this sacred place, the legend grew up that however much stone was taken, the walls were never eroded. Today the grotto holds a **statue of St Paul** donated by Grand Master Pinto in 1748 and a **metal lantern** in the shape of a ship donated by the Order of St John in 1960 to mark the 1,900th anniversary of the shipwreck. Behind the statue is an opening in the wall which takes you into a small **catacomb** (you'll need a torch) with window tombs and an agape table (see boxed text, page 214) – a taster of what can be seen in Rabat's larger catacombs.

From the grotto you can walk through a **passageway**, built in 1680 and designed by Lorenzo Gafá, to St Paul's College/Wignacourt College, now the Wignacourt Museum.

Wignacourt Museum (*Unobtrusive green door at the cnr of Parish Sq & College St or via the 17th-century underground passage from St Paul's Grotto;* ✆ *21454697;* ⊕ *10.00–15.00 Mon–Fri, 10.00–13.00 Sat;* €*2.50, children under 12 go free*) This sizeable museum, with some high-quality exhibits, has never made it onto the main tourist trail. The labelling has recently been improved and catacombs and a World War II shelter beneath the main building have been opened to the public. It is well worth a visit.

The museum The college was originally built at the start of the 17th century but reached its present form in 1749. In the ground floor corridor is one of the museum's prize possessions: a very rare portable wooden **galley altar** used to celebrate Mass on the Knights' ships. At the far end of the corridor is a giant wooden 'rattle' wheel (like a massive version of the rattles football fans used to wave around – but in the shape of a wheel). This is sounded instead of church bells during holy week.

Upstairs, the **picture gallery** runs along the side of the courtyard with views down over the citrus trees. Grand masters and saints in the robes of the Order stare down from the walls, and in the side rooms are several paintings by **Mattia Preti**, including a touchingly beautiful *Madonna of the Sorrows* (probably 1690s) and a *Penitent St Peter*.

The **treasurer's room** still has its chest, and the bed from which the treasurer was expected to guard the college's silver plate and money throughout the night. Just off this room don't miss an interesting little display of 17th-century **ex-voto paintings** (see boxed text, page 280). These small pictures in oil of people in various forms of trouble were mostly given in thanks for what the giver believed was miraculous rescue.

Amongst the many pieces of antique furniture is a sedan chair (1770–80) with the coat of arms of the Knight who had it made, Fra Giovanni Pellerano, Vice-Chancellor of the Order and Bishop of Malta (whose portrait can also be seen). Other exhibits include rare religious books, coins, Roman pottery and early maps of Malta.

The catacombs and World War II shelter Like much of Rabat, the museum sits on a labyrinth of underground tunnels. The extensive catacombs (most of which were once part of the St Paul's complex; see overleaf for details) are only partially cleared of rubble. Usually empty of other visitors, the place is very atmospheric, not to say a little spooky. The tombs are on several levels (possibly suggesting different periods) and of a wide variety of types (see boxed text, page 214). There is one particularly open area with a well-preserved *agape* table (where funerary meals were taken) and just above a small staircase is a graffito of the tree of life.

At a lower level still is the World War II shelter: corridors totalling about 1km in length link some 50 rooms (not all open to the public and many unlit – take a torch). Some 400–450 people hid down here at the height of the bombing.

St Paul's Catacombs (*St Agatha's St/Triq Sant'Agata;* ↘ *21454562;* e *info@ heritagemalta.org; www.heritagemalta.org;* ⊕ *09.00–17.00 daily; €5 adults, €3.50 over-60s/children aged 12–17/students, €2.50 children aged 6–11, children under 6 go free. Audio guide free with ticket & deposit of €20 or ID card.*) The largest, most impressive and most accessible of all Malta's catacombs – this place is a must-see. Over 2,000m² of tombs, the earliest being a small Phoenician burial, the latest dating from shortly before the start of Arab rule in AD870. Most are 4th–8th-century AD Romano-Christian (Byzantine) tombs of various kinds. *Loculi* and *baldacchino* tombs predominate (see boxed text, below) varying from tiny infants' *loculi* in the walls to grand, canopied sarcophagi. It is a real maze too – complete with dead ends and dark corners. Great fun for older kids to explore.

The main catacombs As you descend into the complex, there is a wide open area with two large well-preserved *agape* tables (round stone tables for the funerary meal – see boxed text, below). Each is in a typical C-shaped enclosure that would once have been stuccoed and painted. On the other side of the entrance is a spacious rectangular room that seems to have been used as a chapel in the post-Arab

---

BURIAL AND TOMB TYPES IN MALTESE ROMAN/BYZANTINE CATACOMBS

The Romans buried their dead just outside the city walls, often, particularly in the case of Christians, in substantial catacomb complexes. Usually the shrouded body, perhaps treated with oils and perfumes, was placed directly in the tomb, its head in the rounded shape cut into a stone headrest for the purpose. These headrests allow us to know how many people were buried in each tomb – at least initially. Many tombs are designed for two, but they were often reused with more bodies added at a later date.

After the body was interred and/or on anniversaries of the burial, family and friends would gather for a **funerary meal**, the *refrigerium*, at a round, **stone table** cut from the rock within the catacomb, known as an *agape* table, *triclinium* or *stibadium*. These tables usually have a raised edge and a drainage hole (presumably for cleaning). Most are surrounded by a C-shape of rock-cut benches where the diners would recline. Only in Malta are these structures found underground.

The catacombs were lit partly by *luminaria*, occasional shafts cut through to the surface letting in a beam of natural light, but mainly by small Aladdin-style lamps burning olive oil, placed in the mini alcoves that can be seen along the walls in all the catacombs, and especially around the agape tables.

There are seven main types of tomb, the use of which seems to have depended primarily on wealth and social status. All types have headrests.

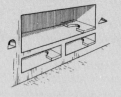

Loculus A simple rectangular recess cut into the wall. Would usually have had a stone or terracotta cover.

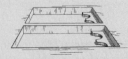

Forma or floor grave A rectangular pit cut into the ground rock. Also had a stone or terracotta lid.

Christian period. In its walls are perfect examples of children's *loculi*, and floor tombs are dug into its floor.

The rest of the catacomb is a chaos of tombs and tunnels. The audio guide, narrated as by a young Romano-Christian woman buried here, is informative if a little slow moving, with a lot of atmospherics between the facts. Whether you listen to all of it or not, following the trail of numbers displayed on the tombs for the audio guide is a good way of ensuring you don't miss anything. At number 10, for instance, is a Phoenician rock-cut tomb shaft that has been broken into by the later catacombs, at 14 *luminaria* (see boxed text, below) and at number 7 a small red ochre painting, though it is hard to see in the semi-darkness.

Smaller tombs There are two small tomb complexes with separate entrances. One of them has a very well-preserved *agape* table in a well-defined chamber. In a side room is a remarkable heavy stone door plug carved with images of surgical instruments that look as if they could have been cut yesterday. The carvings perhaps connect this small hypogeum with a medical guild.

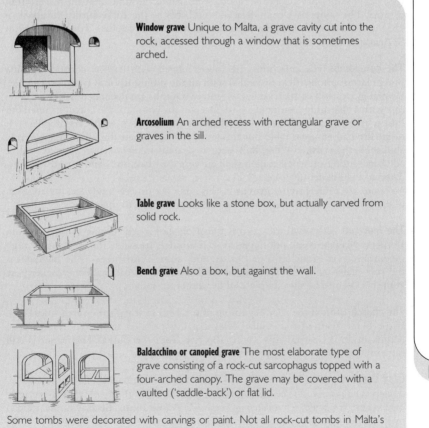

Window grave Unique to Malta, a grave cavity cut into the rock, accessed through a window that is sometimes arched.

Arcosolium An arched recess with rectangular grave or graves in the sill.

Table grave Looks like a stone box, but actually carved from solid rock.

Bench grave Also a box, but against the wall.

Baldacchino or canopied grave The most elaborate type of grave consisting of a rock-cut sarcophagus topped with a four-arched canopy. The grave may be covered with a vaulted ('saddle-back') or flat lid.

Some tombs were decorated with carvings or paint. Not all rock-cut tombs in Malta's catacombs are Christian. There are a few Jewish tombs and Jewish engravings, though none of these is (at the time of writing) are open to the public.

Museum cases The tombs had been looted by the time they were excavated in the 19th century so few objects were found. That said, the museum cases by the ticket office do contain some Roman terracotta figures – including cockerels and men on horseback – as well as decorated oil lamps of the type that would have been used to light the catacombs.

St Agatha's religious complex (*St Agatha's St/Triq Sant'Agata;* ✆ *21454503;* e *catacombs@spmc.edu.mt or camjvictor@hotmail.com; stagathamalta.tk [no www];* ⊕ *09.00–17.00 Mon–Fri (closed 12.00–13.00 Oct–Jun), 09.00–14.00 Sat. Visit is by regular half-hour tour: €3.50 adults, €3 over-60s/students, €1 children under 12.*) Just up the road from St Paul's catacombs is the second-largest tomb complex on the island along with an historic chapel/crypt and church.

The crypt Down a flight of 20 rock-cut steps is St Agatha's Crypt – an underground chapel to the saint who, legend has it, spent some time here around AD250 escaping persecution in her native Sicily (see boxed text, page 206). In St Agatha's time this was a small natural cave. It may have been expanded and embellished as early as the 4th century AD, although the current chapel is medieval. It is decorated with frescoes of saints. St Paul and St Agatha were painted around 1280, the rest are 16th century. The saints have been defaced – probably by the Turks during the attack of 1551 as the Koran forbids the depiction of saints and prophets. For the legend of St Agatha and her part in the 1551 attack, see page 206.

The catacombs The catacombs are low-ceilinged with narrow corridors (much more claustrophobic than St Paul's) with all the different tomb types in evidence. Several graves still contain skeletons, and two tombs are decorated with frescoes – one with a charming picture of a bird. Deep in the complex, the corridors open out into a room – a wealthier tomb chamber or chapel – with carved pillars. It originally had an *agape* table but this was removed when the Church apparently abolished their use. In the wall here is a semicircular alcove painted with a colourful little fresco of a scallop shell curving over two birds and various flowers, dated to the 4th century AD.

There are some **Jewish graves** in this complex (interestingly lacking any sign of *agape* tables) but at time of writing they are not open to the public.

The museum The small museum is a real old-fashioned jumble of objects from Romano-Maltese coins and Egyptian-style amulets (possibly Phoenician) through medieval-carved stone slabs to 19th-century church ornaments. The highlight is the 1666 alabaster statue of St Agatha (with deliberately damaged breasts; see page 206) that used to be the altarpiece of the underground crypt.

The church Built at the very beginning of the 16th century, the church houses the statue of St Agatha (of a similar date) that was paraded around the ramparts of Mdina in 1551, purportedly saving the city from the Turks. This event is still remembered with a special procession every February.

Casa Bernard (*46 St Paul's St/Triq San Pawl;* ✆ *21451888;* m *99844343 or 79444373;* e *casabernard@onvol.net; www.casabernard.com. Hourly tours: 10.00–13.00 Mon–Sat, or by appointment; €8 adults, €5 children up to age 12.*) A tour of this historic house, guided by its owner Georges is a tour through the history of Mdina and Rabat. The 16th-century *palazzo* is built on the foundations of a Roman *domus* that was within the walls of Melite. The well (cistern) is Roman as are the walls and one arch of the cellar which dates to the time of Cauis Verres and Cicero (see St Paul's Square, above).

The dining room is medieval, built around 1350 as part of a one-storey structure with a watchtower (still extant). By this time the site was outside the walls of Mdina, and even in 1580 when the simple pre-Baroque *palazzo* was built, the designer was concerned about defence: the windows are high and tapered towards the outside and the walls are very thick.

The Dominican Monastery and the Chapel of Our Lady of the Grotto (*George Borg Olivier St/Triq Ġorġ Borġ Olivier;* ⊕ *06.00–12.30 & 17.30–20.30*) This is a functioning priory (with ten remaining friars) that opens its doors in daylight hours. The public can wander the peaceful high barrel-vaulted cloisters around a courtyard of citrus trees, and (during the opening times above) visit the chapel and church. If you are lucky, you will be welcomed by one of the friars who will show you round and open up the venerated and highly decorated underground grotto for which the chapel is named. If not, you can see into the grotto through a grille (surrounded by railings) in the floor of the church.

The story begins around 1400 when a hunter is said to have seen a vision of Our Lady in this cave. The grotto quickly became a place of prayer and by 1414 seems to have been established as a chapel devoted to Our Lady of the Grotto. In 1450 the Dominicans came to Malta from Sicily and (wisely) created their mission – and in due course this priory and church – around the sacred cave.

A variety of 'miraculous' events, from a flower that stayed fresh for months to cures for illness, kept the cult alive. In 1999 it received a further boost. The beautiful stone sculpture of Our Lady now in the grotto (which gives Mary a touchingly human look of love towards her son) was by 1980 becoming too delicate to be paraded around at *festa* time, so a copy in white marble was made. This is the one on the altar of the above-ground chapel. Shortly after the *festa* in 1999, the copy-statue was apparently seen – on two consecutive days – to cry a blood-stained tear. Photos were taken on both occasions and, on the second, the tear – which divided into two little streams – was left on her cheek. Look closely and you can still see it beneath the statue's left eye.

Men may also visit the priory upstairs (accompanied by a friar), but women are not allowed.

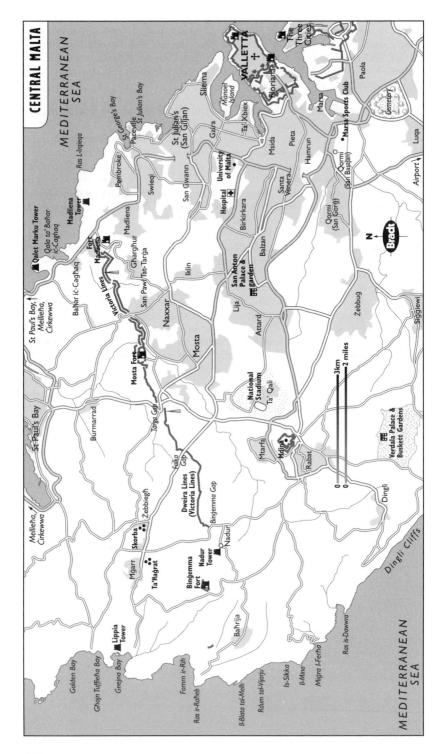

MEDITERRANEAN SEA

MEDITERRANEAN SEA

Bradt

N

Golden Bay
Ghajn Tuffieha Bay
Gnejna Bay
Lippia Tower

Mgarr
Ta'Hagrat
Skorba
Zebbiegh
Bingemma Fort
Nadur Tower
Dweira Lines (Victoria Lines)
Bingemma Gap

Mellieha, Cirkewwa
St Paul's Bay

Burmarrad
Falka Gap
Targa Gap
Mosta Fort
Victoria Lines

St Paul's Bay, Mellieha, Cirkewwa
Bahar ic-Caghaq
Qala ta' Bahar ic-Coghaq
Madliena Tower
Qalet Marku Tower
Fort Madliena

Ras L-Irqieqa
St George's Bay
Paceville
St Julian's Bay
Pembroke
Madliena
Gharghur
San Pawl/Tat-Targa
Naxxar
Mosta

Sliema
Manoel Island
St Julian's (San Giljan)
San Gwann
Swieqi
Gzira
Ta' Xbiex
VALLETTA
Floriana
The Three Cities

University of Malta
Hospital
Iklin
Lija
Attard
San Anton Palace & garden
Balzan
Birkirkara
Santa Venera
Msida
Pieta
Hamrun

Marsa
Marsa Sports Club
Paola
Cemetery

Qormi (San Gorg)
Qormi (San Bastjan)
Luqa
Airport

National Stadium
Ta' Qali

Mtarfa
Mdina
Rabat
Dingli

Verdala Palace & Buskett Gardens

Zebbug
Siggiewi

Bahrija
Is-Sikka
Il-Mina
Migra l-Ferha
Ras is-Dawwra
Dingli Cliffs

Fomm ir-Rih
Ras ir-Raheb
Il-Blata tal-Melih
Rdum tal-Vjarija

0   3km
0   2 miles

MEDITERRANEAN SEA

11

Central Malta

Several key areas of central Malta – the capital Valletta, the old capital of Mdina with its suburb Rabat, and the resort areas of Sliema, St Julian's and Paceville – have been covered in chapters of their own, so this chapter covers the rest of the region, predominantly urban and suburban districts dotted with historic and prehistoric sites. The boundary of the region to the northwest is the Victoria Lines, the defensive wall built by the British across the entire width of Malta, but for reasons of access to some tourist sites, Mġarr, to the north of the lines, is included here.

BIRKIRKARA AND THE THREE VILLAGES

BIRKIRKARA Part of the urban sprawl spreading inland from Sliema and Valletta, Birkirkara (often shortened to B'Kara) is the most populous town in Malta with over 21,500 residents. It is largely untouched by tourism (apart from through traffic) but hidden amongst its maze of streets is Malta's only sight for railway buffs, and the best close-up views of the early 17th-century arched **Wignacourt Aqueduct** which once brought Valletta's water all the way from Mdina (see boxed text, page 220). It runs along much of the length of St Joseph High Road/Triq Il-Kbira San Ġużepp where in some places the arches now form rather grand dividers between the residents' off-road parking spaces.

There are also churches, of course, including the large parish **Church of St Helen** (built 1727–45) with a fine Baroque façade, as well as Malta's ugliest church, the monstrous flaking concrete flying saucer that is St Theresa's. On Wednesdays and Fridays St Helen's is surrounded by a large local market selling just about everything. The **Sanctuary of Our Lady Tal-Ħerba (of Ruins)** – a chapel in the street of the same name – was built in 1610. Heavily remodelled in the 20th century, it contains the largest collection of **ex-voto paintings** in Malta (⊕ *Wed & Sat mornings*, see also boxed text, page 280).

In **Station Garden** (Ġnien L-Istazzjon), a little public park and children's playground, is what was once the Birkirkara Station on the British steam railway that ran from Valletta to Mdina from 1883 until 1931. A little green third-class carriage of the train known by the Maltese as Il-Vapur ta' L-Art ('The Land Steamer') sits next to the original station building which has a sign spelling out the name of the town the British/Italian way, Birchircara. There are several metal plaques telling the story of the railway, its extension to Imtarfa (Mtarfa) to serve the newly built Victoria Lines (see page 231) and its final decline. The British had intended to create a railway network all over the island but, despite the popularity of the train, railways in Malta proved to be financially unviable and this was the only line ever built. For more information and lots of photos for railway buffs, check out *The Malta Railway* by Joseph Bonnici and Michael Cassar (*BDL;* €17.50).

On their very first visit to Malta, the Knights remarked that there was a shortage of fresh water in the country. The problem became more acute with the building of Valletta which stands on a particularly dry peninsula and needed a good enough supply of water to be able to hold reserves in case of siege. The Order ruled that every house built in Valletta had to have a system for collecting and storing rainwater. The old houses still have large cisterns beneath them (see one at Casa Rocca Piccola, page 129).

Yet, as the population of Valletta grew, the city's need for water outstripped what it could collect from winter rains so Grand Master Alof de Wignacourt (1601–22) commissioned an ambitious solution: a 15.7km channel to bring water from natural springs near Mdina all the way to Valletta. Begun in 1610 it took 600 men four years to build the aqueduct. Much of the channel is underground but in order for the water to flow most of the way under gravity, parts of it – mostly through Birkirkara, Santa Venera and Hamrun – had to be raised and were built as a classic arched aqueduct. Stretches of this structure can still be seen, notably on the streets of Birkirkara (see above).

The completion of the aqueduct was royally celebrated in Valletta as the water flowed into a fountain in the square outside the Grand Master's Palace. The fountain now stands in St Philip's Gardens in Floriana (see page 142). Water from the aqueduct also ran to a fountain just outside Porta della Marina, today's Victoria Gate, on the Grand Harbour side of Valletta. Here, ships could fill up with water from a spout in the shape of a cannon barrel (now in the Maritime Museum; see page 153). Above the spout stood the statue of Neptune that now adorns the inner courtyard of the Grand Master's Palace (see page 128).

The Wignacourt Aqueduct went a long way to solving Valletta's water problems but as the centuries passed and Malta's population continued to grow, the whole country was, by the 1970s, once again short of fresh water and new solutions had to be found (see boxed text, opposite).

Getting there and away Birkirkara is very well served by **buses**. Numbers 40, 42, 47, 49, 59, 71, 73, 142, 159 and 169 all come here from Valletta, the 499 from Buġibba and Mosta, and the 560 from Naxxar. **Parking** is free but can be difficult, particularly during shopping hours.

THE THREE VILLAGES AND ST ANTON PALACE AND GARDENS Birkirkara merges
imperceptibly into **Balzan**, which itself merges into **Lija** and **Attard**. These three together are known to tourist guides as 'The Three Villages', though locals rarely refer to them as such. They are not villages anymore, of course, but nor are they bustling modern towns. They retain a certain traditional upmarket calm and charm – a taste of old Malta. There is little tourism here (all to the good), just a very pleasant place to be with some fine buildings, including St Anton Palace and Gardens which sit roughly on the border of Balzan and Attard. The villages have the usual church square at their centres – and each has a *festa* (Balzan in July, Attard on the Feast of the Seven Marys on15 August and Lija earlier in the same month) with Lija's known for good fireworks. Attard's square has a little café with outside tables, and just off the square, the area's best (and smallest) restaurant in a 400-year-old house (see *Where to eat*, below).

Getting there and away Buses 80 and 81 (and, more slowly, the 84) will bring you to this area from Valletta and, in the opposite direction, go to Mdina and Rabat.

The 81 also goes to Buskett Gardens. It is possible to **park** around the Corinthia Palace Hotel. Elsewhere it can be difficult.

Where to stay

Top end

Corinthia Palace Hotel (160 rooms) De Paule Av, Attard; 21440301 or 21465713; e sananton@ palace.corinthia.com; www.conrinthiahotels.com. Opposite the entrance to San Anton Gardens, far from the noise of the tourist areas. Calm & peaceful like the upmarket residential streets around it. Low-rise with attractively landscaped gardens, split-level outdoor pool (no inflatables), garden café (not overpriced), restaurants indoor & out, comfortable rooms, thick carpets, spa with good-sized indoor pool (age 16+), jacuzzi, etc (see *Spas, Chapter 4, page 101*). Helpful staff. Courtesy bus to Valletta & close to a public bus stop, but own transport preferable. *Dbls from €80 (winter), €126 (summer).*

Budget

The University Residence Robert Mifsud Bonnici St, Lija; 21436168 or 21430360; e info@ university-residence.com.mt; www.universityresidence.com. Primarily for people connected with Malta University, the residence also welcomes tourists. Own grounds, swimming pool, launderette, etc. Range of room types. Cheapest are standard student dbls in houses of 7 or 8 rooms with 5 bathrooms & kitchen facilities. Each room has a set of bunk beds, wash basin, desks & wardrobe. Not the most convenient location, but Bus 40 from Valletta stops right outside the residence, there is a large car park & a courtesy bus runs (all day in winter, mornings in summer) to the university 4km away (from where there are buses to the airport, Sliema, etc). Winter €14pppn, summer €21pppn, b/fast €3. The residence also rents out 5 SC farmhouses (about 200 years old) sleeping up to 4. Winter €46 (total), summer €69.

Where to eat

Etienne's 13 Main St, Attard; 21424647; e etiennewines@nextgen.net.mt; 20.00–23.00 Wed–Sun. In a 400-year-old stone house on a corner just off Attard's Church Square (from where, if

---

A THIRSTY ISLAND?   *Hilary Bradt*

How does a small, arid island like Malta provide enough fresh water for its population, and for the influx of tourists during the dry summer months? To find out I visited the Pembroke Reverse Osmosis plant on the northeast coast of the island.

In the old days, Stephen Zerafa (Head of Public Relations at the Water Services Corporation) told me, all Maltese houses had a well, and even rainwater mixed with seawater was drinkable because it was filtered through porous rock so lost its salinity. Indeed, until the 1980s the underground water table was sufficient for all Malta's needs, but the tripling of visitor numbers in three decades required additional supplies and the first reverse osmosis plant was built. There are now three such plants on the island, providing 57% of Malta's water. At maximum capacity, they can provide 94,000m³ of water, with the Pembroke plant doing the lion's share.

The technology is both simple and beautiful, with skeins of what looks like angel's hair – soft and golden – playing a major part. These are actually tiny tubes, through which sea water is forced at high pressure. Salt and other impurities stay behind and pure water passes through the semi-permeable walls. The salt is dumped back on the ocean and the pure water fed into pipes to supply Malta and Gozo.

Despite the recovering of 30% of the energy used, the electric motors needed to run the plant use the same amount of power as a small town. And there are six such motors. Solar power is the most promising source of sustainable energy, or off-shore wind turbines. Meanwhile, as long as Malta has power it has sufficient water for islanders and visitors, and acts as a model for other islands or countries with a limitless supply of ocean, but dry summers.

you are lucky, you will be serenaded by the church choir as you sip a pre-dinner drink), this tiny restaurant has a mini-wine bar downstairs (serving mixed platters & pasta) &, up a narrow spiral staircase, a delightful 1st-floor restaurant with just 6 tables under the stone-slab roof. Regular menu of 5 starters (€9.25–16.50), 5 mains (€21.75–30.90) & 5 puddings (€3.50–9.50) plus specials & a wine tome of 500 wines from all over the world (€10.50–700). Take advice from Etienne – a man who knows his wine & his food.

St Anton Palace and gardens (⊕ 08.00–19.45 summer & until 18.00 winter; take bus 427 from Buġibba) This is the largest and nicest of Malta's public gardens outside the capital, with mature trees (unusual in this dry country) offering shade over a maze of paths that pass colourful flowers and cooling fountains. Ducks, terrapins, fish ponds, aviaries and animals modelled of wire and moss (from a horse to a dragon) make this a good place for a break if you are touring with kids.

The palace was built as a private summer retreat for Fra Antoine de Paule – known for his unpriestly love of luxury and inattention to monastic vows – shortly before he became grand master in 1623. On his death in 1636 the estate passed to the Order of St John and successive grand masters found it a convenient place in which to escape the heat of Valletta.

In 1798 it became the headquarters of the Maltese resistance to French rule and in 1799 HQ for Alexander Ball, the British naval commander sent to help displace Napoleon's troops. It was here in September 1800 that the French capitulation was signed. Throughout British rule, the palace was home to the governor, and the gardens were opened to the public in 1882. When Malta became a republic in 1974, the palace became the official residence of the president.

The main building is not open to the public, but you can walk through the palace precincts. Enter from the gardens beneath the clock and between two stone thrones, passing a plaque listing all Malta's presidents to date. The covered stone walkway runs alongside the president's private garden then out through an (unlabelled) green door onto St Anton Street/Triq San Anton.

NAXXAR

Naxxar is one of Malta's oldest villages. The cart ruts (see box, page 198) just outside the modern town suggest there has been a settlement here since at least Roman times, quite probably earlier, and Naxxar was amongst Malta's first ten parishes listed in 1436. It has now sprawled its way to meet neighbouring Mosta, but **Victory Square** still has a typical centre-of-the-village feel with its Baroque **Parish Church of the Nativity of the Virgin Mary** (1616–30 by Tumas Dingli, with side-apses and façade added in the 20th century). If you are in the area over Easter, this is one of very few churches that still puts up the black damask of mourning on Good Friday. The official line of today's Catholic Church is that Good Friday is not a time for mourning but for celebrating the gift of Christ the Saviour, but this parish has stuck with its traditions. The September *festa* (see page 31) is also very popular.

Opposite the church is the deceptively simple façade of Palazzo Parisio, a late 19th-century confection that its owners like to describe as a mini-Versailles.

GETTING THERE AND AWAY Buses 54, 55, 56, 59 and 159 come here from Valletta (via Birkirkara; the 59 and 159 also go to Buġibba) while the 65 links Naxxar with Sliema, St Julian's and Rabat. Narrow streets make this a difficult place to park.

✕ WHERE TO EAT
✕ **Palazzo Parisio** See opposite for contact details. 2 restaurants open at different times in the same space – a recently renovated section of the palazzo's ground floor in winter & a lovely spot in

Malta is increasingly marketing itself as a place to get married – particularly for Roman Catholics and for those seeking a civil ceremony in a different setting and/or a more amenable climate. There are over 300 Catholic churches on Malta and Gozo in a wide range of architectural styles as well as some wonderful settings. There are, of course, churches or other denominations, as well as two registry offices in Valletta and in Gozo's capital Victoria. For a more interesting non-church setting, for an additional charge, you can choose to have your wedding almost anywhere on the islands. Several of its historic buildings do weddings and wedding receptions including Palazzo Parisio (see below).

Several tour operators offer specific wedding packages which may include a wedding organiser, hairdresser, photographer, flowers, cake, etc. You can even have your dress made locally. It is also possible to organise a wedding in Malta yourself. The Malta Tourism Authority (☎ (UK) 020 8877 6990; e office.uk@ vistimalta.com) produces a weddings information pack.

THE LEGAL STUFF All the forms you need can be obtained from the MTA (as above). The request for the publication of banns (form RZ1) needs to reach the registry office in Malta at least six weeks before the wedding date, along with birth certificates of both bride and groom and the declaration of oath (RZ2). Each of the couple also needs to provide a 'free status certificate' to show they have never been married, otherwise documents are required showing that any previous marriage is legally over. The marriage registry fee is €95 (costs of churches or other locations will of course be in addition and vary) and couples need to arrive in Malta in time to visit the registry office at least once before the wedding to finalise the arrangements.

the gardens during the summer. The same excellent chef looks after both restaurants. **Caffe Luna** (⊕ 09.00–18.00 daily) serves coffee, lunch & tea (sandwiches from €4.50, cakes €7, & at lunchtime a very small selection of international main courses from €18 to €26, English afternoon tea €16.50).
Luna di Sera (⊕ 19.30–23.00 Wed–Sat) is the refined evening restaurant, specialising in Italian food with a touch of French (starters around €15, mains about €25, 6-course tasting menu €75).

WHAT TO SEE AND DO

Palazzo Parisio (29 Victory Sq, NRX 1700; ☎ 21412461; e info@palazzoparisio.com; www.palazzoparisio.com; ⊕ 09.00–18.00 daily (last entry 16.30); guided tours Mon–Fri on the hour 09.00–13.00. Prices without the tour: €6 adults, €4.50 students/children; prices inc tour: €9 adults, €6 students, €4.50 children aged 5–15, children under 5 go free. Also available to hire for weddings (see boxed text, above) & corporate events.) Originally built in 1733 as a country house for Grand Master Manoel de Vilhena (he of the Manoel Theatre), by the end of the 18th century it was in the hands of the Sicilian-Maltese aristocratic Parisio family (who also owned Palazzo Parisio in Valletta). The opulent *palazzo* you see today, however, was created by the grandfather of the family that still owns it, Giuseppe Scicluna (nephew of the Scicluna who built the Dragonara Palace on Spinola Bay). One of the richest families in Malta, the Sciclunas founded the Scicluna Bank, now absorbed into the Bank of Valletta, and Giuseppe was a man of flamboyant taste. For eight years he imported from Italy designers and master craftsmen to work on the house, and landscape gardeners to create a ½-mile-long formal garden (now much truncated).

He died just a year after completing Palazzo Parisio in 1906, leaving it to his four-year-old son, John. In due course, John took over the family bank and under him it became the first bank in Malta to issue cheques, gaining its owner the nickname

'Cisk' (pronounced *chisk* – a mispronunciation of cheques). When he later opened a brewery, he called his beer Cisk – now the bestselling lager in the land.

The house is an exuberant celebration of excess with an eclectic mix of Roman-style wall painting, romanticised classical scenes, marble statues, armour, columns, patterned floors and rich textiles. The peak is reached in the ballroom where golden busts of grand masters are held up by white marble putti, and vast chandeliers light the gilded and mirrored walls.

The first-floor terrace looks out over the formal garden, a pleasant place to stroll with its trees, small lawns, fountains and over 60 species of hibiscus as well as bougainvilleas and citruses. The orangery is from the original 1733 house. The gates at the end of the garden look onto a mess; this area was leased out as a Trade Fair centre. The land has now reverted to the Scicluna family and it is hoped will be developed into something more attractive. There are also plans for a small boutique hotel in one wing of the palace.

San Pawl Tat-Tarġa (St Paul of the Step)
About ten minutes' walk or a very short drive from the centre of Naxxar towards St Paul's Bay is the collection of buildings known as San Pawl Tat-Tarġa, centred on a chapel but with several other historical curiosities too.

The chapel (✆ *21435376/7767; www.maltadiocese.org/in-naxxar?l=1;* ⏲ *only for Mass*) Built in 1696 on a spot where St Paul is meant to have preached. The story goes that he could be heard all the way to Gozo. On a very clear day you can see Gozo from here (hearing is another matter). You can also see the statue of St Paul on St Paul's Island.

16th-century towers Behind the church in this pretty little square is **Torri Gauci (Gauci Tower)** built by the Gauci family in 1548 as a fortified residence. Several members of the family had already been captured by Turkish corsairs and sold into slavery so they weren't taking any more chances. Opposite (across the road) stands **Torri tal-Kaptan (the Captain's Tower)**, an early Knights' watchtower erected under Grand Master Jean Parisot de Valette in 1558 for the Captain of the Maltese Cavalry. The tower looks north towards St Paul's Bay and Salina Bay.

Victorian and World War II fortifications A little further along the road towards St Paul's Bay are remains of the more recent fortifications of the **Victoria Lines** (see page 231), a British wall and military walkway that ran the width of Malta to prevent invaders landing in the north and travelling overland to the more populous parts of the island and the crucial harbours. (For a better preserved stretch of the lines, see *Mosta* page 226, or *Dwejra Lines*, page 231.)

Just below the Victoria lines is a **World War II pillbox**, the only one on the island that has been restored to look exactly as it did during the war, even down to the fake painted windows meant to make it look like an ordinary residence. At least some of the holes in the walls are shell damage.

Looking across the valley from the pillbox you should be able to see a modern satellite dish next to a curved red wall. The wall is a 1930s **early warning sound wall** designed to pick up the sound of aircraft flying out of Sicily. It dates originally from the Abyssinian Crisis of 1936 (when Mussolini invaded Ethiopia).

Cart ruts On open waste ground about 50m below the pillbox (still on the left of the road as you go from Naxxar towards St Paul's Bay) are pairs of ancient cart ruts (see boxed text, page 198). They are a little tricky to spot, but once you have got them they are clearly cart ruts. This set of ruts includes a hairpin bend (not unlike that of the nearby modern road) and some of the deepest ruts in Malta, one of which has been reused to channel rainwater to a cistern.

MOSTA

The second-largest town in Malta, with a population of around 18,700, Mosta was once part of the parish of Naxxar but has now far outstripped it both in size and in the number of tourist visitors. Mosta attracts some 250,000 tourists a year, purely to see its vast domed parish church, although there are also a couple of little-known sights of interest on the outskirts.

GETTING THERE AND AWAY Buses 43, 44, 45, 47, 49, 52, 56, 58 and 157 all come here from Valletta and stop outside Mosta Dome. Also stopping here are the 65 from Sliema, the 86 from Buġibba (which also goes to Mdina) and the 427 from Buġibba going on to Marsaxlokk. Other buses serve Mosta but stop at less convenient parts of the city. There is a **car park** right next to the Mosta Dome in the middle of town.

✖ WHERE TO EAT

✖ **Ta' Marija** Constitution St; ☏ 21434444; e info@tamarija.com; www.tamarija.com; ⊕ 18.30–22.30 daily & also 11.30–14.30 Tue–Sun. This Malta institution glories in its lace tablecloths, twinkly lights, guitars & table-side serenades. This sort of kitsch would be tourists-only in many countries, but Ta' Marija is hugely popular with the Maltese & for 5 years running has won Malta's *Definitive(ly) Good Guide to Restaurants'* top award for Maltese food. All the traditional dishes: *aljotta* (fish soup), *bragioli* (meat dish), snails, rabbit, quail & fresh fish. Maria & son Ben move amongst the diners like the proud host & hostess of a large party. Maltese-sized portions, so be hungry. Great for families, many of whom come for Sun lunch. *Starters €7–10.50, mains €17.50–24.50, buffet (Sat evening & Sun lunch) €19.50, kids' menu €6.*

✖ **The Lord Nelson** 278–80 Triq il-Kbira; ☏ 21432590; ⊕ 19.30–22.30 Tue–Sat (closed 1st week of Jan & 12–31 Aug). In complete contrast to Ta' Marija, this is a traditional, elegant, calm-feeling, intimate & cosy restaurant (especially good in winter) is set over 3 floors of a historic building. A tiny stone spiral staircase links the floors & there is a wonderful (& very popular) table in the 1st-floor *gallarija* with views of the Mosta Dome. French/Mediterranean food. *Starters €6.50–9.50, mains €16.50–22.*

WHAT TO SEE AND DO

Mosta Dome (*Pjazza Rotunda;* ⊕ *usually 09.00–11.45 & 15.00–19.00.* **Festa** *15 Aug, The Feast of the Seven Marys*) The 19th-century parish Church of Santa Marija Assunta (the Church of the Assumption), is known to all as Mosta Dome or, occasionally, the Rotunda. It dominates the town – and often the skyline of Malta – and is claimed to be the third-largest unsupported church dome in Europe. This all depends on what you measure. The Gozitans insist that theirs (the Xewkija Rotunda, page 293) is bigger. It is indeed taller, but at 60m across (45m inside), Mosta's dome is wider.

Partly inspired, it is said, by the Pantheon in Rome, the church was constructed, amidst considerable controversy, between 1833 and 1860. First, money earmarked for the church was diverted to deal with a cholera epidemic, then the French architect, Georges Grognet de Vasse, became embroiled in a bizarre argument in which he insisted that Malta was the tip of the lost city of Atlantis. And finally, the bishop, unconvinced that a round church was really Christian, refused to lay the foundation stone.

The project did eventually get off the ground, however, and its towering Neoclassical façade hides an impressive (and in summer, blissfully cool) interior. The inner surface of the dome is white, blue and gold and the floor is a geometric pattern of marble. The relatively plain walls are dotted with white marble tombs and there are eight murals by Giuseppe Cali.

In April 1942, as a congregation of around 300 attended afternoon Mass, a bomb broke through the dome, thudded to the ground and rolled across the floor. It failed to explode and no-one was hurt, a 'miracle' still celebrated in the sacristy museum where a large bomb (real, but not *the* bomb) takes pride of place in the small museum.

The Victoria Lines and Mosta Fort Just above the town with views back over Mosta is the Ġnien L-Għarusa tal-Mosta public garden, a slightly faded place but with a well-preserved stretch of the British-built defensive wall and walkway, the Victoria Lines (see boxed text, page 231), which runs along the natural ridge. The lines make a great walk with expansive views and an easy path underfoot.

Within the gardens is a milestone, defaced as they all were during World War II when the British feared invasion and wanted to be sure that no enemy would be helped by signposting. The low-lying 19th-century Fort Mosta, a little further along the Victoria Lines, was one of the three main forts linked by the lines. It is now an army and police base, not open to visitors.

Ta' Bistra Catacombs (*Triq il-Missjunarji Maltin; Heritage Malta:* ☎ *22954000;* e *info@heritagemalta.org; www.heritagemalta; free parking or take buses 43, 44, 45, 47, 49, 52, 58, 59 from Valletta or Mosta*) This small site of 4th- to 8th-century catacombs a little way outside Mosta is expected to open to the public sometime in 2011. Beneath a 20th-century farmhouse which will form the visitors' centre, is the start of this catacomb of some 57 tombs in 16 groups (not all of which are visible) along a limestone ridge which runs under the road and continues on the other side. Unlike the catacombs of Rabat these are rural catacombs cut into the side of the rock and this will be the only place where wheelchair users can get to the mouth of a hypogeum tomb. On the far side of the road (reached by a pedestrian tunnel) are several window tombs and a round *agape* table for the funeral meal (see boxed text, page 214). There will eventually be a café and a small children's playground.

TA' QALI

Ta' Qali (pronounced *Ta Ahli*) is Malta's old airport, known by the British RAF as Takali. Built in 1938 as a civilian airfield it was rapidly taken over by the military after the outbreak of World War II and became the most bombed airfield in the world. It is now home to the National Football Stadium, a Craft Village and Malta's Aviation Museum.

GETTING THERE AND AWAY Bus 86 comes here from Buġibba and goes on to Rabat; the 65 runs to Sliema and St Julian's, the 86 to/from Buġibba. If coming by **car**, there is plenty of space to park.

CRAFT VILLAGE (⏰ *09.00–16.00 Mon–Fri, 09.00–13.00 Sat*) Rows of old Nissen huts have been taken over by craftspeople and retailers to demonstrate and sell Maltese crafts. You can watch glassblowing, pottery making, stone polishing, carpentry and filigree work, and buy a mix of tourist tat and genuine crafts.

MALTA AVIATION MUSEUM (*Ta' Qali, RBT 13 (on the former RAF airfield, between the Craft Village & the National Stadium);* ☎ *21416095;* e *info@maltaaviationmuseum.com; www.MaltaAviationMuseum.com;* ⏰ *09.00–17.00 daily;* €*5 adults,* €*3 concessions (inc seniors and students),* €*1.50 children*) Two hangars full of Malta's aviation history. The museum started with one Spitfire – EN199 – that took part in the invasion of Sicily in 1943. The museum exists largely thanks to the energy and enthusiasm of Ray Polidano, who still runs it. Anybody with an interest in things aeronautical should definitely seek him out for a chat.

Apart from the Spitfire, highlights include a Hawker Hurricane discovered by a diver off the Blue Grotto in 1995 (now fully restored), an Aeritalia Fiat G91, a 1950s NATO plane of which there is no example in the UK, and one of only 12 Fairey Swordfish biplanes (nicknamed 'string bags') left in the world. There is also a diminutive forerunner of today's microlights, the Flying Flea (Le Pou du Ciel) built to 1930s designs, and a modern passenger jet cockpit you can climb into.

There is a detailed **guidebook** full of pictures and all the plane-buff facts you could want (*by Anthony Spiteri; €4.70*).

MĠARR

A very pleasant little inland town (not to be confused with Mġarr harbour on Gozo), Mġarr centres (like any self-respecting Maltese settlement) on its church square, with the large silver-domed parish **Church of the Assumption** (*festa* in the third week of August) fronted by a broad raised terrace where a strawberry festival is held each April. The church was begun in 1898 when the people of Mġarr were granted their own parish, breaking away from Mosta, and finished in 1946. Its design is not noticeably modern, but with its Neoclassical columns and plain interior it is an echo of the Mosta Dome. Opposite the church is the unprepossessing **Il-Barri** (The Bull) restaurant. Do not be fooled – this place is more than it looks both culinarily and historically (see below).

GETTING THERE AND AWAY Buses 47 and 52 originating in Valletta come to Mġarr, also going to Birkirkara and Golden Bay. The 52 runs mornings only and also stops in Mosta and St Paul's Bay. There is **parking** on the streets here.

✖ WHERE TO EAT

✖ **Il-Barri** (see below for details) Real inexpensive Maltese home cooking. Excellent *bigilla* (bean & garlic paste) with *galletti* (crackers) & *Ħobż biż żejt* (literally 'bread with oil', but actually also with tomatoes) come as a pre-starter when you order a meal. Locals love this place for its rabbit (*fenek*): starter of spaghetti with rabbit sauce, followed by rabbit in wine, rabbit stew or the very tasty fried rabbit. Other pasta dishes & burgers available. Pizzeria downstairs on w/end evenings. Don't miss the delicious homemade puddings, & if you order rabbit, leave room for the peanuts-in-their-shells that traditionally follow. Great for families. *Starters €3–4, pastas €7, mains €10–11 & for the extra-hungry*

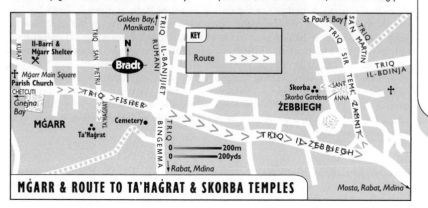

MĠARR & ROUTE TO TA'ĦAĠRAT & SKORBA TEMPLES

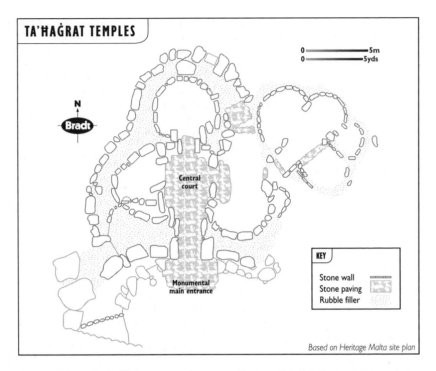

TA'ḤAĠRAT TEMPLES

0 ══════ 5m
0 ══════ 5yds

N

Bradt

Central court

Monumental main entrance

KEY

Stone wall
Stone paving
Rubble filler

Based on Heritage Malta site plan

carnivore, Maltese mix of rabbit in gravy, stewed horsemeat & roast quail (€14.95).

✕ **United Bar & Restaurant** Behind the parish church, Church Sq; ✆ 21572512. The United refers to Manchester United & this bar-restaurant across the square from Il-Barri, is also famous for its rabbit & snails.

WHAT TO SEE AND DO

Mġarr Shelter (*Il-Barri Restaurant, Church Sq;* ✆ *21573235;* ⊕ *09.00–14.00 Tue–Sat & 10.00–11.30 Sun;* €*3 adults,* €*1.50 children under 10*) Behind a nondescript door in the basement of Il-Barri restaurant is a large World War II shelter (see boxed text, page 149). Rediscovered about 12 years ago, the 125m hand-dug tunnel with numerous side rooms descends to some 12m below ground. Up to 400 people sheltered down here during the war including the man who (if you are lucky) will show you round – a member of the family that runs Il-Barri. Born in 1943, he was one of the last babies to occupy the newborns' nursery in the shelter, designed to keep the vulnerable babies away from the overcrowded corridors where disease spread quickly. His elder sister died as a result of scabies at the age of five months.

The shelter originally had no electricity (it does now) and would have been full of smoke from candles and oil lamps. It did, however, have a hygienically tiled hospital area where casualties – civilian and military – were taken, a birth room and even a small schoolroom. Also on show in the shelter is the wing of a Junkers 88 aircraft retrieved from a local field in 1941. It is cool and damp down here so you may need a sweatshirt.

Ta' Ḥaġrat Temple (*Triq Ta' Ḥaġrat;* ✆ *21239545;* e *info@heritagemalta.org; www.heritagemalta.org;* ⊕ *09.30–11.00 Tue only;* €*5 adults,* €*3.50 over-60s/children aged 12–17,* €*2.50 children aged 6–11, children under 6 go free*) If you leave Church Square along Triq Fisher then turn right down Triq Ta' Ḥaġrat and walk to the end, you will find the Ta' Ħaġrat prehistoric temple (see page 228 for a locator map), built between 3600BC and 3000BC (see page 4 and page 78 for more on the temples). You can see a little through the wire fence, but this is just the side of the temple – the back wall of an apse – so it is worth coming when the site is open. At the front of the temple you can clearly see the concave façade, with a bit of bench at its base, facing out over the valley.

The large monumental entrance (partially restored, and with views of the Mġarr church dome behind it) leads into a paved central courtyard surrounded by three apses. The apses have been screened off, probably during the Tarxien phase (3150–2500BC). No decorated stone was found here, but a little model of a temple was discovered (now in the National Archaeological Museum in Valletta; see page 121) which contributed to the debate about how the temples were roofed.

To the right and behind this temple are the remains of another, even smaller, irregular building joined to the first by a flight of steps of unknown date. This may have been a second tiny temple or perhaps as priests' living quarters. The pottery found in excavations suggests that, like Skorba (below), there was a village here for some time before the temple was built.

Skorba Temple (*Żebbiegħ, near Mġarr, about 1.5km from Ta' Ħaġrat; prices & contacts as for Ta' Ħaġrat, but the site is open ⊕ 11.30–13.00 Tue*) Not as attractive as Ta' Ħaġrat and with much less left standing, Skorba yielded a great deal of archaeological information. This is largely because it was first excavated only in the 1960s when archaeology was more careful and more advanced than in the 19th century when most of the temples were unearthed.

Skorba began as a settlement in the 5th millennium BC, before the temples were built in the 4th and 3rd millennia BC. Behind the hedge on the far side of the modern path from the temple enclosure, foundations of two small buildings can be seen. Dr David Trump, who led the 1960s excavation, suggests that they are the foundations of a shrine or shrines pre-dating the temples. Foundations of oval huts were also found (now lost or very difficult to identify), one dating back further than any other unearthed on the islands. Two early types of pottery first identified on this site – the later of which is coloured with red ochre – have been used to

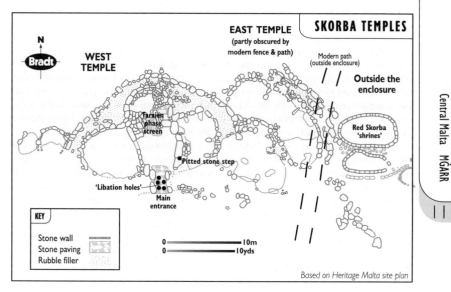

Based on Heritage Malta site plan

name two pre-temple phases in Maltese archaeology: Grey Skorba 4500–4100BC and Red Skorba 4400–4100BC.

Getting there To get here from Mġarr, follow Triq Fisher from Church Square, past the turn to Ta' Ħaġrat, over the roundabout, past Ta' Soldi restaurant, take a sharp left that almost doubles back the way you have come. Signposted 'Skorba', this is Triq Sir Temi Zammit. If arriving by car from Valletta/Mosta/Mdina then take the first right – a fork more than a turn – after the start of the buildings of Mġarr and carry on up the hill towards the children's playground, turn left and you are there. See page 227 for a locator map.

Exploring the site As you enter the enclosure, it is initially hard to make sense of the stones. There are sparse remains of two temples here, but only the west temple (the further from the entrance) is comprehensible to the untrained eye. Built between 3600 and 3000BC, only one megalith of the façade is left standing but you can identify the main doorway by the two standing stones with holes for door bars, the fallen topstone that lies in front of them and the paving either side of it. The paving contains five 'libation holes' (holes perhaps used for making liquid offerings).

You can see quite a bit of the wall of the left apse, while the right apse is barely more than a shape on the ground. There is a step to the right apse that has pitted decoration. This is thought to be a reused stone from the later Tarxien phase (3150–2500BC) during which the apses here are thought to have been screened off from the central 'corridor'. Nowhere else is decoration found on a step or paving. Around this time too, part of the eastern wall of this temple was demolished and a second, four-apse, temple built. The second temple is now very hard to visualise as it is cut across by the modern footpath, its eastern wall incorporated into the modern wall next to the path outside the enclosure.

AROUND MĠARR

Binġemma Gap A couple of kilometres south of Mġarr lies this wonderful little spot where several items of historic and natural interest come together in a small area. The **Chapel of Our Lady of the Way**, more often known locally as Il-Madonna ta' Ittria, built in 1680, marks the spot. There are panoramic views from here back towards Mġarr (with the shining silver dome of its parish church) and on a clear day, all the way to Gozo.

During migration times (spring and autumn), birds – including raptors – pass through here, making it a good spot for **birdwatching** in the early morning and late afternoon. Inevitably this also makes it a good place for hunting and trapping of birds. If you stay around the chapel and the public road and paths you should not have any problems with hunters who mostly patrol the rocky area behind the chapel, but do be sure to read the information on hunting and safety before embarking on any birding (see pages 24 and 48 respectively).

Below the chapel is a cave that was once inhabited, and if you look across the small valley at the hillside opposite, you will see more caves – natural and manmade. These are in fact a **Punic/Roman/Byzantine necropolis** which can be reached by following the little path through the vegetation – including fig, almond and carob trees, and wild fennel. (In spring, when vegetation is thickest, you may want long trousers.) Most of the tombs have some natural light but if you want to see into the depths you will need a torch. There are multiple entrances and everything from small individual tombs to complexes of burials with carved arches and square windows as well as typical stone headrests and little niches for oil lamps. Some of the complexes interconnect and this is a great place to explore (at your own risk, and with care so that nothing is damaged).

The British were worried about enemies landing in the north of the island and travelling overland to attack the more populated Grand Harbour area and the British Mediterranean Fleet. They built a system of defences that spans the entire width of the island, 12km, along a natural ridge from Madliena to Fomm ir-Rih (see below). Work began in the early 1870s with the building of a fort at either end and one in the middle at Mosta (none are open to the public). The forts were later joined together by a strong defensive wall, wide enough for infantry to march along. Complete with batteries, entrenchments, stop walls and emplacements for searchlights and howitzers, the whole system was officially inaugurated in 1897 and named the Victoria Lines for Queen Victoria's Diamond Jubilee.

No invader ever tried to cross the lines, and as early as 1907 military technology had overtaken these defences and they fell into disuse. Recent renovations have rescued several sections of the wall, some of which look very impressive viewed from the north and also make good walks. The wall is itself an excellent path and, being right on the edge of the ridge, affords panoramic views.

At the head of the little valley you will see an impressive defensive wall. This is a part of the **Victoria Lines** (see boxed text, above) known as the **Dwejra Lines**. This stretch has been recently restored and is a great place for a **walk**. Cross the bridge over the little valley and you come to a corner which is another vantage point for surveying the landscape. From here you can walk along the Victoria Lines for more than a kilometre with panoramic views to the north, including of Verdala Palace and Mdina. The MTA booklet, *Malta Countryside Walks: Dwejra Lines Walk* gives more details (download free at *www.visitmalta.com/ebrochures/dwejra_walk.pdf*).

Nadur Tower This 17th-century tower, one of eight built by Grand Master de Lascaris (1636–57) stands at the highest spot on the island after Dingli Cliffs, 242m above sea level. This makes it good for **birdwatching** as well as offering dramatic **views** along the coast and as far as the Ta' Ċenċ cliffs of Gozo. The best views are from the road just before you reach the tower.

THE WEST COAST

Along the west coast of Malta, not far from Mġarr lies a series of bays. All are good **swimming** places, and there are some attractive **walks** along the cliffs either side of the bays too (best outside the heat of the summer). Each bay is different in character. You will need a car to explore these with any ease.

FOMM IR-RIH BAY A large beautiful bay, Fomm ir-Rih ('mouth of the wind'), is surrounded by cliffs and completely undeveloped. A smooth slope of grey clay backs a pebbly beach from which it is possible to **swim** and **snorkel**. You can reach it by boat or by walking down a narrow rocky footpath (about ten minutes from the nearest parking which is down a small road to the left as you arrive at the bay from Baħrija). Because of the walk and its unsuitability for children this place gets relatively few visitors. Quite an isolated spot, it would be unwise to swim here alone, and it is unsafe in windy weather.

There is good **birdwatching** from the headlands on both sides of the bay during migration (spring and autumn). This inevitably also means there are hunters around during the autumn season (see pages 24 and 48).

11

ĠNEJNA BAY Popular with locals, this red sandy beach with rocks to snorkel off, has a car park right next to the water. Known as '**Mġarr's Beach**', it is about 3km from the town (but it is a steep walk back!). There is a pretty row of boathouses (mostly now used as beach huts) cut into the base of the cliffs, and sometimes a not-so-pretty gaggle of caravans that at the time of writing is causing a great deal of local controversy. Above the bay is the **Lippia Tower**, one of the watchtowers built by Grand Master Lascaris in 1636–57.

The water is lovely, although there can be litter on shore and, more importantly, the cliffs are crumbling. A boy was killed here when loose clay was dislodged by a vehicle parked above, and a vast new boulder appeared by the sea in winter 2008–09 having fallen from the cliff; beware of overhangs and think carefully about where you sit.

GĦAJN TUFFIEĦA BAY Although this bay is only just across the headland from Ġnejna Bay, to get between them by car you have to go back into Mġarr and out by a different route. The road does, however, connect directly to Golden Bay. The long flight of steps that leads down from the car park to the bay means that this lovely narrow red sandy beach does not get as crowded as Golden Bay or Ġnejna Bay. With just a **snack bar** and small **watersports** and **sun-lounger** outlets, it is not built up and is a thoroughly pleasant place to relax and swim. Be aware that there can be a dangerous undertow a little way out from the beach here during, or just after, rough weather.

At the far end of the bay from the steps, a clay slope (that can be tricky to cross) divides Għajn Tuffieħa Bay from a smaller beach and flat white rock that attracts naturists and gays (see also page 52 and please note that, despite what may go on here, nude and topless bathing is actually illegal in Malta).

On the tip of the headland by the car park is another of Grand Master Lascaris's watchtowers with a gun emplacement (1636–57) – part of the same defensive system as Nadur Tower and the Lippia Tower on Ġnejna Bay (above). Unless things have changed substantially since the time of writing, signs to 'Roman Baths' should be ignored: they are closed to the public and there is nothing to see.

It is possible to walk from here across the headland to Golden Bay.

GOLDEN BAY (RAMLA TAL-MIXQUQA) Dominated by the Radisson SAS Golden Sands Resort hotel, this is still a lovely beach on which to sunbathe and swim so long as it is not too crowded – which realistically means in autumn and spring rather than summer. The only yellow sandy beach on Malta, it is gently sloping, so good for families (although be aware that after rough weather there can occasionally be a dangerous undertow). In summer, stones are cleared from the water's edge but in spring you may want water shoes, at least for kids. There are plenty of **watersports** available here as well as a **snack bar** and all the facilities of the five-star hotel. There is good **walking** on the coastal clifftops behind (north of) the hotel.

Getting there Buses 47 and 52 run here from Valletta, going on to Mġarr. Bus 652 links to Sliema. There is a small **car park** next to the beach which fills up very fast in summer. Otherwise you have to park up the hill.

Where to stay

⌂ **Radisson SAS Golden Sands Resort & Spa******* (287 rooms, 60 apts) Golden Bay MLH 5510; ☎ 23561000 or 23560001; e goldensands@ radisson.com.mt; www.radissonblu.com/

goldensandsresort-malta. A large modern 5-star resort hotel with loads of activities & facilities, from Maltese lessons for grown-ups to a multi-activity kids' club. Indoor swimming pool &

attractively landscaped outdoor pool overlooking the bay. All rooms have balcony. 3 restaurants. Watersports & sandy beach. Good for families. See also *Spas*, page 101. *Standard dbl ('serene country view') from €125 room-only in Feb, to €280 mid-Aug.*

GAIA Foundation Centre (*Elysium Tree Nursery & Visitors' Centre, Għajn Tuffieħa Road, MLH 5510;* ✆ *21584473/4;* e *elysium@projectgaia.org or director@projectgaia.org; www.projectgaia.org*) Near the Radisson Hotel on the road up to Għajn Tuffieħa overlooking Golden Bay, is the visitors' centre for this conservation NGO. Here you can visit their nursery where plants – native, and in some cases unique to the Maltese islands – are propagated and nurtured, find out more about the conservation of Malta's coast or even volunteer some time and get directly involved (see *Travelling positively*, page 76). There is also an organic **shop** and a **café** where films are occasionally shown.

Central Malta THE WEST COAST

11

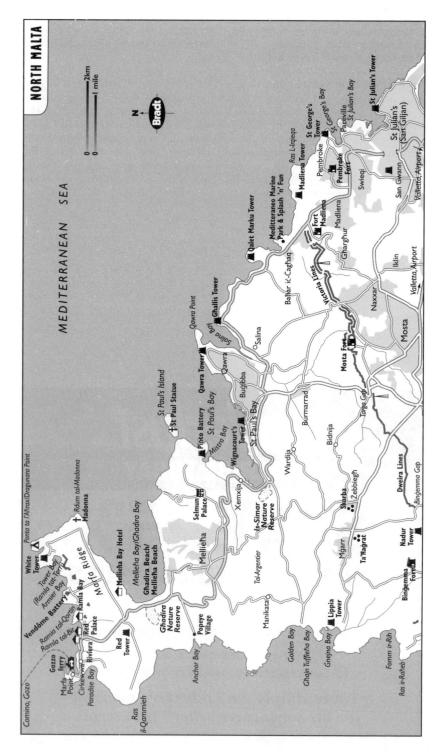

MEDITERRANEAN SEA

Comino, Gozo

Ponta ta l'Ahrax/Dragunara Point

Rdum tal-Madonna
Madonna

White
Tower

Tower Bay
(Ramla tat-Torri)
Armier Bay

Mellieha Bay Hotel

Mellieha Bay/Ghadira Bay

Vendôme Battery

Ghadira Beach/
Mellieha Beach

Ramla tal-Qortin
Ramla tal-Bir

Malfa Ridge

Red
Riviera Palace

Red
Tower

Ghadira Nature
Reserve

Marfa
Point

Gozo
ferry

Cirkewwa

Paradise Bay

Ras
il-Qammieh

Popeye
Village

Anchor Bay

St Paul's Island

St Paul Statue

Pinto Battery

Qawra Tower

St Paul's Bay

Mistra Bay

Wignacourt's
Tower

St Paul's Bay

Qawra Point

Qawra

Buġibba

Selmun
Palace

Mellieha

Xemxija

Is-Simar
Nature
Reserve

Tal-Argentier

Manikata

Golden Bay

Għajn Tuffieħa Bay

Gnejna Bay

Lippia
Tower

Skorba

Żebbiegħ

Mġarr

Ta'Ħaġrat

Nadur
Tower

Bingemma
Fort

Dweira Lines

Bingemma Gap

Ras ir-Raħeb

Fomm ir-Riħ

Wardija

Bidnija

Burmarrad

Salina

Salina
Bay

Salina

Ghallis Tower

Qalet Marku Tower

Mediterraneo Marine
Park & Splash 'n' Fun

Baħar iċ-Ċagħaq

Ras L-Irqieqa

Madliena Tower

St George's
Tower

St George's Bay

St Julian's Tower

Paceville
St Julian's Bay

Pembroke

Pembroke
Fort

Fort
Madliena

Madliena

Gharghur

Victoria Lines

Swieqi

San Gwann

St Julian's
(San Giljan)

Valletta, Airport

Long Gap

Mosta Fort

Mosta

Naxxar

Iklin

Valletta, Airport

Airport

Bradt

N

MEDITERRANEAN SEA

0   2km
0   1 mile

12

North Malta

The north of Malta, divided from the south by rocky ridges, has many small bays, very accessible by sea (in summer). Historically, this made it vulnerable to corsair attack and few people chose to live here during the time of the Knights. The British built a defensive barrier – the Victoria Lines – across the entire width of the country cutting off the north to protect the south, although the Royal Navy also patrolled the northern coasts and as the danger of corsair attack waned, the population of the north began to grow. Come the late 1970s and '80s mass tourism added greatly to the numbers of people here, at least in summer, particularly as the Gozo ferry departs from Ċirkewwa on Malta's northwestern 'hammerhead'. The area is still more sparsely populated than the rest of Malta, however, and there is much more countryside here than elsewhere.

The attractive area around Mġarr and the west coast is, for reasons of access to certain sites, included in *Chapter 11*. So this chapter begins north of there in Mellieħa, moving on to the 'hammerhead' that looks across to Gozo and Comino, before turning southeast to St Paul's Bay, the resort areas of Buġibba and Qawra, and the scenic North Coast Road leading back to Paceville and St Julian's.

MELLIEĦA

Mellieħa perches (in places precariously) on a ridge above the southern side of Mellieħa Bay (Għadira Bay) with **Mellieħa Beach** (Għadira Beach) to its northwest along the head of the bay. This is a classic white-sand beach, the longest in Malta (about 800m) with a lovely gentle slope into clear blue sea. It is just a shame about the busy main road that runs its full length and the ugly buildings at either end. The beach gets very crowded in summer.

It is a steep uphill climb into the village. Just before the shops start, there is an unobtrusive stone doorway on the left which leads down a long flight of stone steps to the underground chapel of **Our Lady of the Grotto** (Il Madonna Tal-Għar). This Madonna is believed to have special powers to help the very young and the grotto walls are hung with baby clothes and votive notes requesting intervention on behalf of sick children or showing gratitude for their recovery. Most of the letters are in Maltese but there are a few in English including one accompanied by a tiny Babygro giving thanks for the arrival of a much-wanted newborn. Heart-warmingly, there is also a photo, clearly added later, of a healthy young boy. Some locals have it that there is (miraculously) one fewer steps going down to the grotto than there are climbed coming up – see what you think.

Mellieħa was one of the first ten parishes in Malta listed in 1436, but by the mid-16th century it had been abandoned due to the fear of corsair attack, only becoming a parish again in 1844. The present parish church (in the square up the steps opposite the entrance to the grotto), dedicated to the Nativity of Our Lady (*festa* 8 September), was built for the 'new' parish towards the end of the 19th century. The neighbouring **Sanctuary of Our Lady of Mellieħa** (*festa* in late September), however, is the oldest Marian shrine in Malta. It is surrounded by legend – including one relating a visit here by St Paul after his shipwreck on Malta in AD60 – and it is still a place of pilgrimage, with a large collection of ex-voto notes and offerings. This is due primarily to the chapel's rock painting of the Madonna and child attributed by believers to Paul's companion St Luke, although its style dates it to the 13th or 14th century.

Back on the main street above Our Lady of the Grotto, if you look up to the left, there are several buildings perched on a rocky ridge looking distinctly unstable. They are in fact undermined by a series of **caves** whose openings you can see in the rock face beneath them. These are a combination of natural caves and manmade extensions. The smaller ones may have been Punic tombs, and several were once inhabited. One was a medieval troglodyte chapel and still contains a Madonna, and the cave with its mouth covered was occupied until very recently and may still be.

GETTING THERE AND AWAY Buses 44 and 45 link Valletta with Mellieħa. Both run via Mosta and on past Mellieħa town to the bay, stopping on the beach road and close to the Għadira Nature Reserve. The 145 links Mellieħa village with Ċirkewwa. The 645 runs from Sliema up the North Coast Road to Mellieħa. Bus 48 will take you to Buġibba, stopping at Mellieħa Church, to the south and Ċirkewwa to the north. All these buses also go to St Paul's Bay.

Parking is free, but can be difficult in the narrow streets of the village. You can park along the road by the beach but it fills up fast on summer weekends.

WHERE TO STAY The Mellieħa hotels are mostly mass-tourism establishments, though generally with a calmer atmosphere than those in Buġibba and Qawra. Most are booked through package deals but they can be booked direct. The Pergola is in town, the rest are on the bay close to the beach.

🏠 **Mellieħa Bay Hotel********** (313 rooms) Għadira 9065; ☎ 21573841; e info@melliehabayhotel.com; www.melliehabayhotel.com. On the quieter north side of Mellieħa Bay. Large resort hotel with swimming pools & paddling pool overlooking the bay. Small private coarse-sand beach. Bright stone-tiled rooms, all facing the sea (though the garden obstructs ground-floor views), interconnecting rooms available. *Dbls B&B from €52 (winter) to €94 (summer).*

🏠 **Mellieħa Holiday Centre********* (150 bungalows) Mellieħa Bay, MLH9064; ☎ 22893000; e info@mhc.com.mt; www.mhc.com.mt. Built by a Danish trade union for its workers, but open to all. A smaller & more basic early version of Center Parcs, with rows of slightly fortress-like limestone bungalows, each with a walled patio & roof terrace. Shared facilities include gardens, terrapin pond, large outdoor pool, shaded kids' paddling pool, table tennis, supermarket & 2 restaurants. There is a tunnel that takes you under the road directly to the beach. Lots of families (many Danish) come here & there it is good for wheelchair users. *2-bedroom bungalow with lounge (& 2 sofabeds, so sleeps up to 6), small kitchen & bathroom from €26.50–46pppn*

B&B, smaller studios €23–33pppn, children 2–12 half-price.

🏠 **Pergola Club Hotel********** (91 apt rooms) Adenau St, MLH 2014; ☎ 21523912/3; e info@pergolahotel.com.mt. Up in the village, 20–30mins' walk from beach. Studios & apt rooms with twin/dbl bed(s), sofabed (sleeping up to 2 extra), kitchenette, table & chairs, also hotel rooms. Small indoor pool, 2 outdoor pools & children's paddling pool. Bar in a cave under the hotel. *SC studio (sleeps up to 4) €40.50–93.20 (depending on season), dbls B&B €42–112. Always email or call for best deals.*

🏠 **Riu Seabank Hotel********** (285 rooms) Marfa Rd, MLH02; ☎ 21521460; e info@seabankhotel.com; www.seabankhotel.com On the south side of the bay near the village, just across the road from the beach. Cool, shady lobby with 2 small aviaries of budgerigars. Indoor pool, pleasant outdoor terrace & pool overlooking fields, kids' club & kids' pool. 'Country view' rooms actually have a country view (albeit marred by a small unattractive building). Rooms are nondescript, but OK. *Dbls B&B from €42 (May), €80 (Aug), €100 (Sep).*

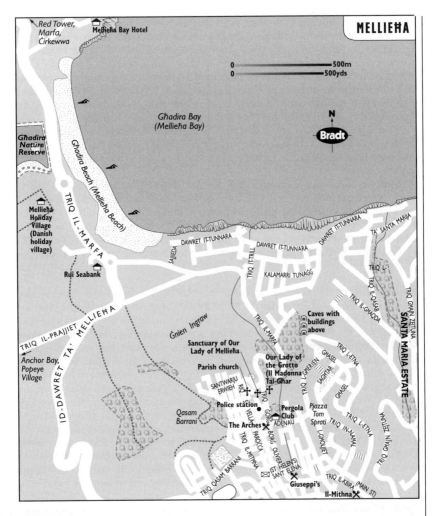

Ghadira Bay
(Mellieħa Bay)

Ghadira
Nature
Reserve

MELLIEĦA

Red Tower,
Marfa,
Ċirkewwa

Mellieħa Bay Hotel

0 ——————— 500m
0 ——————— 500yds

N

Bradt

TRIQ IL-MARFA

Mellieħa
Holiday
Village
(Danish
holiday
village)

Ġhadira Beach (Mellieħa Beach)

Rui Seabank

SAJJIEDA

DAWRET IT-TUNNARA

DAWRET IT-TUNNARA

DAWRET IT-TUNNARA

TRIQ IT-TRILL

KALAMARRI TUNAĠĠ

TA' SANTA MARIA

TRIQ L-

TRIQ IL-QASAB

TRIQ IL-GĦADA

TRIQ GĦAJN ŻETUNA

SANTA MARIA ESTATE

TRIQ IL-PRAJJIET TA' MELLIEĦA

ID-DAWRET TA' MELLIEĦA

Anchor Bay,
Popeye
Village

Ġnien Ingraw

Sanctuary of Our
Lady of Mellieħa

Parish church

SANTWARJU
ERWIEĦ

Qasam
Barrani

TRIQ IL-MARFA

Caves with
buildings
above

Our Lady of
the Grotto
(Il Madonna
Tal-Għar

Police station

The Arches

Pergola
Club

ADENAU

TRIQ L-GĦERIEN

GĦASEL

SAĠITTAR

GĦASEL

TRIQ L-ETNA

TRIQ L-ETNA

Pjazza
Tom
Sprati

TRIQ IN-NAĦAL

TULLIEŻ IWANI

TRIQ GĦAJN ZNUBER

TRIQ QASAM BARRANI

TRIQ IL-MITHNA

BORG OLIVIER

PAROĊĊA

ST HELENS
SANT ELENA

Giuseppi's

TRIQ IL-KBIRA (MAIN ST)

Il-Mithna

North Malta MELLIEĦA

✖ WHERE TO EAT

✖ **Ġiuseppi's** 25 St Helen St, cnr with Ġorġ Borġ
Olivier St; ☎ 21574882 or 27574882; m 99493579;
e mjdiacono@onvol.net; ⏰ 19.30–22.30 Mon–Sat
(closed mid-Aug). A well-established Mellieħa favourite
in a converted townhouse. Small & welcoming with
colourful walls, a mix of different chairs & decorative
oddments. Small menu, changed regularly, plus daily
specials (inc fresh fish). Older children welcome.
Starters €9–10, mains €15–20.

✖ **Il-Mithna** (The Mill House) 45 Triq il-Kbira/Main St;
☎ 21520404; e ilmithna@onvol.net.mt;

⏰ 18.00–22.30 Wed–Sun. Modern Mediterranean food
in a historic setting. Eat in this 17th-century windmill
built by the Knights of St John, or in summer on the
terrace or patio outside. Families welcome; highchairs
available. *Starters €4.50–9, mains mostly €16–18, set
menu before 19.30 3-courses for €14.*

✖ **The Arches** Ġorġ Borġ Olivier St; ☎ 21523460;
e info@thearchesmalta.com; ⏰ 19.00–22.30
Mon–Sat. Innovative French-Mediterranean food in a
smart modern restaurant. Children over 5 welcome.
Starters mostly €9–15, mains €25–38.50.

WHAT TO SEE AND DO AROUND MELLIEĦA

Ġhadira Nature Reserve *(BirdLife Malta;* ☎ *21347646;* e *info@birdlifemalta.org;*
www.birdlifemalta.org; ⏰ *10.00–16.00 w/ends Nov–May or by arrangement with BirdLife*

12

Malta; free entry) Just across the road from the beach at the head of the bay is one of two bird reserves run by BirdLife Malta (the other is on St Paul's Bay, below). It is tiny by British standards with one good-sized hide looking out over a few hectares of wetland and salt marsh, but it is an important place for Malta's birds. It provides a safe haven – a habitat that will not be overtaken by development, agriculture or pollution and where there are no hunters – as well as a source of education for Maltese children that may help them develop an interest in watching living birds. Needless to say the hunting lobby does not like this place and it is surrounded by high fences.

The siege conditions are unfortunately necessary. Hunters have occasionally broken into the site in order to shoot rare birds and the reserve has been damaged on more than one occasion including in an arson attack and by oil being thrown into the water.

BirdLife has a very dedicated staff and the reserve feels very peaceful inside. Little ringed plover breed here (the only place in Malta where they do), along with warblers (Cetti's, fan-tailed, Sardinian), corn bunting and occasionally finches. You may also see Temmink's stint, little stint, turtle doves and a variety of waders (depending on the season). For more on birding in Malta see pages 23, 68 and 97.

From here it is walking distance up to the Red Tower on the Marfa Ridge (see below).

Popeye Village (*Anchor Bay, Mellieħa;* ℡ *21524782/3/4;* e *info@popeyemalta.com; www.popeyemalta.com;* ⊕ *Jul–Sep 09.30–17.30 daily, Aug until 19.00, & Oct–Apr until 16.30;* €*9.50 adults,* €*7.50 children aged 3–15, children under 3 go free*) If you have seen and enjoyed the film *Popeye* (the 1980 live action one directed by Robert Altman, starring Robin Williams) or have young children who have had enough history, you might want to pop into the village of 'Sweethaven' – the original movie set for the film. It is a bit overpriced, but the brightly coloured plasterboard buildings at zany angles linked by zig-zagging wooden walkways are fun to run along if you are aged about five to nine. There is a little boat ride on the hour around the pretty bay, a robotic Christmas scene (year-round), a craftsman making filigree Maltese crosses, wine tasting, a fun pool, a small playground and a terrace of fake grass and sunbeds. Outside the slightly tacky complex is an even tackier (and more expensive) fun fair, a World War II pillbox (free!) and a little coarse sandy beach. It is tempting to swim, but there is apparently a sewage outlet discharging half a mile offshore, so if there is an onshore breeze it is probably best to swim elsewhere.

Getting there Bus 441 from Mellieħa Bay (*on the hour 10.00–17.00 in summer, every 2hrs 10.00–16.00 in winter*) or about a 1.5km walk.

THE MARFA PENINSULA

The Marfa Ridge runs the length of the hammerhead (the Marfa Peninsula) commanding great views, both over the sea towards Comino and Gozo and back over the main island of Malta. You can walk an entire circuit of the hammerhead (about 11 to 12km – see the MTA's excellent booklet, *Malta Countryside Walks: The Marfa Ridge Walk*, http://visitmalta.com/ebrochures/Marfa.pdf). The road runs the length of the ridge so you can also take a scenic drive along here. Down by the water, however, you can only get directly from bay to bay on foot. By car you have to keep going back to the ridge road (not that the distances are very great).

GETTING THERE AND AWAY Buses 45 and 145 from Valletta, 645 from Sliema and 48 from Buġibba – all via Mellieħa and St Paul's Bay (see above for route details) – stop on the main road between Mellieħa Bay to Ċirkewwa before going on to

Ċirkewwa and the Gozo ferry. No buses run along the hammerhead except the 50 which goes to Armier Bay from Valletta on Sundays only. There is no problem **parking** around here.

WHAT TO SEE ON THE MARFA RIDGE
The Red Tower/It Torri L-Aħmar *(Renovated & run by Din L-Art Ħelwa (Malta's National Trust);* ℡ *21215222 or 21225952;* e *info@dinlarthelwa.org; www.dinlarthelwa.org;* ⊕ *10.00–16.00 Mon–Fri & 10.00–13.00 Sat – opened by volunteers;* €*1.50pp, free to British National Trust members, although donations welcome to help with restoration work)* Also known as St Agatha's Tower, the Red Tower was built in 1647–8 by Grand Master Lascaris to defend the Straits of Comino and communicate early warning of attack via other towers to Valletta. It was equipped with four or five cannons and, at times of trouble, up to 49 men. It isn't clear why it was painted red (perhaps to make it easier to see from other towers?), but this was the original colour and it has been retained.

Entrance to the tower is via an impressive flight of steps and a wooden bridge that would probably have been a drawbridge. Inside are two vaulted rooms which may once have been split horizontally to provide sleeping quarters. The roof – with its four corner towers – affords magnificent 360° **views** of most of northern Malta, Gozo, Comino, Mellieħa Bay, Għadira Nature Reserve and a fair chunk of the rest of Malta. The Santa Marija Tower on Comino and the White Tower at the other end of the 'hammerhead' are also easily seen. No wonder the Knights built their tower here. (If travelling with young children, be aware that the roof has only a low wall around it.)

Getting there The tower is **walking** distance (uphill) from Mellieħa Bay. You can take **bus** 145 from Valletta or 645 from Sliema to be dropped off on the main road below the Tower. Alternatively, you can **park** next to the tower.

Beyond the Red Tower From the Red Tower you can walk or drive out over the garigue (limestone rock with low scrubby vegetation) to the tip of the headland at **Ras il-Qammieħ** from where there are **panoramic views** to the Ta' Ċenċ cliffs of Gozo in one direction and right along the west coast of Malta in the other. Keep your back to the (mercifully small) derelict NATO radar station. Sticking out to sea as it does, this headland is a good spot for **birdwatching** during spring and autumn migration. There are therefore also hunters' and trappers' hides here and, in autumn in particular, you may come across men with guns (see *Hunting*, pages 24 and 46 and *Birdwatching*, pages 23, 68 and 97). From here, it is possible to walk down an old military path and stone steps cut by the British to reach **Paradise Bay**, the best beach on the northwest coast (see below). From the beach, footpaths link each bay all the way along the coast facing Gozo and Comino to the far end of the hammerhead where the path leads back up onto the ridge.

By car you have no choice but to double back along the ridge road past the Red Tower to join or cross the main road leading from Mellieħa and the south to Ċirkewwa and the Gozo ferry.

If you cross the main road and keep travelling the **scenic route** along the top of the ridge, you will pass on your left a *girna*, a traditional circular dry-stone hut with a corbelled roof. This is a farmers' shelter often found in Malta's older agricultural landscapes and particularly in this area. Next you come to a small (planted) woodland, popular with hunters and trappers, before reaching the far end of the ridge at Rdum tal-Madonna.

Rdum tal-Madonna On this often windswept spot stands a little white statue of the Madonna (1870) and the **Chapel of the Immaculate Conception**, built in 1961 to replace a 19th-century chapel that had become too close to the cliff edge. The original chapel was built by a fisherman in votive thanks for his safe return as the only survivor of a fishing accident. The cliffs here are eroding fast and it is advisable not to go too close to the edge.

There are great views out to sea and over Mellieħa Bay. The circles in the water are fish farms. On the Mellieħa Bay side there is also a cliff path leading down to a small undisturbed bay, unattractively known as **Slugs Bay** (after a brown sea slug found in the area), with a few square metres of sandy beach. The rare Mediterranean sea daffodil (*Pancratium maritimum*) may be seen here in August. Rdum tal-Madonna is also the centre of a conservation project for the rare seabird, the **yelkouan shearwater**, which breeds in the cliffs here (see boxed text, page 241). A small number of the larger Cory's shearwater also breed here, as do short-toed larks and resident birds, including the blue rock thrush (Malta's national bird) and the spectacled warbler. Other birds are seen during migration (for more on birding in Malta, see pages 23, 68 and 97).

THE NORTHWEST COAST (FACING COMINO AND GOZO)

Dragunara Point/Ponta ta' l'Aħrax From Rdum tal-Madonna there is a scenic cliff path along the end of the hammerhead down to Dragunara Point. Alternatively, return to the road and walk or drive down to Daħlet ix-Xmajjar, turn right, leave the car by the campsite (see *Where to stay* below) and walk a couple of hundred metres.

Dragunara Point is a barren promontory of rough rock with a large hole in it looking straight down into the sea. This is a cave whose roof has collapsed (which makes you wonder a little what you are walking on elsewhere!) and it is particularly impressive when the sea is choppy and waves crash within it (though take care).

The White Tower (It-Torri L-Abjad) and Ramla tat-Torri (Tower Bay) On the next mini-headland is the **White Tower/It-Torri L-Abjad**. No longer white at the time of writing, it is best seen from a distance as the area around it is a grubby mess. However, there are plans to clean the place up and open it to the public complete with historic re-enactors. This is one of the de Redin towers (see page 85) built in 1658 under Grand Master Martin de Redin (1657–60) as part of an early warning communication system that ran from one tower to another all the way down the coast. Straw was burnt to send a warning and a fire at this tower would certainly have been visible from the Red Tower, Selmun, and the tower on Comino. Neighbouring **Ramla tat-Torri (Tower Bay)** has a rather uninviting, muddy sandy beach and a village of boathouses.

Bays and beaches **Little Armier** is a small sandy beach (mixed with a bit of clay) with watersports and a café-pizzeria that also hires out sunbeds (€7.80 for chicken salad with potatoes or pasta, plus a sunbed for the day). It is backed by an old defensive wall now surrounded by boathouses and a gaggle of caravans. A few minutes' walk (or a ten-minute drive) takes you to **Armier Bay** with a larger sandy beach (and less clay), a few food outlets and an unsightly derelict bar. There is a Knights-period redoubt just above the bay and on the headland is the 17th-century **Vendôme battery**, named after the Knight who commissioned it, the brother of Louis XIII of France.

Ramla tal-Bir is dominated by the Ramla Bay Resort (see *Where to stay*, opposite). The sandy beach here can become rather full of seaweed when there is an onshore wind. Another redoubt overlooks the bay. On the Ċirkewwa side is the **Red Palace/Il-Palazz l-Aħmar**, originally a 1657 watchtower extended to its present form in the 20th century. Here too (opposite the Riviera Hotel) is the departure point for some boats to Comino (see *Chapter 13*, page 250).

Malta is home to about 10% of the world's population of the rare yelkouan shearwater (*Puffinus yelkouan*) and about a third of them breed in the cliffs of Rdum tal-Madonna. This has therefore been chosen as the centre of the **LIFE Yelkouan Shearwater Project** which aims to study and protect the species (☎ *21347644;* e *info@lifeshearwaterproject.org.mt; www.lifeshearwaterproject.org.mt/en*).

The yelkouan shearwater, whose name means 'wind-chaser', arrive in Malta from October and breed in burrows in the cliffs. They lay a single egg at the end of February which hatches around the second week in May. In July, when the chicks are old enough, almost all the birds leave the island and head east. Like many seabirds they do not make landfall again until the next breeding season and part of the project here is to tag the birds to find out where they fish and where they spend the winter.

Even when breeding, at least one parent spends the day at sea and in the late afternoon the birds gather in a 'raft' on the surface of the water before flying in to their nests just after dark. They are therefore not easy to see from land but their loud hoarse call (more high-pitched from the male than the female) can be heard, especially on moonless nights between February and April.

In recent years the numbers of yelkouan shearwaters have fallen and a few nest sites have been abandoned; the LIFE project aims to establish what is threatening the species and try to halt the decline. One threat is rats, so please don't leave any edible rubbish lying around. If you would like to know more, there are free **guided walks** with the LIFE project site warden, and if you are really enthusiastic there are opportunities to volunteer (minimum one week; contact the project as above). The **RSPB** also recruits volunteers from the UK (☎ *01767 680551; Irene.Sabiniarz@rspb.org.uk*).

On the other side of Marfa Point, at the tip of which is the Gozo ferry terminal, lies **Paradise Bay**, accessed down a flight of stone steps. It is sandy with clear blue water and a thatched bar and restaurant – easily the nicest beach along this coast (1km from the bus stop – see *Getting there*, above).

All the beaches here become appallingly crowded on summer weekends, when the locals arrive to join the tourists.

WHERE TO STAY
Hotels

⌂ **Ramla Bay Resort****** (194 rooms) Triq Ir-Ramla Tal-Bir, Marfa MLH 7100; ☎ 22812281 or 21580660; e info@ramlabayresort.com; www.ramlabayresort.com. Pleasant garden with thatched seating areas & outdoor pools, small private sandy beach (sometimes seaweedy), small children's playground, indoor pool, watersports, bar with a real *luzzu* boat at its centre, bright rooms, all with balconies. Also 10 family rooms sleeping up to 4 & wheelchair-adapted rooms. The gardens are also wheelchair accessible. *Country-view dbls from €50 B&B in winter to €110 (Aug).*

⌂ **Riviera** **** (250 rooms) Marfa MLH 9069; ☎ 21525900; e info@riviera.com.mt; www.riviera.com.mt. On a pleasant seafront promenade, the former departure point for the Gozo ferry. Reception & bar with large windows looking out at the sea & Comino. Indoor pool, outdoor seawater pools, children's paddling pool, 3 restaurants, spa, watersports. The 'private beach' is a stretch of rocks & concrete accessible to anyone (there are apparently plans to add sand). Rooms are unremarkable but nice, all with balcony. *Standard dbls around €40 in winter to €120 in summer.*

Camping

⋏ **Malta Campsite** Dahlet ix-Xmajjar, Limiti tal-Mellieha; ☎ 21521105, m 99496707; e info@maltacampsite.com; www.maltacampsite.com. Not

much shade, & a long way from public transport (nearest bus stop 1hr walk or €5 via the camp taxi), Malta's only campsite is nonetheless a cheap

North Malta **THE MARFA PENINSULA**

12

accommodation option in a good location for walks. Small shop, café & above-ground swimming pool (surrounded by fake grass), clean showers (€0.70 for 4mins). If renting a mobile home make sure it is a new one & be aware that they get unbearably hot in summer. *Tent pitch €15–25pn depending on tent size (up to 4 people, 5th & 6th person +€5pp), 'furnished tent' (with thin mattresses, plastic table & chairs, fridge, cooker & electricity) up to 4 people €30pn (+€11.50 per extra, children +€3.50).*

ST PAUL'S BAY

This large and beautiful bay, a quiet fishing area until the 20th century, is sadly now surrounded by ugly modern apartments and mass-tourism hotels. Buġibba and Qawra on the southern side are particularly unattractive. These are the areas that have given Malta a bad name as a styleless concrete package-holiday destination.

Out in the bay is **St Paul's Island** which dips in the middle making it look like two islands. On it stands a tall 19th-century statue of the saint who is said to have been shipwrecked on these rocks in AD60 (see *History* page 8 and the boxed text, page 138).

The bay played a bloody part in the end of the Great Siege of 1565. The Turkish fleet, having fled Marsamxett Harbour when fresh troops arrived from Sicily to relieve the Knights, returned, anchoring in St Paul's Bay. Here they faced a rout that some reports say turned the sea red.

The northern side of the bay, around **Xemxija**, is much quieter than the southern side (Buġibba and Qawra) and includes the secluded **Mistra Bay** where there is almost nothing but a sandy, seaweed-strewn (and slightly grubby) beach, the marvellous Palazzo Santa Rosa restaurant (see *Where to eat*, opposite) and, on the small **Ras il-Mignuna headland**, the Pinto Battery, an 18th-century redoubt built by Grand Master Manoel Pinto de Fonseca whose coat of arms can still be seen carved into the stone.

Also on the Xemxija side of the water is the **Selmun Palace**, an 18th-century fortified building that was the base of the Monte di Redenzione degli Schiavi, a foundation that raised money to pay ransoms to retrieve poorer Christians taken into slavery by the Turks. There was always more demand than money so who was rescued was decided by lottery. The building is now part of the Selmun Palace Hotel.

GETTING THERE AND AWAY Buses 43, 44, 45 and 145 come to St Paul's Bay from Valletta. The 48 runs to Ċirkewwa /Gozo ferry, as does the 645 which, in the other direction, goes to Sliema via the North Coast Road and St Julian's. The 652 takes the same route to St Paul's Bay and then goes on to Golden Bay. Take bus 427 to get to Mosta Dome, San Anton Gardens, Tarxien Temples and Marsaxlokk. Please note the Buġibba buses also drop you a short walk from St Paul's Bay (see page 246). **Parking** is free but spaces are at a premium at weekends.

WHERE TO STAY The best deals in this area are likely to be through package-holiday operators and unless you get a very cheap deal or actively like the sound of the area, you would be better off staying elsewhere. One exception, if you are on a budget but have transport, is the Ambassador Hotel on the quieter Xemxija side of the bay.

🏠 ☂ **Ambassador Hotel***** (46 rooms) Shipwreck Promenade, Xemxija; ☎ 21573870; e info@ ambassadormalta.com; www.ambassadormalta.com; ⏱ Apr–Oct. On the edge of St Paul's Bay near a fish farm, this good-value hotel away from the crowds has a rather old-fashioned, but clean, terrace & pool by the bay. Basic but decent rooms, most with bay-view balcony. Divers stay here. *Dbls B&B €39 (low season) to €53.30 (Jul/Aug) B&B, possibly less if you ask.*

✗ WHERE TO EAT

✗ **Palazzo Santa Rosa** Mistra Bay; ➘ 21582737; e psr@maltanet.net; www.palazzosantarosa.com; ⏱ 12.30–15.00 Tue–Sun, 19.30–22.30. Eat on the attractive terrace overlooking the bay or inside what was once the summer house of a wealthy Maltese family. A place to relax over your food. The truly foodie chef-owner, a self-trained ex-journalist, doesn't like rush. He only takes one booking per table for each meal (so you can sit from 12.30 to 15.00 if you want). Chatty menu includes lots of detail about the ingredients (as well as the odd joke). Also a Neapolitan pizzeria at the back. Booking advisable. Highchairs available. *Starters €6.95–12.95, mains €10.95–29 (minimum €20pp).*

XEMXIJA Xemxija is largely made up of modern apartments, but on its rocky fringes are some interesting and unusual unfenced prehistoric and ancient sites.

Prehistoric graves On rocky ground next to Prehistory Street/Triq il-Preistorja on the northwestern edge of Xemxija (the Mellieħa side) you will find a series of holes in the ground marked by cairns. There are six rock-cut tombs here, mostly smaller and less regular than the Punic tombs, consisting of a vertical shaft into the rock (occasionally with steps cut for easier access) and one or more kidney-shaped (or lobed) chambers. Tomb 5 (the one nearest the bottom of the slope) is the largest with five lobes and it was the shape of this tomb that prompted archaeologist John Evans, who led excavations here in 1955, to suggest that such tombs may be precursors to the design of the temples. Most of the artefacts found here date from the earliest temple period (Ġgantija phase 3600–3200BC) though some tombs seem to have been reused in the Bronze Age before being lost to sight for 3,000 years. Take a strong torch if you want to see into the chambers.

There are also some **cart ruts** (see page 198) that run along the rock here. Others are (perhaps appropriately) covered by Prehistory Street!

Apiary, Punic tomb and megaliths Follow signposts to 'archaeological site' from Triq ir-Ridott on the edge of Xemxija to find this cave with its front covered by a stone wall cut through with a regular grid of arched holes. This is an apiary, claimed to date back to the Roman times, but in fact used for beekeeping from early modern times until the 20th century.

If you walk up the steps to the right of the apiary you find yourself on what is dubiously regarded as a Roman path across high rocky scrubland. You will soon see a small sign painted on a cairn pointing right to a Punic tomb and left to 'prehistoric temple'. To the right there is indeed a rock-cut Punic tomb. Walking left, you follow a path through bushes and small trees. There are no further signposts but on your left a few large stones grouped together may once have been part of an apse of a prehistoric temple. There is little left and what remains is difficult to interpret, particularly because bird hunters have built a stone hide in the middle of it.

Heading straight on from the hand-painted sign, the path leads along a rocky ridge with sweeping views. If it's not too hot, this is a very pleasant place for a walk.

IS-SIMAR NATURE RESERVE (*BirdLife Malta;* ➘ *21347646;* e *info@birdlifemalta.org; www.birdlifemalta.org;* ⏱ *10.00–16.00 w/ends Nov–May or by arrangement with BirdLife Malta*) Just outside Xemxija at the head of St Paul's Bay is this tiny bird sanctuary run by BirdLife Malta. Even smaller than their other site at Għadira (Mellieħa Bay – see page 237), it provides a little patch of wetland, reed bed and trees, where migrating birds can settle in safety and resident birds can breed. No hunting is allowed within 500m of the reserve. There are three hides along a little nature trail and a dedicated staff. Little bittern have nested here, rail and kingfisher may be seen, and regular breeding species include reed warbler, coot, moorhen and grebe. To visiting birders these last may not sound very important but to the staff of

BirdLife Malta, 'every new species breeding is a triumph' – a triumph of nature over development, modern agriculture and hunting.

ST PAUL'S BAY Confusingly, the narrow strip of buildings between Xemxija and Buġibba is, like the bay it sits on, known as St Paul's Bay, and here you will find a few mass-market hotels and the oldest of the Knights' towers.

Wignacourt Tower (*Din L-Art Ħelwa (Malta's National Trust);* \ *21215222;* e *info@ dinlarthelwa.org; www.dinlarthelwa;* ⊕ *10.00–13.00 daily (& 12.30 Tue); €2, children under 16 & National Trust members free, but donations always welcome for restoration work*) The oldest surviving coastal defence tower in Malta, this was the first of the towers built by Grand Master Alof de Wignacourt (see *Fortifications*, see page 85). When it was finished in 1610, this tower was the only defensive outpost in the north. Three decades would pass before it was joined by the Red Tower (see page 239).

The Wignacourt Tower was intended to protect the Order's galleys when they were anchored in St Paul's Bay, as well as keeping an eye out for invaders. St Paul's Bay was a known weak point, prone to corsair attack. The tower had two cannons similar to that now displayed on its roof which commands panoramic views over the bay and St Paul's Island (with the great advantage that Buġibba and Qawra are behind you!). In 1715 the coastal battery with three larger cannons was added.

The first floor (where you would originally have entered) has been restored as closely as possible to how it would have been when the master gunner was in charge here, with fireplace, cooking oven, stone latrine, pikes and muskets, and the original wooden main door. The well could also be accessed from here in case it was not safe to go outside. The ground floor, originally a storeroom, now houses a small exhibition on Malta's fortifications by the leading expert in the field, Stephen Spiteri. This is the best display you will find on the subject until the Fortifications Information Centre opens in Valletta (see page 136 for more information).

BUĠIBBA, QAWRA AND SALINA BAY

This is the mass-market tourism centre of Malta: sunnier than Blackpool, but without the beach (or the illuminations). The only sandy beach here is a scruffy man-made patch outside the Dolmen Hotel, otherwise swimming is in the paint-peeling lidos or straight into deep water off the rocks on the seafront, backed by the long parade of bars, dodgems and McDonald's. This is the

---

GRAND MASTER ALOF DE WIGNACOURT

Born in 1547, Alof de Wignacourt was a member of the Knights' French Langue. He enrolled as a Knight in Malta in 1566 and was made Captain of the new city of Valletta before becoming grand master in 1601. His legacy has been lasting: he built six watchtowers of which four remain; he commissioned the aqueduct that brought water from near Mdina to Valletta (see page 220) and still bears his name; he was patron to the painter Caravaggio (see page 125); and he expanded the cult of St Paul, particularly surrounding the grotto in Rabat (see page 211) where he founded the neighbouring 'College' (for officiating priests) that now houses the Wignacourt Museum. He was also the first head of the Monte di Redenzione degli Schiavi, the foundation that raised money to ransom Christians taken into slavery by the Turks. He died in 1622 following a riding accident while hunting in the grounds of Verdala Palace (today's Buskett Gardens) and is buried in the crypt beneath the main altar of St John's Co-Cathedral in Valletta.

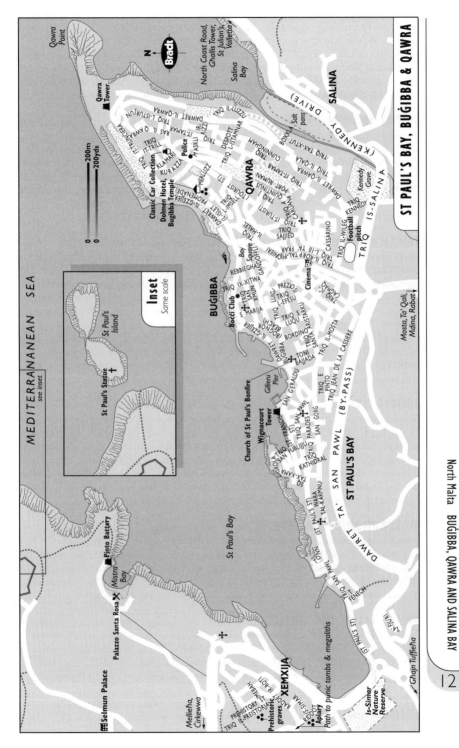

ST PAUL'S BAY, BUĠIBBA & QAWRA

Bradt

N

MEDITERRANEAN SEA

Inset
Same scale

St Paul's Island

St Paul's Statue

200m
200yds

Qawra Point

Qawra Tower

North Coast Road,
Għallis Tower,
St Julian's,
Valletta

Salina Bay

SALINA

Salt
pans

(KENNEDY DRIVE)

TRIQ IL-QAWRA
DAWRET IL-QAWRA
TRIQ L-ISTURJUN
TRIQ IT-TAMAR RAS IL-QAWRA
TRIQ IT-TRILL
TRIQ IL-GĦELEM
IL-ISLET PROMENADE
DAWRET IL-GĦELEM

Classic Car Collection
Dolmen Hotel,
Buġibba Temple

Police
MASKLI
RIŻZI
ST
MERLUZZ
KLAMAR
KURAZZA

QAWRA

TRIQ DESPOTT
TRIQ L-ISTAWAR
NZUL IL-QALA
TRIQ TAX-XTUT

TRIQ
QUINTINUS
PORT RUMAN
TRIQ IT-TAMAR
TRIQ IL-QAWRA
TRIQ IL-GALA
BOXOL
CUNNINGHAM

IS-SALINA
TRIQ KENNEDY

Kennedy
Grove

Football
pitch

TRIQ IL-WILEĠ
TRIQ CASSARINO
TRIQ L-10 TA' FRAR
TRIQ TAL-PIJUNIERI

TRIQ IT-TURISTI
TRIQ SAJJIED
IL-HAZEL
TOURIST ST

Bay

REBBIEGĦA
GANDOFLI
TRIQ IX-XITWA

BUĠIBBA

Bocci Club

TRIQ S
XMUN
S MARIJA
TRIQ
(BOCCI)
BEĊĊ
IL-GŻEJJER
DAWRET IL-
BUĠIBBA

TRIQ
PREZJOSI
TRIQ
LUIGI
LUQU
TRIQ S
EFESU
BORDINO
SANTA ARISTARKU
Cinema

Pier
Gilleru

Church of St Paul's Bonfire
Wignacourt Tower

SAN ĠERALDU
SAN FRANĠISK
TRIQ PARADES
SAN PUBLIJU
TRIQ SAN PAWL
TRIQ TAL-KARMNU
TRIQ SAN GORĠ
SO TRIQ WARBNU
TRIQ KATHIDRAL
TAX-XAMA
TRIQ SAN PUBLIJU
(ST PAUL'S ST)

Toni
BAJJADA
TRIQ IL-MOSTA
TRIQ E
PINTO
TRIQ JEAN DE LA CASSIERE

ST PAUL'S BAY

TA' SAN PAWL (BY-PASS)

DAWRET TA' SAN PAWL

Mosta, Ta' Qali,
Mdina, Rabat

Ghajn Tuffieħa

RUTI
DIRT SAN PAWL
(ST PAUL'S ST)
FENECH

Selmun Palace

Palazzo Santa Rosa

Pinto Battery

Mistra
Bay

St Paul's Bay

XEMXIJA

Mellieħa,
Ċirkewwa

Prehistoric
graves
Apiary

TRIQ SIMGĦA
TRIQ IR-ROTI
PREHISTORIĊI
IL-PREISTORJA
PODOT
TRIQ IX-XGĦAR

Path to punic tombs & megaliths

Is-Simar Nature
Reserve

12

245

downmarket version of St Julian's. One stretch of waterfront is officially named Bognor Beach and the Bognor Bar offers a pint and a chip butty for €2.50. I think you get the picture. The opposite side of Qawra from St Paul's Bay looks over Salina Bay with salt pans and, on the far side of the water, a Knights' tower (see below) and an odd-looking hill. The hill is in fact a vast rubbish dump that can get smelly when the weather is very hot and the wind in the wrong direction.

GETTING THERE AND AWAY Bus 59 comes to Buġibba and Qawra from Valletta and the 70 travels the North Coast Road from Sliema and St Julian's to stop in both places. The 652 runs a similar route from Sliema to stop in Qawra and on to Golden Bay. Other buses run only to Buġibba: the 49, 58 and 449 come from Valletta while the 48 runs to Ċirkewwa (via St Paul's Bay, Mellieħa and Għadira Bay). The 86 goes to Mdina; the 427 and 627 go to Marsaxlokk (the 427 via Mosta Dome, San Anton Gardens and the Tarxien Temples and the 627 via St Julian's, Sliema and the Three Cities). It is only a short walk from Buġibba to Qawra and St Paul's Bay.

CHURCH OF ST PAUL'S BONFIRE At the St Paul's Bay end of Buġibba on Triq il-Plajja tal-Bognor (Bognor Beach Road) is St Paul's Church, generally known as the Church of St Paul's Bonfire (San Pawl tal-Ħġejjeġ), built on what is traditionally regarded as the spot where a fire was lit to warm St Paul, St Luke and their companions after they were shipwrecked in the bay in AD60. This is where he is said to have been bitten by a snake while collecting firewood and, showing no ill effects, been revealed as a saintly presence (see page 138).

This little church was originally built by Grand Master Wignacourt (replacing an earlier church which stood where the Wignacourt Tower now stands) and linked to St Paul's Grotto in Rabat (see page 211). A bomb hit the church in 1943 and what you see today is a 1957 reconstruction.

BUĠIBBA TEMPLE (*Inner courtyard of the Dolmen Hotel, Triq Dolmen, Qawra SPB 2402*) The scant remains of this prehistoric temple have been swallowed up into the gardens of the large Dolmen Hotel but you can wander in and have a look. Incongruous amongst the sunbeds, the prehistoric stones are not a dolmen but the reconstructed monumental entrance to what was once a Tarxien phase (3150–2500BC) temple. A few stones also remain from the façade and a couple of apses. Two decorated 'altar blocks' found here, one carved with fish, the other with spirals, are in the Archaeology Museum in Valletta (see page 121). See also pages 4 and 78.

GLASS-BOTTOMED BOAT TRIP (*Captain Morgan Cruises;* ℸ *23463333;* e *info@ captainmorgan.com.mt; www.captainmorgan.com.mt; €15 adults, €11 children under 12*) Captain Morgan Cruises runs a one-hour boat trip with at least 20 minutes in the glass keel watching the underwater world go by. The boatmen feed the fish so there should be plenty to see, including the occasional octopus. Don't expect a sparkling tropical kaleidoscope though; this is the Mediterranean not the Caribbean.

MALTA CLASSIC CAR COLLECTION (*Tourists St, Qawra (near the bus terminus);* ℸ *21578885;* e *carol@classiccarsmalta.com; www.classiccarsmalta.com;* ⊕ *09.30–18.00 Mon–Fri & 12.30 Sat; €6.40 adults, €4.08 children*) One man's passion for motors turned into a museum: over 100 cars and motorbikes from a 1932 Wolseley Hornet to a 2004 Mercedes SL55 AMG. Also a cinema showing car-related movies and a large collection of model cars.

BUĠIBBA *BOĊĊI* CLUB (*On the promenade next to McDonald's;* ℸ *21577362;* m *99442919*) Boċċi is Malta's traditional game – a bit like *boules* or *pétanque* – and this club organises games for tourists most days between 11.00 and 13.00. For more on the game and its rules see boxed text, page 292.

THE NORTH COAST ROAD

From the edge of Qawra at the head of Salina Bay, the main road runs along the coast as far as the Victoria Lines before turning a little inland *en route* to St Julian's. Once you leave Qawra behind, it is a scenic route and the only real coast road on Malta. There are sparkling sea views and a series of Knights' towers (see below). **Buses** 449 (Valletta–Buġibba), 652 (Sliema–Golden Bay via St Paul's Bay), 645 (Sliema–Ċirkewwa) and 70 (Sliema–Buġibba, Apr–Nov) travel the length of the coast road.

Knights' towers (*Din L-Art Ħelwa (Malta's National Trust);* \ *21225222;* e *info@dinlarthelwa.org; www.dinlarthelwa.org*) In 1658–59 Grand Master de Redin (1657–60) built a series of coastal watchtowers and incorporated earlier towers to create a warning system that ran along the coast from Gozo to Valletta. The towers communicated through flag signalling or by lighting warning fires on the roof. The North Coast Road is the perfect place to see how this worked.

The **Qawra Tower** on Qawra Point was built by the grand master before de Redin, Jean Paul de Lascaris Castellar in 1637, and linked into de Redin's coastal communication system when he built the **Għallis Tower** (1658–59, restored by Din L-Art Ħelwa, open by appointment) just the other side of Salina Bay. This tower in turn has a clear view of Qrejtan Point on the next bay where stands the **Qalet Marku Tower** or St Mark's Tower (de Redin 1658–59, open by appointment with Din L-Art Ħelwa). Looking along the coast from here, you can see the **Madliena Tower** (de Redin 1658–59) near the end of the Victoria Lines.

At this point the road leaves the coast, but the communication line of towers continues with **St George's Tower** (built by de Lascaris) on Paceville's St George's Bay and then **St Julian's Tower** (de Redin, page 85). Several of the towers, including Qalet Marku and Madliena, were reused by the British.

Mediterraneo and Splash 'n' Fun (*Coast Rd, Baħar iċ-Ċagħaq NXR 08; combined tickets for both parks: €22 adults, €15 children/over-60s*) Neither of these two attractions is beautiful and you may not approve of Dolphinaria, but kids are likely to enjoy them. **Bus** 68 from Valletta, via Sliema, St Julian's and Paceville, stops outside, as does bus 70 which starts at Sliema Ferries then takes the same route, before going on to Buġibba. Number 645 does the same, but goes on to Xemxija, Mellieħa and Ċirkewwa (the Gozo ferry). There is a large **parking** lot right outside the parks.

Mediterraneo Marine Park (\ *21372218* or *21376519;* e *mediterraneo@waldonet.net.mt; www.mediterraneo.com.mt;* ⊕ *10.00–17.00; €15.50 adults, €10.50 children aged 4–10/over 65s*) A series of animal shows punctuates the day, featuring sea lions, parrots and dolphins. The rest of the time you can say hello to the animals in their enclosures and, in the case of the parrots, you may get a loud reply. The park also runs a programme for swimming with the dolphins (competent swimmers aged eight and over; €120pp).

Splash 'n' Fun (\ *27374283* or *21374283;* m *79374283;* e *info@splashandfun.com.mt; www.splashandfun.com.mt;* ⊕ *09.00–late; €18 adults, €10 children/seniors*) Fake grass surrounds pools and slides from a little kids' area with a mini tunnel slide, ropes and fountains, to a mega shute with rubber rings to sit on and a terrifyingly steep U-shaped structure like a skatepark half pipe with water. Also a Lazy River to float along in (relative) peace. It all feels a bit run-down and gets crowded on summer weekends.

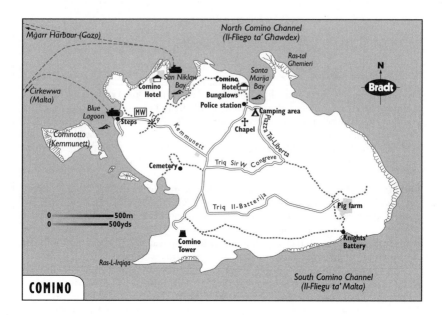

13

Comino

Most people visit Comino (Maltese: Kemmuna) only on day trips and never get further than the Blue Lagoon, Malta's most popular swimming spot. In summer, however, this barren little island – just 2.5km long and with a resident population of four – is a great place to chill out for a few days. Besides simply lazing around, it offers excellent snorkelling and swimming, some watersports (including a small dive centre), a bit of walking and a historic tower and chapel. There is just one hotel (open between April and October), no shops (except the small one in the hotel lobby), no real roads, only a handful of vehicles, and a total ban on hunting (which, in such a small place, actually holds), making it a good place for birdwatching.

HISTORY

Comino may be named for the spice cumin or from the Arabic for 'sheltered place'. Unlike on Malta and Gozo, there is no evidence here of Neolithic settlement, nor indeed of any settlement of any size, until the time of the Knights. Even then, a significant community was only maintained for a few decades. The island quickly reverted to its previous state – a state in which it has since remained: minimally populated except by visitors whether they be pirates, Turkish raiders, smugglers, hunting Knights or, today, tourists.

In the 13th century the island had one resident, Spanish Jewish ecstatic Kabbalistic philosopher and self-proclaimed messiah, Abraham ben Samuel Abulafia, (1240–91) who spent the last years of his life in exile on Comino writing *The Book of the Sign (Sefer ha-Ot)*. He had been driven from Italy after trying to convert Pope Nicholas II to his teachings. The pope's response was, 'burn the fanatic', but it was the pope who, within hours, died of an apoplectic fit.

Legend has it that Abulafia had one visitor, a Maltese hermit. Stoned out of Malta for trying to impose morality on his neighbours, the pious Kerrew sailed on his mantle over the sea to Comino to chat with Abulafia before continuing his unconventional journey to Gozo where he settled in a cave in Qala.

Through the next couple of centuries the island's caves and coves were the haunt of corsairs, pirates and smugglers – convenient places from which to attack passing sea traffic or make brief forays onto Gozo or northern Malta. There was an attempt in the 15th century to get a watchtower built here, but the money went astray and the project foundered. Even the arrival of the Knights in Malta in 1530 seems to have had little impact on Comino, until finally, in 1618, Grand Master Alof de Wignacourt built a system of towers linking Gozo and Malta via Comino. The substantial Comino Tower still stands.

The grand master hoped that incorporating Comino into the defences of Malta and Gozo would encourage people to settle on the island. For a while it did and the population briefly rose to around 200, but by the end of the 17th century Comino was primarily a private playground for the Knights who came here to hunt wild boar and hare. Anyone caught poaching faced up to three years slaving in the Order's galleys.

In 1800, after the British had helped the Maltese to chase the French out of Malta and Gozo, Comino was used as a holding camp for some 2,000 French soldiers waiting to be shipped back to France. It became a place of isolation again in World War I when a small quarantine hospital was built next to the tower and in the 1970s when foot and mouth disease hit Malta, a pig farm was opened on Comino to breed disease-free pigs.

GETTING THERE AND AWAY

Comino is reached from Malta by a small **ferry** taking about 25 minutes from Ċirkewwa (next to the Gozo ferry) or from the Marfa Jetty (near Ċirkewwa, opposite the Riviera Hotel). From Gozo, boats to Comino leave from Mġarr harbour and take 15–20 minutes. Alternatively you can take a **day cruise** from Ċirkewwa or Sliema. You will never have trouble finding a boat to Comino in summer from Mġarr or Ċirkewwa/Marfa and the tourist cruises are widely advertised. Most boats cater primarily for day trippers and run to the Blue Lagoon, but the Comino Hotel has its own boat which lands at San Niklaw Bay right next to the hotel. Hotel guests take precedence if it is busy, but there is usually room for other passengers. It is a ten-minute walk between the hotel and the Blue Lagoon.

Captain Morgan Cruises ✆ 23463333; e info@captainmorgan.com.mt; www.captainmorgan.com.mt. Day cruises from Sliema along Malta's north coast to the Blue Lagoon run 09.30 daily (return 17.30). From €20 (adults, €15 (children under 12 go free). Speedboat tour of the caves costs extra.
Comino Hotel Boat ✆ 21529821; www.cominohotel.com.4 times a day to/from Ċirkewwa, & 6 to/from Gozo. €8.15 adults, €4.08 children.
Ebson Cruises ✆ 21554991; m 79065669; e ebscruises@onvol.net. Hourly trips from Mġarr to

the Blue Lagoon 08.00–18.00 (return trips 08.15–18.15). €8 return, €12 with 20min tour of Comino's caves. Some boats also from/to Ċirkewwa/Marfa, Malta. Also private boat hire.
Mariblu ✆ 21551315; m 99497757; e info@mariblugozo.com; www.maltagozoholidays.com. Ferry plus caves €10pp. Times vary.
Royal C Comino Ferries m 99406529 (Mark), 99408294 (John); e info@cominoferries.com; www.cominoferries.com. Hourly from Marfa Jetty. Including tour of Comino caves on return trip. €10 adults, €5 children, children under 5 go free.

⌂ WHERE TO STAY AND EAT

⌂ **Comino Hotel & bungalows****** (95 rooms & 46 bungalows) San Niklaw Bay; ✆ 21529821 or 21529826; e info@cominohotel.com; www.cominohotel.com; ⏲ Apr–Oct. The hotel is right on the edge of the bay. Small coarse sand 'private' beach, large outdoor swimming pool & children's paddling pool, sand tennis courts. Basic for a 4-star hotel, but clean & relaxed. Most guests are German. HB (with buffet dinner) essential – there is no other source of supper on the island. Lunch is buffet (€20pp) in the restaurant, light meal/snacks from the bar or room service (not too expensive) or bring your own from Malta/Gozo. Watersports equipment for hire (windsurfing, water skiing, canoes,

etc). Bungalows in Santa Marija Bay (10mins' walk or hotel vehicle) are dbl room & sitting room. Own restaurant with pleasant terrace overlooking Santa Marija Bay, swimming pool & tennis courts. Dbls HB €70 (Apr, May, Oct) to €140 (Jul–mid-Sep), cheaper Sun–Thu. Children 3–11 sharing with adults, half price. Or book through Malta Direct (Malta Holidays) or www.expedia.com. Non-residents €39pp, children 2–11 €19.50 for buffet lunch, boat crossing & use of beach & pools.
Å **Camping** Santa Marija Bay. There is a small dusty area used for camping next to Santa Marija Beach. No apparent supervision, small toilet block, hotel bungalows & restaurant/café 100m away.

THE BLUE LAGOON In summer (and even in spring and autumn) tourists flock to the Blue Lagoon (Maltese: Bejn il-Kmiemen, 'Between the Cominos'), a beautiful stretch of turquoise sea over perfect white sand between Comino and the tiny islet of Cominotto (Kemmunett). It is surrounded by handsome caves and is a lovely spot for swimming and snorkelling. The tiny areas of beach and rocky shore can, however, become absurdly crowded from about 10.30 until 16.00/17.00 (later at weekends). If you are coming on your own boat or intending to stay on the island, get here early or late for a glorious swim.

There are **toilets** and a few **kiosks** selling drinks and snacks, but there is no shade except for the handful of umbrellas which can be rented (if they haven't been already). Be aware that cruise boats may not take you right up to the lagoon area (ask them) and boats that drop you off may leave you a bit stranded if you find you have had enough sun, the weather is bad (northwesterly winds have the most impact) or there are too many jellyfish for swimming. Check that you can get a boat back sooner rather than later should you want to. Some cruise-boat operators (but not ferries) will take you to another bay if the Blue Lagoon is not good for swimming.

COMINO TOWER/SANTA MARIJA TOWER (*St Mary's Tower; maintained by Din L-Art Helwa (Malta's National Trust);* ❧ *21225952 (or call HQ: 21220358);* m *9905186;* e *gozo@dinlarthelwa.org; www.dinlarthelwa.org;* ☉ *Apr–Oct 10.30–13.00 & when the flag flies Wed, Fri, Sat, Sun. About 20mins' walk from the hotel, 15mins from the Blue Lagoon.*) The tower has a marvellous dominant position some 80m above sea level with another 8m added by a manmade plinth on which you can walk right round the tower. Built by Grand Master Alof de Wignacourt in 1618, the tower's construction was partly financed by the sale of brushwood from the island. It was part of the Knights' earliest attempt at a national defence system, connecting the Gozo Citadel to Mdina. Being alone on the island, it had to be particularly strong, able to withstand attack for longer than most of the other towers. Its walls are 6m thick and its four corner turrets are topped by a battlement roof. Both the plinth and roof afford panoramic views of the Blue Lagoon, Cominotto, Gozo, northern Malta and Comino itself.

The tower was incorporated into later coastal defences (Lascaris, de Redin, Perellos, see page 85) and has a clear line of sight to the Red Tower on Malta (which could send alarm signals all the way along the coast to Valletta, see page 239), as well as to Fort Chambrai and other parts of Gozo. In 1714 the tower was joined by the battery (see below) built at the other end of the Malta-facing coast. Comino Tower was abandoned by the British in 1829, and the ground floor seems to have been used for animals, but it was brought back into service in World War II and more recently played the part of Chateau D'If in the 2002 film *The Count of Monte Cristo*.

COMINO BATTERY/SANTA MARIJA BATTERY (*Contact details as for the tower, above*) From the tower you can walk right along the south coast of the island on a dirt track at the top of the cliffs with sea views to one side and open unspoilt garigue on the other. It is a lovely walk and leads directly to St Mary's Battery on the island's western tip. This semicircular gun platform with cannons facing out to sea was built in 1715–16 to defend the Gozo channel, part of another round of major defensive upgrading (under Grand Master Ramon Perellos y Roccaful). The garrison slept in the blockhouse which was also the ammunition store. From here you can turn inland, walking past the old pig farm, and carry on across the island to Santa Marija Bay and thence San Niklaw Bay. A full circuit of the island takes about two hours.

13

SANTA MARIJA BAY/ST MARY'S BAY (*10mins' walk from San Niklaw Bay or complimentary hotel transport*) The hotel bungalows are to one side of this bay with their own café and outdoor pool. The **beach** here is larger than at San Niklaw and sandy – and it is where Brad Pitt (as Achilles) meets his mum in the 2004 film *Troy*. The sand is unfortunately often covered in seaweed and there are submerged rocks in the shallows (mind toes and shins). You may prefer to swim off the rocks.

Set back from the beach are a few trees offering rare shade, and a small **camping area**. The pink building is 18th century and is now Comino's diminutive **police station**, manned in summer by two policemen from Gozo – a flag flies when a policeman is on duty. A short way inland is a charming little medieval-style **chapel** with a plain façade topped by bells. There has been a church of some kind on this site since the 12th century – documented by a very early navigational map in the British National Maritime Museum in Greenwich. The present **Chapel of Our Lady's Return from Egypt** was built in the same year as the tower, 1618, and enlarged in 1667 and 1716. Mass is held here – by a priest who visits from Gozo – every weekend in summer.

ST NICHOLAS BAY/SAN NIKLAW BAY (*10mins' walk from the Blue Lagoon*) The **Comino Hotel** fills one side of this bay and its terrace and swimming pool overlook the sea. There are two small patches of coarse-sand beach, technically private to the hotel. The beaches are nothing to write home about, but there is excellent **snorkelling** just a few metres offshore. Well inside the area protected from boats by a string of buoys, six or seven species of fish can be seen within a few minutes. Ordinary swimming goggles will suffice but snorkels are better and can be bought in the hotel shop (€9–19.50). Small yachts and motorboats moor in the bay. The hotel offers day membership which includes boat crossing, buffet lunch and use of beach and pools for €39pp, and €19.50 for children aged two to 11.

DIVING Comino has some dozen dive sites around its coast, including caves, reefs, walls and a couple of wrecks. There is plenty for beginners as well as challenges for the more experienced. The dive centre is next to the hotel but independently run. For more on diving, see pages 66, 90 and 266.

Comino Dive Centre ☎ 21570354; m (Antoine Blanchez) 79945763; e info@cominodivecentre.net or cominodivecentre@gmail.com; www.cominodivecentre.net. PADI courses from children's Bubblemaker (age 8+) to Divemaster & specialist qualifications, as well as accompanied dives from shore & boat, & equipment hire.

BIRDWATCHING Comino, designated a bird reserve, is one of the best places in Malta to birdwatch simply because there is no hunting. This is particularly important in autumn when bird hunting is allowed across most of the rest of the country; Comino is an oasis from which to watch migrating species including passerines which make landfall here.

In spring, common whitethroats, garden and icterine warblers, spotted and pied flycatchers and woodchat shrike are seen and semi-collared flycatcher, rufous bush robin and barred warbler have also been recorded in recent years. **BirdLife Malta** (☎ *21347646; www.birdlifemalta.org*) runs a ringing station and bird observatory on the island during migration periods. In summer, spectacled warblers can be seen on the garigue, along with short-toed larks, chukars (members of the partridge family) and Malta's national bird, the blue rock thrush.

14

Gozo

Arriving in Gozo (Maltese: Għawdex, pronounced *Owdesh*), you may find an involuntary sigh passing your lips as you leave the port and head for the open country. For all its holiday reputation and patches of beautiful landscape, Malta is a busy place. Gozo is more rural and much more laid-back. Residents say it runs on GMT – Gozo Maybe Time – but in fact time-keeping is not significantly more wayward than on Malta. Gozo just feels so much more relaxed. The two islands may be part of the same country and a mere 6km apart, but the atmosphere is completely different.

The Maltese tell some of the same jokes about the Gozitans that the English tell about the Irish, and traditionally life has been tougher on Gozo. But there are no flies on the Gozitans, many of whom seem to do very well for themselves on Malta – returning at weekends to their lovely unspoilt island. Some Gozitans go further afield and you will find houses on Gozo called 'God Bless Australia', 'House of Canada' or 'Old Glory USA' – there is even a kangeroo outside a house near Calypso's Cave – all in gratitude to the nations where the owner earned the money to build or buy the house.

Gozo is only 7km by 14km and has been largely bypassed by the rush to mass tourism that has blighted Malta. There are a few patches of unrestrained building (particularly in Marsalforn) but there is plenty of Gozo that is unspoilt. It is more like Malta was a few decades ago – although the landscape is different. Gozo is made up of small flat-topped hills divided by fertile valleys – green even in summer when most of Malta goes brown. Wild fennel (with its typical aniseed smell), caper bushes, carob and oleander are common sights along with the omnipresent prickly pear.

Church bells ring out over terraces of hillside agriculture and traditional limestone villages, at whose heart is usually an attractive square (sometimes actually a triangle). The square is dominated by an oversized church, often with a tiny police station marked with a traditional British blue lantern, a red phone box and sometimes an old-fashioned British red letter box built into a yellow limestone wall. Many villages have a café and a village shop on or near the square and you may even see an elderly lady sitting on her doorstep making lace.

If you fly over Gozo (which some international flights do) it looks like a cardboard cut-out, so sharply defined are its sheer cliff edges – especially on the northern side. Edward Lear visited the island in 1866 and wrote, 'I drew every bit of it, walking fifteen or twenty miles a day – its coast scenery may truly be called pomskizillious and gromphiberous, being as no other words can describe its magnificence.' He also started a poem, 'Gozo my child is the isle of Calypso', referring to Gozo's identification with Homer's island where the hero of the *Odyssey* spends seven years under the spell of the loving sea nymph (see *Calypso's Cave*, page 289).

Gozo has a couple of beautiful red-sand beaches and a multitude of rocky bays and inlets with inviting clear blue water and great snorkelling, as well as some of

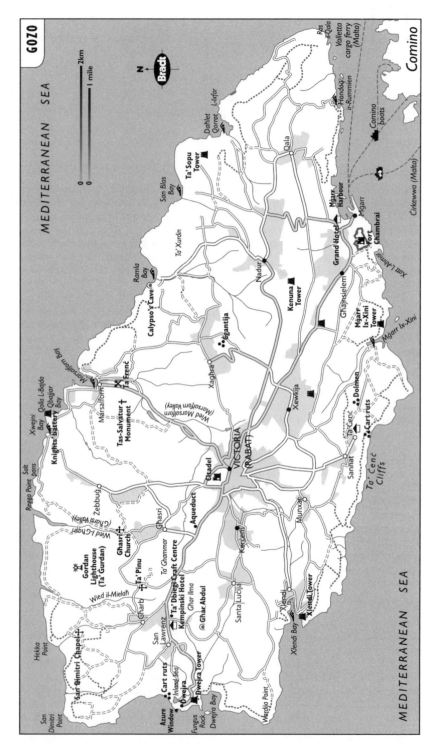

GOZO

MEDITERRANEAN SEA

MEDITERRANEAN SEA

Comino

2km

1 mile

Bradt

N

San Dimitri Point

Hekka Point

Azure Window

Cart ruts

Inland Sea

Dwejra

Dwejra Tower

Fungus Rock

Dwejra Bay

Wardija Point

San Dimitri Chapel

San Lawrenz

Gharb

Wied il-Mielah

Ghar Abdul

Ta' Dbiegi Craft Centre
Kempinski Hotel

Ghar Ilma

Santa Luċija

Gordan Lighthouse
(Ta' Gurdan)

Ta' Pinu

Ghasri Church

Ta' Ghammar

Aqueduct

Ghasri

Żebbuġ

Wied l-Għasri
(Ghasri Valley)

Regga Point

Salt pans

Knights' battery

Xwejni Bay

Qala L-Bajda

Qbajjar Bay

Marsalforn Bay

Marsalforn

Ta' Frenċ

Tas-Salvátur Monument

Calypso's Cave

Ramla Bay

Ta' Xurdin

San Blas Bay

Ta'Sopu Tower

Dahlet Qorrot

L-Xfar

Ras il-Qala

Qala

Valletta cargo ferry (Malta)

Handaq ir-Rummien

Comino boats

Ċirkewwa (Malta)

Mġarr Harbour

Mġarr

Grand Hotel

Fort Chambrai

Xatt l-Aħmar

Għajnsielem

Mġarr Ix-Xini Tower

Mġarr Ix-Xini

Nadur

Kenuna Tower

Wied Marsalforn
(Marsalforn Valley)

Xagħra

Ġgantija

Xewkija

VICTORIA (RABAT)

Citadel

Ta' Ċenċ

Dolmen

Cart ruts

Sannat

Ta' Ċenċ Cliffs

Munxar

Kerċem

Xlendi

Xlendi Tower

Xlendi Bay

254

Malta's (and even the Mediterranean's) best dive sites. And if the wind blows on one side of the island, ruining the swimming and diving, you can hop the few kilometres to the other and will probably find calm, welcoming waters.

There is history here too, of course. One of the oldest temple complexes, Ġgantija (after which the first temple phase is known) sits on a high plateau with commanding views of the Gozo countryside. The Citadel in the capital Rabat (or Victoria) is a mini-Mdina, a tiny impressively walled medieval city, first fortified in the Bronze Age and refortified by every occupier of Gozo since.

HISTORY

Much of Gozo's history is, of course, shared with Malta (see *Chapter 1*). Even as far back as prehistoric times the two islands shared one culture. From medieval times onwards, Gozo has tended to receive less attention than its larger neighbour and so to be less developed. This may have been a disadvantage in times gone by, but in recent decades it is more of a happy escape.

Gozo was less protected than Malta at the time of the Knights and suffered even more from corsair attack. In 1551 the Turks, led by Sinam Pasha and Dragut Reis, captured the Citadel, destroyed much of Rabat and took almost the entire able-bodied population – nearly 5,000 people – into slavery. Some were ransomed or escaped and returned home, but it took over a century for pre-1551 population levels to be recorded again, and Turkish attacks continued until 1708. In the 17th century, the Knights belatedly strengthened the Citadel and built the defensive watchtowers that dot the coast, providing early warning of attack and defence against pirates and smugglers.

Napoleon's troops nonetheless overran Gozo (as they did Malta) in 1798, although once the Maltese rebellion began in Mdina, the Gozitans took up the challenge with gusto and got rid of the invaders more quickly than their larger neighbour. The French holed up in Fort Chambrai and the Citadel and were ousted (with help from the British Royal Navy) by October 1798. Gozo then had almost a year as the independent Nation of Gozo until Malta was freed in September 1799. The two islands were reunited under the British (1800–1964).

In World War II when Malta suffered severely under Italian bombs, Gozo escaped almost unscathed. The Gozitan role in the war was to share its grain – a little reluctantly – with its larger neighbour, helping to keep the population going during the crucial siege of 1942.

GETTING THERE AND AWAY

Despite being a separate island from Malta, it takes no more than about two hours to get from the airport to your accommodation on Gozo – and it can be a very pleasant journey.

BY SEA
By ferry The usual, and by far the cheapest, way to get to Gozo is by the regular 25-minute ferry ride from Ċirkewwa in northern Malta. **Gozo Channel** (❛ 21556114 or 21561622, *Ċirkewwa office:* ❛ 21580435/6, *timetable enquiries:* ❛ 21556016; e *admin@gozochannel.com; www.gozochannel.com*) run a service approximately every 45 minutes throughout the day (and less frequently through the night). They can be a bit less frequent in winter. All fares are return: €4.65 for adults, €1.15 for children under 12 and €15.70 for a car with driver. Should you find yourself short of cash, there is an ATM at each side of the Gozo ferry – at Ċirkewwa and in the Mġarr ferry terminal on Gozo.

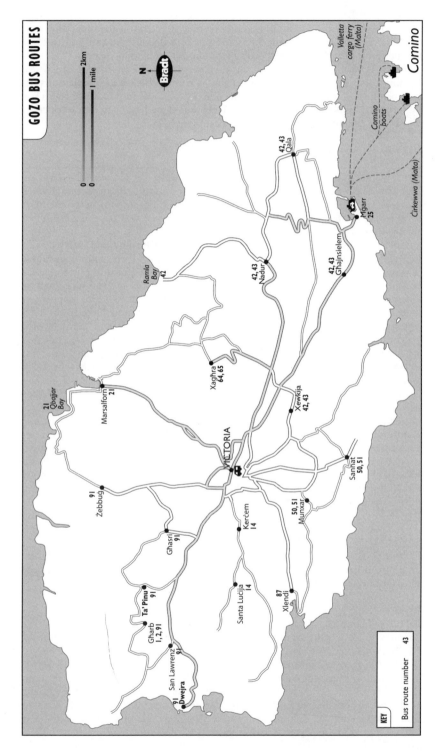

GOZO BUS ROUTES

Comino

Valletta cargo ferry (Malta)

Comino boats

Cirkewwa (Malta)

Mġarr 25

Qala 42, 43

Ramla Bay 42

Nadur 42, 43

Għajnsielem 42, 43

Xagħra 64, 65

Xewkija 42, 43

Marsalforn 21

Qbajjar Bay 21

VICTORIA

Sannat 50, 51

Żebbuġ 91

Munxar 50, 51

Kerċem 14

Għasri 91

Santa Luċija 14

Xlendi 87

Ta' Pinu 91

Għarb 1, 2, 91

San Lawrenz 91

Dwejra 91

KEY
Bus route number 43

2km
1 mile
0

N
Bradt

The ferry can get busy with day trippers at the beginning and end of the day in high season so if you are taking a car across and have a plane to catch allow some extra time. It is most unlikely that a foot passenger would be turned away.

There is also a **cargo ferry** that takes passengers (and cars) from Sa Maison (between Msida and Ta' Xbiex) closer to most tourists' accommodation than Ċirkewwa. It goes three times a week on Mondays, Tuesdays and Thursdays. The trip takes 90 minutes and costs the same as from Ċirkewwa. Departure times vary so call ℘ 22109001 or the numbers above.

By boat via Comino See *Chapter 13*, page 250, for details.

BY AIR

By sea plane If you feel like splashing out (hopefully not literally) the sea plane is a great way to get to Gozo. **Harbourair** (℘ *21228302 or 21228309;* e *info@ harbourairmalta.com; www.harbourairmalta.com*) operates flights to Gozo from the mainland. Board the little 14-seater De Havilland Canada Turbine Single or the 21-seat Twin Otter, and, if you are coming **from Valletta** (10mins, €44 adults, €38 children one-way), take off from the Grand Harbour. The views are fabulous as you fly up the coast of Malta and over Comino before landing just outside Mġarr Harbour in Gozo. For €65 you can get even better views sitting right next to the pilot! **From Malta International Airport** (10mins, €46/35 inc airport tax) or **from Catania in Sicily** (60mins, €100/67) the plane takes off from a runway. Luggage allowance is 10kg per person (€2/kg excess charge).

By helicopter Helicopter transfers between Malta International Airport and Gozo – in a small three-seater – are, at the time of writing, expected to begin soon. See www.heli-link-malta.com to find out more (see also page 57).

GETTING AROUND

As on Malta there are buses to most of the main sights on Gozo, but they are nothing like as regular as they are on the main island and, particularly in winter, may be very few and far between. If you really want to explore Gozo, it is worth hiring a car for a few days (see page 258 for details). See also *Outdoor activities* below for information on cycling, walking and boats.

BY BUS Gozo's bus routes radiate from Victoria/Rabat on Main Gate Street/Triq Putrijal (a few minutes' walk from It-Tokk). Most trips cost 47c for adults, 23c for children. Some routes are infrequent and a few run only in summer or only in the morning so do check you can get back from where you are going. The bus timetable can be found at www.gozo.gov.mt/ pages.aspx?page=896 or call ℘ 21559346 or 21562040, ext 218 (⏱ *05.00–21.00*). The bus numbers that go to each of the villages are listed beneath the place name throughout this chapter.

GOZO JEEP TOURS

If you fancy being taken round the island but want to be in the open air, then you could take a jeep tour. **Gozo Jeep Tours** (*45 St Lucy St, St Luċija, Kerċem;* ℘ *21561817;* m *99456809;* e *eddjul@waldonet.net.mt; www.gozo.com/jeeptours*) organises tours that cover the island quite comprehensively. €40pp, minimum four people, includes pick up from and return to anywhere in Gozo.

CAR HIRE AND TAXIS

Avis Mġarr Harbour; ☎ 25677550; www.avis.co.uk/CarHire/Europe/Malta-Gozo/Mġarr-Gozo; ⏱ 08.00–18.00 Mon–Fri, 08.00–13.00 w/ends. Hire cars, child seats, satnav & roof racks available.

Frank's Garage ☎ 21556814; m 99497565; e franksgarage@waldonet.net.mt; franksgarageltd.com [no 'www']. Taxis & hire cars, self-drive & with driver. They have some good drivers with excellent English & knowledge of the island. Child seats available.

Mayjo Fortunato Mizzi St, Victoria (opposite Arkadia) [270 E3]; ☎ 21556678 or 21551772; m 99423065 or 99890600. Second branch at Marina St, Marsalforn (Apr–Oct) ☎ 21555650; e info@mayjo.com.mt; www.mayjo.com.mt. Family firm with 40 years' experience. Usually 3-day minimum hire. Self-drive or with driver & 24hr taxi service.

St Joseph's m 99496821; e info@stjosephcarrental.com; www.stjosephcarrental.com. Hire cars & taxis.

Xlendi Tourist Services Rabat Rd, Xlendi Bay; ☎ 21560683, 21551175 or 21553302; e info@xlendi.com; www.xlendi.com/carrentals. Minimum age 21. Also rents 50cc & 80cc scooters. Baby seats (€1/day). Book direct or through Europcar (www.europecar.com).

Note: As in Malta, some companies require you to be aged at least 25 to hire a car and may ask for a medical certificate if you are over 70. Some charge extra for a second driver. Check the insurance policy: the likelihood of having a serious accident here is lower than in Malta, but the chances of getting the car scratched is still relatively high. And make sure you are given a parking clock (see *Driving* below).

Driving If driving yourself, note that **petrol** is only available in Victoria, Xagħra, Mġarr, Għajnsielem and Xewkija. There is a petrol station just opposite Arkadia shopping centre at the Mġarr end of Victoria's main street.

The **standard of driving** in Gozo is not dramatically better than in Malta – in that it remains unpredictable – but everything moves much more slowly and drivers are generally more considerate, so it is an easier and safer place to drive. Road surfaces vary enormously. The few main roads are excellent but many of the side roads are very pot-holed.

In the towns, **parking** is sometimes restricted. It does not cost anything but you need to have a parking clock and stays are limited. The cardboard clocks are available from the Gozo Channel Office at the ferry terminal or from the ADT office at the bus station, and one is usually provided with hire cars. Check local signs for what is allowed and when restrictions apply (usually mornings), set your clock for your arrival time and do not overstay – the wardens are zealous! Parking in the villages is free and usually easy.

Finding your way Signposting is generally good, particularly to the main tourist sites. It does occasionally peter out prematurely, but you can always ask. Gozitans are extremely helpful.

It is useful to have a decent **map** especially if you are planning to drive yourself around or walk a lot. The free maps available from many tourist locations are good as far as they go but don't have many roads or any paths. Even the more detailed maps do not cover all minor roads and footpaths. For advice on which maps to buy and where to get them, see page 42 and opposite.

TOURIST INFORMATION

Malta Tourism Authority on Gozo [270 C2] www.visitmalta.com/information-about-the-sister-islands. The MTA's main Gozo office is in Victoria. At time of writing it is at Tigrija Palazz, Level 1, Republic St 300, Victoria; ☎ 21561419; ⏱ 09.00–17.30 Mon–Sat, 09.00–13.00 Sun & public holidays. It is however expected to move to a more prominent position in It-Tokk (the main square). The phone number should stay the same. MTA is also planning to open a tourist office in Mġarr, in the Gozo ferry terminal.

ℹ Gozo Tourism Association [270 D3] 5 George Borg Olivier St/Triq Ġorġ Borġ Olivier, Victoria; ✆ 21565171 or 21565171; e gtagozo@onvol.net; www.islandofgozo.org

ℹ Experience Gozo At time of writing a new website is on the way. www.experience-gozo.com or www.experience-gozo.eu is being designed to bring together small-scale services & activities available on Gozo, particularly the more unusual & personal that will bring visitors & locals together.

Maps and books can be bought in the Agenda Bookshop on the Gozo ferry and at Bookpoint Stationery [270 C3] (*47 Main St/Triq Putrjal, Victoria;* ✆ *21563323;* e *info@bookpointstationery.com; www.bookpoint-stationery.com*). For more on maps please see page 42.

OTHER SOURCES OF INFORMATION
Gozo News www.gozonews.com
Gozo Weather www.gozoweather.com

Ministry for Gozo St Francis St, Victoria; ✆ 21561482; e info.mog@gov.mt; www.gozo.gov.mt

⌂ WHERE TO STAY

There is one genuinely five-star hotel on the island (Kempinski, San Lawrenz, see below) and one other five-star hotel that is in need of some attention (Ta' Ċenċ, below). Numerous three- and four-star establishments (most of which would be three stars in the UK) are joined by a few guesthouses and self-catering apartments concentrated in Xlendi and Marsalforn, as well as a growing number of self-catering 'farmhouses' in the villages – some of which are genuine old farmhouses converted into holiday lets, others new build.

Farmhouses can be a great option, particularly for families, offering space, flexibility, privacy and in many cases your own pool. Most are away from the tourist centres, often in traditional residential village locations, so bear in mind that you will almost certainly need a car.

There are a number of questions worth asking before booking a farmhouse. What is next door? Any potential noise problems? Does it have air conditioning or central heating? (Many do not.) Are there fans/heaters/large windows? How old is the building? Is it in a complex of rented houses? What are the dimensions of the pool? And of the garden/outside area?

Because Gozo is so small, accommodation is all listed together here.

TOP END

⌂ **Kempinski San Lawrenz**★★★★★ (122 rooms) Triq ir-Rokon, San Lawrenz SLZ 1040; ✆ 22110000 or 22116372; e reservations.sanlawrenz@kempinski.com or sales.sanlawrenz@kempinski.com; www.kempinski-gozo.com. Genuinely 5-star, this is a well-designed, well-run, low-rise hotel on the edge of countryside & a traditional Gozitan village. Set in its own landscaped gardens with outdoor pools (the nicest of which is reserved for people age 13 & over) & paddling pool. Excellent food & a well-run spa (see page 101) with a large indoor pool, wonderfully warm in winter (children 2–13 allowed until 15.00, no children under 2). Also tennis, squash, indoor kids' club & twice daily courtesy bus to the coast & Victoria. Staff are friendly & helpful. *Room rates change constantly, but at the time of writing dbl rooms cost about €150 B&B.*

⌂ **Ta' Ċenċ**★★★★★ (96 rooms) Sannat SNT 9049; ✆ 21556819, 21556830 or 21561522/5; e tacenc@vborg.com; www.vborg.com/tacenc. Theoretically 5-star & in a great location opening onto the Ta' Ċenċ cliffs. At the time of writing, most of the rooms are in need of refurbishment. A few have been recently redone & these are reserved for people booking direct with the hotel – so ask for them. The hotel is well designed to fit into the landscape with single-storey buildings of local stone. 2 outdoor pools, spa (see also *Spas*, page 101) with an indoor-outdoor pool, courtesy bus to Mġarr ix-Xini. *Dbl room B&B €130 (winter) to €186 (summer). Call the hotel for best available rates. It may well be cheaper booked through a UK travel operator.*

14

MID RANGE

⌂ **Calypso****** (100 rooms) Marina St, Marsalforn; ↘ 21562000 or 21562012; e info@ calypsogozo.com; www.hotelcalypsogozo.com. Theoretically 4-star but a bit basic & tired. A concrete block with large, rather bare roof terrace with small, shallow pool overlooking Marsalforn Bay. Rooftop restaurant with good views. Room quality variable. Some spacious & clean. Interconnecting family rooms available. *Dbls (land view – a cul-de-sac so should not be too noisy) from €59 (winter) to €94 (peak). Sea view + approx €20. Child 3–11 sharing with parents 50% off.*

⌂ **Cornucopia Hotel****** (50 rooms & 11 bungalows) 410 Ġnien Imrik St, Xagħra XRA 1521; ↘ 21556486 or 21553866; e cornucopia@vjborg.com; www.vjborg.com/cornucopia. Charming garden courtyard leads into this converted farmhouse (part 18th century). Gardens with palms & flowers, 2 small pools & paddling pool, cosy traditional bar, all staff Gozitan. Rooms bright, modern rustic (pine & tiles); bathrooms older in hotel, fresh in newly built bungalows which have views over valley & shared pool. *Dbl rooms from €27.25pppn (low season) to €46pppn (summer) B&B. Bungalows for up to 4 people €72–142 (+€10pppn over 4), b/fast +€4.50pppn.*

⌂ **Grand Hotel****** (93 rooms) Mġarr, GSM 9026; ↘ 21563840; e reservations@grandhotelmalta.com; www.grandhotelmalta.com. Up on the hill overlooking the harbour & ferry terminal (nicer than you would expect). Inviting rooftop swimming pool with a view (no inflatables or balls), indoor pool should be ready by the time you read this. Helpful staff, family rooms sleeping up to 5. *Dbls: internal (views of walls) €23.50–35pppn B&B, country view €28–42, sea view €35–53.50. Children under 5 €5pn.*

⌂ **San Andrea***** (28 rooms) Xlendi Promenade, Xlendi XLN 1302; ↘ 21565555 or 21565400; e info@hotelsanandrea.com; www.hotelsanandrea.com. Very pleasant, welcoming little hotel right on the Xlendi Waterfront. 5th floor lounge with terrace overlooking the bay. All rooms twin with balcony, AC & CH. *Dbls from €22–31pppn B&B (side-view) depending on season, €30–46 (sea view), children under 10 sharing with adults go free. Extra adult 50%.*

⌂ **St Patrick's****** (73 rooms) Marina St, Xlendi XLN 1150; ↘ 21562951/2/3; e stpatricks@ vjborg.com; www.vjborg.com/stpatricks. Right on the Xlendi seafront. Sea-view rooms larger as well as overlooking bay. 6th-floor roof terrace with an oversized bath to cool off in (not a swimming pool). *Dbls from €21–36.50pppn B&B. Sea view €36–61. Children 2–12 sharing with adults 50% off, children under 2 free.*

BUDGET

⌂ **Lantern Guesthouse** (12 rooms) Qbajjar Rd, Marsalforn; ↘ 21556285; m 79566271. Rooms above a little restaurant just off the waterfront. *B&B in dbl room: €25pppn (high season), €19 (winter).*

⌂ **Maria Giovanna Guest House** (15 rooms) 41 Rabat Rd, Marsalforn; ↘ 21553630; m 99821790; e info@tamariagozo.com; www.tamariagozo.com. Basic but clean guesthouse set back from the seafront, a little dark (but therefore cooler in summer), 6 superior rooms spacious & modern. Roof terrace & laundry room. *€20–35pppn B&B, standard dbl room in summer around €55.*

⌂ **Mariblu Guesthouse** (8 rooms) Mġarr Rd, Xewkija; ↘ 21551315; m 99497757; e info@ mariblugozo.com; www.mariblugozo.com Clean, friendly place that smells of good home cooking. Cheerful, brightly painted wine bar & restaurant, small swimming pool, all rooms have kitchenette, 1 family room, 1 2-bedroom apt. Own transport helpful. See page 36. *€20–30pppn B&B, children under 7 free, under about age 12 half price.*

⌂ **Santa Martha Hostel** (10 rooms) Qolla St, Marsalforn; ↘ 21551263 or 21564868; m 79277022; e msalibacini@yahoo.com or saliba.maria@gmail.com; www.santamarthahostel.com. A few mins' walk from the waterfront this very simple but clean & pleasant hostel offers sgl, dbl & trpl rooms (with other configurations possible). *€14pppn B&B.*

⌂ **San Antonio Guesthouse** (13 rooms) Tower St/Triq il-Torre, Xlendi VCT 115; ↘ 21563555 or 21555587; e cgmail@clubgozo.com.mt; www.clubgozo.com.mt. On a quiet residential street about 5mins' walk up the hill from the bay, this delightful guesthouse is fresh & spacious with comfortable, airy communal rooms, chequered tablecloths in dining room & a small swimming pool on a peaceful terrace. Upstairs rooms nicest. *€20pppn B&B (winter), €30 Jul, €35 Aug, €25 the rest.*

⌂ **Ulysses Aparthotel** (14 rooms) Triq il-Gostra/Gostra St, Xlendi XLN 1404; ↘ 21551616 or 21564429; e sales@ulyssesaparthotel.com; www.ylyssesaparthotel.com. Functional clean rooms, studios & 1-bedroom apts above Moby Dives, a few mins' walk from the waterfront. Rooms with AC &

CH. Winebar & restaurant. Includes the only room in Xlendi adapted for wheelchair users. *Dbls €40–70 B&B, studios (dbl with kitchenette) €45–75,*

1-bedroom apt (with sofa-bed so sleeps up to 4) €50–80.

SELF-CATERING ACCOMMODATION

⌂ **Baron Holiday Homes** (40 farmhouses) Karlu Galea St, Victoria; ☎ 21556600; e holidayhomes@barongroupmalta.com; www.barongroupmalta.com/h_homes_home.asp?pmo=0. Nearly 40 farmhouses across the island, all with pool. 3–4 bedrooms from €700/week (winter)–€1,350 (peak). *Also 5 'Exclusive' properties with heated indoor as well as outdoor pool, jacuzzi, Wi-Fi, playstation, full AC & underfloor heating. €980–2,200/week.*

⌂ **Club Gozo self-catering apartments & houses** (3 apts) Contacts as for San Antonio Guesthouse; see opposite. *3 apts 2mins from the guesthouse. €30–44.50/night (1–2 people), €35.50–47 (3–4 people), €41–52.50 (5–6 people); a house with private pool sleeping up to 16 next door to the guesthouse €67 (winter 1–2 people) to €472 (summer, 15–16 people) & 2 rural farmhouses with own pool sleeping 6 & 8.*

⌂ **Cornucopia, Maria Giovanna & Mariblu** All rent out apts & farmhouses (see opposite for their websites & contacts).

⌂ **Gozo Farmhouses** (25 houses) 3 Mġarr Rd, Għajnsielem; ☎ 21561280/1; e info@gozofarmhouses.com; www.gozofarmhouses.com. One of the 1st companies to convert traditional village houses into holiday lets. 25 houses with 1–4 bedrooms, all with washing machine, cable TV, most with pool & BBQ. *Sleeps 2: €65–80pn, sleeps 8: €130–195pn (depending on season). Also estate agent for similar properties.*

⌂ **Gozo Village Holidays** (48 maisonettes) ☎ 21557255/6; e info@gozovillageholidays.com; www.gozovillageholidays.com. **Villaġġ Tal-Fanal** in Għasri is a pleasant complex of 26 newly built, but traditional-style limestone mini-villas (maisonettes) around a landscaped swimming pool in a quiet residential area. Another 22 units share a 2nd pool across the road. Attractively furnished, sleep 2–8, fans (no AC), a heater in winter. **Villaġġ Ta-Sbejha** is a similar complex in Għarb & the company also owns apts in Għasri as well as 8 individual houses (sleeping 2–8, own pools) & the Ta' Frenċ restaurant (see page 262). *1-bedroom unit €50pn (Nov–Dec) to €85 (Aug), 4 bedrooms €95–150.*

⌂ **Moby Dick Complex** Xlendi Waterfront; ☎ 21561518; www.mobydickgozo.com. 6 brand-new modern apts above a good no-frills restaurant overlooking the bay. Clean designer look, AC, fans, lift, back-up generator, flat-screen TV. 1–2 bedrooms plus sofabed & can interconnect 2 apts. *Peak prices around €90pn for 2 people + €15/extra adult. Children under 13 50% off, children under 2 go free.*

⌂ **Unique Gozo Farmhouses** (12 farmhouses plus apts) 'Aldaor', Daleland St, Qala; ☎ 21562957; m 99496975 or 79562957; e uniquegozofarmhouses@gmail.com; http://gozo.com/unique/farmhouses.php. Family business renting out a dozen farmhouses – old & new, with pools & views – & sea-view apts in Marsalforn. *Prices for a couple: farmhouses from €60pn (low season) €116 (peak of peak), apts €35–60.*

Farmhouses, villas and apartments are also listed by location on www.gozo.gov.mt and there is a lengthy list of MTA-approved farmhouses and villas at www.visitmalta.com/farmhouses_gozo and www.visitmalta.com/villas_gozo?l=1.

✖ WHERE TO EAT

When it comes to eating, Gozo is as well provided for in terms of good restaurants as Malta, and if you have a car it should take no more than 20 minutes to get to any restaurant on the island. At lunchtime, or if you do not have your own transport, however, you may want something close by, so the restaurants are listed by location.

GHARB

✖ **Jeffrey's** 10 Għarb Rd; ☎ 21561006; ⏰ Apr–Oct 18.00–22.30 Mon–Sat. On the edge of the traditional village of Għarb, popular Jeffrey's offers Maltese & Mediterranean dishes in the walled garden or AC interior. Book ahead. Family & wheelchair friendly.

MARSALFORN

✗ Il-Kartell Marina St; ☎ 21556918;
✉ ilkartellrestaurant@onvol.net;
www.il-kartellrestaurant.com; ⏰ 12.00–14.30 &
18.30–23.00 daily. A Gozo institution. Come more
for the terrace at the water's edge & the people-
watching (even government ministers eat here) than
for the food, not that the food is bad. Their
delicious antipasti (with Maltese bread) makes a
great light lunch (though they may add a couple of
euros for not having a main course). Live lobster &
mussels in the aquarium, fresh fish daily, special
diets accommodated. *Starters & pasta around €6,*
mains around €13.

✗ Ta' Frenċ Off Marsalforn–Victoria Rd, XRA 9010;
☎ 21553888; ✉ info@tafrencrestaurant.com;
www.tafrencrestaurant.com; ⏰ Apr–Dec
12.00–13.30 & 19.00–22.00 (closed Tue) &

Jan–Mar w/ends only (Fri dinner to Sun lunch).
Gozo's top restaurant. Elegant, atmospheric & with
excellent French & Maltese food. Specialists in
flambé (their crêpe Suzette is to die for) & a wine
book of 700 wines from 19 countries
(€12–€2,000+). Enter through the herb garden.
The restaurant grows its own or sources locally
wherever possible – salt is from Xwejni, honey
from next door, quail, rabbit & chicken from down
the road. Drink in the converted centuries-old farm
building & eat on the covered terrace, or inside
decorated with traditional Maltese clocks & modern
art. Highchairs available at lunch. Booking
advisable. *Starters €11.50–14.25, mains*
€17.50–26.50, daily 4-course 'Market Menu' €28.
Children's menu of pasta & steak, coeliac & veggie
options available.

MĠARR

✗ It-Tmun Mġarr Martinu Garces St; ☎ 21566276;
📱 79446832; ✉ info@tmunmgarr.com;
www.tmunmgarr.com; ⏰ 12.00–14.30 &
18.00–22.30 daily. Newly opened in Mġarr after a
move from Xlendi where it had 25 successful years
specialising in traditional seafood fresh from the
water. Family run with patron Leli Buttigieg at front
of house & wife Jane in charge of the kitchen (their
son Patrick runs It-Tmun Victoria; see opposite). Dine
outdoors or stay inside & watch the chefs at work
in the open kitchen. *Starters €5.25–8.50, mains*
€13.75–19.95.

✗ Portovecchio Martino Garces St, Yacht Marina
(walk right round the edge of the harbour at sea
level until you reach it); ☎ 21563317;
📱 99444999; ✉ portovecchiogozo@gmail.com;
www.portovecchiorestaurant.com. Not cheap, but

with good & interesting food, particularly seafood
(fish in limoncello sauce for instance), a smart
nautical-themed interior & pleasant terrace on the
marina. This relatively new restaurant is getting
itself a great reputation. The Bishop of Gozo
recently wrote in its visitor's book that the food
was 'fantastically delicious'. *Starters €6.25–10.25,*
mains €10–20.

✗ Seaview 15 Shore St; ☎ 21565541;
⏰ 12.00–15.00 & 18.30–22.30 closed Tue &
Jan–Mar only at w/ends. Watch the world go by
from this relaxed, upper-floor restaurant (open-air in
summer, with glass to protect you in winter) next to
the ferry port. Mediterranean food, fresh fish &
steaks. Families welcome. Highchairs available.
Starters €5–7, mains €12–18.

MĠARR IX-XINI

✗ Mġarr Ix-Xini 📱 79854007; ⏰ summer, middle
of the day. Under a couple of trees & a few
umbrellas at the top of this rocky inlet is a tiny
hut kitchen serving cold drinks & fresh fish lunches

(with 2 non-fish dishes) – exactly what is on offer
depends on the day's catch. *Starters around €8,*
mains around €15.

NADUR

✗ Mekren's Bakery Hanaq St (signed to Ramla);
☎ 21552342; 📱 99858249; ⏰ roughly
09.30–18.30. Ring in with orders to collect later. A
small, busy & totally traditional bakery making
bread, ftira (Gozitan pizza) & pizzas. The traditional
closed cheese ftira is especially delicious & the ftira
& pizza are huge & cheap. *Bread around 65c, ftira*
& pizzas €3.50 (margherita €3).

✗ Maxokk Bakery St James St; ☎ 21550014;
www.gozoservices.com/maxokk; ⏰ 10.30–19.00 &
13.00–19.00 Sun. The other side of Church Square
is this even smaller but less traditional place that
also bakes in a wood-burning oven. No bread.
Pizza/ftira, smaller than Mekrens. *€5 each (except*
margherita, €3.50).

SAN LAWRENZ

Tatitas 34 Pjazza San Lawrenz/St Lawrence Sq; 21566482 or 21565099; m 99882810; e tatitas@maltanet.net; Mar–Oct 12.00–14.30 & 18.00–22.30 daily. Maltese limestone interior with white linen tabecloths & subtle modern décor, plus tables out in church square. Very good Maltese/Italian food. Vegetables grown in the garden. Fish direct from Dwejra fishermen. Excellent local ice cream. Families welcome. Highchairs available. *Starters €7–9, mains around €15.*

VICTORIA

Ta' Rikardu 4 Triq Il Fosos, The Citadel; 21555953; 10.00 until at least 19.00 daily. Ricardo not only oversees the cooking of the food, he also produces much of it. The cheeses are from his own sheep & goats, the wines from his vineyard. The large Traditional Platter (€8.75) of cheeses, fresh tomatoes, sundried tomatoes, capers, onion & olives (with bread of course) is delicious & big enough for 2, or even 3 with the addition of a perfect fresh cheese pp (70c each). Wash down with one of Ricardo's own wines (€1.75/glass, €3.50–4.50/bottle to take-away). Also homemade ravioli (€4.20–5.80) & rabbit in Ricardo's wine (€11.50). Wooden tables & friendly staff in an old citadel building. Not to be missed.

Café Jubilee [270 B2] 8 Pjazza Indipendenza; 21558921; e info@cafejubilee.com; www.cafejubilee.com; 08.00–24.00 daily (02.00 at w/ends) food, 12.00–15.00 & 18.00–22.00. Café-bar with wooden tables, old posters & miscellaneous objects all over the walls. Cosy in winter, AC in summer. *Jubilee full English b/fast €4.75, filled croissants €0.75, wraps €4.90.*

It-Tmun Victoria [270 F2] Europe St; 21566667; e info@tmunvictoria.com; www.tmunvictoria.com; 18.30–22.30 daily except Thu. For food, drinks & cocktails until late, & Sun lunch in winter. Book, especially at w/ends. Multi-award-winning restaurant with a modern designer interior but relaxed, informal atmosphere. Excellent innovative European food & a wine book of over 200 wines, specialising in Shiraz. Also wines by the glass from a special temperature-controlled unit. All very much the baby of patron Patrick Buttigieg, whose father runs the more traditional, seafood restaurant It-Tmun Mġarr. Mainly indoor with AC opening to a small outdoor terrace. *Starters €6.50–11.75, mains €14.95–22.95.*

Maji Wine & Dine [270 B2] 6 Sir Adrian Dingli St; 21550878; e info@majiwine-dine.com; 19.00–22.30 Mon–Sat. Ignore the official address & look at the map to find this restaurant. Through an unprepossessing doorway off the main square. An old gentleman's club modernised & trendied up to create a lounge bar, a very cosy winter restaurant & a summer dining terrace overlooking Savina Square & Victoria's rooftops. Chef-manager Michael Buhagiar is a foodie & it shows. *Starters around €8, mains around €15.*

XAGHRA

D Venue Bar & Restaurant Victory Sq; 21566542; m 79557230; e dvenue@onvol.net; 19.00–23.00 daily & lunch 12.00–15.00 Mon, Thu, Sat, Sun. Just opened by the owner of Oleandar (below) a few doors away. Traditional stone exterior belies shiny modern interior with metal bar & football on TV. Restaurant upstairs has one particularly desirable table on the stone balcony overlooking the square. Specialises in steaks. All main courses cooked on the grill. *Starters €6–8, mains €13–25.*

Oleandar Victory Sq; 21557230; m 99459142; e oleander@onvol.net; 12.00–15.00 & 19.00–22.00 Tue–Sun. A small wood-panelled interior, but best when it is warm enough to sit outside on Xaghra's main square (with oleander blossom in summer & heaters when it's cooler). Mainly Maltese food, popular with locals as well as visitors. *Starters €6–8, mains €13–20.*

XLENDI

Ic-Cima St Simon St; 21558407; m 99558407 or 99877510; www.starwebmalta.com/cima.htm; 12.00–14.30 (15.00 in summer) & 18.30–22.30/23.00. Closed Tue. A lovely roof terrace, smart but completely relaxed, with marvellous views over Xlendi Bay & the cliffs, especially good at sunset (birders can even see shearwaters rafting out to sea if they bring bins to dinner!). Delicious Italian (& Maltese) dishes, perfectly cooked & artistically presented.

House-smoked fish & homemade ice creams excellent. Family friendly. Book if you want the best views. *Starters mostly €7–8, mains average €13.* ✕ **Ta' Karolina** m 79564769; ⊕ 11.30–15.00 (except Mon) & 18.30 onwards (closing time depends on number of diners). In the corner of Xlendi Bay, right on the water's edge, Ta' Karolina's tables are next to a tiny sandy beach & mini-bay of shallow sea – perfect for young kids to paddle or splash

about in while you sit over a good meal. Older children can climb the steps up to a path along the rocks leading to a bay once used by nuns to swim in seclusion. Very good Mediterranean/Maltese food with fresh fish & pizzas. Friendly relaxed staff. Book for a table next to the water. *Starters €5–7, mains €12.50–18.50, pizzas from €4.25–6.80, sandwiches from €2.*

SHOPPING

SOUVENIRS Souvenirs from Gozo include **lace** – which you can see elderly women painstakingly making around the island. Handmade lace is usually in small pieces, each slightly different, and very expensive (though not if you price it by the hours required to make it!). There is also lots of machine-made lace available. **Gozo Glass** (like Malta's) is often garishly coloured and not to everyone's taste and **silver filigree** is also made here as on the main island. **Ta' Dbiegi Craft Village** (next to the Kempinski Hotel on the edge of San Lawrenz, see page 277) has a good range of local craft products.

    Food is the other main souvenir. Local honey, carob syrup, prickly pear jam and crystalline salt from the salt pans are all portable, and you can even get Gozitan cheeses shrink wrapped for travel. Try **Gozo Traditions** by the Knights' washhouse in Fontana or get some of **Charlie's** excellent organic products from the wall by the Ġgantija Temples ticket office.

SUPPLIES If you are staying in self-catering accommodation, there will probably be a village shop nearby (unless you are in Xlendi). The following stores in Victoria are nonetheless useful for stocking up:

Arkadia Shopping Centre [270 E3] Fortunato Mizzi St (extension of Republic St); ❟ 22103000, 22103221 or 22103316; ⊕ 09.00–19.00 (supermarket from 08.00). In winter, closes 13.00–16.00. The largest supermarket on Gozo as well as a department store & other retail outlets. Free Wi-Fi in McDonald's.

Parking outside (you need a parking clock in the mornings).
Organika [270 B2] St George's Sq/Pjazza San Ġorġ; e organika@onvol.net; ⊕ 09.00–13.00 Mon–Sat. Gozo's only organic food & ethical products shop.

OTHER PRACTICALITIES
INTERNET CAFÉS AND WI-FI
🖳 **Gozo Business Systems** [270 D4] Triq Ġorġ Borġ Olivier, Victoria; ❟ 21565565; ⊕ 09.00–19.00. A computer business rather than a café so no drinks but well-maintained computers. *€60c/15mins, €1.20/30mins, €2.25/hr, printing 10c/page.*
🖳 **Aurora Band Club** See page 271.
🖳 **Herbees** Rabat St, Xlendi; ❟ 27011153; ⊕ 13.00–01.00. Small fast-food café with a few computers upstairs. *€1/20mins, €2/50mins, €3/90mins.*

🖳 **Extreme Sports Bar & Pizzeria** Qbajjar St/Triq Il-Qbajjar, Marsalforn; ❟ 21550983; e extremesports@gozomail.com; www.starwebmalta.com/extremesports.htm. *€1/20mins, €2/1hr, €3/100mins.*
🖳 **Lantern Restaurant & Guesthouse** Qbajjar St/Triq Il-Qbajjar, Marsalforn; ❟ 21556285; m 79566271. *€1/20mins, €2/1hr, €3/100mins.*

Wi-Fi is available in most of these places as well in some non-internet cafes including the Jubilee Café (see *Where to eat*) and McDonald's in the Arkadia shopping centre (see *Supplies* above), both in Victoria.

Gozo has a lot to offer outdoors – on water and land. It's worth referring to *Part One* of this guide for more general information; what follows is specific to Gozo. The *Adventure Guidebook to the Maltese Islands* by Xavier Hancock (€16.95) has a great deal about outdoor activities in Gozo, including walking, mountain biking, diving, climbing and some more extreme sports. It is available from bookshops or from Xavier's company **Gozo Adventures** (7 *Triq Sant Indrija, Victoria;* ↘ *21564592;* m *99241171;* e *hancock@waldonet.net.mt; www.gozoadventures.com*).

BOAT TRIPS AND FISHING Gozo is a great jumping-off point for boat trips – whether to circle the island for impressive views of the sheer cliffs, to swim and snorkel in harder-to-reach bays, to fish, birdwatch or take a cruise over to Comino with its caves and the Blue Lagoon.

Hey Lampuki 7 Triq Sant Indrija, Victoria; ↘ 21564592; m 99241171; e info@ heylampuki.com; www.heylampuki.eu. Cruises & boat trips in 18-person pilot boat or Adventure RIB. Swimming trips, sightseeing, diving & specialists in extreme adventure trips.
Mariblu Excursions Mġarr Rd, Xewkija (as in Mariblu Guesthouse); ↘ 21551315; m 99497757; e frankie@digigate.net or info@mariblugozo.com; www.mariblugozo.com/excursions.php. Wide range of trips & charters, some on a sailing yacht (with motor). Half- & full-day Comino trips (€35/€65 with lunch & wine & pick-up from & return to anywhere on Gozo or Malta): half-day Comino with half-day Gozo jeep tour (€65pp); private charters; fishing trips in traditional Maltese fishing boats (€150 for up to 6 people); other fishing (€50/hr coastal, €80/hr deep-sea, equipment provided). 10–20% discount for

internet booking (& possibly for quoting this guidebook).
Xlendi Cruises 18 Bakery St, Marsalforn, also has a kiosk on Xlendi Bay; ↘ 21559967 or 21551909; m 99478119 or 99551909 (Angelo), 99427917 (Louis); e info@xlendicruises.com; www.xlendicruises.com. This established company runs regular boat trips as well as hiring out boats, self-drive or with a boatman & offering fishing trips. Regular half-day cruises (about €20pp, children 5–10 half price, under 5s go free) do a full circuit of Gozo or Comino – or a full-day trip goes round both (€25). There are always 2 or more swimming stops (snorkels & masks provided). Optional buffet lunch (usually +€5). Trips leave from Mġarr, but there is free transport from Xlendi & Marsalforn or hotel pick-up & return for €5. You might get 10% discount for quoting this guidebook.

A number of boat companies run to Comino and the Blue Lagoon. See page 250 for details.

WALKING Gozo is a great place for walking – particularly in spring, autumn and early on summer mornings. Bear in mind that in autumn you may be sharing the countryside, and particularly the coast, with bird hunters (see pages 24 and 46), especially first thing in the morning and in the late afternoon/early evening. In summer, the time between sunrise and about 08.30 can be an idyllic time to take a stroll if you can get yourself up that early.

It is possible to walk most places on Gozo (despite some dead-end paths that lead only to fields) including most of the way around the coast. The views are spectacular and the shape of the weathered landscape extraordinary.

Great **coastal** (or part-coastal) walks include Mġarr to Mġarr ix-Xini; Mġarr ix-Xini to Ta' Ċenċ cliffs; along the cliffs from Xlendi Tower (potentially all the way to Sannat); out beyond San Dimitri Chapel (see page 279); from Xwejni Bay past the salt pans and on to Żebbuġ or down into Wied il-Għasri.

Non-coastal walks include up Għammar Hill (with the Ta' Pinu Stations of the Cross) or up Ta' Ġurdan Hill to the lighthouse; Santa Luċija to Dwerja via Għar Abdul (although much of this can also be driven) and Santa Luċija out to

Wardija Point (where there are coastal views and the option to continue walking to Dwejra).

There are four informative **Gozo Countryside Walks** booklets produced by the Malta Tourism Authority available to download free from www.visitmalta.com/walks-around-malta or to buy for about €2. The **Ramblers Association of Malta** (e *ram205@gmail.com; www.ramblersmalta.jointcomms.com*) is also happy to advise walkers, and **Mariblu** (*www.mariblugozo.com/excursions.php*; see also *Boat trips*, above) organise a one-day guided walk starting at the Citadel (not in summer) for up to five people including transport from/to your accommodation and barbecue lunch (€48).

British walking and cycling holiday specialists **Headwater** (❧ *01606 720099;* e *info@headwater.com; www.headwater.com*) offer a one-week self-guided walking holiday in Gozo (*Sep–May, from £609 without flights, £799 with*) including detailed route notes for 14 circular walks.

CYCLING While I wouldn't advise cycling on Malta, Gozo is a different matter. Traffic is much lighter and slower, and drivers more considerate. Manoeuvres can still be unpredictable, however, and you do need to keep a lookout for the many potholes. Bikes can be rented from:

On Two Wheels Mr & Mrs Calleja, 36 Rabat Rd, Marsalforn; ❧ 21561503; m 99421621; e on2wheels@gozo.com; www.on2wheelsgozo.com. Bikes & motorbikes, delivered anywhere on the island. *Mountain bikes cost €10 for 1 day or €5/day for 4 days or longer.*

Victoria Garage [270 C3] Main Gate St, Victoria (opposite the bus station); ❧ 21556414, 21553741 or 21553758; m 99253053; e info@victoriagaragegozo.com; http://victoriagaragegozo.com. Bike, motorbike & car hire. *Mountain bikes €5/day, over 3 days in winter €4/day.*

Cycle Malta & Gozo (*RMF Publishing; €6; available from www.cyclemaltaandgozo.com*) describes three Gozo routes all starting from the Mġarr ferry (making them easy to do on a day trip from Malta). The author, Joseph Montebello (❧ *21826146;* m *99807755;* e *monte620@maltanet.net*) also organises cycle tours. **Mariblu** (see *Boat trips*, above) also run mountain-bike outings.

British holiday operator **Headwater** (❧ *01606 720099;* e *info@headwater.com; www.headwater.com*) offers a one-week cycling tour of Gozo (riding Ta' Ċenċ–Xagħra–San Lawrenz–Ta' Ċenċ). Tours run from September to May, from £709 without flights, £899 with, including half-board in four- and five-star hotels, all maps and detailed route information, bikes and transfer of bags.

DIVING Gozo is one of the most popular places for diving in the Mediterranean and is good for beginners and old hands. It has some 14 shore-diving sites – ranging from Dwejra with the famous Blue Hole (caves, drop-offs, boulder slopes and a chimney) to Ghasri Cave with its cathedral-like dome – as well as many boat-dives. For a guide to some of the top dive sites see, *Chapter 4, page 94*.

There are 11 legitimate dive companies on Gozo, listed at www.visitmalta.com/dive-centres-gozo-comino – make sure you use one of these. Four of the most established are:

Atlantis Diving Centre Qolla St, Marsalforn; ❧ 21554685, m 79710390; e diving@atlantisgozo.com; www.atlantisgozo.com. Well-established Gozitan company offering PADI courses in several languages, accompanied dives & equipment hire & sale. Minimum age 10.

Calypso Dive (est 1985) Marsalforn Bay Seafront; ❧ 21561757; e info@calypsodivers.com; www.calypsodivers.com. Calyspo runs 2 regular dive outings each day at 08.45 & 13.45 & is proud *not* to run on Gozo Maybe Time. Calypso also runs courses – PADI & BSAC & is a BSAC Centre of Excellence. The company tailor-makes programmes of all kinds. Also full holiday packages (exc flights). Minimum age 12. **Moby Dives** (est 10 years) Gosta St, Xlendi Bay; ☏ 21564429 or 21551616; m 99499596; e info@mobydivesgozo.com; www.mobydivesgozo.com. This is the only centre with a training pool (helpful for beginners, though cold). They run all the PADI courses from Bubblemaker (children aged 8+) & introductory adult dives in the pool via Open Water Diver to instructor & specialist qualifications. Also accompanied dives, boats & equipment. Their centre, I block back from the seafront, has its own accommodation (Ulysses Aparthotel see *Where to stay*, page 260) & AC bar-restaurant, The Captain's Table (pizzas from €4.50, sandwiches from €2.90, filled omelette €4.25). **St Andrew's Divers Cove** (est 20 years) St Simon St, Xlendi Bay; ☏ 21551301; e standrew@gozodive.com; www.gozodive.com. Everything from adult beginner courses (in Xlendi Bay) to specialist qualifications (PADI, BSAC, CMAS), accompanied diving, & equipment hire & boat dives. Accommodation can also be arranged within 2mins of the centre.

For more on diving, see *Chapter 3*, page 66, and *Chapter 4*, page 94.

SWIMMING AND SNORKELLING Gozo is a fantastic place for swimming and snorkelling with a good choice of bays, large and small, rocky and a few sandy, all with warm clear water and plentiful fish (almost all of them harmless).

For adventurous enthusiasts, **Swim Trek**, British swimming-tours company (☏ *01273 739713;* e *info@swimtrek.com; www.swimtrek.com*) runs a one-week holiday in Gozo that includes swimming from Gozo to Malta. Six days at San Andrea Hotel, Xlendi, with breakfast, lunch, guiding, coaching and boat support provided (but not travel to Gozo or supper) £700.

For more information on swimming and water safety, see pages 47, 66 and 90.

ROCK CLIMBING Climbers have tended to focus their efforts mainly on Malta, but some are now setting up bolted routes in Gozo, particularly at Mġarr ix-Xini (high grade), Xlendi and Dwejra. **Gozo Adventures** also takes people bouldering and, if you are mad enough, deep-water soloing and coasteering.

Gozo Climbing Association (linked to Gozo Adventures) 7 Triq Sant Indrija, Victoria; ☏ 21564592; m 99241171; e hancock@waldonet.net.mt; www.climbgozo.com

See page 70 for more information on climbing.

BIRDWATCHING Gozo has some great places to birdwatch and, just as on Malta, you are likely to have to share them with hunters during autumn migration, though hopefully not in spring (see page for 48 for more information on safety and page 24 for information on hunting). **Ta' Ċenċ** is probably Gozo's primary birding site being high coastal garigue. Other good spots include **Dwejra** (coast, cliffs and garigue); the **Lunzjata Valley** (especially when northwesterly winds blow during migration) though be aware that much of the land here is private; **Xlendi Valley**; the **Citadel** in Victoria (during migration) because it is so high; and **Marsalforn Valley** (especially in migration time with southeasterly winds). Boat trips are, of course, another way to see birds. The number of birds seen in spring and summer rose in 2009 after two years without spring hunting and the pallid swift, new to Malta, has recently colonised several of Gozo's coastal caves.

For more on birdwatching, see pages 23 and 68, and for the top birding locations, see pages 97–100.

CULTURAL ACTIVITIES

Gozo has its own **opera festival** in October (see *Events*, page 35) as well as occasional **concerts**, and all the villages make the most of their annual *festa* (see page 31). Quite a few contemporary artists work on Gozo, and Hermine Anna Sammut (↘ *21550545*, m *79617746*) has started a private tour, '**On the trail of contemporary Gozitan artists**', a walk from studio to studio visiting Gozo's artists at work (€49pp including lunch, drop-off and pick-up and a handmade souvenir). She also runs half-day hands-on art activities for adults and children.

There is one commercial **cinema** in Gozo, the Citadel by It-Tokk (*Castle Hill;* ↘ *21559955;* e *info@citadelcinema.com; www.citadelcinema.com*). The Kempinski Hotel in San Lawrenz (see *Where to stay*, page 259) is planning to show films shot in Malta (at least in part) including *Gladiator, Count of Monte Cristo, Troy* and *Munich* in its gardens from spring 2010.

MĠARR

(*Bus 25*) Almost everyone arriving in Gozo arrives at Mġarr (pronounced *Imjar*, and not to be confused with Mġarr, Malta). Now dominated by the modern ferry terminal, you can still see how pretty this village and its natural harbour once were. Traditional fishing boats bob on the water, and the road – now edged with small bars and restaurants – sweeps round the bay up to the prominent little church and the Grand Hotel high above the sea.

WHAT TO SEE AND DO
The Church of Our Lady of Lourdes
This small Gothic-style church almost hangs off the edge of the rock above the town. It was built in the 1880s after a traveller commented that the rocks here looked like the grotto of Massabielle in Lourdes where a couple of decades earlier a young girl, Bernadette, had seen visions of Our Lady. This had turned Lourdes into one of the leading destinations for Christian pilgrims, and Gozo's little Lourdes Church, with its fairy-light Madonna is visited by crowds of Gozitans on 11 February, the date when Bernadette saw her first apparition, with some pilgrims returning on the anniversaries of all 18 visions.

Fort Chambray (or Chambrai)
On the sea cliffs above the town is this late attempt by the Knights to build an equivalent of Valletta for the smaller island. The idea had been around a long time but it was left to Jacques François de Chambray (Norman Count and Lieutenant General of the Ships in the mid-18th century) to get around to implementing it. The city was intended to better protect the population and the Gozo Channel from invaders. But by the time the fortified walls were actually built and foundations laid in 1760 it was half a century since the last Turkish attack and the people of Gozo saw little point in purchasing plots and building afresh inside the new city walls.

Work stopped in 1788 with just a barracks and possibly a chapel completed. The fort held out briefly against the French invaders in 1798 but soon gave way, and the French were themselves ousted less than a year later. The British used the fort as a garrison during the Crimean War and World War I and as a military rest home in World War II. It then became Gozo's mental hospital. Today the site is being developed (once again rather slowly) into a luxury housing estate. Only the outside can be seen by the public.

GĦAJNSIELEM

(*Bus 42 & 43 to the village centre or bus 25 to Mġarr Harbour & walk up the hill*) Mġarr blurs into Għajnsielem (pronounced *einseelem*) at the top of the hill. *Għajn* means 'spring', so the village name is 'Salem's Spring', 'Salem' being an Arab name, perhaps a landowner in Arab times or a Turkish corsair reputed to have regularly disembarked his galleys to replenish his water supply here.

The area was little occupied in the 16th century – being too close to possible corsair landings at Mġarr. As the threat diminished in the second half of the 17th century, however, a significant settlement grew up around this source of fresh water. The village once had a stone wash house like that in Fontana (see page 276), but this was pulled down to make way for today's central square, **Pjazza Tad-Dehra (Apparition Square)**, where a local shepherd is said to have seen a vision of Our Lady, commemorated in a monument erected in the square in the 1990s. His vision resulted in the building of a shrine to Our Lady of Loreto which soon became a chapel (1810–20) and is now known as the **Old Parish Church**. As the population grew a larger church was built, the early 20th-century Gothic **Sanctuary of Our Lady of Loreto**.

Just off the main Mġarr–Victoria road is the oldest chapel in Gozo. **St Cecilia's Chapel**, thought to have been built in the 1540s though first documented in 1615, is a simple medieval-style aisle-less stone chapel just 7m square. At the time of writing it is in poor condition but due to be renovated by Wirt Għawdex (*Gozo Heritage NGO;* \ *21563839;* e *info@wirtghawdex.org; www.wirtghawdex.org*).

For more information on the village, see www.ghajnsielem.com.

VICTORIA/RABAT

Gozo's capital Rabat was renamed in honour of Britain's Queen Victoria in her Golden Jubilee year, 1887. It has been known by both names ever since, though locals more often refer to it as Rabat – from the Arabic for 'suburb'. The town is the suburb of the medieval walled Citadel (or Citadella or Il-Kastell) that sits on its northern flank. The impressive Citadel is a must-see and Victoria/Rabat is both pleasant to wander around and a good place to stock up on supplies, from food to petrol, a towel to a new pair of spectacles. **Shops** are concentrated in the centre around the main square (It-Tokk, see below) and the bus station. There are two **banks** (HSBC and Bank of Valletta), both with ATMs and both on the main street (Republic Street) where you will find a **post office** and two **shopping centres** [270 D2 and 270 E3].

Victoria's bus station [270 C3], on Triq Putrjal, off Republic Street, is Gozo's transport hub. You can get from here to most villages on the island (though not necessarily quickly) and will almost certainly end up here if you try to get between any of them. The main car park is next to the bus station, although it is also possible to park on the street (see *Driving* above).

WHAT TO SEE AND DO
It-Tokk/Pjazza Indipendenza/Independence Square [270 B2] Rabat centres on Pjazza Indipendenza (Independence Square), locally known as It-Tokk, meaning 'meeting place' – and it is. There is a market here each morning and open-air cafés in the afternoon. At one end is the semicircular Baroque **Banca Giuratale** [270 B2], built 1773–8 under Grand Master de Vilhena and the seat of local government. It was designed by de Vilhena's French military engineer Charles François de Mondion, who was also responsible for all this grand master's restructuring of Mdina.

At the other end of the square is **St James' Church** [270 B2], a small recently built church on the site of earlier churches. It apparently took some time for the 20th-century congregation to get planning permission, because of their habit of using the church bells to drown out political speakers in the square!

14

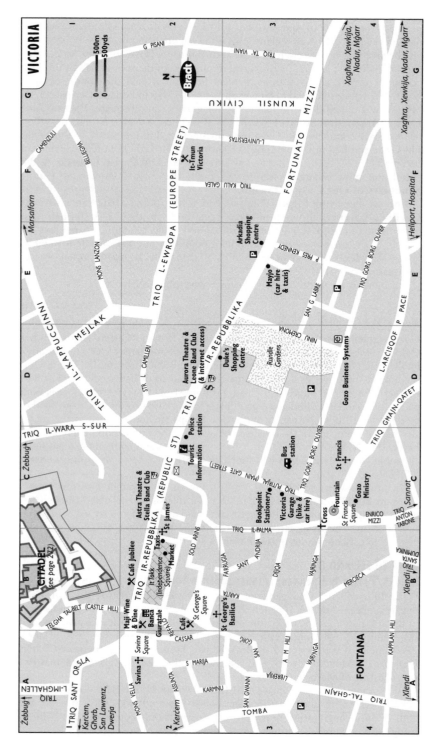

VICTORIA

0 ——— 500m
0 ——— 500yds

N Braċh

G PISANI

A

B CITADEL (see page 272)

TELGĦA TALBELT (CASTLE HILL)

Żebbuġ↑

TRIQ SANT ORSLA

MONS VELLA

Savina Square

Savina †

MONS LANZON

Kerċem, Gharb, San Lawrenz, Dwejra

Żebbuġ↑ C
TRIQ IL-WARA S-SUR

TRIQ IL-GĦAJN

Maġji Wine & Dine ✕ Café Jubilee ✕

Banca Giuratale

Café ✕

St George's Basilica †

RETALO

CASSAR

S MARIJA

ASSUNTA

KARMNU

TOMBA

SAN GWANN

LIBERIJA

A M HILL

VAJRINGA

GORG

SAN

DEJOA

KARITA

SANT ANDRIJA

FARRUGIA

SOLD ARMS

TRIQ IL-PALMA

MERĊIECA

KAPILAN HILL

FONTANA

TRIQ TAL-GĦAJN

Xlendi↓

TRIQ L-IMGĦALLEN→

L-IMGĦALLEN

CAMENZULI

BELLEGHA

IL-KAPPUĊĊINI

MEJLAK

Marsalform→

TRIQ

STR L. CAMILLERI

TRIQ L-EWROPA (EUROPE STREET)

Astra Theatre & Stella Band Club

It Tokk

Taxis

St James' ✕

Independence Square

Market

TRIQ IR-REPUBBLIKA (REPUBLIC ST)

TRIQ IR-REPUBBLIKA (MAIN GATE STREET)

Aurora Theatre & Leone Band Club (& internet access)

Duke's Shopping Centre

$

Tourist Information

Police station

Bookpoint Stationery

Victoria Garage (bike & car hire)

Bus station

Fountain

St Francis Square

† Cross

It-Tmun Victoria ✕

L-UNIVERSITAS

TRIQ TA' VIANI

KUNSILL CIVIKU

FORTUNATO MIZZI

TRIQ KALU GALEA

Arkadia Shopping Centre P

Mayjo (car hire & taxis)

P PRES KENNEDY

NINU CREMONA

Rundle Gardens

SAN G LABRE

P

Gozo Business Systems

St Francis †

Gozo Ministry

ENRICO MIZZI

TRIQ GORG BORĠ OLIVIER

TRIQ GĦAJN-QATET

TRIQ GORĠ BORĠ OLIVER

L-ARĊISQOF P PACE

TRIQ GORĠ BORĠ OLIVER

TRIQ ANTON TABONE

Sannat

Xlendi↓

Xagħra, Xewkija, Nadur, Mġarr→

Heliport, Hospital→

F

E

D

C

B

A

270

The town's main road, Republic Street, runs down one side of the square, while along the other spreads a little maze of narrow alleys (some of them medieval) full of small shops and a couple more church squares including St George's Square.

St George's Square/Pjazza San Ġorġ [270 B2] This traffic-free square is an agreeable place to sit for a Kinnie (or other cold drink), and **Grapes Café** [270 B2] will provide it along with a few Maltese snacks and light meals. The square is dominated by **St George's Basilica** [270 B2], one of Victoria's two parish churches, the other being the cathedral in the Citadel. St George's was built 1672–8, with the façade added in 1818 and the dome, aisle and transepts in the 1930s. It is the most ornate church on the island (and there is plenty of competition), the interior a kaleidoscope of marble, paintings and gilded mouldings. The lavish black and bronze altar canopy is a scaled-down version of Bernini's in St Peter's, Rome. The altarpiece of St George with white charger and felled dragon in the left transept is a 1678 work by Mattia Preti (see boxed text, page 126). The titular statue of St George was carved from a single log of wood in 1838 and was the first such statue in Gozo. It gets its annual outing at the head of the *festa* procession in the third week of July.

Triq ir-Repubblika/Republic Street The main street of Rabat runs east–west through the city and into It-Tokk. It provides banks (including ATMs), small shopping centres, the post office, police station, pharmacies, Victoria's two band clubs and Gozo's main public gardens, **Rundle Gardens/Gnien Rundle** [270 D3], laid out by the British administration in 1910. The park plays host to a busy agricultural show during the St Marija *festa* (mid- August).

Before Malta became a republic, this street was called Racecourse Street and during Victoria's two *festi* (St George's in the third week of July and St Marija) it once again fulfils this purpose as *sulky*, lightweight two-wheeled horse-carts (quite like Roman chariots), are raced uphill along the street.

Band clubs and opera theatres Victoria has two band clubs, between which there is considerable rivalry both at *festa* time and throughout the year. Each club has a building on Republic Street (on opposite sides) with a bar, snooker tables and – more surprisingly – an opera theatre. And each puts on a (usually Italian) opera, as well as other concerts, as part of the **Festival Mediterranea** each autumn (*October to November, www.mediterranea.com*). One year they actually presented the same opera.

The **Aurora Theatre and Leone Band Club** [270 D2], which is linked to the cathedral and the St Marija *festa*, occupies 100 Republic Street which is also home to the **Gozo Billiards and Snooker Club**. **Internet** access is available here for €3/75 minutes (which can be split between several sessions) and live football is shown on a large-screen television. The **Stella Band Club** [270 C2] (for St George's *festa*) and **Astra Theatre** are just up the hill near the main square.

THE CITADEL/IL KASTELL A naturally defensible flat-topped hill in the middle of Gozo (now a few minutes up a steep street from It-Tokk), the Citadel was first fortified in the Bronze Age (and possibly inhabited even earlier). It has been at the centre of Gozitan life (as well as geography) for at least 3,500 years. Expanded by the Phoenicians, the Citadel became a sophisticated fortified town during Roman times when Gozo was a municipality distinct from Malta. By the mid-13th century, it could accommodate the entire population of Gozo – some 366 families – overnight.

14

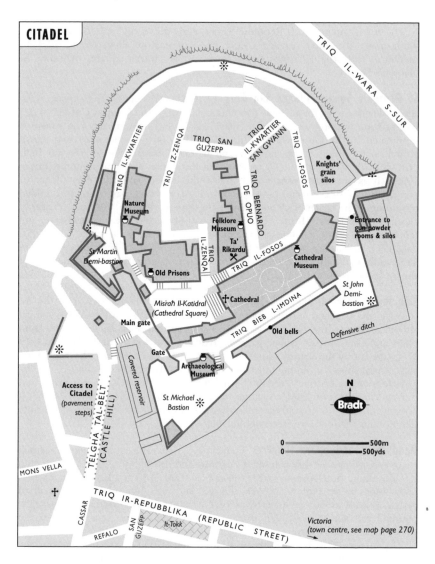

CITADEL

TRIQ IL-WARA S-SUR

TRIQ IL-KWARTIER

TRIQ IZ-ZENQA

TRIQ SAN GUŻEPP

TRIQ IL-KWARTIER SAN GWANN

TRIQ BERNARDO DE OPUO

TRIQ IL-FOSOS

Knights' grain silos

Nature Museum

Folklore Museum

Entrance to gun-powder rooms & silos

Ta' Rikardu

St Martin Demi-bastion

TRIQ IL-ZENQA

Old Prisons

Cathedral Museum

St John Demi-bastion

Miśraħ Il-Katidral (Cathedral Square)

TRIQ IL-FOSOS

Cathedral

TRIQ BIEB L-IMDINA

Main gate

Old bells

Defensive ditch

Gate

Archaeological Museum

Covered reservoir

N

Bradt

Access to Citadel (pavement steps)

TELGHA TAL-BELT (CASTLE HILL)

St Michael Bastion

0 — 500m
0 — 500yds

MONS VELLA

CASSAR

REFALO

SAN GUŻEPP

TRIQ IR-REPUBBLIKA (REPUBLIC STREET)

It-Tokk

Victoria (town centre, see map page 270)

The northern walls seen today were built under the Aragonese (early 15th century) while the southern side of the Citadel overlooking Victoria was reconstructed during the reign of the Order of St John. They came to it somewhat belatedly; closing the stable door after the Turks had attacked in 1551 enslaving most of Gozo's population and devastating the Citadel and Rabat. The grand master of the day, Juan d'Homedes, considered abandoning the Citadel altogether, but by the early 17th century serious rebuilding was under way.

Some of it had to be repeated after the earthquake of 1693 wreaked considerable damage on the Citadel. Fortunately, by this time many of the buildings were empty. The earlier rule that the local population must spend each night in the Citadel (in case of attack) had been withdrawn in 1637 and the people had spread out into Rabat and the surrounding countryside

Despite these vicissitudes, the citadel still boasts the oldest buildings in Gozo, some dating from before the arrival of the Knights, including those that now house the Folklore Museum.

The Citadel remains a marvellous place to wander around with its narrow alleys, historic fortifications and high rampart walls with panoramic views over Gozo and beyond. This tiny fortified city is now home to just a handful of residents, five small museums/historic sites and the best traditional Gozitan lunch going (at Ta' Rikardu – see *Where to eat*, page 263).

The Citadel is approached from Rabat, usually via steps along It-Tegha tal-Belt (known as Castle Hill). The steps are limestone worn smooth by footfall and are very slippery when wet. To either side is a flat area with a few stone lids. This is a 19th-century reservoir built by the British and the nearby obelisk celebrates the arrival of the first water brought by the aqueduct built at the same time, a fraction of which can still be seen on the Victoria–St Lawrence Road (see below). At the top of the steps you enter Cathedral Square via an arched entrance, controversially cut through the citadel walls in 1956 to allow passage of the *festa* statue held at shoulder height.

Cathedral Square/Misraħ Il-Katidral/Pjazza tal-Katidral The square is
dominated by the broad steps leading up to the Baroque façade of the cathedral guarded by two popes: Pope Pius IX and Pope John Paul II (who pops up all over Malta and Gozo because he visited here in 1990 and in 2001). To your right is the cathedral vestry and chapter house added in the 1890s after the removal of the last of the medieval houses that used to surround the square.

The archway now leads to the cathedral ticket office and shop (which also sells some souvenir foods), the Archaeological Museum and, turning left, the old bells of the cathedral cast in the Knights' Valletta foundry between 1639 and 1791. Beyond these is an exhibition of contemporary art that changes monthly and the Gunpowder Room and Silos (see page 275).

On the left side of the square, up some steps, are the law courts, rebuilt in 1687, and the neighbouring Old Prison (see overleaf).

The cathedral and cathedral museum (⏱ *summer 10.00–17.00 Mon–Sat, winter
09.00–16.30; €3pp, children under 10 go free. Audio guide (inc a walk around the rest of the Citadel) available in English, Italian, French & German.*)

Cathedral The present church was built between 1697 and 1711 on the site of an earlier church, which was damaged in the 1551 attack. Plans were made for a new church much earlier in the 17th century with designs by Lorenzo Gafá (who also designed the Mdina Cathedral) but work did not start until after the old church had been further damaged in the 1693 earthquake. During preparations for building, it was found that the church stood on the site of a Roman temple, probably to Juno.

The cathedral is in the form of a Latin cross with eight side chapels. Inside on the left is the splendid font of Gozo onyx (onyx found near Zebugg in 1738) and to the right a copy of it. The floor is covered with multi-coloured marble tombs and commemorative slabs.

Look up at the interior of the dome. Now – especially if you have kids with you – pop outside and have a look at the exterior of the roof before going further into the church. There is no dome. The interior is a remarkably successful *trompe l'oeil*, painted in 1739 by Sicilian artist Antonio Pippi. When viewed from the sides at the altar end of the church, the illusion no longer works.

The cathedral is dedicated to the Assumption of the Virgin Mary (Santa Marija) whose feast day is 15 August (a national holiday). The *festa* statue stands to the right of the main door as you leave.

14

Cathedral museum (*Triq il-Fosos*) Up the alley to the left of the cathedral is the little museum with three floors. The upstairs picture gallery contains mainly 15th–20th-century portraits of priests, and altarpieces from Gozo's rural chapels. The basement silver vault has an impressive collection of ecclesiastical silver, including the vast *festa* candlesticks and the bishop's silver travelling box containing everything needed to celebrate the liturgy. The main hall is a jumble of all sorts of church objects from the bishop's 150-year-old landau, tapestries, mitres and masonry from the pre-1693 church, to a shoe belonging to Pope Pius VII (1800–23) and Pope John Paul II's hats and gloves.

The Citadel museums (*Heritage Malta, Gozo:* ❧ *21564188;* e *info@heritagemalta.org; www.heritagemalta.org;* ☉ *09.00–17.00, last admission 16.30; joint ticket for the following 4 museums:* €*8 adult,* €*5 over-60s/students/children aged 12–17,* €*4 children aged 6–11, children under 6 go free)*

Gozo Archaeological Museum (❧ *21556144*) This little museum occupies the 17th-century Casa Bondi (originally home to the Bondi family, whose Lou Bondi now anchors the main evening current affairs programme *Bondi Plus*). Glance up before you enter to see the attractive stone balcony above the door.

The first room on the ground floor is a bit uninspiring and poorly labelled, but do not be put off – there are some real gems upstairs. First, in the stairwell are two largish chunks of stone. One is a temple slab with a badly weathered snake carved up its side. This was found by the main 'altar' of the larger Ggantija Temple (see page 284). Next to it is a phallic pillar that once stood in the inner left apse of the same temple.

On the first floor are two lifelike human heads carved of globigerina limestone, also found at Ggantija, and two remarkable finds from the nearby prehistoric Xagħra Stone Circle (Xagħra Hypogeum, see page 287). Six amazingly well-preserved stone 'stick' figurines (dated 3150–2500BC) were found tightly packed together as if they had been in a (long gone) container. They may have been 'in production' as some appear unfinished. The figures are like large carefully crafted pegs with the bottom end squared off and in two cases decorated like a skirt. The upper halves have heads, faces and, on some, styled hair or a headdress. The bottom half is the right size and shape for holding in your hand leading to speculation that they may have been carried in some kind of ritual, although so far no others like them have been found. Accompanying them are three smaller models in a similar style, one with a dog-like head and another that might be a crawling baby.

In the same glass case is a beautifully crafted statuette (also 3150–2500BC) of two of Malta's typical prehistoric 'fat ladies' (see *Chapter 1*, page 5) sitting on an intricately decorated couch. The couch is patterned not only on the top and sides but underneath too (look up through the glass shelf). The society that made this must have been quite sophisticated to have furniture, and representations of furniture, like this.

Other prehistoric items include cowry shell jewellery, and various small 'fat ladies' – some of which may in fact be men. Moving forward in time, there is Roman pottery from the villa at Ramla Bay (see below), a stone olive press, as well as amphorae and a painted clay sarcophagus found in Victoria. A large Roman glass jar with two handles is remarkable for being in one unbroken piece despite dating from the first or second century BC, and there is a bizarre sarcophagus found on Comino made of a vertically split amphora.

Back on the ground floor near the exit is an Arab tombstone of a girl buried between Xewkija and Sannat in 1174 (decades after Count Roger of Normandy took the island into Christian administration). The poetic Kufic inscription is translated into English.

Folklore Museum (*Bernardo de Opuo St;* ↘ *21562034*) A maze of traditional small stone rooms and courtyards with Norman-style windows, this museum is worth a visit for the buildings alone. Originally four stone houses probably built in the very early 16th century before the arrival of the Knights, the rooms are now filled with objects large and small related to farming, crafts and day-to-day life on Gozo through the ages.

Amongst the collection is an early flour mill that would have been powered by donkey; a wide range of weights and measures; costumes; wells (water tanks) – one of which has a lid that was the base of a Roman column; agricultural equipment; displays on local crafts including lace-making and weaving, as well as on the cotton industry and fishing. There is a scale model of a traditional boat – an early ancestor of the Gozo ferry – and a room devoted to hunting.

Nature Museum (*Triq il-Kwartieri ta' San Martin (behind the Law Courts);* ↘ *21556153*) In a group of early 17th-century houses, this museum focuses mainly on Gozo's natural resources, although it also includes a tiny piece of moon rock with a diminutive Maltese flag that went to the moon with *Apollo 11*. There is a geological map of Malta, fossils, minerals and stuffed birds (with a note deploring the killing of wild species), a few large shells and corals and a display of Maltese fish. There are small collections of Gozo's butterflies, moths and beetles and, in a room devoted to Maltese flora is a specimen of the plant (not actually a fungus) once so sought after on Fungus Rock in Dwejra (see page 278).

The Old Prisons (*Cathedral Sq;* ↘ *21565988. Note the stocks outside!*) Built in 1548 these six old prison cells held errant knights and locals. And knights did err – usually by duelling or fighting. Even the Grand Master-to-be, Jean Parisot de Valette was imprisoned on Gozo for four months in 1538 for attacking a layman. Other options for punishment included slaving on the Order's galleys or, for lesser crimes, knights and Malta residents were simply exiled to Gozo!

The six cells are full of graffiti: patterns, crosses and particularly ships. Most are of unknown date, though one is clearly marked 1809. Wrongdoers were sometimes sentenced to hard labour and prisoners from here were used in the 1920s to clear the Ġgantija site – not perhaps the help today's archaeologists would choose.

The entrance hall to the museum served as a communal cell in Victorian times and this prison continued to be used into the 20th century.

The Gunpowder Magazine, Low Battery and silos (*Wirt| Għawdex/Gozo Heritage, head office: Dar il-Lunzjata, Wied il-Lunzjata, Rabat;* ↘ *Jay Jones (British volunteer) 21563839;* e *info@wirtghawdex.org; www.wirtghawdex.org;* ⊕ *at least Tue & Sat 11.00–13.00 but hopefully 10.00–13.00 Tue–Sat; entry by donation – they need it for further restoration work*) The Knights' gunpowder magazine was built here between 1599 and 1603. Until then specialist stores for gunpowder did not exist. It now serves as the starting point for an informal mini-tour of a restored corner of the Knights' Citadel including an unlikely visit to their extraordinary **grain silos**. (You may have seen such silos from the outside at Fort St Elmo, see page 132, and in Floriana, page 142).

There may have been up to 100 such conical silos dug by hand in the Citadel to store the town's precious grain. Here it is possible to actually enter three large ones – about 10m deep. We can get into them because of a tunnel built by the British when they converted the silos into water tanks in 1887. Water was piped in (amazingly, under gravity alone) from Ta' Ċenċ and stored here. The red is sediment of red soil. The big black valve you can see as you enter was turned to let water in by night, and to let it out to the town by day – an arrangement that continued until a few decades ago.

14

Next to the silos is a rock-cut corridor with a couple of rooms dug as World War II shelters (perhaps not the best place for them considering the possible effect of a bomb on a vast tank of water!) and a low hole leading to narrow steps. This is the entrance to a secret Knights-period tunnel connecting the Citadel with the town below. Beyond this is the **Low Battery**, a platform jutting out at the eastern corner of the Citadel. It has a stone sentry box and several cannons and overlooks the Citadel ditch and walls.

When you have finished the tour, walk up the steps onto the ramparts above. Here you can see three bumps in the stone floor – the tops of the silos. The plan is to cover these in Perspex to light the silos below and allow people to see in. The ramparts here are also the perfect place to walk along the walls and enjoy the views.

FONTANA A small village on the road to Xlendi that has become a suburb of Victoria, Fontana (meaning 'fountain'), is so called because of its natural spring (*L-Għajn il-Kbir* – the 'Big Spring') that, most unusually in Malta, flows year-round. To make use of the water, the Knights built arched shelters over the spring on each side of the road. The larger **wash house** has two rows of stone basins for washing clothes with stone-carved coats of arms above. A couple of neighbouring buildings have become unobtrusive tourist shops. **Gozo Traditions** sells wine and souvenir food packed for travelling, while the converted slaughterhouse opposite has an old weaving loom and usually a lady making lace, as well as lots of lace and clothing for sale.

KERĊEM AND SANTA LUĊIJA

(*Bus 14, but only 3 times a day*) **Kerċem** (pronounced *Kerchem*) is a quiet village (apart from occasional motorbikes on its fringes) that has become an outer suburb of Victoria. It retains its own central square, however, with a church (late 19th/early 20th century) and well-stocked village shop. The church is the only one in Gozo dedicated to two saints, Pope St Gregory and Our Lady of Perpetual Help, so it has two *festi*: 12 March (St Gregory) and the second Sunday of July.

To the west of Kerċem is **St Luċija** (pronounced *Santa loocheeya*), a tiny village of fewer than 400 people with (for once) an equally diminutive, pretty little church which is visited especially by those who have problems with their eyesight. *Festa* is celebrated in mid-December with a festival of light. This is an active village which also organises other events (*www.santalucija.com*).

From Santa Luċija you can walk through fertile land to **Wardija Point** (taking about an hour) for spectacular views of Dwejra and its famous rock formations. The energetic can continue to walk from here along the coast to Dwejra (approximately 1¼ hours).

NEOLITHIC CAVES AND MODERN QUARRIES Beyond St Luċija is an area of fertile countryside that has been occupied since Neolithic times. It is from this area that water was carried along the British aqueduct to quench the thirst of the people of Rabat/Victoria.

From St Luċija follow signs down a drivable track to **Għar Abdul (Abdul Cave)**. When signs change to 'Dwejra & Quarries' stop and you should find to your right a flat-topped hill with a large cave in it. This is Għar Abdul which was occupied at about the same time as Għar Dalam on Malta – around 5000BC, during the first human settlement of these islands.

You can climb up to the cave (at your own risk) which has clearly not been left unoccupied for the intervening 7,000 years and appears to be used by hunters in the migration season (see *Hunting*, pages 24 and 48). This is indeed a good spot for

birdwatching – spectacled warblers and short toed larks can be seen in summer as well as migratory species in spring (when EU law says there should be no hunting) and autumn (when hunting is allowed).

It is also possible to climb up onto the top of the hill. There are good views down to Dwejra and over to St Lawrence. Other caves in the area were also occupied in prehistoric times but these have been destroyed by quarrying.

To the left of the road is a large modern **quarry** where you can see how the globigerina limestone that is ubiquitous on the island is cut from the living rock. Little has really changed in thousands of years except that cutting the rock is quicker due to mechanisation and the blocks are more uniform.

From here the road leads into St Lawrence and down to Dwejra.

SAN LAWRENZ/ST LAWRENCE

(*Bus 91*) A traditional Gozitan village just above Dwejra, centred on a large square with a domed 19th-century church (*festa* in the first week of August), a small police station with blue lantern, red phone and letter box, colourful oleander trees, a 'central stores' and a good **restaurant** (Tatitas; see page 263), not to mention the headquarters of St Lawrence Spurs FC!

A traditional **blacksmith** often works with his door open on Triq San Lawrenz, between the square and the five-star **Kempinski Hotel** (see page 259), which sits well disguised on the outskirts of the village five minutes walk from the centre. Just beyond it, on the road towards Għarb, is the Ta' Dbiegi Craft Village (see below).

Outside the heat of a summer day, it is very pleasant to **walk to Dwejra** (see below) from here. It can be a circular walk down the road (signed from between church square and the Kempinski) – about half an hour – and back up over the rocks behind the chapel (about 15 minutes). Go up the steps behind the chapel. You may pass cart ruts. Keep roughly above the inland sea (not too close to the edge) until you reach a track. Turn right and you will join a minor road that leads up past a quarry to the village, entering behind and to the side of the church.

TA' DBIEGI CRAFT VILLAGE (🕑 *10.00–17.00 daily though each studio/shop keeps its own hours so some may be open earlier/later in summer & fewer hours/days in winter*) A collection of small buildings where craftspeople make and sell local products including lace; gold and silverwork; stone, onyx and alabaster; woollens and leather; and gozo glass, which you can watch being blown. This is a good place to buy craft souvenirs with prices starting from about €3.

DWEJRA

(*Bus 91*) Dwejra (pronounced *Dwayra*) has become a miniature tourist centre because of its **natural rocky features** but it is still a lovely place to explore, to **swim** (only when the sea is calm: you do not want to be cut up on the rocks), **snorkel** and, for the experienced and well equipped, **dive**. It is considered to offer some of the best deep dives in the region, including the Blue Hole, Fungus Rock and a variety of caves (for more on diving, see pages 66, 90 and 266). For exploring the rocks it is worth having shoes with a decent sole – the surfaces can be very sharp.

There is a little shack **café** (cake €1), a tiny Gozo **glass shop** that also sells a few other souvenirs, usually an ice-cream van, and a few stalls (more in summer than winter). Dwejra is a protected area (though not against hunting) subject to a project by Nature Trust Malta. Their website (*www.dwejra.org*) has lots of information about the area.

Gozo DWEJRA

14

FUNGUS ROCK Just off the coast to the west of here, Fungus Rock is a great solid sentry post to **Dwejra Lagoon**, a lovely place for a deep-water swim or snorkel (especially off a boat). The rock is also called Il-Ġebla tal-Ġeneral, General's Rock (the 'Captain General' of the Knights' galleys was also responsible for coastal defences and hence for this rock). It stands 60m out of the water and is famous for having grown a rare plant, *Cynomorium coccineum* (also known as general's root), whose red juice was treasured for its medicinal properties. So sought after was it that Grand Master Manoel Pinto de Fonseca (1741–73) found it necessary to smooth the sides of the rock to remove footholds, post a 24-hour guard and threaten unofficial pickers with a spell in the galleys. He also installed a basket on a 50m wire to transport legal pickers more easily. The plant (not in fact a fungus but a parasite on salt-tolerant plants) was presented to the monarchs of Europe as well as being used by the Knights against dysentery, bleeding and impotence. In 1800 the British forbade its collection and it has since been found in other locations around the Mediterranean and Asia as well as on Dingli Cliffs (Malta) and Ta' Ċenċ (Gozo).

THE INLAND SEA AND THE AZURE WINDOW The great arch of rock standing out from the cliffs is known as the **Azure Window**, and it does make a great frame for a photo. You can see it from land and, even better, on the little **boat trip** for which most tourists visit Dwejra. This starts from the Inland Sea, a calm, shallow patch of clear seawater inland of the little white 1960s **Chapel of St Anne** (the last rural chapel to be built on Gozo). The **Inland Sea** was once a large cave, but its roof collapsed, opening it to the sky. It is connected with the open sea via a tall, narrow, Gothic-cathedral-like cave some 80m long. For €3.50 per person local boatmen will take you through the cave tunnel and out the other side. The trip continues along the sheer cliffs, around the corner to admire the Azure Window and into a few caves, some of which catch the sun in a way that produces luminous blue water and highlights the orange coral on the rocks beneath the surface of the water. The best light is in the morning and it is good to get here early, especially in summer, to avoid the crowds.

You may come across people swimming and snorkelling (and diving) through the Azure Window and you used to be able to walk across its top. It is now unstable so best seen from a little distance.

CART RUTS A set of Malta's mysterious cart ruts (see page 198) wind 350m down the rock face behind the chapel and the Inland Sea, descending from the top of the rocky hill almost to the cliff edge near the bottom. Some of the track has been weathered away and other parts are too tricky for the untrained eye to identify, but you can certainly find some of the ruts. Walk up the rock-cut path (possibly also very ancient and certainly here since the time of the Knights) behind the chapel until you come to the first steps. Rather than climb them, turn left off the path. After about 25m you should find a pair of cart ruts that are quite deep and clear. Now go uphill until you near the sign saying 'Danger: No Stone Throwing' which is close to the edge of the cliff. Turn right inland and you should come to the clearest ruts on a flat almost vegetation-less rock. You can follow these (allowing for patches of erosion) up towards the top of the plateau.

DWEJRA TOWER/QAWRA TOWER (*Din L-Art Ħelwa:* ☎ *21225952;* e *info@ dinlarthelwa.org; www.dinlarthelwa.org;* ⊕ *09.00–15.00 Mon–Fri, 12.00–15.00 Sun, a flag flies when it is open*) Up a short steep track from the Dwejra road is this 1652 coastal watchtower built under Grand Master Lascaris to guard Dwejra Bay from invaders. It was also later used to keep an eye on Fungus Rock and its precious plants. Recently restored by Din L-Art Ħelwa (the Maltese National Trust), steps lead up to the first-floor entrance. The interior has a well and a staircase to the roof, where the small room is a powder store. There are great views from here of the Azure Window, Crocodile Rock (flat in the sea, named for its shape), Fungus rock and the rest of Dwejra. The bombardier in charge of the tower used to make a little extra income by collecting salt from the salt pans you can see in the rocks below.

The tower was manned until 1873 and used again as an observation post during World War II. From the base of the tower, paths lead off around the cliffs for good **walks** if it isn't too hot. You can walk all the way from here to Wardija Point or more inland to St Luċija, or up to San Lawrenz (see above).

GHARB

(*Buses 91, 2, & 1*) A particularly pretty village of yellow limestone and traditional stone balconies, Għarb (meaning 'west' in Arabic, pronounced *Arb*) is probably one of the oldest villages in Gozo with evidence of settlement since Neolithic times. It is now home to quite a number of holiday lets (and with no apparent ill effect).

The attractive parish **Church of the Visitation** sits beautifully in the space of the charming central square (actually a triangle) alongside the diminutive police station (with blue lantern outside) and red phone box. The church was built in 1699, 20 years after Għarb became a parish, and was (very loosely) modelled on Francesco Borromini's Baroque church of Sant'Agnese in Piazza Navona in Rome. Its two bell towers each have a clock face. On one are the usual numbers, on the other, the words 'Ibni Għożż iż-Żmien', 'My Son, Value Time'.

The village has a very traditional feel and is famous for its craftspeople – blacksmiths, carpenters, lace-makers, weavers and makers of the Għarb blade (*Sikkina ta'l-Għarb)*, still considered an excellent knife. So it is an appropriate place for a folklore museum and for (on the road between here and San Lawrenz) the **Ta' Dbiegi Craft Village** selling local crafts including lace, woollens and blown glass.

WHAT TO SEE AND DO IN AND AROUND GHARB

Għarb Folklore Museum (*99 Church Sq;* 🌂 *21561929;* e *gharbfolkloremuseum@ onvol.net;* ⊕ *09.30–16.00 Mon–Sat, 09.30–13.00 Sun;* €*3.50 adults, children under 11 go free*) In a traditional early 18th-century stone house next to the church, this little museum has 28 small rooms set on two floors around a delightful little courtyard where you can sit and have a cold drink. The rooms are stuffed with objects relating to crafts and day-to-day life in Gozo: tools of the trade of the blacksmith, fisherman, quarryman, stonemason, wine-maker, tinsmith, printer, weaver, candle-maker and baker; as well as old water pumps; and small vehicles including a splendidly painted horse-drawn child's hearse, a sedan chair and a sprinkler cart (for damping dusty roads) with beautifully decorated wheels. On the flat stone roof you can stand behind carvings of St Joseph and two lions and survey the square below.

San Dimitri Chapel Down a narrow country road north of Għarb is a tiny chapel in the middle of fields. The door is unlocked and you can see through an inner grille. The altarpiece is of St Demetrius riding a white horse. At his feet are a woman praying and a chained man. It depicts the legend attached to this chapel: one night corsairs attacked the village, carrying off a local woman's only son, Matthew. The woman, Zgugina, ran despairing to the chapel to ask St Demetrius for help. She promised that if he intervened, she would keep an oil lamp alight for him always. As she wept and prayed, the saint rode out of the picture on his white horse, gave chase to the Turkish galley and returned with Matthew safe in his arms.

The chapel in which she prayed no longer exists. The story continues that it fell into the sea when the cliff under it collapsed in an earthquake. Sailors and fisherman are said to see the light still burning below the water. The present chapel was built in 1736 and a candle always burns in its front hall beneath a copy of a poem about the legend.

The coast beyond Drive or walk on along the rough country road beyond San Dimitri Chapel, then walk down a short track to your left and you come out onto layers of cliffs leading down to the sea, with views over countryside sprinkled with natural megaliths and trappers' huts (see page 24). Continue towards the sea and there are some interesting (and attractive) effects of weathering including wave-shaped rocks and mini cliffs worn smooth and bright yellow like weird stone-hard sand dunes. This is a great place for a **walk**.

It is also a good spot for **birdwatching**, especially for short-toed larks and fan-tailed warbler (zitting cisticola) in summer and migratory birds in spring and autumn (though you will have to share the space with hunters in autumn – see pages 24 and 48).

Sanctuary of Ta' Pinu *(just outside Għarb; bus 91;* ✆ *21556187;* e *rector@tapinu.org; www.tapinu.org;* ⊕ *06.30–12.15 daily (from 05.45 Sun) &* *13.30–19.00. For 15 Weds running up to the festa on 15 Aug* ⊕ *04.30–22.30)* Seven hundred metres out of Għarb towards Victoria stands a substantial church, alone in open countryside. The

EX-VOTO PAINTINGS AND OFFERINGS

There is a long tradition in Malta of ex-voto or votive offerings – paintings, models or objects left in a church requesting, or in thanks for, intercession by the Madonna (or occasionally some other divine figure) on behalf of a devotee in a time of trouble – illness, threat or, most frequently in Malta's history, peril at sea.

The earliest votive offerings here are maritime ex-votos, usually small naive oil paintings (usually less than 50cm across) made either by amateur individuals or specialist painters paid to produce them. The pictures are short on perspective and long on dramatic details of raging seas, figures and their plight. They tend to show a little picture of whichever Madonna has been appealed to (the Madonna comes in many forms in the Catholic Church) and often have the initials 'VFGA', 'Votum Fecit, Gratiam Acceptit' ('Vow Made, Grace Received') or simply 'EV' ('ex-voto', in fulfilment of a vow).

The tradition of ex-votos goes back to well before the arrival of the Knights, although they undoubtedly encouraged such shows of religious devotion and most surviving examples of the art are from post-1530. The oldest ex-voto in Malta with a date on it is a 1631 painting in Żabbar of the mutiny and escape of a group of Christians from slavery on a Tunisian ship.

Ex-votos are not always paintings. Some are small images or models in silver and, as the centuries have passed, real objects (such as crutches and baby clothes) and photographs have become increasingly common. The commissioning of artistic ex-votos came to an end around the middle of the 20th century apparently as a result of a liturgical directive, but the leaving of letters and relevant objects continues.

The best places to see ex-voto offerings include Ta' Pinu, Gozo (particularly modern ones); Żabbar Church Museum, Malta (see page 171); Wignacourt Museum, Rabat, Malta (see page 213); Senglea Parish Church Oratory of Christ the Redeemer (page 156); National Maritime Museum, Birgu (page 153); Sanctuary of Our Lady Tal-Ħerba, Birkirkara (page 219); and Mellieħa (page 235).

Amongst the votive pictures, letters and objects in the Ta' Pinu Sanctuary is this very modern tribute to Our Lady of Ta' Pinu:

My wife Carmen Gatt is from Victoria Gozo. When we visited Malta and Gozo in the summer of 2000 we both went to the beautiful church of Ta' Pinu. I was struck by the beauty and story of Ta' Pinu. When I came back to America I put a magnet statue of her in my security office in World Trade Center Two, 30th floor. When the day of September 11 came I know Ta' Pinu was protecting me. I escaped out of the building just in time and she guided me with her voice out of the building. I pray and thank her.

Sanctuary of Ta' Pinu is Malta's most important pilgrimage site with a remarkable collection of ex-voto offerings, testament to local belief in the intercession of the Madonna Ta' Pinu. Pope John Paul II held Mass on its *parvis* (front terrace) during his visit to Gozo in 1990.

There has been a chapel on this site for centuries. In fact, in 1575, the little church here was so old and derelict it was condemned. The story goes, however, that when the workman enlisted to demolish it struck the first blow, his arm broke. This was taken as a divine signal and the chapel was saved.

Three centuries later a local farm labourer used to stop to pray in the chapel on her way home to Għarb from the fields. One evening in 1883 Karmela Grima heard a female voice calling her from the chapel. Afraid, she nonetheless went in. Here the 'voice of Our Lady' came again telling her to say three Hail Marys, one for each day the Madonna's body lay in its tomb before her Assumption. The woman did as she was asked, then returned home where she became ill and was unable to return to the chapel for a year. When she recovered, she told a friend what had happened and he said that he too had heard voices there and prayed for his sick mother who was duly cured. Word spread and the chapel rapidly became a centre of pilgrimage and prayers for the sick.

So popular was it that the tiny chapel was overwhelmed and in the 1920s, on land donated by the de Piro family (who own Casa Rocca Piccola in Valletta; see page 129), a grand Neo-Romanesque church was built (completed 1931) in front of the old chapel, which is still intact behind the present altar. The arched interior is quite splendid. Note that the rosettes at the base of each arch are all different. All the pictures are mosaic or stonework, except the one in the old chapel, the 'miraculous' early 17th-century painting from which the voice is said to have come.

The narrow rooms either side of the altar, leading to the old chapel, are full of ex-voto offerings, from early naive paintings of ships at sea to crutches, children's clothes and photographs. There is even a letter from an American who worked in the Twin Towers (see boxed text, above).

Way of the Cross (Stations of the Cross) Opposite the church up Ta' Għammar Hill winds a peaceful Way of the Cross. The first station is by the church, the next 12, marked by life-size 3D white marble tableaux, sit alongside the path. The last station, a stone altar that stands in the middle of a hilltop amphitheatre. The walk is steep and can be a little dusty, but it is quiet even when the church is crowded. Lizards criss-cross your path, butterflies flutter in the bushes and the views from the top are spectacular. You can look across to the Ta' Ġurdan (Gordan) Lighthouse on the next hill (which can also be climbed) and down on everything else. There is a cold Kinnie machine at the bottom!

Gozo GĦARB

14

GHASRI

(*Bus 91*) Ghasri (pronounced *Asri*) is the smallest parish in Gozo, though you would not think it by looking at its huge domed church. The traditional church square has this area's usual trio of a little police station with blue lantern, a red British phone booth and an old-fashioned red letter box in the wall. The church, dedicated to Christ the Saviour, does not look modern but is in fact 20th century.

WHAT TO SEE AND DO AROUND GHASRI
Ta' Ġurdan Lighthouse/Gordan Lighthouse On a flat-topped hill above the village is the Gordan Lighthouse built in 1853. Standing 180m above sea level its beam was visible 50km away. You can walk up the hill for 360° views.

Aqueduct Shortly after turning left onto the main road to Victoria from Ghasri, you pass under one of the arches of an aqueduct more of which can be seen on your right. Built by the British in 1839–43 it brought fresh water from Għar Ilma (between here and Dwejra near Għar Abdul, see above) to the reservoirs in the Rabat/Victoria Citadel.

Ghasri Valley (Wied il-Ghasri) A fertile valley runs from the village, between Żebbuġ and Gordan Hill, down to the sea, ending in a narrow inlet flanked by high cliffs. There is a tiny pebbly beach here and the place is popular with **divers** and those looking for a **secluded swim or snorkel**. A dirt track runs along the top of the eastern cliff and there is a steep flight of over 100 steps leading down to the 'beach'.

ŻEBBUĠ

(*Bus 91*) Żebbuġ (which means 'olive'; pronounced *Zeybooj*) is a traditional little village. It sits high between two valleys with commanding views over the surrounding countryside including the Gordan Lighthouse and Ta' Pinu. The pleasant central square (actually triangular) contains a small police station with an old-fashioned British blue police lantern, a damaged red phone booth, a red letter box in the wall, a little bar-café with a few outside chairs and, of course, the church.

The parish **Church of St Mary**, with its plain façade guarded by two cannons, was built in the 1690s and it has been much embellished since. In fields facing the lighthouse, a deposit of onyx (sometimes called Gozo alabaster) was found in 1738 and the church was given an onyx makeover. It now has an onyx altar, pulpit and font, as well as onyx chandeliers and even whole confessionals of onyx!

MARSALFORN

(*Bus 21*) Once a peaceful fishing village and quiet summer retreat, this is now Gozo's main resort town (though Gozo's largest is still pretty small). Slapdash, ill-judged development has done it no favours and the beach is marred by the road running directly behind it along the head of the bay. Yet this remains a popular place to **swim** and hang out in summer. There is a stretch of coarse sand and pebble beach (much larger than at Xlendi, but shelving more steeply so less good for small children) as well as plenty of rocky and concrete shoreline from which to swim. **Water polo** is often played on the western side of the bay.

Several of Gozo's **dive companies** are based here (see *Diving*, page 266) including long-established Calypso Dives, and there are several dives in the area. **Xlendi Cruises** has its head office on the seafront at 18 Bakery Street (near Il-

MEDITERRANEAN SEA

Qbajjar
Bay

Ponta Santa Marija

N

Bradt

0 ————— 200m
0 ————— 200yds

Xwejni Bay,
Salt pans,
Żebbuġ

TRIQ SANTA MARIJA
MEWĠ IL-BAHAR
MIEGEL BAHAR

TRIQ
IS-SALINI

Ġħar Qawqla

TRIQ IL-QBAJJAR

Qolla
s-Saffra

TRIQ SANTA MARIJA

Marsalforn
Bay

ĠĦAR QAWQLA

Water
Polo

XTUT

Harbour

Atlantis
Diving

Santa Martha Hostel
TRIQ TA' WIED L-INFERN
LIFORNA
NAHLA
TRIQ IL-QOLLA (QOLLA ST)
TRIQ IL

MAGRO

Xlendi Cruises office
Il-Kartell
On Two Wheels

Calypso Hotel & Dive Centre

TRIQ IL-BARDA

TRIQ IL-QBAJJAR

Extreme
Sports

TRIQ IL-FORN
(BAKERY ST)

Beach

MARINA

Lantern Guesthouse & internet café

LIZZJU
ULISSE
TRIQ RABAT
TRIQ IL-MUNGBELL
TRIQ IL-ĠWIEH
DE-BONO
LAPSI
TRIQ IL-PLEJJU

TRIQ L-ISQOFPACE

PJAZZA SAN PAWL

TRIQ SAN ĠUŻEPP

Maria
Giovanna
Guesthouse

DAHLET TAL-ĠHAR EJJEX (Track)

TRIQ SAN PAWL
TRIQ ID-DULURI
TRIQ IS-SAJJIED

DAHLA TA' MIELHA

TRIQ IR-RABAT
Wied Marsalforn
TRIQ IL- WED

TRIQ IX-XAGHRA

Ta Frenċ, Victoria↓

Xagħra, Ramla Bay↘

Kartell restaurant; see page 262 for details) where you can book cruises and hire boats (see *Boat trips*, page 265).

Marsalforn's church dates back to the 1730s and is dedicated to **St Paul Shipwrecked**. Local tradition has it that although wrecked on the main island, Paul embarked for his onward voyage to Rome from Marsalforn (why this should be is not related!). The *festa* is celebrated on St Paul's feast day, 10 February.

Just outside Marsalforn on the road to Victoria is **Tas-Salvator** (Christ the Redeemer). The statue of Christ, arms outstretched, on the peak of the hill is a copy of the statue that overlooks Rio de Janiero. Also along this road is Gozo's top restaurant, Ta' Frenċ (see *Where to eat*, page 262).

If you leave Marsalforn in the opposite direction and head north and west along the coast, you will find interesting coastal scenery and good swimming.

XWEJNI BAY AND THE SALT PANS Leaving Marsalforn Bay to the west there is another small bay and popular summer swimming place, **Qbajjar Bay** (bus 21), before you reach **Xwejni Bay** (pronounced *Shwaynee*) – which also fills with locals (and a few foreigners) swimming in hot weather. This bay lies next to an extraordinary clay rock formation, **Qolla L-Bajda**, with a cave beneath it and a late Knights-period battery (built in 1715–16) to its seaward side.

On the other side of the bay stretch a couple of kilometres of **salt pans** below interestingly weathered cliffs of globigerina limestone. The salt pans are chequerboards of shallow rectangular pools cut into the rock, some white with dried salt, others dark with water. Seawater collects in them, either through waves in winter or by being deliberately filled, then as the sun shines the water evaporates leaving the salt crystals, which are collected and stored in the rooms cut into the cliff faces before being sold as Gozo sea salt. Salt has been produced in this way here since Roman times and some of these salt pans certainly go back to the 19th century. They are fun to explore (but please don't tread *in* them or you may contaminate the salt).

You can **drive or walk** along the coast here all the way to Żebbuġ, although the road gets quite narrow and rough in places as you turn inland towards the village. Or you can keep going along the coast until the road turns to a track (still drivable) which leads you to the head of **Wied Il-Ghasri** (see above).

XAGHRA

(*Buses 64, 65*) Xagħra (pronounced *Shara*) means 'wilderness' or 'scrubland'; though the town of this name is anything but. Gozo's largest town outside the capital is a very pleasant place with several visitor attractions. Its fine central square is dominated (of course) by the parish church, the **Basilica of the Nativity of Our Lady**, an early 19th-century building on the site of a much earlier church, with an ornate marble interior. The church is nicknamed Il-Bambina after its 19th-century French white marble statue of the Madonna. Close by is the **Oleander Restaurant** (see *Where to eat*, page 263) with the colourful plants that give it its name brightening up the square in summer.

WHAT TO SEE AND DO

Ġgantija Temples (*Heritage Malta;* ☏ *21553194;* e *info@heritagemalta.org; www.heritagemalta.org;* ☉ *09.00–17.00 daily (last entry 16.30); €8 adults, €6 over-60s/students/children aged 12–17, €4 children 6–11, children under 6 go free; ticket inc entry to Ta' Kola Windmill, see page 288*) Ġgantija (pronounced *Jiganteeya*, meaning 'gigantic' or 'of the giants') is one of the oldest temple sites, giving its name to the first phase of temple building. First excavated in 1827, two temples stand next to each other surrounded by one massive boundary wall. They also share a broad raised forecourt with panoramic views. As you stand with your back to the temples you have Xewkija and its Rotunda on your right, Nadur to the left and in between, Nuffara Hill which was settled in the Bronze Age. The rural area around Ġgantija, Ta' Hamet, is one of the most fertile in Gozo. The farming people who built Ġgantija did not chose this spot for nothing.

You approach the temples from behind. The walls here have some of the biggest megaliths found on Malta, including one thought to weigh some 50 tons. Small wonder legend has it that the temples were built by a giantess. She is said to have eaten broad beans that (like Popeye with his spinach) made her so strong that she could carry her baby on one arm and a megalith on the other.

The outside of the temples is built of the darker, rougher and tougher coralline limestone, while decorative parts of the interiors are of the lighter, yellower, smoother but more easily weathered globigerina limestone (the one from which most domestic Maltese architecture is built). This had to be brought from about a kilometre away. No mean feat without machinery of any kind.

In front of the temples is an **audio information unit** with an introduction in six languages and a helpful ground plan of the temples. There are also **toilets** and a small **shop**. Ġgantija is due to get a proper visitor centre in around 2012.

South Temple The first temple you reach, the one on your left as you face the remains, is the South Temple. It is the larger and older of the two, having been

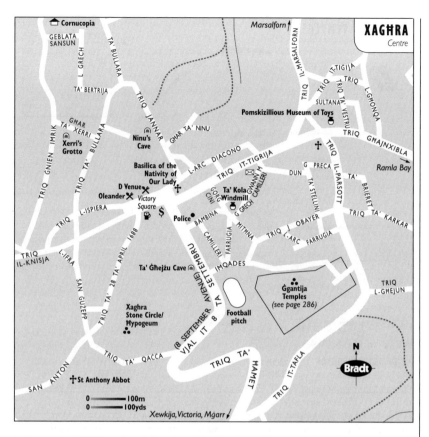

Marsalforn

Cornucopia

GEBLATA SANSUN

TA' BERTRIJA

GHAR TA' XERRI

Xerri's Grotto

Ninu's Cave

GHAR TA' NINU

Pomskizillious Museum of Toys

Basilica of the Nativity of Our Lady

D Venue

Oleander

Victory Square

Ta' Kola Windmill

DUN

G PRECA

Ramla Bay

Police

Ta' Għejżu Cave

IMQADES

Xaghra Stone Circle/ Hypogeum

Football pitch

Ġgantija Temples (see page 286)

St Anthony Abbot

Xewkija, Victoria, Mġarr

0 ———— 100m
0 ———— 100yds

N

Bradt

TRIQ L-GHEJUN

built around 3500BC. The left side of the façade, with **vertical orthostats** topped with horizontal stones, stands over 6m tall, higher than any other surviving temple wall apart from a section of the wall of the inner (second) left apse of this same temple. These megaliths have not been rebuilt or repositioned. They have stood undisturbed at this height for some 5,500 years. The ugly scaffolding is here to ensure that this remains the case! A structural study is under way to assess whether a less intrusive form of support could be employed.

To the right of the temple doorway is the remains of the **façade 'bench'** and to the left are a few stone spheres of the type some experts believe were used to roll the megaliths into place. The **entrance** itself is over a huge threshold stone and is of the trilithon-within-a-trilithon type (see *Chapter 4*, page 79), as is the interior doorway. In the entranceway on the left is a **shallow bowl** which may have held liquid (perhaps for purification purposes).

The doorway has four holes on either side, possibly for bars that could block the entrance, and might have been draped with an animal skin or other curtain. Inside, the passageway is paved with stone (reddened in places by fire) and the walls would once have been smoothed with plaster painted with red ochre. Bits of this plaster were found in the **first left apse** with the low window, an 'oracle hole' (oddly near the ground prompting suggestions that the stone was reused from a different position). The presence of the painted plaster suggests strongly that at least the main part of the temple was originally roofed; such decoration would not have survived being open to the elements.

14

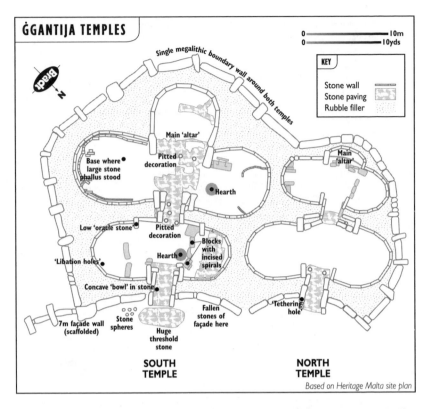

KEY

Stone wall
Stone paving
Rubble filler

Single megalithic boundary wall around both temples

Main 'altar'

Base where
large stone
phallus stood

Pitted
decoration

Hearth

Main
'altar'

Low 'oracle stone'

Pitted
decoration

Blocks
with
incised
spirals

Hearth

'Libation holes'

Concave 'bowl' in stone

Tethering
hole

7m façade wall
(scaffolded)

Stone
spheres

Huge
threshold
stone

Fallen
stones of
façade here

SOUTH
TEMPLE

NORTH
TEMPLE

Based on Heritage Malta site plan

In the **first right apse** is a pattern of construction and decoration very similar to that in the first left apse at Tarxien South (see page 173) – showing the close connections between the temple peoples of the two islands. There are two globigerina stones here decorated with spirals that are now so weathered that the patterns can only be made out by looking very carefully or when the light is at the right angle, a clear demonstration of why most of the decorated stones are now in the archaeological museums in Valletta and Victoria.

You now come to a threshold stone with pitted decoration on it. This divides the first pair of apses from the inner part of the temple. Step over it to reach the second pair of apses. The **left apse** here has a construction of three connected 'altars', originally three trilithons and four uprights. The additional supporting stones in the middle of two of the trilithons are modern additions needed to support the topstones. The snake pillar (now in the Gozo Archaeological Museum; see page 121) was found here, as was the large phallic symbol which once stood on the small stone circle that is still visible in the floor.

In the **fifth apse** you can see that some of the stone at the top of the wall is grey while the rest is more orangey in colour. The grey parts were exposed before excavation in the 19th century, while the rest lay buried. The **main altar** in the middle of the central apse has pitted decoration that is less dense than usual. It has been suggested this could be because it is of an earlier date. Here were found the two lifelike stone heads now in the Gozo Archaeological Museum.

North Temple Sometime around 3000BC part of the north wall of the South Temple was demolished to make way for a second smaller, simpler temple with four apses and a central niche. The boundary wall probably originally ran just around the South Temple and may have been broken and rebuilt to go around the new building, which would explain the kink that is still visible in the wall where the two temples meet.

The **entrance** to this temple, in a concave façade, has a clear threshold stone and a 'tethering point' hole through the rock on the left. The **first two apses** are very plain but beautifully constructed and where smaller blocks are seen here they are not reconstruction, but original. Up another step through the next doorway are two more apses and a central 'altar' with a broken topstone.

At the time of writing the North Temple is closed to the public but it should reopen by the time you are reading this with new walkways to protect it.

The North Cave Just outside the Ġgantija complex on the right of the path as you are leaving, is a cave. Unearthed in 1947, it contained huge amounts of smashed Tarxien period (3000–200BC) pottery. It was probably originally a rock-cut tomb (earlier pottery was also found with fragments of human skull) but seems to have been used as the local dump in the late Temple period.

Charlie Vella's organic produce As you enter and leave the temple site (just before you have to buy a ticket) you walk along the wall of Charlie Vella's orchard where (usually 09.00–16.30) he and his Australian wife sell their excellent organic jams and honey: prickly pear, pomegranate, lemon, fig and orange jam as well as carob syrup (good for coughs) and thyme honey. Small, packable jars cost €2.

Xaghra Stone Circle/Hypogeum (Brochtorff/Brocktorff Circle) (*Bookings via the Ġgantija ticket office (see above) or Heritage Malta Gozo HQ:* ✎ *21564188;* e *info@ heritagemalta.org; www.heritagemalta.org;* €*5 adults,* €*3.50 over-60s/students/children aged 12–17,* €*2.50 children under 12*)

Getting there On the road out of Xagħra towards Xewkija/Victoria, past the children's playground, you follow a street to the right, Triq Ta' Qaċċa, signed to St Anthony the Abbot. On the right is Razzett Xemxi farmhouse and down its right-hand side is a path. Walk round to the back of the house and turn left across a small field (taking care not to damage crops) and the wire gate of the 'circle' is ahead of you. A member of Heritage Malta staff will unlock the site for you.

Exploring the site 'Circle' is something of a misnomer. There was once a circle of stones here, actually the remains of a low perimeter wall, and it can be seen in an 1820s sketch by Charles Brochtorff, a copy of which is in the Gozo Archaeological Museum (see page 274). Hence the site's other name, the Brochtorff Circle. These stones were reused in the building of neighbouring walls and houses later in the 19th century and what you see now is the excavated remains of a hypogeum, an underground burial complex that would once have been a smaller and rougher version of the Ħal Saflieni Hypogeum (see page 176).

Made by extending natural caves, the Xagħra Hypogeum is of a similar date to Ħal Saflieni (4000–2500BC). The site doesn't look like much at first, but look closely and you can spot an 'altar' arrangement in the middle. It was in this area that the remarkable group of **'stick' figurines** now in the Gozo Archaeological Museum was found. The delicate **double 'fat lady' statue** in the museum was also found here. There are a few megaliths, and it is clear that there were once underground 'rooms'. Be aware that some of the stone-coloured lumps on the site are in fact sandbags holding up elements of the structure.

The Xagħra Hypogeum's main contribution to historical knowledge is not in what you can see here but in what was found during the excavations of 1987 to

14

1994 and the fact that the items were undisturbed and could therefore be dated in a way that was not possible at the Ħal Saflieni Hypogeum. On the other hand, due to the fragile geology of the Xagħra plateau, the Gozo site itself is in a much poorer state. Cambridge archaeologist and expert on this site, Caroline Malone, is quoted as saying that while at Ħal Saflieni we have a well-preserved container, but have lost much of information about the contents; at Xagħra we have the opposite.

Other prehistoric sites in and around Xagħra Although Ġgantija is the only temple on Gozo to have remained at all intact, there were once other temples on the island and there are little clumps of megaliths and individual standing stones, particularly in the Xagħra area where there seems to have been an extensive settlement around Ġgantija. Most of the sites are very small, difficult to identify and don't look like much. **Ta' Għejżu Cave**, however, is marked with a sign on a piece of wasteland on the main road into Xagħra (8th September Avenue). It is on your left just after the right turn for Ġgantija. The hole in the ground that is the entrance to the cave is in the middle with a smaller secondary opening at the corner. Ġgantija-phase pottery was found here in 1936 and there was once a megalithic structure above it. The cave lies between Ġgantija and the Xagħra stone circle.

Ta' Kola Windmill (*Heritage Malta:* ☏ *21561071;* e *info@heritagemalta.org; www.heritagemalta.org;* ⊕ *09.00–17.00 (last admission 16.30); entry inc with Ġgantija ticket – see page 284*) Built in 1725 this is one of very few remaining 18th-century windmills. The Knights, conscious of the importance of flour, had a special foundation for the building of windmills which were then leased to millers. When the wind was strong enough, the miller would sound a *bronja* (a large shell) to let villagers know to bring their grain for milling. This windmill, used until about a century ago, is named after its last miller Nikola (Kola) Grech. It has been very well preserved and you can climb up the narrowing spiral staircase to the top and see the whole mechanism including the massive millstones (as well as good views from the tiny window). The lower floor is furnished to recreate the miller's spartan living quarters.

Xerri's Grotto (*Pronounced Sherry's; Triq l'Għar Ta' Xerri/Xerri's Grotto St (from main square follow Church St which is to the right opposite the church, at crossroads turn right into Bullara St, then first left);* ☏ *21560572;* ⊕ *approx 10.00–18.30 daily;* €*2.50*) Ring the doorbell of this ordinary house near Xagħra's main square and follow the owner through her home and down a narrow stone spiral staircase into the ground to visit the cave beneath. Discovered by the grandfather of the present owner in 1923 when he was digging a well, the cave now has a little path and electric lights so you can see the stalagmites, stalactites, rock formations and coloured minerals. It isn't large, but it is quite fun. Nearby on Triq Jannar is another house with a cave beneath – **Ninu's Cave** – but this is less attractive.

Pomskizillious Museum of Toys (*10 Ġnien Xibla St;* ☏ *21562489 or 21567111;* e *sueandedwin@vol.net.mt; www.starwebmalta.com;* ⊕ *May–Oct 10.30–13.00 Mon–Sat, Nov & April Thu–Sat, Dec–Mar Sat only, Jun–Sep 16.00–18.00;* €*2.40 adults,* €*1.40 over-60s,* €*1.10 children/students*) This tiny museum of 19th- and early 20th-century toys includes 'the world's smallest doll' – just a thumb-nail long, made of wood with jointed limbs. There are also several doll's houses, one with wishbone furniture; an attractive Victorian découpage screen and a waxwork of Edward Lear at his desk. Lear visited Gozo in 1866 and described its landscape as 'pomskizillious'; hence the museum's name.

Chapel of St Anthony Abbot There has been a chapel here since at least 1400 though it was rebuilt in 1601. It served as the first parish church of Xagħra until 1692. The 1816 painting (by Dun Salv Bondi) depicts St Anthony with the people of Xagħra living in tents during the plague of 1814 which killed 104 people and led to items from the church being burnt in an attempt at disinfection.

The chapel had to be extensively repaired after World War II and since 1948 its *festa* on 17 January, being the feast of St Anthony, patron saint of the animal kingdom, has included the blessing of pets and animals. At the end of the usual *festa* procession the priest blesses creatures from cattle to guinea pigs giving each owner a souvenir picture of St Anthony, a bag of oats and a rusk.

RAMLA BAY

(*Bus 42, Jul–Sep only*) This lovely red sandy bay is Malta's best beach and so unsurprisingly Gozo's most popular – known locally as Ramla il-Hamra ('the red sandy beach'!). It gets quite crowded in summer but that doesn't change the gentle slope into clear blue water ideal for **swimming**, with rocks at one end for **snorkelling** around. Much of the beach, like many in Malta, has stones at the water's edge so covering for the feet is helpful especially for kids.

You can **park** on the road leading up to the beach (the earlier you arrive the closer you get!). There is also a **taxi** stand here. Two outdoor **cafés** (May–Oct) serve pizzas, snacks, basic meals and ice cream from Portacabins just off the road before the beach. The one further from the beach tends to be marginally the better and a little less busy. By the taxi stand there are also two flagpoles. If a red flag is flying then there are rip currents; a purple flag means 'pests' (usually jellyfish). Either way it is inadvisable to swim. If this happens, head for a bay on the other side of the island (eg: Xlendi or Mġarr ix-Xini).

There is a **manmade reef** just out to sea built by the Knights to block invading fleets. This can be seen as a dark line from the viewing platform of Calypso's Cave (see page 289). The Knights also drilled out large cone-shaped holes in boulders at either end of the beach to use as makeshift mortars called *fougasses*. The one at the far end of the beach from the road can still be clearly seen – and indeed explored (though best done with something on your feet – the rocks are sharp).

The Knights also built a **battery** at the near end of the beach on top of the foundations of a **Roman villa**. The villa was excavated in 1910–12 by Temi Zammit (see boxed text, page 176) revealing a once substantial structure of at least 19 rooms including marble floors and a heated bathing complex. There is nothing to see at the site now, but finds from here can be seen in the Gozo Archaeological Museum in the Citadel (see page 274).

The white **statue of the Madonna** that stands in the middle of the beach is an ex-voto offering from three 19th-century fishermen who, caught in a storm, promised to build a shrine if they returned safe to land.

CALYPSO'S CAVE (*Accessed by road from Xagħra (well signed) or on foot from Ramla Beach; free*) High above Ramla Bay, is 'Calypso's Cave'. Callimachus (310/5–240BC), Hellenistic writer-critic and librarian at Alexandria, identified Gozo as Homer's island of Ogygia where Odysseus (Ulysses) washed up on his way home from the Trojan War and spent seven years under the spell of the sea nymph Calypso. The Gozitans have taken up this identification with enthusiasm. Whether or not this cave has anything to do with the *Odyssey*, evidence has been found of Bronze Age occupation and it is worth a visit just for the views. Clamber down rough narrow steps into the cave and then out onto a rock to look out at the sea (keep hold of young children), or just stand on the viewing platform looking down over the sweep of Ramla Bay with the white Madonna shining against the red sand and the dark line of the Knights' defensive reef running through the blue sea.

NADUR

(*Buses 42 & 43*) Sitting high on a rocky plateau, Nadur is appropriately named from the Maltese word *nadar* – 'to keep watch'. The vast parish **Church of St Peter and St Paul**, with two cannons and two saints guarding its ornate marble-filled interior, was begun in 1760 though its aisle and façade are early 20th-century. The *festa* is around 20 June. The church sits in a traditional village square with its miniature police station (with blue lantern) and British red telephone box, as well as a café, shops and ATM, and around the corner a small maritime museum.

WHAT TO SEE AND DO

Maritime Museum (*Kelinu Grima Maritime Museum, Parish Priest St/Triq Il-Kapillan;* ✆ *21565226 or 21551649;* ◷ *usually 10.00–15.00 Mon–Sat;* €*2.33 adults,* €*1.15 children*) One man's collection of maritime memorabilia gathered over 65 years was donated to the parish priest in 1999 and turned into a small museum. Amongst many photographs and model ships is a shoulder strap that belonged to Lord Mountbatten (worn in Malta in 1949), a 1942 letter from Churchill commending the bravery of one Joseph Grima, a small block of wood from HMS *Victory*, an 1803 letter ordering the burning of USS *Philadelphia* which had been taken by *The Pasha of Tripoli*, pictures of the Gozo ferry from when it was a wooden sailing boat to today, and an old canvas diving suit with lead boots.

Kenuna Tower and botanical garden On the edge of town is a little botanical garden newly created around the renovated Kenuna Tower. The tower was built by the British in 1848 when the telegraph arrived on the islands. This spot had long been used by the Knights to burn bonfires for communication with Comino and Malta and, after years of neglect, the tower is once again being used for communications and is topped with a metal triangle of ultra-modern equipment. As you might expect, the views from here are fabulous: Mġarr and its church, Fort Chambrai, Comino and Malta, Xagħra, and Xewkija with its rotunda are all clearly seen.

Mekren's traditional bakery (*Hanaq St (signed to Ramla);* ✆ *21552342;* m *99858249;* ◷ *09.30–18.30 roughly, but baking from the early hours*) Whether you are hungry or not take a look in here to see a truly traditional Maltese bakery at work. If you are hungry, order Malta's own version of pizza, *ftira* (or just try the normal pizza) in advance. Take a peep into the cavernous wood-burning oven into which the breads are placed with long wooden spatulas.

SAN BLAS

(*No public transport*) A short drive north from Nadur is this beautiful red-sandy bay at the end of one of the most fertile valleys in Gozo. A mini Ramla just along the coast from its larger neighbour, San Blas is more enclosed by cliffs and greenery and much less crowded due to the very steep (repeat, *very* steep) track you have to walk down (and then up!) to get to the beach. It is well worth it as long as there are no jellies about to stop you swimming when you arrive hot and sweaty at the bottom. Like Ramla there can be rip currents here and there is no flag system to warn you so check with locals, especially if weather has been windy, and keep young children and weaker swimmers in their depth. You can park at the top of the steep track and there is a small snack bar at the bottom.

The Maltese are very proud of their bread. Hobż Malti is a crusty sour dough made of durum wheat with a soft inside. Traditionally, each village had a windmill and a baker who cooked the bread in a wood-burning oven. A few of these remain – including the Ta' Kola windmill in Xagħra and Mekren's bakery, Nadur (see pages 298 and 290 respectively). Bread is increasingly produced with modern equipment but daily fresh bread is still regarded as a necessity by most Maltese and it is often delivered by van first thing in the morning.

Bread has been a staple in Malta since the Bronze Age when the Mediterranean triad – bread (grain), olive oil and wine – first became established. Archaeologist Reuben Grima, in his book *The Making of Malta*, points out that these products were probably favoured because the plants from which they are grown thrive in the Mediterranean climate, they ripen at different times of year so a small workforce could produce all three, they can be stored (in case of harvest failure the following year) and all are transportable.

This last was of great importance for Malta whose population rapidly outstripped its ability to grow grain. Malta has not been self-sufficient for many centuries. Today, bread flour is bought by a central co-operative serving all bakers, and comes from as far afield as Iran and the USA. Even in Roman times grain was imported from Sicily, as it continued to be right through the time of the Knights and beyond.

So concerned were the Order not to run out of grain in times of siege that they built huge underground granaries (*fossae* or grain silos) in their fortified cities. The round lids covering these can be seen outside Fort St Elmo in Valletta and in Floriana and you can now walk inside three of the silos in the Gozo Citadel. Those in Floriana were used until the 1980s when a modern grain terminal was built on the Kordin promontory on the Grand Harbour. Today most agriculture on the islands is concentrated on fruit and vegetable production and almost all cereals come from abroad. The bread itself, however, remains Hobż Malti.

Along the coast, on the cliffs between here and Daħlet Qorrot (some 3km from Nadur) is the **Ta' Sopu Tower** (It-Torri Isopu, also known as San Blas Tower and Torre Nuova). It was built in 1667 under Grand Master Nicolas Cotoner. The original staircase to the first-floor drawbridge has gone and the walls are quite weathered. It is not generally open to the public.

DAHLET QORROT BAY

(*No public transport*) A popular swimming spot crowded with locals on summer weekends, Daħlet Qorrot Bay (pronounced *Darlet Or-rot*) is reached by road through a fertile valley to the northeast of Nadur. It is little visited by tourists and the small pebbly beach is marred by quite a bit of dried seaweed. There is, however, good clear water, also accessible from the rocks and down steps from an area of concrete. Caves in the rock face have been extended and converted by local fishermen into a few boathouses.

QALA

(*Buses 42 & 43*) The village of Qala (pronounced *Ahla* and meaning 'port', of which there was probably once one at Hondoq ir-Rummien) is high up to the northeast of Mġarr. It is Gozo's easternmost village with uninterrupted views over the channel to Malta. The little church, known as Il-Madonna tal-blat ('Madonna of

A close relation of *boules*, bowls and *pétanque*, *boċċi* developed in Italy where it is called *bocce*, but the Maltese version is a little different. It is played by two teams of one, two or three players on a marked pitch of coarse sand (or a makeshift flat area of gravel, sand, soil or short-cut grass).

A team of one or two people has seven *boċċi* – three small round balls and four much larger cylinders. A team of three has eleven *boċċi* – three balls and eight cylinders. One team's *boċċi* are red (Team R), the other's green (Team G). There is also one very small marker ball – the jack.

The jack is thrown at the start of each frame and the aim of the game is to get your *boċċi* closest to the jack. This is done both by simply rolling the *boċċi* and by knocking the opposing team's *boċċi* out of the way – or indeed knocking the jack closer to your own *boċċi*. Balls and cylinders can be used interchangeably but the game usually starts with a ball and it is the cylinders – being larger and heavier – that are generally used for displacing opponents' *boċċi*.

HOW TO PLAY

1 Whichever team wins the toss of a coin – let's say Team R – starts.
2 Team R throws the jack. It must land between 15 and 37ft away from the players. If the jack is thrown out of area twice then the other team gets to throw it and start the game. During the game the jack can be knocked anywhere on the pitch and the game continues, unless it lands less than 5ft from the players in which case play stops and the frame starts again.
3 Team R rolls a *bocca* ball trying to get it as close as possible to the jack.
4 Team G takes a turn, trying to get a *bocca* closer than Team R's. Team G continues to roll *boċċi* (balls or cylinders) until it gets one of its *boċċi* closer than Team R's (or runs out of *boċċi*). Play then passes back to Team R.
5 Teams take turns in this way switching over each time a team gets a *bocca* closer than the closest of its opponents' *boċċi*. This continues until both teams have run out of *boċċi*.

Scoring When all the *boċċi* have been used the team with the closest ball to the jack wins and gets a point for each *bocca* (ball or cylinder) that is closer to the jack than the other team's closest ball. If each team's closest ball is the same distance from the jack no points are awarded. The winning team starts the next frame and play continues until one team reaches 21 points and wins the match.

Where to play Xerri Il-Bukket pitch, Qala on Gozo (see below) or games are organised for tourists at the **Buġibba Boċċi Club** (on the promenade next to McDonald's, ask the barman; ✆ 21577362; m 99442919) most days between 11.00 and 13.00.

---

the Rocks') faces Comino and tradition has it that this was so that the people of Comino could be involved in a Mass even when weather prevented a priest from reaching the smaller island.

High on the cliffs on the edge of Qala above Mġarr is a promenade commanding panoramic views across the channel to Comino and the Blue Lagoon, Cominotto and beyond, as well as down over Mġarr and the ferries coming and going. There is a bar-pizzeria here (*Xerri il-Bukkett, Żewwieqa Rd, Qala; pizzas around €5*) that has its own *boċċi* pitch (see boxed text above). Balls are provided and if nobody is playing you can help yourself and have a game.

HONDOQ IR-RUMMIEN BAY

A few minutes' drive from Qala (walkable in under an hour – but beware of the heat in summer) – is Hondoq Bay (pronounced *Hondok*). Directly opposite Comino's Blue Lagoon, this bay is very popular with locals for summer **swimming**. It has a small beach of coarse sand, with smoother sand at the water's edge (so it is good for families) as well as a concrete area with steps into the water and a jumping point much enjoyed by older children. It is not picturesque, but the water is crystal clear and the swimming good. It is also used by divers (especially the less experienced). There is a **café** and **parking**. At the time of writing there is a move to build a massive development here. A small-scale cleaning up of the place would, in the opinion of many, be greatly preferable.

XEWKIJA

(*Buses 42 & 43*) The oldest parish in Gozo outside Victoria (1678), Xewkija (meaning 'thorny wasteland' in Arabic and pronounced *Shewkeeya*) also has the most famous church in Gozo besides the Citadel cathedral: the parish **Church of St John the Baptist** known to all as the **Rotunda**.

THE ROTUNDA (*Church:* ⏁ *05.00–12.00 & 15.00–20.00 (approx), museum & lift 09.30–12.00 Mon–Sat – except if a Mass is in progress; free entry*) This huge church, vies with Mosta (see page 225) to be the largest dome in Malta and both churches claim to have the third-largest unsupported dome in Europe (after St Peter's in Rome and St Paul's in London). For the record, Mosta Dome is wider, Xewkija is taller. The dome here is 27m in external diameter and 75m high and it can be seen from all over Gozo. Information leaflets in several languages are available inside the main door.

The smooth white limestone interior can accommodate three times the population of the village. It is dominated by vast ionic columns, eight of which have ferroconcrete cores supporting the 45,000-ton dome. The church was built between 1951 and 1971 with contributions of money and labour from the people of the parish. It was constructed over the much smaller 17th-century Baroque parish church which was only removed once the new building was complete. Many parts of the old church, including stone carvings, altars, altarpieces and marble tombs, can be seen in the **Sculpture Museum** (⏁ *by volunteers approx 10.00–12.00 & 14.30–16.30*) to the left of the modern altar. The coloured marble altar you pass here is the main altar of the old Baroque church.

Next to the museum is a **lift** (€2) up to a broad **balcony** that runs all the way round the base of the dome (older children should like this). Stand next to vast stone scrolls and above the main door and admire views of Gozo's other spires and domes, as well as the surrounding countryside.

The **feast of John the Baptist** is on 24 June and is celebrated on the nearest weekend.

MUNXAR

(*Buses 50 & 51*) Munxar (pronounced *Moonshar*) village is home to some 700 souls and is centred on a very open church square, with an unusually small Baroque-style, early 20th-century parish church. The last village in Gozo to become an autonomous parish, it lies just south of Rabat and beyond it is the scenic road to Xlendi. The church is dedicated to St Paul but Munxar does not celebrate its *festa* on his feast day in February, but at a time more conducive to outdoor entertainment, the third weekend of May.

SANNAT

(*Buses 50 & 51*) An attractive little village with an early 18th-century parish **Church of St Margaret Martyr** (*festa* 20 July), Sannat is chiefly known as the gateway to the Ta' Ċenċ plateau and cliffs. On the outskirts of the village is the **Ta' Ċenċ Hotel** (see page 259).

TA' ĊENĊ

A marvellous place for a **walk**, the Ta' Ċenċ plateau (pronounced *Ta Chench*) of rough rock and garigue, is home to many of Gozo's most interesting flora and fauna as well as commanding fabulous views off the cliffs that plunge up to 145m into the sea. (Bits of them occasionally literally plunge, particularly in winter, so do not go too close to the edge!). If you walk off the tracks you will want closed shoes with a solid sole as the rocks are sharp and thorny plants common. Lizards are plentiful here and if you are lucky you might even see a black whip snake (the most common of Malta's snake species, all of which are non-poisonous).

This is also a good place for **birdwatching**. Cory's shearwaters nest in the cliffs and can be heard calling and seen through binoculars at dusk in summer. Also in summer there are short-toed larks, corn buntings, spectacled warblers, pallid swifts and Malta's national bird, the blue rock thrush. In spring and autumn, this is a great place to see migrating species as they fly over or make landfall for the first time in hundreds of miles. Be warned, however, that in autumn you are likely to be sharing the cliffs with bird hunters (whose stone hides and used cartridges are here all year round). The EU outlaws spring hunting so this season should be better (see *Hunting*, see pages 24 and 48).

The hunters' many stone huts make it difficult to differentiate the **prehistoric and ancient remains** that dot this rocky plateau from more modern construction in the same materials. However, a couple of sites can be identified. Follow the signs from Sannat to the cliffs and go down the track past some buildings, continuing for about 150m. To the left of the road on the edge looking out at panoramic views towards Xewkija (and the Rotunda) is a small low **dolmen** – a horizontal capstone supported on other blocks. This was probably part of a Bronze-Age tomb complex of which two or three other tombs survive.

The plateau is also criss-crossed with **cart ruts**. Most are very hard to see, but if you walk towards the edge of the cliff along the back boundary wall of the hotel (past their limestone *trulli* – round huts) you will find a patch of open rock about 20m in from the cliff edge (best not to go any closer) with clear cart ruts running across it.

MĠARR IX-XINI

(*No public transport*) Down a narrow, pot-holed road from Sannat or Xewkija (only attempt the final ramp if you are sure your car will make it up again!) is the steep-sided inlet of Mġarr ix-Xini (pronounced *Imjar Ish-Sheeni*). Some of the best **snorkelling** in Gozo is to be had here as well as a usually uncrowded place to **swim** and **dive**, a **historic tower** (open to the public) and a tiny **café** serving excellent fresh fish dinners (see *Where to* eat, page 262). It is also thought to be the place where the Turks hid their galleys while they embarked the captured Gozitans in 1551.

At the end of a fertile valley the road dips down to the head of a long inlet. There is a small stony beach and rocks to swim and jump off. In summer, buoys mark two swimming areas, including a lengthy strip along one side of the rocky gorge. Boats are not allowed inside the buoys.

The fish life here is wonderful. You can see half a dozen species without even getting your face wet, just standing still in a couple of feet of water where sand meets stones on the seabed just off the beach on your left. Snorkelling adds numerous other fish, including tiny luminous blue ones and orange-and-blue peacock wrasse. Fish hide in cracks in the rocks, as do sea urchins, and there is plenty of underwater plant life.

MĠARR IX-XINI TOWER (*Wirt Għawdex, Gozo Heritage, an NGO, head office: Dar il-Lunzjata, Wied il-Lunzjata, Rabat;* ☎ *Jay Jones (British volunteer) 21563839;* e *info@wirtghawdex.org; www.wirtghawdex.org;* ⊕ *10.30–13.30 at least Tue & Sat, but hopefully more often. A flag flies when it is open.*) Climb up the rock-cut steps behind the beach on the opposite side from the road and follow the path – between wild fennel plants – along the rocky side of the inlet until you get to the tower looking out to open sea. Built in 1661 as part of Grand Master de Redin's coastal defence scheme, it also protected against smugglers (who may still use the inlet out of season). It was reused as a watchtower in World War II.

The little rock off the coast is **Ras in-Newwiela**. *Newwel* roughly translates as 'hand over, pass on', said to be the Turks call as they loaded Gozitan slaves from this rock onto their galleys a century before the tower was built.

The tower is entered by a stone staircase to a **first-floor drawbridge**. Inside is a **freshwater well** (to the left) and a **spiral staircase** in the thickness of the wall leading to the roof with two cannons (in a glass cupboard on the first floor is an 8cm limestone sphere that is probably a Knights' cannonball). Unusually there is also an armaments store and a guard's room on the roof, which may also have acted as a protective barrier in case of landward attack. There are great views here, including along the coast towards Mġarr. You can **walk** from here along the coast to Fort Chambrai (and thence Mġarr Harbour) in about 1¼ hours.

XLENDI

(*Bus 87*) On the road down into Xlendi (pronounced *Shlendi*) is **La Grotta disco** (☎ *21551149;* m *99493748;* e *info@lagrottaleisure.com; www.lagrottaleisure.com*), the place to be for the young of Gozo on a summer Saturday night. It is mercifully outside the village which is a surprisingly peaceful place, especially when compared with Gozo's other resort town, Marsalforn, on the north coast. Xlendi also has the great advantage that in summer the seafront is a promenade of cafés, restaurants and small hotels with the road and parking banished to behind the first row of buildings.

The bay is wonderful for **swimming**. There is a very small pebbly beach, not ideal for sunbathing, but offering a gently sloping entry into the water that is fine for all ages. There is also a long stretch of rocks down the Western side of the bay where sunbathers lounge and from which you can swim straight into deep water. Buoys mark the swimming areas. Stay inside them and you do not run the risk of being run over by a boat.

There is great **snorkelling** too – all sorts of fish readily visible in the shallows – and the bay is a popular place for **diving**, good for beginners as well as the more experienced. Xlendi is home to several of the island's dive companies including two of the most established – Moby Dives and St Andrew's Divers Cove (see *Diving*, pages 66, 90 and 266). The **Xlendi Cruises** kiosk organises all sorts of scheduled and tailor-made boat trips (see *Boat trips*, page 265) and rents out pedaloes and simple canoes.

You will find plenty of services in Xlendi including several good restaurants (see *Where to eat*, page 263), cafés, small fast-food outlets, agents ready to book you

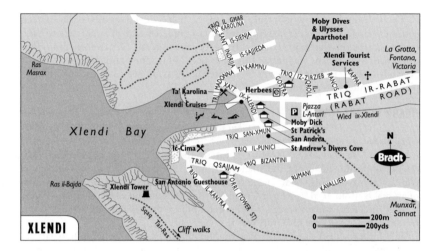

XLENDI

outings, an HSBC with ATM, and an internet café (see page 264). But be warned: unlike almost every other village in Gozo, there is no food shop. If you are self-catering you will be dependent on the small and rather expensive visiting grocery van or you will need to go into Victoria to shop (only 10–15 minutes if you have a car).

XLENDI TOWER At the far end of the rock swimming area, you can walk out to Xlendi Tower, which is also very clearly seen from boats as it guards the entrance to the bay. Built in 1650 in the reign of Grand Master Lascaris, this is the oldest free-standing coastal watchtower on Gozo. It was intended to defend not only against the Turks but also against smugglers and quarantine evaders. It continued to be manned until the 1870s. It is due for restoration with a view to opening it to the public, but for now can only be seen from the outside. It offers a great **viewpoint** and a perfect place for **birders** to set up a telescope to see shearwaters rafting at dusk before they fly in to their nests in the cliffs.

Appendix I

LANGUAGE

With English as one of Malta's official languages, spoken by all but a very few, you will not need a phrase book to get around. It does, however, help to be able to pronounce words and particularly place names in a way that will be understood.

PRONUNCIATION GUIDE Letters we do not have in English or that are pronounced differently:

Written	Pronounced
ċ	'ch' as in 'chop' (note: there is no 'c' without an accent so the accent is often left out. All 'c's in Maltese are pronounced 'ch')
ġ	'j' as in 'jump'
g	'g' like an English hard 'g', as in 'go' (eg: Ġgantija where the first 'g' is soft due to the accent, while the second 'g' is hard so the word is pronounced *jiganteeya*)
għ	Not sounded eg: *għar* (meaning cave) is pronounced *are*
ħ	'h' as in 'house'
h	Hard as in 'ha!' – including when it comes at the end of a word. Or sometimes unsounded.
j	'y' as in 'yam'
q	Not sounded when followed by a vowel although it does give the vowel a hard edge (it is as if you start to say 'k' but do not actually). Eg: Ta' Qali is pronounced Ta 'ali (or '*arli*) with a hard edge on the 'a'.
	At the end of a word or before a consonant it is pronounced a bit more like a 'k' eg: Ħondoq is pronounced *Hondok*. (Just to confuse things, the British colonials in Malta always pronounced 'q' as a 'k', so Ta' Qali was *Takali*)
m	As in English, but when followed by another consonant at the start of a word can be more like 'im', eg: Mtarfa is said almost as *Imtarfa*.
r	May be a little rolled as in Italian
x	'sh' as in 'she'
ż	Soft, as in 'zoo' or 'buzz'
z	A 'ts' sound like in 'pants' (eg: 'pizza') or a 'ds' sound as in suds

The vowels

a	Can be long as in 'path', or shorter like 'u' in 'cut'
e	Short, as in 'egg' or longer like 'ai' in 'pair'
i	Mostly long like 'ee' but sometimes short as in 'pit'
o	Short as in 'pot', or long as in 'aw' in 'saw'
u	Like 'oo' as in 'pool' or 'u' in 'pull'

USEFUL WORDS AND PHRASES
Getting by
Good morning	*bonġu* (pronounced *bonjoo*)
Good evening	*bonswa*
Goodbye	*saħħa*
Thank you	*grazzi*
Please	*jekk joghġox* (pronounced *yek yo-jbok*)
Yes	*iva* (pronounced *eeva*)
No	*le* (pronounced *lé*)

Places of interest
bay	*bajja* (pronounced *buya*)
beach	*plajja* (pronounced *playa*)
castle	*kastell*
cathedral	*katidral* (pronounced *kateedrahl*)
cave	*ghar* (pronounced *are*)
cemetery	*ċimiterju* (pronounced *chimiteryu*)
cistern	*bir* (pronounced *beer*) [for water, usually translated in Malta as 'well' though it is more often a container for water than a source of ground water]
city/urban area	*belt* (*Il-belt*)
cliffs	*rdum* (pronounced *ir doom*)
farmhouse	*razzett*
garden	*ġnien* (pronounced *Janine* – like the girl's name)
harbour	*marsa* (pronounced *marsa*) also *mġarr* (pronounced *imjar*)
inlet	*dahlet* (pronounced *darlet*)
neighbourhood	(like French *quartier*) *kwartier*
parish	*paroċċa* (pronounced *parocha*)
point/headland	*ras* (pronounced *rass*)
spring (of water)	*ghajn* (pronounced *ine*)
square	*misrah* (pronounced *mizrah*)
street/road	*triq* (pronounced *treek*)
suburb	*rabat* (from the Arabic)
tower	*torri* (pronounced *tory*)
valley	*wied* (pronounced *weed*)
wharf	*xatt* (pronounced *shut*)
windmill	*mithna* (pronounced *mitna*) NB: *mitna* means 'we died'!

Signs
Closed	*maghluq* (pronounced *ma'look*)
Open	*miftuh* (pronounced *miftoo*)
Private	*privat* (pronounced *preevat*)

And just to avoid misunderstanding... *Haxix* pronounced *hashish* means vegetables and *Xita* pronounced *shitter* means rain!

Appendix 2

GLOSSARY

The following words are likely to come up in information available in Malta.

Agape table	Round table carved out of the rock in Roman/Byzantine catacombs, usually with benches cut around it. Used for family and friends of the dead to take a funerary meal. Malta is the only place where these are found underground. Also called a *refrigerium* or *triclinium*.
Auberge	The inns or colleges (often translated in Malta as 'hostels') of the Knights where they lived and worked in communities of people speaking the same language (*langues*; see below).
Bastion	A projecting part of a fortified stone wall (in forts built after the advent of gunpowder, bastions are usually pentagonal).
Battery	In the context of fortifications this is an emplacement for heavy guns.
Cavalier	Part of a fortification that is higher than its surroundings, often built up from a bastion or similar, used as a gun platform (see *St James Cavalier*, page 118).
Corbelling	Where each layer of building material (in Malta, stone) projects in from the layer below so that a wall curves inwards at the top. In the case of a room (or a Maltese temple apse) this shrinks the space through which the sky can be seen and, if continued, eventually creates a domed roof.
Corsair	A sea pirate with some official backing.
Curtain	In the context of fortifications, this is the rampart wall joining two neighbouring bastions or towers.
Demi-bastion	A half bastion, consisting of only one face and one flank.
Dolmen	A prehistoric structure of upright stones topped with a horizontal capstone. Usually a burial site.
E-boat	The Allies' name for small, fast technically advanced gunboats developed by the Germans when they were forbidden, under the Versailles Treaty, to build large warships. Very effective at the start of World War II, they were copied by the Allies.
Enceinte	French word for a perimeter wall encircling any work of fortification around a town or castle.
Entrenchment	(Noun) In the context of fortifications, this is an area protected by trenches or other field defences. In Malta it is also used to refer to solidly built sea walls that are part of the bastioned fortifications in some coastal areas.
Festa	Feast day. In Malta, it also means several days of religious and secular celebration surrounding a saint's day.
Fortizza	From the Italian, meaning fort.
Foss	Ditch.

Garigue	Sometimes spelt *garrigue*, this is open scrubland on limestone rock in the Mediterranean region.
Hornwork	A defensive structure outside the main fortification consisting of two demi-bastions linked by a curtain wall, usually very close to, or joined at the rear to, the main fortifications.
Langue	Literally, the French for 'tongue' (language), *langue* refers to one of the eight language groups into which the Knights divided themselves (see boxed text, page 117).
Luzzu	Fishing boat (see boxed text, page 181).
Megalith	A very large stone, particularly those found in prehistoric and ancient monuments/buildings (including Malta's temples).
Orthostat	One of a group of large stone slabs, lined up vertically to form the lower part of a wall in prehistoric and ancient megalithic construction, as in Malta's prehistoric temples.
Parapet	In the context of fortifications, this is an embankment or wall protecting soldiers from enemy fire.
Parvis	Large forecourt of a church, often a raised paved terrace.
Passeggiata (Italian) or *passiggatta* (Maltese)	Both used to describe a stroll or promenade, usually taken on summer evenings before it gets dark.
Pilier	A Knight of St John who heads one of the *langues*.
Ravelin	A V-shaped fortification outside the main fortifications, placed in front of a curtain wall.
Redoubt	A small defensive structure (or mini-fort) generally for the use of infantry defending a position.
Refrigerium	See *agape* table, above.
RTO	Abbreviation of the Italian *riservato*, but usually translated as 'Reserved To Owner', used to mark hunters and trappers hides and private land.
Torba	Crushed and pounded limestone often used for flooring of prehistoric buildings.
Triclinium	See *agape* table above.
Trilithon	A construction of three megaliths – two uprights supporting one placed horizontally across the top (to create something like a doorway).
UNESCO	United Nations Educational, Scientific, and Cultural Organization.

Appendix 3

FURTHER READING

BOOKS

Prehistory and the temples

Malta before History, edited and with photographs by Daniel Cilia, Miranda, 2004. Massive tome of 440 pages; hundreds of illustrations including marvellous colour photos as well as reconstructions of the temples and text by ten experts in the field.

Malta: Prehistory and Temples by David H Trump with photos by Daniel Cilia, Malta's Living Heritage series, Midsea Books, 2002. The key book on Malta's temples. Scholarly, but easy to read and with excellent photos. Includes a site-by-site guide. The author is a Cambridge archaeologist closely involved with excavations in Malta since 1954. This is the only one of these three books you would want to carry around (and much the least expensive!).

Maltese Prehistoric Art 5000–2500BC by Anthony Pace, Midsea, 2002

Human Form in Neolithic Malta by Isabelle Vella Gregory, photos by Daniel Cilia, Midsea Books, 2006. A large, expensive book with lots of photos as well as authoritative text.

Ancient history

Malta: Phoenician, Punic and Roman by Anthony Bonnano with photos by Daniel Cilia, Malta's Living Heritage series, Midsea Books, 2005. The key book on this period. Beautifully produced, scholarly, but approachable with great illustrations. Includes a site-by-site guide.

Medieval Malta

Malta: The Medieval Millennium by Charles Dalli with photos by Daniel Cilia, Malta's Living Heritage series, Midsea Books, 2006. The latest in the excellent Living Heritage series. Expert text and excellent illustrations. Includes a site-by-site guide.

The Knights period

Armoury of the Knights by Stephen Spiteri, Midsea Books, 2003. A comprehensive 400-page guide by the Armoury's one-time curator and leading expert in the field. Includes an annotated catalogue of the collection.

The Art of Fortress Building in Hospitaller Malta by Stephen Spiteri, BDL, 2008. The key book on Malta's remarkable Knights-period fortifications. Spiteri is the top expert and this book is comprehensive and very well and informatively illustrated.

Caravaggio: Art, Knighthood and Malta by Keith Sciberras & David M Stone, Midsea, 2006.

Fortress Malta 360° by Stephen Spiteri, photography by Enrico Formica, Miranda, 2007. Beautifully produced large-format expensive coffee-table book featuring images of Malta's fortifications with text by the leading expert.

Hospitallers: The History of the Order of St John by Jonathan Riley-Smith, Hambledon, 2003. By a leading Cambridge University expert on the crusades.

The Knights Hospitaller by Helen Nicholson, Boydell Press, 2001. Accessible history of the Knights from the beginning through to today.

The Knights of Malta by H J A Sire, Yale University Press, 1994. A thematic history of the Knights (not only in Malta). Well illustrated. Too heavy (literally, not literarily) for the luggage.

The Knights of St John in Malta by Simon Mercieca, Miller, 2005. Easy-to-read, colour-illustrated, short chronicle of the Knights in Malta by a Malta University historian.

Legacy of the Order in Malta 360° by Joseph F Grima, photography by Enrico Formica, 2 volumes (1530–1680 & 1581–1798), Miranda, 2008. Large-format, beautifully produced, expensive hardback of photos.

Malta 1565: Last Battle of the Crusades by Tim Pickles, Osprey, 1998. Short military history of the Great Siege.

Malta: The Baroque Island by Quentin Hughes & Conrad Thake with photos by Daniel Cilia, Midsea, 2003. Large format with glossy photographs and an authoritative survey of the architecture of the Knights of St John in Malta.

Mattia Preti: St Catherine of Alexandria by Cynthia De Giorgio & Sante Guido, Midsea, 2005. Forty-eight pages on Malta's old master and one of his most important works.

The Monks of War by Desmond Seward, Penguin, first published 1972. Covers all the military religious orders with plenty on the Knights of St John. The author has himself become a knight since the book was first published.

The Palaces of the Grand Masters in Malta by Thomas Freller, Midsea, 2009

The Shield and the Sword by Ernle Bradford, Penguin, 2002. Well-written history of the Knights.

The Siege of Malta 1565 by Francisco Balbi di Correggio, translated from the Spanish edition of 1568 by Ernle Bradford, Boydell Press, 2005. Fascinating contemporary account of the Great Siege.

Slavery in the Islands of Malta and Gozo 1000–1812 by Godfrey Wettinger, Book Distributors Ltd, 2002. Some 700 pages on slavery (Muslim, Jewish and Christian).

Understanding Caravaggio and his Art in Malta by Sandro Debono, Insight Heritage Guides, 2007. Short, accessible and copiously colour illustrated.

The British and World War I

Because You Died: Poetry and Prose of the First World War and After by Vera Brittain, edited by Mark Bostridge, Virago, 2008. Including several poems and photographs from her time during World War I nursing in Malta; see also *Testament of Youth*, below.

British Heritage in Malta by Jesmond Grech, Miller, 2003. Ninty-five pages including lots of colour photos. Cross between a history and a guidebook.

British Military Architecture in Malta by Stephen Spiteri, self-published, 1996. Out of print but can still be found. The author is the leading expert on Malta's fortifications.

A Century of the Royal Navy in Malta by Joseph Bonnici & Micheal Cassar, BDL, 1999

The Cross and the Ensign: The Naval History of Malta 1798–1979 by Peter Elliot, Harper Collins, 2009

The Fortifications of Malta 1530–1945 by Charles Stephenson, Osprey, 2004. Short illustrated military history, particularly good on the British fortifications.

The Malta Railway by Joseph Bonnici & Michael Cassar, 1992. Detailed history with lots of photos.

The Royal Navy at Malta 1900–2000 by Ben Warlow, Maritime Books, 2002. A book of black-and-white photos of the ships and life of the Royal Navy in Malta.

Testament of Youth by Vera Brittain, Virago, 1978 and 2008. Memoir which includes her time nursing the wounded of World War I in Malta.

World War II

The Air Battle for Malta by Lord James Douglas-Hamilton, Pen & Sword Books, 2007. A history based on the diaries of the author's uncle, Lord David Douglas-Hamilton, leader of Spitfire squadron in Malta.

Air War Malta by Jon Sutherland, Pen & Sword Books, 2008. The story of the RAF in Malta in World War II.

Faith, Hope and Charity: The Defence of Malta by Kenneth Poolman, Crécy Publishing distributed by Miller, 2004. History of Malta's World War II (*Faith, Hope* and *Charity* were planes).

Fortress Malta: An Island under Siege 1940-1943 by James Holland, Phoenix, 2004. A very human history of World War II in Malta, using survivors tales and diaries to follow a wide variety of people through the war.

Gladiators over Malta: The Story of Faith, Hope and Charity by Brian Gull & Frederick Galea. Wise Owl, 2008.

Malta GC: Rare Images from Wartime Archives by Jon Sutherland & Diane Canwell, Images of War Series, Pen & Sword Books, 2009. Many unseen photos of Malta under siege.

Malta: Island under Siege by Paul Williams, Pen & Sword Books, 2009. Military history with lots of background. Includes a detailed guide to Malta's World War II locations.

Malta: Thorn in Rommel's Side: Six Months that turned the War by Laddie Lucas, Penguin, 1993. The author was the commanding officer of Malta's top-scoring Spitfire squadron so he is writing about people and situations he knew well.

The Ohio & Malta: The Legendary Tanker that Refused to Die by Michael Pearson, Leo Cooper Ltd, 2003. The story of the ship *Ohio* that limped into Malta at the end of Operation Pedestal still miraculously full of fuel.

Pedestal: The convoy that Saved Malta by Peter C Smith, Goodall Publications, 2002

Siege: Malta 1940–1943 by Ernle Bradford, Pen & Sword Military Classics, 2003. Authoritative and gripping history by a man who himself served with the Royal Navy in Malta during the war.

Raiders Passed: Wartime Recollections of a Maltese Youngster by Charles Grech, translated by Joseph Galea Debono, Midsea, 1998. Malta's war from a child's perspective.

The Siege of Malta 1940–42 by David G. Williamson, Pen & Sword, 2007. Very clear, month-by-month account.

Tornado Leader on Malta by Wing Commander Patrick Gibbs, Miller. Written in 1942, before the end of the war, this personal account of flying in World War II – mainly in Malta – is detailed and interesting for not having the benefit of hindsight.

Warburton's War: The Life of Maverick Flying Ace Adrian Warburton by Tony Spooner, Goodall Publications, 2003. English misfit, 'Warby', became one of the most decorated pilots of World War II and, along with his glamorous girlfriend, Christina Ratcliffe, part of Malta's wartime legend. He died mysteriously in 1944.

Women of Malta: True Wartime Stories of Christina Ratcliffe and Tamara Marks by Frederick R Galea, Wise Owl Publications, 2008. Christina Ratcliffe stayed on in Malta after Warburton's death living until 1988.

More books on World War II in Malta can be found at www.pen-and-sword.co.uk (search 'Malta'). There is also an excellent selection at the Malta at War Museum in Birgu/Vittoriosa (see page 147).

General history

A Concise History of Malta by Carmel Cassar, Mireva Publications, 2002. An interesting and unusual account of Malta's history focusing strongly on social history and, although for general readers, often giving documentary detail.

The Making of Malta by Reuben Grima with photos by Daniel Cilia, Midsea Books, 2008. A glossy and beautiful, and also authoritative and informative book looking at Malta through seven themes: sea, rock, water, food, faith, war and celebration.

Malta: History & Traditions by Vincent Zammit with photos by Daniel Cilia, BDL, 2007. A glossy guide to Malta's history with lots of excellent and informative pictures.

Malta: A Panoramic History – A Narrative History of the Maltese Islands by Joseph S Abela, PEG, 2002

The Story of Malta by Brian Blouet, Progress Press, 2004. Accessible history of Malta.

360° Collection A series of large format, beautifully produced and expensive photographic books (weighing over 2kg each) of excellent photos published by Miranda. Some are listed in relevant history sections.

Gozo and Comino, text by Joseph Bezzina, photography by Attilio Boccazzi & Daniel Cilia, 1992

Malta 360° by Geoffrey Aquilina Ross, photography by Enrico Formica, 2003

Malta by Night by Geoffrey Aqulina Ross, photography by Enrico Formica, 2003

World Heritage Sites in Malta 360° by Reuben Grima, photography by Enrico Formica, 2003. Authoritative text and excellent photos of the temples and Valletta.

Underground Malta 360° Vol 1 by Geoffrey Aquilina Ross & Fiona Galea Debono, photography by Enrico Formica, 2004. Includes places not open to the public.

Underground Malta Vol 2 by Edward Said, photography by Encrico Formica, 2005

Fortress Malta by Stephen Spiteri, photography by Enrico Formica, 2007

Arts, crafts, and special interest Note: Books that cover a specific period are listed under that period.

Antique Collecting in Malta by Robert Attard & Romina Azzopardi, Midsea Books, 2008. A guide to Malta's collections.

Antique Furniture in Malta by John Manduca, Midsea, 2002

The Coinage of the Crusaders and the World of Islam by Emmanuel Azzopardi with photos by Daniel Cilia, Midsea, 2006

Costume in Malta: A History of Fabric, Form and Fashion edited by Nicholas de Piro, Midsea, 1998. A large, authoritative account by 21 authors with 300 illustrations.

Gozo Lace: An Introduction to Lace Making in the Maltese Islands by Consiglia Azzopardi, Gozo Press, 1999/2005. One of very few pieces of writing on Maltese lace. Includes some lace patterns.

A Hundred Wayside Chapels in Malta and Gozo by Kilin [sic], Midsea, 2000. The most authoritative guide to Malta's tiniest churches.

The Malta Buses by Joseph Bonnici & Michael Cassar, BDL,1989. The Maltese bus-lovers bible. A history and photographic catalogue of Malta's buses from 1905 to the late 1980s.

The Silver of Malta by Alaine Apap Bologna, Midsea, 1995. Catalogue to an exhibition featuring nearly 1,000 items of Maltese silver dating from the mid-16th to the 19th century.

Wildlife, landscape and the great outdoors

Flora of the Maltese Islands: A Field Guide by Hans Christian Weber & Bernd Kendzior, Margraf, 2006

Limestone Isles in a Crystal Sea: The Geology of the Maltese Islands by Martyn Pedley, Michael Hughes-Clarke & Pauline Abela, PEG, 2002. Summarises decades of research on Maltese geology with colour illustrations and a booklet of geological walks.

Malta Breeding Bird Atlas by André Raine, Joe Sultana & Simon Gillings, BirdLife Malta, 2009. Full-colour guide. The first comprehensive atlas of its kind with a double-page spread of photos, maps and information on each of 32 birds.

Nature in Gozo by John J Borg, Edwin Lanfranco & Joe Sultana, BirdLife Malta, 2007. A guide to Gozo's landscape and habitats, flora and fauna with lots of colour photos.

Walking in Malta: 33 Routes on Malta, Gozo and Comino by Paddy Dillon, Cicerone, 2004. Clear, well-produced little book full of information.

Where to Watch Birds and Other Wildlife in Malta by Alex Casha, BirdLife Malta, 2004. Short paperback with basic advice on what to see and where.

Wild Plants of Malta by Hans Christian Weber, PEG, 2004. Colour-illustrated guide to Malta's rich flora.

Wildlife of the Maltese Islands edited by Joe Sultana & Victor Falzon, BirdLife Malta and Nature Trust, 2002. Nine expert authors cover some 1,000 species of flora and fauna with colour plates and hundreds of line drawings.

Food and cooking
25 Years in a Maltese Kitchen by Pippa Mattei, Miranda, 2003. Cookbook, including recipes for many traditional Maltese dishes.

A Guide to Maltese Cooking by Darmanin Francis, Jumbo Publications, 1997. Traditions, anecdotes and recipes.

The Food and Cookery of Malta by Anne and Helen Caruana Galizia, Pax Books, 2001. No pictures but over 200 pages of highly informed writing and recipes.

Language
Pocket Dictionary and Phrasebook (with pronunciation) by Paul Bugeja, Bay Foreign Language Books, 2004. Easy to use and reliable.

Fiction
Angelo's Eyes and Other Stories by Kilin, Midsea, 2003. A collection of stories by Malta's best-selling author.

Band of Eagles Over Malta by Frank Barnard, Headline Review, 2007. A novel about fighter pilots on World War II.

The Brass Dolphin by Joanna Trollope writing as Caroline Harvey, Corgi, 1998. A romantic novel set in wartime Malta.

Death in Malta by Rosanne Dingli, BeWrite Books, 2005. A writer arrives in Malta to escape home and seek inspiration and becomes embroiled in local life and intrigue. The author was born in Malta but now lives in Australia.

Family Photos by Petra Bianchi, Midsea, 1998. A Maltese author writes the story of a Maltese-Italian family in Valletta and Sliema across a century.

The Information Officer by Mark Mills, Harper, 2009. Thriller set in World War II Malta by bestselling author of *The Savage Garden*.

The Jukebox Queen of Malta by Nicholas Rinaldi, Bantam, 1999 or Black Swan, 2000. American author's novel set in Malta during World War II.

The Kappillan of Malta by Nicholas Montsarrat, various publishers, first published 1973. Set in wartime Malta, this novel about a priest caring for the victims of the war, actually ranges over a great swathe of Malta's history. Montsarrat, a former British naval officer, lived on Gozo from 1959 until his death in 1979.

Koranta and Other Stories from Malta, by Oliver Friggieri, Mireva, first published 1994. Malta's leading contemporary writer, writing in English.

The Sword and the Scimitar by David Ball, Arrow Books, 2004. American historical adventure story set at the time of the Knights' rule in Malta. A Maltese brother and sister are separated when he is taken into slavery by the Ottoman Turks.

Bradt Travel Guides

www.bradtguides.com

Africa

Access Africa: Safaris for People with Limited Mobility	£16.99
Africa Overland	£16.99
Algeria	£15.99
Angola	£17.99
Botswana	£16.99
Cameroon	£15.99
Cape Verde Islands	£14.99
Congo	£15.99
Eritrea	£15.99
Ethiopia	£16.99
Gambia, The	£13.99
Ghana	£15.99
Johannesburg	£6.99
Madagascar	£15.99
Malawi	£15.99
Mali	£14.99
Mauritius, Rodrigues & Réunion	£15.99
Mozambique	£13.99
Namibia	£15.99
Niger	£14.99
Nigeria	£17.99
North Africa: Roman Coast	£15.99
Rwanda	£14.99
São Tomé & Principe	£14.99
Seychelles	£14.99
Sierra Leone	£16.99
Sudan	£15.99
Tanzania, Northern	£14.99
Tanzania	£17.99
Uganda	£16.99
Zambia	£17.99
Zanzibar	£14.99
Zimbabwe	£15.99

Britain

Britain from the Rails	£14.99
Go Slow: Devon & Exmoor	£14.99
Go Slow: Norfolk & Suffolk	£14.99
Go Slow: North Yorkshire: Moors, Dales & more	£14.99

Europe

Abruzzo	£14.99
Albania	£15.99
Armenia	£14.99
Azores	£13.99
Baltic Cities	£14.99
Belarus	£14.99
Bosnia & Herzegovina	£14.99
Bratislava	£9.99
Budapest	£9.99
Bulgaria	£13.99
Cork	£6.99
Croatia	£13.99

Cyprus see North Cyprus	
Czech Republic	£13.99
Dresden	£7.99
Dubrovnik	£6.99
Estonia	£14.99
Faroe Islands	£15.99
Georgia	£14.99
Greece: The Peloponnese	£14.99
Helsinki	£7.99
Hungary	£15.99
Iceland	£14.99
Kosovo	£14.99
Lapland	£13.99
Latvia	£13.99
Lille	£9.99
Lithuania	£14.99
Ljubljana	£7.99
Luxembourg	£13.99
Macedonia	£15.99
Malta	£12.99
Montenegro	£14.99
North Cyprus	£12.99
Riga	£6.99
Serbia	£14.99
Slovakia	£14.99
Slovenia	£13.99
Spitsbergen	£16.99
Switzerland Without a Car	£14.99
Tallinn	£6.99
Transylvania	£14.99
Ukraine	£15.99
Vilnius	£6.99
Zagreb	£6.99

Middle East, Asia and Australasia

Bangladesh	£15.99
Borneo	£17.99
China: Yunnan Province	£13.99
Great Wall of China	£13.99
Iran	£15.99
Iraq: Then & Now	£15.99
Israel	£15.99
Kazakhstan	£15.99
Kyrgyzstan	£15.99
Lake Baikal	£15.99
Maldives	£15.99
Mongolia	£16.99
North Korea	£14.99
Oman	£13.99
Shangri-La: A Travel Guide to the Himalayan Dream	£14.99
Sri Lanka	£15.99
Syria	£15.99
Tibet	£13.99
Yemen	£14.99

The Americas and the Caribbean

Amazon, The	£14.99
Argentina	£15.99
Bolivia	£14.99
Cayman Islands	£14.99
Chile	£16.95
Colombia	£16.99
Costa Rica	£13.99
Dominica	£14.99
Grenada, Carriacou & Petite Martinique	£14.99
Guyana	£14.99
Nova Scotia	£14.99
Panama	£14.99
Paraguay	£14.99
St Helena	£14.99
Turks & Caicos Islands	£14.99
Uruguay	£14.99
USA by Rail	£14.99
Yukon	£14.99

Wildlife

100 Animals to See Before They Die	£16.99
Antarctica: Guide to the Wildlife	£15.99
Arctic: Guide to the Wildlife	£15.99
Central & Eastern European Wildlife	£15.99
Chinese Wildlife	£16.99
East African Wildlife	£19.99
Galápagos Wildlife	£15.99
Madagascar Wildlife	£16.99
New Zealand Wildlife	£14.99
North Atlantic Wildlife	£16.99
Pantanal Wildlife	£16.99
Peruvian Wildlife	£15.99
Southern African Wildlife	£18.95
Sri Lankan Wildlife	£15.99
Wildlife and Conservation Volunteering: The Complete Guide	£13.99

Eccentric Guides

Eccentric Australia	£12.99
Eccentric Britain	£13.99
Eccentric Cambridge	£6.99
Eccentric London	£13.99

Others

Something Different for the Weekend	£9.99
Weird World	£14.99
Your Child Abroad: A Travel Health Guide	£10.95

Index